Insurance Operations and Regulation

Insurance Operations and Regulation

Bernard L. Webb, CPCU, FCAS, MAAA
Consultant

Connor M. Harrison, CPCU, AU, AAM, ARP, AIAF, ARe
Director of Underwriting Education
American Institute for CPCU/Insurance Institute of America

James J. Markham, J.D., CPCU, AIC, AIAF
Senior Vice President and General Counsel
American Institute for CPCU/Insurance Institute of America

First Edition

American Institute for Chartered Property Casualty Underwriters/
Insurance Institute of America
720 Providence Road, Malvern, Pennsylvania 19355

© 2002

American Institute for Chartered Property Casualty Underwriters/
Insurance Institute of America

First Edition • Third Printing • June 2003

Library of Congress Control Number: 2002110459
ISBN 0-89463-102-0

Printed in Canada.

Foreword

The American Institute for Chartered Property Casualty Underwriters and the Insurance Institute of America are independent, nonprofit organizations serving the educational needs of the risk management, property-casualty, and financial services businesses. The Institutes develop a wide range of curricula, study materials, and examinations in response to the educational needs of various elements of these businesses. The American Institute confers the Chartered Property Casualty Underwriter (CPCU®) professional designation on people who meet its examination, ethics, and experience requirements. The Insurance Institute of America offers associate designations and certificate programs in the following areas:

- Accounting and Finance
- Agent Studies
- Business Writing
- Claims
- Global Risk Management and Insurance
- Information Technology
- Insurance Fundamentals
- Management
- Marine Insurance
- Performance Improvement
- Personal Insurance
- Premium Auditing
- Regulation and Compliance
- Reinsurance
- Risk Management
- Surety Bonds and Crime Insurance
- Surplus Lines
- Underwriting

The American Institute was founded in 1942 through a cooperative effort between property-casualty insurance company executives and insurance professors. Faculty members at The Wharton School of the University of Pennsylvania in Philadelphia led this effort. The CPCU designation arose from the same type of business and academic partnership at Wharton as the Chartered Life Underwriter (CLU) designation did in 1927.

The Insurance Institute of America was founded in 1909 by five educational organizations across the United States. It is the oldest continuously functioning national organization offering educational programs for the property-casualty insurance business. It merged with the American Institute in 1953.

The Insurance Research Council (IRC), founded in 1977, is a division of the Institutes. It is a not-for-profit research organization that examines public policy issues that affect property-casualty insurers and their customers. IRC research reports are distributed widely to insurance-related organizations, public policy authorities, and the media.

The broad knowledge base in property-casualty insurance and financial services created by the Institutes over the years is contained mainly in our textbooks. Although we use electronic technology to enhance our educational materials, communicate with our students, and deliver our examinations, our textbooks are at the heart of our educational activities. They contain the information that you as a student must read, understand, integrate into your existing knowledge, and apply to the tasks you perform as part of your job.

Despite the vast range of subjects and purposes of the more than eighty individual textbook volumes we publish, they all have much in common. First, each book is specifically designed to increase knowledge and develop skills that can improve job performance and help students achieve the educational objectives of the course for which it is assigned. Second, all of the manuscripts for our texts are reviewed widely before publication, by both insurance business practitioners and members of the risk management and insurance academic community. In addition, the revisions of our texts often incorporate improvements that students and course leaders have suggested. We welcome constructive comments that help us to improve the quality of our study materials. Please direct any comments you may have on this text to my personal attention.

We hope what you learn from your study of this text will expand your knowledge, increase your confidence in your skills, and support your career growth. If so, then you and the Institutes will truly be *succeeding together*.

Terrie E. Troxel, Ph.D., CPCU, CLU
President and CEO
American Institute for CPCU
Insurance Institute of America

Preface

Without the insurance product, families and businesses would have to live with the uncertainty that their financial well-being could be destroyed. Additionally, few lenders or investors would be willing to lend money without some guarantee that their money would be secure. Those who offer insurance-related services to the public make a valuable contribution to society. Nevertheless, the public has become suspicious of the objectives and operations of the insurance business because of instability in the insurance marketplace, the politicization of insurance, and misunderstandings about the nature of the insurance mechanism. One solution to many of the problems the insurance industry faces today is increased knowledge about how our business works. It is to that end that *Insurance Operations and Regulation* was written.

This edition of CPCU 520 replaces the previous edition, *Insurance Operations*. As the new title implies, the primary change in this revision is the inclusion of a chapter on insurance regulation. The topics for the remaining chapters are the same; however, the material has been updated where necessary to reflect current industry trends.

Despite the changes in this text, it continues to reflect the work of its original authors. Their organization of the material and approach to many topics have been retained. Those original authors are J. J. Launie, Ph.D., CPCU; the late Willis Park Rokes, J.D., Ph.D., CPCU, CLU; and Norman A. Baglini, Ph.D., CPCU, CLU, AU.

To prepare this new edition, we solicited ideas for improvement from course leaders and students. Their comments served as a starting point for this revision. Authors and reviewers urged us to completely revise some sections, eliminate others, and preserve those that required little change. The assistance they provided was indispensable in validating the content of *Insurance Operations and Regulation*. The authors deeply appreciate the critical reviews submitted by the following persons:

Michael J. Apanowitch, CPCU, APA

Ronald E. Arthur, CPCU, ARM

Robert Bambino, CPCU

Michael M. Barth, Ph.D., CPCU

Walter G. Barth, P.E.

Rick Becker, CPCU, CLU, ChFC

Mark Berry, CPCU

Paula L. Bortel, CPCU, CLU, ChFC

Boyd Bruce, CPCU, AIM

Walter G. Butterworth, CPCU

Stephen W. Campbell, CSP, CIH

Michael J. Cascio, FCAS, MAAA

Patricia M. Coleman, CPCU

Deborah Conley, CPCU, AU

James M. Cunningham, CPCU

Paul O. Dudey, CPCU

Linda K. Edgell, CPCU, ARM, AU, ARe

Michael W. Elliott, CPCU, AIAF

Jon L. Elsea, CPCU, CLU, LUTCF, AIM, AAI, AAM

Kevin Flannery, CPCU, AAM, AIS

Edward W. Frye, Jr., CPCU, ARe

William R. Gawne, CPCU

Sandra Gingras, CPCU, AIM, ARP, ARM

George N. Gould, CPCU

Joseph L. Grauwiler, CPCU

Jerome M. Hermsen, CPCU, CIC, ARM, AU, AIM

Kathleen Hinds, FCAS

Don Hurley, J.D., CPCU, CLU, AU, ARM

Anne M. Iezzi, CPCU, AIC

James R. Jones, CPCU, ARM, AIC, AIS

Marcia S. Kulak, CPCU, AIC, ARM, CIC, ARe, CPIW

Kevin G. Kupec, CPCU

Christian J. Lachance, CPCU, CLU, AIC, SCLA

Thomas E. Lyman, CPCU, AIM, ARM

C. Alan Mauch, CPCU

Robert M. McFarland, CPCU, ARP, AAM, AMIM

Kathleen McMonigle, FCAS, CPCU

Thomas R. Michaels, CPCU, SCLA, AIC

Andrew Mulligan

J. Brian Murphy, CPCU, ARM, ARe, AMIM

Jeffrey G. Olmstead, CPCU

Philip E. Olmstead, ARM

John M. Parker, CPCU

Leigh N. Polhill, CPCU, CPIW, AU

Laureen Regan, Ph.D.

Jon A. Rhodes, CPCU, ARM

John F. Russo

Kenneth N. Scoles Jr., Ph.D., CPCU, AIAF

Charles F. Slagle, CPCU, AIM

Andrew W. Snorton, CPCU, AIC, SCLA

Philip N. Spinelli, CPCU, ARM

David C. Sterling, CPCU, CLU, ChFC, CIC

Rodney K. Stoffels, CPCU, ARe, AIS

A. Larraine Stroman, CPCU, ALCM

David J. Swanson, CPCU, CIC, AIAF

William M. Tarbell, CPCU, AU, ARM, AFSB, ARe

Rudolph F. Trosin, CPCU, AIC

Jerome Trupin, CPCU, CLU, ChFC

Jerome E. Tuttle, FCAS, CPCU, ARM, ARe, AIM

Albert G. Wagner III, ASP

Sam Waters, J.D., CPCU, AU

John S. Wemyss, CSP, ARM

Paul Wollmann, CPCU, ARe, ARM

James Wright III, CPCU, AIAF, ARe

Thank you all.

Bernard L. Webb
Connor M. Harrison
James J. Markham

Contributing Authors

The American Institute for CPCU, the Insurance Institute of America, and the authors acknowledge, with deep appreciation, the work of the following contributing authors:

Joseph M. Boslet, PE, CPCU, ARM, ALCM, APA
Vice President of Safety Management
Inservco Insurance Services, Inc.

Kenneth J. Brownlee, CPCU, ARM, ALCM, AIC
Corporate Risk and Claims Manager
Valley Enterprises

Arthur L. Flitner, CPCU, ARM, AIC
Assistant Vice President and Senior Director of
    Curriculum Design
AICPCU/IIA

Larry Gaunt, Ph.D., CPCU, CLU
Professor of Risk Management and Insurance (Retired)
Georgia State University

Joseph F. Mangan, CPCU
Insurance Consultant

Eric A. Wiening, CPCU, ARM, AU, AAI, API
Assistant Vice President and Ethics Counsel
AICPCU/IIA

Contents

Chapter 1

Direct Your Learning

Overview of Insurance Operations

After learning the subject matter of this chapter, you should be able to:

- Explain how insurers have organized to provide property-casualty insurance.
- Explain the risk transfer process.
- Explain insurers' major objectives and the constraints that impede insurers from meeting those objectives.
- Explain and calculate the measures used to evaluate insurer performance.
- Describe an insurer's principal departments and how they interrelate.

Develop Your Perspective

What are the main topics covered in the chapter?

The chapter addresses the types of insurers, the methods insurers use to measure their financial results, departments or functions within insurance organizations, and the interactions among those departments.

Categorize insurers by their structure and form of ownership.

- What activities are restricted based on the form of ownership?
- What pressure might an insurer's executives feel from stockholders or policyholders?

Why is it important to know these topics?

An insurer's financial results are monitored continually to make sure the company is on track with its goals. An insurer might make adjustments that seem arbitrary on the surface, but these adjustments actually help an insurer to align its performance with its goals. An insurer's actions will also be restricted by internal and external constraints.

Consider how your organization's activities are affected by its ownership and the constraints on its activities.

- Which departments within your organization are responsible for making decisions?
- How do constraints and the division of responsibilities affect the way that your organization does business?

How can you use this information?

Interpret your own organization's activities.

- How has its ownership and structure affected its objectives?
- How do departments interact, and who are the decision makers?

Chapter 1

Overview of Insurance Operations

Insurance is a system in which the payments of participants (individuals, businesses, and other entities) are made in exchange for the commitment to reimburse for specific types of losses under certain circumstances. The organization or entity that facilitates the pooling of funds and the payment of benefits is called an insurer. Participants in this mechanism benefit through reimbursement of losses that occur, reduction of uncertainty, and additional services provided by insurers to reduce the possibility of a loss and the resulting consequences.

The principal function of an insurer is the acceptance of risks transferred to it by others. This task is divided into insurer functional areas consisting of marketing, loss control, underwriting, premium auditing, and claims. To reduce uncertainty even further, insurers use reinsurance as a mechanism to spread the consequences of financial loss. Underlying the operation of an insurer is the **law of large numbers** (also known as the law of averages). The operation of the law of large numbers permits insurers to predict their ultimate losses more accurately, thereby enabling them to charge an adequate premium. Adequate product pricing is fundamental to an insurer's continued solvency.

Because of their complexity and the degree of specialized knowledge required, insurer functions are segmented into specialty departments. These departments must work together if the enterprise as a whole is to be successful in performing the task of risk transfer.

To understand the operations of an insurer, one must understand its reason for being, such as to make a profit for its owners, to fulfill a social need, or to satisfy a legislative mandate. How success is achieved or measured directly relates to the nature of the insurer's objectives.

TYPES OF INSURERS[1]

The property-casualty insurance business in the United States can be classified by (1) legal form of ownership, (2) place of incorporation, (3) licensing status, and (4) marketing or distribution system used.

Insurance
A transfer system in which one party—the insured—transfers the chance of financial loss to another party—the insurer.

Law of large numbers
A mathematical principle stating that as the number of similar but independent exposure units increases, the relative accuracy of predictions about future outcomes (losses) also increases.

Legal Form of Ownership

The first insurers in the United States were individuals rather than insurance companies. However, most states in the United States do not now permit individuals or partnerships to act as insurers, although they may act as agents for insurers. Consequently, most U.S. insurers are corporations. Reciprocal exchanges, discussed below, constitute the major exception.

Proprietary Insurers

Proprietary insurers
Insurers formed to earn a profit for their owners.

Proprietary insurers are formed to earn a profit for their owners. Proprietary insurers include stock insurance companies, Lloyd's, and insurance exchanges.

Stock Insurance Companies

Stock insurance companies
Proprietary insurers that are owned by their stockholders.

The principal class of proprietary insurers in the United States comprises **stock insurance companies**. Such companies are owned by their stockholders, who elect a board of directors to oversee the company's operations. In turn, the board of directors appoints officers and employees to conduct the day-to-day operations.

Lloyd's

Lloyd's of London
A marketplace consisting of hundreds of underwriting syndicates, each of them in effect an insurer.

The second category of proprietary insurers consists of Lloyd's of London and American Lloyds organizations (the apostrophe is usually omitted in references to American Lloyds organizations). **Lloyd's of London** is not an insurance company. It is a marketplace, similar to a stock exchange. All of the insurance written at Lloyd's is written by or on behalf of individual or corporate members. The insurance written by each individual member is backed by his or her entire personal fortune. However, each individual member is liable only for the insurance he or she agrees to write, and not for the obligations assumed by any other member. Lloyd's had 2,852 individual members in 2001.[2] Each member belongs to one or more syndicates and delegates the day-to-day management of the insurance process to the syndicate manager. Lloyd's is a major insurer in the United States. Its exact share of the U.S. market is not known, but it probably accounts for 4 to 5 percent of direct U.S. premiums. If its direct insurance and reinsurance operations are combined, U.S. business accounts for approximately 35 percent of Lloyd's total business.[3] Lloyd's now admits corporations as members. Unlike the individual members, the corporate members do not have unlimited liability. The first corporate members were admitted to Lloyd's in 1994. In that year, corporate members accounted for about 15 percent of Lloyd's premium capacity. Their share increased to 82 percent in 2001, with the individual members providing the balance.[4]

American Lloyds are much smaller, accounting for approximately one-tenth of 1 percent of U.S. premiums. Most American Lloyds are domiciled in Texas, although a few are domiciled in other states. Most of the Texas Lloyds have been acquired or were formed by insurance companies because of the favorable regulatory climate under Texas law. They are usually reinsured 100 percent by their parent companies.

Texas laws require that each Lloyds organization have at least ten members (underwriters), and most have slightly more than the minimum. They operate as a single syndicate, under the management of an attorney-in-fact. The attorney-in-fact need not be a lawyer and can be a corporation. The liability of underwriters is limited to their investment in the Lloyds. Unlike the individual members of Lloyd's of London, underwriters for American Lloyds do not have unlimited liability.

Insurance Exchanges

Three **insurance exchanges** were organized in the early 1980s: the New York Insurance Exchange, the Illinois Insurance Exchange, and the Insurance Exchange of the Americas, headquartered in Miami. These exchanges, like Lloyd's, are marketplaces. Any insurance or reinsurance purchased on the exchanges is underwritten by the members. A member can be an individual, a partnership, or a corporation. The members have limited liability. Members belong to syndicates and delegate day-to-day operations to the syndicate manager.

The New York Insurance Exchange and the Insurance Exchange of the Americas have discontinued operations because of financial problems. They wrote both primary insurance and reinsurance. The Illinois Insurance Exchange continues to operate but has discontinued its reinsurance operations.

Cooperative Insurers

Unlike proprietary insurers, **cooperative insurers** are not necessarily formed for profit. They are owned by their policyholders and are usually formed to provide insurance protection to their members at minimum cost. The types of cooperative insurers include mutual insurance companies, reciprocal exchanges, fraternal organizations, and what are here called other cooperative insurers.

Mutual Insurance Companies

Mutual insurance companies constitute the largest category of cooperative insurers. **Mutual insurance companies** are corporations owned by their policyholders. The policyholders elect a board of directors to oversee operations. The directors, in turn, appoint officers and hire employees to carry out the day-to-day operations of the company. Some profits are retained to increase surplus. Profits in excess of those added to surplus are usually returned to policyholders as dividends.

Early mutuals were assessment companies. They collected a small advance premium to cover expenses and levied an additional assessment on members whenever a loss occurred. Very few assessment mutuals remain in operation, and those that do are small and operate in a limited geographic area.

Some mutual insurance companies in the United States avoid the problem of collecting assessments, or even future premiums, by writing perpetual policies.

Insurance exchanges
Marketplaces where insurance or reinsurance purchased is underwritten by their members.

Cooperative insurers
Insurers owned by their policyholders and usually formed to provide insurance protection to their members at minimum cost. Mutual insurance companies, reciprocal exchanges, and fraternal organizations are examples of cooperative insurers.

Mutual insurance companies
Insurers owned by their policyholders and formed as corporations for the purpose of providing insurance to their policyholders. Owners are entitled to elect the directors of the corporation and to receive dividends.

Their members pay a rather large premium deposit initially so that the investment earnings cover the premiums for subsequent years. Only a handful of perpetual mutuals remain in operation.

Most mutuals, and all of the large ones, are advance premium mutuals. Their policyholders pay a premium at the inception and at each renewal of the policy. This premium is intended to cover all expenses and losses during the policy period. Some mutuals retain the right to levy an assessment for additional premiums if they encounter financial difficulties. The larger mutuals issue nonassessable policies, so their policyholders are not subject to such assessments.

Reciprocal Exchanges

Reciprocal exchanges
Associations formed to provide insurance to their members. Risk is transferred to and shared by the other members.

Reciprocal exchanges (also called interinsurance exchanges), like mutuals, are usually formed to provide insurance at minimum cost to members and are owned by their members. However, mutuals and reciprocals have significant differences. When insurance is purchased from a mutual, the risk is transferred to the corporation. In a reciprocal exchange, the risk is transferred to the other members. Also, a reciprocal exchange is managed by an attorney-in-fact. A reciprocal is a nonprofit organization, but the attorney-in-fact can be formed for profit.

Fraternal Organizations

Fraternal organizations resemble mutual companies, but they combine a lodge or social function with their insurance function. They primarily write life and health insurance.

Other Cooperative Insurers

A number of new types of insurers have been formed for specific reasons, usually to make insurance available to a certain organization or group of entities and to make the insurance available at affordable rates. These insurance organizations include captive insurers, risk retention groups, and purchasing groups.

Captive insurers
Insurers formed as a subsidiary of their parent companies, organizations, or groups for the purpose of writing all or part of the insurance on the parent companies.

Captive insurers can take several forms, but the essence of the captive concept is to insure the exposures of the owners of the captive. The ultimate purpose of the captive is to fund the losses of its owners. This approach has sometimes been referred to as "formalized self-insurance." Several states have enacted special captive legislation designed to ease the formation and operation of captive insurance organizations within their jurisdictions.

Special legislation has also allowed the formation of risk retention groups and purchasing groups. These are cooperative insurers. They can be stock companies, mutuals, or reciprocal exchanges, but they are usually organized so that a limited group or type of insured is eligible to purchase insurance from them. These types of insurance organizations are growing in importance in the insurance marketplace.

Other Insurers

Some insurers do not fit neatly into any one of the preceding categories. For example, a health maintenance organization (HMO) can be either nonprofit or for profit. In either case, an HMO provides an agreed schedule of medical services in return for a preset periodic payment by the member. The membership fee is usually payable monthly and does not depend on the health status of the member or the amount of medical services used. A co-payment is usually required for services. For example, one HMO requires members to pay five dollars for each office visit in addition to the regular monthly fee.

The Blues (Blue Cross and Blue Shield) are also difficult to classify. Both are nonprofit. Blue Cross organizations were formed by hospital associations to ensure payment of hospital bills. Although they still perform that function, they are not now controlled by the hospital associations.

Blue Shield covers surgical fees. The Blue Shield organizations were formed by medical associations but are not now controlled by them. Consequently, both Blue Cross and Blue Shield organizations are considered here to be cooperative insurers. Most Blue Cross and Blue Shield organizations were incorporated under special enabling statutes permitting the formation of hospital service plans (Blue Cross) or medical service plans (Blue Shield). A few were incorporated under insurance laws, and, more recently, some have been reincorporated as insurance companies. More than sixty Blue Cross and Blue Shield organizations cover various geographic sections of the country. Collectively, they are the largest insurers of hospital and surgical expenses in the United States.

Other financial institutions have either entered the insurance business or competed with insurers in recent years. Mutual savings banks have engaged in the life insurance business in some states for many years. They act as insurers and not as agents or brokers.

Federal laws and some state laws generally prohibit banks and bank holding companies from acting as insurers, although they may act as insurance agents or brokers under some circumstances. A few holding companies own banks or savings and loan companies along with insurance companies. Some of them started as holding companies for banks or savings and loan organizations and later acquired insurers. Others started as insurance holding companies and later acquired banks or savings and loan companies. Banks are now regularly challenging the prohibitions that have kept them out of the insurance business.

Some banks compete with insurance companies by using traditional banking instruments to serve functions traditionally served by insurers. For example, some banks are promoting letters of credit as substitutes for surety bonds. Letters of credit have also been used as a substitute for municipal bond insurance to protect investors against the failure of a municipality to pay the principal or interest due under its bonds. However, this kind of competition is not yet a major factor in the insurance business.

Pools and Associations

Insurers sometimes encounter exposures that they are unwilling to insure individually because the losses either occur too frequently or are potentially too large. Pools or associations can be formed to handle such exposures, either voluntarily or to meet statutory requirements.

Pool or association
Several insurers, not otherwise related, that have joined to insure risks that the individual members are not willing to cover alone.

A **pool** or an **association** consists of several insurers, not otherwise related, that have joined to insure risks that the individual members are not willing to cover alone. For example, the losses from an accident at a large nuclear power plant might reach several billions of dollars for liability and property damage combined. Because no single insurer is willing to assume such tremendous liability, nuclear energy pools were formed with many member insurers to absorb the losses when they occur. In addition, the pools buy reinsurance from nonmembers to increase their capacity.

Syndicate pool
An association of insurers issuing joint policies to the insured indicating all pool members and specifying the part of the insurance for which each member is responsible.

Pools operate either as a syndicate or through reinsurance. A **syndicate pool** issues a joint (or syndicate) policy to the insured, listing all pool members and specifying the part of the insurance for which each member is responsible. Under such policies, the insured has a contractual relationship with each member of the pool and may sue any or all of them directly if a disagreement arises.

Under a reinsurance pool, one member of the pool issues the policy to the insured, and the other pool members reinsure an agreed proportion of each risk insured. In this kind of arrangement, the insured has a direct contractual relationship only with the company that issued the policy. The policyholder has no direct legal rights against the other members of the pool and may not even know that they exist.

Fair Access to Insurance Requirements (FAIR) plans
Pooling arrangements that provide property insurance to qualified property owners who are otherwise unable to obtain coverage from an insurer in the standard market.

Many pools and associations are required by law. Virtually all states require some kind of pooling arrangement to provide automobile liability insurance for drivers who cannot obtain such insurance from an insurer directly. Similar pools are required for workers compensation insurance in most states. **Fair Access to Insurance Requirements (FAIR) plans** are required by law in twenty-eight states. They provide property insurance to qualified property owners who are otherwise unable to obtain coverage from an insurer. At least two states have joint underwriting associations (JUAs) to provide liquor liability insurance for sellers of alcoholic beverages that are unable to obtain coverage otherwise. Other similar statutory pools or associations for other lines of insurance are required by the laws of some states. Although these pools and associations are required by state law, the protection provided through them is underwritten by private insurers and not by the state governments, although state and federal governments do act as insurers in some situations.

Government Insurers

A number of states have government insurance operations. One-third of the states have state insurance funds that provide workers compensation insurance for some or all employers in the state. Most of the funds compete with private insurers, but several are, by law, the only source of workers compensation insurance in their respective states.

Two states (Pennsylvania and Illinois) have state insurance funds that insure property owners against property damage resulting from collapse of old underground coal mines. Several states provide income-loss disability insurance for workers or medical expense insurance for some segments of their respective populations.

The U.S. federal government has many insurance operations. The largest federal insurance program is the Social Security System, which provides life insurance, annuities, disability income coverage, and medical expense coverage for millions of Americans. A complete discussion of federal insurance programs is beyond the scope of this course, but some of the major programs are as follows:

- Deposit insurance for banks, savings and loan associations, and credit unions
- Export credit insurance
- "All-risks" crop insurance
- Flood insurance
- Crime insurance
- Insurance against expropriation of foreign investments
- Mortgage insurance
- Life insurance for some veterans of the armed forces

At one time, the federal government provided reinsurance to protect private insurers against excessive riot losses, but that program no longer exists.

Place of Incorporation

Classification by place of incorporation categorizes insurers as domestic, foreign, and alien. A domestic insurer within any given state is an insurer that is incorporated within that state, or, if it is not incorporated, was formed under the laws of that state. Reciprocal exchanges are the only unincorporated insurers permitted in most states. Insurance exchanges and Lloyds organizations are permitted in a few states.

A foreign insurer is one that is incorporated or formed in another state of the United States. Alien insurers are incorporated or formed in another country.

Licensing Status

A licensed (or admitted) insurer with regard to any particular state is an insurer that has been granted a license to operate in that state. An unlicensed (or nonadmitted) insurer is one that has not been granted a license. Agents and brokers for primary insurance (except surplus lines brokers) are licensed to place business only with admitted companies. Surplus lines brokers are licensed to place business with nonadmitted insurers, but only if licensed insurers will not write it. Licensing status is also important for purposes of reinsurance.

Marketing Distribution System Used

Insurers can be categorized based on the distribution system used to deliver insurance products to the marketplace. These approaches to the market, discussed extensively in Chapter 3, are the independent agency system, exclusive agency system, direct writer system, and direct response system.

THE RISK TRANSFER PROCESS

Many kinds of entities transfer risks to insurers. Among them are individuals, families, business firms, charitable and educational institutions, and government agencies. Even insurers sometimes transfer risks to other insurers.

Risk management
A process of identifying and addressing loss exposures to reduce the potential adverse effects of those loss exposures on an organization.

The risk transfer process is a part of a larger process called **risk management**, whereby loss exposures are identified and addressed to reduce potential adverse effects on an organization. The risk management process is described in detail in other CPCU texts, so only an outline of it is provided here in the interest of continuity.

The principal steps in the risk management process are the following:

1. Identify the loss exposures to which the entity is subject.
2. Analyze the loss exposures.
3. Examine available risk management techniques.
4. Select the most appropriate techniques to handle the loss exposures.
5. Implement the chosen techniques.
6. Monitor the results of the decisions, and implement necessary changes to the risk management program.

Risk transfer is one of the alternatives in Steps (3), (4), and (5) of the process outlined above. The other alternatives are risk avoidance, risk retention, and loss control. The other steps in the outline are essential to the satisfactory implementation of the risk transfer process.

Many persons or firms play a role in the risk transfer process. For a large corporation, these can include a risk manager, consultants, insurance agents or brokers, and one or more insurers. If the risk involves potentially large losses, the insurer that originally accepts it might transfer all or a part of it to other insurers through reinsurance. The role of each of these entities is discussed below.

Risk Manager

The term risk manager is used here in its broadest sense, meaning the person responsible for identifying and treating risks. Large companies are likely to employ a person with the title of risk manager who devotes full time to the management of risks. In smaller firms, the risk management function might be a part-time duty of a person who has other responsibilities. In either case, the risk manager initiates the risk transfer process by identifying the risks that are present and deciding which ones should be transferred. The risk manager might want or need to seek assistance from consultants or insurance agents or brokers.

Consultants

Many consultants are willing to assist and advise the risk manager in the performance of the risk management process. Many small or medium-sized businesses rely almost entirely on consultants for risk management services. Larger firms, including those with one or more risk management employees, might turn to consultants for advice in unusual or complex situations. Consultants are usually compensated for their services by fees, based on the time required and expenses incurred in providing agreed services. Many insurers have formed subsidiary operations to offer consulting services. These insurers are then able to address the needs of those entities that have the financial resources to self-insure their loss exposures but not the loss control expertise afforded by a commercial insurer.

Insurance Agents and Brokers

Insurance agents and brokers perform a dual role in the risk transfer process. They provide risk management advice to potential insurance buyers, helping them to identify the risks to which they are subject and assisting them in deciding which form of treatment is most appropriate for each of the identified risks. In this role, they compete with consultants.

If a risk is to be transferred to an insurer, the agent or broker assists with (1) finding an insurer that is willing and able to assume the risk and (2) negotiating the terms of the transfer. The agent or broker might also assist with loss adjustment and loss control. Agents and brokers are usually compensated for their services by commissions on the insurance they sell. Compensation by fees based on the effort expended has become increasingly common in recent years. The fees can replace commissions entirely, or the compensation might consist partly of fees and partly of commissions.

Insurers

Insurers are specialists in the risk transfer process. Consequently, they naturally bear the heaviest responsibility for the smooth functioning of the risk transfer process. Among the insurer functions that are necessary to the risk transfer process, or that facilitate the process, are the following:

- Policy contract development
- Pricing
- Marketing
- Underwriting

- Claim adjustment
- Loss control
- Reinsurance
- Investments

Policy Contract Development

The transfer of a risk to an insurer is a contractual matter. Although the laws of most states do not require that insurance contracts be in writing, a written contract helps to facilitate the transaction and reduces the chance of disputes. An agent, a broker, a consultant, or even a prospective policyholder might sometimes draft an insurance contract, but insurers usually perform this task. Insurers may delegate the drafting to an advisory organization, such as the Insurance Services Office, the American Association of Insurance Services, the National Council on Compensation Insurance, or the Surety Association of America. Many insurers develop their own policy forms when addressing the needs of a specific market niche, such as florists or churches, or when an enterprise has insurance needs not exactly suited for standard policy forms.

Pricing

Rate
The price per unit of insurance.

Premium
The total cost for all units of insurance under a policy.

An integral part of the insurance contract is the premium charged. The determination of rates and premiums is therefore an essential function of an insurer. A **rate** is the price per unit of insurance. A **premium** is the total cost for all units of insurance under a policy. For example, in private passenger auto liability insurance, the rate is the price of insurance for a single car, and the premium is the cost for all cars covered under the policy.

Rates for some lines of insurance are determined on the basis of judgment and intuition, with little or no statistical basis. This approach is especially true for lines of insurance that involve wide variations in risks. Ocean marine insurance is an example of such a line. Each ship is different from any other, and the risk also varies with the skill of the officers and crew, the area of operation, and the cargo carried. These wide variations in risk, combined with a limited body of statistical information, require a substantial reliance on judgment in ratemaking.

At the opposite end of the ratemaking spectrum is private passenger automobile insurance. A great mass of statistical information is available, and the risk variation is much smaller. These factors, plus the great public interest in automobile insurance, lead to a much more refined ratemaking system for private passenger auto insurance than for ocean marine insurance.

Custom and tradition might also be important determinants of the ratemaking method to be used. The ratemaking process, like the policy drafting process, might be delegated to an advisory organization.

Marketing

No matter how well the policy is drafted or the rating plan designed, the risk transfer does not take place until the risk manager knows about the exposures and chooses to treat them through insurance. The objective of the marketing function is to inform the risk manager about the policies, rating plans, and services available from the insurer that will address specific needs.

Underwriting

The underwriting function is also essential to the successful operation of the risk transfer process. The purpose of the underwriting function is to determine what risks the insurer will assume and avoid, the premium to be charged for the risks assumed, and the policy terms and conditions under which the risks will be assumed. For most lines of insurance, the underwriter determines the premium to be charged by applying the manual rates and rating plans approved by management. However, for some lines of insurance the rates and premiums are determined by the underwriter and are based on the underwriter's experience and judgment without the benefit of predetermined manual rates and rating plans.

Claim Adjustment

The claim adjustment function is a crucial element in the risk transfer process. A contract of insurance is merely a promise to perform in the future. The purpose of this function is to see that the insured or claimant receives proper payment for covered losses.

Loss Control

The loss control function assists policyholders in the prevention of accidents and the minimization of the losses from accidents that occur. It is an important element in the risk transfer process because it helps to minimize the transfer cost. It also makes some risks acceptable to the insurer that would not be acceptable in the absence of loss control. Loss control personnel also assist the underwriter by providing reliable information for the underwriting process.

Reinsurance

The risk that the risk manager wants to transfer might involve potential losses larger than the insurer is willing to assume. If so, the insurer can pass a part of the risk on to another insurer. This process is known as reinsurance. Reinsurance facilitates the risk transfer process by spreading loss exposures among many insurers.

Investments

The insurer's investment operations might seem at first glance to have only a remote relationship to the risk transfer process. In fact, however, they are an important element in the process. Investment income helps to keep the cost of risk transfer low and makes some risks acceptable to insurers that would not be acceptable on the basis of premiums alone.

All of these insurer functions are explained in greater detail in a later section of this chapter and in other chapters of this text.

OBJECTIVES OF INSURERS

An insurer's management must strive to meet several objectives established by the owners of the company. The major objectives (not necessarily in order of importance) are (1) to earn a profit, (2) to meet customer needs, (3) to comply with legal requirements, and (4) to fulfill the humanitarian and societal duties established for all institutions.

These objectives conflict to a substantial degree. The objective of earning a profit conflicts with all of the other objectives listed. Management must resolve the conflicts in such a way as to provide the most good for the largest number of people.

Profit Objective

The profit objective is most readily associated with proprietary insurers (stock companies and Lloyd's organizations). However, cooperative insurers (mutuals and reciprocal exchanges) must also earn a profit.

Proprietary insurers must earn a profit to compensate the people and institutions that provide their capital. Capital markets allocate funds to those companies, insurers or otherwise, that provide the greatest return consistent with the investment risk involved. Consequently, insurers can attract capital only as long as their profits are comparable to the profits of other companies that are subject to the same level of risk.

Cooperative insurers normally do not compete directly in the capital markets. Their policyholders are the source of their capital. These insurers obtain their capital from the profits they earn on the insurance they provide to their customers. In some infrequent instances, mutuals and reciprocals can obtain capital by borrowing funds under subordinated notes, called surplus notes. These notes can usually be repaid only out of profits, so funds from that source are also likely to depend on the anticipated profitability of the company.

Customer Needs Objective

An insurer's customers need insurance to handle their risks at a cost they can afford to pay. Most of them also need ancillary services, such as loss adjustment, loss control, and risk management advice. Any insurer that wants to achieve long-term success must strive to meet those needs.

Of course, this objective and the profit objective might conflict significantly. Quality insurance at a price that customers can afford might not permit the profit that the insurer needs to attract and retain capital. Conflicts of this nature sometimes result in substantial dislocations in the marketplace. Proposition 103, adopted in California in 1988, is a prominent example of consumer perception that insurers are not providing insurance at a cost consumers can afford.

Subject only to some regulatory constraints, insurers have almost complete control of the quality of the insurance products they offer. Their control of insurance costs is much more limited. The cost of insurance is determined primarily by losses, and losses are largely beyond the control of insurers, especially in the personal lines. Underwriting selection might provide some control of losses for an insurer, but it does so at the cost of denying insurance to some who need it. Savings realized through strict underwriting can be offset, at least in part, by the insurer's increased obligations under JUAs or other residual market mechanisms. Loss control measures and vigorous resistance to fraudulent claims might reduce losses, but the effect of such measures is limited.

The second major determinant of insurance costs is insurer expenses. Insurers have greater control of expenses than of losses, but major expense reductions usually involve a reduction in services provided to customers, perhaps with some failure in meeting customer needs.

The third determinant of insurance cost is the insurer's profit. The insurer has more control over this element of cost than it has over losses, but it might have difficulty attracting capital if the profit margin is cut too low. It might also have difficulty attracting and retaining policyholders if it sets the profit margin too high.

Legal Requirement Objective

Insurers, like other legitimate business firms, want to meet all of the obligations imposed on them by law. This desire to comply with the law stems largely from an urge to be good and responsible corporate citizens. However, insurers might also fear that failure to comply with the law might brand them as irresponsible in the eyes of the public and public officials. It might also be expensive in terms of fines and other penalties.

The cost of complying with regulatory requirements imposed on insurers is, however, substantial. These costs include the expense incurred directly in regulatory compliance, such as accounting and legal costs. They also include the cost of participating in assigned risk plans, FAIR plans, insolvency funds, and similar facilities. To the extent that these expenses increase the cost of insurance, they create a conflict with both the profit objective and the customer needs objective.

Humanitarian and Societal Objectives

Managers of insurance companies, like other responsible members of society, want to avoid human suffering and promote the well-being of society. These societal concerns are expressed in many ways, such as contributions to medical, educational, and other public service organizations and benefits plans established for employees. Although such programs are socially desirable and beneficial, they do involve costs. Consequently, they create conflicts with some of the other objectives discussed earlier.

CONSTRAINTS ON ACHIEVING OBJECTIVES

The conflicts among objectives are not the only reasons that insurers do not always achieve them. There are several other constraints, both within the insurer and in its environment.

Internal Constraints

Several conditions within an insurer might prevent it from meeting all of its objectives. Fortunately, all of these constraints do not apply to all insurers.

Efficiency

For various reasons, all insurers are not equally efficient. The lack of efficiency might stem from inadequate management, insufficient capital, failure to automate processes, inability to adapt to change, or other causes. Less efficient insurers are at a disadvantage in competing with more efficient ones in the marketplace. This competitive weakness might prevent them from meeting their profit objectives and, consequently, their humanitarian and societal objectives. In more serious cases, it can even prevent them from meeting their customer needs objectives. Extreme cases of inefficiency can result in insolvency and consequent failure to meet legal and regulatory objectives.

Expertise

The insurance business is very complex. A considerable amount of expertise is required for the successful operation of an insurance company. Expertise permits an underwriter to select insurance applicants that have fewer losses than the insureds contemplated in the insurance rate. Expertise is evident when a claim is settled for what the claim is worth. A lack of expertise might prevent an insurer from achieving some of its objectives. An extreme lack of expertise might prevent the achievement of any of the objectives. Lack of expertise has resulted in a number of insurer insolvencies in recent years.

Size

The size of an insurer can sometimes make the achievement of its objectives more difficult. Small insurers cannot afford all of the resources available to larger insurers. For example, large insurers can afford to purchase comprehensive information systems for increased efficiency. Such systems are beyond the reach of smaller insurers.

Larger insurers can also afford the personnel and other facilities for greater research efforts to determine customer needs and to develop products to meet those needs. Smaller insurers must operate in more of a seat-of-the-pants mode. Smaller insurers can sometimes compensate for their more limited resources by greater flexibility, but their limited resources remain a handicap.

Financial Resources

Small insurers are usually constrained by limited financial resources, but even the largest insurers sometimes find that their financial resources limit their ability to achieve their goals. In recent years, several large insurers have had their financial resources reduced by underwriting losses, investment losses, or both. These financial reverses have reduced their ability to achieve their profit objectives and their societal objectives.

Miscellaneous Internal Constraints

Other internal constraints can also interfere with the achievement of goals. For example, a newly established insurer might lack the market recognition necessary to achieve its profit goals even if it has the expertise and financial resources to do so. A company that has established an unfavorable reputation in the past might have difficulty overcoming that reputation, even if it currently operates flawlessly.

External Constraints

Factors in a company's environment can also limit its ability to achieve its objectives. These constraints include regulation, public opinion, competition, economic conditions, distribution systems, and others.

Regulation

The insurance industry is one of the most closely regulated businesses in the nation. The regulation extends from incorporation to liquidation and encompasses almost anything an insurer does between those extremes.

Insurance regulators monitor the solvency of insurers to protect the company's policyholders and members of the public that benefit from the existence of insurance. A primary tool to monitor solvency is the National Association of Insurance Commissioners (NAIC) Annual Statement prescribed by regulators in all states. The Annual Statement displays insurer finances based on conservative statutory accounting principles.

The necessity for having rates and policy forms approved by regulatory authorities might hamper an insurer in achieving its profit and customer needs objectives. Regulation might also constrain an insurer from meeting some of its societal objectives if the regulations limit the use of company funds for charitable purposes. The mere complexity of regulation by the fifty states, the District of Columbia, and, to a lesser degree, the federal government might hamper an insurer in achieving its goal to comply with laws and regulations.

Public Opinion

Public opinion sometimes acts as a constraint on achieving objectives. Perhaps the most serious effect of public opinion is achieved through the regulatory process. If the public becomes convinced that insurers are not adequately meeting the needs of their customers, the public outcry pressures legislators and regulatory bodies to take corrective action. In recent years, public dissatisfaction with automobile insurance has resulted in numerous legislative and regulatory measures to stabilize or reduce automobile insurance rates.

To the extent that these measures are effective, they will reduce the ability of insurers to meet their profit and societal objectives. Even if the measures are not effective, the costs incurred in opposing them might interfere with the achievement of objectives.

Competition

The property-casualty insurance industry in the United States consists of about 3,400 companies, of which about 900 operate nationally or in most of the country and write most of the business.[5] This large number of insurers, coupled with a product that is essentially standardized and cannot be effectively protected by patents or copyrights, leads to periods of intense price competition.

These periods of price competition make it difficult for insurers to achieve their profit objectives. The shortage of profits, in turn, makes it difficult for them to meet their societal objectives. Excessive competitive zeal might also tempt insurers to neglect their objective of compliance with legal and regulatory requirements.

Economic Conditions

The demand for insurance is relatively inelastic, so the premium income of insurers is not drastically affected by most downturns in economic activity. An extreme economic depression, such as the Great Depression of the 1930s, might affect premium income severely, however.

Also, economic change might affect insurers in other ways. For example, losses for some kinds of insurance, most notably surety bonds, might be severely affected by changes in economic activity, especially changes in the demand for construction work.

Inflation affects insurance losses. Inflation also affects insurance premiums, but the effect on losses is felt more quickly than the effect on premiums. This difference in timing makes it difficult for insurers to achieve their profit objectives during periods of rapid inflation.

Insurers' investment operations can also be severely affected by economic changes. In recent years, a slump in the real estate market has caused financial strains for some insurers, though life insurers have been affected more severely than property-casualty insurers.

Distribution Systems

An insurer's distribution system might impose some limits on its ability to meet its objectives. Each of the various distribution systems now in use can meet the needs of some insurer customers, but each fails to adequately meet the needs of others. For example, the independent agency system seems to be very successful in meeting the needs of commercial insurance customers, but it has failed to meet the needs of personal insurance customers as well. The other distribution systems now dominate the personal lines markets.

On the other hand, some insurers using the exclusive agency system or the direct writer system have experienced difficulty in reaching personal insurance customers in rural areas. Some have resorted to dealing through independent agents in those areas.

The direct response distribution system is tailored to the needs of those customers who are concerned primarily with price and are willing to settle for less personal service to obtain a lower price.

The limitations of these distribution systems might restrict an insurer's ability to achieve goals in growth and profits. Some insurers have tried to overcome these limitations by using more than one of the distribution systems, but few have been successful. Resistance from elements within the distribution systems, especially independent agents and brokers, is one reason for the failure of mixed marketing systems.

Miscellaneous External Constraints

Other external factors can reduce an insurer's ability to achieve its goals. Some of these factors are natural or manmade catastrophe losses, the breakdown of law and order, changes in the legal system that affect liability claims, technological developments, and other similar factors.

MEASUREMENT OF INSURER PERFORMANCE

An insurer's performance is measured by its success in meeting its goals. The measure of performance for some goals is subjective in some cases. Financial performance is measured by statistical evidence and is generally considered objective, yet some measurements include an element of subjectivity.

Profit Measurement

Several financial figures might be considered in measuring the profitability of an insurer. These include premium volume, expense ratios, loss ratios, combined ratios, investment income, and operating profit and loss.

Problems in Measuring Profitability

Several problems are inherent in the measurement of insurer profit over short periods of time. For example, the occurrence of a major catastrophe, such as a hurricane, might cause the profitability for a single year to be unsatisfactory even though the company's business might be profitable over the long term.

An even greater problem arises from the indefinite nature of loss reserves. An insurer must establish reserves for losses that have already happened but have not yet been paid. These reserves include an amount for losses that have already happened but have not yet been reported to the insurer, called incurred but not reported (IBNR) losses. Because the amount that will eventually be paid for such losses cannot be known exactly, the reserves are simply estimates of ultimate loss payments. Errors in these estimates are common, and insurers must adjust these loss reserves as more concrete information about them becomes known.

These errors in estimating outstanding losses cause distortions in reported profits of insurers, both in the year that improper estimates are originally made and in the years that the improper estimates are corrected. When loss reserves are underestimated, the insurer's profits for that year are overstated. When the inadequate reserves are corrected in a later year, the profit for the year of correction is understated. The opposite effects apply to overestimates. Because reserve corrections of up to a billion dollars or more have been made in a single year by some large insurers, the effects can be substantial. Available methods to adjust for these effects are complex and not completely satisfactory.

Premiums

An insurer's profits heavily depend on the premium income it receives. Even much of an insurer's investment profit depends on premium income, because premium income creates funds for investment. Consequently, a review of an insurer's success in meeting its profit objectives must consider the volume of premium it writes. Companies that do not grow tend to stagnate. Some growth in premiums is desirable. Ideally, the growth should be real, resulting from writing new business, and not merely from rate increases and inflation.

Some growth is desirable, but too much growth might be a warning sign. It might indicate that the company has relaxed its underwriting standards or is charging rates that are inadequate for the risks assumed. In either case, the premium growth might result in lower profits or no profits at a later date.

Of course, premium growth, or the lack thereof, must be evaluated in light of current market conditions. During periods of intense competition, significant premium growth is difficult to achieve.

Exhibit 1-1 shows the total net written premiums for the property-casualty insurance industry for 1991 through 2000. Growth, in current dollars, varied from 1.8 percent in 1998 to 6.2 percent in 1993, reflecting competitive conditions in the market. When measured in constant 1991 dollars, the industry's net written premium growth was flat or declined in six of the ten years during this period.

Establishing reasonable rules to measure the adequacy, inadequacy, or excessiveness of premium growth is difficult. Growth slower than the industry average probably indicates a problem. Likewise, a growth rate substantially higher than the industry average might indicate some changes that might be unfavorable in the long term. Did growth result from some real competitive advantage, or from relaxed underwriting, inadequate rates, or both?

EXHIBIT 1-1

Property-Casualty Insurance Net Written Premiums in the United States From 1991 to 2000 (billions)

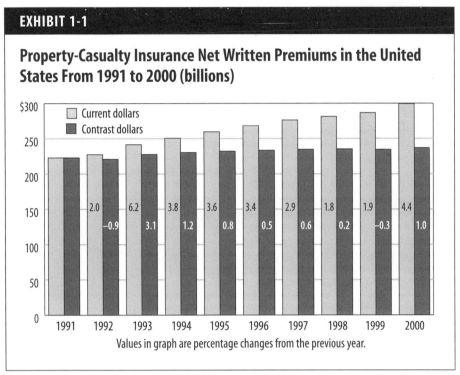

Values in graph are percentage changes from the previous year.

Data for net written premiums in current dollars are used with permission from © A.M. Best Company, *Best's Aggregates and Averages, Property-Casualty, United States,* 2001 Edition, p. 299. The U.S. Bureau of Labor Statistics Consumer Price Index for all urban consumers was used in the calculation of the real rate of premium growth.

Expenses

Insurance company expenses are most conveniently measured by the **expense ratio,** the ratio of expenses to premiums. Exhibit 1-2 shows the expense ratios for all lines combined for the years 1996 through 2000. The loss adjustment expense ratio shown is the ratio of loss adjustment expenses to earned premiums. The other ratios are to net written premiums. The loss adjustment expense ratio is frequently combined with the loss ratio rather than with the other expenses (sometimes referred to as the underwriting expenses). It is shown in Exhibit 1-2 with other expenses. The expense ratio varies rather widely among the various lines of insurance.

As shown in Exhibit 1-2, the expense ratio also varies over time. When rates are rising rapidly, the expense ratio tends to decline because expenses do not rise as rapidly as losses. When competition or regulation holds rates down, the expense ratio tends to increase because expenses, in dollar terms, continue to rise with inflation. This relationship is apparent in a comparison of the total underwriting expense ratio from Exhibit 1-2 with the change in net written premiums from Exhibit 1-1.

Expense ratio
The ratio of an insurer's expenses to premiums. This ratio varies widely among the various lines of insurance.

EXHIBIT 1-2

Property-Casualty Insurance Expense Ratios—All Lines Combined in the United States From 1996 to 2000

Year	Loss Adjustment Expense (LAE)	Commission Expense	Other Expense	Total Underwriting Expense (excluding LAE)
1996	13.0	11.2	14.9	26.2
1997	12.5	11.4	15.5	26.9
1998	13.2	11.3	16.3	27.6
1999	13.3	11.1	16.7	27.8
2000	12.9	11.1	16.4	27.5
5 year average	13.0	11.2	16.0	27.2

Note: Rounding of underlying data prevents the commission expense and the other underwriting expense from summing to the total underwriting expense in the year 1996.

© A.M. Best Company. Used with permission, *Best's Aggregates and Averages, Property-Casualty, United States,* 2001 Edition, p. 107.

In general, a company expense ratio higher than the average expense ratio of the industry might indicate inefficiency. Conversely, a company expense ratio lower than the industry average might indicate superior efficiency. However, such comparisons must be made on a line-by-line basis, since the expense ratio varies substantially by line. For example, the total underwriting expense ratio for fire insurance was 37.7 percent in 2000, and the ratio for medical malpractice liability insurance was 19.8 percent.[6] Additionally, expense ratios differ by the distribution systems used by insurers. Comparisons should be made between insurers operating similarly to best gauge their relative efficiency.

Losses

Loss ratio
The insurer's incurred losses (including loss settlement expenses) for a given period divided by its earned premiums for the same period.

An insurer's success in controlling insured losses is most conveniently measured by the **loss ratio**, the ratio of incurred losses to earned premiums. The loss ratio can be calculated with or without loss adjustment expenses. It is important to know whether loss adjustment expenses have been included, because they can constitute a significant percentage of losses. For example, in 2000, losses alone were 74.4 percent of earned premiums for medical malpractice insurance, and loss adjustment expenses were 36.0 percent.[7]

A company's loss ratio must be evaluated in light of its expense ratio. A company with an expense ratio lower than the industry average can afford a loss ratio higher than the industry average while still earning an acceptable profit. Exhibit 1-3 shows industry loss ratios for all lines combined for the years 1995 through 2000.

EXHIBIT 1-3

Property-Casualty Insurance Loss Ratios—All Lines Combined in the United States From 1995 to 2000

Year	Pure Loss Ratio	Loss Adjustment Expense (LAE) Ratio	Loss and LAE Ratio
1995	65.8	13.2	**79.0**
1996	65.7	13.0	**78.7**
1997	60.6	12.5	**73.2**
1998	63.4	13.2	**76.6**
1999	65.4	13.3	**78.8**
2000	68.6	12.9	**81.5**

Note: Rounding of underlying data prevents the pure loss ratio and the loss adjutment expense ratio from summing to the loss and LAE ratio in years 1997 and 1999.

© A.M. Best Company. Used with permission, *Best's Aggregates and Averages, Property-Casualty, United States*, 1999 Edition, p. 103; 2001 Edition, p. 107.

Combined Ratios

Because the loss ratio and the expense ratio each must be interpreted in light of the other, combining them is convenient. The sum of the loss ratio and the expense ratio is known as the **combined ratio**. A combined ratio of less than 100 percent indicates that the company earned a profit on its insurance operations (often referred to as an underwriting profit), not including any investment profit or loss. A combined ratio in excess of 100 percent indicates a loss on insurance operations.

Two combined ratios are used in the insurance industry: the statutory combined ratio and the trade basis combined ratio. The **statutory basis combined ratio** is calculated in the manner specified in the Annual Statement. It is calculated by dividing the sum of incurred losses and incurred expenses by earned premiums. For a growing company, earned premiums lag behind net written premiums. Because most underwriting expenses are closely related to net written premiums, the statutory combined ratio tends to understate the profitability of a growing company. On the other hand, it tends to overstate profit for a company with a shrinking premium volume.

The **trade basis combined ratio** was developed in an effort to avoid the weaknesses of the statutory combined ratio. In calculating the trade combined ratio, the incurred losses and loss adjustment expenses are divided by earned premiums, and the incurred underwriting expenses are divided by net written premiums.

An example will clarify the difference. Insurance Company reported the financial data for last year as shown in Exhibit 1-4.

Combined ratio
The sum of the loss ratio and the expense ratio.

Statutory basis combined ratio
A ratio calculated by dividing the sum of incurred losses and incurred expenses by earned premiums. The statutory combined ratio appears in an insurer's annual statement, which is filed by an insurer with the state insurance department.

Trade basis combined ratio
A ratio calculated by dividing incurred losses and loss adjustment expenses by earned premiums and then adding the result of dividing incurred underwriting expenses by net written premiums. Financial analysts use a trade basis combined ratio to evaluate an insurer.

EXHIBIT 1-4

Combined Ratio Calculation—Insurance Company

Incurred underwriting expenses	$ 5,000,000
Incurred losses and loss adjustment expenses	14,000,000
Written premiums	25,000,000
Earned premiums	20,000,000

Insurance Company's *statutory basis* combined ratio would be:

$$= \frac{\text{Incurred losses and loss adjustment expenses}}{\text{Earned premiums}} + \frac{\text{Incurred underwriting expenses}}{\text{Earned premiums}}$$

$$= \frac{14,000,000 + 5,000,000}{20,000,000}$$

$$= 0.95 \text{ or } 95\%$$

Insurance Company's *trade basis* combined ratio would be:

$$= \frac{\text{Incurred losses and loss adjustment expenses}}{\text{Earned premiums}} + \frac{\text{Incurred underwriting expenses}}{\text{Written premiums}}$$

$$= \frac{14,000,000}{20,000,000} + \frac{5,000,000}{25,000,000}$$

$$= 0.70 + 0.20 = 0.90 \text{ or } 90\%$$

Insurance Company's premium volume was growing rapidly last year, as shown by net written premiums 25 percent greater than earned premiums. Consequently, its trade basis combined ratio was less than its statutory combined ratio.

Exhibit 1-5 shows the trade combined ratio for all lines combined for the years 1995 through 2000. The industry sustained an underwriting loss in all years of the period, with the combined ratio reaching its peak of 110.4 percent in 2000.

Like the expense ratio and loss ratio, a company's combined ratio must be evaluated with due consideration to competitive conditions within the industry. Also, the combined ratio for a single year might be adversely affected by catastrophic events.

Investment Income

Up to this point, the discussion of insurer profitability has dealt only with underwriting profit or loss, without any consideration of the insurer's investment operations.

EXHIBIT 1-5

Property-Casualty Insurance Trade Basis Combined Ratio—All Lines Combined in the United States From 1995 to 2000

Year	Combined Ratio Before Policyholder Dividends	Policyholder Dividends	Combined Ratio After Policyholder Dividends
1995	106.8	1.5	**108.3**
1996	104.9	1.2	**106.1**
1997	100.1	1.8	**102.0**
1998	104.2	1.9	**106.0**
1999	106.6	1.3	**107.9**
2000	109.0	1.4	**110.4**

Note: Rounding of underlying data prevents the combined ratio before policyholder dividends and the policyholder dividends from summing in years 1997 and 1998.

Insurance operations generate large amounts of investable funds, primarily from loss reserves, loss adjustment expense reserves, and unearned premium reserves. Loss and loss expense reserves are especially significant for liability insurance. The long delay inherent in the liability loss adjustment process generates very large loss reserves. The gradual change from a predominantly property insurance industry to a predominantly liability insurance industry, coupled with rising interest rates, placed greater emphasis on investment earnings. Although interest rates have declined in more recent years, investment income is still the sole source of profit for most insurers. Exhibit 1-6 shows the industry's combined ratio after policyholder dividends, net investment ratio, and operating ratio.

Operating Profit or Loss

Operating profit or loss is the sum of underwriting profit or loss and investment profit or loss. Insurers realize investment earnings from three sources. The first and most stable is investment income, consisting of interest, dividends, and rents derived from bonds, stocks, real estate, and other assets held for investment purposes. The second source is realized capital gains or losses, which result when an investment asset is sold for more or less than its cost. The final source is unrealized capital gains or losses, resulting when the market value of an asset rises above or falls below its cost, but the asset is not sold. The investment profit figures in Exhibit 1-6 do not include unrealized capital gains or losses.

Operating profit or loss
The sum of underwriting profit or loss and investment profit or loss.

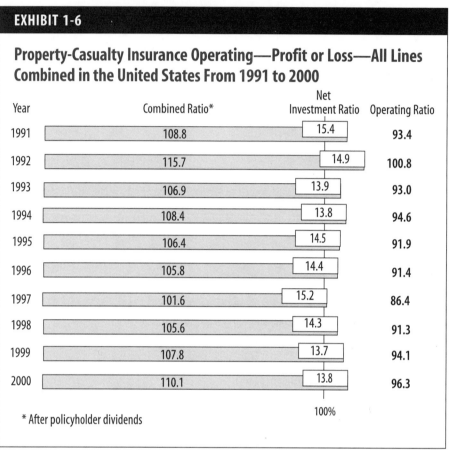

EXHIBIT 1-6

Property-Casualty Insurance Operating—Profit or Loss—All Lines Combined in the United States From 1991 to 2000

Year	Combined Ratio*	Net Investment Ratio	Operating Ratio
1991	108.8	15.4	93.4
1992	115.7	14.9	100.8
1993	106.9	13.9	93.0
1994	108.4	13.8	94.6
1995	106.4	14.5	91.9
1996	105.8	14.4	91.4
1997	101.6	15.2	86.4
1998	105.6	14.3	91.3
1999	107.8	13.7	94.1
2000	110.1	13.8	96.3

* After policyholder dividends

100%

© A.M. Best Company. Used with permission, *Best's Aggregates and Averages, Property-Casualty, United States* 2001 Edition, pp. 264, 266.

Meeting Customers' Needs

How well insurers meet customer needs is difficult to determine. Insurers are more likely to hear from those customers who believe they have not been treated fairly. All insurers receive complaints, and each one should be evaluated. In some instances, there is a real problem the insurer should address. In many more instances, the customer holds expectations that the insurer had not intended to fulfill.

Several state insurance departments tabulate complaints they receive and publish lists showing the number of complaints received for each company. The number of complaints might indicate one company's success or failure relative to other companies in the industry.

Consumers Union periodically surveys its membership to determine their level of satisfaction with the performance of auto and homeowners insurance. The results are infrequently published in that organization's magazine, *Consumer Reports*. It includes a list of the most satisfactory and least satisfactory insurers as indicated by the survey responses. Only a few of the largest insurers are included in the list because smaller insurers are not mentioned in the responses with sufficient frequency to evaluate their performance fairly.

Insurance agents and brokers can also be a source of information for evaluating an insurer's success in this area. They are in frequent contact with consumers and hear their complaints and praise of insurers. Collectively, agents and brokers seldom make formal tabulations of such consumer reactions, so their evaluations are likely to be subjective.

Many insurers emphasize a customer focus to maintain and raise levels of customer satisfaction with the insurer's products and services. Insurers use response cards and phone surveys to determine whether customers feel properly treated by the insurer after a transaction, particularly following a claim.

Insurers marketing insurance through independent agents and brokers usually view this network of producers as their customers in addition to the ultimate insurance consumer. These insurers recognize that producers have many insurance companies available to them and that a competitive marketplace exists within their offices. Being responsive to producer requests and permitting access to insurer policy data and information systems are examples of how insurers maintain and strengthen the company-producer relationship.

Meeting Legal Requirements

An insurer's success or failure in meeting legal requirements is indicated by the number of criminal, civil, and regulatory actions taken against it. These actions are automatically brought to the attention of management and should be evaluated carefully to see whether they result from a consistent pattern of disregard of legal requirements.

State insurance departments monitor the treatment of insureds, applicants for insurance, and claimants, as well as providing oversight to four insurer operational areas: sales and advertising, underwriting, ratemaking, and claim settlement. This regulatory activity, market conduct regulation, is in addition to the state insurance regulation's role in solvency surveillance.

Most states publish a listing of regulatory actions against insurers. This information can be useful in showing how one insurer's performance in this area compares to the performance of its competitors.

Meeting Social Responsibilities

Meeting social responsibilities is the most difficult of all of the major objectives to evaluate. No standards exist for judging an insurer's performance in this area, and very little information on an individual insurer's performance is publicly available. Of course, an insurer can get information from its own records to show its own performance, but comparisons with competing insurers are difficult to make because of the lack of available information.

One possible indicator of social responsibility is the benefits that an insurer provides for its employees. Comparative information for employee benefits is available from the United States Chamber of Commerce and from various insurance company trade associations. Although generous employee benefit plans can be construed as merely another method of competing for good employees, they might also indicate a company's concern for the welfare of its employees.

Another indicator of an insurer's humanitarian concern is its expenditures on loss control activities. Some insurers go beyond the typical efforts in loss control to improve the safety conditions for their policyholders. Many insurers contribute to associations that do research and raise public concern for safety.

Contributions to medical, welfare, and educational institutions and programs are another indication of humanitarian concerns and social responsibility.

FUNCTIONS REQUIRED TO MEET NEEDS

An insurance company consists of many departments, all of which must function properly if the insurer is to survive and succeed. The principal functions or departments of an insurer are the following:

- Marketing
- Underwriting
- Claims
- Loss control
- Premium auditing
- Reinsurance
- Actuarial
- Investments

Marketing

No matter how well the policy contract is drafted and regardless of the accuracy of the rating plan, an insurer cannot succeed without an adequate marketing program. Potential buyers of insurance must be adequately informed of the company's products, including its policies, rating plans, loss adjustment services, loss control capabilities, and other services that make a complete insurance product. Communicating this information to potential customers and producers is the function primarily of the insurer's marketing personnel.

There are several methods for marketing insurance and many variations of each of the principal marketing methods. Many insurers sell through independent agents and brokers, who are independent business people representing several otherwise unrelated insurers. Some market through exclusive agents, who represent only one insurer or a group of insurers under common ownership and management. Others rely on the sales efforts of their own employees. Several very successful insurers advertise through the mail, on television, or in newspapers and magazines to market their services, with no direct face-to-face contact with their customers. All of these and perhaps other methods have been used successfully to reach certain groups of insurance buyers. Some insurers use more than one of the methods mentioned in an effort to reach the widest possible audience.

The objectives of the marketing department must be balanced with other insurer goals. Too much emphasis on marketing might result in compromised underwriting guidelines. Premium growth that sacrifices profitability is not a successful market strategy.

Of course, marketing is more than merely making sales calls. A successful marketing program is likely to include (1) market research to determine the needs of potential buyers, (2) advertising and public relations programs to inform potential buyers about the company's products, (3) training programs to equip the company's employees and agents to meet the public's needs, (4) setting production goals and strategies for achieving them, and (5) effective motivation and management of the producer network.

Underwriting

The functions of the underwriting department are to decide the price and the terms and conditions under which the insurer will provide coverage and to decide which applicants will be insured. Underwriting is, in some regards, a counterbalance to the marketing department. In other respects, it is an aid to the marketing department.

The underwriting department acts as a counterbalance to the marketing department in the development of underwriting guides and the selection of applicants to insure. The primary purpose of these functions is to ensure that the insurer writes a book of business that is profitable and reasonably stable.

Tighter restraints on underwriting policy can lead to fewer applicants being accepted. Over time, an unduly restrictive underwriting policy and an aggressive marketing department will drive up the expenses of the insurer. An increased expense ratio results because the cost of investigating and rejecting applicants is almost the same as processing acceptable business. Additionally, the restricted premium volume produces a lower denominator in the insurer's loss ratio.

The underwriting department aids the marketing department by developing policy forms and rating plans that are marketable and by trying to find ways to insure marginal risks by modifying the policy contract, the rating plan, or the risk.

Claims

An insurance contract is a promise to make a payment to or on behalf of the policyholder if some fortuitous event occurs. The department that has primary responsibility for the loss adjustment function is frequently called the claim department and is staffed by employees who are trained in the skills necessary to negotiate or, if necessary, litigate the settlement of claims by or against policyholders.

Some think the purpose of the loss adjustment process is to minimize losses. Its real purpose is to achieve a fair settlement, neither too high nor too low. Loss settlements that are too high increase the cost of insurance for everybody. Settlements that are too low deprive the policyholder of some of the benefits of the insurance contract. Consistently inadequate loss settlements can hamper the insurer's marketing efforts and can lead to litigation and regulatory actions against the company.

Loss Control

The primary function of an insurer's loss control department is to prevent those losses that can be prevented and to minimize those that cannot be prevented. Loss control has been an important insurer function almost since the beginning of insurance, and it receives even greater emphasis now than in the past.

From an economic standpoint, loss control is preferable to risk transfer because it reduces the waste of valuable resources, both human and material. As a practical matter, both risk transfer and loss control are likely to be used jointly for most large risks because preventing all losses is seldom possible.

The loss control department provides information to the underwriting department to assist in the selection and rating of risks. It might also assist the marketing department in the solicitation of commercial and industrial accounts.

Premium Auditing

When insurers introduced workers compensation and employers liability with a variable policy premium, producers were given the responsibility of obtaining the insured's statement of actual wages paid during the policy period, calculating the premium according to the rate stipulated in the policy, and collecting the additional premium due or returning the excess premium previously paid. This process proved to be unreliable and was replaced by premium auditors to ensure equitable treatment of insureds.

The role of premium auditors has expanded as the number of insurance products subject to variable rating has increased. Compounding the difficulty of this task are the numerous rating bases used in insurance pricing and the size of the commercial accounts subject to audit.

Reinsurance

To the uninitiated, large corporations transferring risk to much smaller insurance companies might seem illogical. For example, all of the nation's

500 largest business corporations are larger than the vast majority of insurance companies, but all of them buy insurance. Reinsurance is the tool that makes such transfers practical. When a primary insurer accepts a risk that is larger than it is willing or able to bear, it can transfer all or a part of that risk to other insurers around the world through reinsurance transactions. For example, the explosion of the Piper Alpha oil rig in the North Sea in 1988 caused total losses of about $1 billion. Many insurers in many parts of the world shared that loss through reinsurance.

Reinsurance also helps cushion the effects of natural disasters on individual insurers and the insurance industries of individual nations. For example, Hurricane Andrew caused more than $15 billion of losses in the United States. It would have been a severe blow if borne by the U.S. insurance industry alone. However, the reinsurance process spread the cost of that catastrophe throughout the worldwide insurance industry, softening its effects substantially.

A well-designed reinsurance program enables a primary insurer to provide insurance for risks that would otherwise be too large. Reinsurance also enables insurance buyers to obtain all of the coverage they need in one or a few policies, rather than buying many smaller policies from many insurers. Reinsurance also protects the financial solvency of primary insurers by enabling them to meet their obligations to policyholders and claimants.

Actuarial

The actuarial department performs the mathematical functions of an insurer. These include the calculation of rates, the development of rating plans, and the estimation of loss reserves. Actuaries might assist in corporate planning. Actuaries are often involved in establishing corporate goals and assessing the company's success in meeting those goals.

Advisory organizations, formally called rating bureaus, once served the insurance industry as a source for final rates. Now, advisory organizations are providing loss costs in lieu of final rates. Insurance company actuaries or actuarial consultants are involved in developing factors (reflecting expenses and anticipated profits) that will convert loss costs to final rates for use with their distribution system.

Investments

At first glance, the relationship between an insurer's investment operations and risk transfer would seem to be remote. Actually, the relationship is quite close for two reasons. First, an insurer's investment operations enable it to earn investment income on the funds generated by its risk transfer activities. The investment income, in turn, reduces the premium that the insurer must charge in exchange for the risks it assumes.

The relationship works in both directions, however. The kinds of insurance risks that an insurer assumes is one of the factors that determine the kinds of investments it acquires. An insurer that assumes only moderate insurance risks might be able to assume greater investment risks, with their higher investment yield. An insurer that assumes very high insurance risks must be more conservative in its investment strategy.

Property insurance losses vary substantially from year to year, in part because of catastrophes such as hurricanes and earthquakes. Also, property insurance losses are paid quickly. Consequently, an insurer that writes mostly property insurance must hold very stable and liquid investments that can be converted quickly to cash to pay losses. Liability insurance is not subject to catastrophic losses and is therefore more stable than property insurance. Liability claim payments are subject to a longer delay between the time of occurrence and the time of payment. Consequently, an insurer that writes mostly liability insurance might be able to hold investments that are slightly less liquid than those held by property insurers. The positive effect of interest rates and investment returns was illustrated in Exhibit 1-6.

Other Functions

Insurers also involve a number of other functions that need not be discussed in detail here. These include accounting, information systems, personnel, legal services, and training.

Though insurers serve society in many ways, their principal purpose is to facilitate the transfer of risk. Their other functions in the economy, such as the preservation of human and material assets and the accumulation of investment capital, are incidental to that principal purpose. All of the foregoing departments of an insurer must work together to serve its principal function and to meet company objectives.

INTERDEPENDENCE AMONG FUNCTIONS

Although each function within an insurer must have some autonomy to perform its work, those functions are far from being completely independent. They must interact constantly if the insurer is to function smoothly and efficiently.

Marketing and Underwriting

Although the underwriting department functions in part as a counterbalance to the marketing department, the two departments must cooperate in many phases of insurer operations. For example, the underwriting department has primary responsibility for deciding what products the insurer will sell and the circumstances under which it will sell them. However, in making those decisions, the underwriting department must give full consideration to the marketing department's opinion about the salability of those products.

In addition, the underwriting department must cooperate with the marketing department in finding ways to make marginal risks acceptable. This can be done by (1) modifying a policy with large deductibles, special exclusions, or other modifications; (2) modifying the rating plan to produce more premium; (3) modifying the risk through loss control; or (4) a combination of all three. In some cases, the underwriting department might be able to use special reinsurance arrangements to make a marginal risk acceptable.

In turn, sometimes the marketing department can assist the underwriting department. Marketing personnel are more likely than underwriting personnel to be in direct contact with policyholders and prospective policyholders. In the course of these contacts, marketing personnel might acquire information that is important in the underwriting process. Such information should be passed on to underwriting.

Underwriting and Loss Control

The loss control department is sometimes called the eyes and ears of the underwriting department. An underwriter who is considering an application for insurance might ask the loss control department to visit the applicant and survey the risks involved in the submission. In providing normal loss control services for existing policyholders, the loss control department might also obtain information that is important to the underwriting process.

Loss Control and Marketing

The loss control department might also be able to assist in marketing. Some insurers feature their loss control activities as a selling point in their advertising and sales presentations. A loss control engineer might accompany a marketing person on sales calls to prospective policyholders who are especially concerned about loss control assistance. Finally, loss control personnel might be able to offer suggestions to improve a marginal risk to make it acceptable to the underwriting department.

Claims and Other Departments

The claim department must also interact with the underwriting, marketing, and loss control departments. It can assist the underwriting department by passing on important underwriting information that arises in the loss adjustment process. In turn, it might ask the underwriting department to interpret the underwriting department's intent when a marginal claim arises.

The claim department can help the marketing effort by providing good claims service to policyholders, thus helping the marketing department to retain existing business and write new business. The claim department can also notify the marketing department before it refuses to pay claims because they are not covered under existing policies.

In the loss adjustment process, the claim department might learn of aspects of the policyholder's operations that need loss control attention. Such information should be passed on to the loss control department. In turn, the loss control department might be able to provide information about a policyholder's operations to assist the claim department in the settlement of a claim.

Actuarial and Other Departments

The actuarial department interacts primarily with underwriting and marketing. Its interactions with claims and loss control, especially the latter, are more limited.

The actuarial department devises most of the rates and rating plans used by the underwriting department. It also prepares the statistical information used to evaluate the performance of the underwriting department. In determining the applicable rates and rating plans, the actuarial department must also consider the views of the marketing department concerning the acceptability of the rates in the marketplace.

The actuarial department has responsibility for the development of loss reserves for Annual Statement purposes. For this function, it must maintain contact with the claims department, since the case claims reserves established by the claims department are an important element in establishing statement reserves.

SUMMARY

Insurance is a system under which risk of loss is transferred to another party (the insurer) for a premium payment. The insurer promises to reimburse the policyholder for covered losses and shares the cost of these losses among all participants in the system. The financial suffering relieved by property-liability insurers is significant.

Insurers can be classified in many different ways. Typical categories are the legal form of ownership, place of incorporation, and licensing status.

The fact that an insurer is a stock insurer (operating for a profit) or a reciprocal exchange (operating for the benefit of the exchange membership) directly relates to the overall set of objectives that guide the insurer in day-to-day operations. The insurer's objectives and the obstacles to those objectives need to be understood by its management and staff so that company strengths can be exploited and weaknesses improved.

The principal function of an insurance company is to accept risks transferred to it by others. Although insurers perform many other functions, all of them are incidental to this risk transfer function.

Many entities might be involved in the risk transfer process. These include risk managers, consultants, and insurance agents and brokers. However, insurers are the principal players in most risk transfers, and without them, most transfers could not be made. Among the insurer functions that are necessary to the risk transfer process are policy contract development, pricing, marketing, underwriting, loss adjustment, loss control, reinsurance, and investments.

Insurers' major objectives include earning a profit, meeting customer needs, complying with legal requirements, and fulfilling the social and humanitarian duties society imposes on its institutions. Insurers must recognize and develop strategies to deal with internal and external constraints that restrain insurers from meeting these objectives.

An insurance company pursues its objectives by segmenting them into functional areas or departments. Those departments must function properly if the company is to be successful and grow. The principal functions are marketing, underwriting, claims, loss control, premium auditing, reinsurance, actuarial, and investments. Each department must have some autonomy to perform its assigned functions, but the departments are far from independent. Each department must interact constantly with other departments if the company is to achieve its objectives.

CHAPTER NOTES

1.   Michael W. Elliott, Bernard L. Webb, Howard N. Anderson, and Peter R. Kensicki, *Principles of Reinsurance*, 2d ed. (Malvern, Pa.: Insurance Institute of America, 1995), pp. 39–47.

2.   Home page of Lloyd's of London, © 2001. World Wide Web: http://lloydsoflondon.co.uk/info/keyfacts.htm (15 April 2002).

3.   Home page of Lloyd's of London.

4.   Home page of Lloyd's of London.

5.   *The Fact Book, 2002: Property Casualty Insurance Facts* (New York: Insurance Information Institute, 2002), p. 5.

6.   A.M. Best Company, *Best's Aggregates and Averages, Property-Casualty, United States*, 2000 Edition, pp. 274, 276.

7.   A.M. Best Company, *Best's Aggregates and Averages, Property-Casualty, United States*, 2000 Edition, p. 276.

Chapter 2

Direct Your Learning

Insurance Regulation

After learning the subject matter of this chapter, you should be able to:

■ Identify three recurring issues in rate regulation

■ Describe the effect each of the following had on insurance regulation:
  • Paul v. Virginia
  • South-Eastern Underwriters Association decision
  • McCarran-Ferguson Act

■ Explain the allegations of the attorneys general lawsuit, and describe the changes regulating from ISO's settlement.

■ Explain the key provisions of the Financial Services Modernization Act.

■ Explain why and by whom insurance is regulated.

■ Describe how insurers are formed and the licensing requirements for insurers and insurance personnel.

■ Explain the goals of solvency regulation and the methods used to meet these goals.

■ Describe the insurance rate regulation process. In support of this objective:
  • Identify rate regulation objectives.
  • Describe the major types of state rating laws and their advantages and disadvantages.

■ Explain why regulating insurance contracts is important and identify common regulatory approaches.

■ Explain what insurance industry trade practices are regulated and how these regulations operate.

■ Identify organizations that act as unofficial insurance industry regulators, and explain how these organizations affect insurance activities.

Develop Your Perspective

What are the main topics covered in the chapter?

The business of insurance is regulated by the states with a few important exceptions. Regulation of insurance protects consumers, helps insurers maintain solvency, and deters destructive competition.

Contrast the jurisdiction of state and federal regulation of insurers.

- What is uniquely state regulated?

- What is the purpose of those federal regulations that have authority over insurance operations?

Why is it important to know these topics?

By understanding how insurance is regulated, you can recognize the restrictions within which your own insurance organization operates. As a consumer of insurance products, you can also appreciate how you are protected against an insurer's insolvency or unfair dealings.

Assess how your organization's activities are directed by state and federal regulations.

- How is competition affected by regulations?

- What activity takes place within your organization to ensure compliance with regulations?

How can you use this information?

Consider possible changes in insurance regulations:

- How would the market and competition change if insurance were regulated federally rather than by the states?

- How might increasing federal control of insurance regulation change the way that your organization operates?

Chapter 2

Insurance Regulation

Currently most insurance regulation is done by the states. This chapter covers how and why insurance regulation evolved and explores the ways in which state insurance departments and other government and private organizations operate to address regulatory goals.

HOW INSURANCE REGULATION EVOLVED

Readers might wonder why we begin the study of insurance regulation by examining the past. Insurance regulation is dynamic, not static, and present circumstances are only today's iteration of practices rooted in the past. Because the same issues come up repeatedly, one cannot understand the present state of insurance regulation without understanding the past.

Recurring Issues in Insurance Regulation

Three issues have been addressed time and again throughout the evolution of insurance regulation. These issues might never be completely resolved, and some that once were resolved have again become critical in recent years:

1. *Whether insurance should be regulated by state or federal governments—or both.* A related question is whether the unique nature of insurance demands some regulatory standards different from those that apply to other businesses.

2. *The extent to which insurance should be regulated.* For example, should regulators control the rates charged by insurers, or should a competitive market allow the laws of supply and demand to determine rates?

3. *Whether to require, encourage, or prohibit collaboration among insurers.* Many facets of this issue are highlighted in this chapter. To greatly oversimplify the basic issue: On the one hand, insurers can price any insurance coverage most accurately when they have full access to statistical information regarding past losses that involve that coverage. When information is limited, covered losses cannot confidently be predicted, and insurers need to add a "risk charge" that increases the cost of insurance. Or, insurers without information can underestimate their expected losses, underprice their insurance, and become insolvent.

On the other hand, the law of supply and demand is violated and consumers are harmed by any activity that stifles free competition. For example, if all insurers charge the same price for a given coverage, the consumer has no choice but to take it or leave it. A fixed price set by sellers is likely to be higher than a competitive price set partly by buyers in a competitive marketplace.

MILESTONES IN INSURANCE REGULATION

From a legal standpoint, the story of insurance regulation in the United States begins with the Constitution and is subsequently punctuated by four key events:

- *United States Constitution.* The United States Constitution gives Congress the right to regulate commerce among the states.

- *Paul v. Virginia.*[1] This 1869 legal decision that insurance is not interstate commerce was the basis for a long-standing belief that insurance is exempt from federal regulation.

- *Southeastern Underwriters Decision.*[2] This 1944 legal decision set the U.S. insurance world on its ear by making insurance subject to federal regulation. In one fell swoop, this decision eliminated the role of state insurance regulators and made insurance subject to federal statutes that prohibit many collaborative activities that had previously been approved and encouraged by the states.

- *McCarran-Ferguson Act.* Congress passed this Act in 1945, restoring most responsibility for insurance regulation to the states. However, the Sherman Act and other federal regulation that deals specifically with insurance would apply to insurers. The Sherman Act applies to boycott, coercion, and intimidation by insurers.

- *Gramm-Leach-Bliley Act.* Also known as the Financial Services Modernization Act, this 1999 legislation was intended to facilitate affiliations among banks, insurance agencies, and investment services. The Act included a reaffirmation of the McCarran-Ferguson Act, making it clear that states will continue to have primary regulatory authority for all insurance activities. At the time this book was written, many implications of the Gramm-Leach-Bliley Act had not yet been clarified.

INSURANCE REGULATION

The story of insurance regulation in the American colonies begins when the first insurance companies were formed there. Because the colonies were subject to British law, colonial insurance companies had to be chartered under the British Crown.

The situation naturally changed following the Declaration of Independence and the founding of the United States. In 1792, Pennsylvania became the first state to charter an insurance company, and by 1797 most states were chartering insurance companies. Throughout the early 1800s, states sporadically enacted state-specific insurance regulations to address problems such as competition, consumer protection, and—especially—solvency. Insurers were subject to the regulation of the states in which they were chartered, and each state had its own regulations.

Until the 1850s, insurance regulation was overseen by state legislatures and various offices within state governments. In 1851, New Hampshire was the first state to establish an insurance board.

Most other states had established boards of insurance regulation by 1859, when New York created the first state insurance department. Eventually, the other states followed suit, and insurance boards were replaced by insurance commissioners.

Paul v. Virginia

Insurance regulation received its first legal test in 1869. Samuel B. Paul, a Petersburg, Virginia, insurance agent, wanted to be licensed in his home state of Virginia, but he wanted to represent New York insurers. According to Virginia law, insurers domiciled in another state were required to deposit a bond with the Virginia state treasurer, but the companies Paul represented had not met this requirement. The state of Virginia therefore denied Paul's application for a license. Paul nevertheless continued to sell insurance for the New York companies. He was indicted, convicted, and fined $50 by the Circuit Court of Virginia, and that decision was upheld by the Virginia Court of Appeals.

Paul continued to fight the charge and, in 1869, the U.S. Supreme Court reviewed the decision. Paul argued that the Virginia licensure law was unconstitutional because only Congress could regulate interstate commerce under the United States Constitution (see sidebar). The U.S. Supreme Court disagreed and affirmed the lower court's upholding of Virginia law.

Commerce Clause of the United States Constitution

The so-called Commerce Clause of Section 8 of the United States Constitution provides that "The Congress shall have power to... regulate commerce with foreign nations, and among the several states, and with the Indian tribes."

The Court determined that insurance is not interstate commerce; insurance is a contract that is delivered locally. The Court's unanimous opinion against Paul concluded by saying:

> Issuing a policy of insurance is not a transaction of commerce. The policies are simple contracts of indemnity against loss by fire. . . . They are not commodities to be shipped or forwarded from one State to another, and then put up for sale. They are like other personal contracts between parties

which are completed by their signature and the transfer of the consideration.... The policies do not take effect—are not executed contracts—until delivered by the agent in Virginia. They are, then, local transactions, governed by local law.[3]

Thus, the U.S. Supreme Court upheld state regulation of insurance. Virginia could continue to regulate its insurance market.

Insurers were not happy with the Paul decision. By 1869, many insurers were operating in more than one state, and they found it difficult to meet the states' varying demands. In a long line of subsequent cases, usually involving an insurance company seeking to defeat state legislation, Paul v. Virginia was cited as the ground for upholding state regulation. By implication, despite few explicit judicial statements, it came to be relied on as supporting the premise that the federal government had no authority over insurance.

Meanwhile, the states had problems determining what areas of the insurance business needed to be regulated and how. In 1871, New York's insurance commissioner met with regulatory representatives from nineteen other states to address their common problems. By 1872, thirty states had become members of this initial regulators' association, known as the National Insurance Convention (NIC).

Rate Regulation

Before the end of the nineteenth century, insurance was considered a private, negotiated contract. Any party who did not like the price did not make the contract. The free market, not the government, determined prices.

Pricing attitudes in American society underwent a fundamental transformation during the period roughly from 1887 to 1916. During those years, major federal legislation, such as the Interstate Commerce Act, the Sherman Act, the Clayton Act, and the Federal Reserve Act, reflected a new business climate in the United States and a new role for the government. The controversies of that time influenced the structure of the insurance business as much as any other business in the United States.

Antitrust Laws

Trusts
Combinations of business firms that attempted to dominate the market and control prices.

Antitrust laws
Laws that prohibit companies from working as a group to set prices, limit supplies, or otherwise engage in activities that would restrict market competition.

A fundamental political question of the time was what to do about the "trusts." **Trusts** were combinations of business firms that attempted to dominate the market and control prices. The market power resulting from such combinations prompted consumer rebellions that spilled over into politics. Many believed these combinations to be an abuse of economic power.

One apparent remedy to the abuse of economic power was to outlaw collusion or conspiracy in restraint of trade. Several states passed **antitrust laws**. In 1890 the U.S. Congress followed suit by enacting the Sherman Antitrust Act (see sidebar), which prohibits contracts, combinations, and conspiracies in restraint of trade and other attempts to monopolize the market. Although first mentioned in this chapter in connection with the history of rate regulation, the Sherman Act is not limited to collusive pricing activities, and it remains in effect today.

Insurance consumers hoped that these state and federal antitrust laws would limit the ability of insurers to raise rates, but it was complicated to apply antitrust laws to insurance.

The Sherman Antitrust Act (1890)—Excerpts

Section 1. Trusts, etc., in restraint of trade illegal; penalty

Every contract, combination in the form of trust or otherwise, or conspiracy, in restraint of trade or commerce among the several States, or with foreign nations, is declared to be illegal. Every person who shall make any contract or engage in any combination or conspiracy hereby declared to be illegal shall be deemed guilty of a felony, and, on conviction thereof, shall be punished by fine not exceeding $10,000,000 if a corporation, or, if any other person, $350,000, or by imprisonment not exceeding three years, or by both said punishments, in the discretion of the court.

Section 2. Monopolizing trade a felony; penalty

Every person who shall monopolize, or attempt to monopolize, or combine or conspire with any other person or persons, to monopolize any part of the trade or commerce among the several States, or with foreign nations, shall be deemed guilty of a felony, and, on conviction thereof, shall be punished by fine not exceeding $10,000,000 if a corporation, or, if any other person, $350,000, or by imprisonment not exceeding three years, or by both said punishments, in the discretion of the court.

. . .

Section 7. "Person" or "persons" defined

The word "person", or "persons", wherever used in sections 1 to 7 of this title shall be deemed to include corporations and associations existing under or authorized by the laws of either the United States, the laws of any of the Territories, the laws of any State, or the laws of any foreign country.

Insurance Rating Bureaus

Insurance rates were probably never determined in an entirely free market. When competition did exist, insurers cut prices to levels that could not support severe losses. Catastrophes wiped out many insurance companies. Insurers often tried to organize the market to control rates and break this devastating cycle.

The normal way to organize the market was to devise a rate "tariff" listing the prescribed rates for different types of loss exposures. Insurers agreed to abide by the tariff. In time, loss statistics helped to refine the tariffs to reflect the degree of risk inherent in the various classes of business.

Antitrust sentiments began to flourish in the United States between the 1880s and 1910s. By 1912, twenty-three states had passed anticompact legislation, designed to prohibit insurer compacts or associations from controlling rates. Such associations were viewed as deterrents to open and free competition—and, in effect, they were. However, they also helped to prevent insurer insolvency.

Eventually, however, states came to support insurance industry control of insurance rates through rating bureaus (see sidebar).

A Brief History of Insurance Rating Bureaus

Early rating bureaus were privately owned, often by only one person, to avoid state antitrust laws.

Eventually state restrictions were removed, and a fire insurance rating bureau was established in every state. The need for uniform approaches to ratemaking and form language led to regional advisory organizations, which eventually took control of the local bureaus in their regions.

In 1960 these organizations were consolidated into the Inter-Regional Insurance Conference, later the Fire Insurance Research and Actuarial Association, and they eventually became part of Insurance Services Office (ISO), formed in 1971.

In addition to the fire rate bureaus, separate rating bureaus developed for inland marine, casualty, surety, workers compensation, and multiple-lines insurance.

Although at one time they were known as rating bureaus that promulgated insurance rates, their successor organizations are now known as advisory organizations that provide statistical data in the form of loss costs for insurers to use in developing their own rates.

In 1923, The National Convention of Insurance Commissioners (NCIC, the renamed NIC) passed a resolution to bring about the repeal of state anti-compact laws. Insurance regulators had reached the conclusion that rate bureaus and insurer compacts or associations were necessary if insurers were to develop and maintain adequate rates and avoid unfair discrimination. By 1925, most insurance regulators were actively pursuing the repeal of their states' anticompact laws.

In a 1925 case not involving insurance, the U.S. Supreme Court affirmed that in certain areas, public policy favors the exchange of cost and pricing information in a competitive environment. With this blessing, states continued to expand their regulation of insurance rates, and rating bureaus became the preferred way to gather the necessary information. The bureaus also imposed considerable structure on the industry.

South-Eastern Underwriters Association Decision

As state antitrust laws were repealed, insurer compacts—often subject to state regulation—once again began to take hold. Among these compacts was the South-Eastern Underwriters Association (SEUA), which comprised nearly 200 private stock insurers that controlled about 90 percent of the fire and allied lines insurance market in six southeastern states—Alabama, Florida, Georgia, North Carolina, South Carolina, and Virginia.

The state of Missouri wanted a federal challenge to rating bureaus, and the SEUA seemed like an ideal target. Even though Missouri had no connection with SEUA, the attorney general of Missouri tried to stop the SEUA's rate fixing and filed a complaint with the Antitrust Division of the United States Department of Justice. A federal investigation ensued, and criminal indictments were brought against the SEUA, twenty-seven of its officers, and all of its members for the following activities:

- Continuing agreement and concert of action to take control of 90 percent of the fire and allied lines insurance market

- Fixing premium rates and agents' commissions

- Using boycott and other forms of coercion and intimidation to force non-SEUA members to comply with SEUA rules

- Withdrawing the rights of agents to represent SEUA members if the agents also represented non-SEUA companies

- Threatening insurance consumers with boycott and loss of patronage if they did not purchase their insurance from SEUA members

The District Court of the United States for the Northern District of Georgia dismissed the case based on the U.S. Supreme Court's decision in Paul v. Virginia. On appeal, the U.S. Supreme Court agreed to hear the SEUA case in 1944. The Court noted that each of the activities, if performed by companies that were not insurers, would have been subject to prosecution under the Sherman Act. The SEUA was not denying this, but contended that it was not subject to the Sherman Act because of the Paul v. Virginia decision.

In analyzing the case, the Court considered the following two questions:

1. Was the Sherman Act intended to prohibit fire insurance company conduct that restrains or monopolizes the interstate fire insurance trade?

2. If so, do fire insurance transactions that stretch across state lines constitute "commerce among the several states" so as to make them subject to regulation by Congress under the Commerce Clause of the U.S. Constitution?

In answer to the first question, the Court determined that the Sherman Act was intended to prohibit the kinds of conduct exhibited by the interstate fire insurers and SEUA. Thus, the second question became crucial. The Court decided that insurance is commerce as referred to in the Commerce Clause of the Constitution and, as such, is subject to regulation by Congress. In support of this determination, the Court advanced these arguments:

- Insurance is not a business that is distinct in each of the states, but is interrelated, interdependent, and integrated across the states. Individuals in several different states can obtain insurance from the same insurance company. The decisions made by insurers consider not only the environment of the state of domicile but also of the states in which products are sold.

- Both before and after the Paul v. Virginia decision, intangible products, such as electrical impulses of telegraph transmissions, were subject to regulation by Congress.

- Other businesses make sales contracts in states where they are not headquartered, and these businesses are subject to regulation by Congress.

Perhaps the Court's entire argument for federal regulation of insurance can be best summed up this way: *No commercial enterprise of any kind that conducts its activities across state lines has been held to be wholly beyond the regulatory powers of Congress under the Commerce Clause. We cannot make an exception for the business of insurance.*

The Supreme Court's decision stunned state insurance regulators and the insurance industry. The system of insurance regulation that had existed for years and that regulators and regulated preferred was now in jeopardy.

The immediate effect of the SEUA decision was that federal legislation now applied to insurance:

- The Sherman Act (1890) prohibits collusion in attempts to gain monopoly power. Any activity that restrains trade or commerce and any attempt to monopolize are illegal. Thus, insurance companies could no longer band together, as in the SEUA and similar groups, to control rates and coverages.

- The Clayton Act (1914) together with its amendment, the Robinson-Patman Act (1936), prohibits practices that lessen competition or create monopoly power. The types of activities declared illegal include price discrimination, tying (requiring the purchase of one product when purchasing another product) and exclusive dealing, and mergers between competitors. The Robinson-Patman Act limited price discrimination only to price differentials that could be attributed to differences in operating costs resulting from competing "in good faith." Thus, insurers could no longer cut premiums to drive out competition unless the insurers could prove that the drop in rates was caused by increased efficiencies in operations.

- The Federal Trade Commission (FTC) Act (1914) prohibits unfair methods of competition and unfair or deceptive trade practices, thus, promoting competition and protecting consumers.[4]

Together, those federal acts meant the end of business as usual for the insurance industry. However, state insurance regulators, as well as those in the industry, believed that some forms of cooperation, especially with respect to establishing the statistical base for adequate rates, were necessary for the insurance mechanism to function effectively. The National Association of

Insurance Commissioners (NAIC; the NCIC was renamed in the 1930s) worked to fight federal regulation.

McCarran-Ferguson Act

In 1945, the year following the SEUA decision, Congress passed the McCarran-Ferguson Act (McCarran). McCarran, which is reproduced in Exhibit 2-1, essentially gave the NAIC and the insurance business what they wanted.

Subject to certain conditions, McCarran returned regulation of the "business of insurance" to the states. Congress justified the legislation on the basis that it was "in the public interest."

One condition of McCarran is extremely important because, if it is not met, Congress can take over the regulation of the "business of insurance." Under sections 1012 and 1013 of McCarran, the Sherman Act, the Clayton Act, the FTC Act, and the Robinson-Patman Act do not apply to the "business of insurance" *unless* the states are not regulating the activities described in the acts. That condition, however, is subject to an exception: The Sherman Act continues to apply to boycott, coercion, or intimidation by insurers.

In other words, states must have their own antitrust legislation and their own unfair trade practices legislation if they want to prevent the federal government from enforcing these Acts. Even then, state legislation does not supersede federal authority regarding boycott, coercion, and intimidation. Furthermore, if Congress passes a law that applies only to the insurance business, not to business in general, the federal law supersedes any state regulation in the areas addressed by the federal legislation.

Section 1014 of McCarran prohibits states from controlling labor relations. Thus, insurers are still subject to federal regulation regarding labor relations.

With the passage of McCarran in 1945, the NAIC and state legislatures began an extremely busy period of developing and implementing various insurance laws that were designed to allow cooperation in setting rates and to keep Congress from interfering rather than to promote competition.[5] Under McCarran, the states had until 1948 to pass legislation to regulate insurance and thus to limit federal regulation.

NAIC's principal concerns were concerted ratemaking and unfair trade practices. In 1946, the NAIC approved two model rate regulation bills—one that applied to liability insurers and another that applied to fire, marine, and inland marine insurers. The purposes of those two bills were as follows:

1. To ensure that rates were not excessive, were not unfairly discriminatory, and were adequate, and

2. To allow cooperation in setting rates, as long as it did not hinder competition.

While most states enacted some form of rate regulation, many states did not closely follow the NAIC models. However, the various state laws met the requirements under McCarran and therefore preempted the provisions of the

EXHIBIT 2-1

McCarran-Ferguson Act
Public Law 15

McCarran-Ferguson Act 15 U.S.C.

Sections 1011-1015 March 9, 1945
Section 1011.

The Congress hereby declares that the continued regulation and taxation by the several States of the business of insurance is in the public interest, and that silence on the part of the Congress shall not be construed to impose any barrier to the regulation or taxation of such business by the several States.

Section 1012.

(a) The business of insurance, and every person engaged therein, shall be subject to the laws of the several States which relate to the regulation or taxation of such business.

(b) No act of Congress shall be construed to invalidate, impair, or supersede any law enacted by any State for the purpose of regulating the business of insurance, or which imposes a fee or a tax upon such business, unless such Act specifically relates to the business of insurance: Provided, that after June 30, 1948, the Act of July 2, 1890, as amended, known as the Sherman Act, and the Act of October 15, 1914, as amended, known as the Clayton Act, and the Act of September 26, 1914, known as the Federal Trade Commission Act, as amended, shall be applicable to the business of insurance to the extent that such business is not regulated by State law.

Section 1013.

(a) Until July 30, 1948, the Act of July 2, 1890, as amended, known as the Sherman Act, and the Act of October 15, 1914, as amended, known as the Clayton Act, and the Act of September 26, 1914, known as the Federal Trade Commission Act, as amended, and the Act of June 19, 1936, known as the Robinson-Patman Antidiscrimination Act, shall not apply to the business of insurance or to acts in the conduct thereof.

(b) Nothing contained in this Act shall render the said Sherman Act inapplicable to any agreement to boycott, coerce, or intimidate, or act of boycott, coercion, or intimidation.

Section 1014.

Nothing contained in this Act shall be construed to affect in any manner the application to the business of insurance of the Act of July 5, 1935, as amended, known as the National Labor Relations Act, or the Act of June 25, 1938, as amended, known as the Fair Labor Standards Act of 1938, or the Act of June 5, 1920, known as the Merchant Marine Act, 1920.

Section 1015.

As used in this Act, the term "State" includes the several States, Alaska, Hawaii, Puerto Rico, Guam, and the District of Columbia.

Robinson-Patman Act, the FTC Act, and the Sherman Act regarding cooperative ratemaking.

In 1947, the NAIC adopted the Act Relating to Unfair Methods of Competition and Unfair Deceptive Acts and Practices in the Business of Insurance. The purpose of that act was primarily to preempt the application of the FTC Act to the insurance industry. The NAIC's model act described certain activities that were deemed to be methods of unfair competition or unfair and deceptive practices and acts. Most states enacted laws that were quite similar to the NAIC model.[6] By the end of 1947, the NAIC and the states felt that they had preempted the federal legislation that would have the most damaging effect on the insurance business.

ISO and the Attorneys General Lawsuit

Insurance Services Office (ISO)

On January 1, 1971, six separate national service bureaus (then known as rating bureaus) consolidated to form Insurance Services Office (ISO). By the end of 1971, nine local or regional property bureaus were also brought into ISO.

ISO's role has changed over the years. As of June 1987, ISO characterized itself as follows:

> a national, non-profit corporation that gathers, stores and disseminates aggregate statistical information to insurance regulators—as required by law—and to insurers for their use. In addition, ISO develops and assists in implementing insurance policy coverage programs that help to define and cover the risks faced by policyholders. ISO also distributes industrywide advisory rate information and, where appropriate, files that information with state insurance regulators.[7]

As of 2002, ISO is a for-profit corporation, and the rating information it provides involves "loss costs" rather than advisory rates. Each insurance company that subscribes to ISO services may base its premium rates on its own expenses, as well as on ISO's loss cost information. ISO continues to develop insurance policy forms and coverage programs that are adopted by a large proportion of property-casualty insurance companies.

Some of the changes at ISO evolved over time, due, in part, to the expanding capabilities of computer technology. Other changes were based on opportunities to provide new services or to consolidate or partner with other related organizations.

The most major changes, however, were the result of a 1988 lawsuit by seven states' attorneys general that once again raised antitrust issues.

The Attorneys General Lawsuit

As noted earlier, antitrust law prohibits companies from working as a group to set prices, limit supplies, or otherwise engage in activities that would restrict competition in the marketplace. Under the McCarran-Ferguson Act, the insurance business had a limited exemption to federal antitrust law to allow joint development of common insurance forms and the sharing of data for the calculation of premiums. However, McCarran did not free insurers from federal antitrust law.

In 1988, the attorneys general of California, New York, and five other states filed antitrust lawsuits in federal District Court in San Francisco, charging that major insurance companies, domestic and foreign reinsurers, and industry associations—thirty-two defendants in all—had conspired to create a global boycott of certain types of commercial general liability coverages, particularly coverage for environmental damages stemming from pollution. Twelve other states subsequently joined the federal suit.

The lawsuit focused on a narrow aspect of the overall insurance market-place—the development of new policy language by ISO. The suit alleged that the defendants engaged in a secret "global conspiracy" to draft restrictive policy language and that the "conspiracy" led to the mid-1980s liability insurance crisis. Six years of litigation ensued.

In October 1994, insurers, the attorneys general from twenty states, and several private plaintiffs reached an out-of-court settlement. Under this agreement, the thirty-two insurance companies and insurance industry organizations would pay $36 million to establish the Public Entity Risk Institute.[8] The Institute would provide risk-management education and technical services and a public entity insurance database for local government agencies. Part of the $36 million would be used to reimburse the states and private plaintiffs for legal expenses.[9]

As part of the settlement, ISO was reorganized. ISO's board was reconstituted to comprise three insurance company executives, seven noninsurers, and ISO's president as chairman. ISO continues its role as a statistical agent for regulators in almost every state. Insurer committees have been dissolved and replaced with insurer advisory panels, whose members make recommendations in their areas of expertise. Rate and form decisions are made, not by insurer committees, but by ISO staff.

In general, ISO continued providing similar products and services for insurers. However, the changes involved in the settlement helped to eliminate a perception that ISO provided a vehicle for collusion among insurers.

Financial Services Modernization

The question of state versus federal insurance regulation has never completely disappeared. Quite the contrary, many times during the last fifty years, it seemed likely to again become a major legislative issue. The issue finally came to the fore during the 1990s, when affiliations between banks and insurers began to take place, and questions arose about who would regulate these "bankassurance" organizations. Banking activities had traditionally been regulated by the federal government and, in some cases, by the states, while insurance was regulated only by the states.

The Gramm-Leach-Bliley Act (GLB) was an attempt to address this issue definitively. However, although GLB answered some questions, it raised many others that have not yet been clearly resolved, at least at the time this is written.

GLB was signed into law by President Clinton in November 1999.[10] Under the Act, each segment of the financial services industry is regulated separately. As to insurance, the functional regulation provisions of GLB reaffirm the McCarran-Ferguson Act, making it clear that states continue to have primary regulatory authority for all insurance activities. However, the Act prohibits state actions that would prevent bank-related firms from selling insurance on the same basis as other insurance agents. Meanwhile, securities activities are regulated by securities regulators, and banking activities are regulated by banking regulators.

GLB also treats insurance underwriting differently from insurance sales and marketing. National banks are prohibited from underwriting insurance through an operating subsidiary. However, they may create an insurance affiliate under a bank holding company structure. This arrangement makes it more difficult for a failing bank to tap insurance assets.

Privacy is a concern frequently raised in connection with information-sharing among banks and insurance affiliates. Privacy issues are addressed in a section of the Act requiring banks to disclose to customers their information-sharing policies and practices. Because states are permitted to have laws that are more restrictive than federal regulations, this provision could lead to some inconsistency in practice.

The new law is also designed to force states to make it easier for insurance agents who want to operate in more than one state. GLB contains a provision that gave the states three years to adopt full reciprocal licensing requirements. If at least twenty-nine states failed to enact reciprocity within this time frame, the law would establish a National Association of Registered Agents and Brokers (NARAB) under which agencies could choose to be federally licensed. As this target has been met, NARAB will probably not be established. The NAIC also responded to the requirements in GLB by creating a Producer Licensing Model Act that satisfies the NARAB provisions. This act requires states to establish either a system of reciprocal producer licensing or uniform standards for licensing. These reciprocity and uniformity issues will continue to evolve over the next few years as regulators, insurers, and producers continue to seek solutions to streamline producer licensing procedures.

An editorial in the *National Underwriter* noted the following:

> On the horizon is a potentially new world of integrated financial services which, if the optimists are correct, will provide consumers with exciting product innovations and lower costs.[11]

At the same time, the editorial noted, financial services modernization might give rise to a new set of issues, including:

- Privacy of personal financial information
- An increasingly critical view of the future of state regulation for an integrated and global financial services industry
- Whether consumers want or need integrated financial services

Commercial Insurance Deregulation

The complexity of state-by-state rate and form regulation created increasing pressure for a simpler regulatory system. Rather than adopting federal regulation, states have begun to deregulate commercial insurance for large corporations that have the expertise necessary to evaluate complex pricing contracts and pricing systems.

By September 2000, some twenty states had enacted laws deregulating commercial rate and/or form filing requirements, and many others were considering similar steps. Regulators also said they would review regulations for personal insurance.[12]

Both the extent of deregulation and the eligibility requirements vary by state. Commercial insureds must generally meet certain specified criteria that establish their size and sophistication as insurance buyers. These criteria may include, for example, a specified minimum insurance premium level, minimum annual net revenues or sales, a minimum number of employees, and the presence of a full-time risk manager.

A bill introduced in the Virginia Senate in January 2000, for example, would exempt "from rate and form filing business involving an entity that employs 'a qualified risk manager' to negotiate insurance coverage on a full-time basis and meets at least two of these criteria:

- Has a net worth of more than $10 million.
- Generates over $25 million in annual revenues.
- Employs more than 50 full-time workers or is a member of an affiliated group with over 100 employees.
- Pays annual aggregate nation-wide insurance premiums (except for professional liability insurance premiums) of over $75,000.
- In the case of a non-profit or public entity, has annual budgeted expenditures of over $10,000.
- Is a municipality with a population of more than 30,000."[13]

WHY IS INSURANCE REGULATED?

Insurers are regulated primarily for the following three reasons:

1. To protect consumers

2. To maintain insurer solvency
3. To avoid destructive competition

Although these objectives clearly overlap, each is examined separately.

Protect Consumers

When people buy food, clothing, or furniture, they can usually inspect the items beforehand to make sure they will meet their needs. Even if they inspect the insurance policies they purchase, most consumers are not equipped to analyze and understand complex legal documents. Regulators help to protect policyholders by reviewing insurance policy forms to determine that they benefit consumers. Regulators can set coverage standards, specify policy language for certain insurance coverages, and disapprove contracts that do not meet with the regulators' approval.

Insurance regulators also protect consumers against fraud and unethical market behavior. Most insurance representatives are honest and ethical, but exceptions such as the following unfortunately exist:

*   Insurance representatives have sold insurance that was not needed.
*   Producers have misrepresented the nature of coverage to make a sale.
*   Insurers have engaged in unfair claims practices, refusing to pay legitimate claims or unfairly reducing the amounts paid.
*   Dishonest insurance managers have contributed to the insolvency of insurers.

Regulation can help to protect policyholders against such abuses.

Regulators often attempt to ensure that insurance is readily available, especially those types that tend to be viewed as necessities. For example, all states now attempt to ensure that continuous auto insurance coverage is available by restricting the rights of insurers to cancel or nonrenew auto insurance policies. However, insurers prefer to avoid unbreakable long-term relationships with insurance buyers whose exposures they would like to reevaluate periodically. Cancellation restrictions aimed at promoting availability can therefore lead insurers to reject more new-business applications, which reduces insurance availability.

Insurance regulators also help to keep consumers informed regarding insurance matters, so that consumers can better protect themselves.

Maintain Insurer Solvency

Solvency regulation seeks to protect policyholders against the risk that insurers will be unable to meet their financial obligations. Consumers and, indeed, even sophisticated business people are in no position to evaluate the financial ability of insurers to live up to their promises. Insurance regulators attempt to maintain and enhance the financial condition of private insurers for several reasons:

*   *Insurance provides* future *protection.* Premiums are paid in advance, but the period of protection extends into the future. If insurers become insolvent,

future claims might not be paid, and the insurance protection already paid for might become worthless.

- *Regulation is needed to protect the public interest.* Large numbers of individuals and the community at large are adversely affected when insurers become insolvent.

- *Insurers have a responsibility to policyholders.* Insurance companies hold substantial sums of money for the ultimate benefit of policyholders. Government regulation is necessary to safeguard such holdings.

Insurance companies have become insolvent despite regulatory reviews. However, sound regulation should minimize the number of insolvencies. Solvency regulation is covered in more detail later in this chapter.

Avoid Destructive Competition

Regulators are responsible for determining that premium levels are high enough to avoid destructive competition. At times, some insurers underprice their products to increase market share by attracting customers away from higher-priced competitors. This practice drives down price levels in the market as a whole. When market rate levels are inadequate, some insurers can become insolvent, and others might withdraw from the market or stop writing new business. An insurance shortage can then develop, and individuals and firms might be unable to obtain the coverage they need. Certain types of insurance can become unavailable at any price.

The insurance business remains very competitive, and insurers have indeed become insolvent because they were unable to handle the competition. Although destructive competition remains a regulatory concern, regulatory attention in recent years seems to have focused more on keeping rates down than on ensuring that rates are high enough.

WHO REGULATES INSURANCE?

The business of insurance is regulated by state insurance departments. State regulators, in turn, are members of the National Association of Insurance Commissioners (NAIC), a nonprofit corporation that has no regulatory authority of its own but plays an important coordinating role. Insurers are also subject to a variety of federal regulations that also affect noninsurance businesses. Although not discussed here, most of the same state and local regulations that affect other businesses, such as zoning laws that restrict insurers' office locations, also apply to insurers.

State Insurance Departments

Every state has three separate and equal branches of government: legislative, judicial, and executive.

- The legislative branch makes the laws.
- The judicial branch (the court system) interprets the laws.
- The executive branch implements the laws.

Day-to-day regulation of the insurance business is done by state insurance departments, which fall within the executive branch of each state government. State insurance departments enforce the various insurance laws enacted by the legislature. These laws regulate the formation of insurers, capital and surplus requirements, licensing of agents and brokers, investment of funds, financial requirements for maintaining solvency, insurance rates that can be charged, marketing and claim practices, taxation of insurers, and the rehabilitation of financially impaired insurers or the liquidation of insolvent insurers.

Under the direction of the insurance commissioner, a state insurance department engages in a wide variety of regulatory activities that typically include:

- Approving policy forms
- Holding rate hearings and reviewing rate filings
- Licensing new insurers
- Licensing agents and brokers
- Investigating policyholder complaints
- Rehabilitating or liquidating insolvent insurers
- Issuing cease-and-desist orders
- Conducting periodic examinations of insurers by field examiners, including claims and underwriting audits
- Evaluating solvency information
- Performing market conduct examinations
- Fining insurers that violate state law
- Publishing shoppers' guides and other consumer information (in some states) in paper form and through the Internet

These activities require professional skill and expertise. However, the states vary widely in the amount of money spent to carry out their activities, even when population and premium volume are similar.

The Insurance Commissioner

Every state insurance department is headed by an insurance commissioner, superintendent, or director appointed by the governor or elected by the voting public.

The duties of a typical state insurance commissioner include:

- Overseeing the operation of the state insurance department
- Promulgating orders, rules, and regulations necessary for administration of insurance laws
- Determining whether to issue business licenses to new insurance companies, agents, and brokers, and other insurance entities
- Reviewing insurance pricing and coverage
- Handling financial and market conduct examinations of insurers

- Holding hearings on insurance issues
- Taking action when violation of insurance laws occur
- Issuing an annual report on the status of the state's insurance industry and insurance department
- Maintaining records of insurance department activities

Most of these tasks are not handled personally by the commissioner but are delegated to others in the state insurance department.

Although most commissioners are appointed, many states now have elected commissioners. Disagreement exists regarding which method of selection better serves the public interest. Proponents of an elective system cite the following arguments:

- An appointed insurance commissioner is subject to dismissal, while an elected commissioner is generally in office for a full term.

- An appointed commissioner might continue regulating in the same manner as his or her predecessor when a different approach is required, but an elected commissioner would more likely change the insurance department's stance.

- An appointed commissioner might not be aware of the public's concerns, but an elected commissioner is keenly aware of the issues important to the public.

- An appointed commissioner might feel inclined to yield to the interests of those responsible for the appointment, while an elected commissioner is not obligated to any particular group or special interest.

Those who favor appointing insurance commissioners raise the following arguments:

- An appointed commissioner has no need to campaign or to be unduly influenced by political contributors.

- An experienced and knowledgeable person can be designated as an insurance commissioner.

- An appointed commissioner is less likely to be swayed by ill-informed public opinion than an elected one.

- An appointed commissioner is more likely to be perceived as a career government employee interested in regulation than as a politician interested in political advancement.

Many commissioners are employed in the insurance business before they enter public office, and many are employed by insurers or insurance-related organizations after leaving office. The expertise necessary to understand insurance operations well enough to regulate effectively can most likely be found in a person who has worked in the insurance industry. Usually, at any given time, a few insurance commissioners are CPCUs. Because of their industry ties, it is sometimes alleged that insurance commissioners have less than an arm's-length relationship with the companies they regulate.

In rebuttal, state insurance commissioners deny they are overly responsive to private insurers. Commissioners frequently regulate in ways objectionable to the industry, such as issuing cease-and-desist orders, fining or penalizing insurers for infractions of the law, forbidding them to engage in mass cancellations, limiting rate increases, and taking numerous other actions that benefit policyholders at the expense of insurers.

Funding for State Regulation

State insurance departments are funded in part by state premium taxes, audit fees, filing fees, and licensing fees, but premium taxes are the major source of revenue. Although state premium taxes are substantial, only a relatively small proportion is spent on insurance regulation. Premium taxes are designed primarily to raise revenues for the states.

The National Association of Insurance Commissioners (NAIC)

The **National Association of Insurance Commissioners (NAIC)**, a forum for insurance regulators, has no direct regulatory authority. However, by providing a forum for the development of uniform policy when appropriate, the NAIC has a profound effect on the nature and uniformity of state regulation.

National Association of Insurance Commissioners (NAIC)
A forum for insurance regulators that has no direct regulatory authority but does profoundly affect state regulation by its actions.

The NAIC meets quarterly to discuss important industry problems and issues in insurance regulation. It assists state insurance departments by developing model laws and regulations and by sharing financial information about insurers. In addition, the NAIC developed uniform financial statement forms that all states require insurers to file.

Model Laws and Regulations

Laws are passed by the state legislature, while regulations are developed and enforced by a regulatory body such as the state insurance department. A **model law** is a draft bill—the suggested wording of a new law—for consideration by state legislatures; any state may choose to adopt the model bill or to adopt it with modifications. A **model regulation** is a draft of a regulation that may be implemented by a state insurance department if the model law is passed.

Model law
A draft bill—the suggested wording of a new law—for consideration by state legislatures. Any state may choose to adopt the model bill or adopt it with modifications.

Model regulation
A draft of a regulation that may be implemented by a state insurance department if the model law is passed.

The laws and regulations of many states follow at least the main idea of NAIC models, resulting in some degree of uniformity among the states. Examples of model laws include model legislation regarding the regulation of risk retention groups, and a model property and liability insurance rating law.

Sharing Financial Information

The NAIC provides important financial information to the states about most insurers that are potentially insolvent.

Accreditation

In 1990, the NAIC implemented an accreditation program to increase the uniformity of insurer solvency regulation across the states. To become accredited, a state must prove that it has satisfied the minimum solvency regulation standards required by the accreditation program.

States must meet three criteria to satisfy the NAIC's Financial Regulation Standards and to be accredited:

1. The laws and regulations the state uses must meet certain basic standards of NAIC models.
2. The state's regulatory methods must be acceptable.
3. Department practices must be adequate.

As of June 2001, all but three states had become accredited.[14]

Federal Regulation

Although the McCarran-Ferguson Act did not completely eliminate federal regulatory authority over insurance, it did return most responsibility for insurance regulation to the states. McCarran gave the states primary regulatory control over the "business of insurance" in most areas, subject to several important exceptions:

1. The federal Sherman Act prohibits boycott, coercion, and intimidation.
2. Federal antitrust laws apply to the extent that state laws do not regulate such activities.
3. Federal laws enacted specifically to regulate the "business of insurance" preempt any state laws applying to the same activities addressed by the federal laws.

McCarran also did not repeal the federal antitrust laws with respect to the insurance industry. Under McCarran, federal regulation, including antitrust legislation, is inapplicable to the "business of insurance," (1) to the extent that the "business of insurance" is regulated by the states and (2) when no boycott, coercion, or intimidation has occurred.

McCarran reverses the usual state-federal allocation of regulatory powers only for the "business of insurance," and the "business of insurance" does not include everything that insurance companies do. For example:

- As employers, insurance companies are subject to federal employment laws just like any other business.
- As businesses that sell their stock to the public to raise capital, stock insurance companies are subject to SEC regulations like any other business.

McCarran did not define what constituted the "business of insurance." For this and other reasons, the antitrust exemption granted to the insurance industry remains somewhat unclear. Based on the court decisions rendered thus far, the meaning of the "business of insurance" appears to involve a three-pronged test.[15] The "business of insurance" is defined as any activity that has one or more of the following three characteristics:

1. The risk of the policyholder or insured is shared and underwritten by the insurer.
2. A direct contractual connection exists between the insurer and the insured.
3. The activity is unique to entities within the insurance industry.

Activities deemed to be part of the "business of insurance" receive the protection from federal intervention allowed under McCarran. That is, they are primarily subject to state insurance regulation if it exists. If states do not oversee these activities, or if the federal government enacts legislation to deal with them, they are subject to federal regulation. However, the Sherman Act applies to any activities that involve boycott, coercion, or intimidation. Furthermore, if activities are not considered part of the "business of insurance" even though they are performed within the insurance industry, federal regulation applies as it would to other businesses in general.

Insurance Fraud Protection Act

The **Insurance Fraud Protection Act** became law in 1994 as part of a federal anti-crime bill titled, "Violent Crime Control and Law Enforcement Act of 1994."[16] This broad legislation was intended to help protect consumers and insurance companies against insolvencies resulting from insurance fraud.

Especially noteworthy is Section (e) of the Act, which applies to:

- Any individual who has been convicted of a felony involving dishonesty or a breach of trust and who willfully engages or participates in the business of insurance whose activities involve interstate commerce

- Anyone engaged in the business of insurance whose activities affect interstate commerce and who willfully permits participation in the business by an individual convicted of a felony or breach of trust

In effect, the Act prohibits anyone who has been convicted of a felony that involved trustworthiness from ever working in the business of insurance unless he or she secures the written consent of an insurance regulatory official. Moreover, it is illegal for insurers, reinsurers, agents and brokers, and others to employ a person who has been convicted of a felony involving breach of trust or dishonesty. Penalties for violating this provision can extend up to five years' imprisonment, plus a fine. "Dishonesty or a breach of trust" is not defined in the Act.

Sections (a) through (d) of the Act create four substantive crimes involving the business of insurance:

- Making false statements or reports to insurance regulators—including overvaluing assets—for the purpose of affecting the regulators' decisions

- Making false entries in books, reports, or statements with the intent to deceive anyone about an insurance company's financial condition or solvency

Insurance Fraud Protection Act
A federal law intended to help protect consumers and insurance companies against insolvencies resulting from insurance fraud. It prohibits anyone who has been convicted of a felony that involved trustworthiness from conducting insurance activities without the written consent of an insurance regulatory official and prohibits insurers from employing such persons.

- Embezzling from anyone who is engaged in the business of insurance
- Using threats or force or "any threatening letter or communication to corruptly influence, obstruct, or impede" insurance regulatory proceedings[17]

For any of these offenses, the Act provides for a possible fine, as well as imprisonment for as long as ten years. If the conduct in question "jeopardized the safety and soundness of an insurer and was a significant cause of such insurer being placed in conservation, rehabilitation or liquidation," the imprisonment can extend to fifteen years.

"Business of Insurance" is defined in this Act as "the writing of insurance, or the reinsuring of risks, by an insurer, including all acts necessary or incidental to such writing or reinsuring and the activities of persons who act as, or are, officers, directors, agents, or employees of insurers or who are other persons authorized to act on behalf of such persons."[18]

Federal Regulations Affecting the Insurance Industry

For activities that are not part of the "business of insurance," federal regulation applies to insurers as it would to any business. In this regard, the insurance industry is subject to federal regulation in many areas—antitrust, employee benefits, securities, taxation, and so on.

Federal Antitrust Laws

Because of McCarran, federal antitrust laws apply to insurance only to the extent that the industry is not regulated by state law. As mentioned earlier, federal antitrust laws generally do not apply to insurance, but the exemption is not absolute. The Sherman Act forbids firms from engaging in any acts or agreements to boycott, coerce, or intimidate; insurers remain subject to federal law in these areas.

Employee Retirement Income Security Act of 1974 (ERISA)

Employee Retirement Income Security Act (ERISA)
A federal law passed by Congress to protect the interests of participants in employee benefit plans, as well as the interests of their beneficiaries.

The **Employee Retirement Income Security Act (ERISA)** was passed by Congress to protect the interests of participants in employee benefit plans, as well as the interests of their beneficiaries. ERISA's complex requirements in many ways directly affect the design of health and life insurance and annuity products that must comply with ERISA. For example, private pension plans subject to the act must meet certain minimum funding standards. ERISA is administered by the Department of Labor and the Treasury Department.

ERISA supersedes state laws, other than insurance regulatory laws, that relate to employee benefit plans. Self-funded employee benefit plans not subject to state insurance regulation are regulated by ERISA.

Securities and Exchange Commission (SEC)

Like other publicly held corporations, an insurance company whose stock is publicly traded must comply with the disclosure requirements of the federal securities laws. Responsibility for enforcing these laws rests with the **Securities and Exchange Commission (SEC).**

While the financial statements filed with state insurance regulators must meet the states' statutory accounting principles (SAP) requirements, financial statements filed with the SEC must be in accordance with the Generally Accepted Accounting Principles (GAAP) standards applicable to corporations in general.

The SEC is responsible for, in addition to accounting requirements, regulating variable life insurance and variable annuities, products sold by life insurers. Because variable annuities are investments, a 1959 Supreme Court decision[19] held that they should be subject to many of the same federal laws and regulations as other securities. Life insurance agents who want to sell variable annuities must be licensed by the SEC; a state life insurance agent's license does not grant authority to sell variable annuities.

Securities and Exchange Commission (SEC)
A federal law that enforces the disclosure requirements of federal securities laws applying to publicly traded stocks.

Internal Revenue Code

Basically, insurance companies are taxed like other corporations. However, special sections of the Internal Revenue Code deal specifically with insurer operations and supersede certain portions of the general tax law, recognizing the unique characteristics of insurance companies. Special treatment is given to the calculation of underwriting income, which is determined as the difference between premiums earned on insurance contracts during the tax year and losses and expenses incurred, an approach that parallels statutory rather than GAAP accounting. Other tax-code provisions apply to methods for ascertaining the reasonableness of estimated loss reserves and to the ways in which investment income and capital gains and losses are calculated.

Other Federal Actions Affecting Insurers

Even without regulating insurers themselves, federal government regulation directly affects the insurance industry in many ways. For example, following are a few federal regulations that require organizations to purchase insurance from private insurers:

- Motor truck cargo carriers must carry compulsory liability insurance purchased from private insurers. The amount of required insurance depends on type of carrier and goods carried. For nonhazardous goods such as meat or produce, at least $750,000 of liability insurance must be carried by for-hire carriers. For hazardous materials such as gasoline or explosives, substantially higher limits are required.
- The Environmental Protection Agency (EPA) requires firms with underground storage tanks to meet certain financial responsibility rules, including carrying third-party liability insurance and coverage for on-site and off-site cleanup. The financial responsibility requirements vary depending on the situation. For example, if the tanks are used in petroleum production, refining, or marketing, the firm must carry at least $1 million of liability coverage for each occurrence.

- Firms that bid on government contracts may be required to furnish surety bonds and to carry certain kinds of insurance.

State Versus Federal Regulation

The question of which level of government—state or federal—should regulate insurance is far from settled. Major arguments for federal regulation of insurers include the following:

- *Federal regulation can provide uniformity in regulation among the various states.* Insurers doing business in more than one state currently are confronted with differing laws, regulations, and administrative rules. Under federal regulation, laws and regulations would be uniform. With only one set of laws, regulations, and administrative rules, insurers might have lower expenses.

- *Federal regulation would be more efficient.* Insurers doing business nationally would deal with only one federal agency instead of fifty different insurance departments. Also, a federal agency might be less likely to yield to industry pressures from local or regional insurers. Federal regulation might also be relatively less expensive than state regulation.

- *Federal regulation could attract higher-quality personnel.* If adequately funded, higher salaries and prestige would attract higher-quality personnel who would do a superior job in regulating insurers.

Opponents of federal regulation present different arguments:

- *State regulation is more responsive to local needs.* Conditions vary widely among the states, and state regulators can respond quickly to local problems and needs. In contrast, federal regulation and government bureaucracy would result in considerable delay in solving local problems.

- *Uniformity of state laws can be attained through the NAIC.* As a result of the model laws and regulations of the NAIC, current state laws are reasonably uniform, with due weight given to local circumstances and conditions.

- *Greater opportunities in innovation are possible with state regulation.* An individual state can experiment with a new approach to regulation. If that approach fails, only that state is affected. In contrast, if a new approach to federal regulation fails to meet its objectives, the entire country might feel its effects.

- *State regulation already exists and its strengths and weaknesses are known.* In contrast, the benefits and possible adverse consequences of federal regulation on the insurance industry are unknown. Moreover, some local regulation is inevitable; thus, increased federal involvement would actually result in more "dual" regulation.

- *State regulation results in a desirable decentralization of political power.* In contrast, federal regulation would increase the power of the federal government and dilute states' rights.

The debate over state versus federal insurance regulation seems likely to persist. The increasing role of electronic commerce raises challenging questions about the regulation of transactions that occur in cyberspace. And the changing role of banks—traditionally regulated by the federal government—in marketing insurance, which is traditionally state-regulated, raises an additional range of questions.

Increasingly, large insurance organizations, national or international businesses, and insurance trade associations are raising their voices in favor of a more centralized insurance regulatory system. The complex, fragmented regulatory system within the U.S. looks archaic to international businesses now that the European Economic Community is breaking down barriers among European countries. In response to these and other pressures, the NAIC has begun to take steps that are likely to result in a simplified regulatory structure, less subject to state variation, while preserving many elements of state regulation.

WHAT AREAS ARE REGULATED?

Insurance regulation focuses mostly on the following areas:

- Formation and licensing of insurers
- Licensing of insurance personnel
- Solvency regulation
- Contract regulation
- Rate regulation
- Market conduct
- Consumer protection

Each area is examined below.

Formation and Licensing of Insurers

By issuing a license to an insurer, the state indicates that the insurer meets minimum standards of financial strength, competence, and integrity. If this evaluation later changes, the license can be revoked. A license indicates that the insurer has complied with the state's insurance laws and is authorized to write certain types of insurance in the state. For a new insurance company, the process of obtaining a license can take months or even years.

Once licensed, the insurer is subject to all relevant state laws, rules, and regulations. An insurer licensed to write auto insurance automatically becomes a member of any state auto assigned-risk plan, which provides a market for insureds who are not good risks. An insurer licensed to write property insurance automatically becomes a member of any property residual market program, such as a state FAIR plan or a windstorm or beach plan. In some states, a workers compensation insurer becomes subject to a state-assigned risk plan for that line of insurance.

As explained below, licensing standards vary somewhat among admitted domestic, foreign and alien, and nonadmitted insurers, and risk retention groups face yet another set of standards.

Domestic Insurers

Domestic insurer
An insurance company doing business in its home state.

Foreign insurer
A United States insurance company doing business in a state that is not its home state.

Alien insurer
An insurance company domiciled outside the United States.

After becoming organized, an insurer must be licensed (authorized to transact business) in its home state, where it is considered a **domestic insurer**. A domestic insurer's license generally has no expiration date. If a domestic insurer obtains licenses in states other than its state of domicile, it is a **foreign insurer** in those states. Licenses of foreign insurers and **alien insurers** (domiciled out-of-country) generally have to be renewed annually.

Domestic insurers must usually meet the conditions imposed on corporations engaged in noninsurance activities, as well as some special conditions imposed on insurers. The organizers file an application for a charter giving the names and addresses of the incorporators, the name of the proposed corporation, the territories and lines of insurance in which it plans to operate, the total authorized capital stock (if any), and its surplus. The state insurance commissioner reviews the application to see whether the applicant also meets the state's special licensing requirements.

An insurer must be financially sound. State laws require that domestic stock insurers satisfy certain minimum capital and surplus requirements before a license will be granted. Traditionally, state capital and surplus requirements were criticized on several grounds:

1. The capital and surplus requirements for stock insurers varied widely among the states.
2. Many states had very low minimum requirements.
3. Some states did not relate the amount of capital and surplus to the premium volume to be written.
4. Economic conditions might change the adequacy of a fixed dollar requirement.

Risk-based capital requirements
Statutory requirements that stipulate that each insurer must have a certain amount of capital based on the level of risk of its insurance and investment operations.

During the early 1990s, the NAIC developed model laws that impose risk-based capital requirements. **Risk-based capital requirements** stipulate that each insurer must have a certain amount of capital based on the level of risk of its insurance and investment operations.

The NAIC's complex formula for property-casualty insurers takes into account four major risk categories:

1. *Asset risk*—the risk that an insurer's asset values will be lower than expected; for example, because of bond issuer default and stock market declines or because of inadequate diversification
2. *Credit risk*—the risk that the insurer will not be able to collect money owed to it; for example, because reinsurance or other receivables become uncollectible

3. *Underwriting risk*—the risk resulting from the volatility of the lines of insurance written by the insurer

4. *Off-balance-sheet risks*—a miscellaneous grouping including, for example, the risks associated with rapid growth.

Basically, the risk-based capital formula requires more capital for property-casualty insurers whose activities are riskier, and less for those whose activities are less risky. A similar formula applies to life-health insurers.

Capital and Surplus Requirements—Stock Insurers

The capital and surplus required to form a domestic stock insurer fall into two categories:

- The *capital stock account* represents the value of the shares of stock issued to stockholders. If 600,000 shares with a $1 par value are issued and outstanding, the corporate books would reflect a capital account of $600,000.

- *Paid-in surplus* represents the amount paid in by stockholders in excess of the par value of the stock. If 600,000 shares of stock with a $1 par value are sold at $1.50 per share, for a total of $900,000, the paid-in surplus would be $300,000.

Minimum initial capital and surplus requirements vary widely among the states with respect to amounts and lines of insurance written.

Surplus Requirements—Mutual and Reciprocal Insurers

Because a mutual insurer has no capital derived from the sale of stock, the minimum requirement applies only to surplus. When a mutual insurer is forming, its initial surplus may be derived from premium deposits paid by prospective policyholders; a portion of the initial surplus may be borrowed. Most states require mutuals to have an initial surplus equal to the minimum capital and surplus requirement for stock insurers writing the same lines of business. Some states, however, have set a minimum surplus requirement for mutuals that is lower than the minimum capital and surplus requirement for stock insurers. In most states, minimum surplus requirements for mutual insurers and reciprocals are the same.

Many states require the organizers of a mutual insurance company to have applications and deposit premiums from a stated minimum number of persons on more than a stated number of separate exposures with aggregate premiums in excess of a certain amount. This requirement provides the insurer with a minimum book of business, and, hence, some stability, the day it opens its doors.

Other Requirements

In addition to tests of financial strength, states impose other formation or licensing requirements For example, the proposed name for a mutual insurer must include the word "mutual," and the proposed name of any new insurer must not be so similar to that of any existing insurer that it would be misleading. The commissioner may have the authority to refuse a license if he or she believes the incorporators or directors of the insurer are untrustworthy. Some states even permit the commissioner to deny a license to an otherwise worthy applicant if he or she believes that there is no need for additional insurers in the state. Once the license has been issued, it can be revoked if the insurer operates in a manner that is clearly detrimental to the welfare of its policyholders (for example, consistent failure to pay legitimate claims or fraudulent business conduct).

Foreign Insurers

To be licensed in an additional state (in other words, as a "foreign insurer"), an insurer first must show that it has satisfied the requirements imposed by its home state (its state of domicile, the state where it is a "domestic insurer"). Second, a foreign insurer must generally satisfy the minimum capital and surplus and other requirements imposed on domestic insurers by the state in which it wishes to do business.

Alien Insurers

Alien insurers (insurers domiciled in other countries) must satisfy the requirements imposed on domestic insurers by the state in which they desire to be licensed. In addition, they must usually establish a branch office in some state and have funds on deposit in the United States equal to the minimum capital and surplus required.

Nonadmitted Insurers

Admitted insurer
An insurer licensed by the state insurance department to do business in the insured's home state.

An **admitted insurer** is one that is licensed by a state insurance department to do business in the insured's home state. A **nonadmitted insurer** is not licensed (not authorized) in the insured's home state; it might or might not be an admitted insurer in other states, and it might even be an alien insurer. A nonadmitted insurer is typically a surplus lines insurer. The surplus lines insurance mechanism allows United States consumers to buy property-casualty insurance from nonadmitted insurers when consumers are unable to purchase the coverage they need from admitted insurers. Although surplus lines insurers are described in terms that sound negative or illegal (nonadmitted, unauthorized, unlicensed), they provide a positive and legal supplement to the admitted insurance market. The business generally accepted by surplus lines insurers includes distressed risks—with unfavorable underwriting problems; unique risks—difficult to evaluate; and high-capacity risks—requiring very high limits. Surplus lines coverages commonly include products liability, professional liability, employment practices liability, special events, and excess and umbrella policies.

Nonadmitted insurer
An insurer not licensed (not authorized) in the insured's home state. Most nonadmitted insurers provide surplus lines insurance under state surplus lines laws.

Surplus lines laws
State laws that permit agents or brokers with a surplus lines license to write business for an "acceptable" nonadmitted insurer when protection from admitted insurers is not available.

Under **surplus lines laws**, a nonadmitted insurer may be permitted to transact business through a specially licensed surplus lines broker if (1) the insurance is not readily available from admitted insurers, (2) the nonadmitted insurer is "acceptable," and (3) the agent or broker has a special license authorizing him or her to place such insurance. The surplus lines agent or broker usually must be a resident of the state.

An "acceptable" nonadmitted insurer generally must file a financial statement that the commissioner finds satisfactory, appoint the commissioner as an agent to receive service-of-process in the state, obtain a certificate of compliance from its home state or country, and, if an alien insurer, maintain a trust fund in the United States. Some states leave the determination of acceptability to the agent or broker. A few states permit brokers or agents to use other nonadmitted insurers if the desired insurance cannot be obtained from either admitted or "acceptable" nonadmitted insurers.

A nonadmitted insurer writing business in the surplus lines market does not face regulatory constraints on rates and forms. However, premium taxes are not avoided, because the surplus lines broker must pay those taxes on the insurer's behalf. From the insured's perspective, a distinct disadvantage of surplus lines insurance is that it is not usually protected by the state's guaranty fund. (Guaranty funds are discussed later in this chapter.)

Risk Retention Groups

A risk retention group is a special type of group captive enabled by the 1986 Liability Risk Retention Act. Once chartered and licensed as a liability insurer under the laws of at least one state, the risk retention group can write insurance in all states. However, in a nonchartering state, a risk retention group may be subject to some state laws, such as unfair claim settlement practice laws, and to premium taxes. It might also be required to become a member of joint underwriting associations (JUAs) or similar associations in which insurance companies share losses in such areas as assigned-risk auto insurance.

Some state regulators have expressed concerns regarding the financial security of risk retention groups, particularly when the group providing the coverage is chartered in another state. Congress went some distance in meeting these concerns by allowing the chartering state to request and to implement, if necessary, an examination of the financial condition of a group even when the commissioner has no reason to believe that the group is financially impaired. However, some state regulators still fear abuses under the Act, and some advocates of the risk retention group concept remain concerned about the possibility of overregulation.

Licensing of Insurance Personnel

States license many of the people who sell insurance, give insurance advice, or represent insurers. These groups include producers (agents and brokers), insurance consultants, and claims representatives.

Agents

Agents and brokers must be licensed in each state in which they do business. Insurance producers operating without a license are subject to civil, and sometimes criminal, penalties. Traditionally, lack of uniformity among the states' licensing requirements has been a tremendous source of frustration and expense for producers licensed in more than one state. As indicated earlier in this chapter, provisions in Gramm-Leach-Bliley (GBL) have led to an increased level of licensing reciprocity among states. The ultimate goal of regulators is to move beyond reciprocity and to resolve issues related to uniformity in the producer licensing process. This will provide greater efficiency in the licensing process while retaining state regulatory authority over licensing.

Brokers

States that issue a separate broker's license might use a different set of examinations to test the competence of candidates, or they might establish higher standards for the broker's license than for the agent's license. Some states prohibit persons from taking the broker's examination until they have been licensed agents for a specified period, such as two years.

Insurance Consultants

Insurance consultants give advice, counsel, or opinions concerning insurance contracts sold in the state. Some states require them to be licensed. Separate examinations usually are required to be an insurance consultant in both life-health insurance and in property-casualty insurance. Requirements for a consultant's license vary among the states.

Claim Adjusters

Some states license claim adjusters who represent insurers. Licensing claim adjusters is justified because of the complex and technical nature of insurance contracts and to protect claimants from unfair, unethical, and dishonest claim practices. Licensing also provides some assurance that adjusters will be aware of prohibited claim practices, have minimum technical skills, and will treat policyholders fairly.

Public adjusters, who represent insureds for a fee, generally are required to be licensed to ensure technical competence and protection of the public.

Solvency

Solvency regulation seeks to protect policyholders and the public by accomplishing two broad goals:

1. Reducing the insolvency risk through monitoring and controls
2. Protecting the public against loss when insurers fail

A delicate balance exists between meeting these goals and increasing the total cost of risk for society as a whole. Insurers' costs are raised by measures that increase the amount of capital they must hold in reserve. Whether directly or indirectly, insurance buyers also pay for the costs of regulation, including regulators' salaries and the costs of collecting and maintaining financial data.

Insurance companies hold large sums of money for long periods of time. Their financial strength must be carefully monitored to ensure their continued ability to pay covered claims, both now and in the future.

Individual consumers and small businesses are not sophisticated enough to analyze claims-paying ability when selecting an insurance company. Even large, sophisticated businesses find it difficult. Some of the analysis is therefore delegated to others. State regulation, independent rating organizations, and state-sponsored insurance guaranty funds all help to protect the consumer. Insurance agents and brokers, who have a vested interest in the long-term relationships with the consumer, can also help consumers avoid purchasing insurance from more risky firms, when an alternative exists. Unfortunately, none of these systems is foolproof.

Methods To Ensure Solvency

Regulators use five principal methods to ensure solvency and measure the financial strength of insurers:

- Financial requirements
- Review of financial annual statements
- Insurance Regulatory Information System (IRIS)
- Financial Analysis Tracking System (FAST)
- Onsite field examinations

Financial Requirements

To obtain and keep its license as an admitted insurer, each insurer must meet certain minimum financial requirements, such as capital and surplus requirements, and comply with restrictions on how loss reserves may be invested. For example, the risk-based-capital requirement, discussed earlier in the context of licensing, is also an ongoing requirement. Indeed, its ongoing application is more important than its effect on an insurer's initial capitalization. Specific financial requirements vary widely among the states.

Review of Financial Annual Statements

Insurers must submit annual financial statements to state insurance departments in a prescribed format: the NAIC **Annual Statement**, which requires detailed information on premiums written, expenses, investments, losses, reserves, and other financial information. These statements are analyzed to assess the insurer's financial position.

IRIS

The **Insurance Regulatory Information Systems (IRIS)**, administered by the NAIC, is used to detect insurers with potential solvency problems. Diagnostic tests are applied to the data submitted by insurers to provide early detection of insurers that might require closer monitoring.

Annual Statement
A form on which every insurer is required annually to submit detailed information on premiums written, expenses, investments, losses, reserves, and other financial information.

Insurance Regulatory Information System (IRIS)
Administered by the NAIC, a system that detects insurers with potential solvency problems by applying diagnostic tests to the data submitted by insurers.

IRIS has two phases:

1. Financial ratios and other reports based on Annual Statement data. Eleven ratios are computed that provide information in the areas of (1) leverage—the amount of business an insurer is writing compared to its capital, (2) profitability, (3) liquidity, and (4) loss reserve integrity. Insurers that do not meet certain criteria in four or more ratios are designated for additional review.

2. The financial ratios and selected Annual Statement data are then analyzed by experienced state examiners and financial analysts.

Based on these reviews, certain insurers may be designated for immediate attention or targeted regulatory attention. Insurers designated for immediate attention must be investigated by regulatory officials in the state where the insurer is domiciled. Insurers designated for targeted attention are examined on a priority basis. Though helpful in setting regulatory priorities, IRIS has limitations as an early detection tool.

FAST

In the early 1990s, the NAIC developed a solvency screening system known as **Financial Analysis Tracking System**, or **FAST**. FAST assigns point values to various financial ratios and produces a total FAST score for each insurer. This score, which is not released to the public, is used to identify companies requiring immediate or priority attention or routine monitoring.

Financial Analysis Tracking System (FAST)
A system that assigns point values to various financial ratios and produces a total FAST score of solvency for each insurer.

Onsite Field Examinations

Regulators conduct onsite field examinations to monitor the financial strength of insurers. State laws usually require that insurers be examined at least once every three to five years. By dividing the country into four geographic zones to avoid duplicate examination of multi-state insurers, the NAIC coordinates the field examinations of insurers that write business in several states.

Liquidation of Insolvent Insurers

If an insurer is insolvent, it is placed in receivership by the state insurance department. With proper management, successful rehabilitation might be possible. If the insurer cannot be rehabilitated, it is liquidated according to the state's insurance code. Many states now liquidate insolvent insurers according to the Uniform Insurers Liquidation Act drafted by the NAIC. The model act is designed to achieve uniformity in the liquidation of assets and payment of claims of a failed insurer. Under this act, creditors in each state in which the insolvent insurer has conducted business are treated equally—creditors in the state where the insurer is domiciled do not receive preferential treatment.

Some states' laws provide for a priority system to dispose of the failed insurers's assets. For example, Nebraska requires payment of the administrative costs of liquidation first and unpaid claims and unearned premiums second. General creditors are paid next, and finally stockholders and surplus noteholders. Stockholders generally lose all or a large part of their original investment. If the insurer's assets are insufficient for paying all claims, the unpaid claims are submitted to the state guaranty fund for payment.

State Guaranty Funds

Guaranty funds do not prevent insurer insolvency, but they mitigate its effects. All states have property and casualty insurance guaranty funds that provide for the payment of unpaid claims of insolvent insurers licensed in the particular state. With the exception of New York, where a pre-assessment system maintains a permanent fund, the assessment method is used to raise the necessary funds to pay claims. Companies doing business in the state are assessed their share of unpaid claims. Although the amounts involved are not trivial—from 1969 through 1999, state guaranty fund net assessments on behalf of insolvent insurers totaled about $6.6 billion[20]— they still represent a very small percentage of total premiums. Insurers can recoup all or part of the assessments by rate increases, by special premium tax credits, and by refunds from the state guaranty fund.

Guaranty funds
State-established funds that provide for the payment of unpaid claims of insolvent insurers licensed in that state. Although guaranty funds do not prevent insurer insolvency, they mitigate its effects.

State guaranty funds vary by state. However, the following characteristics are common.[21]

1. *Assessments are made only when an insurer fails.* As mentioned, New York is the exception. The definition of "failure" varies among the states. Some states regard an insolvency order from a state court as evidence of failure. Others require a liquidation order from the state. All states have limits on the amounts insurers can be assessed in one year.

2. *Policies usually terminate within thirty days after the failure date.* Unpaid claims before termination, however, are still valid and will be paid out of the guaranty fund of the policyholder's state of residence if the insolvent insurer is licensed in the state. Under the NAIC's model act, if the failed insurer is not licensed in the state, a policyholder or claimant cannot file a claim with the guaranty fund but must seek payment by filing a claim against the failed insurer's assets, which are handled by the liquidator.[22]

3. *Claim coverage varies among the states.* No state fund covers reinsurance or surplus lines insurance (except New Jersey).

4. *Claims are subject to maximum limits.* The maximum limit is usually the lesser of $300,000 or the policy limit. Some states have limits under $300,000, and a small number of states have much higher limits, such as $500,000 or $1 million.

5. *Most states provide for a refund of unearned premiums.* However, a few states have no unearned premium claim provision. In these states, a policyholder in a failed company is not entitled to a refund of the unearned premium from the guaranty fund.

6. *A $100 deductible applies to unpaid claims in most states.* Many states exempt workers compensation claims from a deductible.

7. *The majority of states divide their guaranty funds into separate accounts, usually auto, workers compensation, and other lines.* Thus, auto or workers compensation assessments can be limited to insurers that write only that type of insurance.

8. *Recovery of assessments varies among the states.* Thirty-two states permit insurers to recover assessments by a rate increase. The remaining states generally allow insurers to reduce their annual state premium taxes, usually over a period of five years. As a result, taxpayers and the general public, as well as insureds, are subsidizing the unpaid claims of insolvent insurers.

Homeowners and auto insurance claims are covered by all state funds, but some types of insurance, such as annuities, life, disability, accident and health, surety, ocean marine, mortgage guaranty, and title insurance often are not covered. Self-insured groups, including risk retention groups, are not protected by guaranty funds. Only one state has established a special fund for surplus lines.

Reasons for Insolvency

Why do insurers fail? Some insolvencies have occurred when an insurer was overexposed to losses resulting from a major insured catastrophe. Usually, no single event or mistake causes an insurer to become insolvent. Rather, a collection of management blunders and adverse events contribute. Experts have identified some factors that frequently contribute to insolvencies:

- Rapid premium growth
- Inadequate rates and reserves
- Excessive expenses
- Lax controls over managing general agents
- Uncollectible reinsurance
- Fraud

Poor management decisions are at the root of most of these problems. A combination of inadequate rates and lax underwriting starts a deterioration in a book of business. If these problems are not promptly detected and corrected, the decay in the quality of the business accelerates.

Rapid premium growth precedes nearly all major failures. Rapid growth by itself is not harmful, but it reduces the margin for error in the operation of insurers. Moreover, it is usually a strong indication of bargain-basement rates and lax underwriting standards. If rates are inadequate and losses understated, net losses and deterioration of capital rise faster than management can handle.

It can be difficult to tell when a company is financially troubled or even insolvent. Mergers and acquisitions sometimes provide a discreet way for a weak company to cease to exist or to be saved without the world's knowing how bad its condition was or how it became that way. Capital infusions by parent companies or outside investors also clear the slate of past management sins, preventing the event from being viewed as a financial failure or insolvency.

Challenges in Solvency Regulation

Solvency regulation presents some significant challenges. Among them are the time lag in obtaining data, inadequate resources, underqualified personnel, and inadequate sharing of information.[23]

- *Time lag in determining problem insurers.* Annual Statements are submitted two months after the end of the accounting year, and insurance department review can take as long as three months. At this point, certain negative financial trends, such as loss reserve development, might be over a year in progress. This time lag delays detection of a problem and allows insolvent and struggling insurers to continue operating for months. Moreover, most states require field examinations only once every three to five years, and the examinations often take months or years to complete. Meanwhile, problem insurers continue to operate and write new business.

- *Inadequate resources.* Some state insurance departments are understaffed and have insufficient financial resources to monitor the solvency of insurers in an effective manner.

- *Lack of professional qualifications for field examiners.* Some field examiners do not meet NAIC qualification standards for examiners who participate in zone examinations.

- *Inadequate sharing of information by the states.* States vary in the amount of information about problem insurers they share with other states. Some states openly share all information. Other states are reluctant to do so, even though the interstate operations of many large insurers and state responsibility under a guaranty fund make interstate sharing of solvency information absolutely necessary.

RATES

Rate regulation might well be the regulatory activity that receives the most public attention. This section covers the objectives of rate regulation, types of rating laws, the arguments for prior approval and open competition rating laws, and trends in rate regulation. The principles of ratemaking are discussed in further detail in Chapter 10.

Property-casualty insurance pricing has historically tended to move in cyclical patterns. The typical pattern is a few years of low rates, relaxed underwriting, and underwriting losses (soft market) followed by a few years of high rates, restrictive underwriting, and strong underwriting gains (hard market). This pattern is known as the **underwriting cycle**.

The underwriting cycle has strong, generally undesirable, effects on the market and challenges all aspects of rate regulation. A full discussion of the underwriting cycle is beyond the scope of this text.

Underwriting cycle
A cyclical pattern of insurance pricing in which a soft market (low rates, relaxed underwriting, and underwriting losses) is eventually followed by a hard market (high rates, restrictive underwriting, and strong underwriting gains) before the pattern again repeats itself.

Objectives of Rate Regulation

Rate regulation is designed both to maintain insurer solvency and to protect policyholders.

Major Objectives of Rate Regulation

The major objectives of rate regulation are to ensure that rates are:

1. Adequate

2. Not excessive

3. Not unfairly discriminatory

Adequate

Premiums for a specific line of insurance should be high enough to pay all claims and expenses related to those premiums. This requirement helps maintain insurer solvency. If rates are inadequate, an insurer might fail, and policyholders and third-party claimants would be financially harmed if their claims were not paid. The objective of rate adequacy is complicated by the fact that an insurer usually does not know what its actual costs will be when the policy is sold. Premiums are paid in advance, but they might not be sufficient to pay all related claims and expenses that occur later. An unexpected increase in claim frequency or severity can make the premium inadequate.

Many factors can complicate the regulatory objective of adequate rates:

- Insurers might charge inadequate rates in response to keen price competition because otherwise they would lose business.

- State rate approval systems might not approve insurers' requests for adequate rates for political reasons or because of disagreement over the level of requested rates.

- Unanticipated events might lead to higher losses than those projected when rates were set.

Although rate adequacy is a goal of insurance regulation, no method of rate regulation guarantees that rates are adequate.

Not Excessive

A second regulatory objective is that rates should not be excessive. In other words, insurers should not earn excessive or unreasonable profits. Regulators have considerable latitude and discretion in determining whether rates are excessive for a given line of insurance, and they consider numerous factors. These factors include (1) the number of insurers selling a specific coverage in the rating territory, (2) the relative market share of competing insurers, (3) the degree of price variation among the competing insurers, (4) past and prospective loss experience for a given line of insurance, (5) possibility of catastrophe losses, (6) margin for underwriting profit and contingencies, (7) marketing expenses for a given line of insurance, and (8) special judgment factors that may apply to a given line.[24]

Regulators have sometimes used the fair rate of return approach in determining whether an insurer's rates are adequate or excessive. An insurer should expect at least some minimum rate of return on the equity invested in its insurance operations. An insurer's fair rate of return presumably should resemble the rate of return applicable to other types of businesses, especially if insurers are to attract investment capital. Many believe that the insurance business, by its very nature, involves a higher degree of risk than many other businesses, and that higher risks generally should be accompanied by higher returns. To date, there has been little agreement as to what constitutes a fair rate of return for insurers.

Not Unfairly Discriminatory

The word "discrimination," as usually used, carries negative connotations, but the word itself is neutral, implying only the ability to differentiate among things. Discrimination, in the neutral sense, is essential to insurance rating. However, insurers' discrimination must be fair and consistent. This means that *loss exposures that are roughly similar with respect to expected losses and expenses should be charged substantially similar rates.* For example, two men age twenty-five in good health who buy the same type and amount of life insurance from the same insurer should be charged similar rates.

Only **unfair discrimination** is prohibited, not *fair* discrimination. If loss exposures are substantially different in terms of expected losses and expenses, then different rates can be charged. For example, if a woman age twenty-five and another age sixty-five are in good health and purchase the same type and amount of life insurance from the same insurer, it is not unfair rate discrimination to charge the older woman a higher rate. The higher probability of death for a woman at age sixty-five clearly and fairly justifies a higher premium.

Unfair discrimination
Discrimination occurring when loss exposures that are roughly similar with respect to expected losses and expenses were charged substantially different rates.

Types of Rating Laws

The rates that property-casualty underwriters can charge in any state are affected by that state's rating laws. In general, the major types of state rating laws rely on:

- *Mandatory rates.* Under a **mandatory rate law**, rates are set by a state agency or rating bureau, and all licensed insurers are required to use those rates.

- *Prior approval laws.* Under a **prior approval law**, rates used must be approved by the state insurance department before they can be used. Prior approval laws have been criticized by insurers because there is often considerable delay in obtaining a rate increase. As a result, a rate increase may be inadequate by the time it is approved. Furthermore, the statistical data required by the state insurance department might not readily be available.

Mandatory rate law
State law under which rates are set by a state agency or rating bureau and all licensed insurers are required to use those rates.

Prior approval law
State law under which rates must be approved by the state insurance department before they can be used.

File-and-use law
State law under which rates must be filed with the state insurance department but can then be used immediately.

Use-and-file law
State law that allows insurers to put rate changes into effect and later submit filing information that is subject to review by regulatory officials.

Flex rating law
State law that requires prior approval only if the new rates exceed a certain percentage above (and sometimes below) the rates previously filed.

Open competition system
A system under which rates do not have to be filed with the state insurance department.

- *File-and-use laws.* Under a **file-and-use law**, rates have to be filed with the state insurance department, but they can then be used immediately. The department has the authority to disapprove the rates if they cannot be justified or if they violate state law. A file-and-use law overcomes the problems of delay associated with prior approval laws.

- *Use-and-file laws.* A variation of file and use is a **use-and-file law** that allows insurers to put rate changes into effect and later submit filing information that is subject to review by regulatory officials.

- *Flex rating laws.* Under a **flex rating law**, prior approval is required only if the new rates exceed a certain percentage above (and sometimes below) the rates previously filed. Insurers are permitted to increase or reduce their rates within the established range without prior approval. Typically, margins of five or ten percent are permitted. Flex rating permits insurers to make rate adjustments quickly in response to changing market conditions and loss experience, but it dampens wide swings within a short period of time. Flex rating also may restrict insurers from drastically reducing premiums to increase market share. The result should be smoother insurance pricing cycles.

- *Open competition.* Under an **open competition system**, rates do not have to be filed with the state insurance department. Market prices driven by the economic laws of supply and demand, rather than the discretionary acts of regulators, determine the price and availability of insurance. However, insurers may be required to furnish rate schedules and supporting statistical data to regulatory officials, and the state insurance department has the authority to monitor competition and disapprove rates if necessary. The standards of adequate, nonexcessive, and equitable rates still apply.

These laws apply not only to rates for a new line of insurance, but also to rate changes.

Is Strict Rate Regulation Desirable?

In general, consumer groups and politicians tend to support prior approval or other forms of strict regulation, while insurers and economists tend to support use-and-file, open competition, and free markets.

Groups supporting prior approval laws offer several arguments in favor of their position:

- Insurers must justify their requests for rate increases with supporting actuarial data.

- Prior approval laws tend to maintain insurer solvency. Because regulators review rate data, rates can be set at adequate levels to maintain insurer solvency.

- Prior approval laws keep rates reasonable and prevent insurers from charging excessive rates. Many people assume that auto insurers are earning excessive profits and that rates can be reduced only by direct government action.

Those supporting open competition laws advance these arguments:

- In prior approval states, rate increases may be inadequate for writing profitable business. Inadequate rates may force insurers to reduce the amount of new business written or may even force them to withdraw from the market, which could lead to an availability problem.

- Prior approval laws may distort incentives for controlling claim costs. This argument applies largely to auto insurance. To make auto insurance more affordable, regulators may reduce rates for drivers who face the highest premiums by increasing rates for other drivers. They might limit the rates insurers can charge motorists who are in a residual market plan or restrict the use of age, sex, or territory as a ratemaking variable. The result is that high-risk drivers are more likely to drive; they are more likely to purchase expensive cars; and they are less likely to exercise caution in preventing accidents and theft losses than if their rates were not subsidized.[25]

- Prior approval laws may lead insurers to abandon the state, resulting in an increase in the number of drivers in residual market plans. Residual market plans are special government-sponsored plans that make automobile insurance available to motorists who cannot obtain coverage in the standard markets. Considerable evidence exists that in states with strict rate suppression, the proportion of drivers in residual market plans is much higher than in states with competitive rating laws. Under open competition, the equilibrium market price is determined by market forces, not by government regulators. As a result, most motorists can be insured in the voluntary standard market by paying market prices.

- Open competition is less expensive to administer. Regulators are not required to review thousands of rate filings or hold costly hearings. As a result, limited regulatory resources can be devoted to higher priority areas, such as solvency regulation and consumer affairs.

- Open competition tends to overcome the limitations of prior approval laws. Under an open competition law, rates can be adjusted more quickly in response to changing economic and market conditions. Fewer political pressures are encountered, and the need for supporting actuarial data is reduced.

- Price competition among insurers will keep rates reasonable and equitable. Free market forces rather than artificial government intervention will curtail excessive rates.

Deregulation

Many states have now enacted laws deregulating rate and form filing requirements. These laws, in effect, restore open competition for insurance contracts involving larger commercial insureds who meet certain specified qualifications.

Contracts

Insurance contracts present another important area of regulation. Regulation of insurance contracts is considered necessary for at least two reasons:

- *Insurance contracts are complex documents.* Because most insurance contracts are difficult to interpret and understand, it is necessary to regulate their structure and content.
- *Insurance contracts are almost always drafted by insurers who sell them to the public on a take-it-or-leave-it basis.* Regulation can protect policyholders from contracts that are narrow, restrictive, or deceptive.

Insurance contracts are regulated by three principal means: (1) legislation, (2) insurance departments' rules, regulations, and guidelines, and (3) the courts.

Legislation

Regulation of insurance contracts starts with the state legislature, which can pass laws controlling the nature and content of insurance coverages sold in the state. Legislative contract regulation may take one of four approaches: standard forms, mandatory provisions, forms approval, or readability standards.

Standard Forms

Standard policy
An identical policy that all insurers must use if a coverage is sold in the state.

The law may require the use of a standard policy in the state to insure property or liability loss exposures. A **standard policy** is an identical policy that all insurers must use if a coverage is sold in the state.

Mandatory Provisions

Legislation can require that certain standard mandatory contractual provisions appear in certain types of insurance contracts. For example, the states require that certain contractual provisions must appear in all individual health insurance contracts, while other provisions are optional. The required and optional provisions are based on a model bill developed by the NAIC. States usually require that workers compensation insurance, no-fault auto coverage, and often uninsured motorists coverage, for example, contain certain contractual provisions.

State regulations may require that the required policy provisions meet certain minimum standards, providing at least a minimum level of protection.

Forms Approval

Deemer provision
A state regulatory provision that provides that, if a specified period elapses and a filed contract has not been disapproved, the contract is "deemed" (considered) to have been approved.

State law might require that policy forms be filed and approved by the state, in an effort to protect policyholders against ambiguous, misleading, or deceptive contracts. Many states require that a policy form be submitted for approval before it may be used. However, if a specified period elapses and the contract has not been disapproved, the contract is "deemed" to have been approved. (Some states permit the state insurance department to extend the review period.) The purpose of this **"deemer provision"** in state regulatory statutes is to encourage a prompt review of the form, but it can cause the review to be perfunctory.

The NAIC has recently begun exploring some "speed to market" proposals, designed to reduce the time involved in approving forms, so that innovations can reach the market faster. At this writing, the outcome of these proposals remains uncertain.

Readability Standards

Some state laws require that insurance contracts meet a certain test of readability. The law also can specify the style and form of the contract as well as the size of print. Readability legislation has influenced the drafting of both personal and commercial insurance contracts, but readability tests do not necessarily measure understandability.

Rules, Regulations, and Guidelines

State insurance departments carry out specific directives from the legislature, or exercise the general authority they have to regulate insurance contracts. Administrative rules, regulations, and guidelines may be stated in (1) regulations communicated by the state insurance department to insurers, (2) informal circulars or bulletins from the same source, and (3) precedents set in the approval process. For example, the state insurance department may require specific wording in certain policy provisions or make it known to insurers that certain types of policy provisions will be disapproved.

Courts

Although the courts do not directly regulate insurers, they clearly influence them by determining whether insurance laws are constitutional and whether administrative rulings and regulations are legal and consistent with state law. The courts also interpret ambiguous and confusing policy provisions, determine whether certain losses are covered under the contract, and resolve other disputes between insurers and policyholders over contract coverages and provisions.

Court decisions often lead insurers to redraft their policy language and modify various contractual provisions. For example, based on the legal doctrine of concurrent causation, certain courts ruled that if a loss under an "all-risks" policy caused by two perils, of which one is excluded and the other is not, the entire loss is covered. As a result of this doctrine, insurers were required to pay certain flood and earthquake claims they had believed were excluded by their property insurance policies. Subsequent revision of the language in many "all-risks" property policies explicitly excluded coverage for flood and earthquake losses in cases in which an unexcluded peril contributed to the loss.

Market Conduct

Unfair trade practices acts prohibit many abusive practices. Among the most important market conduct concerns for regulators are sales practices, underwriting practices, claims practices, and consumer protection.

Unfair trade practices acts
State laws that prohibit an insurer from using unfair methods of competition and engaging in unfair acts or practices as defined in the acts.

Currently, all U.S. jurisdictions but the District of Columbia and Guam have unfair trade practices acts. State **unfair trade practices acts** regulate the trade practices of the business of insurance as required under the McCarran-Ferguson Act (McCarran).

Unfair trade practices acts prohibit an insurer from using unfair methods of competition and engaging in unfair acts or practices as defined in the acts. Most acts also authorize the insurance commissioner to decide whether activities not specifically defined in the law might result in unfair competition or qualify as unfair trade practices.

Cases involving unfair trade practices may be heard before the commissioner of the state in which the activity occurred. If the insurance company is found in violation of the unfair trade practices act, it is subject to one or both of the following penalties:

- *Fine per violation.* The fine is often significantly increased if the activity is considered to be flagrant, with conscious disregard for the law.

- *Suspension or revocation of license.* This usually occurs if the insurance company's management knew or should have known that the activity was an unfair trade practice.

If an insurer disagrees with the commissioner's findings, generally the insurer can file for judicial review. If the court finds with the commissioner, the insurer must obey the commissioner's orders.

Sales Practices

Agents and brokers are subject to fines, penalties, or revocation of their license if they engage in certain illegal and unethical activities. An agent may be penalized for engaging in practices, like those mentioned below, that violate the state's unfair trade practices act.

- *Dishonesty or fraud.* For example, a dishonest agent might embezzle premiums paid by the policyholders or might appropriate some claims funds.

- *Misrepresentation.* For example, misrepresentation of the losses that are covered by an insurance contract might induce a client to purchase that contract under false pretenses.

- *Twisting.* Twisting is a special form of misrepresentation in which the agent or broker induces a policyholder through misrepresentation to replace one contract (usually life insurance) with another to the detriment of the insured.

Rebating
The practice of giving a portion of the producer's commission or some other financial advantage to an individual as an inducement to purchase the policy. Rebating is illegal in most states.

- *Unfair discrimination.* This could include any act that favors one insured unfairly over others.

- *Rebating.* **Rebating** is the practice of giving a portion of the producer's commission or some other financial advantage to an individual as an inducement to purchase the policy. Rebating is currently illegal in all but two states. The practice is especially problematic with life insurance policies for which the agent's first year's commission is sizable. If an agent rebates part of the commission to one policyholder but not to another, that act is considered unfair discrimination. If the agent rebates the same percentage of the commission to all policyholders, that act is not unfairly discriminatory, but it is still illegal.

Underwriting Practices

Unfair underwriting practices are detailed in Exhibit 2-2. Insurance regulators are concerned that improper underwriting could result in insolvency by the insurer or unfair discrimination against an insurance consumer. To prevent these problems, insurance regulators:

- *Constrain insurers' ability to accept, modify, or decline applications for insurance coverage*. To increase insurance availability, states often require insurers to provide coverage for some exposures they might prefer not to cover.
- *Establish allowable classifications*. Regulators limit the ways in which insurers can divide customers into rating classifications. For example, unisex rating is required in some states for personal auto insurance. This approach promotes social equity rather than actuarial equity.
- *Restrict the timing of cancellations and nonrenewals*. All states require insurance companies to provide insureds with adequate advance notice of cancellation or nonrenewal so insureds can obtain replacement coverage. Insurers are typically allowed to cancel or nonrenew for only specified reasons.

Typical violations discovered under market conduct examinations of an insurer's underwriting function include:

- Discriminating unfairly according to the applicable laws and regulations in the selection of risks
- Misclassifying risks
- Canceling or nonrenewing policies contrary to statutes, rules, and policy requirements
- Using underwriting rules or rates that are not on file with or approved by the insurance departments in the states in which the insurer does business
- Failing to apply newly implemented underwriting and rating factors to renewals
- Failing to use correct forms and rates
- Failing to use rules that are state specific

Claim Practices

All states prohibit certain claim practices by law. Apart from regulatory penalties, failure to handle claims in good faith can lead to claims for damages, alleging bad faith on the part of the insurer.

EXHIBIT 2-2

Unfair Trade Practices With Respect to Underwriting

- Making or permitting unfair discrimination under the following conditions:

  - Among individuals of the same class with equal life expectations in any terms and conditions of a life insurance policy

  - Among individuals of the same class with similar health characteristics in any terms and conditions of an accident or health insurance policy

  - Among individuals or risks of the same class with similar characteristics by refusing to insure or renew or by canceling or limiting the amount of insurance on property-casualty loss exposures solely based on the geographic location of the risk unless such action was necessary for sound underwriting and actuarial principles related to actual or reasonably expected loss experience

  - Among individuals or risks of the same class with similar characteristics by refusing to insure or renew or by canceling or limiting the amount of insurance on residential property, or personal property contained within, solely based on the age of the residential property

- Refusing to insure or to continue to insure or limiting the amount of insurance available to an individual because of his or her sex, marital status, race, religion, or national origin. However, marital status can be considered with respect to eligibility for dependent coverage.

- Terminating, changing, or refusing to issue or renew a property-casualty policy solely based on the applicant's or insured's physical or mental impairment. However, this does not apply to accident and health insurance sold by property-casualty insurers. Furthermore, this provision does not change any other provision of the law with respect to termination, modification, issuance, or renewal of a policy.

- Refusing to insure a risk solely because another insurer has refused to insure or has canceled or nonrenewed an existing policy on the risk. This does not prevent termination of an excess insurance policy due to failure of the insured to maintain underlying coverage.

- Failing to maintain books, records, documents, and other business records so that data is accessible and retrievable by insurance regulators for examinations.

Source: National Association of Insurance Commissioners (NAIC), "Unfair Trade Practices Act," *NAIC Model Laws, Regulations, and Guidelines,* vol. IV, Section 4 (Kansas City, Mo.: NAIC, 1993), pp. 880-4 to 880-6.

Unfair Claim Practices Laws

Unfair claim practices laws prohibit a wide variety of unethical and illegal claim practices. The laws generally are patterned after the NAIC Model Unfair Claims Settlement Practices Act (see Exhibit 2-3). Prohibited insurer practices typically include:

- Misrepresenting important facts or policy provisions relating to the coverage at issue

- Failing to make a good faith effort to pay claims where liability is reasonably clear

- Attempting to settle a claim for less than the amount that a reasonable person believes he or she is entitled to receive based on advertising material that accompanies or is made part of the application

- Failing to approve or deny coverage of a claim within a reasonable period after a proof-of-loss statement has been completed

Strict regulatory controls on claim practices, support the fundamental social and contractual purpose of protecting policyholders. Unfair claim practices tarnish the offending insurer's image and reputation, erode public confidence in the insurance industry, and allow insurers to hide behind the "fine print" of contractual provisions to deny claims to the policyholders' detriment.

Fairness in making claim payments requires honesty on both sides. Payment of fraudulent claims submitted by dishonest insureds should be vigorously resisted, and excessive claim settlements should be avoided. Valid and legitimate claims, however, should be paid promptly and fairly with a minimum of legal formality.

Bad Faith Actions

In some cases, courts have ruled that improper handling of a claim by an insurance company constitutes not only a breach of contract but also an independent tort, the tort of bad faith. An insurer held to have violated good faith standards can be held responsible not only for honoring the intent of the contract (paying the claim) but also for paying additional damages for emotional distress, attorney fees, and other damages. Legal remedies for bad faith actions can give rise to both first-party actions (involving the insured) and third-party actions (involving the claimant). These extra contractual damages—damages over and above the amount payable under the terms of the insurance contract—are payable by the insurer.

Consumer Protection

In a sense, all insurance regulatory activities provide protection for insurance consumers. But some activities are designed specifically to support consumers. For example, state insurance departments respond to consumer complaints, and they also make a great deal of consumer information available.

State insurance departments generally lack direct authority to order insurers to pay disputed claims when factual questions are at issue; such issues are generally best resolved through the courts. However, most state insurance departments investigate and follow up every consumer complaint, at least to the extent of getting a response from the insurer involved.

EXHIBIT 2-3

Unfair Claims Settlement Practices Defined

Any of the following acts by an insurer, if committed in violation of Section 3 [of the Unfair Claims Settlement Practices Model Act], constitutes an unfair claims practice:

A. Knowingly misrepresenting to claimants and insureds relevant facts or policy provisions relating to coverage at issue;

B. Failing to acknowledge with reasonable promptness pertinent communications with respect to claims arising under its policies;

C. Failing to adopt and implement reasonable standards for the prompt investigation and settlement of claims arising under its policies;

D. Not attempting in good faith to effectuate prompt, fair and equitable settlement of claims submitted in which liability has become reasonably clear;

E. Compelling insureds or beneficiaries to institute suits to recover amounts due under its policies by offering substantially less than the amounts ultimately recovered in suits brought by them;

F. Refusing to pay claims without conducting a reasonable investigation;

G. Failing to affirm or deny coverage of claims within a reasonable time after having completed its investigation related to such claim or claims;

H. Attempting to settle or settling claims for less than the amount to [which] a reasonable person would believe the insured or beneficiary was entitled by reference to written or printed advertising material accompanying or made part of an application;

I. Attempting to settle or settling claims on the basis of an application that was materially altered without notice to, or knowledge or consent of, the insured;

J. Making claims payments to an insured or beneficiary without indicating the coverage under which each payment is being made;

K. Unreasonably delaying the investigation or payment of claims by requiring both a formal proof of loss form and subsequent verification that would result in duplication of information and verification appearing in the formal proof of loss form;

L. Failing in the case of claims denials or offers of compromise settlement to promptly provide a reasonable and accurate explanation of the basis for such actions;

M. Failing to provide forms necessary to present claims within fifteen (15) calendar days of a request with reasonable explanations regarding their use;

N. Failing to adopt and implement reasonable standards to assure that the repairs of a repairer owned by or required to be used by the insurer are performed in a workman-like manner.

Reprinted from the NAIC Unfair Claims Settlement Practices Act, copyright National Association of Insurance Commissioners, used with permission.

Many states compute complaint ratios, and some make them readily available to consumers through the Internet. To make consumers more knowledgeable about the cost of insurance, some states publish shoppers' guides and other forms of consumer information, and much of this information can also be found on the Internet. Readers who would like to examine consumer information provided by the various state departments can link to each state insurance department's home page from the NAIC home page at www.naic.org.

UNOFFICIAL REGULATORS

Only the state and federal governments have the authority to regulate insurers. The NAIC plays an influential role, but it has no direct regulatory authority. Other organizations—they can be called "unofficial regulators"—also substantially affect insurer activities. This section briefly examines how four "unofficial regulators" influence insurer activity:

- Financial rating agencies
- Insurance advisory organizations
- Insurer trade organizations
- Consumer organizations

Financial Rating Organizations

Because good financial ratings help to attract and retain customers—and vice versa—insurers try to conduct business in ways that maintain a good rating. Several financial rating agencies provide solvency ratings of insurance companies. The best-known rating agencies are the following:

- A.M. Best Company
- Duff and Phelps
- Moody's
- Standard and Poor's
- Weiss Ratings, Inc.

These agencies' specific approaches are analyzed in other textbooks. In general, each organization provides summary information about insurer financial strength in the form of a financial rating, typically a letter grade similar to those appearing on a student's report card. Corporate risk managers, independent insurance agents and brokers, consumers, and others consult these ratings when choosing an insurer. Many corporate risk managers and public entity risk managers purchase insurance only from an insurer whose financial rating meets or exceeds a specific grade. Contractors and other organizations are often required to furnish a certificate of insurance from an insurance company with at least a specified minimum financial rating. Banks and other lending institutions typically require mortgagees to provide evidence of insurance from an insurance company with at least a specified solvency rating.

Insurance companies whose financial ratings have slipped can find it very difficult to find and retain customers, and a decline in customers often causes financial ratings to slip further. Insurers remain highly aware of the factors considered by financial rating agencies, and they try hard to avoid an adverse rating. When an insurer's financial rating is threatened, remedial measures can involve greater use of reinsurance, a restriction on accepting new business, selling a portion of the company's book of business, selling stock to raise additional capital, or merging with another, more solvent insurer.

Bad financial ratings are not a widespread problem. Also, a "bad" rating does not mean that an insurance company will fail, and a "good" rating does not ensure that the company will never become insolvent. Some of the larger insurers that failed in recent years received high solvency ratings until a year or two before they were declared insolvent. The value of financial ratings is limited by the fact that they are based on past performance and other objective information. Despite these weaknesses, the fact remains that insurance companies work hard to maintain sound financial ratings, to the extent that financial rating agencies have become unofficial regulators.

Insurance Advisory Organizations

Insurance advisory organizations are independent corporations that work with and on behalf of insurance companies that purchase or subscribe to their services. Advisory organizations primarily develop prospective loss costs and standard insurance contract forms. In some cases, they also file such loss costs and forms with the state on behalf of their member and subscribing companies. They often provide other valuable services to the insurance industry and its regulators, such as the following:

- Developing rating systems
- Collecting and tabulating statistics
- Researching topics important to members and the industry
- Providing a forum for discussion of issues
- Educating insurers, insurance regulators, and the public about particular issues
- Monitoring regulatory issues of concern to members

Companies must pay a fee for the services of insurance advisory organizations. Well-known insurance advisory organizations include Insurance Services Office (ISO), the American Association of Insurance Services (AAIS), and the National Council on Compensation Insurance (NCCI).

Even though organizations that use advisory organizations' services are not required to use specific rates or forms, insurance advisory organizations tend to impose a certain degree of uniformity as a matter of practice. Relatively few insurers have the resources to independently develop the statistical information on which to base their own rates or to develop policy forms, endorsements, and rating systems for many different coverages that also comply with a wide array of state regulations. Insurance consumers benefit from competition among insurers who base their rates on sound statistical data. A degree of uniformity in insurance contracts also makes it easier for consumers to comparison shop.

Insurance Professional and Trade Associations

Several national property-casualty industry professional associations and trade associations have developed over the years to provide services to their member insurers and agents and brokers. Some of these associations are listed in Exhibit 2-4.

Trade associations serve an important function for property-casualty insurers and agents and brokers. For a fee, members can have prompt access to legislative developments and can use association personnel as their lobbying forum. They can also participate on committees of the trade association to draft new legislation or to influence changes to pending legislation. Trade associations also continually watch for new regulations promulgated by state insurance departments in response to new or modified state insurance laws. Participation in one or more major trade association can make it possible for insurers—large and small—to exercise influence and gain information without the expense of a large internal staff. It would be difficult for individual insurers to match the scope of coverage and the prompt dissemination of information that the trade associations provide.

Trade associations do not operate solely on the national level. Many state and local associations focus only on the issues important to their members in those jurisdictions. For insurers and agents and brokers doing business solely in one or two states, membership in these associations can be vital and more cost-effective than membership in a national trade association that provides many services the one- or two-state insurer or agent or broker might not need. More often than not, however, insurers join associations on all levels.

Trade associations at the national, state, and local levels exert influence on the NAIC, state and federal legislators, and state insurance regulators. Each trade association has the collective power of its membership behind it. One person speaking on behalf of a major segment of insurers affected by a proposed piece of legislation can have far more influence than the representative of a single insurer voicing the same opinion.

Legislators and state insurance regulators sometimes propose legislation based on incorrect market assumptions and misinformation, or in reaction to crises. Trade associations are often able to provide more accurate information and to educate legislators and regulators on critical issues in time to influence the development of legislation, regulations, and rules. Sometimes, trade associations convince legislators and regulators that the industry can solve a problem without legislation. This type of intervention provides an important service to association membership and is an example of association influence.

EXHIBIT 2-4

Insurance Industry Professional and Trade Associations

Name	Year Founded	Members	Interests
Alliance of American Insurers www.allianceai.org	1922	325 property-casualty insurers	Promotes regulatory, legislative, and legal interests of members and provides public information
American Insurance Association (AIA) www.aiadc.org	1964, with roots in the National Board of Fire Underwriters established in 1866	370 property-casualty insurers	Provides a forum for the discussion of problems; provides safety, promotional, and legislative services.
Council of Insurance Agents and Brokers www.ciab.com	1913	300 of the leading commercial property and casualty insurance agencies and brokerage firms	Takes an active leadership role in crafting the commercial insurance industry's response to issues that affect members and their customers.
Independent Insurance Agents of America (IIAA) www.independentagent.com	1896	34,000 independent insurance agencies handling property, fire, casualty, and surety insurance	Promotes education of agents and promotes regulatory and legislative issues of agents
Inland Marine Underwriters Association (IMUA) www.imua.org	1930	400 member companies	Provides its members with education, research, and communications services that support the inland marine underwriting discipline
National Association of Mutual Insurance Companies (NAMIC) www.namic.org	1895	1,300+ property and casualty insurance companies	Promotes governmental affairs representation; compiles and analyzes pertinent information.
National Association of Professional Insurance Agents www.pianet.com	1931	180,000 insurance agents	Provides educational, representative, and service-oriented activities
National Association of Professional Surplus Lines Offices (NAPSLO) www.napslo.org	1975	800 associate and wholesale brokers and agents	Sets standards for surplus lines industry and provides educational seminars and workshops and internships
Reinsurance Association of America (RAA) www.reinsurance.org	1968	29 property-casualty reinsurers	Promotes the interests of the property-casualty reinsurance industry to federal and state legislators, regulators, and the public
Risk and Insurance Management Society (RIMS) www.rims.org	1950	7,500 individuals representing over 4,000 member companies	Dedicated to advancing the practice of risk management

Sources: *Encyclopedia of Associations, 2000*, 36th ed., vol. 1, part 1, Tara E. Sheets, ed. (Detroit Mich.: Gale Research, Inc., 2000); *The Insurance Information Institute Fact Book, 2001* (New York: Insurance Information Institute, 2001); and organizations' Web sites listed above.

Consumer Organizations

Consumers, through consumer groups, have had a major influence on state insurance departments, state and federal legislators, the NAIC, and insurance consumers. Some consumer groups focus solely on insurance issues. Others tackle a variety of public interest issues, including insurance. Some have adopted a watchdog approach, keeping a careful eye on insurers and their actions. Others take a more activist approach to confront issues and work for change.

One such group, the Consumer Federation of America (CFA),[26] is head-quartered in Washington, D.C. CFA is an advocacy organization that provides information to consumers about auto insurance products and that has worked to improve the safety of household products. Another organization, the Insurance Institute for Highway Safety,[27] conducts research and crash tests to find ways to prevent auto accidents and reduce injuries when accidents occur.

More than a decade ago, one observer stated that the following were the major consumer concerns for the 1990s. As of the early 2000s, at least, these continue to be consumer concerns:

- Consumers believe that automobile rates can be lowered and service, improved.

- Consumers believe that the insurance business is generally exceptionally inefficient.

- Consumers believe that state regulators are too weak.

- Consumers believe that ratemaking has perverse incentives regarding cost cutting and safety.

- Consumers believe that who supplies insurance is less important than that insurance be supplied at reasonable cost and with good service.

- Consumers believe that structural reform is needed in regulation.

- Consumers believe that competition must be increased, particularly in mass-produced personal lines.

- Consumers believe that competition and regulation are not mutually exclusive but, properly structured, work together toward an improved system.

- Consumers believe that health insurance is the number-one insurance crisis to be addressed in this decade.[28]

Complaints made to state insurance departments alert regulators to industry problems and can trigger market conduct examinations, which, in turn, can lead to actions ranging from insurer rebukes to license revocation. In addition, regulators view a high number of complaints as a signal of financial trouble, which can trigger financial examinations. Frequently, consumers and their groups can focus on such complaints to influence state insurance commissioners to call for testimony from the industry on problem issues. The results of such hearings can lead insurers to take corrective action or regulators to develop legislative proposals.

SUMMARY

As noted at the start of the chapter, these issues of insurance regulation continue to recur:

- State versus federal regulation
- The extent of regulation necessary
- The extent to which insurers should collaborate

Milestones in the history of insurance regulation include the following:

- The U.S. Constitution
- Paul v. Virginia
- South-Eastern Underwriters Decision
- McCarran-Ferguson Act
- Gramm-Leach-Bliley Act

Some of the Whys, Whos, and Whats of insurance regulation are listed below:

- *Why?* Insurance regulation is considered necessary to protect consumers, to maintain consumer solvency, and to avoid destructive competition.

- *Who?* Every state has an insurance department, headed by a commissioner, that is responsible for regulating insurance in that state. Insurance regulators belong to a trade association, the National Association of Insurance Commissioners, which has no regulatory authority of its own but provides a substantial influence in coordinating the activities of various state regulators and developing model acts and regulations, as well as sharing financial information. Federal regulation takes many forms, including the insurance fraud protection act, and a variety of regulations that affect insurers and other organizations alike. The question of state versus federal regulation is an ongoing issue, with strong arguments on both sides; the debate is likely to continue for many years to come.

- *What?* Insurance regulators govern the formation and licensing of insurers, the licensing of insurance personnel, solvency, rates, contracts, and market practices, in addition to providing consumer protection.

Other types of organizations serve as unofficial regulators: Financial rating organizations encourage insurers to maintain good solvency ratings; advisory organizations develop standard policy forms and rating systems; professional and trade associations serve many roles, and consumer organizations serve as watchdogs and activists.

CHAPTER NOTES

Portions of this chapter are adapted from three earlier AICPCU/IIA texts: Robert J. Gibbons, George E. Rejda, and Michael W. Elliott, *Insurance Perspectives*, 1st ed., 1992, American Institute for CPCU, Chapters 1 and 3; Kathleen Heald Ettlinger, Karen L. Hamilton, and Gregory Krohn, *State Insurance Regulation*, 1st ed., 1995, Insurance

Institute of America; Justin L. Brady, Joyce Hall Mellinger, and Kenneth N. Scoles Jr., *The Regulation of Insurance*, 1st ed., Insurance Institute of America, 1995.

1. Samuel B. Paul v. Commonwealth of Virginia, S.C., 8 Wall., 168–185 (1869).

2. United States v. South-Eastern Underwriters Association, et al., 322 U.S. 533 (1944).

3. Paul v. Virginia, 8 Wall., pp. 183–184 (1869).

4. Daniel F. Spulber, *Regulation and Markets* (Cambridge, Mass.: The MIT Press, 1989), pp. 464–468.

5. Banks McDowell, *Deregulation and Competition in the Insurance Industry* (New York: Quorum Books, 1989), p. 19.

6. National Association of Insurance Commissioners, "Unfair Trade Practices Act," *Model Laws, Regulations and Guidelines*, vol. IV (April 1994), pp. 880-15 to 880-18.

7. Insurance Services Office, *Insurance Services Office in a Competitive Marketplace: ISO's Role Within the Property/Casualty Insurance Industry* (New York: Insurance Services Office, June 1987), p. 3.

8. The Public Entity Risk Institute's current Web site address is World Wide Web: www.riskinstitute.org (5 June 2002).

9. The foregoing paragraphs under this heading are adapted from *Insurance Issues Update*, Ruth Gastel, CPCU, ed., Insurance Information Institute, November 1994.

10. The complete text of the 41-page act, also known as the Leach-Gramm-Bliley Act, or S.900, may be found at the Library of Congress's Thomas Web site at World Wide Web: http://thomas.loc.gov (15 August 2001).

11. "S.900 Does Not Mean All The Battles Are Over," *National Underwriter*, Life & Health/Financial Services edition, November 22, 1999, p. 42.

12. Ruth Gastel, CPCU, *Insurance Issues Update*, "Rate Regulation and Other Regulatory Issues," Insurance Information Institute, September 2000, p. 3.

13. David M. Katz, "Dereg in Three States May Hinge on Agents," *National Underwriter*, Property & Casualty/Risk & Benefits Management edition, January 31, 2000, pp. 1, 31.

14. National Association of Insurance Commissioners. World Wide Web: http://www.naic.org/1regulator/accreditedstates.htm (15 June 2001).

15. A more detailed examination of this question appears in Justin L. Brady, Joyce Hall Mellinger, and Kenneth N. Scoles Jr., *The Regulation of Insurance*, 1st ed., (Malvern, Pa.: Insurance Institute of America, 1995), Chapter 5, on which this discussion is based.

16. 18 USC Sec. 1033.

17. Ann Monaco Warren, Esq., and John William Simon, Esq., "Dishonesty or Breach of Trust" in 18 U.S.C. § 1033: "Are *You* Criminally Liable on the Basis of an Associate's Record?" *FORC Quarterly Journal of Insurance Law and Regulation*, Fall 1998, September 12, 1998, vol. X, edition III, Federation of Regulatory Counsel, Inc.

18. 18 USC § 1033.

19. S.E.C. v. Variable Annuity Life Insurance Co. of America et al., 359 U.S. 65 (1959).

20. National Conference of Insurance Guaranty Funds, World Wide Web: http://www.ncigf.org (15 August 2001).

21. *Insurer Failures, Property/Casualty Insurer Insolvencies and State Guaranty Funds* (Oldwick, N.J.: A.M. Best Company, 1991), pp. 26–34.

22. *Insurer Failures, Property/Casualty Insurer Insolvencies and State Guaranty Funds*, p. 28.

23. General Accounting Office, Insurance Regulation, Problems in the State Monitoring of Property/Casualty Insurer Solvency (Washington, D.C.: U.S. Government Printing Office, 1989), pp. 2–26.

24. Bernard L. Webb, J. J. Launie, Willis Park Rokes, and Norman A. Baglini, *Insurance Company Operations*, 3d ed., vol. II (Malvern, Pa.: American Institute for Property and Liability Underwriters, 1984), p. 7.

25. Scott E. Harrington, "Competition and Regulation in the Automobile Insurance Market" (paper prepared for distribution at the ABA National Institute on Insurance Competition and Pricing in the 1990s, Baltimore, June 2–3, 1990), p. 6.

26. Consumer Federation of America. World Wide Web: http://www.consumerfed.org (5 June 2002).

27. Insurance Institute for Highway Safety. World Wide Web: http://www.highwaysafety.org (5 June 2002).

28. J. Robert Hunter, "The 1990s—Where Are We Headed," *Insurance Competition and Pricing in the 1990s* (June 2–3, 1990, proceedings of The National Institute), p. 1.

Chapter 3

Direct

Direct Your Learning

Distribution Systems

After learning the subject matter of this chapter, you should be able to:

- Explain how market intermediaries and traditional distribution systems deliver insurance products and services.

- Explain how property-casualty insurance needs are satisfied through alternative marketing mechanisms.

- Compare the branch office and managing general agency systems.

- Describe the typical functions performed by insurance agents.

- Explain the factors to consider in selecting a distribution system.

- Evaluate the market shares of the major types of distribution systems and explain their relative success or failure.

Develop Your Perspective

What are the main topics covered in the chapter?

Insurance companies must reach their customers to sell their policies and deliver services to their customer once the policies have been sold. Four main distribution systems and numerous alternative marketing mechanisms provide channels for insurers to reach customers.

Consider what system your insurance organization uses to distribute its products, information, and services.

- How does the system dictate the service that employees must provide directly to customers?

- What services do agents provide?

Why is it important to know these topics?

Each distribution system provides some benefits and some restrictions for an insurer.

Understand how the distribution systems your organization has chosen operate.

- What are the limitations created by that distribution system?

- What are the opportunities created by that distribution system?

How can you use this information?

Analyze the strengths and weaknesses of the various distribution systems.

- How do they affect other decisions made by your organization?

- Can your organization easily increase its market share of desirable policies by using its current distribution system?

- For your organization's policy-writing objectives, which marketing system(s) would produce the desired results most effectively?

Chapter 3

Distribution Systems

Any firm that sells a product must have a distribution system to deliver its product or service to the customer. The functions of the distribution system depend on the nature of the product sold and the buyers to whom it is sold. The system might be very complex or very simple, again based on the nature of the product and the needs of the buyers and prospective buyers.

This chapter focuses on the insurance market intermediaries that deliver the insurance product to insurance consumers through various distribution systems. The phrase *insurance consumers* is used here in its broadest sense to encompass all buyers of insurance, including individuals, families, businesses, government bodies, and others. There are, in fact, several insurance distribution systems, each designed to meet the needs of a select group of insurers and insurance consumers.

INSURANCE MARKET INTERMEDIARIES

A **distribution system** consists of the necessary people and physical facilities to (1) communicate information between the seller of the product and buyers or potential buyers and (2) move the product between the seller and the buyers. For tangible products, such as automobiles or refrigerators, the distribution system might include extensive and expensive physical facilities, such as trucks, terminals, warehouses, and showrooms. Distribution systems for intangible products, such as the insurance product, are more flexible and adaptable because they are not constrained by large investments in physical facilities.

Because insurance offers an intangible product, the insurance market has special qualities. Understanding these qualities requires a knowledge of the market intermediaries' activities. Representing others in the insurance relationship requires an understanding of the principles of agency.

Unique Characteristics of Insurance Marketing

The marketing of insurance differs substantially from the marketing of other products, especially the distribution of tangible products. The distribution of tangible products usually involves several levels of distribution between the manufacturer and the ultimate consumer. For example, a distributor might

Distribution system
A system that consists of the necessary people and physical facilities to (1) communicate information between the seller of the product and buyers or potential buyers and (2) move the product between the sellers and the buyers.

buy the product from the manufacturer and sell it to a wholesaler. The wholesaler sells it to a retailer, who in turn sells it to consumers.

Insurance is less involved. In most cases, only one intermediary is between the insurer and the consumer. In some cases there are two, but seldom more than two. Often there are none, with the insurer selling directly to the consumer. The levels of intermediaries are discussed in more detail later in this chapter.

Intermediaries in insurance marketing perform several functions. Their principal function is selling. Some kinds of insurance are compulsory, required either by law or by various contractual relationships. For example, workers compensation and auto liability insurance are required by law in most states. Auto physical damage coverage is required by lenders if the car is financed, and homeowners or dwelling insurance is required by mortgage agreements. For these types of required insurance, the principal role of the intermediary is to assist consumers in selecting an insurer and to explain specific details of policies.

Many kinds of insurance are purchased solely at the option of the consumer. For these lines, the intermediary must assist the consumer in determining the coverages needed as well as in selecting an insurer.

Some of the intermediaries might issue policies and collect premiums, though insurers often perform these functions. Many intermediaries adjust claims, most often relatively small property insurance claims.

Legal Status of Agents

Agent
A person or firm in an agency relationship authorized by the principal to act on the principal's behalf.

Most insurers are corporations. As such, they can operate only through agents. An **agent** can be defined as a person or firm authorized to represent another person or firm in the performance of some function. The person or firm represented by an agent is called the **principal**. At law, an agent may be either an employee of the principal or an independent contractor. Within the insurance industry, the term agent is sometimes reserved for independent contractors who represent insurers. The term **broker** is applied to independent contractors who represent policyholders and prospective policyholders in their dealings with insurers.

Principal
The party in an agency relationship that authorizes an agent to act on its behalf.

Another term frequently used in insurance marketing is **producer**, which refers to a person who sells insurance to consumers. It includes brokers, agents of the insurer, employees of insurance companies or of intermediaries, and independent contractors.

Broker
An independent business owner or firm that represents policyholders and prospective policyholders in their dealings with insurers.

Powers and Duties of Agents

Producer
A person or firm that sells insurance products to consumers for an insurance company or companies.

An agent has only the powers conferred by the principal. When an insurer appoints an agent, a written contract is usually executed. The contract usually specifies the powers and duties of the agent. The powers granted usually include the lines of insurance to be written, the agent's authority to bind coverages, claim adjustment authority of the agent, and similar matters. The duties deal with accounting for policies and other supplies furnished by the insurer, accounting for insurer funds in the hands of the agent, adherence to rules adopted by the insurer, and so forth.

The law recognizes certain **apparent authority** of an insurance agent. This apparent authority is a concern only when the agent is dealing with a buyer or prospective insurance buyer who has no knowledge of the agent's **actual authority**, authority conferred by the principal under the agency contract. For example, a property-casualty insurance agent has apparent authority to bind coverage in most states. Thus, an agent can bind coverage even if the agency contract does not specifically mention such action.

Apparent authority
A third party's reasonable belief that an agent has authority to act on behalf of the principal.

Actual authority
Authority conferred by the principal to an agent under an agency contract.

Although insurance agents primarily represent insurers, the law imposes on them certain duties to insurance consumers as well. The extent of these duties depends on the relationship established between the agent and the insurance consumer. If the agent merely agrees to provide one or more specific insurance policies to the policyholder, he or she has only two duties to the client: (1) to provide the agreed policies and (2) to place the agreed policies with a solvent insurer. If the policies are placed with an insurer licensed in the state where the insured exposures are located, it is usually sufficient if the agent has no knowledge of any information to indicate that it is financially impaired. If insurance is placed with an insurer not licensed in the state, the agent might have a duty to exercise greater care regarding the insurer's financial status.

The liability outlined above is the minimum liability imposed on agents. An agent's liability can be expanded substantially through his or her actions or by specific contract. For example, if an agent undertakes to provide risk management advice to a policyholder, the agent might be held liable for overlooking loss exposures. For example, one agent was held liable for failing to advise a client of the need for fire legal liability insurance for a leased building.

Attributes of Insurance Intermediaries

All property-casualty insurance agents, whether company employees or independent contractors, share certain powers and duties. Beyond these shared powers and duties, agents differ greatly in their relationships with insurers and consumers. The principal differences are in (1) their relationship to the insurers with which they do business, (2) how they are compensated for their services, and (3) the degree of control they have over contacts between the insurers they represent and the clients for whom they write coverages, usually referred to as "ownership of expirations."

Relationship With Insurers

The agent's contractual ties to insurers determine the amount of control the insurers can exercise over the agent. Viewed from the opposite perspective, the agency contract determines the extent of the agent's independence from the insurer or insurers represented. Generally, an insurer does exercise greater control over agents who are company employees than it can over independent contractors. In fact, this greater control is one of the characteristics that distinguish employees from independent contractors when a legal distinction must be made. As a general rule, if an agent is an independent contractor, the insurer cannot control the methods the agent uses to accomplish the purposes of the agency. The agent is free to use any legal and ethical methods to accomplish the purposes set forth in the agency contract. For an employee, on the other hand, the employer can control the method, and not merely the goals and objectives of the agency arrangement.

Some insurers specify in their agency contracts that their agents cannot represent other insurers. Thus, those agents are restricted to representing only one insurer or a group of insurers under common ownership and management, even though the agents are independent contractors. Other agents are not subject to such contractual restrictions and may represent as many insurers as they wish, or at least as many insurers as are willing to enter into agency contracts with them.

Some insurers take an intermediate stance between these extremes. For example, an insurance company might permit its agents to represent other insurers provided the other insurers are used only to write business that the company does not want to write.

The level of independence of the agent is an important consideration in distinguishing among the several distribution systems used in marketing property-casualty insurance.

Compensation Methods

The way an agent is compensated is another characteristic of insurance distribution systems. The method of compensation tends to vary with the closeness of the agent's relationships to the insurers represented. Agents who represent several unrelated insurers are usually compensated by a commission on the premiums they write.

Agents who are employees of the insurer might be compensated by salary or by a combination of salary and commissions. Agents who are independent contractors but who are restricted to representing one insurer are usually compensated by commissions. However, some insurers might provide a guaranteed minimum income to such agents during a training period.

Contingent, bonus, and profit-sharing commissions
Commissions paid by an insurer, usually annually, to an insurance agency. These commissions are based on the premium volume and profitability level of the agency's policies with that insurer.

Agents who are compensated by commissions might receive two kinds of commissions. A flat commission, stated as a fixed percentage of premiums, constitutes the principal source of compensation. The commission percentage can vary by line of insurance. The commission rate might differ for new business and renewal business. When the rates are different, a lower commission is usually paid for renewal business, reflecting the lesser effort required of the agent for renewal business.

In addition to the flat commission, agents may receive a variable commission, sometimes called a **contingent commission**, **bonus commission**, or **profit-sharing commission**. The amount of the variable commission usually depends on the loss ratio of the business written by the agent. Sometimes, the variable commission also depends on the increase in the agent's premium volume with the insurer. Thus, variable commissions can be used to motivate agents to write preferred risks, to write more business, or to do both.

Sometimes insurers authorize agents to appoint and supervise subagents. The supervising agent then receives a commission on all business written by the subagents. This commission, called an **override** (sometimes overwrite) **commission**, is usually smaller than the commission paid to the subagents who originate the business. The various commission arrangements are discussed in greater detail later in this chapter.

Override commission
Commission paid to an agent who appoints and supervises subagents.

Ownership of Expirations

Historically, insurers and agents have disagreed as to which of them owns the expirations for policies sold by the agent. Ownership of expirations means ownership of all records showing when existing policies expire, but it also means much more. If the agent owns the expirations, the insurer cannot try to renew the policies, either directly or through another agent. Moreover, ownership of expirations means that the insurer cannot take those policies away or transfer them to another agent.

To illustrate the significance of the ownership of expirations, assume that an agency has been an agent of an insurer for many years. The agency contract specifies that the agency owns the expirations. The agency terminates its agency contract with the company and, on renewal, rewrites all of its policies with another insurer. The original insurance company is powerless to prevent the transfer of the business to another insurer. Because the agency owns the expirations, the insurer is prohibited from soliciting the business either directly or through another of its agents.

Ownership of the expirations is important to both agents and insurers. It provides agents with an important asset with a substantial market value. It gives insurers greater control over their business, because their agents cannot move the business to another insurer either on termination of the agency contract or while the agency contract continues in force.

Of course, ownership of expirations controls only the conduct of the specific insurer and its agents. Ultimate ownership of expirations rests with the policyholders. They can move their business among insurers and agents as they see fit.

The ownership of expirations is usually specified in agency contracts, though some classes of agents may have ownership of expirations as a matter of law in the absence of a contractual provision to the contrary. Practices regarding ownership of expirations vary widely among the various insurance marketing systems. These practices are discussed in greater detail later in this chapter.

TYPES OF INSURANCE DISTRIBUTION SYSTEMS

Four main distribution systems are employed by property-casualty insurers in the United States: (1) the independent agency system, (2) the exclusive agency system, (3) the direct writer system, and (4) the direct response system. The principal characteristics that distinguish one distribution system from another include (1) the extent to which the agent is tied to the insurers represented, (2) the methods of compensating the agents, and (3) the ownership of expirations.

Independent Agency System

Independent agency system
System under which agents, who are independent contractors, sell insurance, usually as representatives of several unrelated insurance companies. The independent agency system uses these agencies as a distribution system.

The **independent agency system** uses agents that are independent contractors. They are usually free to represent as many insurers as they want. Independent agents own the expirations and can switch business among the insurers they represent, subject only to the policyholder's approval.

Insurance brokers represent policyholders rather than insurers, but they are included within the independent agency system. One reason for including them is that the same person can act as an agent on one transaction and as a broker on another. A person must act as an agent when placing business with an insurer for which he or she is licensed as an agent but may act as a broker when placing business with other insurers. Generally, insurance brokers are legally agents for the insured; they are not granted binding authority. The client base for the large broker is very different from that served by most independent agents in terms of sophistication and services required. Finally, compensation schemes may be different for independent agents and for brokers. Brokers perform some or all of their services on a fee basis, whereas independent agents are compensated almost exclusively by commission.

Managing general agents (MGAs)
Independent business organizations that function almost as branch offices for one or more insurance companies. The MGA appoints and supervises independent agents for insurance companies that use the independent agency system.

Managing general agents (MGAs) are also included within the independent agency system. MGAs serve as intermediaries between insurers and agents who sell insurance directly to the consumer, in much the same position as wholesalers in the distribution system for tangible goods. The exact duties and responsibilities of an MGA depend on its contracts with the insurers it represents. Some MGAs are strictly sales operations, appointing and supervising subagents or dealing with brokers within their contractual jurisdiction. That jurisdiction can be specified in terms of geographic boundaries, lines of insurance, or both.

Excess and surplus lines brokers resemble MGAs in that they usually do business primarily with other brokers and agents and not directly with consumers. In fact, some firms operate as both managing general agents and surplus lines brokers.

Excess and surplus lines brokers
Persons or firms that place business with insurers not licensed in the state in which the transaction occurs (nonadmitted carrier).

Excess and surplus lines brokers place business with insurers not licensed in the state in which the transaction occurs. Other brokers and agents are usually limited to placing business with licensed (or admitted) insurers. The circumstances under which business can be placed with an unlicensed (or nonadmitted) insurer through a surplus lines broker vary by state. A reasonable effort to place the coverage with licensed insurers is frequently required. The agent or broker may be required to certify that a specified number (often two or three) of licensed insurers have refused to provide the coverage or to provide letters from the insurers rejecting the coverage. Some state insurance departments maintain lists of coverages eligible for surplus lines treatment without first being rejected by licensed insurers. Some states also maintain lists of eligible surplus lines insurers.

The variety of participants operating within the independent agency system makes it a very flexible distribution system, able to cope with the requirements of a wide variety of insurance consumers. Its flexibility is a great advantage in competing for complex commercial lines business, for which substantial expertise and flexibility are needed. The independent agency system is typically more expensive to operate than other systems. Its cost is a handicap in competing for personal lines business, for which price is often more important than expertise or flexibility from the perspective of the consumer.

The agents and brokers that operate within the independent agency system are compensated by commissions on the business they write. Many of them receive two types of commissions: (1) a flat percentage commission on all business submitted and (2) a contingent or profit-sharing commission earned through volume or by meeting profit goals.

Exhibit 3-1 shows an illustrative contingent commission scale. The contingent commissions shown in Exhibit 3-1 vary only with the agency's loss ratio. Some companies use scales that vary with the amount of business the agency writes with the company as well as the agency's loss ratio. Exhibit 3-2 shows such a commission scale.

Managing general agencies are usually compensated by an override commission on business sold by their subagents. They might also receive a contingent commission based on the profitability, and possibly the volume, of business they write.

Independent agents and brokers own the expirations for the business they write. This ownership is usually clearly stated in the agency contract. However, the ownership exists as a matter of custom and law even in the absence of a contractual provision. The expirations usually constitute the largest and most marketable asset of an insurance agency.

Although independent agents are primarily the sales force of the insurers they represent, they might offer several other services to their clients. Many independent agents adjust some losses under the policies they write. This service might be limited to small property losses, but some agents also adjust small liability claims. Empowering the agent to provide loss adjustment services is advantageous to both policyholders and the insurance company. The principal advantage to policyholders is rapid service; the insurance

EXHIBIT 3-1

Profit-Sharing Commission Based on Loss Ratio

Loss Ratio	Profit Sharing Commission as Percentage of Earned Premiums
0.00	14.00%
0.05	12.05
0.10	10.35
0.15	8.65
0.20	7.15
0.25	5.65
0.30	4.50
0.35	3.30
0.40	2.25
0.45	1.30
0.50	0.60
0.55	0.00

EXHIBIT 3-2

Percentage Increase in Profit-Sharing Commission Based on Premium Volume and Growth Rate

Earned Premiums	Percentage Growth in Premium Volume					
	10%	15%	20%	30%	40%	60%
$ 50,000	3.50%	7.00%	10.50%	17.50%	24.50%	38.50%
75,000	4.69	8.50	12.31	19.94	27.56	42.81
100,000	5.87	10.00	14.12	22.38	30.62	47.12
150,000	8.25	13.00	17.75	27.25	36.75	55.75
200,000	10.62	16.00	21.37	28.37	42.87	64.38
250,000	13.00	19.00	25.00	37.00	49.00	73.00
400,000	20.12	28.00	35.87	51.62	67.37	98.87
500,000	24.87	34.00	43.12	61.37	79.62	100.00

company benefits from lower adjustment expenses and possibly greater customer goodwill.

Independent agents and brokers might also provide risk management advice to their clients, helping them to select the insurance coverages needed and assisting them in obtaining the needed coverage on the most advantageous terms. Many agents and brokers also assist their clients in the establishment and management of self-insurance programs, loss control measures, and other alternatives or supplements to insurance.

Exclusive Agency System

The **exclusive agency system** uses independent contractors called exclusive agents (or captive agents) who are not employees of the insurance company. Unlike independent agents, exclusive agents are usually restricted by contract to representing a single insurance company. Consequently, the insurance company principal can exercise greater control over exclusive agents than over independent agents.

Exclusive agents are usually compensated by commissions. Some of them receive a salary, guaranteed minimum income, or drawing account during an initial training program. Paying one commission rate for new business and another, lower rate for renewal business is common in the exclusive agency system. Independent agents, on the other hand, usually receive the same commission rate for both new and renewal business. Lower renewal commissions might tempt an independent agent to switch business to a different insurer on renewal to get the higher new business commission. This option is not available to exclusive agents because of their exclusive representation agreement.

Exclusive agents do not have ownership of expirations as a matter of custom or law, as independent agents do. Some insurers that market through the exclusive agency system do grant limited ownership of expirations to their agents by contract. Usually, such contracts grant ownership of expirations only while the agency contract is in force. When the agency contract is terminated, the ownership of expirations reverts to the insurance company. The insurer might be obligated to pay the agent for the expirations upon termination of the agency contract, but the agent does not have the option of selling the expirations to anyone other than the insurer.

Exclusive agents might offer loss adjustment services similar to those offered by independent agents. However, their exclusive representation agreements might restrict their ability to offer some risk management services to their clients.

Direct Writer System

The **direct writer marketing system** uses sales agents who are employees of the insurance companies they represent. They are not independent contractors like independent agents and exclusive agents. The agents in the direct

Exclusive agency system
System in which an agent has a contract to sell insurance exclusively for one insurance company or a group of related companies.

Direct writer marketing system
An insurance marketing system that uses sales representatives who are employees of an insurance company.

writer system might be compensated by salary, commission, or a combination of the two. They usually do not have any ownership of expirations and, like exclusive agents, are usually restricted to representing a single insurer or a group of insurers under common ownership and management.

Direct Response System

Direct response marketing system
Any system that does not depend primarily on individual producers to locate customers and sell insurance but relies primarily on mail, telephone, Internet, and/or other media for sales.

In the **direct response marketing system** (sometimes called the mail order system), the insurer does not employ sales agents to make direct, face-to-face contact with policyholders or prospective policyholders. Instead, the insurer offers its services to prospective insureds by direct mail, by telephone, or by advertising through the mass media such as radio, television, newspapers, and magazines.

This marketing system has been used primarily for marketing personal lines of insurance. It has not been widely effective in marketing commercial lines because of the more complex nature of the commercial coverages and rating plans.

Combination Systems

Of the four marketing systems outlined above, no one is most advantageous to all insurance companies or all classes of insurance consumers. The independent agency system is likely to be most satisfactory for buyers who have very complex insurance needs or who consider service more important than cost. Independent agents are also very effective in reaching insurance consumers in rural areas and small towns.

The exclusive agency and direct writer systems have been most successful in dealing with insurance buyers who have relatively simple needs, primarily individuals, families, and small, main-street type businesses. Only a few companies in these systems have been successful in marketing to larger businesses.

Exclusive agency and direct writer systems have also been most successful in reaching urban consumers, though some have specialized in farm and rural consumers. Generally, exclusive agents and direct writers have appealed most successfully to consumers who are more concerned with price than personal service, but many agents among both groups are well qualified to provide the services needed in their markets.

Historically, insurance companies participated in only one of the marketing systems, and most of them marketed through the independent agency system. The other systems have expanded dramatically during the past four or five decades.

Some insurers began to diversify into more than one of the marketing systems as a means of reaching buyers whom their traditional marketing systems had not reached successfully. The first attempts at using mixed marketing systems were probably made by a few direct writers that specialized in commercial coverage. They experimented with selling through independent brokers in order to reach larger commercial insurance buyers who were not being served successfully by their direct writer agents.

Later, some direct writers began using independent agents to sell personal lines and small commercial lines. Their initial objective was to reach the rural and small-town markets not adequately served by direct writer agents and exclusive agents.

Direct writers and exclusive agency companies incur substantial start-up costs and fixed costs in establishing an agent in a new territory. These heavy costs make it difficult for them to market through their traditional methods in rural areas and small towns, where the amount of business available is very limited. Independent agents usually succeed in rural areas because they represent more insurers, offer more products, and, consequently, have a larger market.

Companies that traditionally marketed through the independent agency system have also adopted mixed marketing systems. One large insurer that had participated in the independent agency system for over a century has experimented (with limited success) with all three of the other systems. It purchased a direct writing subsidiary, which it sold about a decade later. It tried direct response marketing but discontinued the program after only a few months. It also entered into contracts with some of its agents providing that the agents would give it first refusal of all business they wrote and would place business elsewhere only if the insurer refused to write it.

Another recent development that seems likely to expand is the movement toward vertical integration in property-casualty insurance marketing. Vertical integration occurs when an organization owns several stages in the process of providing a product to the consumer. For example, an agent or a broker might own an insurance company, or an insurance company might own an agency or a brokerage firm.

Vertical integration seems to have been initiated by the acquisition of insurance companies by the large brokerage firms. Regulatory authorities have discouraged such acquisitions in recent years because of the insolvency of some broker-owned insurers and because of the apparent conflict between the brokers' duties as representatives of the policyholders and their interest in the profits of the insurers they own. Several large brokerage firms have sold off their subsidiary insurance companies.

More recently, several large insurance agencies and brokerage firms have been acquired, in whole or in part, by insurance companies or by holding companies that also own insurance companies. The acquired agencies or brokerage firms are units of the independent agency system. Company ownership of agencies and brokerage firms would seem to be a close approximation of the exclusive agency system. The relationship differs from the exclusive agency system in that the subsidiary agency or brokerage firm is still permitted to deal with other unrelated insurance companies. However, some observers question whether the subsidiary agencies and brokerage firms can deal with unrelated insurers on an equal footing with their parent companies.

Several insurers have been very successful in using mixed marketing systems. The use of mixed marketing systems will probably continue to grow in the foreseeable future.

ALTERNATIVE MARKETING MECHANISMS

Despite the variety of marketing systems that insurers have traditionally used, they have not always been able to satisfy the requirements of all insurance consumers. Various alternative markets have been created to fill the gaps left unmet by traditional insurers.

One of the largest of these gaps consists of consumers who do not meet the underwriting standards of insurers operating in the voluntary market. These **alternative market mechanisms** can also be called shared-market mechanisms because all licensed insurers are required to share in the risks insured through them.

The market mechanisms discussed in the following section do not conform to the traditional meaning of insurance distribution. This section takes a broader approach to describing insurance markets while recognizing that most of these alternative market mechanisms use the same distribution systems as conventional private insurers.

Involuntary Market Mechanisms

Insurers that use one of the marketing systems discussed in the previous section and seek to write insurance exposures they view as desirable are sometimes referred to as the **voluntary market** because they voluntarily provide coverage to entities that meet their underwriting requirements. Several **involuntary market mechanisms** have been developed to provide coverage for entities that do not qualify for coverage in the voluntary market. These mechanisms are *involuntary* in that the insurers have been required to establish them by statute, regulation, or regulatory pressure. The involuntary market mechanisms are sometimes called **residual market mechanisms** because they insure the entities that remain uninsured after the insurers have accepted all insureds who meet the underwriting requirements for the voluntary market.

Involuntary Insurance Market

Perhaps the largest and oldest of the involuntary market mechanisms are those that provide automobile insurance for persons who cannot qualify for coverage in the voluntary market. The total automobile insurance residual market premium totaled over $2 billion in 2000.[1] All states and the District of Columbia have an involuntary market mechanism to ensure automobile insurance availability. In 2000, the involuntary market mechanisms had a 1.5 percent share of the market nationally. The market share varied widely, from less than 0.1 percent to 13.5 percent in Massachusetts.[2] Several states have

Alternative market mechanism
Process in which all licensed insurers are required to share in the risks insured within the program. Sometimes referred to as shared market mechanism.

Voluntary market
That portion of the insurance market that voluntarily provides coverage to individuals and companies that meet their underwriting requirements.

Involuntary (residual) market mechanisms
Mechanisms that make insurance available to those who cannot obtain coverage elsewhere because private insurers will not voluntarily provide such coverage for various reasons.

experienced a decline in private passenger residual market writings. The residual market share in South Carolina, for example, dropped from 29 percent in 1998 to 8.3 percent in 1999 as a result of legislative changes in the state.[3] In 2000, the state market share dropped further, to 2.7 percent.[4]

There are four kinds of auto insurance residual market mechanisms: (1) assigned risk plans, (2) joint underwriting associations, (3) auto reinsurance plans, and (4) state funds.

Assigned Risk Plans

Assigned risk plans are often called *auto insurance plans* in an effort to avoid the perceived stigma attached to the inability to obtain coverage in the voluntary market. The term *assigned risk plan* will be used here because it more clearly distinguishes this type of plan from the other three types.

All states have some kind of involuntary market mechanism for automobile insurance, and most of them are assigned risk plans. Under an **assigned risk plan**, any licensed driver who cannot obtain insurance in the voluntary market is assigned to a specific insurance company. That insurer must then provide coverage for the assigned driver for a specific period of time (usually three years) unless the driver later obtains voluntary coverage. Coverage for the assigned drivers is handled in essentially the same manner as is coverage for the insurer's voluntarily insured drivers.

The number of drivers assigned to each licensed insurer is determined by the insurer's share of the voluntary auto insurance market. For example, an insurer that writes coverage for 10 percent of the cars in the voluntary market would be assigned 10 percent of the cars insured under the assigned risk plan.

In the past, all states had assigned risk plans. The other types of auto insurance residual market mechanisms were developed to avoid or reduce the perceived stigma attached to the assigned risk plans.

Joint Underwriting Associations

Several states now have **joint underwriting associations (JUAs)** to provide auto insurance to those who cannot qualify for coverage in the voluntary market. A JUA resembles an assigned risk plan in that all licensed auto insurers are required to participate in the plan and to share the burden of providing coverage for those who cannot meet the underwriting requirements of the voluntary market.

A JUA differs from an assigned risk plan in that drivers insured under the JUA are not assigned to specific insurers. The JUA provides all coverage, retains all premiums, and pays all losses and expenses. Participating insurers share the profits or (more likely) losses of the JUA in proportion to their shares of the voluntary market.

The JUA appoints several insurers as servicing companies. A driver who is insured by the JUA receives a policy issued by a servicing company, and that

Assigned risk plan
An auto insurance plan adopted in some states to provide automobile insurance to drivers who cannot obtain insurance in the voluntary market. The vehicle operator is assigned to a specific insurance company. That insurer must provide coverage for the assigned driver for a period of time. The proportionate share of assignments to an insurer is based on its percentage of the voluntary auto insurance written in the state.

Joint underwriting associations (JUAs)
Organizations created in a few states that designate servicing insurers to cover high-risk auto insurance customers. All auto insurers in the state are assessed a proportionate share of the JUA's losses and expenses based on their percentage of the voluntary auto insurance premium written in the state.

company adjusts all losses incurred under the policy. The servicing company receives a fee from the JUA to reimburse it for the cost of providing services. The insured driver might not even know that the coverage is being provided by the JUA.

Auto Reinsurance Plans

Auto reinsurance plans
An auto insurance plan under which an insurer that regularly sells automobile insurance cannot refuse to provide coverage for any licensed driver, but it can transfer to the reinsurance plan all or part of a risk. The insurer pays a portion of the premiums to the reinsurance plan, and the insurer is reimbursed for all losses under the policy. The plan's profits or losses are shared proportionately by all licensed auto insurers.

A small number of states have **auto reinsurance plans** instead of assigned risk plans or JUAs. In those states, an insurer that regularly sells automobile insurance cannot refuse to provide coverage for any licensed driver. However, it can transfer to the reinsurance plan all or a part of the risk for any driver who does not meet its normal underwriting standards.

The insurer must issue its own policy to cover the driver. It keeps a part of the premium to cover its expenses and pays the balance of the premium to the reinsurance plan. The originating insurer pays all losses under the policy but is reimbursed by the reinsurance plan. All profits or losses of the reinsurance plan are shared by all licensed auto insurers in the state in proportion to their shares in the voluntary market.

The principal difference between a JUA and a reinsurance plan is the number of *servicing insurers*, although that term is not used in connection with reinsurance plans. Under a JUA, a relatively small number of insurers are designated as servicing companies, and every application for coverage through the JUA must be submitted to one of the servicing companies. Under a reinsurance plan, any insurer licensed to write auto insurance in the state can submit an application for coverage through the plan. Consequently, all licensed auto insurers could be considered to be servicing companies.

State Funds

Maryland Automobile Insurance Fund (MAIF)
An auto insurance fund that collects premiums from the drivers it insures and pays losses on their behalf. If the premiums it collects are inadequate to pay the losses and expenses, the fund can assess all auto insurers licensed in the state to cover its deficit.

Maryland has taken a different approach to the involuntary automobile insurance market. It established a state fund, the **Maryland Automobile Insurance Fund (MAIF)**, to provide coverage for drivers who cannot obtain insurance through the voluntary market. The fund, which is operated by the state, collects premiums from the drivers it insures and pays losses on their behalf. It operates essentially as an insurance company with one major exception. If the premiums it collects are inadequate to pay the losses and expenses it incurs, it can assess all auto insurers licensed in Maryland an amount sufficient to cover its deficit.

Involuntary Property Insurance Market Mechanisms

Fair Access to Insurance Requirements (FAIR) plans
State-run programs that provide basic property insurance coverage on buildings, dwellings, and their contents for property owners who are unable to obtain coverage in the voluntary insurance market.

Involuntary market mechanisms for property insurance have also been established in some states. Two kinds of such mechanisms now exist. **Fair Access to Insurance Requirements (FAIR) plans** now operate in twenty-seven states and the District of Columbia. Beach and windstorm plans operate in seven states.

FAIR plans were established to make property insurance available to persons who cannot obtain it through the voluntary market. The plans provide at least fire and extended coverage insurance. Homeowners coverage is provided in some states. FAIR plans also provide crime coverage in a few states and earthquake coverage in at least one state. FAIR plans operate in a manner very similar to that outlined for auto JUAs above. The FAIR plans provided $113.3 billion of property insurance in 2000.[5]

Beach and windstorm plans exist in the coastal states in the hurricane belt of the Gulf and South Atlantic coasts. Each coastal state from Texas to North Carolina (except Georgia) has a beach and windstorm pool to provide windstorm coverage in the coastal areas. These plans also operate in a manner similar to the auto JUAs. They had a total of $108.0 billion of insurance in force in 2000.[6]

Beach and windstorm plans
State-regulated insurance plans that provide property insurance, both personal and commercial, in coastal areas exposed to heavy windstorm losses.

Workers Compensation Involuntary Market Mechanisms

Workers compensation insurance market mechanisms consist of a national pool, state pools, or workers compensation state funds. The national pool covers thirty-two jurisdictions and includes the high-risk employees in five states with competitive state funds.

The workers compensation involuntary market mechanisms function in a manner similar to the auto JUAs discussed above. In addition, a **National Reinsurance Pool**, administered by the National Council on Compensation Insurance, provides reinsurance for the state pools. These pools, collectively, are the largest writer of workers compensation, with about 20 percent of the market nationally.

National Reinsurance Pool
A pool that provides reinsurance for the state-sponsored involuntary workers compensation pools.

Other Involuntary Market Mechanisms

A number of other involuntary market mechanisms exist. Several states have JUAs for medical malpractice liability insurance. At least two states have JUAs for liquor law liability insurance. Some states have standby JUAs for other lines. These JUAs are not active, but enabling legislation has been adopted so that the insurance commissioner can activate them quickly if they are needed.

Government Insurance

Private insurers provide most property-casualty insurance in the United States. However, a number of government insurers exist at both the state and federal levels.

Supporters justify government insurance programs on several grounds. The first and most convincing argument is the inability or unwillingness of private insurers to provide a form of protection that is necessary for the public welfare. Flood insurance and war risk coverage are examples.

Lower cost to consumers also seems to be a consideration in the establishment of some government insurance plans. Lower cost was probably the major factor in the establishment of the state life insurance fund in Wisconsin and possibly in the establishment of state funds for crop hail insurance.

In some cases, proponents justify government insurance plans on the grounds that it is unfair to enrich private insurers by permitting them to profit on insurance that is required by law. This seems to have been a major consideration in the establishment of state workers compensation insurance funds.

Some government insurance programs seem to have been started to promote social, economic, or scientific developments. For example, mortgage guaranty insurance was established at least in part to encourage home ownership and to provide financial support to the construction industry. A federal agency provides export credit insurance in order to promote exports and thus to foster a healthy national economy.

Whatever the reasons, a number of government insurance programs have been established over the past few decades, and more are under consideration.

State Insurance Funds

State insurance funds
A method for providing workers compensation insurance that would otherwise be written by insurers in the voluntary market. These funds may operate monopolistically or in competition with insurers in the voluntary market.

State insurance funds exist in many states to provide insurance that would otherwise be written by property-casualty insurers. Thirty states have state funds to provide workers compensation insurance. In six of those states employers are required to purchase their workers compensation insurance from the state fund. Private insurers are not permitted to write workers compensation insurance in those states.

In the remaining states, workers compensation state funds compete with private insurers for business. The state with the largest residual market share is Alaska, at 113 percent.[7] Residual market premiums amounted to $485 million, or 3.2 percent of the premium in states with residual markets.[8]

States also have insurance funds for other lines of coverage. The Maryland Automobile Insurance Fund was mentioned previously in this chapter. Several states have funds for crop hail insurance. At least two states have funds to compensate property owners for damage to property on the surface resulting from the collapse of underground coal mines. Several states have patient compensation funds for patients injured as a result of medical malpractice incidents. These funds usually provide coverage for losses in excess of some substantial amount, such as $100,000, with private insurers providing the basic coverage.

Federal Insurance Programs

The federal government has numerous insurance programs. Those most closely related to property-casualty insurance are discussed below.

Flood Insurance

Private insurers debated the insurability of the flood exposure for many years. It was the prevailing belief within the industry that the flood exposure was not commercially insurable. The principal reasons given for uninsurability were the following:

- The catastrophic nature of losses
- The repetition of claims
- Adverse selection (the tendency of only those people in flood-prone areas to buy flood insurance)

Consequently, flood insurance was not generally available in the private insurance market. Some commercial and industrial firms could purchase flood coverage under a difference in conditions policy (DIC), but even that was not usually available to firms located in flood-prone areas.

The National Flood Insurance Act of 1968 established the National Flood Insurance Program (NFIP), which provided a federal subsidy for flood insurance. The program has been subsequently broadened and modified. The NFIP is administered by the Federal Insurance Administration (FIA), which is part of the Federal Emergency Management Agency. The original legislation required state and local governments to adopt land-use control measures to minimize flood damage before they could qualify to participate in the flood insurance program. The program was originally available only to one- to four-family dwellings and small business firms. Now the program has expanded eligibility to include many types of residences and businesses. Coverage limits of $250,000 can be written on residential structures and $100,000 on their contents. Nonresidential structures can be provided coverage limits up to $500,000 on buildings and $500,000 on contents.

Federal flood insurance is marketed through normal insurance marketing channels. Beginning in 1983, under the new cooperative venture called Write Your Own (WYO), participating private insurers began to write flood insurance under their own names and through their normal distribution systems.

The goals of the WYO Program are as follows:

- Increase the NFIP policy base and the geographic distribution of policies
- Improve service to NFIP policyholders through the infusion of insurance industry knowledge
- Provide the insurance industry with direct operating experience with flood insurance[9]

Under this arrangement, the insurers keep part of the premiums for expenses, premium taxes, and commissions, and the balance is deposited in a separate account to pay for losses. Participating insurers have no risk-bearing role in the WYO program.

Federal Crime Insurance

Urban unrest and the sometimes violent disturbances in the 1960s made crime insurance very difficult to obtain in many metropolitan areas of the country. As a part of the Housing and Urban Development Act of 1970, Congress authorized the Department of Housing and Urban Development to underwrite crime insurance in those areas in which it was not available.

Thirteen states and jurisdictions participated in this program, which was eliminated in 1995. Part of this decline in coverage is because of availability in the voluntary insurance market and the creation of state-sponsored residual markets.

The Federal Insurance Administration appoints a private organization to serve as servicing company. Any licensed producer can sell the coverage and be compensated by commission for the services rendered.

FAIR Plans

FAIR plans, like federal crime insurance, resulted primarily from the general deterioration of cities that began in the 1960s. Many city residents found themselves unable to obtain property insurance for their homes and businesses. A federal study commission suggested, as one method of providing such protection, the establishment of FAIR plans and federal reinsurance for riot losses.[10] The riot reinsurance program was terminated in 1983.

The FAIR plans were authorized by the Urban Property Protection and Reinsurance Act of 1968. FAIR plans are associations of insurers formed under state law but required to meet certain minimum requirements established by the U.S. Department of Housing and Urban Development. Persons who cannot obtain property insurance in the voluntary market can apply to the FAIR plan. Some state FAIR plans also provide crime insurance. The FAIR plan cannot refuse coverage solely because of the location of property but *can* refuse coverage if the property is in such poor condition as to be uninsurable and if the insured refuses to restore it to insurable condition. However, these options are unenforceable in some states. The premiums, losses, and expenses of FAIR plans are allocated to participating insurers in proportion to their property insurance premiums in the state.

Insurance Exchanges

Insurance exchanges operate in a manner similar to Lloyd's of London, except that their members can be partnerships or corporations as well as individuals. Also, their members do not have unlimited liability as do Lloyd's members.

The Illinois Insurance Exchange (INEX) is the only such exchange still in existence. It no longer writes reinsurance, but functions successfully as a surplus lines insurer. As of 1995, ten syndicates were active on the Illinois Insurance Exchange. It poses little threat to the U.S. business of Lloyd's in the foreseeable future.

Risk Retention Groups

During the tight insurance market of the mid-1970s, many business firms experienced difficulty in obtaining products liability insurance. In 1981, Congress passed the Product Liability Risk Retention Act, which permitted businesses to join together to form risk retention groups to provide products liability coverage. The act was amended in 1986 to permit risk retention groups to write all kinds of commercial liability coverage except workers compensation.

A **risk retention group** is an insurance company chartered under the laws of a state or other U.S. jurisdiction. Once chartered and authorized by its home state, a risk retention group can operate in all other states without obtaining licenses or meeting the state admission requirements that other insurers must meet. They are, however, required to inform state regulators of their intention to do business in the state. They must also furnish state regulatory authorities with a plan of operation and a feasibility study. The latter must include details of the coverages, rates, and rating plans to be offered in the state.

Risk retention group
An owner-controlled insurance company formed to allow members who engage in similar or related businesses or activities to write liability insurance for the exposures of group members.

If the insurance commissioner determines that a risk retention group is in hazardous financial condition, he or she can seek a court order barring the group from doing business in the state. Also, the risk retention groups are required to comply with state unfair claims practices acts and must participate in JUAs or similar plans. Risk retention groups are exempted under federal law from virtually all other state regulation.

A risk retention group must be composed of members whose business activities are similar, and it must be controlled by its members. It can be organized as a stock insurer, mutual, or reciprocal exchange.

Purchasing Groups

The Risk Retention Act also enabled businesses to form purchasing groups. A **purchasing group** is any group of persons that purchases liability insurance on a group basis, presumably to save premium. The act allows groups to avoid the "fictitious group" laws enacted by various states that prohibit groups from forming solely for the purchase of insurance and also permits purchase groups to avoid state regulation.

Purchasing group
Any group that purchases liability insurance on a group basis to save premium.

As with risk retention groups, purchasing groups can buy all types of commercial liability coverage except workers compensation. In addition, a purchasing group must be composed of members whose business activities are similar, and only members can purchase insurance through the group. A purchasing group can purchase insurance from an insurer that is licensed or admitted in the state where the purchasing group is located. The term "located" has been interpreted to mean every state in which the purchasing group has members. Thus, the underwriter of the purchasing group must be admitted in every state where the group has members. One of the key advantages to a purchasing group is that state insurance commissioners cannot deny rate reductions for a group based on its loss and expense experience.

Mass Merchandising

The term mass merchandising encompasses a wide variety of marketing methods, but they are all characterized by efforts to sell insurance, either personal or commercial, to individual purchasers whose only relationship is membership in a common organization. Although mass merchandising is the generally accepted term for this marketing method, quasi-group marketing would seem to be more descriptive because of the strong resemblance to group marketing techniques used in connection with life and health insurance.

There are no generally accepted definitions for mass merchandising or quasi-group marketing. Because of inherent differences in personal lines and commercial lines, slightly different definitions are used. *Personal lines* programs are categorized according to the following criteria:

- The method of premium collection
- The restrictions, if any, on the insurer's underwriting prerogatives
- The effect of the plan on the cost of insurance to participants

Franchise merchandising
A plan for insuring a number of employees of an employer under a single plan of insurance with premium payment made by payroll deduction.

Franchise merchandising is a plan for insuring a number of employees of an employer under a single plan of insurance. Employee premium payments are made by payroll deduction. Franchise merchandising does not provide participants a discount but rather the convenience of small, regular payments. Insurers offering this type of plan retain the right to decline individual participants.

Mass merchandising
A plan for insuring a number of otherwise independent purchasers of insurance under a single program of insurance at a discounted premium.

Mass merchandising is a plan for insuring a number of otherwise independent purchasers of insurance under a single program of insurance at a discounted premium. As with franchise merchandising plans, the insurer retains the right of individual underwriting selection.

Group marketing
A plan that offers guaranteed policy issuance and discounted premiums to participants.

A **group marketing** plan offers guaranteed issue and discounted premiums to participants. Under this type of plan, no individual underwriting or proof of insurability is required.

Franchise merchandising programs, which were once common, have now become rare. They have been replaced by mass merchandising programs and, in a few instances, by group marketing programs. In general, such programs have been provided most often for employees of a single employer or for members of a labor union. However, some plans have been written for members of social organizations or for customers of a specified business firm, such as a credit-card issuer, a public utility, or a credit union.

Trade association plans
Commercial insurance programs available to any firm within a selected association, provided the firm meets the insurer's underwriting requirements.

The foregoing definitions do not apply to commercial insurance marketing. Franchise marketing, as defined, would be meaningless for commercial insurance programs; at the time of this writing, the authors are not aware of any commercial programs that have been written on a guaranteed issue basis. Consequently, all known programs in the commercial insurance area fall into the mass merchandising category. Unfortunately, within the industry, a mass merchandising program is variously referred to as "a commercial group," "an association/franchise," or "commercial mass marketing."

Safety group plans
Commercial insurance programs available to any firm within a selected industry, provided the firm meets the insurer's underwriting requirements and agrees to a specified loss control program.

Commercial insurance programs can be categorized as trade association plans and safety group plans. Under a **trade association plan**, any member firm of the trade association would be eligible to participate if it meets the insurer's underwriting requirements. **Safety group plans** usually are not restricted to the members of a trade association but are available to any firm in the selected industry, provided the firm meets the insurer's underwriting requirements and agrees to undertake a loss control program specified by the insurer. For example, a trade association plan written for a state restaurant association would be available only to members of that association and only to those members that meet the underwriting standards of the insurer. On the other hand, a safety group plan for restaurants would be available to any restaurant in the state that (1) meets the insurer's underwriting standards and (2) agrees to adopt the loss control program specified by the insurer. Membership in the trade association would not be a requirement for participation in the safety group program. However, adoption of a loss control program might also be required as a condition of participation in a trade association program.

No reliable data are available to indicate the current status of mass merchandising. Less than 1 percent of personal lines insurance seems to be sold through mass merchandising plans. The market share for commercial lines is probably higher, but still well under 5 percent. The development of risk retention groups and group self-insurance has probably siphoned off some commercial lines business that would otherwise have been written through mass merchandising programs.

MARKET DISTRIBUTION SYSTEM MANAGEMENT

An insurer must provide some means of supervising its producers to accomplish the following:

- Motivate them to sell the kinds and amounts of business it wants
- Assist them in handling unusual or difficult insurance situations
- Continually reappraise their performance so that corrective action can be taken promptly
- Recruit additional or replacement producers when necessary

Small insurers operating in restricted geographic areas might be able to provide supervision through the home office. However, larger insurers with more widespread operations usually provide supervision in or near the locality in which each producer operates. In general, two systems are in use in the United States for providing producer supervision: (1) the branch office or regional system and (2) the managing general agency system.

Branch Office System

Under the **branch office system**, the insurer maintains offices in strategically located cities and towns in its operating territory. A small branch office, sometimes called a service office, might consist of only a sales manager, special agent, or field representative (the title varies by company) whose principal duty is maintaining contact with and supervision of producers. Larger branch offices might also include company officers, management personnel, underwriters, claim people, loss control engineers, premium auditors, and other service personnel.

Branch office system
A market distribution system in which an insurer maintains offices in strategically located cities in its operating territory.

Some insurers have two or more levels of branch offices. For example, a large branch office, sometimes called a regional office, might supervise smaller branches scattered throughout one or more states. Regional offices of some insurers are largely autonomous and perform most of the insurance functions, though not the investment functions, usually associated with home office operations. Others function primarily as communications facilities, gathering information from producers, sending it to the home office, and returning home office decisions to the producer.

A great deal of expense is involved in maintaining a widespread system of branch offices. An insurer can afford to maintain such offices only in those territories in which it has or expects to obtain a substantial volume of business.

Managing General Agency System

A managing general agency is an independent business firm that performs for one or more separate insurers some or all of the functions usually performed by company branch offices. A managing general agent might perform such services for a single insurer, though they more commonly represent several insurers. The general agency usually does not sell directly to insurance consumers but appoints and supervises producers throughout the territory. Its territory might consist of an entire state or several states. A few managing general agencies cover very large territories, though frequently for specialty lines of insurance.

The advantage to an insurer of operating through a managing general agent is the low fixed cost. The general agency is compensated by an overriding commission on the business sold by the producers it appoints. Consequently, the insurer does not have the large fixed cost of maintaining a branch office. The general agency, by writing relatively small amounts of business for each of several insurers, earns enough commissions to cover its expenses and earn a profit.

The managing general agency system was a major marketing system for property-casualty insurers in the nineteenth century when most insurers were small and much of the nation was sparsely populated. As the population and insurers grew larger, many insurers accumulated sufficient premium volume to operate through branch offices in many areas. In some cases, the insurers merely terminated their relationships with managing general agencies and established their own branch offices staffed with their own personnel. In other cases, insurers purchased the general agencies and converted them to branch offices.

As a result of additional insurers moving to the branch office system, the total number of managing general agencies has been declining. Those that remain have had their underwriting authority restricted as insurers increased their producer supervision activities at the home office level. As a result, most managing general agencies were forced into the excess and surplus lines and into specialty markets such as mobile homes, snowmobiles, nonstandard automobile, and other lines not normally sought by the majority of insurers.

FUNCTIONS PERFORMED BY AGENTS

The functions to be performed by insurance agents are generally specified in the agency contract. They vary rather widely from one distribution system to another and also from one agent to another within a given distribution system. Several of the functions sometimes performed by agents are discussed below. Some agents perform all of the functions discussed; others perform fewer functions.

Prospecting

Virtually all agents prospect. This function consists of locating persons, business firms, and other entities that might be interested in purchasing the insurance services offered by the agent's principals. Prospects can be located by several methods:

- Referrals by present clients
- Advertising of various kinds, including media advertising and direct mail
- Telephone solicitations
- Cold canvass

Large agencies might have employees who specialize in locating prospective clients. However, in most agencies, the individual agent is responsible for his or her own prospecting operations. Insurance companies might also assist in the prospecting function, especially in the exclusive agent and direct writer systems.

Sales

Selling is the principal function of an insurance agent. Commission on business sold is the principal source of income for agents, and the ownership of expirations on business sold is the principal asset of an insurance agency. The steps in selling include contacting the prospective client, determining the prospect's needs, preparing a proposal, and closing the sale.

Risk Analysis

As noted earlier, determining the prospect's needs is usually an important step in the sales process. Risk analysis is the principal method of determining the prospect's insurance needs. For an individual or family, the process of risk analysis might be relatively simple. A brief questionnaire might provide the information needed for the analysis, and only an hour or two might be needed to perform the analysis. The risk analysis process for business firms is likely to be much more complex. Much time is required to develop and analyze risk information for a large firm with diversified operations.

Policy Issuance

Historically, most agents assembled policies using printed forms provided by the insurers. A copy of the policy, called the declarations "daily report" or simply the "daily," was sent to the insurer. In recent years, the trend has been for insurers to assemble the policies and either mail them directly to policyholders or send them to the agent for delivery.

The change to company issuance was undertaken primarily as a cost-cutting device. Insurers believed they could issue the policies at less cost, especially with the advent of computerized policy management systems.

Collection

Agents who issue policies might also prepare the bills and collect the premiums. After deducting their commissions, they send the premiums to the insurers. If the insurer issues the policy, the insured is usually directed to send premium payments to the company, bypassing the agent. In **direct billing**, the insurer sends the premium bill to the policyholder, collects the premium, and sends the commission to the agent.

Direct billing
A billing system in which an insurer sends premium bills to the insured, collects the premium, and pays commissions to the agent.

Agency billing
A billing system in which an agent sends premium bills to the insured, retains the commissions, and sends the remainder of the premium to the insurer.

For business that is **agency-billed**, the three widely used bases for transmitting the premiums to the insurer are (1) the item basis, (2) the statement basis, and (3) the account current basis.

Under the item basis method, the premium (less commission) is forwarded to the insurer when it is collected by the agent or becomes due. It is the least complex of the three bases.

Under the statement method, the insurer sends a statement to the agent showing the premiums that are due. The agent is obligated to pay the premiums indicated as due or to show that the statement is in error.

Under the account current method, the agent prepares a statement periodically, showing the premiums due to the insurer, after deducting appropriate commissions, and transmits that amount to the insurer. The agency contract indicates how often the agent must submit the account current statement. Monthly is most common.

Under the item basis, the agent is usually not required to pay the insurer until the premium is actually collected. Under the other two methods, the agent is required to pay the insurer when the premium is due, even if the policyholder has not paid the agent. To provide the agent some protection against the credit risk, premiums are usually not due to the insurer until thirty or forty-five days after the effective date of the policy. This delay also permits the agent to invest the premiums collected until they are due to the insurer. The resulting investment income might be a significant part of the agent's remuneration. This investment income is not available to the agent under direct billing or under the item basis of agency billing.

Claim Handling

All agents are likely to be involved to some degree in the handling of claims under the insurance they sell. Because the agent is the policyholder's principal contact with the insurer, the insured naturally contacts the agent first when a claim occurs.

In some cases, the agent might simply give the policyholder the telephone number of the claim department and possibly the name of a person to call. Alternatively, the agent might obtain some basic information about the claim from the policyholder, relay it to the insurer, and arrange for a claim person to contact the insured.

Finally, many agents are authorized by their principals to adjust some kinds of claims. Most often, the authorization is limited to small property claims, for example, property losses under $5,000. Some agents are also authorized to settle small liability claims, especially auto property damage liability claims. A few large agencies that employ skilled claim people might be authorized to settle larger, more complex claims. The limitations on the agent's claim-handling authority should be specified in the agency contract.

Claim handling by qualified agents offers two major advantages: quicker service to policyholders and lower loss adjustment expenses to the insurer. Of course, if the agent is not qualified to handle claims, overpayment of claims might offset the expense savings.

Consulting

Many insurance agents offer consulting services for which they are paid on a fee basis. Such services are usually performed on the agent's own behalf. Such services might be provided for a fee only, or the agent might set a maximum fee, to be reduced by any commissions received on insurance written because of the consulting contract. Laws in some states prohibit agents from receiving both commissions and a fee from the same client.

Other Services

Agents also provide other services to current and prospective policyholders. As policyholders' circumstances change, the agent must be able to advise them regarding desirable policy changes and process those changes selected.

The agent must also be able to answer questions regarding policyholders' existing coverage and additional coverage requirements. Also, questions frequently arise regarding premium billings and other accounting issues.

Finally, agents are expected to facilitate contacts between policyholders and insurer personnel, including premium auditors and loss control representatives.

DISTRIBUTION SYSTEM DECISIONS

An insurer usually selects a distribution system before it begins writing business. Changing distribution systems for existing business is very difficult and possibly expensive because of the existing agency contracts and possible ownership of expirations. However, an insurer that has previously elected one of the distribution systems might decide to use a different one when entering a new territory or launching a new insurance product. Several factors, discussed below, should be considered in selecting a distribution system.

Geographic Location

The geographic location of prospective policyholders must be considered in selecting a distribution system. The principal concern with regard to geographic territory is the population density. An insurer's fixed costs for establishing an exclusive agent or direct-writer agent in a territory are substantial. Consequently, those marketing systems can be employed satisfactorily only when a sufficient number of prospects exist within a relatively small geographic area. The fixed cost of appointing an independent agent or using the direct response system is much lower, so those systems can be used in sparsely populated areas. Several insurers that traditionally used either the exclusive agency system or the direct-writer system have elected to use the independent agency system in rural areas and small towns because of the lower fixed costs.

Expertise and Reputation of Producers

The level of expertise required of a producer depends on the types of insurance written. Generally, commercial lines require greater producer expertise. Some exclusive agency and direct writer producers have been successful in selling commercial lines, especially to small, main-street-type businesses. However, the medium- to large-size commercial lines business is still dominated by the independent agency system. This domination is especially notable in specialized lines, such as surety bonds and ocean marine insurance. Commercial lines requires a level of service that cannot be handled satisfactorily by the direct response marketing system. Consequently, an insurer that wants to market medium- to large-size commercial accounts should probably use the independent agency system. An insurer that wants to sell personal lines could use any of the systems. Of course, it would need to consider the resources required and the high fixed costs associated with the exclusive agent and direct writer systems during the start-up period. An insurer that expects to sell to small business firms could use any of the systems, assuming there are adequate resources to meet the fixed costs of the system selected.

Nature of Existing Business

The characteristics of an insurer's book of business must be considered in any change in distribution system. As noted, the independent agency system seems to have an advantage in marketing medium- to large-size commercial lines.

The other systems are very successful in marketing personal lines and small commercial lines, except for the direct response system. Another factor that should be considered is the ownership of expirations. If the producers own the expirations, the insurer must either give up the business and start over or purchase the expirations from producers. Either option might be expensive, depending on the quality of the existing business.

Ability To Service Products

The amount of service required varies among lines of insurance. Personal lines generally require the least service, while commercial lines require greater direct involvement by the producer and insurer representatives. The producers available in the distribution system selected by an insurer must have the expertise required for the lines of insurance offered and the clients to whom insurance is offered. Although many producers within the other systems possess substantial expertise in handling complex insurance products, the independent agents, as a group, have an edge, both actual and perceived, in the expertise needed for such lines.

Markets To Be Targeted

The nature of the markets to be targeted might be a significant factor in choosing a distribution system. The personal-commercial dichotomy and geographic spread of prospects were mentioned earlier. The level of price consciousness is also important. Some insurance consumers are more interested in price than service, and others emphasize service more. The direct response system is likely to enjoy a significant advantage in cost in comparison with all of the other systems. It is likely, however, to offer less service than the other systems. Consequently, it is most effective in reaching buyers whose paramount concern is price.

At the other extreme, the independent agency system probably offers better service than any of the other systems, but it does so at a higher cost. Consequently, it is most effective in reaching buyers whose paramount consideration is service.

The direct writer and exclusive agent systems are approximately equal in both cost and service. They reach a wide middle audience for whom price and service are equally important.

Insurer Characteristics

The three characteristics of the insurer that should influence the selection of a distribution system are the following:

* The existence and nature of the current business, as discussed above
* The buyers it wants to reach, also discussed above
* Its financial resources

The initial fixed cost of entering the market through the exclusive agency system or direct writer system is greater than doing so through the independent agency system. The insurer must hire, train, and financially support the direct writer and exclusive agency producers at substantial cost before they become productive. The cost of appointing independent agents or conducting a direct response campaign is much lower. Consequently, insurers that enter the market through the exclusive agency or direct writer system require greater initial financial resources to reach a given level of production.

Degree of Control Required or Desired

The extent of control that the insurer wants to exercise over its marketing operations might influence its choice of a distribution system. An insurer can exercise the greatest control over producers in the direct writer system. Under that system, the producer is an employee of the company, and the company can exercise control over both the results achieved and the methods used to achieve them.

Under both the independent agency system and the exclusive agency system, the producers are independent contractors. As such, the insurer can control only the results they produce, not the means by which they produce them. In addition, independent agents can represent several insurers and can switch business among them. Ownership of expirations by the producer, more common in the independent agency system, also reduces the amount of control available to the insurer.

There are no producers involved in the direct response system. Consequently, the insurer has complete control of its distribution system.

MARKET SHARES

One way of evaluating insurer distribution systems is by measuring the relative market shares of each system. A.M. Best data do not distinguish among the types of distribution systems in the same way this chapter does. A.M. Best categorizes insurers as either "agency writers" or "direct writers." The first category includes companies using the independent agency system. The latter category encompasses what this chapter has described as the direct writers, exclusive agents, and direct response systems. For continuity with previous discussions, the exhibits used in this section simply distinguish between "independent agency" and "other."

A historical analysis of this century shows the dramatic rise of the direct writer, exclusive agency, and direct response distribution systems. Throughout the period of those systems' growth, many industry analysts have questioned the viability of the independent agency system. Despite predictions to the contrary, the independent agency system persists. Actually, the rate of erosion in the independent agency system market share has slowed. In many lines of insurance, the independent agency system remains the dominant distribution system.

Exhibit 3-3 shows the market share for all lines combined for 1996 to 2000. In 1991, the independent agency systems market share was 53.1 percent as compared to a 2000 level of 50.7 percent. Although the overall trend has been down for the independent agency system, additional insight into these trends is revealed when market share is segmented between personal and commercial lines as shown in Exhibit 3-4. The direct writer, exclusive agency, and direct response systems have a dominant market share in personal lines insurance. Although the independent agency system has seen its role in the personal insurance market decline substantially since the other distribution systems entered the marketplace, the rate of that decline has decreased significantly. In commercial insurance, the independent agency system continues to lose market share, yet it remains the market leader.

EXHIBIT 3-3

Market Shares by Marketing System
All Property-Casualty Lines Combined

Market Share as a Percentage of Industry Net Written Premium

System	1996	1997	1998	1999	2000
Agency	50.5	50.5	50.6	50.8	50.7
Direct	49.5	49.5	49.4	49.2	49.3

Insurance Information Institute. Used with permission, *The Fact Book 2002*, p. 11.

EXHIBIT 3-4

Market Shares by Marketing System
Personal Lines Versus Commercial Property-Casualty Lines

		Personal			
System	1996	1997	1998	1999	2000
Agency	32.0	32.6	32.8	32.1	31.7
Direct	68.0	67.4	67.2	67.9	68.3
		Commercial			
System	1996	1997	1998	1999	2000
Agency	66.7	66.6	66.6	65.5	64.5
Direct	33.3	33.4	33.4	34.5	35.5

Insurance Information Institute. Used with permission, *The Fact Book 2002*, p. 34.

Exhibit 3-5 shows the relative market share for selected personal and commercial lines. The direct writers, exclusive agents, and direct response systems dominate the private passenger automobile market. They have also recently grown in the homeowners market. Commercial lines have remained the domain of the independent agency system. The direct writers, exclusive agents, and direct response systems, however, have been successful in making inroads into the insurance market for small business owners. This fact is not disclosed in the combined data collected from the Annual Statement.

EXHIBIT 3-5

Market Shares by Marketing System
Selected Personal and Commercial Property-Casualty Lines

Market Share as a Percentage of Industry Net Written Premium

Private Passenger Automobile Liability Insurance

System	1996	1997	1998	1999	2000
Independent	32.0	32.8	33.4	32.8	32.1
Other (Direct)	68.0	67.2	66.6	67.2	67.9

Homeowners Multiple Peril

System	1996	1997	1998	1999	2000
Independent	35.2	35.2	34.2	32.7	32.0
Other (Direct)	64.8	64.8	65.8	62.3	68.0

Commercial Automobile Liability Insurance

System	1996	1997	1998	1999	2000
Independent	73.7	73.1	74.0	73.2	71.8
Other (Direct)	26.3	26.9	26.0	26.8	28.2

General Liability Insurance (Including Products Liability)

System	1996	1997	1998	1999	2000
Independent	77.4	72.2	76.0	74.2	74.6
Other (Direct)	22.6	22.8	24.0	25.8	25.4

Workers Compensation (Excluding State Funds)

System	1996	1997	1998	1999	2000
Independent	76.4	76.3	76.4	75.7	74.3
Other (Direct)	23.6	23.7	23.6	24.3	25.7

© A.M. Best Company. Used with permission, *Best's Aggregates and Averages, Property-Casualty, United States,* 2001 Edition, pp. 313, 321, 322, 325, 326.

The direct writers, exclusive agents, and direct response systems have emphasized personal insurance for several reasons. First, private passenger auto insurance, to which they first turned their attention, is the major property-casualty insurance line, accounting for about 40 percent of the industry's total premium volume. Direct writers, exclusive agents, and direct response systems have experienced exceptional growth. These insurers were able to address the needs of automobile owners when private passenger auto insurance rates were increasing significantly. They were later able to cross-sell homeowners insurance to their cost-sensitive policyholders. Second, because of its relative simplicity when compared with commercial insurance, personal insurance can be sold successfully without the extensive involvement by insurance company personnel that is needed for most commercial insurance. The combination of a large market and relative simplicity permitted these distribution systems to build large sales forces with minimum training delays and expenses. One reason the independent agency system was less competitive on price than other distribution systems was the lower or no commission paid to other agency systems. Lastly, these insurers were early users of policy issuance automation, thereby reducing their underwriting expenses and creating efficiencies that independent agency insurers have had difficulty matching.

The long-term future of the independent agency system continues to remain in doubt. A study conducted by Conning & Company predicts that the number of independent agencies will fall about 19 percent over the next decade.[11] This study echoes the evidence presented in the exhibits in this section; the independent agency system is better positioned to compete in the commercial market than in the personal market. The study suggests that those independent agencies that try to defy this trend will lose. This view of the future of the independent agency system market share is not universal. Independent Insurance Agents of America suggests that declines in the number of agencies reflect agency consolidations and that the number of independent producers overall has not declined.[12]

SUMMARY

Distribution systems provide a means through which products are delivered to the ultimate consumer. In the case of insurance and other financial products, the marketing intermediary usually adds value to the nature of the product in terms of additional services. That is also a good way to view the insurance product—as a bundle of goods and services.

Distribution systems are typically categorized by the existence or degree of independence of the insurance agent, how agents are compensated, and the control that producers can exercise over client listings.

The independent agency system played a significant role in the development of the U.S. insurance industry. Because of independent agents' entrenchment as an institution, the newer forms of distribution are frequently compared to those of independent agents. Exclusive agents, direct writers, and direct response marketing systems have made substantial inroads in the market once dominated by independent agents.

The traditional markets do not meet all needs. Insurers have created new market mechanisms when they have had little opportunity for profit or where governments have determined that an unmet need exists. Those mechanisms include the following:

- Involuntary market mechanisms providing auto, property, workers compensation, and other kinds of insurance
- Government insurers at both the state and federal levels
- Insurance exchanges
- Risk retention groups
- Various mass merchandising systems

In general, the two systems in use in the United States for providing producer supervision are (1) the branch office or regional system and (2) the managing general agency system.

The functions to be performed by insurance agents are generally specified in the agency contract. These include prospecting, sales, risk analysis, policy issuance, collection, claim handling, consulting, and other services.

An insurer's selection of a distribution system is based on the following factors: geographic location, expertise and reputation of producers, nature of existing business, ability to service products, the nature of the buyers to be reached, insurer characteristics, and the degree of control required or desired.

An analysis of the independent agency system with the combination of exclusive agency, direct writer, and direct response systems indicates that the independent agency system has been displaced as the leading writer of private passenger auto and homeowners insurance. However, it is too early to judge the success of the other systems in penetrating the commercial markets.

CHAPTER NOTES

1. *AIPSO Facts 2001/2001* (Johnston, R.I.: AIPSO, 2002), p. 11.
2. *AIPSO Facts, 2001/2002*, p. 21.
3. *The Fact Book 2002* (New York: Insurance Information Institute, 2002), p. 45.
4. *AIPSO Facts, 2001/2002*, p. 21.
5. *The Fact Book 2002*, p. 45.
6. *The Fact Book 2002*, p. 63.
7. *Residual Markets, Workers Compensation, 2000 Experience* (Downers Grove, Ill.: Alliance of American Insurers, 2002), p. 5.
8. *Residual Markets, Workers Compensation, 2000 Experience*, p. 5.
9. Federal Insurance Administration, Federal Emergency Management Agency, World Wide Web: www.fema.gov/nfip/wyo.what (6 June 2002).

10. National Advisory Panel on Insurance in Riot-Affected Areas, *Meeting the Insurance Crisis in Our Cities* (Washington, D.C.: GPA, 1968). See also Richard F. Syron, *An Analysis of the Collapse of the Normal Market for Fire Insurance in Substandard Urban Core Areas* (Boston, Mass.: Federal Reserve Bank of Boston, 1972).

11. Victoria Sonsine Pasher, "Agency Ranks To Fall 19% By 2006," *National Underwriter—Property & Casualty/Risk & Benefits Management*, February 3, 1997, p. 1.

12. Jeffrey M. Yates, "Independent Agent Renaissance Defies Critics," *National Underwriter—Property & Casualty/Risk & Benefits Management*, March 17, 1997, p. 29.

Chapter 4

Direct Your Learning

Underwriting

After learning the subject matter of this chapter, you should be able to:

- Explain the purpose of underwriting.

- Describe the underwriting functions performed by most insurers. In support of this objective:

  - Explain how underwriting activities are organized.

  - Contrast line and staff underwriting activities.

- Explain how insurers distribute authority for underwriting decisions.

- Describe the considerations in establishing and communicating underwriting policy.

- Describe qualitative underwriting performance measures, and calculate financial performance measures.

- Given a case, illustrate how the underwriting decision-making process guides an underwriter to make consistent decisions and to identify acceptable business.

- Explain how monitoring an account and a book of business influence an insurer's results.

Develop Your Perspective

What are the main topics covered in the chapter?

The underwriting department in an insurance company is responsible for developing and maintaining a profitable collection of policies.

Examine the activities required to achieve the insurer's underwriting profitability objectives.

- What policies must be developed?

- What processes must be in place?

Why is it important to know these topics?

Although an underwriting profit is never a certainty, an underwriting department's objective is to select and maintain those policies that are most likely to be profitable for the insurer.

Consider the effort required to achieve and maintain underwriting profitability goals.

- What are the underwriting profitability goals for your organization?

- What activity is required by underwriting in your organization to achieve profitability?

- What regulations restrict your company's underwriting department's ability to accept or reject applications?

How can you use this information?

Examine your own organization's underwriting objectives.

- Is your organization's underwriting department achieving its objectives? How could line and staff underwriters correct any failure to achieve its objectives? How could they be more efficient?

- What activity is required by underwriting to prepare to write policies for a new insurance product?

Chapter 4

Underwriting

Underwriting is the process of selecting policyholders by recognizing and evaluating hazards, establishing prices, and determining policy terms and conditions. Yet, underwriting includes more than merely selecting policyholders. It also includes determining the insurer's selection criteria and the markets for the insurer's products. Underwriting is crucial to the success of any insurance company. Favorable underwriting results are necessary for the profitable growth and even the survival of the insurer. Although many insurance activities, such as marketing, loss control, ratemaking, and claims, are occasionally subcontracted to outside companies or individuals, underwriting is not likely to be delegated to others because of the importance of its success to the insurer.

Before the corporate form of insurance emerged, the underwriter was the insurer. This personal "risk-bearing" persists to this day at Lloyd's of London, where each individual participant or "name" at Lloyd's bears whatever portion of a risk the "name" has accepted. Although underwriting in modern insurance corporations has been delegated to specialized underwriting departments, the ultimate underwriters remain the top corporate officers of the insurance company.

THE PURPOSE OF UNDERWRITING

The purpose of underwriting is to develop and maintain a profitable book of business. A **book of business** is all of the policies that an insurer has in force or some subgroup of those policies. For example, a book of business can refer to all the general liability policies or all commercial policies. A book of business can also refer to business produced in a specific geographic area or produced by a particular branch office or agency.

For underwriting to achieve its purpose, insurers must avoid adverse selection. **Adverse selection** occurs when the applicants for insurance present a higher-than-average probability of loss than is expected from a truly random sample of all applicants. In flood insurance, for example, those persons and businesses that expect flooding, rather than all persons and businesses, are more likely to purchase flood insurance. The term "adverse selection" is often used incorrectly to refer to the effects of competition in the selection process. If one insurer practices selective screening, accepting the best risks and declining the

Underwriting
The process of selecting policyholders by recognizing and evaluating hazards, establishing prices, and determining policy terms and conditions.

Book of business
Also called a portfolio, a group of policies with a common characteristic, such as territory or type of coverage, or all policies written by a particular insurer, producer, or agency.

Adverse selection
A situation that occurs because people with the greatest probability of loss are the ones most likely to purchase insurance.

others, then the other insurers must practice selective screening or be prepared to suffer poor loss experience. Insurers have taken the stance that they must actively select applicants or, in effect, be selected against by those applicants. To appreciate the role of the modern underwriter in achieving the goal of underwriting, understanding how this discipline has evolved and the resources available to underwriters today is helpful.

Evolution of Underwriting

Monoline policies
Policies that contain only one line of coverage, such as fire or general liability.

Before the 1950s, when states began enacting multiple-line rating laws, separate **monoline policies** provided particular types of insurance, such as fire, general liability, crime, or inland marine. Underwriting departments were compartmentalized and operated on a monoline basis. An underwriter was trained as a fire underwriter, a marine underwriter, or a casualty underwriter, for example.

The typical career path of the underwriter of forty or fifty years ago was different from an underwriter's career path today. Fire underwriters often began as "map clerks" who worked with the large, leather-bound volumes of the Sanborn Maps then in general use. Those maps, which contained scale drawings of all buildings, streets, and fire mains, showed the concentration of insured property in a single geographic area. After serving as a map clerk, the future underwriter served a type of apprenticeship as a junior underwriter or an assistant underwriter, working with and learning from an experienced underwriter.

Describing how the training process typically worked, a publication noted the following:

> [An underwriter] knew his craft. He had worked at this desk for 35 years—apprenticed there for 20 of those years at the elbow of a senior underwriter. When his senior retired, he slipped into that slot and, like his former boss, he, too, would retire there. But he wasn't worried about a replacement. For the past eight years a young assistant had worked at his side, learning everything there was to know about his particular line of underwriting. In another 10 years or so—maybe more—this lad would be ready to step into his shoes.[1]

This system produced underwriting specialists who could quote rates from memory and knew all of the intricacies of the contract provisions and coverage for their particular line. The system was disadvantageous for assistant underwriters because senior underwriters often blocked promotion for many years. Moving to another line of coverage would mean beginning the entire "apprentice" process again.

Multiple-Line Underwriting

A multiple-line insurance policy is one that insures more than one line of insurance, such as property and liability. For nearly a century, states believed that multiple-lines underwriting was too great a danger to insurer solvency and therefore limited the lines of insurance that one insurer could write. With the passage of the McCarran-Ferguson Act in 1945, the regulatory environment began to change. Multiple-line laws appeared in several states, and in the 1950s, insurers began offering package policies that included more than one line of coverage. As package policies became more popular, underwriters who specialized in one line soon proved to be ill-prepared to underwrite package policies.

Many insurers changed both the structure of their underwriting departments and the training of their underwriters to deal with the multiple-lines innovations. Those changes, together with an increasing mobility in the insurance labor force, created more flexibility in underwriting organizations. Long apprenticeship programs gave way to intensive training programs. Today, underwriters must often learn the nuances of several lines of insurance in a relatively short period of time. An underwriter's training is further complicated because coverages, hazards, and exposures have changed rapidly in recent years. Technological advances have introduced both new materials and new industrial processes that have drastically altered the hazards in such lines as commercial fire, commercial liability, and workers compensation. Changes in the legal environment have profoundly affected products liability and professional liability coverage exposures. Regulation can also restrict the underwriter's ability to price the exposure properly. Those factors, combined with inflation, have placed heavy demands on today's underwriters. Rather than having the benefit of a lengthy apprenticeship to learn a single line of insurance in a stable technological, legal, and cultural environment, the modern underwriter must master several lines of insurance in a continually changing environment in a relatively short period of time. Underwriters, if they are to remain viable in the profession, must regularly educate themselves on matters that affect the business of insurance and factors that affect their book of business.

Underwriting Developments

Insurers have developed a variety of responses to the challenges of modern underwriting. Many insurers have developed intensive, ongoing training programs to provide underwriters with the necessary techniques and knowledge in the shortest possible time.

Advancements in computer hardware and software systems along with their widespread availability have revolutionized the daily work flow of underwriters. To a great extent, the use of paper files has been reduced in servicing policyholders and processing both new and renewal business. Computer terminals are connected to on-line databases that provide immediate access to policyholder information and to massive amounts of company and agency data. Underwriting decision support systems are emerging as tools to assist underwriters in making better informed decisions. These systems hold promise for streamlining and enhancing the process of treating every underwriting decision comprehensively. The tremendous advances in technology have increased productivity and efficiency in service. Additional advances in service quality can be expected as new technologies continue to emerge; among them is image processing, which involves transforming paper documents to digital images that can be stored electronically and recalled easily.

Despite the technological advances and increases in information availability, the key to successful underwriting remains sound, informed judgment. "Underwriting intuition," a trait often attributed to good underwriters, should be recognized for what it truly is—the ability to apply a rational (although internalized) decision-making process to a group of diverse policyholders.

UNDERWRITING ACTIVITIES

There are no hard and fast rules about how underwriting activities should be performed. Nor are there constraints on how underwriters or underwriting departments should be organized to conduct those activities. However, there is usually a relationship between how underwriting activities are segmented and how the underwriting group is physically organized.

An insurer organizes itself to make the best use of its strengths. Factors influencing this organization include the size of the insurer and the scope of the insurer's operation. A large national insurer, for example, might make major underwriting policy decisions at the home-office level. A regional insurer, on the other hand, might grant individual branch offices significant leeway in determining underwriting policy in their territories. In both cases, the authority granted affects where specific underwriting activities are performed in an insurance company.

Line underwriters
Those responsible for evaluating individual applicants and policies subject to renewal.

Staff underwriters
Those who assist underwriting management in making and implementing underwriting policy.

A commonly used dichotomy distinguishes between activities performed by individual line underwriters and staff underwriters. **Line** (or desk) **underwriters** are responsible for evaluating individual applicants and policies subject to renewal. Line underwriters are generally located in branch or regional offices of insurers, where day-to-day underwriting tasks are performed. **Staff underwriters** assist underwriting management in making and implementing underwriting policy.

Line Underwriting Activities

Line underwriters are responsible for the following activities:

- Selecting insureds
- Classifying risks
- Determining proper coverage
- Determining the appropriate rate or price
- Providing service to producers and policyholders

Certain hazardous classes of business or unusually large amounts of insurance often require review by a higher underwriting authority. That higher authority might be an underwriting manager or other senior staff underwriter in the branch office, regional office, or home office.

In addition to engaging in the preceding activities, some line underwriters also analyze insurance needs, design insurance coverages, set rates, and market products, including making visits with producers to present or prospective clients.

Selecting Insureds

The insurer must select those applicants it desires to insure. If an insurer does not select insureds carefully, some insureds will be able to purchase the insurer's products at prices that do not adequately reflect their exposures to loss. The selection process enables the insurers to ration available capacity to obtain the optimum spread of loss exposures by geographic distribution, class, size of risk, and line of business.

Selection is an ongoing process. Once an account has been placed on the books, the account must be monitored to determine that it *continues* to be acceptable. Corrective action might be necessary for those accounts with excessive losses or for accounts subject to adverse selection. Many consider the selection of insureds as a negative process, that is, the declining of unacceptable business. However, the selection process has positive aspects: the creation of risk management and insurance programs that enable insurers to attract desirable applicants for their products.

Classifying Risks

Correct classification is necessary to properly rate policies and to determine the risk. Accurate classification ensures a pooling of insureds whose expected loss frequency and loss severity are similar. Such a pooling of insureds enables the insurer to develop an adequate rate to pay the incurred losses and operating expenses and to produce a profit. Misclassification can have several adverse results, including insufficient premium to cover losses and expenses, the inability to sell policies because prices are higher than competitors' prices, and charges of unfair trade practices by regulatory authorities.

Determining Proper Coverage

Responsibility for determining the appropriate coverage that best meets the insured's needs rests with the risk manager and the agent or broker, but the underwriter can frequently offer invaluable assistance. The underwriter's role in this process can range from simply ascertaining that the policy is issued with the appropriate forms and endorsements to drafting manuscript policies and endorsements for complex or unique risks. The peculiar characteristics of each submission must be evaluated and related to policy provisions that deal with the potential loss characteristics.

In addition, producers and insureds might depend on the underwriter to determine whether the policy requested is appropriate for the applicant. For example, suppose an applicant has requested a building and personal property coverage form with the causes of loss broad form to insure a manufacturing location. While reviewing the applicant's operations as described in the inspection report, the underwriter discovers that the applicant also has an acceptable transportation exposure. The underwriter discusses this exposure with the producer and offers to provide the coverage. In this situation, the underwriter's actions exemplify a *positive* approach to underwriting.

An underwriter's knowledge of insurance contracts and ability to relate contract provisions to individual policyholders or applicants benefit producers and applicants. Producers often request broader coverage for a particular applicant than the underwriter is willing to provide. Rather than decline the application altogether, the underwriter might offer a more limited but adequate form of coverage through higher deductibles or limiting covered causes of loss. As a result, the producer has an opportunity to provide an adequate level of protection to the client.

Determining the Appropriate Rate or Price

The appropriate rate must be not only adequate to permit the insurer to continue to write profitable business, but also competitive with other insurers. In most types of personal insurance, workers compensation, and some other commercial insurance, proper classification automatically determines the appropriate rate. For major commercial lines, such as general liability, in which competitive pressures on individual accounts are often more focused, the underwriter might have the option to adjust the rate based on the individual characteristics of the insured. Many insurers operate through a number of subsidiary insurers. Each subsidiary has rates filed at different levels to reflect different groups of insureds in the marketplace. Personal insurers frequently have "good," "better," and "best" companies, and their underwriters can place an applicant with the company considered most appropriate. The underwriter must be assured that the characteristics justify the adjustment and must document that the adjustment was in accordance with the insurer's rating plan when filed with the regulatory authorities.

Providing Service to Producers and Policyholders

The extent of the line underwriter's responsibility for producer and policyholder service varies considerably. Many insurers using the independent agency marketing system allow their agents to issue certain types of policies and endorsements. Usually, an insurer's policyholder service department issues policies and necessary endorsements. The underwriter's responsibility in policy issuance often includes preparing the file for the policy typist or for data entry.

All underwriters prepare quotations and assist with proposals for agents and brokers. Underwriters are often a major source of technical expertise for the producers. The skill and efficiency with which the line underwriters perform this task help determine the insurer's success in the marketplace.

Staff Underwriting Activities

Although staff underwriting activities are usually performed at the home office, some regional underwriting managers have staff assistants. The major staff underwriting activities are as follows:

- Formulating underwriting policy
- Evaluating experience
- Researching and developing coverages and policy forms
- Reviewing and revising rating plans
- Preparing underwriting guides and bulletins
- Conducting underwriting audits
- Participating in industry associations and advisory organizations
- Conducting education and training

Formulating Underwriting Policy

Underwriters must continually research such fundamental issues as which markets the insurer should attempt to reach. This research includes evaluating the following:

- Adding or deleting entire lines of business
- Expanding into additional states or retiring from states presently serviced
- Determining the optimal product mix (the makeup of the book of business, such as general liability or workers compensation)
- Determining potential premium volume goals

For most insurers, the responsibility for those research activities is shared with actuarial and marketing departments. Determining present and prospective capacity to write business helps insurers achieve premium volume goals. Capacity is the volume of premium an insurer can safely write in a given year based on its policyholders' surplus (retained earnings). The overall underwriting policy is ultimately communicated to line underwriters and others through changes in underwriting guides, bulletins to producers, and home office directives.

The formulation of underwriting policy is influenced by how an insurer's underwriting management views the insurance marketplace and its desired position in it. Most insurers see their role as "standard lines" insurers. That is, they seek out better-than-average accounts. Some insurers, however, see an opportunity to offer coverage in areas of the market that are underserved by the standard market. The nonstandard or specialty insurers may use loss control, more restrictive coverage forms, or price to make "marginal" or "unacceptable" accounts in the standard market profitable. Either approach to the insurance marketplace can succeed or fail; neither approach is the "right" or "wrong" one. It is important to recognize this dichotomy in the insurance marketplace and that it reflects underwriting management's attitude toward risk bearing.

This chapter and the two that follow focus on characteristics and conditions that distinguish the average risk from risks that are better or worse than average.

Evaluating Experience

Staff underwriters also analyze the loss and premium data of their own books of business and of the industry by line, class, size of risk, and territory to discern trends. That analysis is then used to determine whether changes must be made in the company's marketing or underwriting strategies. The necessary changes are usually communicated through the underwriting guide, but sometimes underwriting bulletins or bulletins sent to the insurer's producers describe special situations.

Researching and Developing Coverages and Policy Forms

As in many other businesses, researching and developing new products are vital to continued growth and prosperity in insurance. New coverages are developed to meet changing legal, social, economic, and technological conditions. Development activities by staff underwriters also include modifications in coverage to meet changes in market conditions or changes in various state statutes. Staff underwriters might also serve on industry or association committees that study policy forms and recommend changes.

Reviewing and Revising Rating Plans

Rates and rating plans must be continually reviewed and updated to respond to the effects of changes in expected loss experience, competition, and inflation. The review and update must occur whether the insurer files rates independently or belongs to an advisory organization. Until fairly recently, advisory organizations were known as "rating bureaus." An **advisory organization** is an organization of insurers formed to assist its members and subscribers in gathering the data necessary to calculate rates. The role of the advisory organization continues to evolve in response to regulatory and consumer group pressures. Most advisory organizations no longer publish final rates. Instead, they develop historical and prospective loss costs that they file with the appropriate regulatory authorities. The insurer must then examine its own operational costs and profit requirements and combine them with loss costs to create the final rates charged to policyholders. Production efficiencies or a superior risk-selection process can justify a lower rate that gives an insurer a competitive advantage in the marketplace.

For those coverages and lines of business for which advisory organizations do not develop loss costs, the insurer must develop its own rates completely. In such situations, the review and revision of rating plans become even more crucial.

Advisory organization
An organization of insurers formed to assist its members and subscribers in gathering the data necessary to calculate rates. These organizations develop prospective loss costs that they file with regulatory authorities.

Preparing Underwriting Guides and Bulletins

Underwriting guides and bulletins describe the underwriting practices necessary to implement underwriting policy. Staff underwriters periodically update the underwriting guides to reflect changes in underwriting policy. Underwriting guides, which distinguish between acceptable and unacceptable business, will be considered in detail later in this chapter.

Underwriting guides and bulletins
Publications that describe the set of parameters or limitations on the applications and existing accounts that are acceptable to the insurer. Guidelines are established by each insurer for each line of business written.

Conducting Underwriting Audits

Staff underwriters are usually responsible for monitoring line underwriting activities to ensure compliance with the insurer's underwriting philosophy and practices. That monitoring is partially accomplished by analyzing underwriting results by line, class, size of risk, and territory and by conducting field audits. The typical field audit consists of a staff underwriter or a team of staff underwriters visiting a branch or regional office and checking individual underwriting files. The audit focuses on proper documentation, adherence to procedure, classification and rating practices, and conformity of selection decisions with the underwriting guide and bulletins.

Participating in Industry Associations and Advisory Organizations

Most insurers are members of national and state associations and advisory organizations that address industry concerns and issues. Staff underwriters are usually selected to participate in the activities of those organizations on behalf of their employers. In addition to advisory organizations, staff underwriters often work with trade associations that represent their members in legislative and other matters, automobile insurance (assigned risk) plans, and JUAs that deal with residual markets and pools for covering specialized risks.

Conducting Education and Training

Staff underwriters are usually responsible for determining the educational needs of line underwriters. The training department implements the resulting training program and continuing educational activities. If an educational need involves a technical insurance area, staff underwriters often develop the course and serve as instructors.

Centralized Versus Decentralized Underwriting Authority

A key element in any decision-making process is determining whether the decision-maker has the authority to make the decision. **Underwriting authority** is a degree of latitude granted individual underwriters or groups of underwriters (which might be organized in a department or branch). The authority granted varies by position, grade level, and experience.

Insurance companies vary considerably in the degree to which underwriting authority is decentralized. In the distant past, when most insurers

Underwriting authority
The degree of latitude granted to individual underwriters or groups of underwriters. An underwriter's authority defines the limit on decisions that the underwriter can make without receiving approval from someone at a higher level.

operated out of a single office, underwriting authority was centralized in the home office. As insurers expanded their service areas geographically, some underwriting authority was moved out into regional and branch offices. Some insurers have even extended underwriting authority to specific producers.

The degree of decentralization of underwriting authority varies considerably by insurer and by line of business. Underwriters of specialty lines such as surety bonding, aviation, and livestock mortality operate with relatively centralized underwriting authority. On the other hand, some insurers delegate a substantial amount of underwriting authority to specific producers. Proponents of that type of decentralization believe that it eliminates duplication and capitalizes on the producers' familiarity with local conditions. When producers have underwriting authority, their compensation for the additional expense of underwriting, issuing policies, and handling claims is a high commission rate and a large percentage of profit sharing (contingent commission).

The amount of underwriting authority given to producers depends on the insurer's philosophy, the experience and profitability of the producer, the line of business involved, and other factors. Most insurers extend binding authority to the producer but reserve policy issuance for the company in order to preserve control over final underwriting and pricing. A notable exception is that most insurers provide their producers with a supply of homeowners and dwelling fire policies to be used for real estate closings when required by the mortgage company. A contingency commission agreement that provides the producer with an additional commission based on the loss ratio of the book of business and on the increase in premium volume can be further motivation for proper underwriting.

In certain lines of business, the producer might have no underwriting authority. High limits of insurance, specialized classes of business, and unusually hazardous classes represent instances when the producer is required to submit the account to the underwriter, who then makes the underwriting decision.

When granted underwriting authority, the producer uses an underwriting guide that shows those classes and lines of business that the insurer finds acceptable and unacceptable. The producer's experience and areas of expertise often determine the scope of the producer's underwriting authority. The insurer's underwriting policy governs cases that the producer must refer to higher underwriting authority.

ESTABLISHING UNDERWRITING POLICY

An effective underwriting policy translates the objectives of an insurer's owners and executive management into rules and procedures that will guide individual and aggregate underwriting decisions. Underwriting policy determines the composition of the book of business.

The composition of a book of business includes both the particular types of insurance products the insurer will offer as well as the amount of business to insure. Individual types of insurance or product lines are referred to as "lines of business." The Annual Statement, which is prescribed for financial reporting in all states, divides property-casualty coverages into thirty-eight separate lines of business. Examples of those statutory lines of business are fire, allied lines, workers compensation, commercial multi-peril, and ocean marine. A complete listing appears in the Annual Statement. Insurers can group lines of business into related product lines or product mix. For example, an insurer that markets commercial auto insurance will have to offer the following Annual Statement lines of business: commercial auto no-fault (personal injury protection), other commercial auto liability, and commercial auto physical damage. Underwriters who use the term "line of business" are generally mentally combining the separate Annual Statement lines into a single reference such as "commercial auto."

Establishing an underwriting policy involves making compromises among underwriting objectives. Every insurer would like to expand premium writings, increase market share, and obtain profitable results. Conservative accounting rules prescribed by the NAIC prevent the immediate recognition of new insurance sales. Statutory accounting procedures (SAP) require that a liability be created on the balance sheet equal to the premiums written by the insurer. As the insurer earns premiums over time, the liability is reduced, and cash is freed up for use by the insurer. The dilemma faced by the insurer is that acquisition expenses are required to be charged off immediately according to SAP rather than being amortized, as premium income is. That accounting requirement creates a cash flow problem that the insurer can alleviate only by drawing on its retained earnings or capital (policyholders' surplus). Unlike other businesses, an insurer's successful expansion of business can lead to a technical insolvency. For an insurer to be successful in the long term, it must maintain a balance of factors.

The principal dimensions of an insurer's underwriting policy, depicted in Exhibit 4-1, are (1) the lines of business and classes to be written, (2) territories to be developed, and (3) forms, rates, and rating plans. The major constraining factors of underwriting policy are (1) capacity, (2) regulation, (3) personnel, and (4) reinsurance. Those factors affect the various dimensions along which underwriting policy is structured.

Any suggestion to change the current underwriting policy should be evaluated to determine its effect on the other dimensions and the constraining factors that might apply. For example, an insurer might decide to begin writing a new line of business. The insurer must determine the effect of that decision on other dimensions of underwriting policy. Which states and producers within those states will have the opportunity to sell the new line? Which combinations of forms and rates will be developed to create the product contemplated by management? Introducing a new product or expanding into a new jurisdiction will also necessitate changes in underwriting policy. Similarly, decisions to withdraw from lines of business, territories, and products should be evaluated

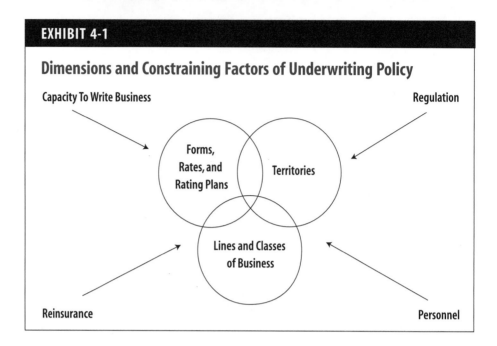

EXHIBIT 4-1

Dimensions and Constraining Factors of Underwriting Policy

Capacity To Write Business

Regulation

Forms, Rates, and Rating Plans

Territories

Lines and Classes of Business

Reinsurance

Personnel

using the framework. Underwriting policy will also change when decisions concerning the following are made:

- The emphasis placed on a particular territory
- Specific coverage options to offer
- Coverage limits to offer
- Policyholder acceptance guidelines
- Classes of business to write or avoid
- Pricing standards to employ
- Rating schedules to use
- Payment plan options
- Competitive need to offer new coverages and rating plans

All aspects of these topics should be described in detail in the insurer's underwriting guidelines.

Any change in underwriting policy must account for the effect of constraining factors on decisions in the insurance marketplace. The following discussion describes each constraining factor and illustrates some of the ways in which the factor constrains underwriting policy changes.

Capacity To Write Business

Capacity to write business
The amount of business an insurer is able to write. Capacity is usually based on a comparison of the insurer's written premium to the size of its policyholders' surplus.

An insurer's **capacity to write business** refers to the relationship between premiums written and the size of policyholders' surplus. That relationship is critical in evaluating insurer solvency. The NAIC has created a series of eleven statistical ratios that are used in conjunction with analytical evaluations to identify insurers that should receive financial scrutiny by regulators. Premiums to surplus (net premiums written divided by surplus) is one of those key ratios and is considered too high when it exceeds 300 percent, or 3-to-1.

One way to exceed the premiums-to-surplus ratio is through rapid growth of premiums written. As mentioned, growth increases written premiums and reduces surplus to pay for immediate expenses. That constraint often precludes insurer expansion unless reinsurance is purchased.

Changes in surplus caused by underwriting gains and losses, and unrealized capital gains and losses, can also affect the premium-to-surplus ratio. Profitable growth permits additional expansion in subsequent years. Failure to underwrite successfully will produce losses that must be paid from surplus, thereby reducing the insurer's ability to write business in succeeding years. Generally accepted accounting principles (GAAP) do not recognize investment gains and losses until they are realized when the security or asset is sold. Statutory accounting procedures (SAP) require insurers to carry common stock on the balance sheet at market value (or association value) as of December 31.[2] Changes in the value of securities are immediately reflected in the insurer's surplus. An external method of increasing surplus and thereby improving the ratio is the infusion of new capital. That infusion could occur when the insurer sells additional stock or obtains a loan.

Insurers recognize that they have limited capacity to write business and must make prudent use of the capacity they have. Allocating that capacity is a matter of policy that insurers must evaluate on a regular basis. For example, an insurer might decide that commercial property insurance should be increased and that certain segments of the commercial general liability line should no longer be pursued. A particular class of general liability insureds might be experiencing a level of losses that exceeds the losses anticipated by the rate. Sometimes, the insurer might decide to stop writing a line of business or to add a line not previously written as a means of optimizing allocation of scarce capacity. Alternatively, the insurer might decide to limit its writing of a given line of insurance in a particular territory. In the past, for example, inadequate rate levels and rising benefit levels for claimants in many states have led some insurers to develop restrictive acceptance criteria for workers compensation insureds.

Regulation

States promulgate insurance regulations, which to some extent are coordinated under the auspices of the NAIC. State regulation takes the form of specific legislation enacted by the state legislatures and state insurance department regulations. Insurance regulation prescribes or affects virtually every major element of an insurer's operation. Regulation affects underwriting policy in several ways. Insurers must obtain licenses to write insurance by individual lines of insurance within each state. Rates, rules, and forms must be filed with state regulators. Some states, such as Florida, specifically require underwriting guidelines to be filed. In response to complaints by consumer groups, the federal government and the NAIC are considering the issue of insurance availability in geographic areas that consumer groups believe the insurance industry has not adequately served. In addition to financial audits, mentioned earlier, regulators perform market conduct examinations to determine whether insurers adhere to the classification and rating plans they have filed. When a market conduct examination discloses deviations from filed forms and rates or improper conduct, the insurer is subject to penalties.

The effect of regulation on underwriting policy varies by state. In some jurisdictions, insurers might be unable to get rate filings approved, or approval might be granted so slowly that rate levels are inadequate in relation to rising claim costs. Insurance, particularly personal auto and workers compensation insurance, has increasingly become a political issue. Some insurers have determined that regulation is too restrictive in some jurisdictions and have chosen to withdraw from those jurisdictions.

Personnel

Insurance requires the talents of specialists to market the product effectively, underwrite specific lines of insurance, service the account through loss control efforts, and adjust losses that occur. An insurer must have a sufficient number of properly trained underwriters to implement an insurer's underwriting policy. No insurer, for example, should pursue aviation, boiler and machinery, or ocean marine insurance without a sufficient number of experienced underwriting specialists in those lines of insurance.

In addition to having the skilled personnel to perform the job, the insurer must have the personnel *where* they are needed. All things being equal, insurance theory suggests that premiums should be obtained from a broad range of insureds to create the widest possible distribution of loss exposures. As a practical matter, policyholder service requirements and expenses related to regulatory requirements preclude small insurers from national operations in which efficiencies will be difficult to achieve with low volumes of business in each territory.

Reinsurance

The price and availability of reinsurance treaties can limit what the insurer can write. Reinsurance involves a contractual relationship through which risks are shared with another insurer. Reinsurance is an essential tool in reducing the effect of expanded writings on an insurer's surplus. Through reinsurance, an insurer can shift the financial consequences of a loss and legal obligations for reserves, thereby increasing its own capacity.

The availability of adequate reinsurance and its cost are important considerations in implementing underwriting policy. Reinsurance treaties might exclude certain lines or classes of business, or the cost of reinsurance might be prohibitive. Reinsurers are also concerned with the underlying policy forms offered by the insurer. A reinsurer might have no reservations concerning an insurer's use of forms developed by advisory organizations but might expressly exclude reinsurance coverage for manuscript forms developed for a particular insured or forms developed independently.

IMPLEMENTING UNDERWRITING POLICY

Once underwriting policy has been set, it must be communicated and implemented. The instruments used for this purpose in most cases are the underwriting guides and bulletins. After underwriting policy has been in place for a period of time, underwriting audits are conducted to determine whether underwriting policy is being followed. Underwriting results, properly measured, indicate the effectiveness of underwriting policy.

Underwriting Guides and Bulletins

Underwriting policy is reflected in a statement of objectives. Underwriting guides specify ways to achieve those objectives and are usually structured by major lines of business and class of business, and modified to meet changing conditions. Underwriting guides contain standards for eligibility and acceptability and establish underwriting authority requirements.

Some insurers have extensive underwriting guides with step-by-step instructions for handling particular classes of insureds. Such guides might identify specific hazards to evaluate, alternatives to consider, criteria to use in making the final decision, ways to implement the decision, and methods to monitor the decision. The guides might also provide pricing instructions and information pertinent to the reinsurance program. An excerpt from an underwriting guide with many of these characteristics is shown in Exhibit 4-2.

Some insurers take a less comprehensive approach to underwriting guides. For example, some underwriting guides might list all classes and indicate their acceptability by line of business. Codes are then assigned to indicate the desirability of the exposure and the level of authority required to write the class. An example of this type of underwriting guide appears in Exhibit 4-3.

Underwriting guides do the following:

- Provide for structured decisions
- Ensure uniformity and consistency
- Synthesize insights and experience
- Distinguish routine from nonroutine decisions
- Avoid duplication of effort

Provide for Structured Decisions

Underwriting guides provide structure for underwriting decisions by identifying the major elements that should be evaluated with each type of insurance written. For example, an underwriting guide for a contractors equipment floater coverage would indicate that the use of the equipment is of paramount importance in determining acceptability and would specify the premium to be charged. The underwriting guide would therefore indicate that two identical bulldozers are exposed to different hazards if one is used in road construction on flat terrain and the other is used to clear fire breaks in a mountainous region.

EXHIBIT 4-2

Commercial Property Underwriting Guide

RISK EVALUATION
UNDERWRITING EVALUATION EXHIBIT

This exhibit presents in schedule form the most important elements that might categorize a risk as "Below Average," "Average," or "Good." It is emphasized that there will be few risks that are totally "Below Average" or totally "Good" for all categories. Most risks will be subject to variations of one degree or another for each of the underwriting elements. The final classification by the underwriter will be determined by weighing the relative importance of each characteristic as applied to the risk.

IMPORTANT: IF THE RISK CLASSIFIES AS "BELOW AVERAGE" IN RESPECT TO "OWNERSHIP," IT IS
UNACCEPTABLE IRRESPECTIVE OF ANY OTHER
FAVORABLE RISK CHARACTERISTICS.

	BELOW AVERAGE	AVERAGE	GOOD
O W N E R S H I P	Abnormal loss history or unsatisfactory adjustment record	Loss record satisfactory	Little or no loss history
	Moral instability	Morally sound	Morally above reproach
	Criminal record	No criminal record	No criminal record
	Dishonest	Honest	Unquestionable integrity
	Illegal business	Legitimate business	Legitimate business
M A N A G E M E N T	Poor credit or bankruptcies	Good credit	Excellent credit
	Business unprofitable	Business profitable	Business highly profitable
	New venture and/or lack of experience	In business 3-5 years	In business 5 years
	Heating, wiring, plumbing over 20 years old	Heating, wiring, plumbing remodeled within last 20 years	Heating, wiring, plumbing less than 10 years old
	Poor control of common hazards	Minor common hazards	Common hazards well safeguarded
	Poor housekeeping/maintenance	Adequate housekeeping/maintenance	Good housekeeping/maintenance
	Usually careless	Reasonably careful	Exceptionally careful

	BELOW AVERAGE	AVERAGE	GOOD
C O N S T R U C T I O N	More than 25 years old	Less than 25 years old	Less than 10 years old
	No fire-stops where advisable	Minimum fire-stops	Effective fire-stops
	Poorly suited to occupancy	Basically suitable for occupancy	Especially suitable for occupancy
	Converted risks	Built for occupancy	Built for occupancy
	Large undivided area	Standard fire divisions	Important hazards cut off
	Poor design	Architecturally sound	Very well designed
	"Short-cut" construction	Good basic construction	Excellent construction and engineering
O C C U P A N C Y	Vacant, unoccupied	Occupied	Occupied
	Contents highly combustible (Cl. C4 & 5)	Contents moderately combustible (Cl. C3)	Contents low combustibility (Cl. C1 & 2)
	Contents highly susceptible (Cl. S4 & 5)	Contents moderately susceptible (Cl. S3)	Contents low susceptibility (Cl. S1 & 2)
	Extra-hazardous process for class	Normal processes for class	Processes well safe-guarded
	Ordinary hazards not guarded	Ordinary hazards guarded	All hazards well guarded
	Obsolete merchandise or products	Merchandise and products saleable	Products or merchandise in demand
	Run-down equipment	Good equipment	Excellent equipment
	Undesirable tenancy	All occupants acceptable	Owner occupancy or all desirable tenants
	Susceptible to quick-spreading or flash fires	Quick-spreading fire unlikely	Quick-spreading fire unlikely

Continued on next page.

	BELOW AVERAGE	AVERAGE	GOOD
P R O T E C T I O N	No first aid	Minimum first aid	Private protection good
	Public protection at risk deficient	Public protection equal to town protection	Public protection excellent
	No watch service	Ordinary public police patrol	Private watch service
	Delayed alarm probable	Normal alarm expected	Early alarm probable
	Inefficient public fire department	Normal public fire department operations	Very effective public fire department
E X P O S U R E	Severe	Ordinary	Light or none
	Large frame exposures	Frame exposure limited	No frame exposure
	Large concentrated values	No large concentration of values	Values well spread
	Unprotected wall openings or no parapets	Parapets and protection of exposed wall openings inadequate	Exposed wall openings protected and exposed walls adequately parapeted
	Neighborhood declining	Neighborhood stable	Good environment
	Poor location for type of business	Acceptable location for type of business	Especially desirable location for type of business
	Outmoded business location	Stable or good business location	Prime business location economically prosperous
	Shore-front or hurricane exposure	No extraordinary storm exposure	No weather exposure
R A T E	Inadequate	Satisfactory	Satisfactory
I N S U R A N C E T O V A L U E	Less than 80%	At least 80%	At least 80%

UNDERWRITING ANALYSIS FORM 97-1564 GUIDELINES

Underwriting Analysis Form 97-1564 has been designed to set forth the underwriter's analysis of the risk elements that affect the quality of the risk. The purpose of the form is to document and record the underwriter's reasons for the risk grading so that the analysis will be available to managerial and supervisory staff and to other underwriters who may have occasion to handle or review the risk. The analysis form also provides a means to ensure that the necessary disciplines for risk selection will be observed.

Completion of this form is required for:

1. All risks written as "Exceptional Selection." (See section 15 of this Guide.)

2. All mono-line risks with limits of $100,000 or more.

3. (a) All new commercial multi-peril risks with total property limits exceeding $150,000. *The analysis must be completed, however, for occupancies with combustibility gradings of 4 or 5 or occupancies listed on pages 12.1 and 12.2 of this Guide.*

    (b) All renewal commercial multi-peril risks with total property limits exceeding $300,000. The analysis must be completed, however, for exposures under $300,000 if there has been a significant change in the character of the risk, such as change of location or change of occupancy.

4. All risks that require special surplus, facultative pro rata, or facultative excess of loss reinsurance.

5. All risks rated under individual risk premium modification, schedule rating, or similar plans.

6. All other risks not falling within the above criteria for which a completed Underwriting Analysis Form is required by your delegation of authority.

7. Any classes or limits of risks that may, from time to time, be required by national or branch underwriting managers.

It should be remembered that the Underwriting Analysis Form is the record of your evaluation of a risk. *The same mental process and discipline for risk evaluation must be followed even though completion of the form is not required.* A profitable experience can be attained only by a consistent assessment of each risk to determine quality. Careful consideration of the eight underwriting elements shown in the Underwriting Analysis Form is vital to such an evaluation.

EXHIBIT 4-3

Risk Selection Guide

A. GENERAL:

The Risk Selection Guide is a comprehensive alphabetical listing by class of business showing what the IIA Insurance Companies believe to be the desirability of insuring an average risk in the class. The Guide grades each class for Property, Commercial Automobile, Workers Compensation, Burglary and Robbery, Fidelity, Premises/Operations Liability, and Products/Completed Operations Liability. In addition, the final column titled "Form" indicates whether the General Liability coverage must be written on a Claims-Made Form (indicated by a "C"), or whether the Occurrence Form is available (indicated by an "O"). Please remember the risk selection guide is only a guide. The company retains final authority regarding the acceptance or rejection of any specific risk.

B. CLASSIFICATION ACCEPTABILITY RATINGS:

The Risk Selection Guide is being published as a section of this agent's manual to answer the question: "Are risks within a particular class likely to be accepted by the IIA Insurance Companies?" In light of this question, the risk grades as found in the Risk Selection Guide are defined as follows:

E—Excellent

This class of business is considered to have excellent profit potential. Unless a specific risk in this class has unusual hazards or exposures, it will rarely present any underwriting problems. Risk graded as "E" may be bound by the agent without prior underwriting consent.

G—Good

This class of business is considered to have good profit potential. Normally this risk may be written before obtaining an inspection or developing additional underwriting information other than that present on the application. The agent may bind risks graded as "G" without prior underwriting consent.

A—Average

Potential for profit is marginal due to high variability of risks within the class. It is understood that the underwriter might think it is necessary to inspect the risk before authorizing binding. In all instances, it is recommended that the agent call the underwriter and discuss the risk before binding.

S—Submit

The account presents little potential for profit. These risks will require a complete written submission before binding. The underwriter *must* obtain a complete inspection and evaluate any other underwriting information deemed necessary before authorizing the binding of this risk.

D—Decline

Due to the lack of potential for profit, this class of risk is prohibited and will not be considered. Under no circumstances may a risk classified as "D" be bound without the prior written approval of the Vice President of Commercial Underwriting.

C. FOOTNOTES:

Footnotes sometimes are indicated as applying to an individual classification for a specific line of insurance. These footnotes are displayed at the bottom of each page and are designed to make you aware of certain hazards or exposures that are unacceptable or need to be addressed in an acceptable manner.

We hope the Risk Selection Guide will be valuable in understanding the types of business our companies want to be writing. However, please do not hesitate to call your underwriter if you are unsure as to how to classify a particular risk, or if you feel the factors associated with a specific risk make it considerably better or worse than the grading assigned by this guide.

DESCRIPTION	PROPERTY	AUTO	WC	BURG. & ROB.	FIDELITY	PREM & OPS	PROD & CO	FORM
Abrasive wheel manufacturing	S	A	D	A	G	S	D	C
Abrasives or abrasive products manufacturing	S	A	D	A	G	S	D	O
Abrasives or abrasive products manufacturing—Artificial	S	A	D	A	G	S	D	O
Adhesives manufacturing	S	A	S	A	G	A[1]	S[1]	O
Adhesive tape manufacturing	S	A	S	A	G	A[1]	S[1]	O
Advertising sign companies—outdoor	A[2]	G	S[3]	G	G	A[3]	G[3]	O
Aerosol container manufacturing	S	A	D	G	G	A	D	C
Aerosol containers—filling or charging for others	D	A	D	G	G	A	D	C
Agate or enamelware manufacturing—Workers Compensation only			D					
Air conditioning equipment manufacturers	A[2]	A	S	A	G	A[1]	S[1]	O
Air conditioning equipment—dealers or distributors only	G	G	A	G	G	G	G	O
Air conditioning systems or equipment—dealers or distributors and installation, servicing or repair	G	G	A	G	G	G	G	O
Air pressure or steam gauge manufacturing—Workers Compensation only			D					
Aircraft or aircraft parts manufacturing	A	G	S	A	G	D	D	O
Airport control towers—not operated exclusively by the Federal Aviation Administration	D	A	D	D	D	D	D	O
Airport—lessees of portions of airports engaged in the sale of aircraft or accessories, servicing or repairing of aircraft, or pilot instructions	D	A	D	D	D	D	D	O
Airports—commercial	D	A[4,5]	D	D	D	D	D	O
Airports—private	D	A[4]	D	D	D	D	D	O
Airport runway or warming apron—paving or repaving, surfacing, resurfacing or scraping	A	G	S	G	G	D	D	O
Alarm manufacturing—burglar	A[2]	A	A	A	G	A	D	C

1 Acceptability will depend upon specific nature of the operation and specific types and uses of the products.
2 The risk is unacceptable if any painting or finishing is done inside without an approved spray booth.
3 Work done above two stories in height is unacceptable.
4 No vans, mini-vans, or buses. Any automobile used in public or private livery is unacceptable.
5 Emergency use vehicles, such as ambulances and rescue vehicles, are unacceptable.

By identifying the principal hazards associated with a particular class of business, the underwriting guides ensure that underwriters consider the primary hazard traits of the exposures being evaluated. In addition to orienting underwriters who are unfamiliar with the class, underwriting guides also serve as a reminder for experienced underwriters.

Ensure Uniformity and Consistency

Underwriting guides help to ensure that underwriting policy and thus selection decisions are made uniformly and consistently throughout all geographic regions. Ideally, submissions that are identical in every respect should elicit the same underwriting response at each of the insurer's branch offices. Underwriting management cannot review every decision made by line underwriters. Underwriting guides instruct and inform individual underwriters of an acceptable approach to evaluating applicants and the overall desirability of a particular type of risk or class of risks. These guides also assist in maintaining anticipated exposures commensurate with underwriting policy to develop a book of business with exposures that the planned rate level can cover.

Synthesize Insights and Experience

Underwriting guides also synthesize the insights and experience of seasoned underwriters and assist those less familiar with particular lines and classes. Each industry and industrial process has its own unique set of hazards and exposures. Underwriting guides summarize the most pertinent observations that have been accumulated from the insurer's past experience.

In addition to insurer underwriting guides, a few commercial publications contain a wealth of underwriting information. One such publication is *Best's Underwriting Guide*, which concentrates on the significant hazard areas of each classification reviewed. Commercial publications usually supplement the insurer's underwriting guide. Although those publications contain useful underwriting information, they do not reflect any one insurer's underwriting philosophy.

Distinguish Routine From Nonroutine Decisions

Another purpose of the underwriting guides is to distinguish routine from nonroutine decisions. Line underwriters are given authority to make selection decisions on routine submissions. Generally, nonroutine submissions must be referred to higher underwriting authority (in some cases, the home office) for approval. Underwriting guides usually indicate that a particular class of business must either be declined or submitted to a higher level of authority for approval.

Avoid Duplication of Effort

Many underwriting situations recur. If the problems inherent in a particular situation have been identified and solved, the solution should apply to all similar situations recurring in the future. Underwriting guides contain the information necessary to avoid costly duplication of effort.

Other Uses of Underwriting Guides

Underwriting guides also provide information to assist underwriters in policy preparation. Rules and eligibility requirements for various rating plans are also included. Specialized information, such as eligibility for experience and retrospective rating together with appropriate rating formulas, also often appears in the underwriting guide. Many underwriting guides describe specialized procedures required by the insurer. Underwriting guidelines also support compliance with state regulatory requirements.

Underwriting Audits

The **underwriting audit** is a management control tool used to determine whether underwriters in branch and regional offices are properly implementing underwriting policy. The larger and more decentralized the insurer's operation is, the more difficult is the task of achieving uniformity and consistency in underwriting standards and adhering to a particular underwriting philosophy. Audits also disclose whether underwriting guidelines cause undesirable results. If they do, the underwriting guidelines should be reviewed and revised. The audit might reveal that existing underwriting guidelines are perceived as being unrealistic and are not being followed. The audit should also identify unused guidelines and multiple or standing exceptions. Audits should disclose those situations in which underwriters have exceeded the authority granted through the underwriting guidelines. Most large insurers can conduct audits on personal policies through the insurer's computer system. Audits on commercial accounts are usually performed using paper files.

Underwriting audit
A process in which members of an insurer's home office underwriting department examine files to see whether underwriters in branch or regional offices are following underwriting guidelines.

The typical underwriting audit in a branch or regional office is conducted by one underwriter or a team of staff underwriters from the home office who visit the branch office and review selected files. Evaluating the quality of underwriting decisions is difficult, but the underwriting audit can determine whether proper procedures and policies are being followed. The simpler the line of business being underwritten is, the easier the audit task becomes. In personal lines, because the attributes of desirable insureds can easily be enumerated, the auditing team can identify lack of compliance quickly. Some companies use a point system to grade underwriters, assessing a penalty point for each violation of underwriting standards or procedure uncovered.

If underwriting data have been computerized, computers can evaluate the composition of a book of business to determine whether underwriting policy is being properly implemented. The audit teams can then explore problems identified in this manner in the field.

Measuring Underwriting Results

The success of underwriting is measured by the results obtained. The insurer's combined loss and expense ratio indicates the effectiveness of its underwriting program. Of course, inflationary trends, catastrophic losses, and adverse political and economic trends can distort these ratios in the short run. Evaluating results by line of business, territory, and source of production (that is, by agency) will identify problem areas. The preceding factors also affect the interpretation of underwriting results. In addition, because the insurance business has proved to be cyclical over the years, the underwriting results of a particular insurer can be measured against the average performances of the industry during a given phase of the cycle.

Insurance Industry Trends

Countrywide underwriting results have indicated the presence of a continuing underwriting cycle. Within the past several years, extreme periods of both good and poor underwriting results have occurred, although investment income has offset underwriting losses in many years.

The exact causal mechanism for this cycle has not been defined; however, certain forces appear to significantly affect the cycle. Those forces include inflation, investment results, competition, and the effect of regulation. Slow regulatory responses to rate increase requests in periods of inflation might have been an important determinant of the subsequent unsatisfactory underwriting results. Delayed, reduced, or denied rate increases in recent years have reduced written premiums by hundreds of millions of dollars. The major component of loss costs are increasing rapidly because of inflationary factors, so the poor underwriting results are not surprising. At the same time, rate increases might be lower than necessary to respond to rising loss costs because of regulatory decisions or competition among insurers.

Additional factors influencing underwriting experience include automobile insurance plans, JUAs, and similar residual market plans to solve social as well as insurance problems. Once limited to substandard private passenger auto, residual market plans have expanded to include FAIR Plans and a variety of state-sponsored mechanisms, such as assigned risk plans for workers compensation and medical malpractice JUAs.

Competitive forces can also increase the amplitude of underwriting cycles. During periods of seemingly favorable results, insurers try to increase their premium volume, writing commercial business at less than adequate rates. Contributing to this problem is the belief on the part of certain managers that they can write increased volumes of commercial insurance at an underwriting loss, which they can make up with superior investment results. This practice is called cash-flow underwriting. Although those tactics can be effective in the short run, they have resulted in disastrous operating losses for some insurers long term.

Difficulties in Interpretation of Results

The evaluation of underwriting results based on an insurer's loss and expense ratio is made more difficult because several complicating factors reduce the ratio's efficiency as a measurement device. The most significant of those factors are premium volume considerations and loss development delay.

Premium Volume Considerations

Premium volume and underwriting policy are directly related. Adherence to stricter underwriting standards than those previously employed usually causes premium volume to decline. Conversely, loosening underwriting standards typically results in an increase in premium volume. The interpretation of an insurer's combined loss and expense ratio, both on an aggregate basis and by line, should take into account the extent to which the insurer's premium volume goals have or have not been met. The *extreme* example shown in Exhibit 4-4 shows the two approaches used to determine underwriting profitability and the effect that changes in premium volume can have on insurer underwriting results.

In statutory accounting, the loss ratio is calculated by dividing incurred losses by earned premiums. The expense ratio also relates underwriting expenses to

---

EXHIBIT 4-4

Underwriting Results—Financial and Trade Bases

This exhibit shows a hypothetical example of an insurer experiencing a 25 percent drop in written premium as a result of following a much more restrictive underwriting policy. On a *financial basis,* the combined results have improved from 102 percent to 96 percent. On a trade basis, however, the insurer's experience deteriorated from 99.9 percent to 102.2 percent. Analysis of underwriting results should be done on both bases to evaluate the effect of changes in premium volume correctly.

	Year 1	Year 2
Written premium	$10,000,000	$7,500,000
Earned premium	9,500,000	9,000,000
Underwriting expenses	3,990,000	2,790,000
Incurred losses	5,700,000	5,850,000

Financial Basis

Loss ratio:

$$\frac{\text{Incurred losses}}{\text{Earned premium}} \quad \frac{\$5,700,000}{\$9,000,000} = 60\% \qquad \frac{\$5,850,000}{\$9,000,000} = 65\%$$

Expense ratio:

$$\frac{\text{Underwriting expenses}}{\text{Earned premium}} \quad \frac{\$3,990,000}{\$9,500,000} = 42\% \qquad \frac{\$2,790,000}{\$9,000,000} = 31\%$$

Financial basis combined ratio   102%   96%

Trade Basis

Loss ratio:

$$\frac{\text{Incurred losses}}{\text{Earned premium}} \quad \frac{\$5,700,000}{\$9,500,000} = 60\% \qquad \frac{\$5,850,000}{\$9,000,000} = 65\%$$

Expense ratio:

$$\frac{\text{Underwriting expenses}}{\text{Written premium}} \quad \frac{\$3,990,000}{\$10,000,000} = 39.9\% \qquad \frac{\$2,790,000}{\$7,500,000} = 37.2\%$$

Trade basis combined ratio   99.9%   102.2%

earned premium. The sum of those ratios is the financial basis combined ratio. The combined ratio as calculated by A.M. Best Co., which is also referred to as the trade basis combined ratio, uses the same loss ratio but divides underwriting expenses by written premium.

The rationale for relating underwriting expenses to written premium is that most expenses are related to placing business on the books rather than maintaining it. The effect of the trade basis combined ratio is to recognize the "equity" in the unearned premium reserve.

Analyzing on a trade basis has some limitations, however. First, the extent to which expenses are related to written premium rather than earned premium varies by line. Commissions and acquisition expenses also vary by line. Certain specialty lines such as boiler and machinery have significant continuing inspection expenses, which are actually related more to earned premium. This is also true to a lesser extent for workers compensation insurance. For this reason, comparisons between insurers with different mixes of business on a trade basis can be misleading.

Loss Development Delay

In certain lines of business, particularly the liability coverages, a considerable amount of time elapses between the occurrence of a loss and the settlement of the claim. Although reserves are established as soon as the loss is reported, significant inaccuracy exists in estimating ultimate loss costs. That inaccuracy is known as loss development delay, or as the "long tail," and it has two major components: changes in the reserves for reported losses and changes in the reserves for incurred but not reported (IBNR) losses.

In lines of business written on an occurrence basis, which can have an extended discovery period between the time of the occurrence of the insured event and the discovery and subsequent suit by the claimant, the IBNR greatly affects the accuracy of current reported loss results. The change on the part of many professional liability insurers to claims-made forms and the introduction of the claims-made commercial general liability policy were intended to alleviate this problem.

If a policy is written on an occurrence basis, the insurer provides coverage for injuries that occur during the policy period even if claims for such injuries are not actually brought against the insured until years after the coverage has expired. If a policy is written on a claims-made basis, the insurer provides coverage only for claims made against the insured during the policy period. Thus, in theory, a pure claims-made policy does not cover losses that have not been reported by the end of the policy period. In practice, however, claims-made policies often cover losses reported after the policy period by virtue of "extended reporting periods." Thus, IBNR losses can be a problem under either type of policy.

In all liability lines, where several years can elapse between the notification of a claim and the final settlement, changes in reserves occur frequently. Because the incurred losses used to compile loss ratios include both paid losses and outstanding loss reserves, the loss ratio as an indicator of underwriting performance relies heavily on the accuracy and realistic evaluation of the reserve estimations. The more time that elapses between notification and settlement, the less accurate the estimation is. Exhibit 4-5 shows an example of a loss development delay for a particular group of general liability policies on a calendar-accident-year basis.

Standards of Performance

One technique that can be used to evaluate the performance of an underwriting department is to set standards of performance regarding several crucial areas of underwriting. Those standards of performance include the following:

- Selection
- Product mix
- Pricing
- Accommodated risks
- Retention ratio

EXHIBIT 4-5

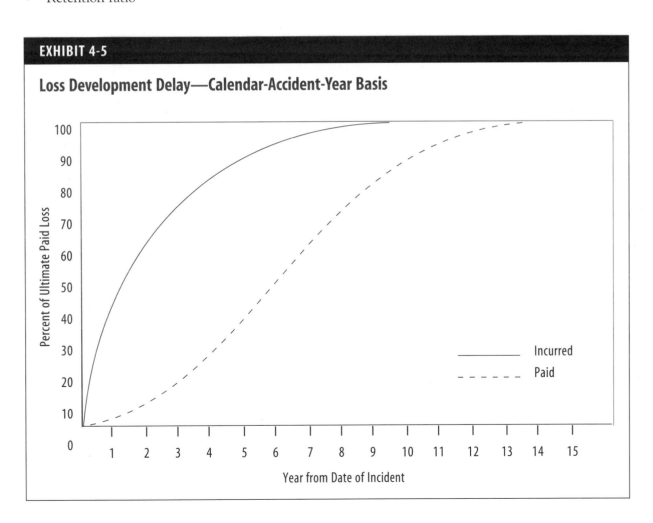

Loss Development Delay—Calendar-Accident-Year Basis

- Success ratio
- Service to producers

Although some of those standards clearly apply only to commercial lines underwriting departments, others can be used for both personal and commercial lines.

Selection

To implement this monitoring technique, establishing well-defined selection rules in the underwriting guide is necessary. Those selection rules should define highly desirable, average, and below-average types of insureds, and each underwriter, branch, or region should have a goal specifying the balance of the three types of insureds. During an underwriting audit or review, the business written by a particular underwriter, branch, or region can be segmented into the various categories, and the percentages of the book of business in each category can be evaluated.

Product Mix

This monitoring technique requires a statement within the underwriting guide of the desired product mix for new and renewal business. For example, if product liability losses are causing an adverse effect on the entire book of business, the product mix standard might require a reduction in manufacturing classes but a concerted effort to increase the writing in the contractor, service, and mercantile classes. The comparison of the actual book to the desired one provides a straightforward evaluation of performance.

Pricing

Pricing standards are used to gauge the adequacy of the premiums being charged relative to some standard. In commercial insurance, insurance rates are typically modified to reflect features specific to the account being underwritten. Pricing standards provide guidance by indicating the extent to which these departures from the premium would be charged to the "normal" account. An underwriting audit might find that profitability in a line of insurance is being sacrificed for growth. Pricing standards are one way insurers communicate their pricing policy to line underwriters.

Accommodated Risks

Accommodation
An application or an existing policy that does not adhere to underwriting guidelines. Such policies may be accepted in return for other, more potentially profitable business.

This standard of performance requires a log in which all "accommodated risks" are entered along with the reasons for the accommodation. An **accommodation** is usually the acceptance of a substandard exposure in return for other, more profitable business. During regular underwriting audits and reviews, evaluation of the log can determine whether accommodations are being granted too often and can ensure that the producer has delivered increased volume or fulfilled some other promise.

Retention Ratio

Retention ratio
The percentage of policies renewed at an anniversary.

The **retention ratio** is the percentage of business renewed. Since most, if not all, of the underwriting investigation work has been performed for existing policies, keeping those policies offers more profit potential than acquiring new business. An unfavorable percentage of renewals might indicate serious deficiencies, including poor service to producers, noncompetitive pricing, or unfavorable claims service. This standard requires careful monitoring of the renewal rate and evaluation of any trends discerned.

Success Ratio

The **success ratio**, sometimes called the "hit ratio," is the ratio of business written to business quoted. This standard is usually employed in commercial lines. Data must be gathered for a large number of quotations to determine the average range for this ratio. Ratios that are either inordinately high or low might require follow-up and further investigation. A high ratio might indicate any of the following:

- Easing of competition
- Rate inadequacy or rates lower than other insurers
- Broader coverage than other insurers
- Deterioration in selection criteria

Low success ratios might indicate one or more of the following:

- Increasing competition
- Rates that are too high
- Coverages or forms that are too restrictive
- Selection criteria that are too high
- Poor service

Service to Producers

Because producers usually rank insurers on the basis of service received, the insurer must be able to evaluate its own performance. This standard requires establishing a set of minimum acceptable standards for certain types of service to producers. The actual performance of each underwriter, branch, or region being evaluated is then compared with the targeted level of performance. An example of one such standard appears in Exhibit 4-6.

THE UNDERWRITING PROCESS

Underwriting has been defined as the selection of policyholders through hazard recognition and the evaluation, pricing, and determination of terms and conditions. The **underwriting process** specifies the steps underwriters generally follow when evaluating a prospective policyholder.

Underwriters have traditionally resisted admitting that their underwriting intuition is actually the internalization of a decision-making process that can apply to a variety of loss exposures. They argue that it is difficult to identify one process that adequately addresses the many facets of underwriting decision making. Perhaps the skill described as "underwriting

Success ratio
The ratio of insurance policies written to those that have been quoted to applicants for insurance.

Underwriting process
The steps underwriters generally follow when evaluating prospective policyholders. These steps include (1) gathering information, (2) identifying alternatives, (3) selecting an alternative, (4) implementing the decision, and (5) monitoring the results.

EXHIBIT 4-6

Example of "Service to Producers" Underwriting Standards

Category	Minimum Acceptable Standard
1. Quotations	3 working days
2. New policies	3 working days
3. Replies to correspondence	2 working days
4. Cancellations, endorsements, certificates	5 working days
5. Direct cancellation notices	Same-day service
6. Renewals	No later than 10 days before expiration

intuition" would be better described as the creative application of the underwriting process.

The underwriting decision-making process can be described as consisting of the following five steps:

1. Gathering information
2. Identifying, developing, and evaluating alternatives
3. Selecting an alternative
4. Implementing the decision
5. Monitoring the exposures

Gathering Information

Underwriters would like to have a comprehensive knowledge of the activities, operations, and character of applicants. That ideal objective cannot be achieved, however, because of the necessary tradeoffs required to minimize underwriting expenses. Concentrating too much time on a particular account is also impractical. Despite those limitations, underwriters try to balance the degree of hazard with how much information is needed and the cost to obtain it. For example, an underwriter would require an extensive investigation of a manufacturer. Conversely, the underwriter might require much less information for a low-hazard risk like a gift shop.

The underwriter draws together information from a number of sources to develop a profile of the applicant. The profile is a composite of information about the applicant that describes the nature of the operation, financial condition, and characteristics of the risk.

Sources of Information

The principal sources of information are the producer, the application, consumer investigation reports, government records, financial rating services, loss data, independent inspection reports, field marketing personnel, premium auditors, claim files, and production records.

The Producer

Typically, it is the producer who has personal contact with the applicant, has firsthand knowledge of the applicant's operations, and knows the applicant's reputation in the community. The producer usually performs the investigation required to determine the coverage needs of the applicant. The producer using this knowledge to provide the insurer with an acceptable applicant is serving to "pre-qualify" or **field underwrite** the applicant.

The degree to which an insurer depends heavily on the producer to evaluate thoroughly the acceptability of the applicant varies by producer and type or class of business and might differ based on the marketing system employed.

Direct writing and exclusive agency insurers are explicit about the characteristics of the ideal applicant. Producers for these insurers screen applicants with full knowledge of the parameters used by the underwriters in evaluating the applicants' hazard characteristics.

Producers for independent agency insurers have a number of markets available to them. Their task is more complex because they must understand the marketing goals and underwriting guidelines of the various insurers they represent. Additionally, independent agents must balance the placement of their business among their insurers to maintain preferential treatment and meet obligations under agency contracts. The ability to match applicants with an appropriate market (insurer) is an essential skill for independent producers.

The Application

Information about the applicant and information obtained by the producer to further entice the insurer to accept the prospective insured are combined in the application. Insurance applications gather general information required to process, rate, and underwrite the applicant. Usually, a different application exists for each line of business. Each insurer may develop its own application or use the ACORD standard applications. ACORD applications were developed by industry committees to reduce the amount of paperwork agents must handle when working with several insurers. In either case, the application attempts to target specific information necessary to properly evaluate the acceptability of the applicant. In the case of an ACORD application, individual insurers may take advantage of some free-form areas on the application to obtain unique information that the company believes is crucial to sound decision making.

Despite the completeness of the application, the underwriter usually finds it necessary to obtain additional information concerning the applicant. This information can be loosely categorized as internal or external, and objective or subjective. The underwriter needs to be aware of the insurer's internal sources of information because they can often be obtained quickly and economically.

Field underwriting
The pre-qualification investigation an insurance producer performs before submitting an application to an underwriter.

Likewise, external information might be expensive to obtain and delay processing of the application. Objective information consists of facts that have been recorded and can be verified. Subjective information consists of opinions or personal impressions. The underwriter needs to be able to distinguish between the two and be able to identify subjective influences that could exist in objective information.

Consumer Investigation Reports

Several independent reporting services provide background information on prospective policyholders. On personal coverages such as private passenger auto, these reports usually include a description of the neighborhood and environment of the applicant, and information for verification of proper classification assignment. Various types of reports are also available for most commercial coverages.

Government Records

Government records include motor vehicle reports; criminal court records; and civil court records, including records of suits filed, mortgages and liens, lists of business licenses, property tax records, and bankruptcy filings.

Motor vehicle records (MVRs) are a fundamental information source for auto underwriting. Some states require insurers to obtain MVRs each year so that driver violations can be incorporated into the rating scheme of each policy.

Most underwriters use independent services to obtain civil and criminal information even though they can obtain that information directly from court records. Civil and criminal reports will show any previous bankruptcies or judgments that are on record.

Financial Rating Services

Dun & Bradstreet (D&B), Standard & Poor's, and TRW are some of the major financial rating services. They provide data on the credit ratings of individual businesses, together with industry averages for purposes of comparison. Although the use of one or more of these financial rating services is almost universal in surety bond underwriting, the services are also used in many other commercial lines. They can be used to verify a financial statement provided by an applicant as well as to provide an overall picture of the applicant's financial stability and strength. A financially weak business might present an unacceptable hazard. Use of the data provided by the financial rating services is greatly enhanced if the underwriter is familiar with financial ratios used to evaluate a firm's liquidity, profitability, and debt structure. In addition, the 10-K form filed with the Security and Exchange Commission (SEC) contains a wealth of information on public companies.

Loss Data

Underwriters usually have loss experience on policyholders and producers and also on an aggregate basis by class, line of business, and territory, both for the insurer and the industry. The loss experience of a commercial policyholder might be extensive enough to have statistical significance on its own, while in personal insurance it is the loss experience for the class or territory that has more significance.

Loss frequency, loss severity, and the type of loss are all important in analyzing loss data. The cause of loss and the date of loss provide further insights. There might be a possibility of either reducing the hazards through loss control measures or adding or increasing a deductible if these causes of loss can be identified. The date of loss provides information on possible seasonality or trends in loss experience. Results for a given line, class, or territory, as well as insurance industry results, might indicate rate inadequacy, causing a modification of underwriting policy pending approval of higher rate levels.

Inspection Reports

Inspection or loss control reports prepared by loss control personnel provide information on the physical condition of property, the safety of business operations, and the insured's management.

Most inspection reports in commercial insurance contain lists of both mandatory and suggested recommendations. A follow-up on the degree of compliance provides the underwriter with insight into the attitude of management toward safety.

Field Marketing Personnel

In most companies, field marketing personnel (such as field representatives or special agents) can provide both specific and general information. Field marketing personnel can frequently obtain information that a producer omitted from an application or a submission. In territories that are sparsely populated or in other situations in which qualified loss control personnel are not available, many insurers use field marketing personnel to make simplified inspection reports. The field marketing person can also provide detailed background information on the producer and sometimes on the applicant. In some insurers, this function is fulfilled by sales managers, managing general agents, or the producer.

Premium Auditors

The premium auditor examines the policyholders' operations, records, and books of account to determine the actual insurance exposure for the coverages provided. The usual procedure is for the premium audit to be conducted after a provisional premium has been collected and the policy term has expired. It is increasingly common for the insurer to conduct a pre-audit so that policyholders will be aware that premium adjustments will be made after the term and that the information will be required to complete the audit. In either case, the premium auditor has the opportunity to gather information concerning the policyholders' operations that might have underwriting implications, including moral and morale hazards.

Claim Files

When underwriting renewals of existing policies, an underwriter can often obtain insights into the character of the policyholder by reviewing the policyholder's claim files. Claim adjusters frequently develop significant underwriting information during the course of their investigations. For example, an adjuster investigating a small fire loss at a machine shop might uncover evidence of poor housekeeping and a disregard for loss control on the part of the policyholder. Some insurers have an information system whereby claim adjusters notify the underwriter any time they obtain pertinent information on physical, moral, and morale hazards on any policyholder. For personal policies, the adjuster can often identify through an investigation an insured who is making many small claims that most people would attribute to normal wear and tear. In commercial accounts, such as a workers compensation policy, a review of claim files might indicate the presence of dangerous conditions requiring loss control engineering.

The claim adjuster is one of a few employees of the insurer who has an opportunity to make a firsthand appraisal of the locations insured. The value of his or her observation is so great that maximum effort is justified to ascertain that nothing inhibits full communication with underwriting. An example of a report that could facilitate communication is shown in Exhibit 4-7.

Production Records

Records are usually available on individual producers, indicating loss ratio, premium volume, mix of business, amount of supporting business, length of service, and industry experience. In the case of an independent agent, the number of insurers represented by the agency is also relevant. In auto underwriting, for example, the production records on the mix of business would indicate whether a particular producer is submitting an inordinately large percentage of young drivers or drivers with poor driving records. In commercial lines, the production records would indicate the producer's familiarity with complex or unusual classes of business. The background and experience of the producer might be of concern to the underwriter in the case of a large boiler and machinery application or a complex manufacturing submission. Such a submission from a producer whose book of business is 95 percent personal insurance would raise questions in the underwriter's mind about the producer's familiarity with the coverage and his or her ability to service the account properly. In all marketing systems, producer results over a reasonably extended period of time (usually three to five years) are a good measure of his or her capability as an effective field underwriter.

Hazard
Any condition that has the propensity to increase either the frequency or the severity of a potential loss.

Hazard Evaluation

A **hazard** is any condition that increases the expected frequency or severity of loss. Hazards can result from almost innumerable sources and can be classified in many ways. One such classification is to identify hazards as physical, moral, and morale. Much underwriting information is developed to enable the underwriter to identify and evaluate hazards. The underwriter is primarily concerned with whether the hazards in the applicant's operations or activities are greater than normal, unusual, or uncontrolled. The loss control representative can be directly involved in assessing those hazards for the underwriter.

Physical Hazards

Physical hazards are tangible characteristics of the property, persons, or operations to be insured that affect the probable frequency and severity of loss resulting from one or more causes of loss. Physical hazards can be attributes of the applicant, of the property to be insured, or of the environment in which the property is located. An untrained driver, damageability of cargo being shipped, and the quality of public fire protection are all examples of physical hazards.

Physical hazards
Tangible characteristics of the property, persons, or operations to be insured that affect the probable frequency and severity of loss.

Moral Hazards

Moral hazard is a condition that exists when a policyholder tries to cause a loss or exaggerates a loss that has occurred. Although most information on moral hazard is subjective, objective data might be available, such as a history of past financial difficulties or a criminal record. Potential indicators of moral hazard include weak financial condition, undesirable associates, and poor moral character.

Moral hazard
A condition that exists when a person might intentionally cause a loss or exaggerate a loss that has occurred.

Weak Financial Condition   The owners of a financially weak commercial enterprise might intentionally cause a loss to obtain desperately needed cash. For example, the Persian Gulf War of 1991 and fear of domestic terrorism presented a backdrop for a failed insurance fraud attempt. The owners of two million gallons of sodium hydrosulfate stored near the Norfolk, Virginia, Naval Base planted pipe bombs after doubling their property insurance. Had the owners been successful, they would have been able to eliminate their back debts and make a $1 million profit.[3] Ocean marine underwriters are particularly aware that during periods of overcapacity, the owners of an idle or obsolete vessel might try to "sell it to the underwriters" by intentionally causing a loss.

Because the financial condition of a business can change quickly, detecting the hazard caused by weak financial condition requires constant monitoring. Changes in consumer tastes or innovation by competitors can leave a business with a sizable obsolete inventory. Economic downturns can postpone essential maintenance to vital services such as electrical, plumbing, and heating systems.

Undesirable Associates   A policyholder's association with criminals is another indicator of potential moral hazard. A business that is frequented by members of the underworld or other undesirables does not reflect well on the character of the proprietor.

EXHIBIT 4-7

Claim Report to Underwriter

CLAIM REPORT TO UNDERWRITER

CONFIDENTIAL—FOR INTERNAL USE ONLY

Adjuster — Use this form when accident frequency, loss cost, conditions, or type of risk should be brought to attention of the Underwriter

DATE OF ACCIDENT/LOSS	INCURRED COST OR RESERVE $		CLAIM NUMBER	
PRODUCING BRANCH OFFICE	UNDERWRITING DEPARTMENT	CAUSE CODE	POLICY NUMBER	
TO:			INCEPTION	EXPIRATION
CLAIM OFFICE		LIMITS	PRODUCING AGENT	
FROM:			COMPANY	AGENCY CODE
INSURED'S NAME		INSURED'S MAILING ADDRESS (STREET)		
			CITY	STATE	ZIP CODE
LOCATION OF ACCIDENT/PREMISES INVOLVED (STREET ADDRESS)		CITY		
			STATE	ZIP CODE

FULL NAME OF DRIVER OF INSURED VEHICLE (AUTO OR MOTOR TRUCK CARGO) OR INJURED EMPLOYEE (WORKERS COMP.)

☐ ANY ACTION DEEMED NECESSARY WILL NOT AFFECT THE DISPOSITION OF THIS CLAIM.
☐ ANY ACTION DEEMED NECESSARY MAY AFFECT THE DISPOSITION OF THIS CLAIM.

INSTRUCTIONS TO ADJUSTER: Check applicable blocks below and explain each item checked under REMARKS.

A. AUTOMOBILE	B. WORKERS COMPENSATION OR GENERAL LIABILITY	C. FIDELITY OR, BURGLARY OR, PLATE GLASS OR, FIRE MARINE AND MULTI-LINE
☐ 1. Physical disability	☐ 1. Hazardous physical condition	☐ 1. Inadequate safeguards or training
☐ 2. Vehicle in poor condition	☐ 2. Machinery	☐ 2. Inadequate records
☐ 3. Evidence of drinking	a. Defectively manufactured	☐ 3. Loss frequency
☐ 4. Reckless driving	b. Poorly designed	☐ 4. Possible illegal activities
☐ 5. Uncooperative	c. Does not meet industry standards	☐ 5. Questionable loss
☐ 6. Loss frequency	d. Inadequately labeled	☐ 6. Vacant premises
☐ 7. Poor driving record	☐ 3. Poor location	☐ 7. Underinsured
☐ 8. Driver under age 25*	☐ 4. Uncooperative	☐ 8. Questionable physical condition
☐ 9. Indiscriminate loan of vehicle	☐ 5. Poor management or supervision	☐ 9. Late notice
☐ 10. Driver fell asleep	☐ 6. Inadequate records	☐ 10. Poor housekeeping
☐ 11. Gross negligence	☐ 7. Loss frequency	☐ 11. Uncooperative
☐ 12. Total loss of insured vehicle	☐ 8. Late notice	☐ 12. Possible financial problems
☐ 13. Late notice	☐ 9. Pollution loss	☐ 13. Exposure from adjoining risks
☐ 14. Owned vehicle not on policy	☐ 10. Other	☐ 14. Fire protection/first aid system impeded
☐ 15. Other		☐ 15. Carelessness
*Personal auto policy not so classified		☐ 16. Other

REMARKS

_____

_____

_____

ADJUSTER'S SIGNATURE

C.R.U. DATE

Poor Moral Character   Moral hazard can arise from the poor moral character of the policyholder even when the financial condition is sound. Previous questionable losses, a criminal record, or evidence of moral turpitude can indicate a moral hazard. A reputation for unethical or illegal business practices would also indicate moral hazard.

Morale Hazards

Morale hazard
A condition that exists when a person with insurance is not as careful as he or she would be if there were no insurance.

Morale hazard is a condition that exists when people are less careful than they should be because of the existence of insurance. That hazard arises out of carelessness or indifference to loss and is usually more subtle and more difficult to detect than moral hazard. Morale hazard might better be termed "lack of motivation hazard" because it exists in policyholders that are poorly motivated to avoid and minimize losses. Morale hazards might be indicated by poor personality traits or poor management.

Poor Personality Traits   Personality traits such as carelessness and thoughtlessness indicate morale hazard. Careless persons might not intentionally cause a loss, but they can exhibit a cavalier attitude toward valuable possessions, increasing the likelihood of loss. Someone who thoughtlessly leaves his or her keys in the car exhibits this hazard. The absence of pride of ownership can indicate the existence of morale hazard.

Poor Management   Poor or inefficient management can also indicate morale hazard. Sloppy housekeeping and indifferent bookkeeping are overt manifestations of this condition. Indifference to loss can result in neglecting the maintenance of fire extinguishers and other safety devices. Poor or nonexistent internal control systems invite theft and embezzlement by employees. Failure to comply with recommendations or to cooperate with loss control personnel is a further indication of morale hazard.

Identifying, Developing, and Evaluating Alternatives

After all the essential information on a particular submission has been gathered and hazards have been evaluated, the underwriter is ready to make a decision. The underwriter must identify and develop the alternatives available regarding the submission and, after carefully evaluating each alternative, choose the optimal one under the circumstances.

Two alternatives are easily identified: the underwriter can accept the submission as is or reject it. In addition, the underwriter can accept the submission subject to certain modifications. Determining the appropriate modification to best meet the needs of the insurer, producer, and applicant can be a challenge.

The four major types of modifications that can be made are as follows:

- Adopt loss control programs or devices
- Change rates, rating plans, or policy limits
- Amend policy terms and conditions
- Use facultative reinsurance

Adopt Loss Control Programs or Devices

One alternative available to the underwriter for a submission that would otherwise be unacceptable is to reduce the hazards. Such loss control programs as the installation of sprinklers, addition of guard service, and improvements in housekeeping and maintenance are means of reducing physical hazards. Further examples are the requirement of clear space for insureds in brush or wooded locations or the installation of machinery guards to reduce employee injuries. Some of these programs are relatively inexpensive and simple to implement, while others, such as sprinklers, require considerable capital investment.

From the applicant's viewpoint, insurer recommendations to reduce hazards might have a very positive, long-term effect on the ultimate costs of doing business, or they might be viewed as wholly unnecessary expenses. A significant function of underwriting is the making of sound recommendations accompanied by well-reasoned and convincing explanations to the applicant.

Change Rates, Rating Plans, or Policy Limits

A submission that is not acceptable at the rate requested might be desirable business at a higher rate, on a different rating plan, or with a lower limit. In private passenger auto, for example, a submission may not be eligible for the "safe driver" program for which it is submitted but might qualify for inclusion in another program at standard rates.

The rate modification could be either positive or negative. A producer might submit an account that is particularly desirable, with the recommendation that a rate deviation would increase the producer's likelihood of obtaining the account. In commercial insurance, where more discretion in pricing is permitted, pricing of submissions is crucial to obtaining profitable accounts in a competitive market. For instance, "a" rated (estimated loss potential) general liability policies are those classes in which the underwriter is given a range of possible rates, or suggested rates due to the statistical uncertainty of these classes. Judgment is used to select a rate that will earn a reasonable profit and be competitive enough to obtain the account. Pricing modifications also play a key role in judgment-rated lines such as inland and ocean marine. A number of rating plans are available for commercial applicants. The principal ones come under the category of merit plans and include experience rating, schedule rating, and retrospective rating.

Experience Rating

Experience rating uses the policyholder's actual loss experience to develop a premium modification factor to adjust the manual rate that would normally be applied. These plans are sometimes referred to as *prospective experience rating plans* because the premium modification is calculated before the inception of the policy to which it is applied. Experience rating is available for general liability risks that develop a specific premium level (which varies by company) and have at least one year of experience. In application, the experience rating plan uses three years of past loss experience, when available, and a credibility factor based on the size of the policyholder's premium to determine the actual modification. In comparison to other individual rating plans, experience rating has a formal methodology and must be applied without discrimination to all risks that meet experience rating eligibility requirements.

Schedule Rating

Schedule rating provides for the awarding of debits and credits to a risk based on specific categories such as the care and condition of the premises and the training and selection of employees. The credits or debits vary by insurer and are limited by insurance statute (usually between 25 and 40 percent). When applied, they reflect the underwriter's estimate of the degree of potential risk an insured presents, and the underwriter uses debits and credits to appropriately adjust the manual rate upward or downward. Insurance statutes require that insurers apply these plans to all eligible risks without discrimination and that adequate documentation be kept on file to justify the pricing decision.

Retrospective Rating

Retrospective rating is an individual experience modification program that uses the current year as the experience period to develop the experience modification factor. Under this plan, a provisional premium is charged at the beginning of the policy period. At the end of the policy period, the actual loss experience for *that* period is determined, and a final premium is charged. The insured's premium is adjusted after the end of the policy period to cover the expenses and losses developed by the insured during the policy period subject to specified minimum and maximum premiums. These plans have several variations that protect the policyholder from fluctuations in the final premium.

Policy Limits

Underwriting policy usually specifies the maximum limits of liability that can be written. For property insurance, the underwriter must be alert to over-insurance situations that could lead to a fraudulent loss. Underinsurance might be a more common problem. Adequate insurance limits are essential to meet loss settlement and coinsurance requirements. The limits on liability coverage afforded usually reflect reinsurance limitations or reinsurance availability and a possible catastrophic loss from a single exposure.

Amend Policy Terms and Conditions

A problem submission might be made acceptable by modifying the policy form to exclude certain causes of loss or to add or increase a deductible. An insurer might not be willing to write replacement cost coverage on a run-down home but might be willing to provide the limited HO-8 or a dwelling form. In small commercial accounts in which a large number of small losses might have caused unsatisfactory experience in the past, increasing the deductible might greatly improve the viability of the coverage.

The degree of flexibility available to the underwriter varies considerably from one line of insurance to another. In situations in which the coverage forms have been filed subject to approval by state regulatory bodies, coverage modifications are seldom possible. Even in those cases, it might be possible for the underwriter to suggest an alternative coverage form to the insurance applicant or producer when the requested form cannot be provided.

Use Facultative Reinsurance

If the applicant is in a class of business that is not covered by the underwriter's reinsurance treaty or if the amount of insurance needed exceeds net treaty capacity, the underwriter might be able to transfer the exposure that exceeds its capacity to a facultative reinsurer. Facultative reinsurance should not be used as a method to pass along a bad risk to a reinsurer. An alternative to purchasing facultative reinsurance is to suggest that the producer divide the insurance among several insurers.

Selecting an Alternative

The selection decision involves determining whether to accept the submission as offered, accept it with some modification, or reject it. Although rejection is sometimes unavoidable, underwriters should try to determine which modifications are necessary to make the submission acceptable, because one of the insurer's goals is to produce profitable business. Rejections produce neither premium nor commission, only expense.

Selecting an alternative involves weighing the positive and negative features of a submission. The underwriter must identify and evaluate the exposures, assess the degree of risk relative to the average exposure contemplated in the rate, review the controls and protection features in place, and assess management's commitment to loss prevention. Additional factors that need to be considered before a decision is made include the following:

- Amount of underwriting authority required
- Presence of supporting business
- Mix of business
- Producer relationships
- Regulatory constraints

Amount of Underwriting Authority Required

Before accepting an applicant, an underwriter must determine whether he or she has the necessary amount of underwriting authority. The underwriter's task differs when he or she has sufficient authority to decide and when the underwriter prepares the file for submission to higher underwriting authority.

Thus, the underwriter should check the underwriting guide before promising a producer a quick answer on a submission because referral to higher underwriting authority is often time-consuming.

Presence of Supporting Business

An application that is marginal on its own might become acceptable on an account basis if the rest of the account is desirable. Premium volume alone might be unacceptable to an insurer, since the premiums from five separate marginal insureds are probably not comparable to one superior account. On the other hand, the prospect of obtaining some above-average business in other lines might make a marginal submission viable if the supporting business is profitable enough to subsidize the marginal business.

In account underwriting, all of the business from a particular applicant is evaluated as a unit that must stand or fall on its own merits. The account underwriting approach evaluates both the submission for a given type of insurance and its supporting business.

Mix of Business

Mix of business
The distribution of individual policies comprising the book of business of a producer, territory, state, or region among the various lines and classifications.

The **mix of business** is the distribution of individual policies comprising the book of business of a producer, territory, state, or region among the various lines and classifications. Underwriting policy, as determined by management and as specified in the underwriting guide, frequently indicates the insurer's goals regarding the mix of business. Particular classes, such as youthful drivers in private passenger auto insurance or restaurants in property fire coverage, might be overrepresented in the present book of business. Consequently, the insurer might decide to raise the criteria for acceptability or to prohibit new business.

Producer Relationships

Often an important producer pressures an underwriter to accept a marginal prospect as an accommodation. Usually, the producer assures the underwriter of the delivery of some outstanding business later. Underwriters should keep accommodation files to enable them to detect excessive requests for accommodations and to determine whether the promised business materializes.

The relationship between the insurer and the producer should be based on mutual trust and respect. Differences of opinion are common, particularly since some of the goals of producers and underwriters conflict. Nevertheless, the long-run goals of producers and insurers are growth and profit. Mutual accommodation and willingness to see the other's viewpoint are essential to building a satisfactory working relationship.

Regulatory Constraints

State regulatory authorities are increasingly constraining the freedom of underwriters to decline new business or refuse to renew applicants. Underwriters must know those constraints, usually codified within the state's unfair trade practices laws. If regulation limits reasons for cancellation or refusal to renew, the selection decision on new submissions should be very carefully evaluated. Many states also limit the time within which an underwriter can decline a submission or provide notice of refusal to renew. Therefore, a timely decision must be made to avoid a mandatory acceptance or renewal of an otherwise unacceptable risk.

The so-called privacy laws that several states have enacted also restrict underwriting. The effect of those laws is to restrict the type and the amount of information about an applicant that an underwriter can obtain.

Implementing the Decision

Implementing underwriting decisions generally involves three steps. The first step is communicating the decision to the producer, if necessary, and to other insurer personnel. If the decision is to accept with modifications, the reasons must be clearly communicated to the producer or applicant, and the applicant must agree with the modifications. The insurer must establish controls to verify that modifications requested are implemented, particularly loss control recommendations. If the underwriter decides to reject the application, the underwriter must communicate this decision to the producer in a positive manner to avoid damaging their long-term relationship. Underwriters must present clear and logical reasons stipulating why the particular applicant does not meet the insurer's underwriting requirements. Effective communication of both positive and negative decisions clarifies insurer standards as market conditions change.

The second step is developing appropriate documentation. The underwriter might need to issue a binder or send a policy work sheet to the policywriting department. In some lines of business, the underwriter might need to prepare certificates of insurance.

The third step involves recording information about the policy and the applicant for accounting, statistical, and monitoring purposes. Data entry personnel extract essential information so that the system contains the policy information details on each policy written. For example, the premium must be posted to bill the producer. Data about the policyholder include location, limits, coverages, price modifications, class, and risk features. Those data must be coded so that the insurer and the industry can accumulate information on all accounts for ratemaking, statutory reporting, financial accounting, and book of business evaluations. That information is also used to follow the progress of the account and to trigger renewals and situations requiring special attention. For example, expiring policies will be identified so that updated information can be obtained. One purpose of the policy information system is to alert underwriters to claims activity during the policy period, other problems, or substantial changes with the policyholder. A claims referral system can immediately refer the file to the underwriter if the frequency of losses exceeds a predetermined limit or if a severe loss occurs.

Monitoring the Exposures

After an underwriting decision has been made on a submission or renewal, the underwriter's task is not complete. He or she must monitor the activity on the policies to ensure that satisfactory results are achieved.

Underwriters must be alert to changes in the loss exposures of insureds. Changes in the nature of the policyholder's business operation, for example, could significantly raise or lower the loss potential of the policyholder. Underwriters do not have the resources necessary to constantly monitor all policies written and underwrite new submissions at the same time. Therefore, monitoring usually occurs when policy changes or losses are brought to the underwriter's attention.

Adding a new location for a property policy or a new driver to an auto policy can cause the underwriter to investigate further to determine whether the character of the risk will change significantly. A notice of loss provides the underwriter with another opportunity to review the policyholder and determine whether the nature of the loss that occurred is commensurate with the type of loss exposures the underwriter expected. Summary information about the claim or a review of the claim file will provide valuable information concerning the nature of the loss and the operations of the policyholder.

Other opportunities to review individual policies come from loss control and premium audit reports. The loss control and safety inspection could have made specific recommendations that were to be implemented as a condition of policy issuance. A follow-up investigation could reveal that only some of the requirements have been met. Premium audits usually lag behind the issuance of a renewal policy by several months. The audit report could disclose larger exposures than originally contemplated, unacceptable operations, new products, new operations, or financial problems.

Once a claim has occurred or a premium audit has been conducted, the underwriter has the opportunity to contact insurer personnel who have first-hand knowledge of the insured. They can often provide information on new exposures or uncover additional hazards or operations that will help the underwriter reevaluate the account and determine its continued acceptability.

A second aspect of monitoring requires evaluating an entire book of business. Underwriters use premium and loss statistics to determine where aggregate problems lie in a deteriorating book of business. The review of the book of business can determine whether underwriting policy is being complied with and can detect changes in the type, volume, and quality of policies that might require corrective action.

Relationship Between Decisions and Outcomes

Monitoring the quality of decisions affecting a book of business is complicated because underwriting decisions and results are not directly related. Since underwriting decisions are made under conditions of uncertainty, what appears to be a good decision might result in a poor outcome. An underwriter can accept a perfectly "clean" application, only to suffer a major loss. On the other hand, an underwriter might make a poor decision, such as accepting a substandard insured, and have no losses. Over the long run, however, the better the quality of the underwriting decisions are, the better the results are.

Monitoring a Book of Business

Monitoring a book of business means evaluating the quality and profitability of all business written during a specific period of time covering a certain territory for a specific type of insurance. To be effective, that evaluation should identify specific problems within a line of business. A line of business can be subdivided into class of business, size of account, territory, and producer for the purpose of evaluation. In each phase of the evaluation, the insurer is primarily concerned with the loss ratio that develops. The insurer is also concerned that sufficient premium volume be developed to cover fixed costs and overhead expenses.

Class of Business

A poor loss ratio in a particular class can indicate inadequate pricing or a disproportionate number of high-hazard policyholders relative to the average risk in the classification. Classes with poor or deteriorating experience can be identified and corrected through rate increases, coverage restrictions, or more stringent selection standards. Changes in technology, materials, and operations, as well as the social and legal environment in which they are employed, can have a significant effect on the desirability of a class.

Territory

A territory can be defined in various ways to reflect an insurer's operations. For example, territory could encompass the three-state area over which a branch office has domain, or a single state. Another definition of a territory is the rating territory used in pricing policies within a state. However defined, territories identify geographic areas where profits are or are not realized. Identifying areas can guide the insurer in future agency appointments for profitable regions or areas experiencing growth. If results are poor, the information could indicate areas where the insurer might withdraw if rate relief is not forthcoming.

The regulatory and legal climate for insurance varies by state. That climate alone can affect the desirability of conducting business in a state and the possibility of achieving a profit. Basic considerations in territorial analysis are physical differences in terrain, degree of urbanization, and the potential for natural disasters.

Producer

Ideally, each producer's book of business should be evaluated annually. The producer's premium volume, policy retention, type of business, and loss ratio are evaluated both on an overall basis and by line and class of business. That evaluation should include the balance desired between personal and commercial business and the projected growth factor. Key considerations are the goals the insurer and producer established and the progress made toward those goals. If the producer has a small premium volume with the insurer, a single large loss can distort the loss ratio. A similar situation can occur in a small line of business. For example, a producer might appear to have an unprofitable workers compensation experience based on loss ratio when he or she actually has only one policy with an unsatisfactory loss ratio.

SUMMARY

Underwriting is selecting policyholders through hazard recognition and evaluation, pricing, and determination of policy terms and conditions. The practice of underwriting insurance policies began when insurance emerged as a commercial enterprise. In modern practice, underwriters strive to develop a larger market share of profitable business. Adverse selection, a natural opponent of this objective, occurs when the applicant for insurance presents a higher-than-average probability of loss than is expected from a truly random sample of all applicants. Underwriting activities are typically described with a distinction between day-to-day activities (line functions) and management activities (staff functions). Although that distinction is not universal, it helps differentiate between underwriters who make individual risk decisions and those who establish general policy guidelines for the insurer.

Establishing underwriting policy is a key objective of senior management. Effectively implementing underwriting policy is a criterion for the success of any insurer. An insurer's underwriting policy promotes the type and classes of insurance anticipated to produce a growing and profitable book of business. Although almost any restriction on acceptable business can be imposed, there are limitations on what an underwriting policy can contain and real-world limiting factors to that policy.

Implementing an underwriting policy means communicating the standards to line underwriters and following up periodically to ensure that standards are being met. Underwriting guides and bulletins are the primary tools for disseminating underwriting policy. Underwriting management conducts underwriting audits on a regular basis to determine how well individual underwriters, branch offices, and agents are adhering to standards.

As in most businesses, financial ratios are used to indicate the success of the underwriting effort. Key ratios are the loss ratio, expense ratio, and combined ratio. Combined ratios of less than 100 percent indicate profitable underwriting results, and unprofitable underwriting results are indicated by ratios over 100 percent. The combined ratio ignores investment income—an important component of an insurer's overall profitability.

An underwriter can make what appears to be a good underwriting decision but end up with poor results. The reverse of this is also true. The more common problems with evaluating individual underwriting results are the span of time between the decision and the results, and the occurrence of factors beyond the control of the underwriter. Several underwriting performance measures are more subjective and do not rely on account profitability.

The underwriting process can be viewed as consisting of a five-step decision-making process:

1. Gathering information
2. Identifying, developing, and evaluating alternatives
3. Selecting an alternative
4. Implementing the decision
5. Monitoring the exposures

This chapter discussed each of those steps in a manner that can be applied to any specific line of business or insurance product.

CHAPTER NOTES

1. "Is Underwriting a Lost Art?" *Producer*, Crum and Forster Insurance Companies, Winter 1976, p. 13.
2. Association values are set by the Securities Valuation Office (SVO), which is a unit of the NAIC. The SVO catalogs the values of all securities held by insurers and determines values in difficult situations. For example, the SVO would peg a value for a bond whose issuer had defaulted on repayment or on a security issue that is not publicly traded.
3. "Three Arrested in Fraud Scheme," *Business Insurance*, February 18, 1991, p. 11.

Chapter 5

Direct Your Learning

Underwriting Property Insurance

After learning the subject matter in this chapter, you should be able to:

■ Explain the importance of fire underwriting to other causes of loss that affect property.

■ Given a case, evaluate fire hazards using the COPE factors.

■ Given a case, evaluate the account's exposure to various causes of loss.

■ Given a case, explain the major underwriting considerations in each of the following:
- Time element insurance
- Commercial crime insurance
- Marine insurance

Develop Your Perspective

What are the main topics covered in the chapter?

In this chapter, a wide range of direct and indirect causes of loss to property is addressed from an underwriting perspective. Some causes of loss, such as fire, require extensive evaluation.

Consider the underwriting evaluations for each cause of loss.

- What are the unique factors for each cause of loss?

- How can underwriters make accurate policy-selection decisions based on these factors?

Why is it important to know these topics?

Causes of loss, or loss exposures, are the focus of an underwriting review. An underwriter will gather information to determine the extent of the potential losses for a new application or for an existing policy.

Identify direct and consequential loss exposures and the factors that can increase their frequency and severity.

- What types of direct and consequential loss exposures do businesses face?

- How can risk management and insurance address potential losses?

How can you use this information?

Analyze direct and indirect causes of loss for property exposures.

- What might be done to minimize the potential loss frequency or severity for your own organization?

- Compare the loss potential for two or more properties considered for purchase or lease. Include the loss potential for each property as a factor in the purchase or lease decision.

Chapter 5

Underwriting Property Insurance

Chapter 5 focuses on underwriting selected types of property insurance. Property underwriters have traditionally emphasized fire as a cause of loss. Analyzing the insured property's susceptibility to loss by fire is an appropriate approach to underwriting property insurance because fire is the covered cause of loss that has the greatest potential to inflict a *total* loss on the insured property. In addition to examining fire, this chapter analyzes the nature of and underwriting concerns associated with other causes of loss included in most property policies, as well as those insured by crime, inland marine, and ocean marine policies. This chapter also addresses underwriting other types of property-related loss, such as business income losses. Chapter 6 similarly treats liability loss exposures.

FIRE INSURANCE UNDERWRITING

Whether written monoline or as part of a package, fire is generally the most important cause of loss to underwrite in property insurance. Fire insurance is one of the oldest types of property coverage, dating back to the seventeenth century. Fire insurance was an outgrowth of destructive conflagrations such as the fire of London in 1666. Early fire insurance contracts were written on property at a fixed location and provided little off-premises coverage and few, if any, additional causes of loss. Although loss frequency for a given insured is usually low and most losses that do occur are partial losses, fire always contains the potential for a total loss, a possibility that greatly influences underwriting practices.

Underwriting fire as a cause of loss focuses on the physical hazards presented by a particular loss exposure. To ensure a thorough review of these hazards, property underwriters use an approach that scrutinizes four specific areas, traditionally referred to as COPE: construction, occupancy, protection, and external exposures.

Construction

The construction of a building that is insured or that contains insured property is a primary consideration when property insurance is underwritten. The building's construction relates directly to its ability to withstand damage by fire and other perils and to protect its contents against loss.

The policy application and a personal inspection by the producer or loss control representative can provide specific data on the construction of a particular building. For buildings subject to specific rating, advisory organizations publish information on building construction. If additional information is needed, independent inspection companies can perform a property survey.

Construction Classifications

Insurance Services Office (ISO) divides building construction into six classifications:[1]

1. Class #6—fire resistive
2. Class #5—modified fire resistive
3. Class #4—masonry noncombustible
4. Class #3—noncombustible
5. Class #2—joisted masonry
6. Class #1—frame

Those classifications are based on the following:

1. The materials used for the components of the structure that bear the weight of the building and its contents
2. The materials used in the roof and floors of the building, especially the supports for the roof and floors
3. The fire-resistance rating of the materials used in the building construction

Construction classifications are based on the ability of the materials used in constructing a building to resist damage by fire. Ratings consider the characteristics of (1) the vertical load-bearing members that ultimately support the weight of the building and (2) the materials used in the roof and floors, which spread the weight across the vertical load-bearing members.

Fire Resistive

Fire-resistive construction
Building construction that incorporates load-bearing members that can withstand damage by fire for at least two hours.

The characteristic that defines **fire-resistive construction** is the ability of the load-bearing members of the structure to withstand damage by fire for at least two hours. This is a higher standard than one requiring that the structure itself not burn. The load-bearing components of a fire-resistive building will not buckle or collapse as might the members of other construction types.

Fire-resistive construction is superior to other types of building construction but is not "fireproof." Fire-resistive ratings are assigned to construction material based on laboratory evaluations in test furnaces. Evaluations certify that materials will withstand damage by fire under certain weight loads regardless of whether materials can be repaired or reused. The performance of such materials may differ significantly under actual fire conditions.

From an underwriting standpoint, fire-resistive construction is the best type for most causes of loss. The strength of the structure gives it superior resistance to causes of loss such as windstorm, earthquake, and flood. The construction materials are either (1) noncombustible with a fire-resistance rating of at least two hours or (2) protected by a noncombustible covering such as concrete, masonry, plaster, or gypsum that provides at least a two-hour fire-resistance rating.

Modified Fire Resistive

A building of **modified fire-resistive construction** has bearing walls (walls supporting the weight of the upper floors and roof) and columns of masonry or reinforced concrete construction. It is similar to fire-resistive construction, except that the fire-resistance rating of the materials is one to two hours.

Masonry Noncombustible

In the **masonry noncombustible construction** class are buildings with exterior walls of fire-resistive construction with a rating of not less than one hour or buildings of masonry construction. The roof and floors must be of noncombustible or slow-burning materials. The typical masonry noncombustible building has a masonry nonbearing wall surface, a concrete floor, a metal deck roof, and an unprotected metal frame. Low initial cost and low maintenance have made this type of construction extremely popular.

Noncombustible

A building of **noncombustible construction** has exterior walls, a roof, and a floor constructed of and supported by metal or other noncombustible materials. Although these buildings are noncombustible, they are not fire resistive. If this type of building is filled with combustible contents, structural failure is extremely likely in the event of a serious fire. The unprotected steel structural supports in this type of building will twist and bend when subjected to the heat of a typical fire. Even though these structures are constructed of noncombustible material and will not contribute fuel to a fire, their susceptibility to damage makes them only marginally safer from an underwriting perspective than joisted masonry or frame construction (described below).

Joisted Masonry

Joisted masonry construction has load-bearing exterior walls made of brick, adobe, concrete, gypsum, stone, tile, or similar materials, with floors and roofs of combustible materials. Joisted masonry construction is also referred to as ordinary construction, ordinary masonry, brick, wood joisted, and brick joisted. Exterior walls may be of fire-resistive construction with a fire-resistance rating of at least one hour or of masonry construction. The walls are self-supporting, meaning that they stand without support from the building's frame. Because the exterior walls are load bearing, many underwriters regard them as part of the building's frame. Interior columns and floors are of combustible material, usually wood.

Modified fire-resistive construction
Construction that has load-bearing walls and columns of masonry or reinforced concrete construction. The fire-resistance rating of these construction materials is one to two hours.

Masonry noncombustible construction
Construction that includes exterior walls of fire-resistive construction with a rating of not less than one hour or masonry construction.

Noncombustible construction
Construction that has exterior walls, a roof, and a floor constructed of and supported by metal or other noncombustible materials.

Joisted masonry construction
Construction that has load-bearing exterior walls made of brick, adobe, concrete, gypsum, stone, tile or similar materials, with floors and roofs of combustible materials.

Joisted masonry buildings are found in most major metropolitan areas, especially in northern states. The need for the exterior walls to support the weight of the structure places practical limits on the height to which these structures can be built. Joisted masonry construction is rarely used for buildings higher than five stories and is used in many areas only for buildings of three stories or less.

Mill construction is a type of joisted masonry construction that uses heavy timbers for internal support of the floors and roof. In this construction type, there are no concealed areas under the roof and floors that might permit a fire to go undetected. The heavy wood floors serve as a firestop, thereby slowing the spread of fire.

The size of the wood members used in mill construction gives these buildings structural strength. Fires that would engulf the light joists used in typical joisted masonry might only char the heavy timber beams used in mill construction.

Frame

Frame construction
Construction that has load-bearing components made of wood or other combustible materials.

In **frame construction**, the load-bearing components of the building are wood or other combustible materials. In addition to the direct damage caused by a fire, frame construction can suffer structural damage because the weight-bearing supports are combustible. Many dwellings and small mercantile buildings are frame. Buildings of mixed construction, such as wood frame with brick veneer, stone veneer, aluminum siding, or stucco, are properly classified as frame buildings.

Construction Materials

The construction of the weight-bearing members of a building is a basic consideration in fire underwriting. Additionally, the construction materials used in partition walls and other components of the structure affect its combustibility and desirability from an underwriting standpoint.

Interior Finish

The interior finish of a structure affects its underwriting acceptability. A fire-resistive office building, for example, may have an interior finish that is highly combustible. Underwriters have to consider several characteristics of interior finishes, including their ability to spread fire, the fuel provided for a fire, and the smoke and noxious gases emitted while burning. Each of these characteristics affects the overall property loss potential of the structure and the safety of the occupants.

Fuel load
The expected amount and type of combustible material in a given area. Also called fire load.

Relatively noncombustible interior finishes include wall coverings such as plaster, gypsum, and wallboard. Combustible interior finishes include wood or plywood, fiber ceiling tiles, and plastic wall coverings. Surface coatings such as certain paints, varnishes, and wallpapers, when added to other combustible finishes, could contribute significantly to the fuel load. The **fuel load** (also called the fire load) measures the expected amount and type of combustible material in a given fire area. Even the adhesives used in floor or ceiling tile can substantially affect a building's capacity to sustain or fuel a fire.

A fire that consumes combustible interior finish can generate highly toxic gases that can circulate quickly throughout a building. A fairly severe fire that started in the lobby of a hotel provides an example. As the highly combustible finishing materials on the wall and ceiling burned, they generated a large volume of hot smoke and gases. The smoke and gases seeped into a stairwell, quickly finding an open door twelve floors above the fire. People entering this twelfth-floor area perished even though the hotel sustained little damage to its structure overall. These deaths occurred not only because the interior-finish fumes were toxic but also because unprotected vertical openings allowed hot smoke and gases to travel upward.

Insulation

Just as the interior finish of a structure greatly affects its combustibility, insulation may also add problems. A common form of insulation is fiberglass, which is often installed with a paper backing. Insulation material may also include combustible substances such as finely chopped paper treated with fire-retardant chemicals. Insulation also serves as a sound barrier, and, therefore, combustible insulation can be found in the interior walls of otherwise highly fire-resistive buildings.

Whether the insulation is installed to conserve heat or to suppress sound, an attempt should be made to determine its flame spread, fuel contribution, and smoke contribution characteristics. This information should be available from the manufacturer of the insulation.

Rising energy costs in the 1970s led to renewed interest in conserving the energy consumed in heating and cooling buildings. As a result, insulation has been added to many existing structures. This insulation can contain the heat of a fire within a building, concentrating it on structural members. Such an insulated building may, therefore, weaken and collapse more quickly than anticipated.

Roofing

The exterior surface of a roof serves as a weather seal, but it also provides a barrier against exposure fires. Roofs are subject to attack from sparks and embers falling from fires outside the building. The combustibility of either side of the roof is important in retarding the spread of interior fires. Untreated wooden shingles invite the spread of exposure fires. Roof coverings vary in the fire resistance they provide. Underwriters Laboratories, Inc., evaluates and classifies roofing materials.

Asphalt shingles are probably the most common roof covering for residential buildings. Although they are somewhat combustible, they are excellent barriers to severe fire exposures when properly constructed and installed. Conversely, combustible materials such as wood shake shingles or tar paper afford almost no protection. In the presence of high winds, a wood shake roof may send firebrands downwind.

Other Construction Considerations

In addition to the fire resistance of a building's construction, underwriters have to consider other factors, including age, building height, fire divisions, building openings, and building codes.

Age

Property underwriters have to consider several factors that are directly related to the age of older buildings they insure or to buildings that contain covered property. Those factors concern the following:

1. A different building code was probably in effect at the time the building was constructed. As a result, the building may lack protective features and systems generally considered essential by today's standards.

2. The heating, cooling, electrical, and fire protection systems may have become obsolete.

3. The building may have been intended for a different occupancy and may not be suitable for its current use.

4. Conversion and remodeling may have created concealed spaces in which fire may burn undetected and spread rapidly.

5. Over the years, alterations and repairs may have left unprotected openings in vertical and horizontal firestops.

6. The need to comply with current building codes may increase the cost of making repairs following a loss.

7. The condition of the building may have deteriorated for numerous reasons, including normal wear and tear, hard use, or lack of maintenance.

8. The value of an older building is often difficult to determine, especially if the builder used construction techniques and materials that are no longer available.

Although proper maintenance mitigates the effects of age and deterioration, all buildings will eventually wear out. The degree of obsolescence or deterioration is directly related to the type of construction, occupancy, physical abuse of the building, and quality of the owner's maintenance.

A frame structure, for example, will normally show its age more quickly than a joisted masonry building. However, an office occupancy in a frame structure with good maintenance may be preferable to a fire-resistive building occupied by a foundry with minimal maintenance.

Construction methods and materials have changed over time. Building materials that were in use in the 1920s or 1930s have long been abandoned. Electrical systems of forty, fifty, and sixty years ago were designed primarily for lighting, while modern wiring systems are designed to accommodate space heating, air conditioning, computer systems, and heavy appliances.

A building that was designed for a dry-goods retailer fifty years ago might be inadequate for the laundry, printer, or beverage distributor that occupies the structure today. The weight of equipment, stock, and storage associated with the business may have increased since the building was designed and built. In addition to the increase in hazard that occurs because of the change in occupancy, the structural integrity of the building has probably deteriorated over time.

Building Height

The height of an insured structure is an important consideration. Buildings present unique problems when their height restricts the capability of the local fire service to fight a fire from outside. The National Fire Protection Association (NFPA) defines a high-rise building as one that is at least 75 feet tall. The tallest extension ladders in use today can reach 120 feet, but many municipal fire services are not capable of fighting a fire from the exterior of a building that is in excess of 100 feet (eight or nine floors).

In a high-rise building, the fire department has to fight the fire from inside. Firefighters must consider the fire-resistive characteristics of the structure and the presence or lack of approved horizontal and vertical barriers used to confine the fire to its area of origin. In one high-rise fire, the fire department could not approach the building because of flying glass caused by heat-shattered windows. Firefighters were forced to enter the building through a parking garage that permitted access to the basement.

Controlling combustible contents in high-rise buildings is crucial. The building should not contain occupancies that create a high fire hazard or a heavy fuel load. The most common uses of high-rise structures are as offices, apartments, and hotels. These occupancies present a light fire hazard. However, office occupancies often store highly combustible paper files, which create the potential of a severe fire.

High-rise structures sometimes have restaurants or bars on the upper floors. In that location, restaurants are a hazardous occupancy, and without adequate control or private protection, they constitute a significant hazard.

The effect of elevation on a fire is also an important consideration. When a fire starts, it becomes necessary to vent the smoke and toxic gases it produces and to introduce fresh air for firefighters and occupants who may be unable to escape. A state-of-the-art heating, ventilating, and air conditioning (HVAC) system can accomplish this. If mechanical ventilation fails, it may become necessary to open or break windows. This action, however, exposes the fire floor to winds that are much more intense at the height of upper floors than at ground level. In addition to the damage the wind causes directly, strong winds may assist in spreading the fire and may hamper fire-fighting efforts.

More important than property damage in a high-rise building is the safety of human lives. A structure of 100 stories might have as many as 25,000 occupants. If a severe fire occurs on the fiftieth floor, more than 12,000 people may be located above the fire and may, therefore, be subjected to potential injury from flame, smoke, and gas. The first priority of fire department personnel is the safety of a building's occupants. To the extent that lives are endangered, firefighters must concentrate on human safety before fighting the fire.

Fire Divisions

A different type of problem may be found in large horizontal buildings. Many structures have a total horizontal area approaching one million square feet. Vertical integrity is the solution to many fire problems in high-rise structures, and fire divisions are the corresponding solution for fires in large horizontal areas. A **fire division** is a section of a structure so well protected that fire cannot spread from that section to another.

Fire division
A section of a structure so well protected that fire cannot spread from that section to another.

A **fire wall** restricts the spread of fire by serving as a fire-resistive barrier. Interior walls may or may not be of sufficient fire resistance to qualify. Generally, fire walls must consist of at least eight inches of masonry material; however, fire wall adequacy also depends on the combustibility of building contents. A fire wall must also be free standing, which means that it has to support its own weight without assistance from other building components. A load-bearing wall, on the other hand, might not be a fire wall.

Fire wall
Wall that restricts the spread of fire by serving as a fire-resistive barrier.

Fire walls cannot be effective if fire can easily spread over or around them. To prevent fire from spreading, fire walls have to extend above a combustible roof and through exterior walls. Vertical extensions of a fire wall above the roofline are called **parapets**. The Factory Mutual Research Corporation (FMRC) recommends that parapets extend at least thirty inches. Parapets may be higher or lower depending on local building codes.[2] Extensions of the fire wall through the outer walls are known as **fender walls**. They are common in frame construction that uses interior fire walls to create fire divisions. In many frame apartment structures, fender walls also provide privacy to terraces and patios.

Parapets
Vertical extensions of a fire wall above a roofline.

Fender walls
Extensions of a fire wall through an outer wall.

A definite firestop is a special class of fire wall that is of substantial construction. At a minimum, such a wall must have a minimum fire-resistance rating of four hours with no openings, even if protected.

Some underwriters apply a similar concept to multiple-story buildings of fire-resistive construction. By doing so, they recognize the existence of vertical as well as horizontal firestops. They reason that a floor with a two-hour fire-resistance rating is effective in preventing the vertical spread of fire just as fire walls are effective in preventing the horizontal spread of fire. However, because fire spreads more readily upward than horizontally, very few underwriters will give the same weight to fire-resistive floors as they do to horizontal fire walls.

Building Openings

Building openings may increase the potential for loss by fire. Although the construction type may be appropriate for the intended occupancy, subcontractors, such as electricians and heating and air conditioning contractors, may have installed equipment that penetrates vertical and horizontal firestops. For example, a high-rise structure nearing completion in New York City had noncombustible structural members that were adequately protected and that afforded it at least a two-hour fire rating. Subcontractors subsequently diminished the protection by removing the insulation from the structural steel members and resurfacing them with a protective coating. When a fire occurred, the steel members were weakened and required replacement. Although the damage to these members was minimal and their original cost was not inordinate, a multimillion-dollar loss resulted from replacing major building supports in a structure nearing completion.

Buildings contain many openings that without additional protection can violate the basic integrity of a fire division. These openings include doors between fire divisions, floor openings for stairs between floors, elevators, dumbwaiters, and conveyor belts. In most circumstances, fire doors can protect these openings. The most common causes of unprotected openings are oversight and poor loss control.

Openings in fire walls are sometimes needed if a building is to serve its intended purpose. If a fire wall is to perform its function, fire doors must protect those openings. Fire doors are classified based on their ability to resist fire. The classification scheme used by NFPA ranges from doors that withstand fire for three hours to those that withstand fire for one-third of an hour. Approved doors have a rating seal on the door's edge.

A fire door in a fire wall must be capable of withstanding the same fire as the wall itself. A one-hour fire door in a two-hour fire wall, for example, reduces the fire protection rating of the entire wall to one hour. A vertical opening such as an elevator or a stairwell is protected only when it is completely segregated into a separate fire division. A properly constructed elevator shaft or stairwell constitutes a building within a building.

A fire door cannot be effective if it is propped open. Each door must be automatically self-closing and unobstructed. Doors that must be left open to permit efficient industrial operations are fitted with fusible links that melt and release the door when the temperature reaches a predetermined level. This permits the doors to close automatically when exposed to the heat of a fire.

Building Codes

Building codes are local ordinances or state statutes that regulate the construction of buildings within a municipality, county, or state. Studies have shown that well-designed and properly enforced building codes can reduce insured losses, especially from such causes of loss as windstorm and earthquake. In most areas of the country, however, underwriters must rely on their own resources to evaluate the effectiveness of building code enforcement. Assessing the effectiveness of building codes requires either extensive research or first-hand knowledge. Either alternative is time-consuming and expensive.

Building codes
Local ordinances or state statutes that regulate the construction of buildings within a municipality, county, or state.

ISO and the Insurance Institute for Property Loss Reduction (IIPLR) developed the Building Code Effectiveness Grading Schedule (BCEGS). This program completed a five-year phased introduction in 2001. The BCEGS program includes grades from 1 to 10, indicating the effectiveness of a community's building code. The schedule places special emphasis on mitigation of losses resulting from natural hazards, such as wind and earthquakes. A BCEGS grade of 1 indicates a municipality with exemplary commitment to building code enforcement.[3]

Occupancy

The occupancy of a building affects the frequency and severity of losses. Factors affecting frequency and severity vary by occupancy and can be grouped under three headings: (1) sources of ignition or fire causes, (2) combustibility, and (3) damageability. In addition to these generic classifications of occupancy hazards are hazard concerns common to all occupancies. Specific occupancy classes such as restaurants have their own special hazards.

Ignition Sources

Ignition sources or causes provide the means for a fire to start. Underwriters must know the principal sources of ignition that an insured occupancy or the use of the covered building produces. Potential ignition sources include the following:

1. Friendly fires that escape containment. They can result from open flames and heaters, smoking, torches, lamps, furnaces, ovens and heaters, and welding and cutting torches.

2. Friction that generates enough heat to ignite nearby combustible material. Sources of friction include hot bearings, rubbing belts, grinding, shredding, picking, polishing, cutting, and drilling.

3. Electricity that produces either sparks or heat that can ignite exposed combustibles. Static electricity frequently causes sparks. Lighting fixtures, overloaded circuits, and worn wiring can release potentially damaging amounts of heat.

4. Certain chemical reactions, called exothermic reactions, that produce heat sufficient to cause ignition.[4]

Although certain industrial occupancies present obvious hazards with respect to sources of ignition, some hazards are more subtle. The fire hazard presented by smoking and lit cigarettes, for instance, relates directly to the number of persons passing through the premises and the building's prevailing policy on smoking. Health concerns unrelated to fire potential have led many buildings to prohibit occupants from smoking indoors, but smoking materials remain a significant cause of fire losses.

Combustibility

A building's occupancy indicates to underwriters the type of property the building is likely to contain. The combustibility of contents depends on how quickly the material will ignite, the rate at which a fire will spread, and the intensity or amount of heat a fire will generate. Gasoline, for example, is easily ignited, spreads fire quickly, and burns with explosive intensity.

The major classifications of materials that are highly combustible include the following:

1. Light combustible materials such as thin plywood, shingles, shavings, paper, cotton, and other fibers
2. Combustible dusts such as those produced when refinishing bowling alley lanes or refining flour
3. Flammable liquids
4. Combustible gases such as hydrogen
5. Materials subject to spontaneous combustion
6. Explosive materials, acids, and oxidizing agents[5]

The combustibility of a building's contents affects the underwriting desirability of that building. Management practices by the insured can make a significant difference in the acceptability of the insured regardless of the content's combustibility.

Damageability

The damageability of contents is a major underwriting consideration and is necessary for determining the probable maximum loss to contents should a fire occur. Even a small and quickly extinguishable fire can result in a severe loss to highly damageable contents, such as expensive clothing or furniture.

Hazards Associated With the Occupancy

The physical hazards that an occupancy presents can be classified into two categories: common hazards and special hazards.

Common Hazards

Certain hazards, called **common hazards**, exist in almost every occupancy. For convenience in analysis, underwriters generally recognize several broad (though not mutually exclusive) categories of common hazards.

Common hazards include the following:

1. Housekeeping
2. Heating equipment
3. Electrical equipment
4. Smoking materials

Housekeeping Every occupancy generates waste and trash. Underwriters have to consider three aspects of the exposure this creates: uncollected litter, storage, and disposal.

Common hazards
Hazards that exist in almost every occupancy. They include (1) housekeeping, (2) heating equipment, (3) electrical equipment, and (4) smoking materials.

Waste and trash in the form of uncollected litter can significantly contribute to the spread of fire. Paper, oily items, packing materials, and discarded smoking materials are common examples of this hazard.

Many industrial operations use lubricants in significant amounts, so the waste and litter they produce are often oily. Janitorial work frequently uses oily substances or is performed where oil and grease are present. An accumulation of greasy soot in vents and flues, particularly over cooking stoves, is a significant hazard.

Most commercial and institutional occupancies require that wastes be temporarily stored. Depending on the material and the nature of the storage, the concentration and confinement of the waste may increase or decrease the hazard. When neatly stacked and enclosed, paper and cardboard, for example, resist burning better than the same material piled haphazardly and loosely. In a confined space, oily materials are subject to spontaneous combustion.

Good housekeeping also requires the separation of materials that may react with one another. Trash and waste should be stored in noncombustible containers.

Disposing of waste by incineration on the insured premises requires special precautions. Incinerators constitute an additional source of heat and heat byproducts. Mixtures of wastes present special problems, since some explode when burned or give off toxic gases. A properly designed and operating incinerator can control these hazards.

Heating Equipment   Furnaces and other heating equipment provide a potential source of ignition. The hazard exists primarily in the burners or heating elements of the equipment; however, the equipment itself and the pipes, ducts, and flues leading from it also radiate heat. Some sources of heat present greater hazards than others. Wood-burning stoves and salamanders (portable heaters), for example, present a greater hazard than a gas furnace because fuel cannot be controlled or withdrawn once added to the fire. Sparks could also ignite combustible material in the vicinity of wood-burning stoves and portable heaters.

Electrical Equipment   NFPA reports that most of the fires started by electrical motors and appliances are caused by careless use, improper installation, or poor maintenance. Management's interest in regular maintenance is a major factor in fire loss prevention.

Smoking Materials   Controlling fire caused by smoking and matches involves prohibiting smoking in certain areas and ensuring the safe handling of cigarettes, cigars, and matches where smoking is permitted. Management's smoking policy and its enforcement are important considerations in controlling this hazard.

Special Hazards

Each occupancy class creates its own special hazards. In addition, individual businesses sometimes contain hazards that are neither common to all occupancies nor usual for the class. In analyzing special hazards, underwriters usually identify two distinct types: special hazards of the class and special hazards of the risk.

Special Hazards of the Class   Potentially hazardous conditions that increase the likely frequency or severity of loss but which are typical for the type of occupancy are called **special hazards of the class**. Examples include cooking in a restaurant or using volatile chemicals in a manufacturing plant. Almost every occupancy has a hazardous activity that can reasonably be expected based on the nature of the occupancy. Underwriters must be familiar with the operations and hazards that are typical of the classes they entertain.

Special hazards of the class
Potentially hazardous conditions that increase the likely frequency or severity of loss but are typical for the type of occupancy.

Special Hazards of the Risk   Some businesses engage in activities that are not typical of other businesses with which they would be classed. Those activities, termed **special hazards of the risk**, often create hazards neither contemplated by the underwriter nor charged for in the rates. A maintenance garage for a large fleet of trucks or taxicabs, for example, might contain a small body shop or welding equipment. The garage is a special hazard of the class, but the auto body work, typically performed by an auto body shop, would constitute a special hazard of the risk. Identifying special hazards of the risk usually requires a physical inspection of the insured's business.

Special hazards of the risk
Hazards created by activities in which a business engages that are not typical of other businesses with which they would be classed. These hazards are not contemplated by the underwriter or charged for in the rates.

Types of Occupancies

Underwriters have traditionally grouped occupancies into broad categories to aid in analyzing the hazards that might be present. The six categories that are frequently used are as follows:

1. Habitational
2. Office
3. Institutional
4. Mercantile
5. Service
6. Manufacturing

Habitational Occupancies

Habitational occupancies include apartments, hotels, motels, and nursing homes. Habitational occupancies are often in the control of someone other than the building owner, so detecting or controlling the presence of hazards can be difficult. Often, the hallmark of a superior habitational occupancy is the extent of building maintenance performed by the owner. Such activity demonstrates to the tenants that the owners care about the condition of the building. Also, regular maintenance permits the owner access to occupant-controlled areas that might have become substandard because of tenant neglect. Situations, once identified, can then be corrected.

Habitational occupancies are often affected by ups and downs in the economy. A proxy for the financial stability of the owner is the vacancy rate of the business. The vacancy rate of an account can be compared with the average vacancy rate of similar operations in the area.

Office Occupancies

The office occupancy is a relatively low-hazard classification. Materials found in offices are usually of limited combustibility and only slightly susceptible. Buildings used for office occupancies might have unusual features, such as restaurants or heliports. Office occupancies can be found in any type of structure and often share a building with other occupancies.

Institutional Occupancies

Institutional occupancies include schools, churches, hospitals, and property owned by governmental entities. Governmental entities often operate habitational properties such as public housing and nursing homes. Institutional occupancies also include special-purpose facilities such as prisons and police and fire stations.

During the liability insurance crises of the 1970s and 1980s, many institutional properties shifted to retention programs. Risk retention groups for public entities are commonplace in today's insurance market. The trend toward privatizing public functions has led many of these public facilities back to the insurance market.

Mercantile Occupancies

Mercantile occupancies include accounts whose primary business is buying and selling goods, wares, and merchandise, whether wholesale or retail. Department stores, clothing stores, hardware stores, specialty shops, and grocery stores are examples of mercantile occupancies.

The combustibility of a mercantile operation's contents varies with the type of merchandise sold. For example, a sporting goods store might stock ammunition and camping-stove fuel. Hardware stores and home centers normally have large quantities of flammables and combustibles, such as paints, varnishes, solvents, lumber, curtains, and wallpaper.

The stock of mercantile occupancies is usually of significant value and is susceptible to fire, smoke, and water damage. For example, clothing is especially subject to severe loss from smoke and water damage, and the stock of a hardware store will rust from the water used in fighting a fire. Health authorities usually require food exposed to fire and smoke to be withdrawn from sale. In these classes, a small fire can produce a large loss.

Service Occupancies

Service occupancies include businesses that perform an activity for the customer rather than create or sell a product. This category includes dry cleaners and automobile service stations.

The hazards presented by a service occupancy are usually specific to the service being performed. Dry cleaners, for example, have several occupancy hazards. Lint accumulation presents a fire and an explosion hazard. Dry cleaners also have large boilers for the hot water used in cleaning, and irons and presses could serve as ignition sources. Many of the solvents used in dry cleaning are flammable and need to be handled and stored properly.

Manufacturing Occupancies

Manufacturers are in the business of converting raw stock into finished products. The special hazards of occupancies in this category vary with the nature of the product being manufactured. For example, a steel manufacturer has blast furnaces, rolling mills, and associated steel processing equipment, while a pasta manufacturer has an extensive drying process and a severe dust hazard.

Protection

Fire protection is of two types: (1) public or municipal protection provided by towns and cities or (2) private protection provided by the property owner or occupant. Public and private protection consist of three elements: prevention, detection, and suppression. The quantity and quality of fire protection available to individual properties vary widely. Although some exceptions exist, dwellings and small commercial buildings depend almost entirely on public protection, while larger commercial building owners are able to supplement public protection with private fire protection systems.

Public Protection

Public fire protection is defined as fire protection equipment and services made available through governmental authority to all properties within a defined area. The organization of public fire protection varies by community. Municipalities and sometimes counties often provide protection to all properties within their boundaries. In many areas of the country, however, the most effective use of available equipment and personnel dictates fire district boundaries.

ISO independently evaluates public fire protection and publishes its findings in the form of a public protection classification (PPC) for each community in the United States. The PPC is an integral part of the property insurance pricing process. Although most underwriters need only a basic understanding of the municipal grading system, a more extensive knowledge permits them to evaluate private protection efforts relative to available public protection.

The PPC system rates the quality of a public fire service on a scale of 1 to 10. The classification measures the adequacy of the equipment available to the public fire service, the water supply, and response time. Class 1 represents the ideal; it is not reasonable to expect any community to achieve this rating. Classes 1 through 8 define protected properties, while properties in classes 9 and 10 are unprotected. Properties that are located too far from a water supply adequate for fire suppression fall into Class 9. Public protection class 10 applies to properties that have no public fire protection service available.

A single public protection classification does not always apply to an entire municipality or fire district. Geographic features sometimes prevent prompt fire service response to some areas, and water mains and hydrants may not extend to all properties a fire service protects. These considerations produce a higher public protection classification (indicating lower-quality public protection).

Public fire protection
The equipment and services made available through governmental authority to all properties within a defined area. Public fire protection is often rated by public protection classifications (PPC) on a scale of 1 to 10 with 1 representing the ideal protection and 10 representing no protection.

A property may also take a public protection classification inferior to the community as a whole for two principal reasons. First, the property may present an exposure to more challenging fires than the fire service is equipped to handle, such as flammable metals or large quantities of flammable liquids. Second, the fire service may lack adequate year-round access to the property, especially when the property owner maintains private roads. The owners of some seasonal properties in colder climates, for example, maintain private roads but make no arrangements for snow plowing because they are closed for the winter. An accumulation of snow on the roads periodically makes such locations inaccessible to fire services. The PPC would take this into account and produce a classification of 9 or 10 for those locations.

Private Protection

The existence of private protection systems is a significant factor in under-writing. Although all three elements of prevention, detection, and suppression are important, this section focuses on detection and suppression. The loss control personnel of insurers often assist commercial policyholders with their prevention activities. Loss control is discussed in Chapter 7.

Detection

Early detection is important to fire suppression because the size of a fire increases exponentially with time measured in seconds, and larger fires are more difficult to suppress. Because most fires start when the premises are unoccupied, mechanical detection systems are crucial for limiting the extent of fire damage. The major detection systems include (1) a guard service with a clock system, (2) a private patrol service, (3) smoke and heat detectors, (4) an automatic local alarm, and (5) a central station alarm or remote station system. In addition, certain sprinkler systems have an alarm that is triggered by the flow of water within the system.

The effectiveness of a guard service depends on the alertness of the guard. A clock system encourages the guard to make regular rounds. Each guard carries a device that time-marks the route through the premises. The disadvantage of a basic clock system is that the watchman's attention or lack thereof cannot be determined until the device is reviewed. Many businesses have connected certain locations to a central station. If these locations are not checked by the watchman, the personnel of the central station follow up.

Small merchants or businesses often employ private patrol services to check for break-ins. In many areas of the country, business and industry associations provide private patrol services as a benefit to their members. A guard visits each business several times during the night to ensure that all doors and windows are secure and that fire has not broken out. Although they provide some security, private patrols are unlikely to discover a fire on a timely basis. Some private patrol services employ a clock system to verify that guards complete their assigned rounds on schedule.

The use of smoke detectors in private residences and businesses has increased significantly with the development of inexpensive, battery-powered smoke detectors. NFPA standards now require that smoke detectors be wired directly to an AC power source in all newly constructed dwellings or buildings. NFPA 74 also recommends for residences that smoke detectors be located outside each sleeping area, on each floor serving as living quarters, and in the basement. Most smoke detectors perform independently, sounding an alarm only at the location of the detected smoke. More advanced systems interconnect the alarms so that all the units go off simultaneously. Often, these advanced systems also serve as burglar alarms by sounding a different alarm tone to indicate a break-in.

Heat detectors may be operated independently of suppression devices but are most frequently combined into devices like automatic sprinkler systems. Heat detectors are slow to activate, which makes them less desirable than smoke detectors in most areas. Heat detectors are used when other detection devices are not effective or are triggered too easily. Small storage rooms in which heat buildup would be rapid or kitchens in which some smoke is a usual byproduct may be better protected by heat detectors.

Heat detectors activate when heat causes a physical or an electrical change in a material or gas. They may be set to respond to a specific temperature or to a predetermined rate of rise in the ambient temperature. Automatic sprinkler systems commonly use a fusible material that melts rapidly at predetermined temperatures. Electric heat detectors are triggered similarly, but the melted link frees a spring-loaded mechanism, which completes an electrical circuit. Continuous line heat detectors activate the alarm when the heat-sensitive insulation surrounding paired steel wire is melted to complete an electrical circuit. Rate compression detectors respond when air temperature exceeds a specified level. Rate-of-rise detectors react to rapid changes in air temperature.

To perform their intended function, smoke and heat detectors must be connected to an alarm, which may be local, central station, remote station, or proprietary. A **local alarm system**, triggered by smoke or heat, sounds a siren or gong inside or outside the building. It relies on occupants or pass-ersby to report the alarm to fire or police officials. For that reason, local alarms are not considered effective in reporting fires.

Local alarm system
A detection system, which can be triggered by smoke or heat, that sounds a siren or gong inside or outside the building.

A **central station system** is a private service with personnel who monitor the systems of several commercial establishments and sometimes residences. Depending on the type of alarm received, the service either calls the appropriate authorities or dispatches its own personnel to investigate. A central station alarm, with or without sprinklers, greatly increases the likelihood of a rapid response to an outbreak of fire and should greatly reduce both insured and uninsured losses. Central station alarm systems eliminate the need for human intervention at the scene and offer a better solution to fire detection than a local alarm. The disadvantage of this method is its relative cost.

Central station system
A private detection service with personnel who monitor the systems of multiple businesses and residences. The service may either call appropriate authorities or dispatch its own personnel to investigate a premises when an alarm is triggered.

Remote station systems and proprietary alarms are similar to central station systems, except that they do not signal a commercially operated central station. A remote alarm directly signals the local police and fire stations. A proprietary system transmits an alarm to a receiving station located on the protected premises.

Suppression

Private fire suppression falls into four categories: (1) portable extinguishers, (2) standpipes and hoses, (3) automatic sprinkler systems, and (4) private fire brigades.

Every business and residence should have some type of portable fire extinguishers available. To be effective, extinguishers must receive regular maintenance, and users must be trained to operate them. Most fire extinguishers are classed as "ABC," meaning they can be used on all types of fires. Class "D" extinguishers are designed for fires involving flammable metals. NFPA publishes standards that indicate the number and type of portable fire extinguishers that the size and occupancy of a property require.

Standpipe and hose systems consist of water supply pipes located inside buildings and equipped with standard fire department connections at regular intervals. In a multistory structure, standpipes are commonly located in stairwells or fire towers with a hose connection at each floor landing. When the building covers a large horizontal area, standpipe outlets are typically spaced at regular intervals throughout the floor. Standpipe systems usually have fire hoses attached so that both the fire service and the occupants of the building can use them. A valve at the standpipe station controls the flow of water to the hoses. Even without attached hoses, standpipes are an invaluable aid in fighting a fire. They deliver water to the interior areas and upper floors of a building, eliminating the need for the fire service to drag charged hoses long distances to reach the fire.

Standpipe systems may draw their water from the building water supply, but they do not always contain water. All standpipe systems have a fire department connection, sometimes called a "siamese connection," on the outside of the building. This allows the fire service to introduce additional water into wet standpipe systems and to increase the operating pressure for more effective fire suppression.

Automatic sprinkler systems provide the most effective means of controlling damage caused by fire. They consist of a series of interconnected valves and pipes with sprinkler heads attached. In the most common type of system, each sprinkler head contains a heat-sensing element and responds individually to the heat generated by a fire. Automatic sprinkler systems respond more quickly than any other fire suppression system and deliver water where it is needed. Sprinkler systems always require their own water supply, but they also come equipped with an external fire department connection to supplement water and pressure.

Most automatic fire sprinkler systems are **wet pipe systems**, meaning that the pipes always contain water under pressure. The water is released immediately when a sprinkler head opens. In areas in which the sprinkler lines are exposed to temperatures below freezing, a dry pipe system may be appropriate. The pipes in a **dry pipe system** contain compressed air or a similar inert gas that holds a valve in the water line shut. The opening of a sprinkler head allows water into the previously dry piping. Dry pipe systems respond more slowly to fire than wet pipe systems because the gas must leave the system before water can flow through.

Many property owners have **Halon extinguishing systems**. Halon gas disrupts the chemical reaction in a fire, thereby eliminating the extensive damage to contents caused by water from sprinkler systems. However, because Halon is a chlorofluorocarbon (CFC) and depletes the ozone layer, the United States and other countries producing Halon agreed to phase out its production. Maintaining and replacing the extinguishant in Halon systems will therefore be expensive in the future.

Pre-action sprinkler systems consist of a sprinkler system equipped with an automatic valve controlled by a fire detection device, such as a smoke detector or heat detector. The valve remains closed until the smoke or heat detector opens it in response to fire conditions. Before the system will discharge water, the detection component has to detect a fire and heat has to actuate a sprinkler head. A dry pipe system is *not* advisable if water damage to sensitive property is a concern. When a fire can be expected to involve flammable liquids or live electrical equipment, extinguishants like dry powder and carbon dioxide are appropriate and effective. Well-protected restaurants, for instance, use dry chemical or CO_2 extinguishing systems, often called Ansul systems (the leading manufacturer of such systems), to protect hoods over cooking equipment and ducts that carry away the heated air and products of combustion. Water is not an appropriate extinguishant in these areas, where heavy accumulations of grease are commonplace.

Both sprinkler and standpipe systems can be connected to an alarm, called a water motor alarm, that will alert a monitoring station to the flow of water through the pipes. A sprinkler alarm may be connected directly to the fire department. Both sprinkler and standpipe alarms may be connected to a central station that will monitor them constantly and respond to any water flow. Sprinkler and standpipe alarms provide early notification of both fires and sprinkler leakage. Some alarms may still be connected only to a local gong on the outside of a building. Because they rely on passersby to notify the police or fire service, local gongs have never been effective as primary protection.

Private fire brigades are found only in the largest industrial businesses, such as petrochemical plants and rural areas in which municipal fire protection is unavailable or considered inadequate. Underwriters should evaluate private fire departments in the way that they evaluate public fire departments. They should develop information on the number and training of personnel as well

Wet pipe systems
Automatic fire sprinkler systems with pipes that always contain water under pressure. The water is released immediately when a sprinkler head opens.

Dry pipe systems
Automatic fire sprinkler systems with pipes that contain compressed air or other inert gas that hold a value in the water line shut until an open sprinkler head allows water into the previously dry pipe.

Halon extinguishing systems
An extinguishing system that disburses chlorofluorocarbon, disrupting the chemical reaction in a fire.

Pre-action sprinkler systems
Sprinkler systems that include an automatic valve controlled by a fire detection device, such as a smoke or heat detector.

as on the amount and type of equipment and its location within the industrial complex. More than likely, ISO has already evaluated the characteristics of a private fire department.

External Exposures

External exposures are those outside the area owned or controlled by the insured. These exposures fall into two categories: (1) single-occupancy exposures and (2) multiple-occupancy exposures. Each of these categories presents different underwriting problems.

External exposures
Exposures outside the area owned or controlled by the insured.

Single-Occupancy Exposures

When the property being underwritten consists of a single building, fire division, or group of buildings, all owned or controlled by the policyholder, a single-occupancy exposure exists. The external exposures in this case come from adjoining properties. Examples include buildings close enough to permit a fire in the exposing property to spread to the insured premises and fuel such as brush, woodlands, or trash left out in the open on adjoining properties. External exposure hazards differ in one significant characteristic from those previously considered. The policyholder's own loss control activities can correct deficiencies in construction, occupancy, and private protection on the insured premises. External exposures, on the other hand, are by definition outside the control of the policyholder. Often little can be done from an engineering standpoint to reduce or minimize external exposures.

Exposing Buildings

An exposing building may be considered present when another building significantly increases the possibility of a fire in the insured building. Factors that influence the severity of an exposure fire on a building, in addition to the intensity and duration of the exposure fire, include the following:

1. Type of construction of the exposing and exposed buildings
2. Height and width of the exposure fire
3. Openings in the exterior walls of the exposing and exposed buildings
4. Type of combustible contents in the exposure fire
5. Protection for openings in the wall of the exposed building
6. Interior finish of the exposing and exposed buildings
7. Distance between the exposing and exposed buildings
8. Shielding effects of noncombustible construction between the exposing and exposed buildings
9. Wind direction and velocity at the time of the fire
10. Public and private fire protection[6]

Fire walls, fire doors, special barriers, and parapets reduce the probability that an external fire will spread to the insured property. Clear space between buildings, good water supply, quick response from the fire department, and internal and external automatic sprinkler systems are additional methods of controlling external exposures. The methods by which the exposure hazard between two buildings can be reduced include the following:

1. Complete automatic sprinkler protection
2. Blank walls of noncombustible materials facing the exposure
3. Barrier walls (self-supporting) between the building and the exposure
4. Extension of exterior masonry walls to form parapets or fender walls
5. Automatic outside water curtains for combustible walls
6. Elimination of openings by filling them with construction equivalent to the wall
7. Glass block panels in openings
8. Wired glass in steel sash windows (fixed or automatic closing) in openings
9. Automatic or deluge sprinklers outside over openings
10. Automatic (rolling steel) fire shutters on openings
11. Automatic fire doors on door openings
12. Automatic fire dampers on wall openings[7]

Adequate clear space enables firefighters to respond properly to a fire in an adjoining building and reduces the likelihood that the heat from the fire will ignite the exposed structure. Clear space should be free of fire fuel. An alley filled with trash, for example, would not provide adequate clear space.

Other Exposures

A variety of exposures other than structures can markedly increase the likelihood of a fire loss. Examples include lumberyards, gasoline storage tanks, brush, or woodlands. An underwriter might not recognize the exposure presented by an open area containing brush surrounding a structure, but significant brush fires have swept through developed areas with catastrophic results.

Multiple-Occupancy Exposures

In a multiple-occupancy building, persons other than the policyholder own or control portions of the fire division that contains the insured property. If the policyholder in question occupies part of a building that is divided from the rest of the building by an approved fire wall, that section is considered a single occupancy. The rest of the building is then treated as an exposing fire division. If the policyholder, on the other hand, occupies part of a building with combustible walls separating the insured property from the other occupancies, a multiple-occupancy exposure exists. Shopping centers commonly have walls that can be moved to resize store areas to meet the needs of new occupants. Most office buildings occupied by more than one tenant are also multiple-occupancy structures.

A factor to consider in evaluating a multiple-occupancy commercial location is the occupancy class of the other occupants. In a typical commercial shopping center of ordinary construction, a craft store may be exposed by a restaurant or a paint store in adjacent portions of the same fire division.

Another factor to consider is the amount of protection available against fire originating in exposing occupancies. Although there is no approved fire wall between occupancies, there may be a noncombustible wall that does provide some protection. Alternatively, the walls separating occupancies could be no more than drywall partitions with continuous attics throughout the fire division.

Other Fire Underwriting Considerations

Construction, occupancy, protection, and exposure are the basic tools underwriters use to analyze the risk of loss by fire and related causes of loss. One of the most important applications of those tools is to craft the available information into an estimate of the most severe loss the insurer can expect the policyholder to sustain. Such judgments require underwriters to consider policy provisions that can affect the ultimate amount of loss that might be paid by the insurer. The two most commonly used measures of loss severity are amount subject and probable maximum loss (discussed below).

Policy Provisions Affecting the Amount of Loss

How much an insurer will have to pay when loss occurs is a significant consideration to property underwriters. The factors that determine that amount include the insurable interest of all persons insured, policy provisions for establishing the value of insured property, the relationship of the amount of insurance to that value, and the most severe loss the underwriter anticipates.

Property insurance forms limit recovery to the amount of the insured's insurable interest at the time of loss. The most common interest in property comes from its outright ownership. Other forms of ownership exist in which the insured may have something less than an insurable interest in the entire property or may have an insurable interest for only a period of time. For a given property, several persons or entities may have an insurable interest, and the insurable interests of all these parties may exceed the value of the property. Underwriters need to recognize that the amount of coverage provided may be less than the total insured amount or more than anticipated because of additional interests in the property and additional insureds added to the policy.

Policy valuation provisions determine, in part, the amount of loss that will be paid under a policy. Actual cash value (ACV) was once considered the best measure of a loss. Under that valuation approach, the insured received payment for the value of property replacement less depreciation. Underwriters liked this approach because the insured was essentially being restored to the same position it was in before the loss occurred. With an ACV valuation provision, the insured has few incentives to cause the loss and many incentives to maintain the property. Replacement cost valuation provisions do not deduct for depreciation. Under the ACV approach to valuation, depreciation was a real and uninsurable exposure that the insured should have included in budgeting but more than likely did not. Replacement coverage is considered a necessity by insureds and is readily provided by insurers.

Another approach to property valuation is functional replacement cost. This approach measures the amount of loss by the cost of similar property that performs the same function. These alternative approaches to property valuation can serve to reduce the amount potentially paid on a loss.

Another policy provision affecting an insurer's ultimate payment under a property policy is the coinsurance provision. Coinsurance provisions reduce the amount an insurer pays on partial losses if the insured has failed to buy an amount of insurance close to the value of the property. Because of the coinsurance provision's punitive nature, underwriters have insisted that insureds buy the proper amount of coverage so that this provision does not affect partial loss claim payments. Many underwriters simply decline accounts that do not buy adequate amounts of insurance to properly insure what is owned.

An insurer's ultimate loss exposure is affected when an insured uses blanket insurance, the alternative to specific insurance. With the specific insurance approach, an amount of insurance coverage is indicated for each location. The blanket insurance approach can insure several locations and types of property with one limit. There are several advantages to this approach to determining insurance coverage needs, and it works well for the policyholder if the properties insured are at separate locations. For the underwriter, blanket insurance means that the limits overall must be kept within 90 percent of the total value to avoid penalizing the insured on partial losses.

Measures of Potential Loss Severity

The size of the largest loss an underwriter can anticipate is an important consideration in property underwriting. Most insurers use three related measures to estimate the largest loss a property is likely to produce:

1. Policy amount
2. Amount subject
3. Probable maximum loss (PML)

The policy amount refers to the coverage limits requested on the account. Amount subject and probable maximum loss are more valuable measures to underwriters but are, by their nature, subjective.

Amount subject measures the exposure to a single loss and varies by cause of loss. Amount subject represents a worst-case scenario—the total value exposed to loss at any one location from any one event. Amount subject can vary by cause of loss and may be different for the insurer and the insured. The insured might, for example, have two locations near one another. Although a single fire might not affect both locations, they both might be susceptible to total loss in the same tornado. Assuming that each location contains only a

Amount subject
A measure of the exposures to a single loss representing a worst-case scenario—the total value exposed to loss at any one location from any one event.

single fire division, the amount subject for fire insurance at each location would be the total value at risk at that site. The amount subject for a tornado, however, would be the sum of the values exposed at both locations. If the business insured each location with a different company or retained a substantial share of the property risk, the amounts subject would not be the same for the policyholder and the insurer.

Probable maximum loss (PML)
An estimate of the largest likely loss.

After evaluating the individual risk characteristics of an account, an underwriter uses experience and judgment to determine the largest likely loss, or **probable maximum loss (PML)**. For example, an underwriter may decide that a total loss to a high-rise fire-resistive structure is conceivable but unlikely. The underwriter would therefore set the PML at less than the full value of all insured property at that location.

Many underwriters regard PML as meaningful only for fire-resistive buildings and their contents. These underwriters assume that other types of construction will not effectively resist damage and will result in a total loss should a loss occur. Other underwriters take a more conservative approach by assuming that if a fire occurs it will breach at least one fire wall. Some underwriters apply this logic only when fire walls are breached by protected openings. This approach yields a PML that includes at least two fire divisions. Some underwriters develop a PML that is less than the full value of the exposed property in a single fire division. Those underwriters anticipate that detection and protection are adequate to limit the loss.

Determining the amount subject and probable maximum loss requires "best" guesses of what an insurer's exposure might be. Underwriters following similar logic in amount subject and PML calculations might develop different values because judgment plays a crucial role in their determination. Likewise, insurers calculate the values differently and place varying importance on them. Some insurers, for instance, view PML relative to the policy premium and ask, "How many years will it take for us to be repaid should the probable maximum loss occur?" For those insurers, PML is just another way of measuring loss severity. Some insurers integrate PML with their reinsurance program so that a PML above a specified amount indicates that reinsurance is required on an account. Underwriters must remember that probable maximum loss calculations, regardless of their apparent sophistication, are just subjective estimates. Actual losses commonly exceed the PML that an underwriter has determined for a location.

UNDERWRITING OTHER CAUSES OF LOSS

In addition to fire, property underwriters have to consider other causes of loss that the policy forms cover. Not all covered causes of loss receive equal treatment. Some occur so infrequently or cause damage so slight that including them in the process would only waste time. Underwriters have to decide which causes of loss need investigation and focus their limited resources on those "key perils."

Lightning

Almost from its origin, insurance of fixed property on land has paired lightning with fire in coverage forms. Lightning frequently causes fire, and the two causes of loss produce damage so similar that even trained observers cannot always determine which caused the loss. Early court decisions held that lighting was "fire from the sky" and, therefore, part of the peril of fire. Only within the past few years have commercial lines forms listed lightning as a separate cause of loss. Homeowners forms continue to cover "fire or lightning" as a single peril. This does not mean, however, that lightning cannot or does not cause insured damage independently of fire.

Underwriters usually pair fire and lightning together when evaluating an account. Lightning is a significant source of ignition for fires, but it can also be controlled by properly installed and maintained lightning arresters. When lightning is the source of ignition, the analysis of the fire cause of loss is generally applicable.

Lighting can cause significant damage even when a fire does not ensue. For example, lightning can strike an electric transmission line and generate a power surge. The surge can then enter buildings the affected line serves and cause extensive damage. Such an event rarely causes fire, but damage by high voltage to an insured's electrical system can destroy it. Protection from electrical surges is usually provided by grounding the electrical service. The property owner can enhance surge protection by installing an external surge protector on power lines entering the building. Many types of electrical equipment, such as computers and electric motors, warrant interior surge protectors.

Explosion

Explosion is another cause of loss closely related to fire. Explosion is any violent expansion of gases into the atmosphere. The most common causes are the following:

- Ignition of flammable clouds (combustion explosions)
- Rupture of confined spaces (pressure explosions)

Combustion Explosions

Fire that develops so rapidly that the normal expansion of gases proceeds at a violent pace produces a combustion explosion. Events of this type occur when a flammable cloud of dust, vapor, mist, or gas encounters an ignition source. Combustion explosions are classified as either deflagration if they develop slowly or detonation if the rate of combustion exceeds the speed of sound. Gases, dust, mist, and low explosives (like black powder) generate deflagrations. Clouds of gas or dust and decomposition of unstable materials (including high explosives) produce detonations. Both types can be highly destructive. Detonations are much more severe than deflagrations, partly because they produce a shock wave that contributes to the overall damage.

Preventing the formation of combustible clouds is the surest protection against combustion explosions. Fire can occur only when the mixture of fuel and oxygen falls within its flammable range. The two most effective strategies for preventing combustion explosions are to limit the amount of fuel in the atmosphere and to restrict the oxygen supply that reaches the fuel. Controlling explosion losses also requires managing the sources of ignition. Electricity and friction are the most common sources of ignition for combustion explosions. They are easy to overlook and can be difficult to control. Limiting the potential of electricity to ignite a combustible cloud requires using explosion-proof electrical fixtures in hazardous environments and managing static electricity to prevent it from creating sparks. Techniques include grounding or bonding all electrical apparatus, using floor materials and coverings that do not conduct electricity, connecting ground wires on machinery with moving parts, and requiring nonconductive clothing.

Friction is inherent in the operation of machinery and presents few problems in an ordinary atmosphere. In potentially explosive environments, on the other hand, friction that would ordinarily pass unnoticed may generate enough heat to trigger an explosion. Techniques for containing friction to manageable levels include lubrication of moving parts, proper alignment of moving parts to minimize rubbing, and a comprehensive preventive maintenance program. Belts, pulleys, and rollers demand special care.

Because no amount of care can prevent all combustion explosions, making provision to minimize damage from those that inevitably occur is also important. Venting and isolation provide effective damage control. Venting incorporates design features to minimize explosion damage by relieving pressure on the structure itself and directing the force of the explosion away from property susceptible to damage. Isolation places space or barriers between the potential source of an explosion and property that it might damage.

Pressure Explosions

A second type of explosion, a pressure explosion, occurs when a confined space cannot contain internal pressure and bursts. Although any confined space may explode under sufficient pressure, explosion of pressure vessels is the principal concern. Pressure vessels common to most occupancies include water heaters, tanks, boilers, and process equipment. In commercial lines, boiler and machinery insurance covers explosions of steam boilers and piping, while commercial property forms insure explosions of other pressure vessels. Homeowners forms protect against both.

Pressure in fired vessels occurs when heat causes the contents of the vessels to expand. Fired vessels include water heaters, fired kettles, and hot water boilers. Steam boilers also provide pressure to unfired apparatus, such as steam jacketed kettles and other process equipment. Other unfired pressure vessels rely on mechanical means, such as compressors, to build and maintain internal pressure.

The leading cause of pressure vessel explosion is equipment failure in one of three areas: primary controls, safety devices, or the structure of the vessel. The main function of primary controls is to maintain optimal operating conditions. If primary controls perform as intended, the unsafe conditions that lead to a pressure explosion will not develop.

Safety devices may be secondary controls or pressure relief devices. Secondary controls shut equipment down as soon as an unsafe situation begins to develop. They are often identical to primary controls, except that they require manual reset. That feature demands operator intervention and calls attention to potential hazards. Pressure relief devices vent excessive pressure to prevent an explosion when all controls have failed and temperature or pressure builds to unsafe levels. Safety valves are the most common. They open when pressure reaches their rated capacity, closing again when it drops.

The structure of a pressure vessel may fail and cause an explosion for several reasons. Corrosion, erosion, or wear and tear can gradually thin the surface. Thermal expansion and contraction or excessive vibration may introduce cracks that weaken the shell and end sheets. Good maintenance and timely replacement of obsolete equipment offer the only protection against these types of failures.

Fire that reaches a pressure vessel can cause an explosion in two ways: (1) the vessel's contents, already under pressure, expand as fire drives the temperature up, and (2) the heat simultaneously causes even noncombustible materials to lose strength. Internal pressure increases while the vessel's ability to contain it diminishes. Although fire is the cause of loss in both instances, underwriters should evaluate this loss potential as part of the explosion exposure.

Windstorm

Underwriters have to give windstorm careful consideration because it is a major cause of loss and possesses the potential to generate a catastrophe. Virtually all personal and commercial property insurance policies include windstorm among the covered causes of loss. Although every part of the United States is subject to some form of severe wind, hurricanes and tornadoes are the two most significant sources of windstorm damage. Windstorm is a difficult cause of loss to underwrite. Short of identifying particular susceptible geographic areas and not writing property insurance or excluding windstorm as a cause of loss in those areas, underwriters can do little to limit the consequences of a windstorm, should one occur. Windstorm coverage is generally available in most parts of the United States because property owners with little exposure to windstorm damage purchase coverage. Additionally, reinsurance spreads the catastrophic effects of windstorm losses to others.

Hurricanes

Hurricanes are tropical storms, and few natural phenomena can approach their destructive power. The Saffir/Simpson scale, shown in Exhibit 5-1, is the most familiar gauge of hurricane intensity. That scale, which has categories from 1 to 5, is useful in assessing potential hurricane damage for underwriting purposes.

Since 1989, the number of severe hurricanes making landfall in North America has increased. Such storms principally affect the southern Atlantic and Gulf Coasts of the United States, the Gulf Coast of Mexico, and islands in the Caribbean. Pacific Ocean hurricanes (called typhoons) also threaten Hawaii but rarely reach the continent. The most damaging hurricane on record is Hurricane Andrew. It struck South Florida and Louisiana in August 1992, causing more than $15.5 billion of insured losses. Hurricane Iniki, which struck the island of Kauai in Hawaii the same year, helped make 1992 the worst year of natural disasters the insurance industry has ever experienced.

Types of Hurricanes

Penetrating storm
A storm that strikes the coastline at approximately a right angle and moves directly inland. These storms typically cause damage over a relatively small area.

Raking storm
A storm that parallels the coast. Such a storm can maintain its intensity for a long time and can cause damage over a wider area.

Hurricanes that make landfall may be either penetrating storms or raking storms. A **penetrating storm** strikes the coastline at approximately a right angle and moves directly inland. These storms typically cause heavy wind damage over a relatively small area. Once the eye of the hurricane is over land, the storm quickly decreases in intensity. A **raking storm** parallels the coast. Because this type of storm can maintain its intensity for a long time if the eye remains over the ocean, it can inflict damage on a wider area. Storm surge damage is usually more serious in a raking storm.

Hurricane Damage

Hurricanes cause damage in several ways. Most hurricane damage results from the effect of high wind on exposed property. Wind-driven rain can also penetrate structures and can cause significant damage. Most of that rain enters buildings through holes the wind creates in the roof or walls and is therefore insured as windstorm. When a hurricane comes ashore, it drives a wall of high water before it. That storm surge threatens primarily coastal properties, but it may also impede drainage, raising the water level in rivers, streams, and bays. Finally, the heavy rains that a hurricane produces cause flooding alone or in combination with the storm surge.

More tropical storms are forming, and more of them are becoming hurricanes. Atmospheric scientists believe that severe tropical weather occurs in a natural cycle that extends over several decades, perhaps as long as forty years. The length of this cycle has bred complacency that promotes the heavy commercial and residential development of coastal areas. This development has dramatically increased the value of property exposed to a single storm. By making flood insurance readily available in coastal plains, the National Flood Insurance Program has encouraged this trend. Many scientists also believe that the climate is becoming permanently warmer, a phenomenon known as the greenhouse effect. The higher temperatures that result may contribute to the growing severity of storms and the losses they produce.

EXHIBIT 5-1

Saffir-Simpson Hurricane Disaster-Potential Scale

CATEGORY 1	Central Pressure	Winds	Storm Surge
	Greater than 980 millibars	74–95 mph	4–5 feet

Winds of seventy-four to ninety-five miles per hour. Damage primarily to shrubbery, trees, foliage, and unanchored mobile homes. No real damage to other structures. Some damage to poorly constructed signs. Storm surge four to five feet above normal. Low-lying coastal roads inundated, minor pier damage, some small craft in exposed anchorages torn from moorings.

CATEGORY 2	Central Pressure	Winds	Storm Surge
	965–979 millibars	96–110 mph	6–8 feet

Winds of 96 to 111 miles per hour. Considerable damage to shrubbery and tree foliage; some trees blown down. Major damage to exposed mobile homes. Extensive damage to poorly constructed signs. Some damage to roofing materials of buildings; some window or door damage. No major damage to buildings. Storm surge six to eight feet above normal. Coastal roads and low-lying escape routes inland cut by rising water two to four hours before arrival of hurricane center. Considerable damage to piers. Marinas flooded. Small craft in unprotected anchorages torn from moorings. Evacuation of some shoreline residents and low-lying island areas required.

CATEGORY 3	Central Pressure	Winds	Storm Surge
	945–964 millibars	111–130 mph	9–12 feet

Winds of 111 to 130 miles per hour. Foliage torn from trees; large trees blown down. Practically all poorly constructed signs blown down. Some damage to roofing materials of buildings; some window or door damage. Some structural damage to small buildings. Mobile homes destroyed. Storm surge nine to twelve feet above normal. Serious flooding at coast and many smaller structures near coast destroyed; larger structures near coast damaged by battering waves and floating debris. Low-lying escape routes inland cut by rising water three to five hours before hurricane center arrives. Flat terrain of five feet or less above sea level flooded inland eight miles or more. Evacuation of low-lying residences within several blocks of shoreline possibly required.

CATEGORY 4	Central Pressure	Winds	Storm Surge
	920–944 millibars	131–155 mph	13–18 feet

Winds of 131 to 155 miles per hour. Shrubs and trees blown down; all signs down. Extensive damage to roofing materials, windows, and doors. Complete failure of roofs on many small residences. Complete destruction of mobile homes. Storm surge thirteen to eighteen feet above normal. Flat terrain ten feet or less above sea level flooded inland as far as six miles. Major damage to lower floors of structures near shore due to flooding and battery by waves and floating debris. Low-lying escape routes inland cut by rising water three to five hours before hurricane center arrives. Major erosion of beaches. Massive evacuation of all residences within 500 yards of shore and of single-story residences on low ground within two miles of shore.

CATEGORY 5	Central Pressure	Winds	Storm Surge
	Less than 920 millibars	+155 mph	+18 feet

Winds greater than 155 miles per hour. Shrubs and trees blown down; considerable damage to roofs of buildings; all signs down. Very severe and extensive damage to windows and doors. Complete failure of roofs on many residences and industrial buildings. Extensive shattering of glass in windows and doors. Some complete building failures. Small buildings overturned or blown away. Complete destruction of mobile homes. Storm surge greater than eighteen feet above normal. Major damage to lower floors of all structures less than fifteen feet above sea level within 500 yards of shore. Low-lying escape routes inland cut by rising water three to five hours before hurricane center arrives. Massive evacuation of residential areas on low ground within five to ten miles of shore possibly required.

Hurricane Andrew, for example, was not the most powerful storm to make landfall in the United States. The extent of the destruction it caused was the result of development that placed a large amount of property at risk. Building codes that were not enforced and inadequately designed structures also influenced the extent of the damage.

Hurricane damage is typically caused by a combination of wind and water. Hurricane Andrew was an exception to this because very little storm surge accompanied it.

Controlling Wind Damage

Studies of hurricane damage provide valuable insight into effective means of controlling wind losses. Several lessons for controlling wind damage were learned from the buildings affected by Hurricane Andrew:

1. Windstorm is a more serious consideration for personal than commercial lines underwriters. One- and two-family dwellings sustained most of the damage in Hurricane Andrew, while fully engineered structures fared very well overall.
2. The key to a building's survival in a windstorm is maintaining the integrity of its envelope, the outer walls, and the roof, all of which keep weather out.
3. Well-designed building codes can protect property from windstorm damage. In Hurricane Andrew, maximum sustained winds probably did not exceed 125 miles per hour,[8] only slightly higher than the design requirement of the South Florida Building Code, which applied to the entire affected area. Structures built to code should have weathered the storm with no more than nominal damage.
4. Building code enforcement is essential in coastal areas.

A comprehensive evaluation of building codes and their enforcement requires extensive local knowledge that insurers can acquire only by maintaining a staff in every area of the country or by costly research, making it impractical for most insurers. The Building Code Effectiveness Grading Schedule (BCEGS), described earlier, will help to resolve this dilemma.

Other Underwriting Considerations for Hurricanes

Because losses from hurricanes frequently affect a large number of insured properties, underwriters have to do more than evaluate individual submissions. Managing a book of business is essential to successful underwriting in areas subject to hurricane losses. Hurricanes Hugo and Andrew each claimed the solvency of several insurance companies and weakened the financial condition of many more. Reinsurance has been an essential element in protecting the solvency of insurers. Significant catastrophes like those caused by Hugo and Andrew have raised the price of catastrophe reinsurance and have caused reinsurers to limit the amount of reinsurance they want to make available. Likewise, insurers are extremely aware of the aggregate exposures they have exposed to a single storm.

Computer models are available to measure the exposure to a single storm for an entire book of business. Staff underwriters have to use those models to contain total exposure to a level that does not impose financial hardship on the insurer. To achieve that objective, an insurer has to restrict the number of risks it writes in those areas. An insurer may elect to restrict its writings by establishing a target expressed as a desirable market share, policy count, or total insured value.

Tornadoes

Tornadoes are small but especially violent windstorms. They form in warm, humid, and unsettled weather and are often spawned by thunderstorms and tropical storms. Tornadoes consist of winds rotating at speeds that may reach 300 miles per hour; this creates a partial vacuum at the center of the storm, called its vortex. Upward velocity at the vortex wall can exceed 200 feet per second. Condensation around the vortex produces a pale cloud that gives the tornado its characteristic funnel shape. When the tornado makes contact with the ground, it draws debris into the circulating air, and the funnel cloud darkens. Scientists are not sure how tornadoes form, but they do know the storms pack awesome destructive power. The average tornado path is only one-quarter of a mile wide and rarely extends more than sixteen miles. Most paths are considerably shorter and narrower. A tornado can touch down in a backyard, pick up a lawn shed and its contents, and lift off again without damaging the fences bounding the yard. On the other hand, a tornado path may be up to a mile wide, and the longest on record extended over 300 miles. Tornadoes move forward at an average of forty miles per hour but have been clocked at seventy.

Incidence of Tornadoes

Tornadoes occur worldwide but most frequently in the United States. No part of the country is immune, but the Great Plains of the Midwest and Southeast are most prone to tornado damage. Exhibit 5-2 illustrates the distribution of tornado activity across the nation. Tornadoes occur year-round but exhibit a seasonal pattern with a peak in the spring. Beginning in March, the peak moves from the southern coastal states through the southern plains states into the northern plains states and Great Lakes area. Incidence declines from June to its low point in December. The appearance of tornadoes is random and unpredictable.

Tornado Damage

Tornadoes owe their destructive power to their compact size, powerful winds, and the upward movement at the vortex wall. Their winds exceed any reasonable design load. Tornadoes also subject property to rapid changes in the direction of wind stress and uplift forces no other phenomenon can produce. Tornadoes can lift cars and heavy farm machinery from the ground and deposit the remains miles away. The most common effect of a tornado is total destruction of any property squarely in its path. Substantial buildings and property at the edge of a tornado's path may escape with serious structural damage. Property close to the path can sustain minor to severe damage.

Hail

Destructive hail falls almost exclusively during violent thunderstorms. Hailstones can be more than five inches in diameter and weigh over one and one-half pounds. Damage to growing crops accounts for nearly 80 percent of all hail losses, but hail can also cause severe damage to auto and home windows, neon signs, and fragile structures such as greenhouses. Aluminum siding and roofing materials are particularly susceptible to hail damage.

Riot or Civil Commotion

Even the most basic property insurance forms cover loss by riot and civil commotion, which includes any disruption of public order. The distinction between the two perils varies by state because riot is a crime, and its definition depends on the penal code. Nevertheless, property insurance covers the two events as a pair. The two principal causes of riot losses are fire and looting. Simple and often inexpensive risk management measures can be effective in controlling losses from riot and civil commotion.

Vandalism and Malicious Mischief

Vandalism can occur anywhere, but it is particularly evident in urban areas. Children and young adults commit most acts of vandalism. In fact, FBI statistics show that over 41 percent of vandalism arrests are of persons under eighteen years old.[9] Schools, churches, parks, playgrounds, and youth centers are examples of properties that present a possible vandalism exposure. Since groups of children are more likely to commit vandalism than adults, areas containing many children, such as urban areas, are likely to have a higher incidence of vandalism than are areas in which residents are mostly older adults.

Other types of vandalism can occur during labor disputes or when an organization becomes the target of violence because of social protest. Violent protest has caused vandalism damage to home offices of multinational corporations, major banks, offices of foreign airlines, and the homes of public officials.

Because it produces relatively small losses, vandalism rarely attracts much of an underwriter's attention. Frequency is more of a consideration than severity with vandalism, so an appropriately set deductible will reduce the insurer's loss payments.

EXHIBIT 5-2

Total Number of Tornadoes by State—2000

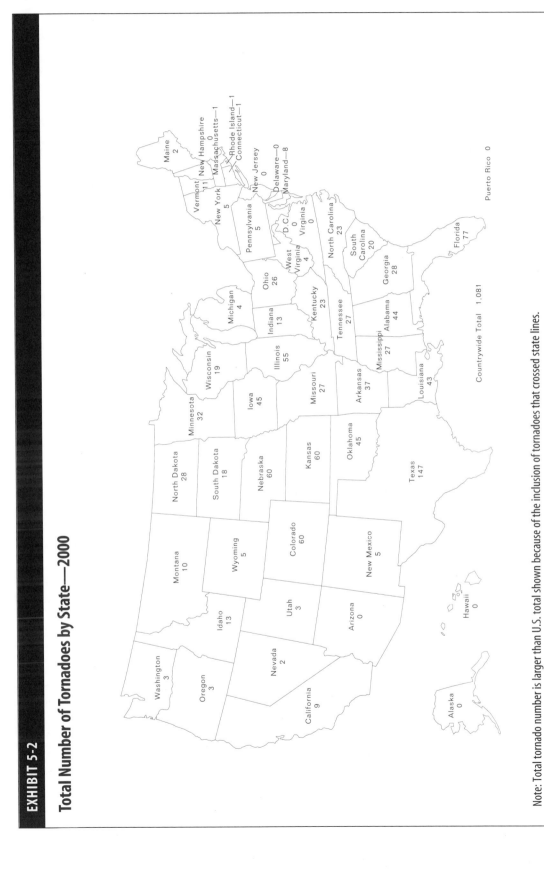

Note: Total tornado number is larger than U.S. total shown because of the inclusion of tornadoes that crossed state lines.

Adapted with permission from *The Fact Book 2002: Property/Casualty Insurance Facts* (New York: Insurance Information Institute, 2002), p. 89.

Water Damage and Sprinkler Leakage

Homeowners and commercial property coverage forms frequently insure certain types of water damage. Direct damage caused by accidental discharge, overflow, or leakage of water or steam from plumbing, heating, and cooling systems is the most common. Water damage caused by flood is usually excluded because of its catastrophic nature, and policy writers have taken great care to distinguish the circumstances when coverage applies. Poor maintenance is the cause of most water damage losses, so underwriters rarely write this cause of loss specifically.

Flat roofs are another source of water damage losses because water can soak through the roof covering. That happens most often when water accumulates or "ponds" in low areas. In cold weather, packed snow and ice may block roof drains, keeping melted snow from running off.

Sprinkler leakage losses occur when water or other extinguishing agents escape from sprinkler systems. Losses occur infrequently, and damage is likely to be severe only in exceptional cases. The most common causes of sprinkler leakage losses are freezing, mechanical injury, poor maintenance, and excessive temperature at sprinkler heads. Sprinkler heads exposed to physical damage should have guards over them, and both the pipes and risers should be protected from accidental rupture. Forklifts present a special danger to sprinkler heads, risers, and lines.

Underwriting sprinkler leakage concentrates on two elements: (1) the damageability of the contents and (2) the physical condition, maintenance, and design of the sprinkler system itself. When the contents of the structure protected by a sprinkler system are highly susceptible to water damage, sprinkler leakage may result in a severe loss. Frequent inspections should be performed to determine the condition and maintenance of sprinkler systems. Many underwriters rely on periodic inspections of sprinklered properties by ISO. Underwriters should be leery of fully sprinklered buildings that take a nonsprinklered rate. This situation usually indicates that the sprinkler system was installed improperly or is deficient. A water motor gong that activates when water flows through the system reduces the likelihood of a severe loss to highly susceptible property.

Sinkhole Collapse and Mine Subsidence

Collapse of sinkholes is relatively new as an insured cause of loss. Underwriters are fortunate that typical losses in this area are usually neither frequent nor severe. Sinkholes occur where underground rivers and streams have carved channels out of solid limestone bedrock. The caverns formed are relatively weak, but the water they contain supports the weight of the cavern roof and the earth above it. Because community growth has placed increased demands on water tables, some have begun to drop. When no longer supported by the water pressure, caverns can collapse, causing sinkholes.

Sinkholes often occur in Florida. Florida has a great deal of limestone and a rapidly growing population that increases the demand on the water table. Sinkholes occur in other parts of the country as well. Evaluating a sinkhole exposure requires an extensive knowledge of local topography and the demographic growth trends of an area. Few underwriters possess such specific knowledge and therefore rarely analyze sinkhole collapse as a cause of loss.

Mine subsidence and sinkhole collapse are similar causes of loss. Underwriters have difficulty determining whether a structure is built over the site of an abandoned mine shaft or tunnel in the same way they have difficulty determining sinkhole exposures. States with serious mine subsidence exposures have made mine subsidence a required coverage option for years.

Volcanic Action

Volcanic action was traditionally part of the earth movement exclusion. The eruption of Mount St. Helens in 1980 made insurers reconsider that exclusion, and many insurers made claim payments for claims stemming from the eruption anyway.

Insurers considered volcanic eruption subject to adverse selection. That is, the eruption of a volcano is a local event, and those people who need coverage the most are the ones who purchase it.

State insurance departments expected insurers to pay volcanic action losses and let the insurers and the public know it. Some insurance commissioners required coverage after the fact. One simply found coverage under the explosion cause of loss. Insurers took the course of least expense and paid the losses, then amended their forms to include volcanic action losses.

Weight of Ice, Snow, or Sleet

During the winter months, ice, snow, and sleet can accumulate on roofs. When that happens, more weight may be added than the structure can carry, causing partial or total collapse. Structures in areas exposed to regular cold winters are most susceptible. Cold snaps can also extend deep into the Sun Belt, where roofs might not be designed to withstand heavy snow. Controlling these losses requires properly designed and well-maintained structures. Roofs with large open spans are particularly susceptible to collapse under a snow load. Design defects contributed to the roof collapse of the Hartford Civic Center after a rather ordinary snow and ice accumulation built up on the roof.

Ice Damming

Pitched roofs help resolve the problem of heavy ice, snow, or sleet by allowing a structure to shed some of the load. They prevent excessive weight from accumulating. The most significant problem with pitched roofs is the formation of ice dams. When melting snow and ice run down a roof and freeze near the edge, especially along overhanging eaves, that ice blocks the flow of additional snow melting off the roof. Such an ice blockage is called an ice dam. Losses occur when heat escaping from a building melts the snow accumulation from the bottom, forcing the runoff to occur beneath the built-up snow and ice on the roof. The best way to control this type of loss is to provide good insulation and adequate ventilation under the roof, which can help to prevent the melting of snow and ice along the roof surface. Insulation above the top-floor ceiling limits the amount of heat that escapes from the interior. Ventilation disperses the heat before it can cause melting. The underside of the roof stays cool, limiting snowmelt to the top of the built-up snow and ice, from which it runs off easily.

Collapse

Buildings collapse for several reasons other than the weight of ice, snow, or sleet, including defective design or construction; deterioration; and the weight of people, personal property, or water on a roof. Poor construction caused the collapse of a ceiling in the Port Authority Trans Hudson (PATH) Transportation Center at Journal Square in Jersey City, New Jersey. The plaster on the metal lath ceiling hung suspended from the reinforced concrete structure and collapsed under the weight of two PATH employees doing maintenance above it. The design contemplated this load, but the contractor had cut corners, omitting every fourth suspender and spreading the rest out. Vibration from passing PATH trains combined with the weight of the maintenance workers, whose equipment caused the collapse.

Any weight on a roof can cause it to collapse. Water that accumulates on flat roofs from rainfall when drains are blocked is a common cause. Regular inspection and good maintenance should prevent such losses. Many roof structure designs do not contemplate the load of property or people, but that is not always apparent to the users of a building.

Some buildings have collapsed from the cumulative effect of vibration. Those buildings are usually very old structures whose builders could not anticipate modern traffic. For example, a nineteenth-century hotel near Cooper Union in New York City collapsed without warning. Engineers identified vibrations from a subway line below the street and passing trucks as the cause.

Anticipating all potential causes of collapse is impossible. Underwriters might do better to concentrate on the quality of a structure's design, construction, and maintenance. Novel or unusual designs are more prone to collapse than traditional ones. The Hartford Civic Center used an innovative design that failed under conditions the builders could reasonably anticipate. The ceiling of the PATH Transportation Center embodied a standard design widely used in building lobbies. Its collapse resulted in numerous inspections to make sure that poor quality of workmanship did not affect similar ceilings. When a building's roof collapses because rain cannot run off it, poor maintenance or design is the cause. Other parts of the building are likely to be affected by similar maintenance or design defects.

Flood

Flood is a common event in large areas of the country, recurring at regular intervals. Some locations flood every year, but others face no known flood hazards. Floods result from greater precipitation than the land can drain and sometimes seem to occur unpredictably. The spring and summer of 1992 brought flooding to the Mississippi River system. Local residents thought they had experienced the worst possible flooding with the 100-year flood in 1972. Even though the Army Corps of Engineers can show that floods of this magnitude occur on average every 500 years, predicting the years in which those floods will occur is not possible. Seven types of flood are common:

1. Riverine floods occur when rivers, streams, and other watercourses rise and overflow their banks. They can result from either heavy rainfall or snow melt upstream in their drainage basins.

2. Tidal floods arise from high tides, frequently driven by high winds offshore, and from tropical storms making landfall or passing close offshore. They affect bays and the portions of rivers along the coast.

3. Wind floods can occur wherever a strong wind holds back a large body of water from its normal drainage course and raises the water level. Back bays behind barrier islands are especially susceptible to wind floods. Water that cannot escape through normal channels can flow out of these bays across the barrier islands.

4. Rising water levels downstream may prevent drainage upstream, causing a backwater flood. Backwater floods can extend for a substantial distance upstream.

5. Ice jams sometimes develop as ice thaws and begins to move downstream. They block the flow of water, causing it to back up and to flood upstream areas. If the ice jam breaks suddenly, it can cause flooding downstream.

6. Accidental floods are caused by the failure of flood control systems. A dam might break, causing flooding downstream. Blocked floodgates and spillways cause upstream flooding.

7. Topographic changes brought about by development can also cause floods. For example, instead of being absorbed into the soil, rain water can accumulate on concrete and asphalt parking lots. If storm sewer drains have inadequate capacity or are blocked, water can build up and flood adjacent properties.

The National Flood Insurance Program (NFIP) administered by the Federal Emergency Management Agency (FEMA) is the largest flood insurance underwriter in the United States. Homeowners insurers that write flood insurance almost always do so on behalf of NFIP through the "Write Your Own" program. Some commercial insurers provide coverage for flood under commercial policies. Information on known flood hazards is widely available, and protective measures can be taken. Underwriting flood exposures successfully requires analyzing the known probability that a flood will occur at a certain location and establishing a rate adequate to the risk of loss the insurer assumes.

Earthquake

Earthquake underwriting is difficult because many geographic regions have significant exposures. Underwriters need to control their total earthquake writings to protect against a catastrophic loss from a single seismic event. The underwriting analysis of earthquakes considers the following three major factors:

1. Areas of earthquake activity
2. Soil conditions
3. Building design and construction

Areas of Earthquake Activity

The Pacific Coast from Alaska to California is the most seismically active area of the United States, and 90 percent of all earthquakes in the United States occur in California and western Nevada. The most severe earthquake ever recorded, however, occurred along the New Madrid Fault in Missouri in 1811.

The United States Office of Science and Technology has measured the chance of damaging seismic activity for each area of the country, dividing the country into four zones. Earthquake risk is almost nonexistent in Zone 0. In Zone 1, minor damage from earthquakes may occur. Zone 2 is exposed to moderate damage, and Zone 3 represents areas of significant damage potential. The map of seismic risk is shown in Exhibit 5-3.

Soil Conditions

Earthquake waves travel at smaller amplitudes in bedrock, so structures built on bedrock or supported on piling driven into bedrock are less susceptible to earthquake damage. Consolidated soil of long standing (thousands of years), such as limestone and some clay, will stand up better than unconsolidated soil, such as sand, gravel, silt, and some clays. Filled land, common in many large cities, represents a particularly hazardous type of unconsolidated soil from an earthquake standpoint. Unconsolidated filled land (as well as certain other types of unconsolidated soils) is subject to **liquefaction** during an earthquake, becoming so unstable that it acts like a liquid. For example, during the 1985 earthquake in Mexico City, the underlying soil that had once been a lake bed liquefied and contributed significantly to the extensive damage. San Francisco's marina district experienced extensive damage in the 1989 Loma Prieta earthquake primarily because it was built on landfill.

Liquefaction
Condition occurring during an earthquake when unconsolidated soils become unstable. The land can become so unstable that it acts like a liquid.

Building Design and Construction

Most buildings (of nonseismic construction) are designed to carry a vertical load, the weight of the structure and its contents. An earthquake causes horizontal stresses that weight-bearing columns and walls are not designed to bear. An earthquake-resistant building has all its structural members tied together securely so that the building moves horizontally as a single unit

EXHIBIT 5-3

Seismic Potential for the Contiguous United States

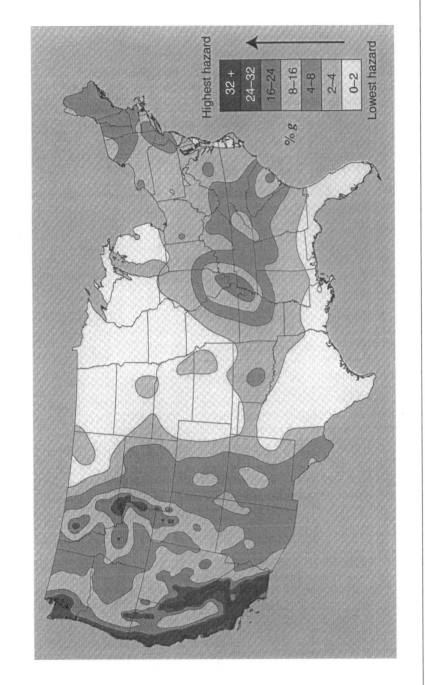

Source: National Seismic Hazard Mapping Project, U.S. Geological Survey, World Wide Web: http://www.geohazards.cr.usgs.gov.

when subjected to earthquake forces. If not tied together, walls and columns can be moved out from under the floors they were designed to support, causing the building to collapse.

Joisted masonry construction is rigid and particularly susceptible to structural failure during earth movements. A frame building, on the other hand, is relatively flexible and "gives" during earth movement, often sustaining relatively minor damage, such as cracked plaster. Brick-facing or other stone veneer and tile roofs often sustain earthquake damage. Tilt slab construction, which is sometimes found in light industrial buildings and warehouses, is also susceptible to earthquake damage. Fire-resistive construction survives most earthquakes with slight damage.

UNDERWRITING TIME ELEMENT COVERAGES

Direct property insurance coverages are readily understood because grasping the tangible nature of a financial loss is easy. More difficult to understand are the related losses of reduced income and extra expense associated with a direct property loss. These *indirect* or *time element* losses are a consequence of the policyholder's inability to use the covered property immediately following a loss. The longer the interruption in activity—rebuilding the structure or residence and preparing it for use or occupancy or replacing key or specialized production machinery—the greater the loss.

Time element coverages are available for personal and commercial policyholders. The homeowners policy offers "loss of use" coverage, which provides indemnification to the policyholder for either additional living expenses incurred or the fair rental value of the property when made uninhabitable by a covered cause of loss. Additional living expense compensates the policyholder for extraordinary expenses incurred while the residence is being repaired. Fair rental value is the amount of rent that could have been fairly charged for the premises had there been no covered direct loss. Loss of use coverage also indemnifies the policyholder when a civil authority prohibits the policyholder from occupying the residence because of a covered cause of loss to other property. The dwelling fire policies contain similar coverages.

The commercial counterpart of this coverage is the business income coverage form, which has two variations. One version provides business income coverage alone, and the other adds extra expense coverage. Both versions of the business income coverage form include coverage for extra expenses that helps to reduce the business income loss. The insuring agreement of the business income coverage forms commits the insurer to pay the policyholder the actual loss sustained because of a necessary interruption of the policyholder's operation arising from direct physical damage to property caused by a covered cause of loss. Extra expense coverage provides for the additional expenses incurred by the policyholder to minimize the interruption of operations regardless of whether the insured reduces the loss of business income. Insureds who are more concerned with uninterrupted operation than with loss of business income can purchase extra expense coverage separately.

Three "optional coverages" are available to eliminate or suspend the coinsurance clause provided in the business income coverage forms. These optional coverages are maximum period of indemnity, monthly limitation of indemnity, and agreed value. Another alternative is a nonstandard valued form that bases recovery on a mutually determined dollar amount payable each day operations are suspended up to a specified maximum number of days. Those optional forms are appealing because coinsurance calculations, which affect the adequacy of coverage, are complex. The simplicity of these alternative coverage forms does not guarantee adequate coverage. Income projections must be performed to ensure that the limits selected are adequate.

Determination of Probable Maximum Loss

Determining the applicant's probable maximum loss is an involved task. The first step is to determine the magnitude of the loss by projecting expected earnings for the period of coverage. This evaluation is crucial in determining the amount of coverage necessary. The second step is to select a coinsurance percentage that will approximate the expected period of interruption should loss occur.

Coverage Needed

Any projection of income is at best an estimate that may vary significantly from the actual results. With that in mind, the recommended approach has three steps:

1. Project the firm's net income and expenses for the next twelve to twenty-four months, and pinpoint seasonal fluctuations.
2. Estimate the probable period of maximum interruption (this involves determining the probable time to rebuild a damaged facility or, in the case of a manufacturer, the time it takes to return the goods in process to their pre-loss level).
3. Determine whether to cover ordinary payroll, and identify all charges and expenses that would not necessarily continue after loss occurs.

The most recent year-end financial statement is one source for this analysis. If the fiscal year has ended more than six months previously, an evaluation of the most recent twelve months of earnings would be in order. Because the recent past is some indication of the short-term future trend for sales and earnings, an analysis of current net income and expense is necessary before making a projection.

Significant seasonal fluctuations in sales and/or earnings directly affect the calculation of not only the proper amount of insurance needed to cover the probable maximum loss but also the amount of insurance required to comply with the coinsurance clause.

Coinsurance Selection

To encourage insurance to value and to simplify ratemaking, business income forms contain a coinsurance clause that operates in essentially the same way as the coinsurance clause in direct damage property insurance policies. Instead of using the value of the property as a base against which the coinsurance percentage is applied, the business income form uses the policy year's net income and all operating expenses, not just those that would continue during a shutdown. The policyholder may choose 50, 60, 70, 80, 90, 100, or 125 percent coinsurance.

The chosen coinsurance percentage is roughly related to the expected period of business interruption. For example, a business that anticipates a maximum period of interruption to be six months might select a 50 percent coinsurance clause. Businesses requiring more than a year to recover from a loss should consider a 125 percent coinsurance clause.

Four important caveats should be remembered when using this rule of thumb:

1. The coinsurance percentage does not apply to the maximum loss exposure. Business income is defined as net income plus continuing expenses incurred during the interruption, but the coinsurance clause applies to net income plus *all* operating expenses that would probably have arisen during the twelve-month period following the inception date of the policy.
2. Seasonal fluctuations in sales and expenses should be charted so that coverage limits and coinsurance percentages selected provide sufficient coverage for the worst possible occurrence in terms of severity and timing.
3. To comply with the coinsurance clause, the policyholder may have to purchase more business income coverage than seems necessary. Distinguishing in advance of the loss which expenses will continue and at what magnitude is difficult. The consequences of overinsurance are often offset by rate credits.
4. Because the determination of business income coverage and the *base* used to calculate the satisfaction of the coinsurance differ, establishing proper coverage amounts and coinsurance percentages is confusing and difficult.

Underwriters should be instrumental in assisting producers and applicants in determining appropriate limits and percentages.

Determination of the Probable Period of Interruption

A business income loss requires that there be direct damage to the insured premises by a covered cause of loss. Analysis of the physical and moral hazards of the risk therefore begins with an analysis of the direct damage exposure. If the business income form is added to a direct damage policy, this analysis has presumably already been completed. In those instances when business income coverage is written separately, analysis of the COPE factors is required to determine the direct damage loss exposure.

The severity of a business income loss is not directly related to the severity of the underlying direct damage loss. A relatively minor property loss destroying only 5 percent of the structure might result in a total business income loss up to the policy limit if the destroyed property included a machine vital to the manufacturing process that could not be replaced in less than one year.[10] Time is the principal element in business income coverage and is the additional dimension in underwriting time element coverages. Determining probable periods of interruption is difficult. The underwriter must evaluate the seasonality of the business, the time it will take to rebuild, bottlenecks, long production processes, and disaster contingency plans.

Seasonality and Rebuilding Time

The degree of seasonality in the policyholder's operations is a major factor in determining potential exposure. This is an important underwriting consideration because a highly seasonal business with 80 percent or more of its business concentrated in a three-month peak season could suffer a severe business income loss from a relatively short shutdown.

Similarly, the time period required to rebuild the insured premises is a major factor in determining exposure. Specialized structures requiring long construction periods, the possibility of lengthy delays in obtaining permits, severe climatic conditions inhibiting construction during certain times of the year, and congested urban locations are all factors increasing exposure to loss.

Bottlenecks

Manufacturing and mining risks are particularly susceptible to bottlenecks. The term bottleneck refers to a machine, process, or building that is essential to the continued operation of an entire facility or manufacturing plant. A relatively minor direct damage loss can lead to a severe business income loss in the case of a bottleneck. The existence of a potential bottleneck can be determined by using a flow diagram of the production process. Some manufacturing processes use machines that must be custom manufactured, and the reinstallation process takes many months. If the process is vital but is duplicated on machines in separate fire divisions, the exposure is greatly reduced.

Although bottlenecks are usually found in processing or manufacturing risks, a congested area or an unusual building configuration can result in a bottleneck during the reconstruction period.

Long Production Processes

If the manufacturing or processing operation takes an unusually long time to complete, the business income exposure could be extended. If a product must be aged or seasoned, destruction of the facility could lead to a lengthy interruption, because this time would be added to the period necessary to restore the structure and machinery to operating condition. The time required to get the stock in process to the point where it had been before the loss must be considered, because the business income form covers actual loss sustained.

Disaster Contingency Plans

Although the business income form requires reasonable speed in the restoration of the operation, proper planning can further reduce the length of interruption. A disaster contingency plan would include detailed written plans for the restoration of the operation if part or all of the buildings and equipment were destroyed. The disaster contingency plan should be tied into the flowchart of the firm's operation, indicating the actions that would be necessary in the event of the destruction of each part of the process. This type of plan could also indicate whether continuation of the operation would be feasible in the event of certain types of damage. If that were the case, extra expense insurance might be indicated, either in lieu of business income coverage alone or in a combined form.

UNDERWRITING CRIME INSURANCE

Crime is a significant cause of loss for both personal insureds and commercial insureds. The crime loss exposures for most individuals and families are covered under their homeowners policy. (Theft coverage can also be added by endorsement to a dwelling policy.) The ISO homeowners policy does not define "theft," but it is generally understood to include burglary, robbery, and larceny. The policy does identify specific limitations in theft coverage. For example, missing property must have been taken by others, not simply misplaced. (ISO's HO-8 provides even more limited coverage for theft than ISO's other homeowners forms.)

The homeowners policy has special limits on certain kinds of personal property, many of which are particularly susceptible to theft. For instance, money, bank notes, bullion, gold other than goldware, silver other than silverware, and platinum coins and medals are subject to a $200 limit. The homeowners policy singles out other personal property for a special coverage limit but only from a theft loss. These property categories and the per-item loss limitations that apply are as follows.

- Jewelry, watches, furs, and precious and semiprecious stones $1,000
- Firearms of any type $2,000
- Silver and silver-plated ware, gold and gold-plated ware, and pewterware $2,500

Many personal insureds have personal property in those categories, and the coverage provided under an unendorsed homeowners policy is inadequate for them. For example, a homeowner may discover that a $4,000 tennis bracelet and a mink stole were taken by thieves. Recovery in this instance would be limited to $1,000 total. For insureds owning property in those categories, the ISO homeowners policy permits the insured to add the items to the policy for an additional charge with a scheduled personal property endorsement. The coverage provided for the separately listed item is the total amount of insurance provided under the policy—not in addition to the category limitation.

A significant benefit is afforded the insured by scheduling this property. The ISO scheduled property endorsement provides "all-risks" coverage, with no deductible, anywhere in the world (except for fine arts). The addition of the personal property replacement cost endorsement provides protection, up to the scheduled limit, for those categories of property subject to depreciation.

The crime coverage needs of commercial insureds are extremely varied, so many coverage options are available to address their individual crime loss exposures. Commercial crime losses can arise from two areas. The first is crimes committed by employees, called "employee dishonesty" or "fidelity." Thefts by insureds are excluded in the personal lines forms. The second is crimes committed by others, which can be categorized as burglary, robbery, or theft, depending on the nature of the crime. Because of the diversity of property and coverage needs of commercial insureds, the balance of this section is devoted to commercial crime. Many of the loss control measures discussed below and character issues regarding the insured are just as relevant for personal lines insureds.

Employee Dishonesty

Employee dishonesty covers theft by employees. It is unique among crime insurance coverages and owes its unique character to the following factors:

- Employees have ready access to valuable property. They can learn the company's routines and schedules and the habits of fellow employees. They can discover what controls management has in place and how well the controls work.

- Losses can be hidden from discovery. Unlike burglary and robbery, which by definition are visible crimes, employee theft is by stealth. The act of theft can be deliberately obscured or covered for varying lengths of time.

- Large losses are common. The thief's access to property continues until the crime is discovered. The length of time of access, in turn, contributes to the size of loss.

- The insured might be reluctant to face the facts. Employers are often unwilling to believe that an employee might steal from them. That reluctance to accept reality leads to practices that contribute to opportunities for theft and greatly increases exposures to loss.

- Management might be reluctant to prosecute employees who steal. Many employers will not sign complaints or testify at criminal proceedings against their employees. They may wish to avoid bad press; to accept the culprit's "hard luck" story; or to have the affair end quickly, especially when the employee promises restitution.

The following characteristics of employee dishonesty crimes pose additional problems for underwriters:

1. Losses might be frequent, but they are usually hidden until they become large losses. For example, an embezzler typically takes small sums of money over a long period of time and is caught only when the total is too large for the embezzler to continue to hide it.

2. Employer reluctance to accept that some employees are dishonest creates a problem of adverse selection. Most financial institutions purchase fidelity coverage, but only a small percentage of mercantile establishments do so. Employee crime losses are significant, and they are estimated to cost businesses more than any other form of crime. Nonetheless, employee dishonesty insurance is a profitable line for insurers and available for most insureds.

Underwriting Employee Dishonesty Exposures

By tradition, insurers have written employee dishonesty insurance for an indefinite term. Insurers rerate employee dishonesty policies each year but assume that the relationship with the insured will be long term. Underwriters must be satisfied that certain conditions, such as the following, exist before issuing the policy:

1. Management of the insured organization must exhibit the highest moral character. A moral hazard, in other words, must not exist.

2. The insured should be profitable. Profits indicate competence within the company's market spheres. Management planning and control systems should work well. The company should be financially able to respond to recommended loss control expenditures. The corporate culture should reward positive performance.

3. Burglary and robbery loss control systems should be in place and maintained, because appropriate defenses against external crime also deter employee crime.

4. Amounts of insurance should fall within the limits prescribed by the insurer's underwriting guidelines.

5. Management controls should exist and be maintained. Management controls are evidence of management's care and concern.

Controlling Employee Dishonesty Losses

Stemming employee dishonesty losses requires strict adherence to management controls. Listed below are controls, applicable to almost all organizations, that can be considered minimum standards for acceptability:

• The insured screens new hires and checks their references.

• Before they are promoted, seasoned employees are reviewed, especially for promotions or transfers into sensitive positions.

- A substance-abuse screening program is in place. Underwriters regard this as a positive sign because substance dependency creates potential for employee dishonesty.

- Underwriters normally request a list of all employees, their positions, and their hire dates. The rate and level of employee turnover can contribute to an increase in the insured's exposure to loss.

- Termination procedures are well defined. The computer passwords of employees who had worked in sensitive areas are revoked, and keys or access cards are returned.

- Management remains sensitive to all employee behavior. Dramatic changes in lifestyle might indicate employee dishonesty.

- Periodic audits test accounts receivable, cash accounts, inventories, and disbursements.

- Bank reconciliation is done to ensure that company and bank records agree.

- A division of authority between employees exists so that employees monitor one another.

- Annual vacations are required, since some methods of embezzlement require a daily adjustment of records.

- Duties are rotated to discover irregularities or defalcations.

- There is two-person or dual control on some items, such as the vault, cash, and other items that could be converted quickly.

Other Crime Exposures

Crime committed by others includes acts such as robbery, burglary, and theft. The definitions used in crime insurance polices are often different from those in general usage. Because the difference in terminology can be confusing, the crime-insurance definitions of "burglary," "robbery," "theft," "disappearance," and "inventory shortage" are discussed below.

Burglary is the forcible entry into or exit from premises, a building, a safe, or a vault, with the intent to commit theft. Burglary policies limit this definition by covering only when the premises are not open for business. The definition of "forcible entry or exit" includes thieves who hide within a fenced area or in a building during business hours to take property and force their way out after closing.

> **Burglary**
> The forcible entry into or exit from premises, a building, a safe, or a vault, with the intent to commit theft.

Robbery means illegally taking property by violence or threat of violence against a person. Crime forms describe the person who has custody of the property as a custodian while on the premises and as a messenger elsewhere. This facilitates a distinction between coverage on and away from the insured's premises. Robbery also includes taking property from a messenger or custodian who has been kidnapped for that purpose.

> **Robbery**
> The illegal taking of property by violence or threat of violence against a person.

Theft means any act of stealing. It includes burglary, robbery, shoplifting, and other acts of stealth.

> **Theft**
> Any act of stealing.

Disappearance
The loss of property with no reasonable explanation.

Disappearance is the loss of property with no reasonable explanation. When disappearance is a covered cause of loss, coverage is extended to include situations in which the insured simply misplaces property. Coverage forms no longer use the term "mysterious disappearance," but the term persists in general usage. "Mysterious disappearance" implies an opportunity for theft even if there is no evidence of one.

Inventory shortage
A loss that can be proved only from inventory records.

Inventory shortage is a loss that can be proved only from inventory records. "All-risks" policies that cover theft exclude loss from inventory shortage because "shrinkage" is considered a normal event in any business and one that the insured can control. The inventory shortage exclusion prevents the insured from transferring this ordinary cost to the insurer.

Underwriting Other Crime Exposures

The process of underwriting commercial crime insurance requires considering the following five factors:

1. Property susceptibility
2. Location of the property
3. Nature of the occupancy
4. Public protection
5. Modifications of coverage and price

Property Susceptibility

Every piece of property has characteristics that make it more or less desirable to thieves. Those characteristics are usually considered together, but an underwriter should be able to recognize them separately. The characteristics are determined by three questions:

1. Is the property susceptible to crime?
2. Is the property fungible?
3. Is there a ready market for it as stolen property?

The size, weight, portability, visibility, and accessibility of goods determine how susceptible they are to theft. The emphasis given to each of these characteristics is relative. An object's size or weight does not in itself preclude its theft. A forty-ton steel truss bridge was stolen from a West Virginia creek in the late 1950s. Despite that occurrence, bulky items like bridges and buildings are viewed as having low susceptibility to theft. Jewelry, clothing, small electric appliances, precious metals, books, and hand tools, on the other hand, are highly susceptible. The higher the property's value is relative to its bulk and weight, the more attractive it becomes to thieves.

Fungibility measures a property's value as an item of exchange. Money, securities, and other negotiable instruments are highly fungible. Bulk gas, bridges, and the like are considered essentially not fungible. That is, they might meet a rare exchange demand, but they are not regularly traded goods.

A semitrailer truck loaded with name-brand golf balls has low fungibility. It is, however, susceptible. A ready market probably exists for the load of golf balls.

A combination of several factors determines a commodity's marketability. Goods that are in widespread use have more potential customers. Goods that are difficult to trace are more marketable. The economy often plays a key role, making a surprising variety of goods very marketable for some period of time.

As a last resort, thieves may turn to the original owner as their market. Once several boxcars filled with automobile and truck engine blocks "disappeared." After months had passed with no trace of the boxcars, the thieves contacted the manufacturer. After price and delivery negotiations, the engines arrived at their original destination.

After considering the above issues, underwriters must ask themselves the larger question: How likely is the property to be stolen?

Location of the Property

Such things as topography, neighborhood, climate, and the local crime rate can tell underwriters what kind of losses to expect. Seasonal occupancy, typical of a resort, for example, makes loss by crime more likely. Crime occurs more often in some areas than in others, and underwriters should use this type of information. Conventional wisdom holds that cities have a higher rate of crime than suburbs and rural areas. Although this remains true, the gap might be closing.

Statistics on local crime rates often reflect the experience of entire cities or counties, which is of little value to underwriters. They are not complete because many victims do not report crimes, especially in areas where they occur most often. Underwriters who want accurate information in a form they can use have to develop their own data. The need to avoid unfair discrimination in underwriting makes reliable data especially important.

Nature of the Occupancy

A reporter once asked Willie Sutton, a notorious bank robber of the 1940s and 1950s, why he chose to steal from banks when there were easier targets. His answer was, "Because that's where the money is." Then and now, some occupancies are more attractive to crime than others.

Some occupancies generally have a great deal of cash or other valuable property on hand. Those occupancies include banks, savings and loans, credit unions, check-cashing services, grocery stores, stadiums, arenas, churches, and buildings where charity events are held.

Some businesses are conducted in locations that are removed from the public or operate during off hours, when few people are around to deter criminals. Those include twenty-four-hour convenience stores and service stations, and public warehouses.

Public Protection

Public protection reflects the quality of the local criminal justice system. How soon do police officers respond to alarms and reports of crime? How often do prosecutors obtain convictions? How well does the system deter crime? Effective public protection means lower rates of crime and fewer crime losses. In gauging the quality of public protection, there is no substitute for local knowledge.

Modifications of Coverage and Price

Commercial crime insurance underwriters have some latitude in modifying the proposal for insurance. In many instances, an applicant knows the coverage that he or she wants and will turn to another insurer when the requested coverage is not provided. In many more instances, however, the applicant chooses not to prolong the insurance-purchasing decision and accepts the broadest coverage at the lowest price. Because insureds who usually request crime insurance need the coverage, they are likely to consider and accept counteroffers made by an underwriter who is trying to write the account. Possible modifications include changes in coverage, limits, pricing, the deductible, and the use endorsements requiring protective safeguards.

Coverage   Requests for policies providing broad coverage do not always fit within the underwriter's guidelines. Rather than reject the account outright, the underwriter might offer coverage that is less generous. Many requests for broad crime coverage must be negotiated. An account might be ineligible for crime coverage under a commercial property form with a special causes of loss coverage form. As a counteroffer, the underwriter might offer to provide coverage under the causes-of-loss broad coverage form in combination with the applicable crime coverage form. This approach to controlling exposures for the entire account does little to control commercial crime exposures. Overall, transforming marginal accounts into acceptable accounts for crime insurance using coverage modification is a difficult process.

Coverage Limits   For most other types of insurance, the insured purchases an amount of insurance close to the value of the exposed property. In the case of crime insurance, most insureds assume that only small crime losses will occur. This assumption and the desire to reduce premiums tend to reduce the policy limit and to increase problems associated with underinsurance. In the case of crime insurance, the underwriter might be satisfied with providing policy limits much lower than the amount of the values insured. Because of the moral hazard that too much insurance might create, most underwriters do not want to provide coverage to full value even if the insured requests it.

Pricing   Because crime forms do not contain a coinsurance clause, the insured is not penalized for having inadequate limits. Losses will probably be partial and still exceed the policy limits. Underinsurance can lead to underpricing, so underwriters must consider the risk of loss when pricing crime coverage.

Because policy limits tend to be low relative to the amount at risk, probable maximum loss usually equals the amount subject. Underwriters who provide commercial crime coverage should expect that losses will exceed the policy amount.

Deductibles Deductibles in crime insurance serve the same purposes as they do in other types of insurance. They eliminate small, more predictable losses, therefore preventing an erosion of the loss portion of the premium, and tend to make the insured more conscious of the benefits of loss control.

Deductibles are not used as underwriting tools in crime insurance as often as they might be. Larger, more sophisticated policyholders recognize the value of retaining small, frequent losses that can often be readily contained through loss control techniques and financed with current cash flow.

ISO's business personal property coverage forms contain a standard $250 deductible. The deductible for crime insurance should be at least equal to the deductible amount that applies to other types of losses to the insured's business personal property.

Protective Safeguards A protective safeguards endorsement is a form of warranty. It is the insured's promise to take certain steps to protect against loss. That promise becomes part of the policy and becomes a condition precedent to coverage. If the insured fails to protect the property as promised, the insurer need not pay any losses that result.

Courts have adopted varying attitudes toward warranties. Some courts almost choose to ignore them. In the case of crime safeguards, however, courts are more likely to rule that breach of warranty negates coverage. The subject of the insured's promise is clearly material to the underwriting decision, which makes enforcement by the courts more likely.

Underwriters cannot assume that courts will insist that the insured fully comply with the warranty. A good faith effort to comply is almost always sufficient. For example, the failure of a central station alarm service solely because of a power or telephone service outage does not breach the promise. The situation is different, however, if the utility cuts off electrical service because the insured has failed to pay its bills. The intent of a warranty is not to create a loophole through which an adjuster can deny liability. The warranty imposes the duty to make a good faith effort to maintain the level of protection specified in the endorsement.

The rules and rates filed by insurers almost always require a warranty for any protective system that earns a rate credit. Underwriters might also regard a system as essential even when it does not qualify for a reduced rate. Warranties ensure that the risk the underwriter accepts and the loss exposure are the same. If the underwriter demands that protective systems be present, the crime policy with the protective safeguard endorsement should be used to enforce their maintenance throughout the policy period.

Controlling Other Crime Exposures

Crime loss exposures respond well to loss control efforts. As mentioned earlier, implementing loss control measures and using them diligently are two of the most telling characteristics of a good prospect for crime coverage.

Private protection systems to prevent or control loss include the following:

- Safes and vaults
- Cages, special rooms, and limited access areas
- Indoor and outdoor lighting
- Fences and walls
- Protection of openings on the premises (gates, doors, windows, and skylights)
- Guard services
- Alarm systems
- Electronic surveillance systems
- Inventory control and other management activities

Loss control, or protection devices and systems, are generally thought to serve at least two important functions: to preclude crime losses and to deter crime.

A dedicated thief can break through protection systems if given enough time. In other words, safes, vaults, fencing, and so on, rarely preclude access when a thief is strongly motivated. However, protection devices and systems do make an invaluable contribution to deterrence. They frustrate, confuse, and slow down criminal processes, frequently causing a thief to seek an easier target.

Although even the best protection systems do not eliminate loss, their value cannot be overemphasized in reducing the probability of loss. After moral hazard, private protection is the most important consideration in crime insurance underwriting.

Underwriting guidelines should indicate the acceptable level of protection that a particular class or location demands. Because private protection is known to reduce risk of loss by crime, the level of private protection required depends on the judgment of an insurer's staff underwriters. Line underwriters might feel more or less secure with the level of private protection recommended by the underwriting guide for a particular account and might adjust the insurance proposal, perhaps by reducing the amount of coverage provided.

The two main categories of private protection devices are barriers to criminal access and detection devices. Barriers include devices that protect the premises, safes, and vaults. Detection devices are guards, alarms, and surveillance systems.

UNDERWRITING MARINE INSURANCE

Ocean marine is one of the oldest forms of insurance. Ocean marine underwriters have historically insured both oceangoing hulls and their cargoes.

The "warehouse-to-warehouse" clause added land transportation as well. Inland marine insurance, peculiar to the United States and Canada, grew out of a willingness of ocean marine underwriters to provide coverage for goods and equipment in transit within the North American continent. Using the marine tradition of broad insuring agreements, inland marine coverages grew rapidly and began competing with fire and casualty insurers. This conflict led to the development of the **Nationwide Marine Definition** in 1933, amended in 1953 and 1976, which defined those areas within which inland marine coverage could be offered.

Nationwide Marine Definition
Definition of the kinds of risk and coverages that can be classified under state insurance laws as marine and inland marine insurance.

Ocean Marine Insurance

Ocean marine insurance is divided into four major categories: (1) yachts, (2) commercial hulls, (3) protection and indemnity, and (4) cargo.

Some differences exist between the underwriting considerations for yachts and those for commercial hulls and cargoes. Although the term yacht usually brings to mind a seventy-foot luxury vessel, all sailboats and inboard-powered boats are also considered yachts.

Yachts

Underwriting considerations for all yachts from twenty-foot sailboats to one-hundred-foot oceangoing powerboats can be grouped under three headings: (1) seaworthiness, (2) navigable waters and season, and (3) operator experience.

Seaworthiness

The soundness of a vessel for its intended use is reflected in its age, manufacture, construction, and maintenance. Typically, the older a vessel becomes, the lower is its value and the greater is the chance of a constructive total loss should any damage occur. Most insurers place age limitations on vessels insured. Construction quality varies by manufacturer, so a manufacturer with a good reputation is an important underwriting characteristic. Fiberglass construction has proved to be a significant improvement over wooden construction. Modern fiberglass construction is lightweight and includes foam interlayers that significantly reduce the hazard of sinking. Fiberglass hulls also eliminate much of the hull maintenance required for wooden vessels. All vessels, regardless of their construction, require regular maintenance to remain fit. A marine survey is the most effective way for underwriters to obtain information on a particular vessel. The survey provides a comprehensive evaluation of the value and condition of the vessel.

Navigable Waters and Season

Underwriters have traditionally used a navigation warranty as a major underwriting tool. The **navigation warranty** restricts coverage to the area for which the yacht, equipment, and experience of the operator are appropriate. The perils of the seas differ greatly by area and by season within the same area. Putting to sea during the hurricane season in the Caribbean or during the

Navigation warranty
Part of an insurance contract that restricts coverage to the area for which the yacht, equipment, and experience of the operator are appropriate.

winter in Maine is not prudent. A navigation warranty suspends coverage when a vessel is used under conditions other than those agreed to with the underwriter.

Operator Experience

An experienced operator is an extremely important underwriting consideration. Many insurers give credit to operators who have completed Power Squadron or Coast Guard Auxiliary courses. Membership in an organized yacht club generally indicates the policyholder's dedication to his or her pastime and often implies sound experience and training. Many insurers use automobile motor vehicle records as an indicator of an operator's ability. The finest construction and equipment are useless if an operator does not possess sufficient seamanship to use the vessel properly.

Commercial Hulls

When evaluating commercial hulls, underwriters must consider some of the same basic types of information that they consider for yachts: the construction of the ship, its equipment and maintenance, the area within which it is used, and the expertise of the master and mariners. Although similar in kind, commercial hull underwriting differs from yacht underwriting in the sources of information. Various registers of shipping provide the physical characteristics of a vessel. The "flag" or nation in which a ship is registered determines the safety regulations under which the ship is operated and the frequency of inspections. An inspection should determine the state of maintenance.

In commercial hulls, the cargo is a major consideration. Some cargoes, such as oil, chemicals, and coal, present serious hazards to the hull.

Protection and Indemnity

Protection and indemnity (P&I) coverage is a special type of liability insurance. It covers the liability of a vessel owner for bodily injury, illness, death, and damage to the property of others arising out of the ownership, use, or operation of the vessel. Admiralty law sets certain limits on the liability of vessels when an owner does not have privity to its operation. This limitation is usually applicable in commercial hull situations but seldom applies to yachts, whose owners are usually onboard.

Protection and indemnity coverage includes the following:

- *Loss of life and bodily injury*—This applies to persons injured aboard the vessel or elsewhere, including members of the crew if such injury is deemed to be the responsibility of the owner.

- *Property damage*—This covers the owner's liability for loss of or damage to the property of others aboard the owner's vessel, fixed objects, and other vessels and property onboard them (insofar as the collision clause in the hull policy does not apply).

- *Other coverages*—A vessel owner whose craft sinks in private waters or obstructs a channel or otherwise constitutes a menace to navigation may be faced with the legal responsibility of marking or removing the wreck, or destroying it. Insofar as the expense of this procedure constitutes a legal liability of the owner, it is covered by P&I.

- *Clean-up expense*—Clean-up costs incurred because of pollution incidents are insured. Insurers commonly exclude the pollution exposure altogether or issue a separate policy on that exposure.

- *Defense costs*—The defense cost of litigation, including necessary bonds for release from court seizure, is covered whether against the vessel (*in rem*) or against the owner (*in personam*).

- *Fines*—The liability of the insured shipowner or operator for fines that may be imposed for violating the law is also covered (sometimes subject to a deductible).[11]

One serious area of exposure under P&I coverage is pollution from oil tankers. The tanker Exxon Valdez ran aground on March 24, 1989, spilling eleven million gallons of oil. This, the largest spill in North American history, caused over $2.2 billion in pollution losses. Pollution coverage is generally included in P&I sold by "P&I clubs" (mutuals) but often not in P&I sold by domestic U.S. insurers.

Cargo

Many firms today import components, raw materials, and finished goods from overseas, and others are involved in exporting goods. All of these firms are prospects for ocean cargo insurance. By use of the "warehouse-to-warehouse" clause, ocean cargo coverage also includes land transit from the originating warehouse to the dock and from the dock at the port of destination to the consignee's warehouse, which usually involves thousands of miles. In the area of cargo insurance, the quality of the policyholder and his or her business reputation are important. He or she must have as a primary interest the safe arrival of the product at its destination. A policyholder who tries to save money by reducing the amount of packing cannot be profitably underwritten.

Underwriters are asked to insure a wide variety of commodities. Commodities such as ingots of pig iron offer very low susceptibility to loss or damage, but others, such as fine glassware and china, can be easily damaged. Shipments of fishmeal or burlap can present extraordinary fire hazards. Auto parts and liquor are very attractive to thieves. Any bulk shipment or any shipment of raw materials presents its own unique problems. Some chemicals, for example, become worthless if they are exposed to air, and certain electronic devices require expensive recalibration if they are even slightly damaged. A few commodities and their special hazards are shown in Exhibit 5-4.

The ports between which goods will be shipped and the land transportation that will be used from "warehouse-to-warehouse" are also major underwriting concerns. In some ports, ships must be unloaded by lighters, which are small, self-propelled vessels or barges. This increases the probability of damage to the cargo. Some ports are known to have high crime and damage rates.

Excluding bulk shipments, much of today's cargo is shipped in large, enclosed metal boxes known as containers. These are similar to semitrailers without their chassis. They can be "stuffed" at the original point of shipment and unloaded at destination, thus eliminating extra handling at the port. Much of the most recent tonnage has been vessels constructed solely to transport containers.

Containerization may reduce pilferage and fresh water damage losses, provided the container is watertight and carries the merchandise from warehouse to warehouse. Because at least one-third of all containers are shipped on deck, however, the risk of exposure to heavy weather and washing overboard is greatly increased. The threat of a hijack of an entire shipment and the danger of breakage from shifting cargo are additional serious perils.

A final but important point is the location of goods on a ship. Deck cargo is subject to wind, water, and wave damage to a much greater extent than cargo stowed below decks. Certain cargoes such as rough lumber are usually unaffected by shipment on deck.

Inland Marine Insurance

Filed classes
Those inland marine classes for which advisory organizations are required to file loss costs, rule, and forms.

In terms of forms and rates, inland marine insurance is divided into filed and nonfiled classes. Those inland marine classes for which advisory organizations are required to file loss costs, rules, and forms are defined as **filed classes**. Filed classes have been selected for relatively greater regulatory scrutiny than other inland marine classes because they are considered to have many policyholders with reasonably homogeneous loss exposures. Most filed policies are relatively inflexible in terms of coverage or rates. Typical filed classes include the commercial articles coverage form, equipment dealers coverage form, physicians and surgeons equipment coverage form, sign coverage form, theatrical property coverage form, film coverage form, floor plan coverage form, jewelers block coverage form, mail coverage form, accounts receivable coverage form, and valuable papers and records coverage form. Two major categories of filed classes are jewelry and furs, which are also the two largest personal lines classes. **Nonfiled classes** are developed and rated in accordance with the underwriting practices of an individual insurer.

Nonfiled classes
Those inland marine classes rated in accordance with the underwriting practices of an individual insurer.

About one-half of all inland marine coverage is written on nonfiled forms. Nonfiled classes include a vast array of exposures—from bridges and tunnels to power tools. Depending on company practice, an underwriter can freely modify any nonfiled forms, thereby providing a great deal of flexibility. In many circumstances, a "manuscript" policy must be designed to cover an unusual or a one-of-a-kind exposure.

The diverse coverages inland marine encompasses have the common trait of being historically undesirable to fire underwriters. Property in transit, "all-risks" coverage, and property in the care, custody, and control of others make these coverages the domain of inland marine underwriters. The following sections discuss some of the nonfiled coverages that generate the largest premium volume.

EXHIBIT 5-4

Some Commodity Characteristics

Auto parts	Pilferage and theft in certain areas of the world where new cars are not readily available
Automobiles	Marring, denting, and scratching
Canned goods	Rusting, denting, and theft
Chemicals in paper bags	Shortage and contamination from torn bags
Fine arts	Handling damage and theft
Fishmeal	Highly susceptible to heating damage and fire
Fresh fruit	Extremely sensitive to temperature change and difficult to keep from spoiling
Glass	Breakage and staining
Grain	Shortage and weevil damage
Household effects	Breakage, marring, chipping, scratching, shortage, and water damage
Liquids in bulk	Leakage, shortage, contamination
Lumber (cut)	Shortage, staining, and handling damage
Machinery	Rust and breakage of parts
Paper in rolls	Chafing, cutting, and water damage
Rags	Fire and shortage
Refrigerators and stoves	Marring, scratching, chipping, and denting
Scrap metal	Alleged shortage due to difference in scale weights at origin and destination
Steel products	Rusting, bending, and twisting
Television sets	Breakage of picture tubes
Textiles	Hook damage, theft, and water damage

Contractors Equipment

Contractors equipment policies can be used to insure almost any type of mobile equipment used by contractors, including hand-held power tools, mobile cranes, excavators, and bulldozers. Such equipment is used in a variety of construction projects by both small contractors and businesses engaged in tunneling projects worth hundreds of millions of dollars.

The typical coverage form provides direct physical damage coverage on an "all-risks" basis. A key factor in underwriting this coverage is knowing the use of the equipment and the scope of its operations. Other factors to consider include the following:

1. The size and value of the individual items of equipment
2. The type, age, maintenance, supervision, operating characteristics, and protection of the equipment
3. The experience and accident record of the equipment operators
4. The financial status of the policyholder
5. The concentration of equipment at a single site
6. Past loss history
7. Labor relations[12]

Builders Risk/Installation

Builders risk coverage can be purchased by attaching the appropriate coverage part to the ISO commercial property form. Many producers prefer instead to advise their clients to use nonfiled forms that permit flexibility in rating and coverage. Those forms include transit coverage for building materials brought to a site.

Buildings under construction face the same exposures as completed structures but are often more vulnerable because protective safeguards are not yet in place. Underwriters should be aware of the following conditions that might increase the hazards for a fire loss:

1. Water mains that might not be completed
2. Fire hydrants that are operational but that might not be near the structure
3. Standpipes that might not be connected in high-rise structures
4. Sprinkler systems that might not be installed or activated
5. Heat and smoke detectors that might not be installed
6. Construction activities that introduce new heat sources, such as welding or brazing
7. Salamanders that are used for heat

Construction sites are susceptible to theft and vandalism unless security precautions are taken. Those precautions include installing fencing, lighting, and alarm systems on trailers and storage sheds and employing security guards.

Structures with large roof spans have an increased chance of collapsing before all of the needed supports are in place. Structures are particularly susceptible to wind damage before the exterior walls and roof are in place. Coverage for flood and earthquake, subject to sublimits and higher deductibles, is usually available as an optional coverage under a builders risk policy.[13]

Transportation

Goods shipped by truck, air, rail, and mail are the most logical candidates for inland marine coverage. The covered causes of loss are usually very broad, are frequently "all-risks," and routinely include flood and earthquake. Transportation insurance can provide coverage for the following interests:

1. The shipper, who is any party who hires another to transport cargo
2. The carrier, who actually transports (or carries) goods for another
3. The consignee, who is the person designated for delivery

The details of the transaction and common law determine which party bears the risk of loss in transit. The underwriter has to consider who bears the risk of loss, how susceptible the cargo is to damage, and what steps have been taken to protect against foreseeable losses.

At common law, a contract carrier is liable as an ordinary bailee, and a common carrier is liable as an insurer of the goods, subject to five exceptions: acts of God, acts of public enemies, exercise of public authority, fault or negligence on the part of the shipper, and inherent vice or nature of the property. The contract between the shipper and the carrier, called a bill of lading, frequently departs from common law principles. Deregulation of the trucking industry has made it common practice to place the risk of loss on the shipper or consignee. Terms of sale usually make provision to transfer title to the goods and the risk of loss from the seller to the buyer at a defined point. The underwriter has to be aware of the arrangements that cover insured shipments and their implications.

Instrumentalities of Transportation and Communication

The principal instrumentalities of transportation and communication include bridges; tunnels; pipelines; wharves, docks, and piers; radio and TV towers and stations; and dry docks and marine railways and cranes. Although much of inland marine insurance deals with property in transit or capable of being transported, those subjects of insurance are *related to* transportation. Instrumentalities of transportation and communication are fixed location structures and present many of the same hazards as any other type of real property. In addition, because of their specialized nature, such structures are subject to some unique hazards.

The primary areas of concern for underwriters of these instrumentalities include the construction and maintenance of the structure and any unique hazards or exposures that may exist. Bridges and tunnels, for example, may be exposed by trucks carrying gasoline or explosives. Television towers are susceptible to ice buildup in severe winter storms, increasing the likelihood of a collapse in high winds. Pipelines are particularly susceptible to earthquakes. Wharves, docks, and piers may be damaged by high waves as well as by ships colliding with them.

Bailee Coverages

Bailee coverage is provided in many inland marine policies, either as a section of coverage in a policy providing other coverage, such as the jewelers' block, or as a separate policy. The cleaners and dyers customer's policy generally provides bailee coverage only. That policy provides direct damage coverage for the customer's goods that the cleaner or dyer has in bailment, and all losses by insured causes of loss are covered whether or not the policyholder was legally liable for the loss. In that way, bailee's insurance goes beyond any type of legal liability coverage. Bailee insurance also serves to close a gap in coverage that would otherwise be created by the common wording in liability policies that excludes coverage for the property of others in the insured's "care, custody, or control."

SUMMARY

Modern property insurance had its beginnings in catastrophic fires that swept European cities in the late seventeenth century. Loss by fire was originally the only covered cause of loss. As demands for additional coverages were made, additional causes of loss and broader coverages were added. Property insurance causes of loss may now include fire, windstorm, hail, aircraft, vehicle damage, riot and civil commotion, explosion, smoke, vandalism, sprinkler leakage, water damage, sinkhole collapse, volcanic action, earth movement, flood, and crime.

Most of the tools underwriters use to evaluate exposures relate to the fire cause of loss. Because fire is a predominant cause of loss, properly underwriting that exposure to achieve profitability increases the likelihood that an account will be profitable overall.

The acronym COPE is used by property insurance underwriters to remind them of the four basic areas they should investigate in every submission—construction, occupancy, protection, and external exposure.

Building construction is divided into six classifications—fire resistive, modified fire resistive, masonry noncombustible, noncombustible, joisted masonry, and frame.

Occupancy is described in terms of combustibility and damageability. Hazards fall into two categories: common hazards found in most commercial buildings and special hazards unique to the specific occupancy. Occupancy hazards and the degree of their control must be evaluated to determine to what extent they increase or decrease the expectation of loss.

Fire protection can be classified as private or public and consists of three elements—prevention, detection, and suppression. Private protection is provided by the property owner or tenant and ranges in sophistication from hand-held fire extinguishers to a fully equipped fire station at a manufacturing facility. Private protection detection systems include private patrol services, guard services with clocks, smoke and heat detectors, automatic local alarms, and automatic central station alarms. Private suppression systems fall into the following categories: portable extinguishers, standpipes and hoses, automatic sprinkler systems, and private fire brigades. ISO's public protection classification groups communities into one of ten categories based on the fire protection present.

A consideration of external exposures broadens an underwriter's perspective to include areas and buildings adjacent to the risk being evaluated. Availability of clear space, presence of surrounding brush, heights of exposing structures, and the occupancies of those structures are examples of the concerns underwriters have.

Other causes of loss—and, thus, concerns—are lightning; explosion; windstorm; hail; riot or civil commotion; vandalism and malicious mischief; water damage and sprinkler leakage; sinkhole collapse and mine subsidence; volcanic action; weight of ice, snow, or sleet; ice damming; collapse; flood; and earthquake.

Time element underwriting includes measuring the largest loss of net income and estimating the probable period of interruption. The size of the net income loss is reflected in the selection of the coverage limits and the coinsurance percentage. The likely length of interruption is determined through sales projections and tempered by seasonal cycles and general economic conditions. Other considerations are the estimated rebuilding time, the time needed to return to the same level of production, and the presence of a disaster contingency plan that could reduce the period of interruption.

Crime insurance covers intentional losses caused by persons other than the policyholder to money and securities and to property other than money and securities through causes of loss such as employee dishonesty, burglary, robbery, and theft. Evaluating crime potential involves examining the characteristics of the property subject to crime losses—susceptibility, fungibility, and marketability. Other aspects that indicate loss potential include location of the property, nature of the occupancy, and public protection.

Marine insurance is the predecessor of all forms of insurance. Ocean marine is divided into four major categories—yachts, commercial hulls, protection and indemnity, and cargo. The underwriting criteria used to evaluate yachts include the seaworthiness of the vessel, the waters navigated, the season, and the experience of the operators. Commercial hull insurance involves the same concerns as yachts, but the values involved are more significant. Protection and indemnity (P&I) is liability insurance that provides coverage for claims arising out of the ownership and use of a vessel. Also covered is liability for injuries to members of the crew. Ocean cargo insurance involves the import and export of a wide variety of goods and raw materials. Underwriting considerations focus on the susceptibility of the cargo to damage and the manner in which it is packed.

Numerous coverage forms provide inland marine insurance. The ones discussed in this chapter represent the largest classes based on premium volume. The next chapter completes the discussion of the underwriting function. Like this chapter on underwriting selected property lines, Chapter 6 introduces liability underwriting basics for several important lines.

CHAPTER NOTES

1. Insurance Services Office, *Commercial Fire Rating Schedule* (New York: Insurance Services Office, 1983), pp. 3–4.

2. *Fire Protection Handbook*, 17th ed. (Quincy, Mass.: National Fire Protection Association, 1991), p. 6–23.

3. Insurance Services Office, Mitigation Online, World Wide Web: www.isomitigation.com/bcegs.html (6 November 2002).

4. *NFPA Inspection Manual*, Charles A. Tuck, Jr., ed., 4th ed. (Boston: National Fire Protection Association, 1976), p. 20.

5. *NFPA Inspection Manual*, p. 20.

6. *Fire Protection Handbook*, 17th ed., p. 6–8.

7. *Fire Protection Handbook*, 17th ed., p. 6–9.

8. Gary G. Nichols and Sam Gerace, "A Survey of Hurricane Andrew" (Birmingham, Ala.: Southern Building Code Congress International, 1993).

9. *Statistical Abstract of the United States 2001*, Table 308. Persons Arrested, by Charge and Selected Characteristics: 1999, p. 191.

10. Robert B. Holtom, *Commercial Fire Underwriting* (Cincinnati: The National Underwriter Co., 1989), p. 140.

11. E. P. Hollingsworth and J. J. Launie, *Commerical Property and Multiple-Lines Underwriting*, 2d ed. (Malvern, Pa.: Insurance Institute of America, 1984), pp. 404–405.

12. Roderick McNamara, Robert A. Laurence, and Glen L. Wood, *Inland Marine Insurance*, vol. 2 (Malvern, Pa.: Insurance Institute of America, 1987), pp. 170–171.

13. McNamara, Laurence, and Wood, pp. 242–243.

Chapter 6

Direct Your Learning

Underwriting Liability Insurance and Package Policies

After learning the subject matter of this chapter, you should be able to:

■ Explain the legal concepts underlying liability insurance.

■ Given a case, explain the major underwriting considerations for different insurance products and types of coverage.

Develop Your Perspective

What are the main topics covered in the chapter?

The scope for liability and the factors considered in underwriting are described for auto liability, general liability, workers compensation, professional liability, personal liability, umbrella and excess liability, package policies, small accounts, and surety bonds.

Consider the legal basis for liability in the United States.

- How does this legal foundation create liability exposures in all of the various forms described in the chapter?

Why is it important to know these topics?

However unintentional or unexpected liability losses might be, some factors increase the chance that an organization or individual might cause injury or harm to others and be the subject of a liability claim or lawsuit.

Analyze these factors and the role of underwriting.

- How does underwriting select and price policies to reflect the exposures presented?

- What does underwriting do to protect the financial stability of your insurance organization?

- What regulations restrict an underwriter's ability to freely select and price policies?

How can you use this information?

Judge the general liability exposures for a local business.

- What property or activities increase their potential for loss?

- How could the business decrease its potential for being the subject of a liability claim or lawsuit?

Chapter 6

Underwriting Liability Insurance and Package Policies

This is the last of three chapters describing how underwriters perform policy-holder selection. As in the chapter on property underwriting, specific lines of insurance are discussed to illustrate the liability underwriting process. Although not all lines are discussed, this chapter covers the major personal and commercial liability lines and addresses the major underwriting concerns for those lines.

It is commonplace today to purchase property and liability coverages in a combined contract. The commercial package policy (CPP) represents a modular approach to policy design. Given the right combination of policy components, the policyholder is entitled to an overall package discount. The homeowners policy and businessowners policy both contain multiple lines but are offered as indivisible policies.

THE LEGAL BASIS FOR LIABILITY

The U.S. legal system provides remedies by which citizens can assert their legal rights, which are legally protected interests. These rights include freedom from injury to a person or damage to his or her property caused by the intentional or negligent acts of others. To protect these rights, the law recognizes two classes of wrongful acts, criminal and civil. A crime against a person is also an offense against society, generally punishable by fine or imprisonment. A **civil wrong** invades the rights of an individual, either by breach of contract or by tort. The principal legal remedy for civil wrongs is damages. **Liability** is created when the law imposes an obligation on the wrongdoer to compensate the injured party for the financial consequences of the wrongful act. Liability insurance exists to protect against liability that the insured may incur through the legal process, such as a trial. The two main sources of liability that insurance covers are torts and statutes that impose liability without regard to fault.

Torts and Negligence

A **tort** is a wrongful act (other than a breach of contract) committed by one person against another for which a civil lawsuit in a court can provide a remedy. The person who feels wronged and who files suit seeking relief is

Civil wrong
An act that invades the rights of an individual, either by breach of contract or by tort.

Liability
An obligation imposed by law on a wrongdoer to compensate an injured party for the financial consequences of a wrongful act.

Tort
A wrongful act (other than a breach of contract) committed by one person against another for which a civil lawsuit in a court can provide a remedy.

called the plaintiff, and the person the plaintiff charges with committing the tort is the defendant. A body of law has developed from common law, which is decisions of courts, and from state and federal statutes, which are written laws enacted by legislative bodies.

Torts may be intentional or negligent. Liability insurance protects the insured against the financial consequences of negligence but rarely covers intentional torts. **Negligence** is the failure to exercise the degree of care that a reasonably prudent person would exercise to avoid harming others. It requires the following:

Negligence
The failure to act in a manner that is reasonably prudent or the failure to exercise the appropriate degree of care under given circumstances.

- A legal duty owed to the plaintiff to use due care
- A failure to conform to the standard of care required in the situation, with the defendant's conduct creating an unreasonable risk of harm
- A causal connection between the negligent act and the plaintiff's injury
- Actual loss or damage to the plaintiff

Traditionally, courts have recognized three classes of persons whose rights the law protects. An **invitee** is a person who enters a premises for the financial benefit of the owner or occupant. A customer who comes into a store is an invitee. A **licensee** is any other person who enters the premises with permission, such as a social guest. Anyone who enters the premises without permission is a **trespasser**. This hierarchy produced three levels of duty to others, with the highest degree of care owed to an invitee and the lowest to a trespasser. Although an understanding of these three categories is helpful in understanding degrees of care, most courts have abandoned this hierarchy in favor of a rule that holds a person liable for any injury that is reasonably foreseeable, regardless of the victim's status as invitee, licensee, or trespasser. Whether they apply the traditional measure of duty or the newer doctrine of reasonable foreseeability, courts measure the conduct of a defendant by the standard of the reasonable person. This is a figurative person who represents the standard of conduct the community expects.

Invitee
A person who enters a premises for the financial benefit of the owner or occupant.

Licensee
A person who enters a premises with the owner's or occupant's permission.

Trespasser
A person who enters a premises without the permission of the owner or occupant.

Absolute liability
Liability that arises from inherently dangerous activities that result in injury or harm to another, regardless of how much care was used in the activity. Absolute liability does not require proof of negligence.

Strict liability
A concept applied by the courts in products liability cases in which a seller is liable for any and all defective or hazardous products that unduly threaten a consumer's personal safety. No proof of negligence is required.

Liability Without Fault (Absolute Liability)

Society permits certain extremely hazardous activities because of the benefits they provide. The use of explosives in construction projects, for instance, is an example of a hazardous activity. Keeping dangerous animals in a zoo or a safari park and operating aircraft are other examples. No matter how careful people engaged in these activities may be, a certain number of losses are likely to occur. To compensate innocent victims of these accidents, common law devised the doctrine of **absolute liability**. This rule of law applies only to certain exceptionally dangerous activities. Any person who engages in such activities becomes liable for any damage that results without regard to fault. The term **strict liability** has also been applied to this doctrine. To avoid confusion with the rule of strict liability in tort, this text uses only the term absolute liability to describe liability that the law imposes in the absence of fault. Workers compensation statutes apply this rule to injuries to employees that arise out of and occur during the course of their employment. The employer is liable, regardless of who is at fault.

Vicarious Liability

In some situations, the law holds one person liable for the torts of others. This is called **vicarious liability**. Relationships that may create vicarious liability include the following:

1. A principal-agent relationship
2. An employer-employee relationship
3. A parent-child relationship
4. A contractual relationship
5. A partnership

A principal may be liable for the torts of an agent (employee) acting within the scope of the agency. An agent is one who acts for another person, called the principal. A contract defines the agent's authority to act for the principal. The same rule imposes liability on an employer for the acts of employees in the course of their employment under the doctrine of *respondeat superior*, or "let the master respond." As a general rule, a parent is not liable for the torts of a minor child merely because of the family relationship, but the law recognizes exceptions. A child sometimes acts as the parent's agent or employee. Parents may also fail to exercise reasonable care in controlling a child for the safety of others.

Damages

Damages are the remedy the law provides for torts. They consist of money the law entitles the plaintiff to recover for personal injury or property damage. In addition, a court may order the plaintiff to mitigate damages by protecting against further damage or injury. Money damages that courts award are usually classified as compensatory or punitive. The purpose of **compensatory damages** is to compensate the injured party for the harm caused by the defendant's wrongful act. Courts award **punitive damages** to punish defendants whose conduct is willful, wanton, or grossly negligent. Liability insurance always covers compensatory damages but follows state law on punitive damages. State law varies as to whether punitive damages are covered by liability insurance.

Forms of Liability Insurance

There are three principal forms of liability insurance. Automobile and general liability insurance forms protect the insured against the financial consequences of real or alleged torts. Workers compensation insurance protects employers against liability imposed by statute for injuries to their employees that arise out of and occur during the course of their employment. Underwriters often base their decisions on an assessment of all lines of business that make up an account. They can reach an intelligent risk selection decision, however, only by evaluating each line separately.

Vicarious liability
Legal responsibility that occurs when one party is held liable for the actions of another party.

Respondeat superior
A legal doctrine that holds the principal liable for harm done by its agents while acting within the scope of their agency.

Damages
Monetary awards that one party is required to pay to another who has suffered loss or injury for which the first party is legally responsible.

Compensatory damages
Damages intended to compensate a victim for harm actually suffered.

Punitive damages
Damages awarded by a court to punish wrongdoers who, through malicious or outrageous actions, cause injury or damage to others.

UNDERWRITING AUTOMOBILE LIABILITY INSURANCE

Most people in the United States regard driving a car as a right rather than a privilege. In some parts of the country where public transportation is poor or nonexistent, driving a car is a virtual precondition for employment. For this reason, powerful public pressure is brought to bear on any institution or system that tries to limit the ability of a person to own and operate a motor vehicle.

Although they provide an important source of transportation, motor vehicles also cause the death and disability of thousands of people each year. If the head of a household is killed or disabled in an accident, his or her dependents will suffer serious economic loss. Insurance to meet those losses may be the only thing that stands between the innocent victim and dependence on the general welfare system. The public's demand for unlimited access to automobiles, combined with autos' capacity to cause injury, places tremendous pressure on automobile underwriting.

Exhibit 6-1 shows that the death rate from traffic accidents in the United States between 1996 and 2000 has declined slightly. Conversely, economic losses from accidents increased from $115.6 billion in 1995 to $230.6 billion in 2000.[1] Increases in the cost of automobile repair and medical treatment have outpaced the improvement in highway safety.

The automobile accident problem is complex. Automobile and highway design, operator licensing, traffic density, vehicle inspection, and enforcement of traffic laws all affect underwriting results.

The Regulatory and Legal Environment

Automobile underwriting must comply with an array of regulatory requirements that often infringe on an underwriter's freedom. Underwriting discretion is especially limited with regard to underwriting personal automobiles. Some insurers believe that regulation is becoming so restrictive that it will eventually preempt the risk selection process in personal automobile insurance.

One objective of regulation has been to make insurance available to all motor vehicle operators. The goal has been to ensure that financial resources are available to compensate the innocent victims of automobile accidents. No single approach or combination of methods has been successful in achieving that goal. The legislated approaches include the following:

1. Financial responsibility laws
2. Compulsory automobile liability insurance
3. Shared automobile market mechanisms
4. Mandatory uninsured motorists coverage
5. No-fault automobile laws
6. Restrictions on cancellations and nonrenewals

Each of these techniques alters the environment in which an underwriter has to make risk selection decisions.

EXHIBIT 6-1

Traffic Deaths, 1996–2000

Year	Deaths	Annual % change	Death rate per 100 million vehicle miles	Death rate per 100,000 motor vehicles
1996	42,065	+6.2	1.7	20.86
1997	42,013	−0.1	1.6	20.64
1998	41,501	−1.2	1.6	19.95
1999	41,717	+0.5	1.6	19.61
2000	41,821	+0.2	1.5	19.27

Insurance Information Institute, *The Fact Book 2002*, New York, p. 97.

Financial Responsibility Laws

Financial responsibility laws require the owner or operator of a motor vehicle to show proof of financial responsibility in one of three instances:

1. After an automobile accident that causes bodily injury or property damage greater than a preset dollar amount
2. After conviction for serious offenses, such as reckless driving, driving under the influence of alcohol, or leaving the scene of an accident
3. After failure to pay a final judgment arising from an automobile accident

Financial responsibility laws ensure that motorists can pay the victims of any accident in which they are at fault. Advocates of financial responsibility laws argue that they increase the number of insured motorists but do not impose heavy enforcement costs. The filings required after conviction for a serious offense place a burden on only the reckless but financially responsible motorist.

Financial responsibility laws suffer from the defect that the laws come into operation only *after* the motorist has been involved in an accident or convicted of a specific violation. Although insurance is the usual mechanism for ensuring financial responsibility, states usually permit the posting of a bond or a deposit with the bureau of motor vehicles as an alternative method of compliance.

The requirement for filing proof of insurance affects underwriting. The insurer may have to file a form verifying that the owner or operator who had an accident and did not have insurance at the time now has coverage. The financial responsibility laws provide that insurance is in effect until a notice of termination is filed with the department of motor vehicles. Financial responsibility laws also extend insurance coverage to all vehicles owned by the insured. This applies regardless of whether all of the insured's cars appear on the insurance policy.

Financial responsibility laws
Laws that require motorists, under certain circumstances, to provide proof that they have the ability to pay, up to certain minimum amounts, for damage or injury they might cause as a result of their operation of a motor vehicle. Furnishing proof of automobile liability insurance is one way to satisfy such laws.

Many financial responsibility laws have failed because they lacked an effective enforcement mechanism. It is very difficult to remove an irresponsible driver from the road, even after his or her driver's license has been suspended or revoked. If that person continues to drive, unlicensed and uninsured, the financial responsibility system provides no assistance to any future innocent victims.

Compulsory Automobile Liability Insurance

Compulsory automobile liability insurance laws require the registered owners of all motor vehicles to carry insurance with minimum limits specified by law. States handle the enforcement of these laws through a variety of methods or checkpoints to ensure compliance. Some typical examples include the following:

* Signing a sworn statement when applying for license tags
* Providing evidence of insurance when registering an automobile
* Providing evidence of insurance when meeting the state requirement for annual safety inspection
* Requiring all motorists to carry evidence of insurance that can be verified by police at the scene of an accident
* Requiring insurers to notify the department of motor vehicles when a policy has been cancelled
* Checking a random percentage of all licensed drivers in a state[2]

The minimum auto limits vary by state. A typical state minimum is 20/40/10. This means the driver should have at least $20,000 per person bodily injury coverage, $40,000 per accident bodily injury damage, and $10,000 property damage coverage. Most insurance professionals would agree that these minimums are much too low.

Shared Automobile Market Mechanisms

A law that requires automobile liability insurance does not guarantee that every driver can find an insurer willing to provide coverage. Every state has developed a means to meet the insurance needs of those drivers who cannot obtain coverage in the voluntary market. Such arrangements are referred to as the *residual market*. It includes automobile insurance plans, joint underwriting associations, reinsurance facilities, and state funds.

Automobile Insurance Plans

An automobile insurance plan (AIP), also called an assigned risk plan, assigns drivers to insurers that are members of the plan. The law usually requires each insurer to accept assignments based on its share of the voluntary market in the state. The AIP requires plan applicants to be rejected by the voluntary market before they may apply. In theory, policyholders in the plan pay a higher rate than those available in the voluntary market. Sometimes, however, plan rates for drivers with good records have been lower than those in the voluntary market. For insurers, this market arrangement does not guarantee an even distribution of rejected drivers among insurers. The experience of individual insurers will vary based on the luck of the draw from the pool of rejected drivers.

Joint Underwriting Associations

Joint underwriting associations (JUAs) operate as insurers in their own right. They appoint servicing carriers to handle all the functions of an insurance company. As it does for AIPs, the law usually requires all insurers that write automobile coverage to participate in a JUA. Profits and losses from the residual market are evenly distributed among insurers based on their share of the voluntary market.

Reinsurance Facilities

States with reinsurance facilities require all voluntary insurers to be servicing carriers of the residual market. Insurers may *cede* a percentage of their policies to the facility. The profits or losses on those policies are shared evenly among all insurers. Insurers treat their ceded policies as their own for rates and claims handling. One often-cited advantage of this approach is that drivers are not aware that they have been rejected and placed in the residual market. Reinsurance facilities have consistently operated at a deficit that has been funded by increased premium rates for all insureds. In the past, the subsidy has been hidden in the rates, but state laws now require insurers to itemize this charge.

State Funds

Maryland operates a state fund as its residual market. Deficits from the fund are charged to insurers and included in rates for all drivers. Other states have occasionally considered a similar arrangement.

Mandatory Uninsured Motorists Coverage

Some states, as an alternative to or in addition to compulsory automobile liability insurance, require all drivers to carry uninsured motorists coverage. Uninsured motorists coverage compensates the policyholder for medical expense and loss of income (and in some states property damage) for injuries (and damages) arising out of the use of an uninsured motor vehicle. This coverage is activated when the owner of an uninsured motor vehicle is at fault in an accident with the policyholder or when the policyholder is the victim of a hit-and-run driver.

No-Fault Automobile Laws

No-fault automobile laws represent a modest departure from and addition to the tort-law system. The majority of the states with no-fault laws require first-party and liability insurance and restrict in some way the right of an injured party to sue. States with no restriction on lawsuits are referred to as "add-on" states. Pennsylvania and New Jersey permit individual policyholders to choose to waive their right to sue in return for a reduced premium. The remaining states have no restrictions on lawsuits and vary as to whether the insurance is compulsory.

The idea of no-fault auto insurance first appeared in a book by law professors Robert Keeton and Jeffrey O'Connell in 1965.[3] Since then, about half of the states have adopted some form of no-fault auto insurance. These plans require insurers to cover a defined package of benefits known as personal injury protection (PIP). A variety of no-fault plans are now in effect. The typical plan provides first-party medical coverage and loss of earnings coverage for automobile accident victims in all cases. Many states also provide survivors' and funeral benefits, as well as payment for replacement services required by the injured party.

Slightly more than half of the no-fault plans limit the injured party's right to sue. PIP benefits become the exclusive remedy for injuries sustained in an automobile accident until the injuries exceed a threshold defined in the statute. The threshold may be either a monetary threshold or a verbal threshold. A **monetary threshold** is a specific dollar amount that medical costs or other economic damages must exceed before a tort claim may be filed. A **verbal threshold** is measured by the seriousness of an injury as expressed in words such as "permanent disfigurement." Monetary thresholds have not been particularly effective in reducing the number of lawsuits. In many cases, the dollar values are set so low that any visit to a hospital emergency room exceeds the threshold, and very few monetary thresholds have been adjusted to keep pace with inflation. Verbal thresholds have effectively reduced both the number of lawsuits and the rate at which automobile insurance premiums increase.

Like financial responsibility laws, no-fault laws are difficult to enforce. Some car owners purchase no-fault insurance only to obtain a vehicle registration and promptly cancel coverage.

Restrictions on Cancellations and Nonrenewals

In response to public pressure, most states have enacted statutes that restrict the reasons for which insurers may cancel or nonrenew automobile policies. In some states, the restrictions apply to both personal and commercial policies, but in most states, they affect only personal automobile policies. Some statutes specify the acceptable reasons to cancel or nonrenew. Others rely on the insurance department to set the ground rules. The implication for an underwriter is that once a policyholder has been put on the books, it may be difficult or impossible for a company to abandon that policyholder in the future.

Private Passenger Automobile Underwriting Factors

Insurers usually measure the desirability of an account by the characteristics of the insured drivers. The underwriting guide reflects management's evaluation of these factors, which are also used to classify and rate the account. Many systems are used to evaluate the loss potential of private passenger automobile

Monetary threshold
Under a no-fault system, a limit below which a person injured in an automobile accident collects only from his or her own insurer rather than seeking compensation from the party at fault.

Verbal threshold
A provision in some no-fault laws that restricts the right of a person injured to seek compensation from the party at fault to cases involving automobile accidents that result in death or certain specified injuries, such as disfigurement or dismemberment.

applicants. The major underwriting factors considered in most private passenger automobile underwriting guides are the following:

1. Age of operators
2. Age and type of automobile
3. Use of the automobile
4. Driving record
5. Territory
6. Sex and marital status
7. Occupation
8. Personal characteristics
9. Physical condition
10. Safety equipment

Age of Operators

The age of the operator is important in determining the likelihood of suffering losses. Data compiled by the National Safety Council indicate that although only 5.1 percent of all drivers were under age twenty in 2000, they accounted for 16.1 percent of all accidents and 14.0 percent of all fatal accidents. This disproportionate relationship of age and accident frequency does not change until operators reach age thirty-five.[4] Exhibit 6-2 presents complete accident frequency by age for 2000.

Rating plans in virtually all states take age into account and charge considerably higher rates for young drivers. Whether the higher rate offsets the increased loss potential remains for the underwriter to judge.

Age and Type of Automobile

The age of an automobile may be used as a general indication of its mechanical condition. Although some old automobiles are in outstanding mechanical condition, there is nevertheless a correlation between age and mechanical condition.

The type of automobile also has a bearing on underwriting acceptability. Sports and luxury cars tend to produce higher losses than other models. Passenger vans and full-size station wagons are more likely to produce lower loss payments than most models. The physical damage premium should reflect the damageability and cost of repair of the automobiles. To the extent that the premium structure does not account for damageability, the desirability of the type of automobile is affected. Studies are made annually of the cost of repairing various makes and models of automobiles.

Use of the Automobile

Other things being equal, the longer an automobile is on the highway, the greater the probability of its being in an accident. Long commuting distances or

EXHIBIT 6-2

Accidents by Age of Driver

Accidents by Age of Driver, 2000

Age group	Number of drivers	% of total	Drivers in fatal accidents	% of total	Drivers in all accidents	% of total
Under 20	9, 624,000	5.1	8,600	14.0	4,030,000	16.1
20-24	16,081,000	8.5	7,200	11.7	2,560,000	10.2
25-34	35,915,000	18.9	11,600	18.9	5,540,000	22.1
35-44	41,815,000	22.0	12,200	19.9	5,240,000	20.9
45-54	36,573,000	19.3	9,300	15.1	3,690,000	14.7
55-64	22,778,000	12.0	5,000	8.1	1,960,000	7.8
65-74	15,741,000	8.3	3,700	6.0	1,190,000	4.7
Over 74	11,273,000	5.9	3,800	6.2	890,000	3.5
Totals	189, 800, 000	100.0	61,400	100.0	25,100,000	100.0

Note: Percent of total columns may not add due to rounding.
Source: National Safety Council.

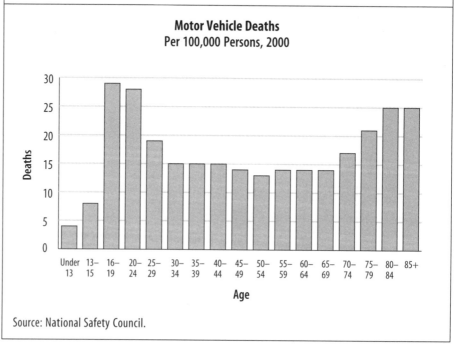

**Motor Vehicle Deaths
Per 100,000 Persons, 2000**

Source: National Safety Council.

Reprinted with permission from *The Fact Book 2002:* (New York: Insurance Information Institute, 2002), p. 100.

business use of an automobile results in high annual mileage. As is the case with most of these characteristics, rates attempt to reflect the increased loss potential. A typical rating plan contains separate classifications for the following:

1. Pleasure use only
2. Cars driven to work in a carpool in which drivers rotate
3. Cars driven to work more than three miles but less than ten miles one way
4. Cars driven to work more than ten miles one way
5. Business use

The classification for pleasure use only usually includes driving to work less than three miles one way. Underwriters must determine whether the driving mileage indicated is excessive in view of the rate that applies.

Driving Record

Both prior accidents and prior moving violations are important in evaluating a private passenger automobile applicant. The prior loss history of the driver may indicate poor driving habits, recklessness, or simply a lack of skill. Certain moving violations indicate a disregard for safety, while others indicate carelessness.

Territory

The probability of both liability and physical damage losses is related to the principal place of garaging. Furthermore, theft and vandalism occur at a higher rate in congested urban areas, with parking on the streets, than in less populated areas. Drivers are more likely to be involved in an automobile accident in an urban area but more likely to be involved in a fatal accident in a rural area. Higher driving speeds and greater distance in mileage and time to reach medical help have been presented as possible explanations.[5]

Other territorial variations are unrelated to population density. Some areas of the country have severe winter weather, which causes dangerous icing conditions. In other areas, sandstorms frequently cause comprehensive coverage losses to paint and windshields.

Sex and Marital Status

Underwriters have long recognized the ability of gender and marital status to predict future loss experience. The value of these two factors varies considerably with the age of the applicant. For example, young female drivers were generally considered to be better than young male drivers. For many years, young female drivers paid the same premiums as adult drivers. However, in recent years, young females have paid more than adult drivers in most states, but still considerably less than young males.

Exhibit 6-3 illustrates that there are more male than female drivers, that female drivers have a higher involvement in all accidents, and that male drivers are more likely to be involved in fatal accidents.

EXHIBIT 6-3

Sex of Drivers Involved in Accidents, 1996–2000

| | Drivers in all accidents | | | | Drivers in fatal accidents | | | |
| | Male | | Female | | Male | | Female | |
Year	Number	Rate*	Number	Rate*	Number	Rate**	Number	Rate**
1996	11,400,000	73	7,500,000	84	42,300	27	15,100	17
1997	14,300,000	90	9,600,000	103	43,600	27	16,100	17
1998	12,700,000	77	8,600,000	90	40,800	25	15,300	16
1999	10,600,000	63	7,400,000	74	30,400	18	11,800	12
2000	15,200,000	90	9,900,000	100	45,600	27	15,800	16

* Number of drivers in all accidents per 10 million miles driven.

** Number of drivers in fatal accidents per 1 billion miles driven.

Source: National Safety Council.

Adapted with permission from *The Fact Book 2002* (New York: Insurance Information Institute, 2002), p. 101.

The marital status of younger drivers is a factor in both rating and underwriting. Married male drivers under thirty usually pay less than their single counterparts because married persons in that age group generally tend to be more mature and responsible than single persons of the same age. Their marital situation also suggests that they spend more time at home.

Some states regulate the use of sex and marital status for underwriting purposes. A few states prohibit price discrimination on the basis of sex or marital status.

Occupation

The relationship between a person's occupation and driving habits is controversial. Some underwriting guides make distinctions on this basis; others do not. Certain occupations, such as traveling salespersons, require extensive driving and increase the probability of loss. This should be accounted for in the rates that reflect use of the vehicle.

Personal Characteristics

Underwriters often order consumer investigation reports to provide information on the personal characteristics of insured and other drivers. This information is subjective and must be carefully evaluated.

Many insurers use credit information to evaluate the stability of insurance applicants. Underwriters have demonstrated a correlation between poor credit risk and poor insurance risk. Critics of insurers' use of credit information suggest that the connection between the two factors is nonspecific and that the connection may mask factors that are prohibited for evaluation purposes, such as race.

Physical Condition

Physical impairments may be a problem if allowances for the impairment have not been made. Modifications of a car to accommodate a driver with physical impairments and a demonstrated mastery of the vehicle usually make the applicant acceptable.

Safety Equipment

Since the 1980s, many new cars have come equipped with advanced safety systems. Underwriters have begun to take these features into consideration. They allow rate discounts for antilock braking systems that reduce the number of accidents, and for passive restraint systems or air bags that reduce injuries to vehicle occupants.

Commercial Automobile Underwriting Factors

Public attitudes toward commercial automobiles differ from those held toward private passenger automobiles. The public knows that commercial firms usually carry insurance with high liability limits. Accordingly, an accident involving a commercial auto is likely to generate larger claims than a similar accident involving a personal automobile.

With most insurers, an analysis of a commercial automobile risk closely follows the characteristics used in rating the policy. Information that is key to policy pricing is essential to underwriting the exposure.

All commercial automobile policies are class-rated initially. Policies that develop enough premium are eligible for experience rating that modifies current premium to reflect past losses. Schedule rating is used to modify the premium for characteristics the rates do not fully reflect.

Trucks, tractors, and trailers, as well as those truckers hauling exclusively for one concern, are classified and rated using four factors:

1. Weight and type of vehicle
2. Use of the vehicle
3. Radius of operation
4. Special industry classifications

Weight and Type of Vehicle

The damage resulting from an accident is related to the size, or weight, and speed of the vehicles involved. Commercial tractor-trailer rigs can weigh 80,000 pounds or more when loaded and often travel at the maximum legal speed, so commercial vehicles are more likely than other vehicles to cause severe damage when an accident occurs. Large trucks are also difficult to maneuver in heavy traffic or on small inner-city streets. The vehicle weight and type are reflected in the primary rating classifications of commercial vehicles.

Use of the Vehicle

Commercial vehicles vary significantly in the intensity of use as well as how they are used. Some may be used almost continually in hauling goods, while others may be used only to travel to and from a job site, remaining parked most of the time. The ISO *Commercial Lines Manual* (*CLM*) divides business use into service, retail, and commercial use. Each of these classifications is described in the *CLM* and reflected in determining the primary classification to which the vehicle is assigned. The use classification measures the intensity with which the vehicle is driven.

Service use
A description of vehicle use that applies to vehicles used principally to transport personnel or material to a job site.

Retail use
A description of vehicle use that applies to vehicles used primarily for deliveries to and pickups from households.

Commercial use
A description of vehicle use that applies to any vehicle that does not fall into the service or retail use categories.

Service use applies to vehicles that are used principally to transport personnel or material to a job site. These vehicles are often driven to a job site at the start of a shift and remain there until the shift is over. Because they are used less intensely, service vehicles receive the lowest rate. **Retail use** means that the vehicle is used primarily for deliveries to and pickups from households. Drivers frequently follow unfamiliar routes and operate on tight schedules. This use class receives the highest rate. **Commercial use** applies to any vehicle that does not fall into one of the above two classes.

Radius of Operation

Radius of operations is significant in determining the primary classification because distance traveled (as well as the nature of travel) can affect accident frequency. Trucks operated over long distances may have more, and more severe, accidents than those operated locally. There are probably several reasons for this. A driver who operates a truck over long distances may not be as familiar with the route and its hazards as are drivers who operate trucks locally. Second, long-distance trucking is more likely to be more strictly scheduled. If drivers are rushing to meet a delivery deadline, resulting fatigue and excessive speeds can increase accident frequency. Finally, because long-haul trucks are large and usually travel at high speeds, they are typically involved in more severe accidents than trucks used within a city or town. (However, the expectation of a higher frequency of accidents for long-haul trucks is partly offset by the number of accidents that occur as a result of congested city traffic and the stop-start nature of city driving.)

The radius of operation is measured *on a straight line* from the street address of principal garaging. Over-the-road mileage is not used. Local is regular operation within a radius of 50 miles. Intermediate is regular operation within a radius of 51 to 200 miles. Long distance is regular operation in excess of a 200-mile radius.

There is no prescribed definition of regular operation. Some insurers use an 80 percent rule when the highest rate use applies, unless a lower-rated classification is used 80 percent of the time. An average of once a week has become an accepted standard in the absence of a ruling to the contrary by a state authority or the insurer involved. This interpretation does not preclude correcting a vehicle's classification for an extended change in use caused by seasonal factors or if the vehicle use has permanently changed. Underwriters should be familiar with the definition of regular operation used by their own companies.

Special Industry Classifications

Special industry classifications, or **secondary classifications**, consist of seven major industry classifications, each of which is further divided into subclassifications. The numerous classifications permit the capture of meaningful data by specialized use even though most of the subclassifications within an industry grouping carry the same rate. The major categories are as follows:

Secondary classifications
Commercial auto classifications that permit the capture of meaningful data by specialized use.

- *Truckers*—Vehicles used to transport the goods or materials of others; the category does not include moving household goods, office furniture, or fixtures and supplies.
- *Food delivery*—Vehicles used by wholesale food distributors and by food manufacturers to transport raw and finished products.
- *Specialized delivery*—Delivery vehicles such as armored cars or autos for delivering film, magazines or newspapers, mail and parcel post, and similar items.
- *Waste disposal*—Vehicles transporting waste material for disposal or resale.
- *Farmers*—Vehicles owned by farmers and used in farming operations.
- *Dump and transit mix trucks and trailers*—Vehicles are placed in this category when no other classification appropriately includes a vehicle's incidental dumping operation.
- *Contractors*—All vehicles used by contractors other than dump trucks.
- *Not otherwise specified*—Vehicles that cannot be classified in any other group.

Commercial Automobile Loss Control

The loss control activities of an insurer are important in achieving and maintaining the underwriting profitability of an account. Loss control representatives (LCRs) serve to make both drivers and managers more safety-conscious. In addition, they assist policyholders in developing vehicle inspection programs to address problems identified in loss control reports and create a positive approach to safety through safety programs.

Loss Control Reports

The loss control report can be a very important source of information for the underwriter. It confirms and supplements information (estimates of the cost of hire; type, scope, and efficiency of operations; physical condition of autos; losses; list of autos; and so on) found on the application.

For economic reasons, underwriters cannot inspect the operation of every commercial policyholder. Insurers usually establish certain criteria as to which risks are inspected and how often, but in any specific case, the commercial underwriter usually has the option of ordering a survey, either from the loss control department or from an outside firm.

Policy size and/or premium amount are important, but they are not the only criteria for requesting inspections. Autos handling liquefied petroleum gas, acids, corrosive chemicals, flammable materials, or explosives are usually inspected before being bound. Inspections are routine when extremely high limits of liability are requested. The type or size of the autos frequently causes a commercial auto underwriter to seek additional information from an inspection.

The policyholder's accident record is an important factor considered by the loss control representative in making recommendations to the policyholder for improving his or her desirability as a risk. Several backing losses may indicate a need for additional loss control systems. Better rearview mirror systems help, but they cannot always let the driver see well enough to avoid backing losses. The solution may lie in having a walking ground guide direct the driver in backing up. Several proximity alarms are also on the market that alert drivers to hazards in blind spots directly behind the vehicle and to the sides. They are more effective than mirrors.

A high frequency of theft or vandalism claims may indicate a need for better vehicle protection. The type and extent of protection would be at least partly determined by the location of vehicles when stolen or vandalized. Finally, the location of losses reported by the loss control representative may alert the underwriter to the fact that the actual radius of operations is greater than that indicated on the application.

For these reasons, the policyholder's system for recording losses, including those losses that are not covered by insurance (for example, below the deductible amount), is important to the loss control representative when conducting the loss control survey. An application for insurance often lists only the insured losses that the applicant has had. Perhaps the applicant keeps records only of the losses large enough to report to the insurer or has received a list of losses from the present insurer and has included that list with the application.

In addition, because of higher physical damage deductibles ($500 to $1,000 or more) usually written on commercial autos, many small accidents are not reported. This makes the loss frequency appear better than it is. The vehicle condition also deteriorates if damage from small accidents is not repaired. For these reasons, the ability of the loss control representative to report the uninsured losses on the loss control survey is important to the underwriter. Loss control representatives can often assist the policyholder in establishing an effective record-keeping system or improving the current system.

Safety Programs

Policyholders with a fleet of autos should have a formal, written safety program. An underwriter can learn a good deal about a policyholder by examining the details of the safety program and the records associated with that program. Smaller commercial auto risks should also have some plan, even if it is informal and not written.

The following are seven essential elements of a good fleet safety program that an underwriter should take into consideration:

1. Driver selection
2. Driver training and motivation
3. Equipment control
4. Accident reporting and review
5. Periodic checking of drivers and vehicles
6. Enforcement and reinforcement of the program
7. Management support of the program

An important point to remember is that although industrial safety programs depend on the first-line supervisors to monitor and help implement safety procedures, fleet safety programs rely almost entirely on the auto operators, not fleet supervisors, to supervise their actions behind the wheel. Nevertheless, fleet supervisors can schedule occasional trips with each driver as a check on the driver's habits and as a show of managerial support.

Some policyholders also conduct periodic on-the-road evaluations of their drivers to see whether they are obeying the laws and following company procedures. This is a positive factor, but it must be followed up with corrective action. It does little good to find out which drivers are speeding if the policyholder does not do anything about it. These evaluations and their results should be included in the safety program records that the underwriter reviews.

There are firms that specialize in road patrol (that is, on-the-road spot-checks of drivers). Companies may hire such firms to check their vehicles. In some cases, they give the "engineer" for the road patrol firm the authority to pull over the drivers (where laws and highway conditions permit) to check further into the driver's and the truck's conditions. Underwriters cannot require policyholders to use such firms. However, underwriters view applicants that use such firms as more desirable because of their concern for safety.

One factor the engineers often uncover is the presence of unauthorized personnel in truck cabs. In addition, of the many factors they examine— speed, entries in the driver's log, vehicle condition, time of observation, and location—the last two items might prove important if drivers are taking unauthorized routes.

Using a road patrol is a positive factor in the underwriter's evaluation of a risk, but only if the firm uses the resulting reports to take corrective action. Underwriters should request the reports filed on drivers and ask what corrective action, if any, was taken.

Insurance Requirements for Commercial Automobiles

The Motor Carrier Act of 1980 requires certain motor carriers to meet financial responsibility requirements and to demonstrate that they do so. Although motor carriers can meet financial responsibility requirements by obtaining a surety bond, most satisfy this requirement through insurance. Most states have financial responsibility requirements for intrastate motor carriers.

The Motor Carrier Act imposes this financial responsibility requirement on motor carriers based on their operation and the type of commodity they carry. The Motor Carrier Act divides motor carriers into four categories and requires different financial responsibility limits for each category. The regulations provide extensive detail on the types of carriers and commodities. Motor carriers not carrying hazardous materials in interstate or foreign commerce and motor carriers carrying hazardous materials must comply with the Motor Carrier Act. The financial responsibility limits range from $1,000,000 for motor carriers engaged in interstate commerce but not carrying hazardous materials to $5,000,000 for motor carriers that haul explosives, poisonous gas, or radioactive materials. There are also provisions for small freight carriers, not falling within the categories mentioned above, that carry specific commodities to meet a financial responsibility requirement of $300,000.

Motor carriers meeting the financial responsibility requirements through insurance must get their insurer to add a specified form to their commercial automobile insurance. The MCS-90, or "Endorsement for Motor Carrier Policies of Insurance for Public Liability Under Sections 29 and 30 of the Motor Carrier Act of 1980," imposes additional responsibilities on the insurer. The MCS-90 amends the insurance policy to comply with the act and removes some of the defenses that the insurer would normally have without the presence of the form. For example, the insurer would be responsible for injuries caused by insured-owned vehicles not identified on the policy or from trucking routes not described in the application. Additionally, the Motor Carrier Act requires insurers to give motor carriers thirty-five days' notice of cancellation and thirty days' notice to the Department of Transportation. Insurer payments for claims not normally covered by the insurance policy but required because of the presence of the MCS-90 can be recovered from the insured. Unfortunately for the insurer, it is unlikely that the insured will repay. Underwriters usually analyze a motor carrier's financial stability when evaluating an account.

UNDERWRITING GENERAL LIABILITY

General liability insurance has developed into a package of coverages including the following:

1. Liability for bodily injury and property damage that arise out of the insured's business operations or premises
2. Personal and advertising injury liability
3. Premises medical payments
4. Fire legal liability
5. Liability the insured assumes under contract

Commercial general liability coverage forms also include products and completed operations liability. Because both the coverage and the factors the underwriter considers in the risk selection decision are materially different from other exposures, this section treats products and completed operations liability as a separate line of business.

The exposure for general liability insurance is based on the exposure of the public to the hazards of the insured's business premises and operations. Underwriters often refer to the components of this exposure as hazards. They speak of the premises hazard, the operations in progress hazard, and the personal injury hazard. This use of the term "hazard" refers to potential liability exposures that can lead to legal action against the insured. The analysis of liability exposures usually tracks the coverage forms most likely to provide satisfactory coverage.

The public includes customers, representatives of suppliers, anyone else associated with the business, and the general public. Although all businesses have this liability exposure, the extent of the exposure varies widely. An underwriter will want to know whether the exposure is common for the classification and how much variation in the exposure is likely.

Occurrence and Claims-Made Coverage

The commercial general liability policy (CGL) has two versions: occurrence and claims-made. The feature that distinguishes the two forms is the definition of the event that triggers the coverage, called a coverage trigger. The occurrence form uses the traditional coverage trigger found in most liability policy forms. The insurer agrees to pay damages for bodily injury or property damage that occurs while the policy is in force. It does not matter when the claim is made. Under the claims-made form, the insurer agrees to pay damages for bodily injury or property damage for which a claim is first made during the policy period. Claims-made policies were designed to eliminate the long delay between the time a loss occurs and the time it is settled. A pharmaceutical manufacturer, for instance, can expect to receive claims in many future years from injuries that occur in the current year. Claims-made policies enable insurers to capture final claim data more quickly for ratemaking purposes. The claims-made policy has never been used to the extent insurers once envisioned, but underwriters need to understand the differences between the forms and how they operate.

Premises and Operations Exposures

The premises and operations hazard has two distinct components. **Premises liability exposures** arise from the ownership or possession of real property. **Operations liability exposures** arise from a policyholder's business activities conducted away from its own premises and from work uncompleted. To distinguish the *operations* hazard from the **completed operations hazard** (injuries arising from finished work), underwriters frequently refer to the former as *operations in progress* (injuries arising while the work is being performed).

Premises liability exposures
Liability exposures that exist when there is ownership, occupancy, or use of property (the premises).

Operations liability exposures
Liability exposures arising from a policyholder's business activities conducted away from its own premises and from work uncompleted.

Completed operations hazard
Hazards or exposures arising from an organization's finished work or products sold.

The liability exposures most businesses face arise principally from either the premises they own or occupy or the operations the businesses conduct. This has led underwriters to divide premises and operations exposures into two classes, *premises* and *operations*. Underwriters think of a retail store, for example, as a premises exposure. A building contractor presents an operations in progress hazard. Underwriters recognize that insureds whose exposure is mainly related to their premises also face liability for their operations in progress. Underwriters treat the operations exposure as incidental to the premises hazard. By the same token, when the operations in progress hazard is dominant, underwriters recognize an incidental premises hazard. This is a useful technique for analyzing the exposures and does not reflect a perception that the exposure is exclusively premises or operations.

The level of exposure to liability varies with the type of business. Some differences in the extent of exposure may be a result of location, type of business, time in business, or a combination of the three. For example, a store with a good reputation and steady business is more likely to attract customers than a new store or one that is on the decline. The increase in customer traffic increases the exposure. Location may create a similar increase in traffic and, thus, in the extent of exposure. A downtown electronics store may open up a new branch in a suburban shopping mall. A mall usually has several well-known large stores that attract traffic to other, smaller stores in the mall. People who are in the mall to shop are much more likely to enter the electronics store premises than pedestrians on city streets would be. In addition, because of differences in store hours and customers' shopping habits, a greater percentage of mall customers are likely to be present at nights or on weekends. Even if the total number of customers were average for the class, the mall electronics store would have a relatively high concentration of customers at certain hours. Fire exposure also increases in extent because the setup of a mall and higher customer traffic make it less likely that customers would be able to exit the premises quickly. In contrast, the extent of most weather-related exposures would decrease for a store located in a mall, because the quality of mall maintenance usually helps to eliminate such premises hazards as icy walkways or sidewalks. Each risk must be underwritten individually so that the exposure can be evaluated.

Nevertheless, a concentration of people does not necessarily indicate excessive exposure. What may create an underwriting problem for the electronics store would not do so for a theater. The rate for the store may be inadequate, while the rate for the theater may be sufficient because it anticipates concentrations of people.

Consideration must also be given to the legal status of persons likely to be on the premises. What is the policyholder's legal duty to these persons, and what standards of care are expected? The policyholder must demonstrate behavior that is consistent with the standard of care required. A comparison must be made between the duties owed by the policyholder and an average risk in the same classification. If the results of the comparison are the same, there is usually no problem, but if they vary, the underwriter must account for the difference. For example, a retail store with mostly adult customers may need to exercise reasonable care, but a toy store attracting a large number of children may need to exercise additional care.

Bodily injury usually receives the primary emphasis in underwriting because it tends to produce larger losses. An underwriter cannot, on the other hand, ignore the potential for property damage losses. Property damage losses include claims not only for the value of the damaged property but also for the loss of its use.

Physical Hazards

Physical hazards are as important to underwriting liability coverage as they are in any other line of business. Underwriters classify physical hazards into the same classes used for other lines of business. Many physical hazards, such as those that induce slips and falls, are common to many premises. They are common hazards. Other physical hazards, such as chemicals, dust, and explosives, occur only in certain types of businesses. These are the special hazards of the class. Some businesses conduct operations that are not typical of the class to which they belong; they are considered to be special hazards of the risk.

Many types of accidents likely to occur within a building (slipping, falling, tears, cuts, and burns) are the result of conditions or hazards that may be present on the premises. The causes of the injuries are what is important to the underwriter. The underwriter tries to determine what hazards or conditions increase the likelihood of injury or damage for which the owner or lessor of the premises will be held liable. Some of the more common hazards are uneven stairs, tears in carpets, inadequate lighting, congested aisles, poor housekeeping, and defective heating or electrical equipment. Other hazards, such as the presence of sharp objects, flammable liquids, explosives, toxic gases, and welding equipment, are usually found only on premises at which specific operations are located. The potential number of hazards at various premises is almost unlimited.

When evaluating the physical hazards of a premises exposure, underwriters have to consider the entire premises. When the principal exposures arise from the interior of the premises, underwriters cannot afford to overlook exposures to loss associated with the exterior. Injuries can be caused outside the building by broken or icy sidewalks, parking lots in poor condition, falling signs, building collapse, playground equipment, swimming pools, and other features of the property. Mobile equipment could cause injury inside or outside the building, depending on the type and use of the equipment.

Generally, businesses with heavy premises exposures like apartment houses and office buildings have minimal operations exposures. Businesses with small premises exposures, such as service businesses and contractors, have substantial operations exposures. An electrical contractor is likely to have a place of business, but it is not likely to be a significant factor in risk selection. A store and shop where electrical fixtures are sold and repaired, on the other hand, would constitute a premises exposure that an underwriter would have to assess separately. Typical contractors have little premises exposure, but they have substantial operations exposures because of installation and repair work. An electrical contractor who has a sales and repair operation on the premises has both a premises and an operations exposure.

The hazards related to an operations exposure vary more than do those related to a premises exposure. Each service or contracting risk uses different tools. Some have heavy machinery or mobile equipment; some use flammables and blowtorches; some rent or lease equipment; and some blast, excavate, or erect. The builders of both single, ranch-style residences and high-rise apartments do similar work, use similar tools, and create attractive nuisances at construction sites, but the similarity ends there. The high-rise building contractor works with steel girders, land leveling equipment, deep excavations, and hoists, often in heavily populated areas. The variation in hazard as a result of these differences is great.

In addition to the bodily injury exposure of premises-type risks, an underwriter must also consider the physical hazards that can cause property damage losses. Torn or stained clothing and damage to vehicles in parking lots are the most common property damage losses. Pollution has become one of the most important sources of severe losses. This is a factor to consider when the insured requests limited pollution coverage under the general liability coverage form. A premises exposure, such as an apartment house, may appear innocuous. The building may, however, have an oil-fired heating system fed from an underground storage tank. This presents a serious exposure that most underwriters prefer to leave for specialists in environmental impairment liability.

Operations-type risks generally have a greater potential for causing property damage losses than do premises-type risks. A contractor, for example, was hired to repaint the exterior fixtures on a fire-resistive building. A painter at the same site was using a propane torch to remove scaling paint from the cooling tower on the building's roof. When the painters broke for lunch, the painter failed to turn off the torch. The unattended flame ignited the flammable fill of the cooling tower, causing a fire and a six-figure property damage liability loss. Leased equipment can damage a customer's property if it is not kept in good repair or if a customer misuses it. Use of heavy equipment is likely to cause serious property damage, but the major sources of property damage losses are fire, collapse, water damage, and, in some cases, pollution.

Premises—An Example

A department store presents many of the hazards inherent in a premises exposure. This store is located in a multistory, fire-resistive structure in an urban shopping district. Although the exposure is primarily a premises one due to the number of people who visit the store, an operations exposure arising from store deliveries and installation work also exists.

Common hazards such as uneven stairs, congested aisles, loose wires, worn floors, and poor lighting can present bodily injury hazards in a department store. Even well-maintained department stores have premises hazards, such as elevators, escalators, and revolving doors, that are simply a function of normal department-store construction. Other areas and items in the store, like the toy department, playrooms, pools and fountains, and glass showcases, might be hazardous, and the underwriter must evaluate them. Sidewalks and parking lots, especially if they are not well maintained, create external premises exposures.

Many department stores have cooking demonstrations to show new products. If a propane tank were to explode, injuries would likely result not only from the explosion but also from the ensuing fire. Fire, in fact, is usually the primary cause of severe loss in a department store. When fire breaks out, customers may be trampled in the rush to escape the danger, or the crush of the crowd may block exits and trap a large number of people inside. The best way to control this hazard is to prevent fire from breaking out, but if a fire does start, it must be controlled. Adequate means of egress are also essential, so exit routes should be clearly marked. Swinging doors that open outward on either side of revolving doors can facilitate a quick and easy exit in the event of an emergency.

For most department stores, property damage exposures are not as great as bodily injury exposures. Frequent slips and falls often involve minor property damage claims for damaged clothing, but they could also result in severe losses. If the store has a parking lot, the possibility of auto damage exists. Department stores that provide services such as equipment installation and repair have, in addition to a premises exposure, an operations exposure that increases the potential for property damage.

If loss experience shows that a department store has a high frequency of injuries caused by falls, the underwriter must determine the reason. Are the falls due to poor surface conditions, such as torn carpets? Do they occur principally in the aisles, on the escalators or elevators, or at the entrances and exits? Are the stairways well lighted? Do the elevators stop evenly with the floors or move suddenly? After the hazard has been identified, the under-writer must make sure the insured addresses the hazards. Accident statistics are available for many industries. By comparing them to the insured's loss experience, underwriters determine how a store compares to the "average."

A department store might have a substantial frequency of "struck by object" and "struck against object" accidents. Are these accidents caused by narrow or congested aisles, poor housekeeping, or stockroom personnel pushing carts? Whatever the hazard, the underwriter must determine whether it can be controlled; otherwise, the frequency of claims can be expected to continue.

Operations—An Example

Consider a firm that sells, repairs, and installs home security systems. The primary exposure for this business is the possibility of loss arising out of operations conducted in the homes of customers. Bodily injury losses could result from service personnel who carelessly leave tools where customers can trip over them. Generally, however, the underwriter would not expect a high frequency of bodily injury claims from a home security system sales and repair business. Instead, such a business would be expected to generate a high frequency of property damage losses. Installing a security system usually involves sliding wires through attics, basements, and walls so that every window and door is tied to the alarm system. This installation process can result in property damage losses.

Just as with the department store example used above, the underwriter can review past loss experience. Losses can be categorized to identify trends.

The frequency and severity of property damage losses depend primarily on the nature of the operations of the particular business. If most of the installations are done on homes in the process of construction rather than on completed homes, the frequency of loss should be reduced. A key factor in evaluating loss severity is the quality of workmanship. Are the installation personnel well trained? How long have they been performing their jobs? How much supervision do they get?

This kind of operation exposure can also create severe as well as frequent losses. In addition, frequent losses increase the likelihood of random severe losses. A given hazard may produce widely different levels of loss severity. For example, wiring a security system incorrectly might produce an electrical short that starts a house fire.

Unexpected Physical Hazards

Underwriters must consider an additional and rather unpredictable factor in reviewing an account for general liability insurance. Special hazards of the risk may exist. The business may have exposures to loss that are not characteristic of the class as a whole. This may present a greater exposure of loss than the rates for the class contemplate. Underwriters must identify for a particular account any special hazards of the risk and decide whether they present unacceptable liability exposures. These hazards could evolve from an incidental operation, a "one-shot deal," a gradual diversification of operations, or an assumption of operations not contemplated when the risk was originally insured and priced.

As mentioned, some department stores provide special services that add operations exposures to a normally premises-only type of business. Many stores also have an auto service area, a grocery section, or a restaurant. Department stores or any business can sponsor sporting events either as a promotional activity or for the benefit of employees. Such activities are not inherent in the operation of the business, and therefore, any related hazard is relatively unexpected; yet such activities could significantly increase the likelihood of a liability loss.

Exposures in the home security systems business can also deviate from the norm. The owner could enter into a contract with a contractor who builds large residential developments. This may mean hiring extra employees without having the benefit of training them completely or burdening the regular employees with rush jobs, which may result in carelessness or lower-quality workmanship. The home security system operation could also expand into other types of work, such as installing telephone and television cabling. Do the employees have the ability and expertise to perform these tasks? Peak seasons, demonstrations, exhibits, and hiring subcontractors are other conditions that might create unexpected hazards that could increase the liability exposure of department stores and home security systems businesses beyond the scope of their particular class.

Contractors and Subcontractors

The policyholder may be liable for the negligent acts of contractors or subcontractors hired to perform work. Generally, a property owner or contractor who has hired an "independent contractor" is not liable under common law for the independent contractor's negligent acts. An independent contractor performs his or her work without specific direction as to *how* the work is to be performed. In some instances, courts have held that an independent contractor is a de facto employee. This eliminates the common-law immunity the principal or contractor enjoys. Determining who is responsible for activities that cause injury is particularly a problem when contractors and subcontractors are individuals without employees. It is easy for the injured party to claim that work was directed by the property owner.

The law also holds the insured vicariously liable for duties that cannot be delegated to others. A principal has a duty to select a competent independent contractor and provide a level of general supervision adequate to protect the public from injury. Thus, either an owner of land (as an employer of a general contractor) or a general contractor (as an employer of a subcontractor) may be held liable to third persons for the negligent acts of contractors or subcontractors. The underwriting implications of this exposure could be significant. Admittedly, the policyholder's liability for the acts of others is less significant than liability for its own acts.

However, the potential exposure exists, and coverage is included in the general liability coverage forms. For all business classifications other than contractors, there are no special classification and rating rules because the potential exposure is minimal. For contractor classes, subcontractors need to be evaluated to determine whether they carry adequate insurance. If they do, only a small charge is made to cover those circumstances when the policyholder may be held liable for the work of the subcontractor. The underwriter should treat subcontractors who fail to provide evidence of insurance as the insured's employees.

An insured does not know at the outset of the policy term which subcontractors will be hired during the year, so this is a major concern for the underwriter. The underwriter is therefore placed at a disadvantage, since the subcontractors cannot be evaluated before writing the policy. The underwriter has to rely on the policyholder's reputation for being selective in hiring subcontractors. When the subcontractors are known, the insurer can require certificates of insurance from the subcontractors.

Contractual Liability Coverage

Commercial general liability coverage forms contain a contractual liability exclusion that serves to define coverage for liability the insured assumes under a contract or an agreement. They provide what was once known as broad form contractual liability coverage. With a few exceptions, it covers any liability the insured assumes under a contract related to the business.

Hold Harmless Agreements

Hold harmless agreement
A contractual provision that obligates the indemnitor to assume the legal liability of the indemnitee.

Indemnitor
The party in a hold harmless agreement who assumes the legal liability of the other party.

Indemnitee
The party in a hold harmless agreement whose legal liability is assumed by the indemnitor.

A contract under which one party assumes the liability of another is called a **hold harmless agreement**. The name derives from the customary language in which one party, the **indemnitor**, agrees to *save, indemnify and hold harmless* the other party, the **indemnitee**. Like an insurance policy, a hold harmless agreement is a contract of indemnity. The principal differences are that the indemnitor in a hold harmless agreement is not in the business of assuming risk, and that a hold harmless agreement is rarely a separate contract. It is usually a clause in a contract that has a broader purpose.

Insured Contracts

ISO commercial general liability forms define an "insured contract" as follows:

a. A contract for a lease of premises. However, that portion of the contract for a lease of premises that indemnifies any person or organization for damage by fire to premises contract while rented to you or temporarily occupied by you with permission of the owner is not an "insured contract";

b. A sidetrack agreement;

c. Any easement or license agreement, except in connection with construction or demolition operations on or within 50 feet of a railroad;

d. An obligation, as required by ordinance, to indemnify a municipality, except in connection with work for a municipality;

e. An elevator maintenance agreement;

f. That part of any other contract or agreement pertaining to your business (including an indemnification of a municipality in connection with work performed for a municipality) under which you assume the tort liability of another party to pay for "bodily injury" or "property damage" to a third person or organization. Tort liability means a liability that would be imposed by law in the absence of any contract or agreement.[6]

The first five sections of this definition cover incidental contracts. General liability forms have always included coverage for these contracts. The sixth section provides broad form contractual liability coverage. It covers liability the insured assumes under almost any contract relating to the operation of the business.

Limiting coverage to the tort liability of another person the insured assumes under contract addresses a problem some risk managers perceived in older forms. A business sometimes signs a contract under which it assumes only its own liability imposed by law in the absence of a contract. This raises the question of whether liability is assumed under a contract. Some risk managers could imagine an insurer's rejecting a claim based on the insured's negligence because it was also the subject of a hold harmless agreement. This issue was important when a contractual liability exclusion was common, but it has little meaning today.

Risk managers began to perceive another problem with the definition of contractual liability. They assumed that contractual liability coverage in the older forms included defense. Although this is not true, and the newer forms actually provided broader coverage, insurers responded to the perceived problem. Since March 1996, contractual liability has also covered the cost of defending the indemnitee against claims for which the insured would be liable in the absence of a contract. This coverage does not apply when the indemnitee's interests are in conflict with the insurer's. This situation occurs most often when a suit alleges negligence of both the indemnitor and the indemnitee. Each party's best defense is often to shift responsibility to the other. Coverage for defense of the indemnitee also requires that the insurance company be able to assign the same counsel to defend both the indemnitee and the insured.

Underwriting Contractual Liability

An underwriter cannot know at inception what liability an insured will assume during the policy term. This is similar to the situation that exists when an insured employs independent contractors. When evaluating this exposure, an underwriter can rely on the insured's reputation and past practices.

The two parties to a hold harmless agreement often presume that one party assumes the entire liability of the other. They rely on the indemnitor's insurance to protect both parties from liability losses. This is especially true when a certificate of insurance lists contractual liability coverage. Certain types of hold harmless agreements, however, fall outside the scope of contractual liability coverage. Statutes in most states also limit using hold harmless agreements in certain situations. Courts in some instances have found that hold harmless agreements are so vague that they are meaningless. Extremely broad assumptions of liability may violate public policy. In these instances, the indemnitee has not transferred the exposure, despite the contract.

Products and Completed Operations Exposures

Any business may incur liability for injuries caused by products it makes, sells, distributes, or even gives away. Many service businesses, such as builders and repair shops, face a similar exposure from the work they perform for others.

Sources of Products Liability

Liability for the sale, manufacture, and distribution of products can arise from breach of warranty, the tort of negligence, and strict liability in tort. It is not uncommon for the plaintiff to assert all three causes of action in a products liability suit.

The oldest basis for imposing liability on the maker or seller of a defective product is **breach of warranty**. This is a cause of action based on breach of contract. In every sale of merchandise, the law implies warranties of merchantability and fitness for the product's intended use. The seller may also

Breach of warranty
A cause for legal action based on laws that provide protection for consumers who purchase products that do not perform as expected.

make an express warranty of fitness for a specific purpose. Breach of warranty suffers from inherent limitations as a basis for a product liability action. This has led courts to recognize other grounds for products liability.

Negligence extends protection to a broader range of persons who may suffer injury from a defective product, but it is often difficult to prove. A plaintiff can rarely point to a specific act of negligence in a products liability action. In order to permit plaintiffs to recover for legitimate injuries, the courts recognize the **doctrine of *res ipsa loquitur***. This rule of law shifts the burden of proof from the plaintiff to the defendant when the following are true:

Doctrine of *res ipsa loquitur*
("The thing speaks for itself.")
Doctrine that applies when direct evidence of negligence is lacking, but the facts of the occurrence may warrant an inference of negligence.

1. The event that is the proximate cause of injury does not ordinarily occur in the absence of negligence.
2. Sufficient evidence exists to eliminate other possible causes.
3. The circumstances indicate a negligent act that falls within the defendant's duty to the plaintiff.

Res ipsa loquitur creates a presumption of negligence when the facts suggest that there is no other possible explanation. The defendant has the opportunity to rebut the presumption of negligence.

Many products essential to maintaining the quality of life cannot be made free of danger. The hazards of these products, however, are not always obvious. The makers of these products have a duty to warn potential consumers of any danger that is not generally known to the public. Failure to give adequate warnings is the most common charge of negligence in products liability suits.

The most frequent basis for products liability suits is a relatively new doctrine, strict liability in tort. This rule of law is sometimes referred to as simply strict liability and is often confused with the doctrine of absolute or strict liability that imposes liability in the absence of fault. It first appeared in a 1963 California case,[7] and almost every state has adopted this doctrine since then. Strict liability in tort imposes liability on any person who releases an unreasonably dangerous product into the stream of commerce. It is difficult to imagine how this could occur in the absence of negligence or an intentional act.

Products Liability Underwriting Considerations

The evolution of the law of products liability requires the underwriter to place emphasis on the product itself. The underwriter has to be concerned with the potential exposure of the public to products hazards. The frequency and severity of losses a product is likely to cause are the primary concerns. Although many factors can affect the product's exposure, if the product is not inherently hazardous, there is significantly less exposure to loss. To illustrate, consider two products: a power lawn mower and a pillow. The lawn mower is a much more hazardous product than the pillow because of its inherent characteristics that increase the likelihood of loss. Determining the inherent hazards of the product is therefore the first and most important step in underwriting a product. This would be followed by an analysis of the exposure of the public to these product hazards.

The quantity of information needed by the underwriter varies with the nature of the product. Much of the information presented earlier in the text regarding premises and operations underwriting also applies to underwriting products coverage. The business of the applicant, the limits of liability, and the size and scope of the business are important in underwriting both types of coverage. As in underwriting premises and operations liability, the first source of information for products underwriting is the application. However, most applications have a section (or the insurer has a separate questionnaire) that requires information about products liability exposures.

The underwriter must consider other information in order to get a complete picture of the applicant's exposures. This information either supplements or verifies what is shown on the application.

The underwriter should also ask the following questions:

- What are the inherent hazards of the product?
- What representations or promises are made to the consumer in the sales material and advertising?
- Do technical manuals for complex products accurately reflect the safety precautions required in the product's assembly and repair?
- Does the product's packaging adequately protect the product so that it will operate properly when used?
- Are the instructions easy to read and understand?
- Does the product's warranty overstate the capability of the product?
- Are loss control efforts introduced into the product's design and production phases of product development?
- Is a complaint-handling system in place to identify flaws and prevent further injuries?
- Are quality control checks incorporated into the product's manufacture?
- Are accurate records kept of products and components so that defective products can be identified and recalled?
- Have product lines changed to increase the inherent hazards?
- What is the applicant's position in the channel of distribution?
- Who is the ultimate consumer of this product?

The bases on which courts assess products liability are not independent. Plaintiffs increase their chances of winning a products liability case when they assert more than one ground for recovery. This increases the product liability losses underwriters have to pay. The owner of a sport utility vehicle, for instance, was injured when the car overturned on a road. A court found that the propensity to overturn did not render the product unreasonably dangerous. It was a reasonable hazard for an off-road vehicle. As a result, the plaintiff lost the strict liability in tort action. The manufacturer's advertising, however, had portrayed the vehicle as a suitable family car. An appeals court ruled that this allowed a jury to infer that the manufacturer had breached an express warranty of fitness for a specific purpose. The court upheld the award against the manufacturer on those grounds.[8] This case turned on the insured's advertising rather than on the hazards inherent in the product.

Completed Operations Underwriting

Completed operations are characterized by a wide range of possible hazards. Activities that generate completed operations hazards include construction, service, repair, and maintenance. The characteristic that distinguishes completed operations from products liability is the existence of the insured's completed work that may cause injury or damage.

There are relatively few completed operations classifications as compared to other lines of business. Lack of sufficient claims data sometimes accounts for this. Completed operations exposures are also included within other exposures. Products classes often include completed operations. Some premises and operations classifications also include the completed operations hazard. These include nursing homes, photographers, printers, and swimming pool installers.

As in the case of the other general liability sublines, the underwriter must classify the completed operations exposure correctly. An incorrect classification will not generate the proper premium for the exposure. If the rate is too high, it will drive away profitable business. If the rate is too low, underwriters can expect to sustain losses they cannot afford.

Businesses that perform services generally have an operations rather than a premises exposure. Consequently, such businesses are likely to have completed operations exposures. The activities or operations, particularly those performed off-premises, that could cause a loss are the basis of operations underwriting. Thus, the manner in which the job is performed is important to the underwriter in evaluating the exposure to loss. Quality of workmanship and equipment, supervision of employees, technical skill, reputation, and years of experience are all factors that help the underwriter evaluate the operations exposure. If any of these qualities is lacking to any significant degree, the underwriter would conclude that the loss potential arising out of the operations has been increased. These same risk characteristics are important in evaluating the completed operations exposure. For example, faulty workmanship is likely to cause a loss while the work is being performed, but it will also increase the potential of loss occurring after the work is completed.

A home security system installer who has careless work habits or lacks technical knowledge could damage the customer's premises and even cause a fire. The same conditions could also cause a loss after the installer finishes the work and leaves the premises. The damage or injury that results falls within the completed operations exposure. The underwriter has to assess the increase in the overall liability exposure from the completed operations hazard. Lack of technical knowledge or faulty workmanship is likely to increase loss frequency to the same degree for both.

The nature of the operation affects the severity of the losses it will produce. The hazards the underwriter has to consider may be different for each subline and class. A contractor building high-rise apartments is an example. While constructing the building, workers can cause extensive property damage from fire, collapse, or water, as well as bodily injury from falling objects, the operation of equipment, and the use of construction materials and tools. After the apartments are inhabited, fire or collapse could cause even more serious injuries and damages. If the cause could be traced to the faulty workmanship of the contractor, the insurer who underwrote the completed operations exposure would be responsible for the loss. In this particular case, the characteristics affecting loss frequency are greatly reduced once the building is completed, but the potential severity is greatly increased. At the other extreme, a piano tuner could cause damage to the customer's property while in the process of performing the work, but it is extremely unlikely that injury or damage would occur after the work is completed. Logically, piano tuning is an operations classification in which the completed operations exposure is included in the rate.

In evaluating an applicant for completed operations coverage, the underwriter must determine the likelihood and severity of potential losses by evaluating the nature of the applicant's business. The completed operations exposure may be considerably different from the operations exposure for a class, just as the exposure to loss as a result of the operations hazard varies from one risk to another within a class.

WORKERS COMPENSATION UNDERWRITING

Workers compensation insurance includes statutory workers compensation coverage and employers liability coverage for employers whose employees may be killed or injured or may acquire an occupational disease in the course of their employment. It is compulsory in all states except New Jersey, South Carolina, and Texas. Even in those states, most employers carry workers compensation coverage. Benefits include death benefits, disability income, medical expense, and rehabilitation expense as required by the applicable workers compensation laws. Employers liability insurance covers employers for their legal liability to an employee for injury arising out of and in the course of employment that is not covered under the workers compensation law.

Workers compensation is a major line of insurance in the United States. It represents 8 percent of all property-casualty insurance premium income, second only to auto insurance.[9] The loss experience in this line of business is closely related to the prevailing economic and political environments. For several years, workers compensation was an unprofitable line of business. Rising costs of medical treatment increased the claims insurers had to pay. Wages, the base used for premium determinations, did not keep pace with rising medical and litigation costs. Insurers sought to pass the increased costs on to employers in the form of higher rates. This generated political pressure to limit rate level adjustments. Many observers believed that workers compensation coverage would never again generate a reasonable profit.

When insurers focused their attention on controlling losses, their results improved. They began a program of case management to control loss costs. When state statutes were an impediment, they worked for reform. In 1994, these efforts met with success. Insurers earned an operating profit on workers compensation for the first time in ten years. Sound underwriting and proactive loss control succeeded in improving their results, and the trend shows every indication of continuing.

The workers compensation and employers liability policy is probably the most standardized liability insurance policy. The form is designed to provide complete coverage for employee injuries except for specified exclusions. The policy combines blanket coverage for obligations imposed by the state workers compensation law and broad coverage for other employers liability. This broad coverage and the additional flexibility provided by endorsements spare policyholders the necessity of revising the insurance program every time a new location is established or when some other change in the business occurs.

An interesting feature of this policy is that it contains uniform provisions, even though workers compensation benefits vary by jurisdiction. The same policy can be used for basic coverages in various states without endorsements because the compensation laws of those states, not the policy provisions, control the conditions of coverage. The workers compensation laws are specifically incorporated into the policy contract by the reference in the policy. Thus, an underwriter analyzing the coverage and benefits provided must read the applicable statutes as well as the policy. The use of the standard policy by all insurers, together with uniform underwriting rules, also enables rating bureaus to calculate sound rates.

Workers Compensation Underwriting Considerations

Underwriting workers compensation insurance is similar to underwriting general liability insurance. The difference is that general liability insurance deals with injuries to the general public, while workers compensation responds to injuries to one's own employees. In many businesses, the general public and employees share the same environment, as is the case with retail stores. Businesses such as manufacturers have a closed environment so that the activities within the workplace can potentially be more controlled. To a large extent, general liability underwriting and workers compensation have many of the same hazards and the same type of analysis required to evaluate those hazards.

Beyond the physical hazards, general liability and workers compensation lines differ drastically in their perception by insurer management. Not all insurers offer workers compensation insurance coverage. Of those insurers that do, most have fairly regimented procedures that guide underwriters in making individual decisions on applicants within classes approved by underwriting management.

To make a profit or minimize their losses, most insurers have established strict underwriting guidelines. The most desirable situation occurs when workers compensation coverage is provided as part of an overall account. Many insurers, however, continue to write workers compensation on its own merits.

Some insurers restrict their writing to those applicants who are eligible for experience rating. This requirement relates less to the effect of experience rating than to other factors. The experience rating plan of the National Council on Compensation Insurance (NCCI) is used in most states. The eligibility requirements vary by state, but in general, the applicant's payroll that developed in the last year or the last two years of the experience period must have produced a certain premium. If an applicant is eligible for experience rating, the experience rating program is mandatory. Many insurers do not believe that they can underwrite accounts that do not meet the minimum requirements for experience rating. Their fixed costs make it difficult to earn a profit on very small accounts. Larger accounts that are not eligible have usually been in operation less than two years. That is a negative underwriting indication for any line of business.

Some insurers use the experience rating modification as an index of the account's desirability within its class. A modification greater than 1.00 requires investigation. It may be the result of one large loss. The insured may also have implemented loss control procedures to prevent similar losses in the future. If an experience-rated policy does develop adverse results during the year, the experience rating mechanism ensures that the policyholder will be penalized in future policy terms. It does not matter who provides coverage, which provides a financial incentive for effective loss control. The experience rating process provides an accurate method to capture statistics about an applicant. Loss records show both past losses and the direction in which those losses are going.

Insurers that offer workers compensation insurance must also participate in the assigned risk program. This is a residual market similar to those discussed for automobile coverage. Employers who have been rejected by private insurers may apply to the plan. NCCI administers the National Workers Compensation Reinsurance Pool, a voluntary association of insurers. Member companies act as servicing insurers and receive a fee for the services they provide. This relieves insurers that do not service assigned risk accounts of the burden. It reduces costs because NCCI can select more efficient insurers as servicing carriers. It also creates economies of scale that reduce costs. The premiums and losses of a business in the plan are pooled. They are then allocated by state to all members of the pool in proportion to each member's workers compensation premium volume. The pool operates in thirty-three states and provides some coverages in nine other states. In addition, the NCCI manages the statutory pool in two states. In some states, the state fund serves as the assigned risk plan.

Underwriting Guidelines for Individual Classes

Underwriting management evaluates individual classes and decides which to accept and which to reject. Management communicates the insurer's preferences in underwriting guidelines and bulletins. A conservative insurer may want to avoid all high-hazard occupations, such as steeplejacks or window washers. This same insurer may be willing to write some contractors but avoid roofing and insulation contractors. Other insurers may target their marketing efforts to high-hazard classes. Just as in other lines of business, there is no single correct way to underwrite workers compensation.

Underwriting Considerations for Individual Applicants

Line underwriters use the insurer's guidelines to evaluate individual accounts. The primary factors they consider are on-premises and off-premises hazards. Other factors also demand special attention. These factors include the number of part-time and seasonal workers, the premium for workers compensation relative to the balance of the account, and subcontractors the insured may engage.

Temporary and Seasonal Workers

A business may employ a large number of temporary or seasonal workers who are generally not as well trained as permanent workers. This lack of training increases the risk of injury. These workers also present a potential moral hazard. They may fake injury on the job in order to receive workers compensation benefits until they return to school or find a long-term position.

Premium Size

Insurers often seek to write accounts of a specific size. They may target the middle market or Fortune 100 accounts. Underwriting guidelines often use premium size to identify the accounts an insurer wishes to write. The relative premium for each line of business may also be a factor. A guideline may be to accept certain accounts only if the workers compensation premium is less than 50 percent of the total amount of premium generated by the account. These guidelines may lead an underwriter to decline an account that is acceptable by all other measures.

Subcontractors

Most workers compensation laws hold a contractor responsible for workers compensation benefits to employees of its uninsured subcontractors. The standard workers compensation policy automatically insures this exposure. Underwriters must therefore ascertain whether this exposure exists and, if it does, evaluate it and include the appropriate premium charge if coverage is written. The policyholder must either prove that the exposure has been insured or pay a premium based on the subcontractor's payroll as well.

Management Attitude and Capability

A successful workers compensation insurance program requires active cooperation between policyholder management and the insurer. The underwriter must determine the willingness and ability of management to cooperate in the effort to minimize hazards and reduce losses.

If the firm does not have a safety program, or if the program exists only on paper with no management effort directed toward its implementation, managerial indifference can usually be assumed.

A firm that has insufficient financial resources or believes that it is at a competitive disadvantage may be unable or unwilling to implement a safety program. Some of the first areas cut back in an economic recession are worker training, maintenance, and safety.

Employee morale and claims consciousness often reflect management attitude toward workers compensation and industrial safety on the one hand and the degree of managerial skill on the other hand. A poorly managed firm is likely to have below-average workers compensation loss experience. If employee morale is low, grievances against management may motivate workers to file false or exaggerated claims for workers compensation as a means of escaping from an unpleasant work environment.

On-Premises Hazards

There are a variety of on-premises hazards. Some of them are found in virtually all occupations, such as housekeeping and maintenance. Others are peculiar to a particular operation or industry. Occupational disease and cumulative trauma disorders are two other on-premises hazards that, while not as common, should be evaluated for each occupation.

Housekeeping

From an underwriting standpoint, housekeeping refers to the quality of planning for the workplace, cleanliness, and efficiency of operation. This includes such factors as the arrangement of machinery, the placing and adequacy of aisles, the marking and cleanliness of stairs and freight elevator openings, and overall cleanliness.

Maintenance

Poorly maintained machinery presents an inherent danger. A good program of plant and machinery maintenance indicates a positive attitude toward work safety. The absence of such a program indicates carelessness or a lack of awareness, which can severely affect future work injuries.

Although general hazards are present in all types of firms, specific hazards may be present in a particular firm as a result of the type of machines, equipment, materials, and processes used in its operation. These specific hazards require specific controls, such as machine guards, exhaust systems, and materials-handling devices designed to meet the requirements of the particular situation.

Most accidents occur as a result of either an unsafe act (88 percent) or an unsafe condition (10 percent).[10] An unsafe act or practice on the part of an employee might include failing to use the proper personal protective equipment. Workers may, for example, fail to wear dust masks or air-supplied respirators in dust-laden atmospheres. The management of the firm can influence employee behavior. Its hiring policy, safety program, and enforcement of safety rules can increase or reduce injuries on the job. Premises inspections can indicate the extent to which the insured appears to tolerate unsafe actions. Unfortunately, there is always the danger that employees may act differently during an inspection than at other times. Losses can also occur when supervisors do not enforce safety rules continuously.

Unsafe conditions are generally easier to identify than unsafe acts. In an office, there is usually a minimum exposure to dangerous conditions, such as those involving machinery, chemicals, and similar hazards. There may be some potential for slips and falls and even for back strain from improperly lifting files, boxes of paper, and similar heavy objects.

New types of injuries are developing in office environments. The pace of business and the demands placed on workers have given rise to increased numbers of stress-related workers compensation claims. Other occupations, such as school teachers and police officers, set the precedent for stress being a compensable injury. The increased use of computer keyboards has caused some office workers to lose feeling in their hands. That injury, called carpal tunnel syndrome, results from cumulative trauma. Another computer-related concern is the effect of radiation emitted by video display terminals (VDTs). Despite twenty years of investigation and study, researchers have found no conclusive link between devices emitting electromagnetic fields (EMFs) and cancer in humans. The uncertainty about the effects of EMFs have led many workers to file claims in the belief that they have suffered an injury on the job. Long periods of work with a VDT may cause eye fatigue and physical ailments.

In a factory, the manufacturing process and the type of materials used are important. The loss history of the policyholder and others in the same industry provides information on the types of losses that might occur. In woodworking, for example, sharp cutting tools operating at high speeds can result in serious lacerations. In other processes, the potential for burns is inherent in the operation.

The rating structure takes into account the differences in relative hazards among occupational classes. A machine shop is more hazardous than an office, for example. The underwriter must attempt to determine to what extent the policyholder is typical of its class. The machine shop must be evaluated relative to some guidelines that indicate the conditions usually found in a typical machine shop. The presence of additional hazards not found in other machine shops or the heightening of normal hazards due to poor maintenance or housekeeping would indicate a substantial exposure.

Occupational Disease

Workers compensation statutes provide benefits for certain diseases in addition to injuries from accidents on the job. Although the definition varies by state, an occupational disease is generally one that arises from causes the worker faces on the job and to which the general public is not exposed. It is more difficult to predict the frequency and severity of occupational diseases than of work-related accidents. Accidents are easy to identify. Exposure to unfavorable conditions at work, on the other hand, does not always cause occupational disease. Changes in the state workers compensation statutes have broadened coverage for occupational disease. The interpretation of compensable diseases has become more liberal.

Some of the occupational diseases covered by the various state workers compensation laws are silicosis (exposure to silica dust), asbestosis (caused by inhalation of asbestos fibers), radiation (including ionizing radiation), tuberculosis, pneumoconiosis (black lung), and heart or lung disease for certain groups, such as police or firefighters.

In an industrial setting, hazard analysis involves monitoring the working environment for the presence of industrial poisons. These poisons may enter the body by ingestion, inhalation, or absorption through the skin. Analyzing the toxicity of the various chemical compounds used in a particular process provides a means of evaluating the occupational disease hazards due to that source.

Cumulative Trauma Disorders

Cumulative trauma disorders arise from a series of minor stresses that occur over a period of time. These relatively minor injuries combine to cause disability or create a need for medical treatment. Examples of cumulative trauma disorders include deafness as a result of a long exposure to high noise levels or kidney damage from a lifetime of jolting in the cab of a truck. Most states now recognize cumulative trauma disorders as compensable injuries.

The major problem associated with determining compensability for these injuries is distinguishing between conditions brought on by the normal aging process, or those to which the general public is subject, and those that are truly job related. Determining financial responsibility is another concern.

Experience in the red meat industry demonstrates that employers can control cumulative trauma disorders. Workers in this industry suffered so many injuries caused by repetitive movements that OSHA made it the target of special attention. This led to the development of new safety rules that employers adopted and enforced. As a result, injury rates fell dramatically. Several years after making the red meat industry the target of its first special campaign, OSHA praised employers in this industry for the improved loss rates they had achieved.

Off-Premises Hazards

Individual firms differ in the extent to which they present off-premises hazards. In some firms, the employees carry out all their employment duties on the premises. In other firms, a great deal of travel is done in the course of employment. There are two elements to the off-premises hazard: (1) the duration of travel and the mode of transportation and (2) the types and extent of hazards at the remote job sites.

Two accounting firms with identical payrolls are presented here as examples of the first type of off-premises hazard. In Firm A, the accountants do all their work on the firm's premises. In Firm B, which does a great deal of auditing for firms in the construction business, the accountants travel much of the time in the course of employment. This travel is done in private automobiles as well as in commercial and corporate aircraft. Traffic accidents or plane crashes could result in serious workers compensation losses for Firm B from this off-premises exposure, which is not present in Firm A.

Corporate aircraft may result in a multiple-fatality workers compensation loss in the event of a crash. The potential for multiple losses is also present when several employees share the same car or truck when traveling on business for their employer.

The same techniques previously mentioned to evaluate on-premises hazards may be used for off-premises hazards. The separate evaluation of off- and on-premises hazards is necessitated by the fact that the number of workers exposed to off-premises hazards may be only a small fraction of the total work force.

Occupational Safety and Health Act

The Occupational Safety and Health Act (OSHA) of 1970 was designed to assure all workers a safe and healthy workplace. This act set safety standards for employers and imposed penalties for violations of the standards.

The Department of Labor has the task of enforcing the act. Safety inspectors may enter the working premises at any reasonable time to inspect the premises, equipment, and environment of the work force. When a violation is detected, a citation is issued describing the exact nature of the violation. The employer has fifteen working days after receiving written notice of the violation to notify the Department of Labor that either the citation or the penalty assessed will be contested. Any willful violation that results in an employee's death is punishable by a fine of up to $10,000 or imprisonment of up to six months. The second conviction carries double penalties.

Each of the large number of employers subject to the act is required to keep occupational injury records for employees. Every employer must maintain a log of recordable occupational injuries and illnesses and supplementary records of each occupational injury or illness. OSHA defines a recordable case as one involving an occupational death, occupational illness, or occupational injury involving loss of consciousness, restriction of work or motion, transfer to another job, or medical treatment (other than first aid). OSHA safety inspections and logs are no substitute for underwriting inspections of the various locations. Rather, they should be viewed as a source of additional data and inspection assistance. The information in the log can be used to identify the types of losses that are occurring, their frequency, and their duration in terms of lost workdays. It can also be used to verify other loss information submitted with the application.

Maritime Occupations

Some employee injury claims come within federal rather than state jurisdictions. Federal laws entitle certain groups of workers to compensation for work-related injuries without regard to fault. The effect of these laws is similar to state workers compensation laws. The difference is that the schedule of benefits and administrative procedures are established by federal laws. As a result, there can be differences in loss costs and, thus, the applicable rates for insurance coverage under the federal laws. The principal federal laws covering on-the-job injuries are the United States Longshore & Harbor Workers (USL&HW) Act and the Merchant Marine Act. The latter is more commonly known as the Jones Act.

Maritime compensation exposures often appear unexpectedly. These surprises may result from the producer's or underwriter's limited familiarity with the nature of the operations insured, from insufficient underwriting information when the coverage was written, or from the policyholder's venture into a new operation with a maritime exposure after the inception of the policy. The problem is complicated by the fact that most of these situations concern maritime employments for which distinctions between land and water areas and between crew members and harbor workers are especially difficult to draw.

Some insurers avoid any workers compensation exposures falling under federal jurisdiction because of insufficient underwriting expertise or reinsurance restrictions. Employments covered by the United States Longshore & Harbor Workers (USL&HW) Act require expertise in underwriting, claims handling, premium auditing, and loss control. Even an underwriter with many years of experience, but no experience in handling maritime exposures, would find it difficult to evaluate such exposures. Reinsurance treaties may also contain restrictive provisions regarding coverages such as those that insure the USL&HW Act exposure.

An underwriter may discover USL&HW Act exposures in many typical construction and erection operations. Too often, this discovery results from a claim. Underwriters must always be alert to the existence of maritime exposures. They may be indicated in many ways, including persons to whom certificates of insurance are issued, the type of equipment owned, a list of jobs in progress, claims under other coverages, and so on. Some producers located near navigable waters attach a Longshore & Harbor Workers Compensation Act coverage endorsement to every workers compensation policy, just to be safe, even if such exposures are not contemplated when the policy is issued. In those situations, the underwriter must instruct the producer to clearly indicate when a maritime exposure is anticipated.

PROFESSIONAL LIABILITY UNDERWRITING

A professional possesses the special knowledge and skill necessary to render a professional service. Typically, this special knowledge and skill result from a combination of the person's education and experience in a particular branch of science or learning. For tort law purposes, those whom the law has recognized as professionals include physicians, surgeons, dentists, attorneys, engineers, accountants, architects, insurance agents and brokers, and many others.

Underwriters have also developed professional liability forms for special exposures that fall outside the traditional scope of professional services. Some accounts, for instance, face a severe exposure to personal injury claims. General liability forms exclude some of these exposures. Underwriters will decline to offer personal injury coverage for others. This has led to the development of professional liability forms that cover personal injury hazards. Examples include media liability, law enforcement agencies, and security guards.

Other professional liability forms insure exposures that have traditionally fallen within the business risk exclusion. Underwriters at one time did not feel that they could insure these exposures. A new class of professional liability forms insures against liability for faulty advice or workmanship. Data processing firms can now obtain coverage for the failure of their software or systems to perform as expected. Consultants in all fields can insure their liability for losses clients sustain as a result of the consultant's advice.

Professional liability, by its nature, is subject to large and relatively infrequent claims. Additionally, these claims are usually filed and settled many years after the date of the event from which the claim arose. Thus, it is often difficult to determine whether a line of business is profitable until many years after the premium has been collected. To alleviate this problem, some professional liability policies have been changed from an occurrence basis to a claims-made basis.

In the past, professional liability policies almost always included a condition that required the professional to consent to any out-of-court settlement. In most areas of professional liability, claims have become so large and so serious that insurers insist on the right to settle out of court without the consent of policyholders. At present, some professional liability policies contain the traditional condition, and some do not. The difference is significant to the underwriter.

The legal environment of professional liability has greatly changed in recent years. Both frequency and claim severity have increased as courts have held professionals liable for damages in a wide variety of circumstances.

The medical professional liability exposure is not limited to doctors in private practice, hospitals, and clinics. Many manufacturing plants have first-aid facilities, nurses, or even doctors in attendance. Although these facilities improve the account from a workers compensation standpoint, underwriters should not overlook the professional liability exposure this presents. Other professional liability exposures found in many industrial and commercial firms are directors' and officers' errors and omissions and fiduciary liability for pension plan administrators.

The type of specialty practiced by the particular physician is an important underwriting consideration. Those generally considered in the high-risk category are anesthesiologists, neurosurgeons, plastic surgeons, obstetrician-gynecologists, and cardiovascular surgeons. The general practitioner has much less exposure, particularly if surgery is not performed.

Professional liability underwriters should consider the following attributes of physicians: degrees and/or licenses held, membership in professional organizations, certification, recertification (continuing education), years in practice, type of clientele, associates (that is, fellow workers), and whether the physician practices as an individual or as a member of a professional association. All of these indicate something about the doctor's position within the medical community, which will often play a major role in the defense of suits. This is not to say that a well-known doctor will be found innocent because he or she is popular with other doctors. Nevertheless, the professional reputation of the doctor will be important in malpractice cases, and the insurer is looking for other doctors to speak on behalf of the doctor's professional competence.

The principle that exposure is related to areas of specialty extends to lawyers' professional liability as well. A law office that specializes in corporate practice involving many complex cases at one time has much more exposure to loss than a firm dealing exclusively in small probate and real estate work. Once again, the consequences of a mistake must be considered.

This analysis of the professional's clientele may be extended to insurance agents' errors and omissions, real estate brokers' errors and omissions, and accountants' and auditors' errors and omission. Several large accounting firms have had losses resulting from their certification of the financial statement of a publicly held company. The courts held that the auditing process that preceded the certification was conducted negligently and resulted in losses to stockholders and others. The exposure is greater for a firm auditing large public companies than for one keeping the books for a number of small, privately held firms.

PERSONAL LIABILITY UNDERWRITING

Personal liability insurance was designed for the average individual and his or her family. It covers liability that does not arise out of the policyholder's business or profession or out of the use of an auto, an airplane, or a large watercraft. The policy applies to the premises where the policyholder maintains a residence and to the nonbusiness activities of the policyholder and members of the household. Personal liability is part of every homeowners policy and can be purchased with a dwelling fire policy or alone.

Residence Premises Exposures

All property owners, or tenants in control of property, have certain obligations in relation to injury caused to people who come onto the property. A great many residence premises losses are caused by an attractive nuisance on the premises. An **attractive nuisance** is an alluring or unusual object or structure (usually man-made), such as a swimming pool or a treehouse, that may entice children to trespass. These hazards are in addition to the basic premises hazards of uneven or icy sidewalks, poorly maintained steps and porches, and poorly lighted hallways. Large sliding glass doors have produced

Attractive nuisance
A potentially harmful object or structure so inviting or interesting to a child that it would lure the child onto the property to investigate.

substantial losses when guests have walked or run through them. A significant underwriting factor is the attitude the policyholder exhibits toward his or her home, as evidenced by how the premises are kept and maintained. The underwriter can evaluate these conditions through photographs or personal inspections conducted by the producer or inspection services.

Residence liability losses are infrequent but may be severe; therefore, loss experience can be extremely volatile in all except the larger books of business. The policy is usually sold as a package, but even when sold alone, it commands a relatively low premium. The expense factor of this low premium does not permit extensive investigation and inspection of the individual premises. The result is that the underwriter is faced with a highly unpredictable loss situation that must be underwritten on the basis of scanty information. To combat this problem, some insurers have developed supplementary applications to capture additional information. These forms may ask some of the following questions:

- Are large or potentially vicious dogs present?
- Does the policyholder own or keep horses?
- Does the residence have objects or structures that may attract children, such as a swimming pool, hot tub, backyard gym, swings, slides, or climbing bars?
- Is there an incidental office occupancy exposure?
- Is the residence under construction or being renovated?
- Does the policyholder rent all or part of the dwelling to others?

Personal Activities

A major loss exposure is the personal activities of the policyholder and the resident members of the household. Personal activities are not limited to the residence premises; a personal liability policy extends its protection broadly to all activities not specifically excluded. Insured incidents might include injuries or damages caused by an unlicensed recreational vehicle or property damage intentionally caused by children.

Sports liability is one area of major concern. Injuries caused while golfing, hunting, fishing, and playing team sports are typical of the exposures expected. The off-premises operation of large watercraft and snowmobiles is excluded from coverage unless the policy has been appropriately endorsed. It is usually impossible for the underwriter to find out the activities of the policyholder or the skill with which those known activities are conducted. The only possible resource for this information is the producer, who may know that the applicant has a particularly strong interest in an area that may present a greater-than-expected risk. If available, such information is merely subjective.

Underwriting Considerations

The underwriter should investigate several avenues that are not directly related to the premises or the activities of the policyholder, including occupation, claims history, and credit history.

The occupation of the applicant may indicate possible business exposures on the premises. Some occupations such as sales are conducted to some extent on the premises. Occupations that could possibly increase the traffic and therefore the exposure are less desirable.

Past losses may indicate future losses. For that reason, applications usually request information on all losses during the past several years.

Many insurers have begun using credit information to evaluate applicants. Credit information indicates the extent to which the applicant is in debt, whether bills are paid on time, and the existence of outstanding judgments. Poor credit can indicate an overall lack of responsibility. If an applicant is declined or canceled based on consumer credit information, the insurer must notify the policyholder of this fact in writing and offer him or her the opportunity to review the information with the credit collection information service. Insurance regulators have recently questioned the relevancy and propriety of this use of credit information. Such information will likely be restricted in the future for insurance purposes, unless a direct cause-and-effect relationship can be proved between creditworthiness and loss potential.

UNDERWRITING UMBRELLA AND EXCESS LIABILITY POLICIES

Many policyholders find that they need high limits of liability coverage not offered in standard liability policies. Businesses and individuals may have significant assets that need protection from potentially catastrophic liability claims. Many situations may cause severe losses, such as multiple passenger auto accidents, gasoline truck explosions, building collapse, hotel fires, and defective products.

Umbrella Policies

Umbrella liability insurance, both commercial and personal, is designed to cover large, infrequent losses. It does not provide primary insurance, nor does it cover all losses. Most umbrella policies have a deductible or self-insured retention that the policyholder must pay. The retention for commercial forms is usually $10,000, and the retention for the personal form is usually $250.

Umbrella policies are not standardized. The contract language and underwriting rules and guidelines vary from one insurer to another. In most cases, umbrella policies have three basic characteristics. They are designed to do the following:

1. Provide excess liability limits above all specified underlying policies
2. Provide coverage when the aggregate limits of the underlying policies have been exhausted
3. Cover gaps in coverage in the underlying policies

The umbrella policy requires as a condition of coverage that agreed limits of liability be maintained on the underlying policies. If this is not done, the umbrella will respond as though the limits existed. This could potentially create a tremendous uninsured loss.

Underwriting umbrella policies requires a careful analysis of the same exposures covered by the underlying policies. Underwriters must have a thorough knowledge of the coverage provided by underlying contracts and how the particular applicant in question has had its policies modified through endorsements.

Providing an umbrella policy above a private passenger automobile policy may raise some additional concerns. State statutes may require uninsured motorists coverage equal to the bodily injury liability limits of the policy unless rejected by the policyholder. The insurer may not be willing to provide such high limits on uninsured motorists coverage or leave the decision to the discretion of the policyholder. A similar problem exists in those states that permit the stacking of policy limits. In those states, the courts have permitted the policyholder to combine the limits for each vehicle insured under the policy.

Excess Policies

Excess policies are written only to increase the limits of liability on a particular policy. Umbrella policies go one step further by providing coverage even when underlying coverage does not exist. Excess insurance is frequently written on a layered basis, with several policies used to provide very high limits.

As in the case with umbrella policies, loss frequency is not a problem with specific excess insurance, but severity is a potential problem. Reinsurance for both umbrella and specific excess policies usually alleviates the problem. Specific excess policies are seldom underwritten in the sense of traditional risk analysis, but pricing is important. The philosophy is usually that if the primary insurance is acceptable, then the excess is acceptable also. The excess insurer often relies on the underwriting judgment of the primary insurer.

PACKAGE POLICY UNDERWRITING

Package policies
Policies containing two or more property and liability coverages in a single policy.

Package policies consist of policies containing two or more property and liability coverages in a single policy. Examples abound today, but this was not always the case. Traditionally, then by regulatory mandate, insurers were restricted from combining property and liability coverages into a single policy. States passed legislation in the 1950s that enabled the creation of multi-line policies. Multi-line laws permitted coverage combinations, which better meet the needs of policyholders. Package policies usually provide a discount reflecting the reduced cost of issuing several policies. Policyholders are also less likely to have gaps and overlaps in coverage.

Not all of a policyholder's exposures can be combined in a single policy. Account underwriting is a more appropriate approach. It considers all of the insured's needs as a unit and treats the policies that satisfy those needs as a single account. Insurance producers have encouraged insurers to take an account approach to offering insurance. Producers want to maximize the potential commission available from a single client by providing all of that client's insurance coverages, as well as being assured that client needs are met.

Package and account underwriting make a great deal of sense from an underwriting standpoint. The reduced expenses associated with selling and processing increase the profit potential. More importantly, the larger total premium generated by an account makes it possible to do more in-depth investigative work on the character of the policyholder and the nature of the risk. Many of the factors that distinguish good accounts from bad ones do not relate to any one coverage. Underwriters have learned that the characteristics that make a good property account also make a good account for other lines. Account underwriting allows them to use this knowledge to their advantage.

Combining coverages into a single policy also enhances the spread of risk, reduces adverse selection, and provides an opportunity for greater premium growth. By internally organizing to underwrite package policies and accounts, the insurer can increase its level of service to producers and insureds by creating a single source for all service needs.

The disadvantage of package and account underwriting is that underwriters cannot be selective in the coverages offered to the applicant. Applicants and producers want the insurance program accepted as a whole. As a result, underwriters are forced into a choice between all or nothing. Underwriters placed in this position may have to accept some marginal exposures in order to write the more profitable parts of the account.

Kinds of Package Policies

Underwriting package policies depends to some degree on the kind of package policy. Package policies may be described as (1) a simple combination package policy, (2) a minimum requirement package policy, (3) indivisible package policies, or (4) nonstandard package policies.

A simple combination package policy includes two or more standard coverages in one convenient format for the policyholder. There is no package discount, and the underwriting is the same as if separate coverages were requested. This approach provides maximum flexibility to the underwriter, who may choose not to issue the requested form but instead offer a more restricted form if necessary. Each coverage is priced separately, and the package premium is simply a total of the premiums for the individual coverages.

A minimum requirement package policy requires the insured to purchase certain minimum coverages. An example is the ISO CPP (commercial package policy) that requires a direct damage coverage form in the commercial property coverage part (or the inland marine physicians and surgeons coverage form) *and* premises and operations liability for the same premises insured under the direct damage coverage.[11] A combination of forms that do not meet these requirements may be referred to as a package but is not eligible for the package discount.

Requiring certain minimum coverages reduces adverse selection. The policy writing, accounting, and billing expenses are less with one package policy than with three or four separate monoline policies. On an entire book of business, this reduces expense costs. The benefits of reducing expense costs and adverse selection are passed along to the insured in the form of a package discount.

Because of this package discount, most insurers try to select above-average risks for these package policies. The underwriting guide usually specifies what is above average in terms of type of business and physical hazards. One inspection may provide sufficient information for property, liability, and crime loss exposures. Since there is a minimum requirement of property and liability coverages, inspections are coordinated. Separate policies often require separate inspections that increase costs.

A package policy requires underwriters to do more than analyze each of the individual coverages. Underwriters have to accept or decline diverse exposures as a unit. A single larger premium must reflect a combination of smaller premiums of varying levels of adequacy.

An indivisible package policy provides a broad range of coverages for a single indivisible premium. The businessowners policy (BOP) and homeowners policies are examples of this type of package. Unlike the minimum requirement policy, the premium is shown only in total. It cannot be separated by coverage. Indivisible package policies permit little coverage selection by the policyholder. This reduces adverse selection, but it also permits almost no flexibility in pricing and coverage. Individual package policies require a large group of insureds whose exposures to loss are essentially identical. This makes them suitable only for personal lines and small commercial accounts. The underwriter's challenge is to evaluate the sum of the various exposures presented by a risk against the single premium to determine acceptability.

Nonstandard package policies are usually manuscript contracts written to the policyholder's and the underwriter's specifications. Maximum flexibility is achieved by eliminating minimum coverages, and pricing tends to be on an individual risk basis. This approach is limited to large policyholders.

Underwriting Considerations

Underwriting decision making is simple on a submission with no adverse exposures. Likewise, the decision is clear if the submission has no redeeming values. The decision becomes difficult when part of the package is acceptable, but the balance is not. Perhaps the property loss exposures of a small manufacturer are minimal because of loss control devices, but the products liability exposure may be great because of the nature of the product. The premises and operations liability exposures of a dry cleaner may be excellent as demonstrated in its loss-free history. The property exposure, on the other hand, may be questionable because the operation uses a solvent with a low flash point.

In these cases, the underwriter must weigh the strengths against the weaknesses, identify any appropriate alternatives, and choose the best one. To do this, an underwriter may ask questions such as the following:

1. What are the limits of liability of each of the sections of the package policy?
2. What are the premiums for each policy section? (This question is inappropriate if the package policy has an indivisible premium, thus complicating the underwriter's decision.)
3. What is the expected frequency of loss for each major policy section?
4. What is the expected severity of loss for each major policy section?

Sometimes conflicting exposures are those in which a low hazard for one line of coverage increases the hazard of another coverage. This may be compounded by the fact that an underwriter may wish to offer suggestions to further lower the exposure in the first category, which increases the exposure in the second line of coverage.

The underwriter also has to determine whether the premium for the low-hazard exposures offsets the inadequate premiums of the higher hazard exposures. Most rating plans contain minimum rates and premiums by coverage for low-hazard risks. They have been developed to cover the expenses of underwriting and issuing a policy, which may account for the majority of the cost in some instances. When a number of coverages are combined into a single package, the minimum rates, being primarily for expense purposes, may provide more than adequate premium when added to other line premiums.

In indivisible premium policies, the underwriter must use imagination to identify unusual exposures for which an indivisible "class rate" does not develop sufficient premium. For example, one such package provided "all-risks" coverage on liquor stores at a premium less than that for mercantile open stock burglary alone.

Package underwriting also provides the opportunity to investigate management abilities and techniques as they relate to the total loss control of the account. Management influences all areas of loss potential to ensure the continuing profitability of the operation and the development of programs for the recognition and control of loss exposures. The package policy analysis, because it has more expense dollars available from the larger premium, enables the underwriter to look more closely at many aspects of management, including its ability to make a profit. A profitable operation will have both the resources to invest in loss control and the desire to do so.

Package policies are more than just a combination of monoline coverages. Underwriters should be aware of the differences between the monoline version and the package version of forms and the type of applicant each version attracts. Some package policies have altered the usual monoline policy provisions to broaden the coverage. For example, the businessowners policy does not contain the coinsurance provisions found in the commercial property coverage form. The package credit provided under the commercial package policy program may give too steep a discount, based on the insurer's own experience, thereby making packaging undesirable. Applicants eligible only for dwelling fire and personal liability policies may present a greater exposure to loss than those eligible for coverage through the homeowners program.

UNDERWRITING TECHNIQUES FOR SMALL ACCOUNTS

Insurers are facing continuing pressure to become more efficient and reduce their expenses. This pressure is especially keen in personal lines, where individual account premiums are small. As a result, expenses tend to consume a larger share of the premium these accounts generate. Small business accounts face similar pressure. In response to pressure from the public and to improve their market share, insurers have sought techniques to reduce the cost of underwriting small accounts.

Screening
A process of categorizing applicants to allow underwriters to concentrate only on those applicants that require a decision. It involves comparing customers' risk characteristics with the insurer's underwriting guidelines to identify customers who match the characteristics specified as desirable by the guidelines.

This effort has produced a process known as **screening**. Underwriting management develops a profile that represents the ideal account in a particular class. Support staff then use this profile to screen new applications and renewals of policies in force. If the account matches the profile closely enough, the insurer issues a policy. A large discrepancy between the account and the profile results in declining the account. Marginal or questionable accounts are referred to an underwriter for a final decision. Some insurers have devised scoring systems to enhance the screening process. Others use a simple count of attributes that match the profile.

Some insurers screen accounts using custom computer software. Others employ customer service representatives or underwriting assistants for this purpose. Agents can also use the profile to evaluate new prospects quickly. Screening has three principal advantages. First, it provides quick answers for most submissions. If the account fits the profile, the insurer can accept quickly. Only a few border-line accounts will have to wait for the underwriter to review the application and make a decision. Screening also reduces costs. Computers or less skilled personnel handle routine processing and make routine decisions. This frees the underwriters to do what they do best, make decisions when acceptability or rejection is not clear-cut. In this way, insurers use their most expensive talent only when there is a real need for it. If agents use the profile to screen new submissions, the share of acceptable accounts the insurer receives will increase. This will reduce the cost of processing applications the insurer will decline in the end. Finally, screening allows agents to get to know the insurer's target market better. Agents can use the profile to evaluate new accounts without having to submit an application or call the underwriter with questions. This helps the insurer build a better rapport with its producers.

SURETY BOND UNDERWRITING

Suretyship is a technique used to provide assurance to one party, called the obligee, that another party, called the principal, will fulfill an obligation he or she has undertaken to perform. Suretyship is not insurance but is a type of guarantee that insurers often offer in addition to their insurance products.

Insurance companies are the leading surety underwriters. Surety bonds may guarantee (1) faithful performance, (2) financial strength, or (3) ability or capacity to perform.

Unique Features of Bonds

Unlike insurance, a surety has recourse for losses to the principal. The principal is primarily responsible to fulfill the contractual obligation—not the surety. Since insurance contracts are between two parties, either may cancel unilaterally. But surety bonds are written for the benefit of a third party to the bond and may be terminated only with the consent of the obligee. Thus, the initial surety underwriting decision must reflect this situation. Surety bonds are often written for an indefinite period, and little rate flexibility exists for some types of bonds. If the surety pays a loss, the principal is usually legally liable to reimburse the surety for the loss, but underwriters must be concerned with the ability of the principal to meet this financial obligation.

Types of Surety Bonds

Surety bonds can be grouped in many different ways. Generally, they are divided into four major categories: (1) public official bonds, (2) court bonds, (3) license and permit bonds, and (4) contract bonds. This section concentrates on contract bond underwriting since it is by far the largest line of surety bonds.

A knowledge of financial analysis is of paramount importance in underwriting contract bonds. Audited statements for at least the past two years provide a starting point, but if the latest statements are more than six months old, an interim statement may be requested. In addition, the underwriter should carefully evaluate the following:

1. *Business experience of the contractor*—This should include the experience of the owners before their association with the firm as well as the business experience of the firm itself.

2. *Performance record*—The underwriter must check the size and growth pattern of individual jobs. A contractor that is growing too rapidly or is bidding on a job that is much larger than or different from his or her customary work must be scrutinized.

3. *Plant and equipment*—The need for a plant may be nonexistent for a road contractor, but a sheet metal shop is essential for an air conditioning contractor. A physical inspection can determine the age and condition of equipment.

4. *Financial resources not included in financial statements*—The status of work in process (or work on hand) is not truly reflected in the financial statements. The profit (or lack of it) from these uncompleted projects is not shown and requires further investigation. The terms and conditions of the line of credit available from banks should also be investigated.

SUMMARY

Liability underwriting continues to be the most challenging underwriting area. Legislation and court decisions require frequent changes to policy forms and underwriting guidelines. This changing environment requires the underwriter to continually update his or her knowledge and skills to keep up with situations that may arise.

Effective automobile underwriting requires an appreciation of the regulatory and legal environment that affects this line of business. The residual market and how those costs are spread or shared have created a highly charged political environment for insurers in many states. The latitude often granted insurers in underwriting private passenger automobile insurance is minimal. Several states do not permit the rejection of applicants. Some states limit the underwriting criteria to just a few factors.

Commercial automobile underwriting uses fewer controversial factors but is influenced to some extent by regulatory requirements on personal automobiles. Underwriters look at the weight of the vehicle and its use, including the radius of operation and type of materials carried. Effective loss control programs can significantly affect the profitability of a commercial automobile risk. Motor carrier laws may impose responsibilities on insurers that were not contracted for as part of the insurance. Reimbursement for such claims is permitted but may not be realistically possible given the circumstances.

Until recently, workers compensation insurance has been largely unprofitable. Insurers that write workers compensation coverage reduced the restrictions on the circumstances under which coverage will be offered and on which classes are desirable. Even with the legal changes and rate increases, the underwriter must extensively investigate and evaluate the hazards present to ensure that the applicant can be priced profitably. The Occupational Safety and Health Act has not affected the work environment as its writers had envisioned. The act has created a resource of statistics that an insurer can use to evaluate a class of business and that an underwriter can use to evaluate an individual applicant. Many insurers purposely avoid policyholders who have maritime-related occupations. Insurers may not discover that these exposures exist until a claim is presented.

Many of the hazards identified in workers compensation exposures are also present for the general liability underwriter. The principal difference is that the general public rather than the policyholder's employees is exposed to injury. Underwriters need to know the hazards presented by the policyholder's premises, products, and operations. The CGL includes coverage for liability assumed under incidental contracts.

The standard of care required of a professional is greater than that of an ordinary individual. Professional liability insurance covers those incidents that arise out of a policyholder's professional responsibilities. Because of the expertise required in writing this coverage, a relatively small number of insurers is actively involved in providing this coverage.

Umbrella and excess policies are available to provide extra large limits. Personal and commercial umbrella policies provide liability coverage over certain required policies as well as coverage when no coverage exists. Excess policies are usually found only in the commercial market and provide high limits only for specific policies.

Several definitions of package policies exist. However defined, package policies present the underwriter with a number of challenges and opportunities. One challenge is to evaluate several diverse exposures in a single account. The underwriter must weigh the loss potential from these hazards to determine whether the account will be profitable overall. An opportunity is to perform a thorough investigation on the entire account, which may not have been cost-justified if the account had been written on a monoline basis.

Surety bonds are not insurance contracts but are so often sold by insurers that their discussion is pertinent here. There are a number of different types of bonds. This chapter highlighted the underwriting of one of these types, contract bonds.

This chapter focused on the considerations that an underwriter should make in evaluating liability and package policies. It is by no means exhaustive in its approach. An underwriter should have a good grasp of exposure analysis and insurance coverages as well as an appreciation of the role of the loss control engineer and the claims process.

CHAPTER NOTES

1. National Highway Traffic Safety Administration, The Economic Impact of Motor Vehicle Crashes, 2000, World Wide Web: www.nhtsa.dot.gov (11 June 2002).

2. *FC&S Bulletins*, Personal Lines, Personal Auto, February 1996, D. 1-2.

3. Robert E. Keeton and Jeffrey O'Connell, *Basic Protection for the Traffic Victim* (Boston: Little, Brown and Co., 1965).

4. National Safety Council Website, World Wide Web: www.nsc.org/library/facts/yngdrive.htm (11 June 2002).

5. *1997 Property/Casualty Insurance Facts*, p. 90.

6. Commercial General Liability Coverage Form, Insurance Services Office, CG 00 01 0196, p. 11.

7. Greeman v. Yuba Power Products, Inc., 59 Cal 2nd 57 (1963).

8. Denny v. Ford Motor Co., 84 NY 2d, 1018 (1995).

9. *The Fact Book 2000* (New York: Insurance Information Institute, 2002), p. 15.

10. W. Heinrich, *Industrial Accident Prevention*, 4th ed. (New York: McGraw-Hill, 1959), p. 13.

11. *Commercial Lines Manual*, Section Nine Multiline (New York: Insurance Services Office, 1994), p. 2.

Chapter 7

Direct Your Learning

Loss Control and Premium Auditing

After learning the subject matter of this chapter, you should be able to:

- Explain the objectives of the loss control function.
- Illustrate how loss control supports other insurer functions.
- Given a case, recommend how loss control services can be used to improve an account.
- Illustrate how loss control activities can be organized.
- Explain reasons for conducting premium audits.
- Given a case, illustrate the activities at each stage of the premium audit process.
- Explain how premium audit supports other insurer functions.
- Explain the consequences of a premium audit error.
- Illustrate how premium audit activities can be organized.

Develop Your Perspective

What are the main topics covered in the chapter?

Loss control works with customers to lower the frequency and severity of losses. Premium auditing determines the actual insurance exposures for coverage with variable premium bases.

Recognize how these departments provide information that is vital in meeting underwriting profitability goals.

- Without these departments, how would insurers investigate loss exposures and actual premium exposures with certainty?

Why is it important to know these topics?

The two functional departments of loss control and premium auditing interact directly with policyholders. In doing so, they obtain information that might be unattainable by other departments within an insurance organization.

Consider how the information gathered by loss control and premium auditing benefit the insurer and the customer.

- What information do these departments share with other functional areas of the insurance company, and what information do they obtain from other departments that helps them perform more effectively?

How can you use this information?

Investigate your own organization's loss control and auditing departments.

- How has the loss control department helped to change the loss exposures of unacceptable applicants into those of acceptable applicants?

- How has the premium auditing department improved underwriting profitability results?

Chapter 7

Loss Control and Premium Auditing

An insurer's success often depends on the quality of its loss control and premium auditing functions. Both of these functions involve direct contact with the policyholder and provide the insurer with additional information about the quality of the business written. Such contact also presents opportunities to provide service to the policyholder and build a stronger relationship over time. Loss control and premium auditing, which were briefly introduced in prior chapters of this text, are described in more detail here.

LOSS CONTROL

Loss control measures may be directed toward lowering loss frequency, lowering loss severity, or a combination of the two. **Loss prevention** is defined as those measures intended to lower the frequency of losses—in other words, to prevent losses from occurring. **Loss reduction** is defined as those measures intended to lower the severity of the losses that do occur. The term **loss control** refers collectively to loss prevention and loss reduction.

Loss control has been a function of property-casualty insurers throughout most of the history of the industry. Some early fire insurers even maintained organizations to extinguish fires in the properties they insured. Although modern insurers no longer maintain fire extinguishment services, they continue to play a major role in fire prevention by inspecting insured properties and providing advisory services to policyholders. Moreover, insurers engage in many other loss control activities that relate to the increasingly complex loss exposures confronting modern society.

Objectives of Insurer Loss Control Activities

Insurers conduct loss control activities for several reasons. These reasons correspond to the overall objectives of insurers stated in Chapter 1.

Profit Objectives

An insurer's loss control activities can help the insurer to reach its profit objectives in several ways.

By inspecting the premises and operations of those who apply for insurance, trained loss control representatives (also known as safety engineers or loss

> **Loss prevention**
> A type of loss control that seeks to lower the frequency of losses (to decrease the number of losses).

> **Loss reduction**
> A type of loss control that seeks to lower the severity of losses that occur (to decrease the dollar amount of the losses).

> **Loss control**
> A risk management technique that attempts to reduce loss frequency (how often losses occur) or loss severity (the amount of damage caused by losses).

control engineers) can improve the information on which the underwriting department will base its decisions about whether to accept or reject applicants and about how to price coverage. Better underwriting information enables the insurer to do a better job of selecting policyholders at a price that will produce an underwriting profit.

Apart from supporting the underwriting decision-making process, loss control personnel can recommend loss control measures to change a marginal risk to an acceptable risk, thereby increasing the insurer's premium volume. Unless the insurer can reach its targets for premium volume, it probably cannot reach its profit objectives.

Once the decision is made to insure an applicant, the loss control function can continue to monitor the policyholder and suggest appropriate loss control measures as the policyholder's loss exposures change. By assisting policyholders in this manner, loss control personnel can reduce losses that the insurer must pay, thereby helping to keep the insurer's book of business profitable.

The loss control representative, through the influence of the insurer, can encourage policyholders to pursue loss control activities. The representative accomplishes this objective by working with policyholders to identify additional loss control opportunities and safety improvements.

For some insurers, the loss control function might actually serve as a direct source of income. Traditionally, insurers provided loss control services only to their policyholders and did not charge a fee in addition to the policy premium. Many insurers today offer their loss control services on a fee basis to firms that have chosen to retain, or "self-insure," their losses. Similarly, some insurers provide their own policyholders with supplemental loss control services for a fee in addition to the policy premium. These services can be sophisticated. Several major insurers offer a "cafeteria" type plan in which the policyholder has access to a variety of experts such as nurses, ergonomic specialists, engineers, attorneys, and chemists.

Because loss control services are sold separately from insurance coverage, they are sometimes referred to as being "unbundled." Insurers offering unbundled loss control services view their sale as a new source of income to bolster profits and help support the sophisticated personnel and equipment needed to cope with the complex loss control problems brought about by modern technology and modern law.

Meeting Customer Demand

Recently, many insurers have substantially increased their loss control activities because of an increased demand from insurance consumers, particularly commercial and industrial firms. This increased demand has resulted partly from an increased awareness of the cost of accidents and partly from the pressures of legislation such as the Occupational Safety and Health Act, the Consumer Products Safety Act, the Comprehensive Environmental Response Compensation and Liability Act, and the Americans with Disabilities Act.

The rapid increase in the size of liability judgments, especially for products liability, has also contributed to the increased demand for loss control services.

Some of the benefits policyholders may realize from implementing a proactive loss control policy include improving the account's desirability to underwriters; lowering insurance premiums; reducing disruption to operations following accidents; fulfilling occupational safety and health standards; complying with local, state, and federal laws; and improving the account's financial performance.

By satisfying customer needs for loss control services, insurers can attract new customers, retain satisfied customers, and gain a competitive advantage over insurers that do not provide the services that customers need and want.

Meeting Legal Requirements

Some states require insurers to provide a minimum level of loss control service to commercial policyholders. Compliance with the law supports the insurer's overall objective of fulfilling all legal requirements of the jurisdictions in which the insurer operates.

Another objective related to compliance with the law is to provide loss control services competently to minimize the possibility of errors and omissions claims by policyholders or others alleging injury because of the insurer's negligence. This errors and omissions liability exposure also may influence an insurance company's decision about what types or levels of loss control services to provide. A later section of this chapter discusses this factor in more detail.

Humanitarian and Societal Concerns

Accidental losses affect society at all levels. An occupational injury may cause pain, suffering, and loss of income for one individual, or a fire loss to a large factory may cause loss of business income, employee layoffs, and contingent business income losses for suppliers of the firm. The sum of all accidental losses has a profound adverse effect on society in general.

By assisting policyholders in preventing or lessening accidental losses, insurers pursue humanitarian objectives and benefit society at large. Although an insurer's payment of insurance proceeds for accidental losses can help an individual, a business, or society to recover from accidental losses, preventing the same losses is generally a preferable alternative.

Cooperation Between Loss Control and Other Functions

An insurer's loss control efforts are most effective when they complement the activities of other departments within the insurer. Loss control's principal opportunities for cooperation are with underwriting, marketing, premium auditing, and claims.

An insurer and its policyholders can also benefit from cooperative relationships between the insurer's loss control function and organizations outside the insurer.

These outside organizations include independent agents or brokers, as well as trade associations that engage in activities related to loss control.

Loss Control and Underwriting

As described above, loss control personnel can provide information to underwriters that enables them to make better underwriting decisions. Principally, this information consists of field inspection reports on the premises and operations of new applicants and existing policyholders who wish to renew their policies. In addition, loss control can provide technical support to underwriting on a variety of subjects, such as fire hazards of new building materials, health hazards of materials or production processes, and new techniques or equipment for materials handling.

Loss control representatives are often the only ones in the insurance company who have met the new insured. This contact helps produce a personal bond that can later be important when difficult situations arise or if specific information is needed from the policyholder.

Loss control can also assist underwriters in modifying an applicant's loss exposures to meet eligibility limits. After an applicant has been accepted, loss control can be instrumental in helping the policyholder to remain within underwriting guidelines and thereby qualified for policy renewal. In some instances, loss control may even be called on to "rehabilitate" a marginal account that underwriting has already accepted because of competitive considerations.

To provide these support services to underwriting, loss control personnel, in addition to possessing technical skills, must be effective communicators. Inspection reports should provide a clear picture of the applicant's hazards in terms that the underwriter will understand. Loss control personnel must also be able to communicate effectively with policyholders. In many cases, a loss control representative is the main communications link between the underwriter and the policyholder.

Loss Control and Marketing

Loss control can be an important ally in helping the insurer's marketing staff meet its objectives. By inspecting an applicant's premises and recommending ways of reducing hazards, loss control personnel can make the difference between the applicant's being rejected or accepted by the insurer's underwriting department. By making marginal accounts acceptable, loss control helps marketing to reach its sales goals. Loss control can also help marketing by proving to the policyholder that it understands the insured's process and the hazards associated with it. The loss control representative can offer tangible advice on improving safety. This expertise is particularly important for accounts that are eager for this type of help.

After applicants become policyholders, loss control can play a key role in retaining them as customers of the insurer. In fact, a commercial policyholder may actually have more regular contact with the insurer's loss control representatives than with any other employee of the insurer. By providing professional and courteous service that the policyholder perceives as an added value of the insurance policy, loss control personnel can create customer goodwill.

Finally, through their direct contact with policyholders, loss control representatives can learn what insurance coverages or services policyholders need or want. If loss control representatives convey this information to the appropriate marketing or sales personnel, it can assist the marketing department in either meeting the specific needs of a single policyholder or developing product enhancements that will appeal to many insureds.

For example, a loss control survey may reveal that the policyholder has acquired new property that is not adequately covered under the existing policy. If conveyed to the appropriate marketing staff, this information might lead to the sale of additional coverage to that policyholder. If the same problem is experienced by several insureds, that information could lead to a decision to revise the insurer's policy forms to provide better coverage for newly acquired property.

Loss Control and Premium Auditing

In one respect, the jobs of loss control representatives and premium auditors are similar, since both visit the policyholder's premises and have direct contact with the policyholder. The difference in the information each develops is that loss control representatives typically visit the policyholder at the beginning of the policy term, while premium auditors visit at the end of the policy term. Because premium auditors often arrive after it is too late to correct record-keeping deficiencies resulting from the policyholder's ignorance or misunderstanding, loss control personnel can use the opportunity provided by the inspection visit to pave the way for the premium audit.

To exploit this opportunity, however, premium auditors must communicate their needs to the loss control representatives. If aware of the need, for example, loss control representatives can note the location of the accounting records and the name of the person to contact at audit time. They can also record the names, titles, and duties of active executive officers. Their description of operations could be a starting point for the auditor's classification of exposures. Loss control representatives might even estimate the payroll by classification or at least the number of employees per department. They can report the existence of any new operations. If properly informed, they can also advise the policyholder concerning record-keeping requirements and the need for certificates of insurance. Finally, they can offer the assistance of the insurer's premium auditors to deal with any complex questions regarding the necessary audit. Potential problems can therefore be prevented before it is too late.

Loss Control and Claims

A partnership between loss control and claims can be just as valuable to an insurer as the relationship between loss control and underwriting, marketing, or premium auditing. The loss control department needs claims experience information to direct resources and efforts to crucial areas. The claim department relies on the loss control function for exposure data and background information that may support the adjusting process if a loss occurs. Claim and loss control personnel should regularly communicate to discuss common concerns and to review loss cases.

The claims experience information that can be useful to the loss control function includes frequency and severity of losses by line of insurance, by cause of loss, by kind of business engaged in by the insured, and by worker occupation. Regarding individual accidents, particularly in the workers compensation line, the loss control function can also benefit from information about the type of accident, the body part injured, how the accident occurred, and perhaps other details from the adjuster's report. The loss control staff can use this information to (1) identify areas for research, (2) target loss exposures for additional attention, (3) identify characteristics associated with particular types of losses, and (4) develop possible alternatives to control losses.

Loss control personnel are usually well informed in engineering, mechanical, and technological areas that may not be familiar to claim personnel. Thus, loss control specialists can assist claim personnel in solving technical problems that accompany claims. The loss control department can provide codes, standards, technical opinions, laboratory analyses, and other assistance to the claims department in the investigation and settlement of losses. A loss control specialist can design product recall procedures to assist claims personnel and insureds in controlling specific product losses.

Loss Control and Agents and Brokers

The traditional role of producers with regard to loss control was to encourage the support of the policyholder's loss control activities and to coordinate the efforts of the insurer's loss control personnel with those of the insured. This traditional role is still filled by producers and may be the only role played by many small to medium-sized agencies or brokerage firms. However, larger producers have progressed well beyond this traditional role.

Many large agencies and brokerages maintain their own loss control departments, and some are able to furnish services on a par with those offered by insurance companies. If a policyholder is receiving loss control services from both the insurer and its agent or broker, the loss control entities of both organizations should strive to coordinate their efforts for the mutual benefit of all parties involved, particularly the policyholder.

Loss Control and Trade Associations

Apart from their individual efforts to reduce the losses of their policyholders, many insurers work collectively to improve the effectiveness of loss control throughout society by participating in certain industry associations. General trade associations promote loss control in addition to performing many other functions; specialized trade associations are devoted almost entirely to loss control.

General Trade Associations

The loss control activities of general trade associations are usually restricted to (1) lobbying for loss control laws, (2) sponsoring public information campaigns to encourage loss control, and (3) conducting research in loss prevention and reduction. Such functions can be illustrated by some of the activities of one of these trade associations, the American Insurance Association (AIA). Other associations perform similar functions.

The AIA's Engineering and Safety Service provides educational materials and educational conferences for member companies. It also provides material to legislators and other government officials. Among its services is the National Building Code, a model code designed for adoption by local governments. The code requires building features that would reduce the loss of both lives and property. A second model code published by AIA, the Fire Prevention Code, emphasizes hazards not directly caused by building features, including the hazards resulting from the manufacture, handling, and storage of toxic or highly combustible materials.

Other insurer trade associations involved in loss control, lobbying, public information programs, or research include the Alliance of American Insurers, the National Association of Independent Insurers, and the Insurance Information Institute. Producer trade associations, such as the Independent Insurance Agents of America and the Professional Insurance Agents, also support loss control efforts through lobbying activities and public information programs, such as fire or theft prevention campaigns.

Specialized Trade Associations

Several trade associations are devoted exclusively or almost exclusively to loss control. One such organization is the Insurance Institute for Highway Safety (IIHS). The IIHS is supported by general insurance trade associations and several individual insurers. Its purpose is to identify, evaluate, and develop ways to reduce human loss and property loss caused by traffic accidents. The results of IIHS research are made available to legislators, other government officials, and persons interested in traffic safety.

Other specialized loss control organizations supported by insurers include the National Automobile Theft Bureau, which conducts stolen vehicle recovery and auto theft prevention activities, and the Insurance Committee for Arson Control, which serves as a catalyst for insurers' anti-arson efforts and a liaison with government agencies and other groups devoted to arson control.

Insurers, along with other contributors, also support loss prevention agencies not directly affiliated with insurance. Examples of such organizations are the National Safety Council (NSC) and the National Fire Protection Association (NFPA). The NSC publishes safety materials of all kinds and conducts a public information and publicity program in support of safety. The NFPA serves as a source of information on fire prevention and protection, develops and publishes fire safety standards, and sponsors public educational programs.

Loss Control Services Provided by Insurers

An insurer's loss control efforts generally correspond to three levels of professional safety practice: (1) physical surveys, (2) risk analysis and improvement, or (3) safety management programming. These general levels of service should be viewed as points of reference on a continuum of services. In actual practice, the level of service an insurer provides to a particular policyholder is often somewhere between two of these reference points.

Physical Surveys

Physical surveys
Loss control services consisting of collecting underwriting information on a customer's loss exposures.

The first level of service—**physical surveys**—mainly consists of collecting underwriting information on a customer's loss exposures, such as building construction, worker occupations, site diagrams, fire protection systems installed, and so on. This level of service does not require highly trained or experienced loss control representatives. Consequently, less experienced personnel are often assigned to this type of work.

On a typical survey, a loss control representative inspects the customer's premises on a walking tour and interviews the customer's management to discover details that may not be apparent from the tour. The loss control representative seeks to evaluate physical hazards affecting the customer's exposures to the following:

- Fire, windstorm, water damage, burglary, and other causes of property loss
- Legal liability arising out of premises, operations, products, completed operations, automobile, mobile equipment, environmental impairment, and other sources of liability
- Employee injuries relative to working conditions, machinery hazards, and employee safety practices

In addition to evaluating physical hazards, the loss control representative seeks to evaluate management commitment to loss control and employee attitudes toward appropriate safety behavior patterns. Thus, the loss control representative may obtain insight into the possibility and extent of both moral and morale hazards.

At the conclusion of the tour, the loss control representative holds a general review with the manager responsible for these types of concerns to ask questions, discuss loss exposures, and share suggestions for controlling hazards identified during the survey. After leaving the customer's premises, the loss control representative organizes the information in a formal report. An example of a loss control report is shown in Exhibit 7-1.

Many insurers will also generate recommendations, suggestions that can help the customer eliminate or control loss exposures. Typically, recommendations are generated when a loss control representative identifies a condition that falls below a satisfactory level. With mercantile risks, for instance, a common recommendation is to control slip-and-fall perils by improving the maintenance program for aisles, steps, and stairwells. To organize the suggested improvements, each recommendation is identified by the month and year and given a unique identification number. A review of this list for an account will indicate the cooperation of the insured in improving its loss exposures.

If the customer has requested insurance on a building or buildings valued in excess of a particular threshold, such as $100,000 or $250,000, the survey report may also include a property valuation. Typically, property valuations are performed by using construction cost estimating systems that are available from various vendors. The characteristics of the building that are needed for applying the construction cost information are obtained in the process of the physical survey. By determining the building's actual cash value, functional value, or full replacement cost (depending on which of these measures will be the basis for insurance), the appropriate amount of insurance can be determined.

Several benefits are derived from physical surveys. The insurer's underwriters can read the survey report and gain a better understanding of the loss exposures being insured. The policyholder can also gain a better understanding of its loss exposures and what steps could be taken to prevent or minimize losses, comply with applicable laws and regulations, and provide a better working environment for employees. All of these factors can contribute to higher employee morale and productivity. If a property valuation is part of the survey, the policyholder can be more certain of an adequate recovery in the event of a total loss and less likely to incur a coinsurance penalty in the event of a partial loss.

Risk Analysis and Improvement

The second level of insurer loss control service—risk analysis and risk improvement—advances the first level to what might be considered the normal practice for most insurers. In addition to completing a physical survey and hazard evaluation, as described above, the insurer's loss control personnel analyze the customer's loss history and submit formal written recommendations to the business owner or manager on ways to reduce hazards. Ordinarily, a loss control representative will contact the policyholder within sixty to ninety days to check the policyholder's progress in complying with the insurer's recommendations.

To support the risk analysis and improvement process, the insurer's loss control personnel may provide one or more of a variety of training, informational, or counseling services. Some common examples of these services are described below. Other, more specialized services are available from some insurers.

Safety Programs

A **safety program** is a series of presentations on any of various safety-related subjects that is intended to raise workers' awareness of loss exposures and appropriate safety behaviors. Typical subjects are fire safety, driver safety, and machine operation safety. The selection of subjects is based on an analysis of the policyholder's loss exposures or trends in loss experience. Priority is given to subjects that could significantly improve the policyholder's loss experience. Films, slide shows, and videotape programs may be shown in conjunction with training programs or lent to policyholders as requested.

Safety program
A series of presentations on various safety-related subjects.

EXHIBIT 7-1

Short Form Loss Control Report

IIA Insurance Companies
720 Providence Road, Malvern, PA 19355

INSURED
Terry's Casual Wear

MAILING ADDRESS
4814 Hwy. 17 South, N. Myrtle Beach, S.C.

LOCATION SURVEYED
SAME

PERSON INTERVIEWED
Theresa Mason

SURVEY DATE
6/28/X1

LOSS CONTROL REPRESENTATIVE
John Henderson

POLICY NUMBER
CRO7234525

EXPLAIN OR MAKE RECOMMENDATIONS FOR ALL CIRCLE ○ ANSWERS

A. RISK OVERVIEW

RISK HAZARD	HAZARD CONTROL	PREMISES CONDITION	HOUSEKEEPING	PRIOR LOSS	OPINION OF RISK
☐ Low	☐ Good	☐ Good	☐ Good	○ Yes	☐ Good
☑ Medium	☑ Fair	☑ Fair	☑ Fair	☑ No	☑ Fair
○ High	○ Poor	○ Poor	○ Poor		○ Poor

B. DESCRIPTION OF OPERATIONS

1. Description of business and/or operations:
   Retail clothing store

C. GENERAL DATA

1. Insured is: ☑ Owner ☐ Tenant ☐ Lessee
2. Insured is: ☑ Corporation ☐ Partnership ☐ Individual
3. Yrs. in business 5   At this location 3
4. Business hours: 10 to 11
5. Estimated gross annual sales $ 225,000
6. Neighborhood is: ☑ Commercial ☐ Rural ☐ Residential ☐ Industrial
7. Neighborhood is: ☑ Stable ○ Other
8. Does business appear successful? ☑ Yes ○ No
9. Management attitude satisfactory? ☐ Yes ○ No
10. Other occupants in building? ☐ Yes ☑ No
    If YES, describe

BUILDING

1. Year built   3
2. Building height (stories & ft./story):   1
3. Exterior wall construction: Frame   Wood   Cover   Wood shingle
4. Floor construction   Wood
5. Roof const.: Support   Wood   Deck   Metal   Cover   Metal
6. Area (include basement only if finished): sq. ft.   1,320
7. ☐ Fire Resistive   ☐ Ordinary
   ☐ Non-Combustible   ☑ Frame

8. Vertical openings:
   Stairways protected?   ☐ Yes   ○ No   ☑ None
   Elevators protected?   ☐ Yes   ○ No   ☑ None
   Elevators: # of passengers _____ # of freight _____
9. Int. finish: Walls   Wood   Ceiling   S/R
10. Building condition satisfactory?   ○ Yes   ○ No
11. Basement in building?   ☐ Yes   ☑ No
    If YES,   ☐ Full   ☐ Partial   _____ %
              ○ Finished   ☐ Unfinished

HAZARDS

1. Heating type: FA central loc elsewhere
   A. Fuel   ☐ Gas   ☑ Electric   ☐ Wood/Coal   ☐ LP Gas   ☐ Oil
   B. Appears safely arranged?   not seen   ☐ Yes   ○ No
2. Air Conditioning?   ☐ Yes   ○ No
   Type: ☑ Central   ☐ Package   ☐ Portable   ○ Other
3. Electrical type: ☐ Conduit   ☑ Romex   ☐ _____
   A. Overcurrent Protection: ☑ Cir. Brkrs.   ☐ Fuses
   B. Appear safely arranged?   ☑ Yes   ○ No
4. Are the following satisfactory?
   A. Housekeeping   ☑ Yes   ○ No
   B. Maintenance   ☑ Yes   ○ No
   C. Trash Removal   ☑ Yes   ○ No
   D. Smoking Control   ☑ Yes   ○ No
   E. Flam./Combust. liquids   ☐ Yes   ○ No   ☑ None noted
   F. Welding/hot work   ☐ Yes   ○ No   ☑ None noted
   G. Other special hazards   ☐ Yes   ○ No   ☑ None noted

FIRE PROTECTION

1. Risk within city limits?   ☑ Yes   ○ No
2. Fire Department: ☐ None   ☑ Paid   ☐ Volunteer
3. Distance to fire dept.   1/3   Miles
4. Number of hydrants and distance   1 at 50'; 1 at 370'
5. Adequate fire extinguishers?   ☑ Yes   ○ No
   Size and type: 2A
6. Extinguishers properly tagged and serviced?   ☐ Yes   ☐ No
7. Sprinkler system?   ☑ Yes   ☐ No
   A. Coverage: ○ Partial   ☐ Full   _____ %
   B. Alarm: ☐ Central Station   ☐ Local
8. Fire detection/alarm system?   ☑ Yes   ☐ No
9. Watchman service?   ☑ Yes   ☐ No
10. Fire Dept. name and class: N. Myrtle Beach

Continued on next page.

LIABILITY—ARE THE FOLLOWING SATISFACTORY?

1.	Yard and walks	☑ Yes	○ No	☐ None noted
2.	Parking areas	☑ Yes	○ No	☐ None noted
3.	Public	☑ Yes	○ No	☐ None noted
4.	Stairs, balconies	☐ Yes	○ No	☑ None noted
5.	Handrails, guardrails	○ Yes	○ No	☑ None noted
6.	Floors	☑ Yes	○ No	
7.	Sales displays	☑ Yes	○ No	☐ None noted
8.	Exterior/interior lighting	☑ Yes	○ No	☐ None noted
9.	Signs	☑ Yes	○ No	☐ None noted
10.	Elevators # _____	☐ Yes	○ No	☑ None noted
11.	Exits	☑ Yes	○ No	
12.	Other liability hazards	○ Yes	☑ No	
13.	Chargeable parking area sq. ft. _____ none			

"ALL-RISKS"

#	Item	YES	NO
1.	Any structural damage noted (walls, foundation, floors, roof, ceiling)?	○	☑
2.	Any evidence of water damage?	○	☑
3.	Any heavy equipment mounted on roof (tanks, signs, etc.)?	○	☑
4.	Potential for excessive snow/water buildup on roof?	○	☑
5.	Drainage adequate?	☑	○
6.	Evidence of floor overloads?	○	☑
7.	Plumbing in good condition?	☑	○
8.	Area prone to flash flooding?	○	☑
9.	Unusual exposure to landslide and/or erosion?	☑	○
	on waterway		

EXPOSURES

COMPLETE ONLY WHEN DIAGRAMS NOT REQUESTED

	DISTANCE	HEIGHT	CONSTRUCTION	OCCUPANCY
N				
S				
E				
W				

COMMERCIAL COOKING (if applicable)

1.	Volume of cooking: ☐ Light ☐ Moderate ☐ Heavy	YES	NO
2.	Metal hood over grease-producing equipment?	☐	○
3.	Frequency of filter cleaning adequate for cooking exposure?	☐	○
4.	Hood, filter, ducts clean?	☐	○
5.	Cleaning company contracted?	☐	○
6.	Proper clearance from combustibles?	☐	○
7.	Automatic fire extinguishing system?	☐	○
8.	Service contract for property maintenance?	☐	○
9.	Current tag?	☐	○
10.	Automatic fuel shut-off?	☐	○
11.	Full surface protection?	☐	○
12.	Portable extinguishers adequate and serviced?	☐	○

OPEN STOCK BURGLARY (if requested)

1. Type of merchandise
2. Stock values: Avg. $ _____ Max. $ _____

	YES	NO
3. High crime area?	☐	○
4. All building openings (doors, windows, etc.) properly protected and secured?	☐	○
5. Adequate night lighting?	☐	○
6. Police patrol adequate?	☐	○

7. Burglar alarm ☐ Full ☐ Partial
   ☐ Cent. Sta. ☐ Local Gong ☐ None

   Alarm Co. Name _____

INSIDE/OUTSIDE ROBBERY (if requested)

1. Daily receipts: Avg. $ _____ Max. $ _____
2. Frequency of bank deposits Avg. $ _____ Max. $ _____

	YES	NO
3. High crime area?	○	☐
4. Cash/receipt buildup in registers controlled?	☐	○
5. Checks stamped "FOR DEPOSIT" as received?	☐	○
6. Hold up alarm on premises?	☐	○
7. Safe on premises?	☐	○

Manufacturer _____
Location _____ Class _____ (B.C.E. etc.)

COMMENTS/RECOMMENDATIONS:

_____
_____
_____

PLATE GLASS

	YES	NO
1. Any hazards due to neighborhood?	○	☐
2. Any plates cracked and/or pitted?	○	☐
3. Frames and settings in good condition?	☐	☐
4. Unusual hazards due to crowding or high value of window display?	○	☐
5. Glass endangered by vehicle traffic or vandalism in area?	○	☐
6. Any thermal, tempered, stained or lettered glass?	○	☐

APARTMENTS/CONDOS/MOTELS (if applicable)

1. No. of units _____
2. Occupancy _____ %
3. Rent $ _____
4. Est. market value $ _____
   Source of information _____

	YES	NO
5. Are the following satisfactory?		
Playground	☐	○
a. Housekeeping	☐	○
b. Grounds	☐	○
c. Access	☐	○
6. Swimming Pool?	☐	☐
Protected?	☐	○

Continued on next page.

Operations

Your insured is a corporation that has been in business for five years. It has been in business at the present location since the shopping mall was constructed three years ago. The mall has numerous small shops and restaurants built up on a boardwalk over a small inlet, approximately 3,000 feet from the Atlantic Ocean. Insured leases this space for a clothing store, selling ladies moderately low-priced casual wear and a few accessories, such as purses, belts, etc. Also, there is a small line of costume jewelry in one case at the counter.

Building

The building is three years old, of wood frame construction, and found to be in good condition and well maintained. The building is on wood pylons, and a portion of the building is above the actual water (see diagram and photo).

Heating and Air Conditioning

Heat and air conditioning are ducted from elsewhere in the mall and are said to be water-controlled and thought to be electric; however, the actual unit was not located. The insured said she believes the actual units are near Hwy. 17, several hundred feet from the building.

Wiring

Wiring is romex with breaker protection. This appears to be in good condition and is three years old.

Protection

Insured is located in North Myrtle Beach, and the North Myrtle Beach fire department will respond there. No unusual fire department obstructions were noted.

Portable extinguishers were posted all around the mall area, and these were properly tagged and serviced. Also, there is a Z100 Moose digital alarm system protecting the shop. This has heat detectors, as well as infrared motion detectors, and insured states she believes this is directly monitored by the fire department. The alarm system was installed by the owners of the mall, and apparently these are present in every location.

Much of the mall is sprinklered, and there is a PIV valve 50 feet outside of insured's location; however, this particular shop is not sprinklered.

There are security guards employed by the mall, and the insured said that they patrol this area 24 hours a day.

Liability

The shop was in good condition from a liability standpoint. Stock is neatly stored and arranged in a clutter-free manner. Floor covering, lighting, and egress are good, and there are marked exits. All parking is controlled by the mall, and there is no parking area controlled by the insured.

Losses

Ms. Boykin states no losses have occurred under these coverages. They did have one business interruption loss during Hugo in 1989.

Comments

Due to premises and building conditions, as well as good controls and the nature of insured's operation, this risk rates good for all coverages surveyed.

Note

Initially, we visited insured on 6/20; however, Ms. Boykin was not in. We phoned back on several occasions before she contacted us on 6/28 to obtain loss and other information.

Recommendations

None are deemed necessary at this time.

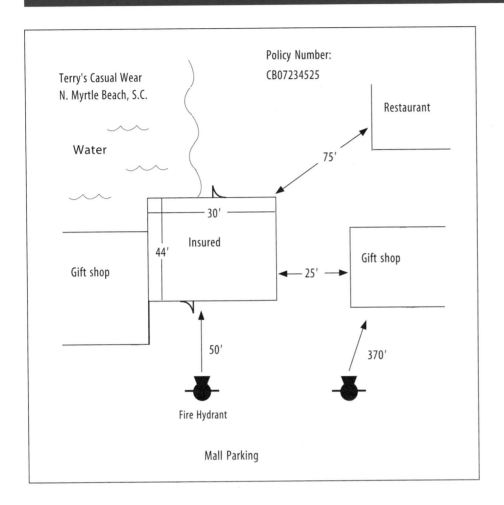

The objectives of safety programs are to develop positive safety attitudes among all workers, to improve workers' understanding of safety-related matters, and to help workers accept responsibility for their role in the organization's safety program. Ultimately, the policyholder may be expected to integrate these objectives into its own goals and not to rely on the insurer's personnel except for special or more complex topics.

To prepare the policyholder's managers for assuming a leadership role in loss control matters, the insurer may also conduct supervisory safety training sessions in addition to the training programs for all employees.

Technical Information Resources

Many insurers support their policyholders' loss control efforts by serving as a convenient source of technical information. The information sought by the policyholder might relate to specific hazards and appropriate controls, the interpretation of standards, or particular safety management products or suppliers. By providing technical information needed by the policyholder, the insurer helps the policyholder save time and effort in obtaining data needed to make informed loss control decisions. The insurer also builds a working relationship with the policyholder that can help to retain the policyholder's account.

Fire Protection Systems Testing and Evaluation

Fire protection (and detection) systems must be regularly tested in order to ascertain their reliability during emergencies. Many insurer loss control departments enter into service contracts with their policyholders or other clients to provide periodic testing and maintenance for such systems. The insurer's principal concerns are whether the system will respond in an emergency and whether the system is properly designed for the client's current loss exposures.

Pre-Construction Counseling

When business owners are considering expanding existing facilities or constructing new structures, they often overlook the connection between construction features and insurance rates. Generally, rating credits may be given for noncombustible or fire-resistive construction, sprinkler systems, smoke detectors, burglar alarms, security hardware, and other features. A pre-construction review of the drawings and specifications by the insurer allows the policyholder to see how its insurance rates and underwriting acceptability will be affected by the new construction. Any plan alterations desired by the policyholder can then be made at minimal cost before construction begins.

Safety Management Programming

The third level of insurer loss control services—safety management programming—has become more prominent among advanced loss control operations. This activity is usually coordinated by senior staff members, often called loss control consultants, who have the advanced technical and communications skills needed for this type of work.

Safety management programming
A complete evaluation of the policyholder's operations and the establishment of loss control objectives, selection of appropriate loss control measures, implementation of chosen loss control measures, and a monitoring program.

The **safety management programming** process begins with a complete evaluation of the policyholder's operations, just as in risk analysis and improvement loss control activities. After reviewing the evaluation with the policyholder, loss control consultants assist the policyholder in establishing loss control objectives, selecting appropriate loss control measures, organizing the resources necessary to implement the chosen loss control measures, and setting up procedures for monitoring the program.

Ordinarily, the customer is responsible for actually implementing the program, without direct assistance from the loss control consultant, because of several concerns. These concerns include errors and omissions liability, lack of authority to exercise a management role in the customer's business, and the need for management to have "ownership" of the program. After being implemented, the plan must be monitored to see whether adjustments are needed. The consultant can provide a great deal of technical assistance in the monitoring phase of the program.

The consultation process normally requires frequent visits to the customer's premises for gathering initial information, planning the review with management, and following up to monitor the program. The support services described above in connection with risk analysis and improvement are typically included in safety management programming as well. In most situations, program results are apparent within three to six months after the formalized safety management program has been implemented.

Factors Affecting Service Levels

Every insurer must decide what levels of loss control service to provide. Few insurers provide the same level of service to all policyholders, so the question perhaps is what levels of loss control service to provide to which customers. Apart from the basic reasons for practicing loss control described at the beginning of this chapter, several factors may affect insurers' decisions on what levels of loss control service to provide.

Personal Versus Commercial Insurance

An insurer that writes only personal insurance is unlikely to provide extensive loss control services. The relatively small premium for a typical personal auto or homeowners account does not justify the expense necessary to conduct on-site safety inspections by trained loss control personnel.

During the personal insurance underwriting process, insurers may in some situations request their agents or sales employees to photograph a house or verify the vehicle identification number of a car. Insurers may provide producers with checklists to ensure that certain items are either requested specifically of the applicant or looked for during the producer's drive-by. An example of a checklist is shown in Exhibit 7-2. In this and other circumstances, producers can effectively carry out loss control programs when provided with explicit instructions from home office loss control personnel. When insuring exceptionally high-valued property—such as a mansion or a yacht—the insurer may use trained loss control representatives to develop underwriting information or recommendations for reducing physical hazards.

Apart from on-site inspections, an insurer can promote loss control among its personal lines policyholders by publishing educational bulletins or by offering rate discounts for home alarm systems, deadbolt locks, automobile anti-theft devices, driver education, or other loss control measures undertaken by policyholders. An insurer may also provide financial assistance to industry associations that disseminate information, conduct research, lobby legislators, or otherwise support loss control efforts to benefit society as a whole. Fire safety and highway safety are two major areas addressed by such associations.

At the other end of the loss control spectrum are insurers that offer industrial policies in which loss control activities are an essential part of the services purchased by the policyholder. The most extreme example of this insurance type is boiler and machinery insurance, a market dominated by a few insurers who conduct frequent inspections to avert losses.

EXHIBIT 7-2

Personal Lines Property Report

PERSONAL LINES PROPERTY REPORT

DATE   November 1, 20XX
POLICY NUMBER   PCA 123 4579
NAME   Willis Bethea
MAILING   900 Jeffries Bridge Road
ADDRESS   West Chester, PA 19380
PROPERTY
LOCATION
(IF OTHER THAN ABOVE)

PHOTOS
☑ ATTACHED
PHOTOS _____
(IF MORE THAN ONE)
☐ NOT AVAILABLE

AMT. OF COVERAGE $ 194,000

OBSERVATIONS	VALUES

DIAGRAM—SHOW DIMENSIONS

1. Apprx. Year Built ___1977___   OTHER: _____
2. Number of Stories   ☐ 1   ☑ 2   ☐ 3   ☐ _____
3. Occupancy:
   ☐ Single Family   ☐ Two Family   ☐ _____
4. Predominant Constr. Material:
   A. Dwg.   ☑ Frame   ☐ Brick   ☐ Solid   ☐ _____
   Veneer   or Stone   Brick
   B. Roof   ☑ Comp.   ☐ Tar &   ☐ Wood   ☐ _____
   Shingle   Gravel   Shingle
   C. Outbuildings   ☐ None   ☑ Frame
   ☐ Masonry   ☐ Metal   ☐ _____
5. Condition:
   A. Dwg.   ☑ Good   ☐ _____
   B. Roof   ☑ Good   ☐ _____
   C. Outbuildings   ☐ None   ☑ Good   ☐ _____
6. Neighborhood:
   A. Type   ☑ Residential   ☐ Commercial
   ☐ Rural   ☐ _____
   B. Status   ☐ Improving   ☑ Stable   ☐ _____
7. Protection:
   Approximate Distance in Feet to Nearest Hydrant   100 ft
   Approximate Distance in Miles to Nearest
   Responding Fire Department   1 1/2 mi
8. Liability Hazards
   ☑ Outside Pool   ☑ Fenced   _____
   ☐ Horses   ☐ Unfenced
   ☐ Large Dogs   ☐ Business use
9. Hazards Noted: ☐ None
   ☐ Vacant or   ☐ Isolated or   ☐ Difficult Access
   Seasonal   Hidden   for Fire
   Property   ☐ Wood Stove   Department
   ☐ Dead Trees   ☐ Combustible   ☐ Open
   or Limbs   Brush or Debris   Foundation
   ☐ Adjacent   ☐ Flooding or
   Property   High Water   ☐ Other

Utility shed

Deck

Covered porch   Two-car garage

Estimated replacement cost using:
☑ Room count method
☐ Square foot method
$ 210,000

CUSTOM HOME FEATURES:
_____
_____
_____
_____

Date of Report ___9/1/X2___
Agency: F.A. Smith, West Chester
Inspector: Bill Smith

REMARKS—RECOMMENDATIONS FOR IMPROVEMENT
_____
_____
_____
_____
_____

Size of Policyholder

The larger premiums generated by commercial policyholders and the greater values at risk permit the allocation of loss control services to those policyholders.

The level of service rendered to a commercial policyholder can depend on the size of the account, as measured by policy premium. Typically, an insurer devotes greater resources to larger accounts than to smaller accounts. The loss control department and the underwriting department can determine in advance what loss control services to provide to the various premium levels.

In some cases, policyholders may want a higher level of service than the insurer provides as part of the basic insurance product. Satisfying customers in these situations is one of the reasons that some insurers offer unbundled loss control services. Policyholders who want supplemental services can purchase them for a fee in addition to the basic policy premium. In that way, those who do not want or need supplemental services are not required to subsidize the costs of these services through the basic policy premium.

Types of Exposures Insured

The loss control services an insurer will provide depend to some degree on the types of exposures the insurer is willing to cover. An insurer that covers large and complex industrial firms needs the skilled personnel and sophisticated equipment to meet the loss control requirements of such firms. It needs, for example, personnel and equipment to do the following:

1. Test and evaluate the effects of noise levels on employees
2. Appraise the hazards to employees of solvents, toxic metals, radioactive isotopes, and other substances
3. Assist in the design of explosion suppression systems or fire-extinguishing systems for dangerous substances or easily damaged equipment
4. Evaluate products liability exposures and prepare programs to minimize such exposures
5. Deal with many other complex and specialized loss control problems

On the other hand, an insurer that deals primarily with habitational, mercantile, and small manufacturing exposures might be able to maintain a much less sophisticated loss control department.

Potential Legal Liability

The possibility of being held legally liable for negligence in providing loss control services may cause some insurers to avoid or minimize the exposure by not offering loss control services or by restricting their loss control activities. This concern arose principally after the 1964 case of Nelson v. Union Wire Rope Corporation,[1] in which the court ruled that an insurer could be held liable to any person (not just the policyholder) who might reasonably be expected to be injured as a result of the insurer's negligence in rendering loss control services.

Insurers have attempted to minimize liability for loss control services by adding disclaimers to their inspection report forms or policies. Typically, these disclaimers state that any inspections, surveys, or recommendations made by the insurer are for underwriting purposes only; the insurer does not warrant that conditions are safe or healthful or comply with laws or regulations. Although such disclaimers may help to inform the policyholder of the nature of the insurer's services, they are not likely to protect the insurer against a suit by any person, such as an employee or a customer of the named insured, who is not a party to the insurance.

As a result of the Nelson case and similar cases, some states amended their workers compensation laws to provide insurers with some protection for job-connected loss control efforts. However, such statutory protection extends only to liability arising from loss control inspections related to workers compensation. It does not, for example, provide immunity to the insurer for inspections related to general liability or property insurance.

At the time of the Nelson case, many insurers feared that a flood of similar suits and judgments would follow. As the years passed and the flood of cases failed to materialize, insurers' concerns diminished substantially. The effect of the Nelson case and other similar cases has been minimal. Most large insurers with loss control operations feel they can address the liability issues and maintain staff in areas subject to liability questions.

Organization of the Loss Control Function

An insurer's loss control function is largely a field operation because loss control representatives must visit the policyholder's premises in order to conduct surveys and consult with policyholders. Thus, if the insurer maintains a system of field offices for sales, underwriting, and claims, loss control personnel will also likely be situated in some or all of these offices. As with sales, underwriting, or claims, loss control field operations are typically supported by personnel in the home office. An insurer must therefore decide on an organizational structure that most efficiently accommodates the loss control function at both the home office and the field levels.

Because loss control has always had a close working relationship with underwriting, insurers traditionally placed the loss control function within their underwriting departments. In more recent years, insurers show considerable variation in how they organize the loss control function. Some of the typical patterns in which the loss control function may be performed include the following:

- Separate department
- Department combined with premium auditing
- Part of the underwriting department
- Part of an administrative department
- Independent contractor

Loss Control as a Separate Department

The loss control function may be set up as a separate department with its own line of reporting and management control. In this form of organization, a loss control department at the home office has responsibility for the loss control function throughout the company. Depending on the management structure, the head of the nationwide loss control function at the home office may be a vice president, perhaps reporting to an executive vice president. Although the head of the underwriting function has no authority over loss control operations, cooperation between the two departments is a key objective.

In the case of a large national insurer with a number of regional and branch offices, the loss control department has lines of authority and responsibility at the regional and branch office levels, all reporting to the home office department. Exhibit 7-3 illustrates this type of organization.

In this arrangement, loss control representatives and clerical support personnel in the branch report to the loss control manager. The branch loss control manager has two lines of reporting. One is within the functional area, where the branch loss control manager reports to the regional loss control manager if the insurer is large enough to warrant this level of management. If not, the branch loss control manager reports directly to the home office loss control vice president. The second line of reporting is to the branch manager. This dual reporting is characteristic of an insurer branch organization. The branch underwriting and claim managers have similar dual lines of reporting. In most insurers, the branch manager is directly responsible for marketing. This branch organization is shown in Exhibit 7-4.

EXHIBIT 7-3

Loss Control as a Separate Department

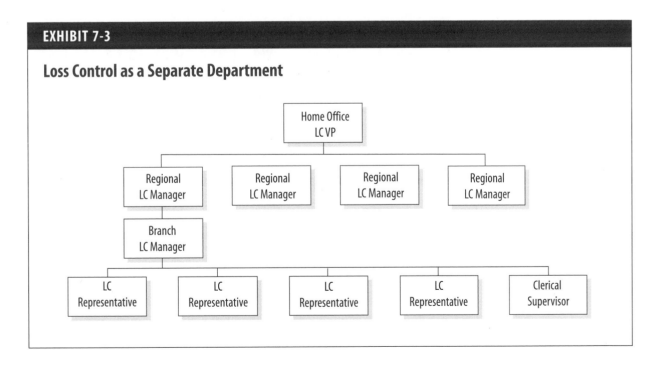

EXHIBIT 7-4

Branch Office Organization—Loss Control as a Separate Department

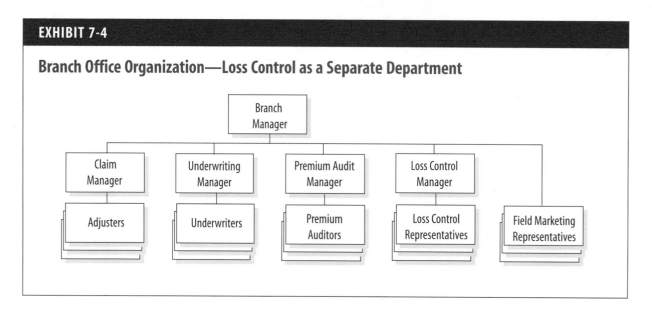

The following are several possible reasons for establishing a separate loss control department:

1. The insurer wishes to provide unbundled loss control services from a separate department.

2. The insurer's loss control services have become so complex and geographically dispersed that they cannot be adequately managed by the manager of another department with other priorities.

3. A separate loss control department allows greater independence of judgment concerning loss exposure evaluation.

4. A separate department makes it easier to segregate budget expenditures so that specific costs for loss control services can be identified and managed separately.

Combined With Premium Auditing

An alternative form of organizing the loss control function combines loss control with premium auditing. At the branch office level, such a department may be called a policyholder services department. Exhibit 7-5 depicts this pattern of branch office organization.

In this organizational structure, the policyholder service manager supervises those employees most frequently calling on the insurer's commercial customers. Both the loss control personnel and the premium auditors provide technical services to the policyholder. There are, however, substantial differences in the training and duties involved in loss control and those involved in premium auditing. Because it is extremely unlikely that a manager has previous field experience as both a premium auditor and a loss control representative, the policyholder service unit manager probably has a background in one or the other of the functional areas. Problems in communication and understanding

EXHIBIT 7-5

Branch Office Organization—Loss Control Combined With Premium Auditing

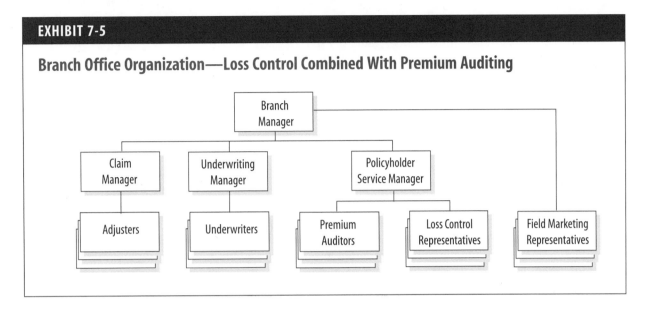

can arise because the manager may not be able to relate well to the differences between the two functional areas or to understand the problems faced by the field personnel in discharging their duties.

Part of Underwriting

In some companies, the loss control function falls within the underwriting area. If the insurer divides underwriting into separate personal lines and commercial lines departments, then loss control is usually part of the commercial lines department. Exhibit 7-6 illustrates this organizational structure.

EXHIBIT 7-6

Loss Control Reporting to Underwriting

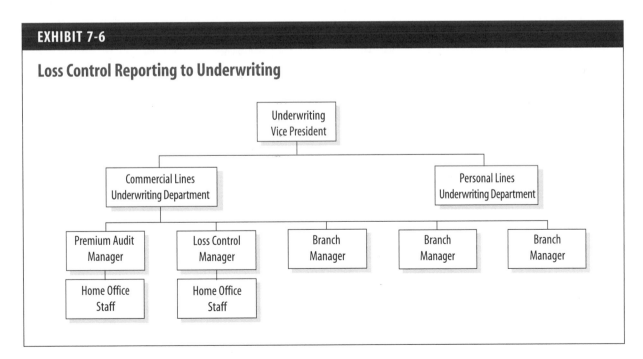

At the branch office level, loss control departments may report to the branch office underwriting manager. In this type of organizational structure, branch premium audit personnel may also report to the branch underwriting manager. This type of branch organizational structure is shown in Exhibit 7-7.

When the loss control function is part of the underwriting department, the manner in which the underwriting manager views loss control is of paramount importance. If the underwriting manager can maintain a balanced management perspective, the arrangement usually works well, because the underwriting manager controls both functions and can create an environment of mutual support. However, if the manager chooses to place a lower priority on loss control activities, the insurer's loss control efforts can suffer. In many cases, the manager of the underwriting department can be distracted from loss control matters by other priority interests, such as agent relations, production of premium volume, and underwriting profitability. As a result, loss control may not receive the attention or active support it needs to be effective.

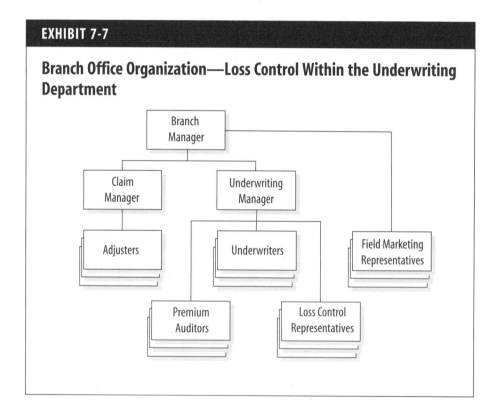

EXHIBIT 7-7

Branch Office Organization—Loss Control Within the Underwriting Department

Part of Administrative Department

Some insurers find it more convenient to combine the loss control function with such administrative functions as accounting and credit. This structure best serves the needs of small insurers or those with a relatively small proportion of commercial lines business. It may also suit insurers who rely heavily on outside firms to provide loss control services. Exhibit 7-8 depicts a branch office organization following this pattern.

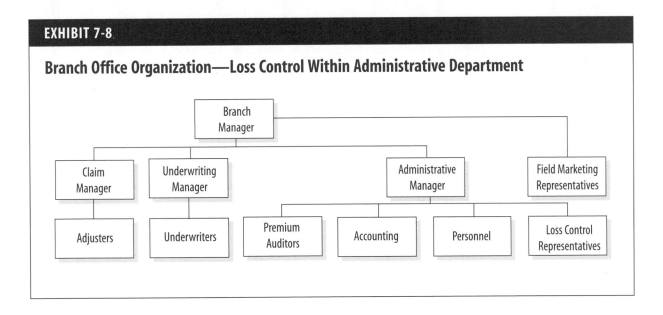

EXHIBIT 7-8

Branch Office Organization—Loss Control Within Administrative Department

Independent Contractors

Independent loss control firms perform their services as independent contractors of the insurer rather than as employees. Independent loss control firms are similar to the independent claims adjusting firms used by insurers. Some insurers rely heavily on independent loss control firms; others rarely use them.

An insurer may use an independent loss control firm to provide service to a commercial account located some distance from the insurer's nearest loss control representatives. If the policyholder is located in a territory where the insurer has few commercial lines policyholders, significant expense savings may be possible by using the services of an independent firm. Independent firms may also be used to perform specialized work that is beyond the technical expertise of the insurer's personnel.

Another reason for using independent firms is to provide additional capability to meet peak level demands when the insurer's management determines that adding more full-time staff is not warranted. The independent services may also be used to meet requirements during periods when the insurer's loss control staff is depleted because of vacations, illness, or turnover.

Home Office Activities

To manage field activities and provide support services to field representatives and consultants, an insurer conducts a variety of activities within its loss control function, typically in its home office. These activities can be classified into three general categories: (1) management, (2) research and publications, and (3) technical backup.

Management

Management functions related to loss control differ only in detail from management functions relative to any other insurer operation. They include establishing policies and objectives; hiring, training, and supervising personnel to carry out policies and achieve objectives; and evaluating departmental performance.

The major policy decisions that must be made concern the scope of the insurer's loss control activities. Should the loss control department be staffed with the necessary engineers, industrial hygienists, and other professional persons required to perform those activities? Should it be the eyes and ears of the underwriting department, devoting its efforts primarily to developing underwriting information? Or should it perform a combination of the two functions? The factors that may influence management's decision were discussed earlier in this chapter.

Of course, there are many other policy decisions to be made. For example, what kinds of loss control services should insurer personnel and outside consultants provide? What kinds of service should be provided at the field office level rather than at the home office level? Should loss control services be furnished only as an ancillary service incidental to the marketing of insurance, or should loss control services also be provided on a fee basis to firms that do not buy insurance from the company? Many other examples could be cited.

Establishing objectives for loss control operations is not dramatically different from establishing objectives for other insurer operations. In fact, loss control management is likely to adopt or be subject to some of the general objectives applicable to underwriting. However, some specialized objectives for loss control personnel might include the following:

1. Completing a certain number of surveys, consultations, and safety programs
2. Meeting the time frames for completing underwriting surveys and other tasks
3. Operating within the loss control department's budget
4. Achieving a specified number of "saves" (that is, situations in which loss control measures recommended by the insurer and implemented by the policyholder prevented or reduced actual losses)
5. Satisfying policyholders with the services to be provided
6. Cooperating with underwriting or other departments of the insurer

Departmental performance can be measured by comparing actual results with stated objectives. Some objectives, such as policyholder satisfaction, may be harder to quantify than others, such as the number of underwriting surveys conducted.

An insurer's practices in hiring and training loss control personnel depend on its staffing needs. An insurer whose loss control personnel are limited to surveying uncomplicated premises and operations does not need the same level of expertise as a large insurer that provides unbundled loss control services to a wide range of customers with complex loss exposures.

In some cases, an insurer may concentrate on hiring recent college graduates with little or no background in loss control who can be trained on the job. In other cases, an insurer may seek to hire experienced practitioners possessing all of the skills needed to perform highly specialized work.

To assist in training personnel, the home office staff typically develops training and reference manuals for conducting field operations. The major subject areas covered in such manuals could include the following:

- Basic loss control practice
- Workload management
- Conducting site visitations and surveys
- Completing field reports and other documentation
- Hazard identification and evaluation
- Errors and omissions liability
- Conducting safety management consultations
- Individual performance evaluations
- Expense accounts and related administration

Research and Publications

Another major activity of the home office loss control staff is research into the techniques of loss prevention and reduction. Such research may consist of basic scientific research into the causes of loss or searches of existing literature to find new developments that can be applied in loss control.

Examples of basic scientific research include such projects as (1) analyzing the effectiveness and adverse characteristics of various extinguishing agents that might be used on computer fires, (2) testing the irritant or toxic characteristics of solvents, and (3) developing new techniques for guarding particularly troublesome machinery. As noted earlier, basic research is often conducted at the association level in order to spread the rather substantial cost over a wider base. However, some research is conducted at the insurer home office level, either by employees or by consultants.

Most research conducted at the insurer level is oriented toward direct applications. That is, it consists of constantly reviewing basic research conducted by trade associations, government agencies, and others to find new discoveries and developments that can be applied to the insurer's loss control efforts. For example, the home office staff may encounter medical research indicating that vapors from a particular solvent may cause lung cancer. Such information must quickly be disseminated to loss control representatives in the insurer's field offices, along with possible measures to cope with the danger. Such measures might include better ventilation techniques or the suggestion of an alternative solvent that would serve the same purpose but involve less of a health hazard.

In addition to conducting research and disseminating the findings internally, the home office staff may publish loss control information for policyholders and others in the form of books, manuals, or checklists. These publications are not intended to replace the services provided by the insurer's loss control function. However, they do provide a valuable supplement to such services and assist the policyholder in effectively administering the loss control program on a daily basis.

The home office staff may also develop reporting forms to assist its field representatives in gathering underwriting and loss control information. Such forms are developed in the home office unit to achieve a consistent format and to coordinate the forms with those of other functions, such as underwriting and claims. Examples of these reporting forms include checklists, site diagrams, and insurance-to-value forms.

Technical Backup

In addition to its managerial and research activities, the home office loss control staff usually provides technical backup services for field office inspectors. These backup services may consist of advice and counsel to field representatives on specific problems, actual field assistance in inspecting complex operations, or both.

A common area for home office technical backup is industrial hygiene. Many insurers do not have sufficient demand to justify maintaining industrial hygiene personnel and equipment at the field office level, especially the personnel and equipment required to evaluate the hazards associated with radioactive isotopes, exotic metals (such as beryllium), and other industrial materials. Such personnel and equipment may be maintained at the home office and dispatched to the field offices on temporary assignment. Products and environmental liability loss control are other areas for which qualified personnel are more likely to be found only at the home office level.

PREMIUM AUDITING[2]

In several commercial lines of insurance, specialists called premium auditors play a vital role in the insurance mechanism. Their knowledge of accounting procedures, as well as insurance principles, enables them to obtain the information needed to calculate premiums and to establish future rates for insurers. In safeguarding the accuracy of the information on which insurance premiums are based, premium auditors help to make the insurance mechanism work as it is intended.

Insurance premium audit
A methodical examination of a policyholder's operations, records, and books of account to determine the actual insurance exposure for the coverage provided.

An **insurance premium audit** is a methodical examination of a policyholder's operations, records, and books of account. Its purpose is to determine the actual insurance exposure for the coverages provided and to render a precise report of the findings.

Reasons for Premium Audits

The need for a premium audit arises from the existence of insurance policies with a variable premium base. In an insurance policy, the insurer promises under certain conditions to indemnify the policyholder for particular kinds of losses during the specified policy term. In return, the policyholder pays a premium that equals the applicable rate times the number of exposure units involved. An exposure unit is the fundamental measure of loss potential that is used to compute both probability of loss and premium. In fire insurance, the exposure unit is each $100 of insurance; in workers compensation insurance, it is each $100 of payroll. Other exposure bases (or premium bases) include gross sales, area, admissions, vehicles, and many other such variable items. The rate, which is the price per unit of exposure, depends on the classification. Different classes of exposure have different rates, depending on the probability of loss for that class.

Because an insurance contract provides protection for a specified period in the future, policyholders might have difficulty predicting the number of exposure units that will be covered by the policy. An insurance contract defining the premium in terms of exposure units simplifies this task and spares policyholders the necessity of purchasing more insurance protection than they need. A business seeking workers compensation coverage, for example, does not know how many employees it will have during the coming year. The policy, however, sets the premium as the manual rate for the applicable classification per $100 of payroll for the year. At policy inception, the policyholder pays a deposit premium based on an estimate of the annual payroll, and a premium auditor might examine the policyholder's records following the end of the policy period to determine the actual payroll for each applicable classification. The insurer then calculates the actual earned premium. If it is greater than the deposit premium, the policyholder receives a bill for the additional premium due. If it is less, the policyholder receives a refund.

In lines other than workers compensation, the premium might be based on any one of a number of items other than payroll. General liability coverages are written with premium bases such as gross sales, payroll, or other measures of fluctuating exposures. Business auto policies require premium auditors to verify a schedule of covered vehicles. Reporting forms used with fire or marine insurance are audited at the discretion of the insurer. Blanket commercial property coverages provide for an audit to adjust the premium for property that the policyholder acquires or disposes of during the policy term.

Although an actual premium audit is not feasible for every policy with a variable premium base, there are several distinct reasons for an insurer to audit the records of the insured. The primary reason is to obtain and verify the information necessary to compute the actual earned premium for the policy period. In addition, audits are required to comply with regulation and to collect ratemaking data. Beyond that, there are sound business reasons for premium audits, such as inhibiting fraud, obtaining greater insight into the policyholder's operations, and reinforcing a mutually beneficial relationship. In assigning policies for audit, the audit manager may have any or all of these considerations in mind.

Determining Correct Premium

When a policy is written subject to audit, the actual premium can be calculated only at the end of the policy term when the exact exposure is known. Even then, more than a routine calculation is usually necessary to determine the premium. In most cases, the applicable manual for the line of insurance involved strictly defines the procedure, specifying inclusions and exclusions in the premium base and defining distinct rating classifications. Mastery of these rules requires considerable effort and practice. Insurers avoid many potential errors by assigning the task to specialists whose knowledge of the rules is current and accurate.

Policyholders have the information to determine the premium base but usually lack sufficient understanding of manual rules to present the information in the necessary form. Consequently, the insurer usually determines the actual earned premium. Either way, the insurer should be satisfied that the premium information is reliable and properly classified. The fundamental rule in collecting information is the following: the closer to the source, the more reliable the observation. Even if there were never any question of the insured's ability to provide the premium data, the insurer would gain confidence in the accuracy of the data by physically inspecting the original books of account and testing the data obtained.

The insurer also bears a responsibility to determine the premium correctly. Unless premiums are commensurate with the exposures covered, the insurer cannot operate profitably. If, however, the insurer overcharges, it will probably lose the business when the insured discovers the error. The interest as well as the obligation of the insurer therefore requires as much certainty and precision in the premium adjustment as possible. A premium audit serves this function.

Meeting Regulatory Requirements

Although the rules vary from state to state, they often require premium audits of workers compensation accounts. Compared to other lines of insurance, the regulation of workers compensation insurance is usually much more prescriptive. This tendency follows from the compulsory nature of workers compensation coverage. It can be argued that in requiring workers compensation coverage, the state has also assumed an obligation to guarantee its availability to all and to ensure that such coverage is administered fairly and equitably. Therefore, even most states that allow open competition to set rates in other lines of insurance prescribe uniform workers compensation rules and class rates. As an added protection, the rules in some states stipulate that the insurer must audit the records of policyholders who meet certain size and time conditions.

Collecting Ratemaking Data

Calculating actuarially credible class rates depends on accurate data regarding claims payments, earned premiums, and insured exposures for each class. Although claims reports reveal the necessary information on claims for a given period, the premium volume and total insured exposures by class cannot accurately be determined without the compilation of data from premium audits. The detailed class-by-class breakdown of exposures obtained by a premium audit is necessary for the insurer's statistical report to the advisory rating organizations (rating bureaus), as well as for billing purposes. When the rating bureau has accumulated statistics showing the premium volume, the loss experience, and the total insured exposures for each class, the actuaries can calculate appropriate rates or loss costs. The rating bureau's rate filing is based on this information.

Inhibiting Fraud

Occasionally, business owners deliberately attempt to reduce their insurance premiums by presenting false or misleading information to the insurer.

Although uncovering fraud is not the purpose of premium auditing, diligent premium auditors have contributed to uncovering deceptive practices. Policyholders are far less likely to submit erroneous information to the insurer when they know that such information might be checked and independently verified by a premium auditor. Thus, even when performed only randomly, premium audits are an effective control on the integrity of the premium computation and collection process.

Reinforcing Policyholders' Confidence

The vast majority of policyholders seek fairness in their dealings with insurers. Competent premium audits, therefore, contribute to the policyholders' confidence in fair treatment. A premium computed from a meticulous audit has more credibility than one computed in some way entirely outside the knowledge of the policyholder. There is less reason to fear a mistake when the auditor has obviously exercised due care in collecting and verifying the data. Observing the audit process counters the notion that premium adjustments are arbitrary and conveys the impression that all policyholders are, and in fact must be, treated according to uniform and equitable procedures. Finally, the auditor can explain the audit procedure to the policyholder so that the premium bill will not be a surprise when it arrives.

There are longer-range benefits for the insurer. A policyholder with a favorable impression of the insurer is less likely to look for another insurer at renewal time or when the need for additional coverage arises. Having gained from the audit procedure a greater appreciation for how the premium is determined, a policyholder might make a conscious effort to keep better records in the future, especially when properly segregated records will reduce the premium charges. The policyholder might also be more receptive to loss control advice or other services the insurer can provide.

Obtaining Additional Information

A premium audit might generate additional information about the policyholder. Such information can be extremely useful in determining whether to renew a policy. Premium audit information can also identify marketing opportunities. Information collected from several audits can support an analysis of insurer underwriting policy or overall operations. Finally, it is a source of feedback on the insurer's image and effectiveness.

Thus, the premium audit leads to greater certainty and, therefore, more efficient operations. The insurer becomes more certain of the actual exposures assumed, the classification of exposures, the characteristics of policyholders, and the amount of premiums earned. The policyholder becomes more certain of the nature of the relationship with the insurer, the protection provided under the policy, and the cost of the protection. And ratemaking organizations become more certain of the validity of their rate filings.

The Premium Auditing Process

The work of premium auditors requires accurate and complete information. To be sure that their information is accurate and complete, premium auditors should follow a systematic process for each audit. Premium audits require countless individual decisions, and premium auditors should reach these decisions in an orderly, methodical fashion.

Judgment in Premium Auditing

Auditors cannot make premium audits in cookbook fashion. There is no single recipe that produces a perfect audit every time. At each stage of the audit process, premium auditors must make judgments about the particular case and decide how to proceed. Sometimes they need more information about the operations, more records, or an explanation for an apparent discrepancy. These individual judgments are necessary because premium auditors must satisfy themselves that the information they obtain is reasonable and reliable.

Stages of the Premium Auditing Process

If there is no substitute for the premium auditor's individual judgment, there is also no substitute for logical thought and systematic procedure. Premium auditors can apply a process to all audits, large or small, regardless of the coverages involved. Consistently following this systematic process ensures that every audit is thorough. The stages of the auditing process provide a framework for organizing the countless individual decisions auditors must make.

Planning

Premium auditors must consider several questions in the auditing process. Once these questions are answered, the insurer can implement guidelines for determining which policies should be audited and the approach to be taken on each.

Because insurers cannot afford the expense of auditing every auditable policy every year, they must decide which policies to audit. This decision is influenced by legal requirements, premium size, operations of the insured, prior audit experience, nature of the policy, cost of auditing, geographical factors, and staffing requirements. For example, legal mandates might not permit the insurer the option of whether to perform a workers compensation audit. Bureau rules usually require audits of all policies involving a premium above a certain amount and might restrict audit waivers to no more than two in a row. Bureau rules also restrict classification changes, except under specific circumstances. Changes, such as the discovery of new exposures, might be used only for the policy in force rather than the one subject to audit, unless an interim audit has been performed.

The insurer might determine that the audit is not worth the cost and elect (where permissible by the bureau) to waive the audit. In doing so, the insurer will consider the policy and its endorsements, prior audit reports, and the potential success of a voluntary report from the policyholder.

A **voluntary report** (also called a policyholder's report) is a form the policyholder completes and returns by mail. The insurer includes instructions to assist the policyholder in capturing the pertinent exposure information required to adjust the premium for the expired policy period. An example of a policyholder's report is shown in Exhibit 7-9. Once the insurer receives the voluntary audit, it might choose to accept the voluntary audit, perform a two-year audit at the end of the next policy term, or initiate an immediate field audit to confirm the voluntary audit.

Voluntary report
A form the policyholder completes and returns by mail.

Field audits (also called physical audits) are personal examinations of the policyholder's books and records. Field auditors must judge how long each audit will take and decide how to schedule audit appointments efficiently. For each audit, they must anticipate the classification and exposure questions that might be involved and determine the premium base and any necessary allocations of it. They then must plan how to approach the audit, what records to use, where the records are located, whom to contact, and which questions to ask. Such advance planning greatly improves the efficiency and the quality of the premium audit.

Field audits
Personal examinations of the policyholder's books and records.

Reviewing Operations

Skilled premium auditors observe many characteristics of a policyholder before they see the books. They determine the nature of the entity insured; observe the nature of the operation and compare it to similar enterprises, looking for classifications that might not be shown on the policy; assess the quality and cooperation of the management to judge how to proceed with the audit; and report any significant information to the underwriting department. In addition, they note changes in the organization and new exposures and are always alert to other clues about the nature and trend of the insured's business.

EXHIBIT 7-9

Policyholder's Voluntary Report

POLICYHOLDER'S REPORT

Your Insurance Policy was issued on an **estimate** of the premium bases listed below. We now need the **actual amounts** so we can figure the premium. Please fill in the amounts for the period of time shown in the section called **Reporting Period**. If you have any questions, **please contact your agent.** We will appreciate your response by the **due date**. Thank you.

NAME AND ADDRESS OF AGENT		NAME AND ADDRESS OF COMPANY			
Elliott B. Arnold Agency P. O. Box 1224 Atlanta, GA 30301	AGENCY CODE 3207	IIA Insurance Company P. O. Box 1000 Springton, PA 19809			

NAME AND ADDRESS OF INSURED	POLICY NUMBER	KIND OF POLICY	
John's Sporting Goods, Inc. 1972 Olympic St. Atlanta, GA 30301	WC 1234	Workers Compensation	
	POLICY PERIOD MONTH-DAY-YEAR TO MONTH-DAY-YEAR 6-6-X5 TO 6-6-X6		DATE 6-7-X6
	REPORTING PERIOD 6-6-X5 TO 6-6-X6		DUE DATE 7-6-X6

CODE	DESCRIPTION/LOCATION	PREMIUM BASE	AMOUNT	RATE	PREMIUM
8017	Retail Stores N.O.C.	Remu- neration		3.73 per $100	

☐ COMPLETE ☐ DO NOT COMPLETE THIS SECTION EXECUTIVE OFFICERS/PARTNERS/PROPRIETORS

TITLE	NAME	SPECIFIC DUTIES	EARNINGS
			DO NOT INCLUDE IN UPPER SECTION

Who keeps your records? ___David Schneider___   Signature ___David Schneider___   Title ___Treasurer___
                              NAME

Where are they kept? ___178 Trimmings Ct.___   Phone Number ___522-3054___   Date ___7-1-X6___
                              ADDRESS

RETURN TO ☑ COMPANY ☐ PRODUCER

Determining Employment Relationships

After analyzing the policyholder's operations, premium auditors must determine who the policyholder's employees are for those lines of insurance whose premiums are based on payroll. The manner of answering that potentially intricate question, however, depends on its purpose.

The status of various people working for the policyholder has an important bearing on the premium basis of workers compensation policies. The premium basis includes the payroll of every person considered an employee under workers compensation laws. Therefore, the premium auditor must distinguish between employees and those persons correctly identified as independent contractors. Although the employees' payroll might constitute the premium base for both workers compensation and general liability policies, the definition of employee is not necessarily the same for both coverages. The question becomes more involved when the premium auditor must answer it according to the applicable workers compensation laws, which vary by state. Many policyholders do not realize that they must obtain certificates of insurance from their subcontractors; otherwise, premium auditors must include the subcontractors' payrolls in the premium base. If the premium base is not payroll, employment status loses much of its significance for the premium auditor, but it can still be a clue to the nature of the operations.

Finding and Evaluating Records

Premium auditors can examine all books or records of the policyholder that relate to the insurance premiums. They must decide, however, which records will provide the necessary information most efficiently and reliably. They must evaluate the accounting system to determine how much confidence to place in the accuracy of particular records and what alternative sources exist to confirm the premium data obtained.

In addition to meeting basic bookkeeping standards, insureds should set up their records to take full advantage of insurance rules and requirements. Insureds should separate their payroll records by classification and arrange their records so that auditors can easily identify previously nonreported classifications. Payroll records should identify the bonus part of overtime pay, which is not includable in the premium basis. The basis of premium includes other forms of remuneration, such as vacation pay, tool allowance, bonuses, commissions, sick pay, the value of boarding and lodging, and other money substitutes. During a pre-audit meeting, the auditor can often assist in setting up the appropriate bookkeeping procedures.

Auditing the Books

When premium auditors examine the policyholder's accounting records, they must select a procedure for obtaining the premium data as readily as possible. They must determine how much evidence suffices to ascertain the exposures and classifications with a reasonable degree of confidence. If the evidence is not readily available, they must balance the time and expense of obtaining it against its potential effect on the audit. Sound audit tests might allow premium auditors to rely on more readily available records.

When the policyholder uses an automated accounting system, premium auditors must evaluate the capabilities of the system as well as the reliability of the accounting process. They must decide what output to accept for premium determination purposes and what additional data to request. If the output does not include all the necessary data, they must determine what steps to take to obtain it. Time spent arranging for the computer to produce the necessary data can save significant audit time.

Analyzing and Verifying Premium Data

Once premium auditors have obtained the necessary data for calculating the premium, they must decide whether the data are reasonable. Do they add up? Do they seem complete? Do they reflect every step of the policyholder's operations? Are they consistent with industry averages? For example, are the ratios of payroll to sales or labor to materials reasonable considering the nature of the operation? Can deviations from expected amounts be explained? Auditors should verify premium data in the general accounting records and reconcile any discrepancies. Premium auditors must use considerable judgment in analyzing and verifying premium data to ensure the validity of the audit findings.

Premium evasion
An insurer's loss of premiums due to the intentional acts of a policyholder through underreporting or misclassifying exposures.

In some instances, policyholders attempt to reduce their insurance costs through premium evasion. **Premium evasion** is the loss of premiums due to the intentional acts of the policyholder through underreporting or misclassifying exposures. Moral or fraudulent evasion involves withholding or distorting facts with the intent to deceive. More common premium evasion involves providing incorrect or misleading information whereby the policyholder rationalizes this action to get a better deal or gain a competitive advantage.

Reporting the Findings

No premium audit is complete until the auditor summarizes the results in writing and transmits them to the billings and collection unit. Naturally, the auditors should record the data so that the insurer can bill the premium adjustment. Billing data should be clearly summarized so that the audit can be processed without delay. In addition, premium auditors must show how they obtained the data. They must decide how to present the data in a manner that enables others to retrace their steps. The premium auditor should describe the policyholder's operations succinctly and explain any deviations from normal expectations. Premium auditors must also identify other significant information obtained during the audit and communicate it effectively to the appropriate people. An example of a premium audit report is shown in Exhibit 7-10 along with an explanation of each item contained in the report.

EXHIBIT 7-10

Suggested Format for Audit Report

① Insured   Any Company   Policy No.   WC 102030
                 112 Broad Street   Policy Period: 7-1-X5 to 7-1-X6
                 Wichita, KS   Audit Period: Same
       (Records at Able Accounting, 50 Riverside Drive, Wichita, KS 39301)

② Operations: Masonry contractor, new houses and commercial buildings. No subcontractors. No drivers. Part-time office help.

	Gross Payroll	Clerical-8810	Masonry-5022	Verification
③ 7-X5	2050	④ 200	④	③ (941 Reports)
8	2210	200		3Q X5 6668
9	2408	200		4Q X5 6564
10	2396	200		1Q X6 3660
11	2368	200		2Q X6 7183
12 (Bonuses included)	1800	300		Total 24075
1-X6	1260	250	Balance	Audit 24075
2	1200	250		-0-
3	1200	250		
4	2015	250		
5	2550	250		
6	2618	250		
⑤	24075	2800	21275	
⑤	(1280)		(1280)	Overtime premium
⑥	-0-		-0-	Limitation excess
	1600		1600	To bring Vice President Applegate to required minimum
⑦	620		620	Casual labor, cash payment
⑧	-0-		-0-	Subcontractors
	25015	2800	22215	

⑨ Other exposures: No USL&HW No special jobs

⑩ Ownership: President—S. Arnold   12,000   Included 5022
                Vice President—S. Applegate   3,600   Included 5022
                                        +1,600   Added to equal minimum
                Secretary-Treasurer—E. Clinton   No salary, not active

⑪ Billing Summary

     Kansas Masonry - 5022 $22,215
     Kansas Clerical - 8810 $2,800

⑫ No other entities

⑬ No other classifications

⑭ No other states

⑮ No deviations

⑯ No notes for other departments

⑰ Records examined: payroll journal, cash book, individual earnings records, 941 Forms

     Note: Oklahoma work expected next year.

⑱   *Shelly Arnold*   7-15-X6
        Signature of Insured   Date

Continued on next page.

Suggested Format for Audit Report

1. Name, address, policy number(s), policy period, audit period, location of records, and phone number.

2. Description of operations. Ideally the description should process the record examination and figure extraction process, since the classification should fit the description, rather than the description fitting the classification.

3. Gross payroll and verification.

4. Analysis by classification.

5. Deductions (overtime, limitation excess, etc.).

6. Additions (board and lodging, amounts necessary to bring to minimum, etc.).

7. Additions (miscellaneous or casual labor not previously shown).

8. Additions (uninsured subcontractors).

9. Exposures for special jobs, increased limits, waivers, U.S.L.&H.W., and maritime exposures.

10. Ownership (names, duties, amounts included, and classification).

11. Recapitulation by classification and state, observing rate changes and exposure breaks. This section might be called the "billing summary." Normally it should appear on a separate page so that there can be no doubt regarding which figures to use in extending the premium.

12. Clearing of entities shown on policy. For each entity, the report should either show the exposure or show that no exposure exists.

13. Clearing of classifications shown on policy. Similarly, the report should account for all classifications.

14. Clearing of states shown on policy. Again, the report should account for every state shown.

15. Explanatory remarks and notes concerning any policyholder peculiarities or deviations from normal auditing or classification procedures and reasons therefor.

16. Notes for other departments.

17. Listing of records examined and notes for other auditors.

18. Insured's signature.

Cooperation Between Premium Auditing and Other Functions

The auditor might be the only insurer representative who comes into actual contact with the policyholder and who views the operations first hand. The auditor is also the only insurer representative who has access to the policyholder's confidential records. Consequently, auditors usually have access to more direct information concerning the policyholder than do any other of the insurer's departments. An important secondary objective of the auditor's report is therefore to provide other departments with information relating to their functions.

Because the auditor is responsible for correct premium determination, he or she must possess a high degree of initiative, resourcefulness, and technical competency in the areas of accounting and insurance. Insurers are more

frequently turning to premium auditors as a source of information for developing classification and rating information as well as information that supports the underwriting, marketing, claims, and loss control functions.

Premium Auditing and Underwriting

The underwriter's fundamental responsibility is to select a book of business that will produce a profit. This responsibility involves reviewing the information available and often obtaining additional information so that a rational decision can be made. This selection process involves determining the proper classifications and price; reviewing the policyholder's past performance; evaluating hazards in relation to the operations, equipment, and materials used; and analyzing the character and experience of employees and management.

In addition, the underwriter in some lines of business can modify the price by special filings or through the exposure to loss by restrictive policy conditions. The underwriter must also consider possibilities for loss control. Once an underwriter has accepted a policyholder, the underwriter must periodically monitor the account to determine continuing desirability and future action. Throughout this process, most of the underwriter's analysis must be based on information furnished by someone else. Seldom does the underwriter have the opportunity to inspect the policyholder's premises. Therefore, premium audit reports constitute a valuable source of the underwriter's information. Effective teamwork between underwriters and premium auditors is essential in ensuring that existing accounts remain profitable.

Incorrect Classification

A crucial part of the auditor's job is to classify the insured exposures correctly. Often the audit is the only source of information for proper classifications. For large accounts, auditors frequently visit a prospective policyholder before the insurer actually accepts the account, or shortly after acceptance. During this pre-audit survey, the premium auditor confirms the information on the application. The auditor does not become involved until the policy has been written and the first interim audit or annual audit is due.

The premium auditor can classify the operation, verify the estimated premium base, and, if possible, observe the operation. Such visits also provide an opportunity to explain to the policyholder the record keeping required for insurance purposes. Suggestions for keeping overtime records, excess payroll records, and records segregated by classification can lead to a more efficient audit at the expiration of the policy term.

Although the underwriter must establish the classifications when the policy is issued, the information submitted is occasionally incomplete or erroneous.

Properly classifying an account can be complex. The rating manuals contain numerous rules and exceptions. Operations of policyholders also change over time. In such situations, particularly when the policy does not generate sufficient premium to justify an inspection or loss control report, a premium audit can bring to light any classification changes necessary to update the policy. The premium auditor's expertise in classification questions can help underwriters maintain the proper classifications on the policy and thus keep the deposit premium in line with the exposures assumed under the policy. Premium auditors notify the underwriting department of any discrepancies among the classifications on the policy and those that are proper for the operation.

If the classification and rate on the policy are too high, the policyholder is being overcharged and might thus be placed at a competitive disadvantage when bidding for jobs or pricing products. Such a situation could have serious legal ramifications if negligence on the part of the insurer is a factor. If the classification and rate on the policy are too low, then an account is less likely to be profitable. Claims or expenses do not diminish because a policyholder is classified incorrectly.

Inadequate Exposure Estimate

Another potential threat to underwriting profits arises when the policy is written with inadequate exposure estimates. Even though the proper exposure will be developed and charged on an audit, the additional premiums might never be collected. Any delay causes a loss of potential investment income. The **pre-audit survey** is probably the best tool in preventing underreporting on new business.

Pre-audit survey
A form completed by the insured at the request of the insurer that provides exposure information required to adjust the policy premium for the expired policy period.

When the insured exposure has been underestimated or incorrectly classified, an inadequate deposit premium will result. Some policyholders might deliberately underestimate exposures to reduce the deposit premium. Also, producers may use low initial exposure figures to capture an account in a competitive quote situation. Policyholders who expect a return premium are usually quick to make records available, whereas policyholders expecting a large additional premium might resort to numerous stalling tactics.

The auditor might not be in a position to rectify the problem of inadequate exposure estimates completely; however, full exposure data can and should be given to the underwriting department in those cases in which the estimates are inadequate. The underwriter is usually responsible for updating the exposures on the current policy and has a business interest in doing so.

New Exposures

New exposures might be another important area in which underwriting information is deficient. New exposures can result from a change in the policyholder's prior operation or from an entirely new venture. The policyholder often does not communicate such changes or new operations to the producer or the insurer, and, even if it is reported, the information might be sketchy, faulty, or otherwise insufficient for underwriting purposes. A premium auditor should not attempt to underwrite the new operation, but he or she should supply sufficient details regarding ownership and operations to provide complete rating information. The auditor should also indicate the proper classifications for such new exposures. Other items of interest to the underwriting department include the experience of the new operation's management, its financing, the marketing of its product, the derivation of its income, and any other information pertaining to unusual hazards.

Observations Concerning the Desirability of the Account

From every point of view, underwriting desirability is a highly complex subject. The auditor is in a position to observe and to communicate to the underwriting department many items that affect the overall desirability of the account. For instance, the premium audit report might indicate the experience, caliber, and attitude of the policyholder's management. Business information reported by premium auditors also includes a list of officers, the number of employees, payroll, real estate ownership and values, stock values, and annual sales. This information can be valuable to the underwriter in better understanding the operations of the policyholder and in confirming that the coverage options selected and coverage amounts are appropriate. A brief discussion of the types of underwriting information premium auditors can obtain, categorized by type of hazard presented, follows.

Physical Hazards   Premium auditors should exercise common sense in notifying the underwriting department when substandard physical conditions exist. Auditors should not bother underwriters with inconsequential information. How auditors evaluate physical hazards and determine when they should report them is a matter of judgment and experience. Premium auditors recognize their role in overall insurer profitability and can take the responsibility to report hazards that will adversely affect underwriting results.

The auditor might have the opportunity to observe buildings under construction, poor housekeeping, careless storage of combustibles, and so on. Additional hazards might arise out of the business environment, such as the surrounding geography, exposure to flood, and exposure to potentially hazardous neighboring businesses or industrial plants.

The list of potential hazards could go on indefinitely; for the auditor, however, the important point is to develop a habit of taking a careful look at potential loss-causing hazards and to inform the underwriter about them.

Moral Hazards   Moral hazards arise from financial instability, a failing business or industry, undesirable associates, and poor moral character on the part of the policyholder or management. Illegal or unethical business practices, questionable losses, unreported exposures, and a poor reputation in the community are examples of possible moral problems. The insurance contract is based on complete honesty by both parties; an insured of poor moral character violates that good faith principle. The auditor must therefore report any observations indicating possible moral hazards.

Morale Hazards   Morale problems might be indicated by a cavalier attitude toward loss or by poor business attitudes. Indifference to normal protective measures and to proper maintenance of property and equipment may indicate possible morale hazards. The premium auditor can easily spot slipshod record keeping, which may indicate that other areas are also poorly managed.

Cooperation of the Policyholder   The uncooperative policyholder presents unique challenges to the auditor. Unless the lack of cooperation arises from a misunderstanding, which can be resolved, or from ignorance, which can be eliminated, it is doubtful that the auditor will ever be able to review sufficient records to make a proper premium adjustment. The failure or inability to obtain the proper premium for the policy adversely affects underwriting performance, and the auditor must communicate this to the underwriting department.

Condition of Records   Poor records might also indicate a morale problem and greater exposure to loss. Besides contributing to loss potential, poor records consume the auditor's time and might obstruct a proper premium adjustment. Although poor record keeping can be remedied by educating the policyholder, in many cases the insurer will have to expect premium adjustment problems stemming from inadequate records to persist indefinitely. Continuation of this condition, the probable premium effect in overcharge or undercharge, and the extra time and expense involved in auditing are all areas that the underwriter should consider in determining an account's desirability.

Many other areas of underwriting exist to which the auditor can contribute significant information. The foregoing examples are only a few of the more important and common ones. An auditor should develop the habit of taking an underwriter's view of an account and using the auditor's report, or an acceptable substitute, to convey the desired and needed information.

Premium Auditing and Marketing

The auditor can also play a significant role in the area of production. To many policyholders, the auditor *is* the insurer. The auditor's conduct and skill are often important factors in retaining an account. Auditors must often demonstrate their proficiency by convincing a policyholder of the correctness of an audit when the policyholder would prefer to have a cheaper classification and a lower premium. The premium developed and explained by a professional auditor might make a major difference in the profit margin.

In addition to this opportunity, the auditor can directly serve the production or agency staff by being in tune with its needs. This means diligently reporting and promptly communicating pertinent information.

Notification of Undisclosed Exposures

The producer has a vital interest in the business and operations of the policyholder. Ideally, the policyholder will communicate all changes in operation and all new operations to the producer. Often, however, in the rush of business pressure, the policyholder completely overlooks notifying the producer of these changes. The auditor is in an excellent position to fill this void by notifying the producer of any changes or new operations. This serves two purposes. First, it builds valuable rapport between the auditor and the producer. Second, it gives the producer additional time to contact the policyholder for information about the new operation and to provide insurance counseling. Because the auditor's notice to the underwriting department will precipitate an inquiry, the producer will be better able to respond and perhaps to arrange additional coverage immediately.

Notification of Classification Changes or Large Additional Premiums

Producers do not like to receive, without advance notice, a premium audit billing with a large additional premium because of a classification change. The advantage of giving the producer sufficient notice is that the producer has time to plan the best way to collect the additional premium and to explain the classification change to the policyholder. The producer has that ultimate responsibility; therefore, it makes good business sense to give as much advance notice as possible.

Advance notice also gives the producer an opportunity to express an opinion about a classification change. At times, the producer might be aware of bureau inspections or other information that would have an important bearing on the proposed change in classification.

Ideally, the auditor should tell the producer of any classification change of consequence, whether it results in a major premium difference or not. The auditor should also inform the producer of large additional premiums for other reasons, such as a policyholder's underreporting or inadequate exposure estimates or deposits. The auditor's report should indicate that such communication has occurred and that the response has been received. Company policy will determine when, how, and by whom this should be done.

Problems of Inadequate Records or Uncooperative Policyholders

The producer may be the auditor's most valuable helper in solving the problems of inadequate records or uncooperative policyholders. The producer is often in a position to influence the policyholder to cooperate and thus to solve the problem before it involves the underwriting department.

Whether producers can solve such problems, they are at least entitled to try, since they have a financial stake in the policyholder's retention. Therefore, the auditor should tell the agency or marketing staff about inadequate records or uncooperative policyholders.

Possibility of Additional Business (or Economies in the Present Insurance Program)

The auditor should be sure to give to the producer any information pertaining to potentially uninsured or underinsured risks. Perhaps fine art objects in the policyholder's office are currently uninsured. The auditor, by being alert to that possibility, might pass along to the producer many leads for potential new business.

Another opportunity for communication with the producer concerns economies that can be effected in the present insurance program without sacrifice of coverage. Perhaps installing a partition might qualify an employee for another classification and achieve a reduction in workers compensation premium. Or maybe by only a slight modification in process, an interchange of labor could be avoided, thereby saving premium. Countless other ways exist for the auditor to supply valuable service to the policyholder's insurance program. A professional concern for the interest of others regularly leads to such opportunities.

Premium Auditing and Claims

Claim information can be valuable to the auditor in verifying claimants' employment and in assigning classifications. The auditor can provide an even greater service, however, by reviewing claim abstracts in order to verify or correct the classification codes assigned by the claim coder. Various insurance regulators have recently emphasized the importance of ensuring more accuracy in claim coding. No one is in a better position to review and to correct those codes than the auditor. This review also ensures that claims and premiums are matched in the same classifications, thus improving the credibility of rates.

Auditors should also review claim abstracts to verify that claimants were employees of the policyholder and were injured during the period of coverage. If claimants were not employees, the auditor should notify the claim department accordingly.

Values of inventories, contractors' equipment lists and values, and automotive equipment values are other important facts that the auditor can furnish to the claim department. For example, the claim department might request a premium auditor to review crime and fidelity losses—a line of business that usually has no auditable exposures. The auditor can determine that the amount claimed is accurately calculated from the policyholder's books and records; that the amount claimed is determined in accordance with the policy provisions relating to loss valuation and adjustment; that the loss claimed does not exceed the actual loss sustained; and that the loss is not partly or fully attributable to some cause other than that for which coverage is provided. In addition, the auditor can assist claims adjustments by verifying periods or dates of employment and by providing or verifying average earnings for individual claimants.

Premium Auditing and Loss Control

The loss control or safety engineering department also has an interest in the auditor's observations. Obviously, the loss control representative cannot visit every policyholder, but the auditor can serve as an additional source of information for the loss control department. Auditors should forward information about unsafe procedures and working conditions and observations of policyholders' vehicles on the road to the loss control department for further investigation and recommendations.

Consequences of Premium Audit Errors

Although the insurance mechanism relies on them to measure and classify exposures correctly, premium auditors can make mistakes. A premium audit error can have lasting and far-reaching consequences. Errors can distort the insurer's rating structure and cause significant problems for both the insured and the insurer. Correcting the mistake requires considerable additional time and effort. Sometimes, the insurer can never regain the goodwill lost.

Consequences for the Insured

If audit errors occur without detection, policyholders do not pay the proper premium for their insurance. Some policyholders pay more than their proportional share for the exposures covered; others pay less than their share. Insureds paying excessive insurance premiums are placed at a competitive disadvantage and might experience financial problems. Other insureds, however, might continue to operate despite unusually hazardous working conditions, because audit errors lead to a subsidy in the form of underpriced insurance coverage.

Errors in audits also result in incorrect experience modifications. Experience rating bases an insured's current premium on the insured's past experience (exposure units and losses). When those exposure units and losses are incorrect, the experience modification will be incorrect, resulting in the insured's paying incorrect future premiums. In addition, if an error in an audit is detected, the experience modification cannot be calculated until the final, correct audit is conducted and the correct data are submitted to the bureau. Depending on the modification (that is, whether the correct modification will be higher or lower than the one being used), the insured is either overpaying or underpaying for insurance until the bureau calculates the final, correct modification.

Finally, errors in premium audits reduce the confidence an insured has in auditors and in the insurance mechanism in general. The loss of confidence might make the insured reluctant to buy insurance and to cooperate with insurers.

Consequences for the Insurer

Incorrect or merely incomplete premium audits affect the insurer in a variety of ways. Each error impairs the efficiency of the insurer's operations, even when the errors are corrected. Although some of the damage might be invisible, the more obvious costs are described below.

Deterioration of Underwriting Results

If the undetected premium audit errors cause overcharging of some policyholders and undercharging of others, the overcharged policyholders might switch to another insurer to obtain coverage at a lower premium. The insurer loses premium volume as a result while retaining the policyholders whose premium is not commensurate with the exposures.

Loss of Goodwill

When policyholders discover errors in the premium audit, the image of the insurance company suffers. The policyholders lose confidence in the insurer's competence and might consider switching to another insurer. Policyholders who continue their coverage with the insurer despite their consternation over an incorrect audit might be unwilling to cooperate in the investigation of a claim or the implementation of loss prevention measures. Perhaps the biggest cost, however, is the marketing and underwriting effort expended to secure the business subsequently lost because of mistakes in premium audits. Of course, other departments also have the responsibility to avoid errors, which can similarly consternate the policyholder when discovered at the time of the audit.

Additional Effort

Incorrect or incomplete audits also cause extra work for several departments of the insurer. Redoing the audit taxes the resources of the premium audit department. Other departments might become involved in attempting to explain the error and mollify the policyholder. Underwriters have to correct their records and might therefore be drawn into the controversy. The accounting department must make the appropriate adjusting entries and issue a corrected bill. When premium audits are complete and correct, these tasks are not necessary.

Premium Collection Problems

Policyholders are not likely to pay premium bills they believe or suspect to be incorrect. Even when the problem is eventually resolved, the insurer's cash flow suffers as a result. A perceived or an actual error in the determination of an additional premium might result in a re-audit of the policyholder's books to confirm or refute the initial audit. When this situation is combined with the traditional premium payment time lags, the insurer has lost the use of any of its money for the period.

Consequences for Insurance Rates

An equitable insurance premium requires that insurers treat all exposures in the same fashion. Thus, all policyholders subject to the same degree of hazard belong in the same rate classification. An inconsistency in the audit classification of exposures not only causes inequity in the level of current premium paid but also distorts the class loss results that determine future rates. Particularly in lines such as workers compensation, in which a large volume of the business is audited, the results of premium audits substantially affect rate equity and accuracy. No matter which ratemaking method insurers or bureaus use to develop the manual rates for the various workers compensation classes, the accuracy of the underlying class rate can be no better than the data provided by the premium audits.

Premium audits affect the equity and accuracy of class rates in two ways. The first is in the consistency and accuracy of classification determinations. If premium auditors in one area of a state consider a particular industrial class to be in classification X, while the premium auditors in another part of the state consider it to be in class Y, then the inconsistency distorts the resulting loss data from *both* classes and leads to inequitable rates for all policyholders in the state for those two classes. Equally important in the ratemaking procedure is accurately classifying claims. By notifying the claim department when additional classifications are assigned and by reviewing the classification of past claims at the time of an audit, premium auditors can assist the claims department in accurately classifying losses as well as exposures.

The second manner in which premium audits affect the equity and accuracy of class rates is the measurement of the exposure base. An audit error, not in classification but in determining the amount of exposures, also distorts the rate structure. Whether on a loss ratio basis using exposure units or on a loss ratio basis using premium, underreporting or overreporting the proper exposures affects the rate for that class. However, distortions of rates from misreporting exposure units are likely to be minor. This conclusion is supported by the statistics collected in rating bureau test audit programs.

ORGANIZATION OF THE PREMIUM AUDITING FUNCTION

A description of how the premium audit could be organized within an insurer is very similar to that of the loss control function. Exhibits 7-4 through 7-8 showed how the premium audit function would fit in various organizational schemes. Likewise, Exhibit 7-3 could easily be transformed into an organizational chart showing how the premium audit function could perform as a separate department within an insurer.

In some insurers, the premium audit manager might also be responsible for the credit function. This task includes billing and collecting additional premiums determined through the audit as well as the return of excess premiums paid. The premium audit manager might be better able to coordinate these activities than if they were handled by a separate department. When this organizational arrangement is in place, the insurer needs to establish and enforce controls to prevent employee dishonesty.

The use of independent premium auditing service firms varies by insurer. Some insurance companies rely exclusively on outsiders for premium auditing, citing the ability to identify and control expenses. Other insurers use their own personnel for premium auditing, because of the importance they attach to the ancillary functions performed by premium auditors. As a practical matter, insurers typically use their own premium auditing personnel in their regular operating territory. For premium audits outside a given geographic region, they employ the services of an independent auditing service firm. Additionally, independent auditing service firms might be used to supplement the insurer's regular premium auditing staff during high demand times during the year, such as January and July, when many policies are renewed. It has been estimated that independent auditing service firms perform as many as half of all premium audits.

SUMMARY

Loss control and premium auditing are often viewed as extensions of the underwriting function. As the underwriting function evolved to deal more exclusively with the risk selection process, other functional departments were created to handle certain crucial tasks.

Loss control measures are directed at reducing the frequency and severity of losses. Loss control activities are motivated by greater insurer profits, the loss control service needs of insurance customers, satisfying legal requirements, and humanitarian concerns.

The loss control function usually complements several other insurer departments. Loss control representatives usually serve as the eyes and ears of the underwriting department. Through their reports, they enable underwriters to make sound decisions on the applications and renewals they underwrite. In addition to verifying declared exposures, loss control representatives may be able to identify previously undisclosed hazards. The recommendations of loss control representatives are considered essential in writing an account at a profit or reforming a marginal risk.

Making a marginal account profitable also supports the insurer's marketing function. Insurers are continually encouraging their producers to develop new accounts. Underwriters can frequently be critical of new business to the point that producers become frustrated. The loss control representative can mitigate these tensions by offering an objective evaluation of the applicant. The loss control representative can offer tangible and practical suggestions that often satisfy all parties. In particular, the policyholder may recognize that the insurer has a genuine interest in reducing injuries and damages that give rise to claims and is not just resistant to paying claims.

The claim examiner and loss control representative can exchange valuable information about specific policyholders insured and the circumstances giving rise to claims. Loss control representatives can then generalize their experience to help producers and insured trade associations better understand situations that can lead to a loss.

Loss control services can be provided at various levels. Three identified levels are physical surveys, risk analysis and improvement, and safety management programming. The extent of these services provided by any one insurer depends on the insurer's mix of business between personal and commercial lines, the size of the policyholder, the types of exposures insured, and the potential legal liability for not providing loss control services.

In the home office, staff members of the loss control function coordinate overall operations, provide technical assistance, and communicate their findings through in-house publications.

Because of the number and size of policies now written with a variable premium base, premium auditors play a vital role in the commercial insurance business. Several insurers annually develop net additional premium approximating $100 million as a result of premium audits. In order to develop the correct premium for the exposure assumed on an adjustable policy, premium auditors must possess highly technical skills and wide knowledge. They must be experts on rating manual rules and classifications, continually assimilating the latest changes. Because they have access to sensitive financial information, they must always act discreetly and professionally. Their findings must be recorded and communicated thoroughly and precisely to serve as the basis of premium billing as well as of future ratemaking statistics.

Because of their direct contact with policyholders, premium auditors have an opportunity to refer specific observations to the underwriting department for further investigation. Such instances include incorrect classifications, inadequate exposure estimates, previously unidentified exposures, and other factors that would affect the overall desirability of an account. Similarly, premium auditors can alert the marketing department to specific circumstances found at the policyholders' locations. For example, premium auditors may discover exposures that are not being addressed in the existing insurance program, thereby creating an additional sales opportunity. Other functional departments that interact with premium auditors include claims and loss control.

Errors in premium audits can result in policyholders' paying more or less than their fair share for exposures covered. Consequences of faulty audits for insurers include deterioration of underwriting results, loss of goodwill with the policyholder, additional effort to redo the audit, and potential premium collection problems.

Loss control and premium audit functions share many of the same organizational characteristics. Both are primarily field operations that may fit into the insurer's organizational structure in various ways. With both functions, many insurers choose to employ independent contractors under appropriate circumstances.

CHAPTER NOTES

1. 199 N.E. 2nd 769, Ill.
2. This material is adapted from Everett D. Randall, *Principles of Premium Auditing*, 3d ed., vol. 1 (Malvern, Pa.: Insurance Institute of America, 1995), Chapter 1.

Chapter 8

Direct Your Learning

Reinsurance

After learning the subject matter of this chapter, you should be able to:

■ Demonstrate how insurers use reinsurance to achieve their objectives. In support of this educational objective:

- Explain the functions of reinsurance.

- Explain the reinsurance contractual relationship.

- Given a case, evaluate an insurer's reinsurance needs; determine how premiums and losses would be shared under the major types of proportional reinsurance; and determine how losses would be paid under the major types of nonproportional reinsurance.

- Explain how insurers use financial reinsurance.

- Describe the sources of reinsurance.

Develop Your Perspective

What are the main topics covered in the chapter?

Reinsurance serves the insurance industry, and ultimately insurance consumers, by stabilizing loss experience. It improves a primary insurer's ability to write more coverage. This chapter describes these functions and the types of reinsurance that serve these functions.

Contrast reinsurance with primary insurance.

- What is unique about the reinsurance market and its products?
- Who are a reinsurer's customers?
- How do reinsurers serve their customers?

Why is it important to know these topics?

Without reinsurance, most privately owned primary insurers would be unable to operate successfully. Potentially catastrophic losses and the uncertainty of widely fluctuating loss results would restrict their ability to write coverages. Reinsurance stabilizes an individual insurer's results and effectively spreads the financial effects of losses globally.

Identify the functions of reinsurance that are most beneficial to your organization.

- What types of reinsurance serve these functions?

How can you use this information?

Determine how reinsurance affects your organization's financial results.

- What types of reinsurance does your organization purchase?
- Why has it selected the reinsurance that it has?
- How has reinsurance affected its financial results in the last two years?

Chapter 8

Reinsurance

An insurer, like any other business firm, obtains insurance for loss exposures that are too great for the insurer to retain. Such exposures might include those inherent in the insurer's own business operations, such as fire damage to the home office building, or those of others assumed under insurance contracts. This chapter discusses only the transfer of loss exposures assumed under insurance contracts. The practice is known as reinsurance. (In life insurance, this practice is referred to as reassurance.)

Reinsurance can be defined as a contractual agreement under which one insurer, known as the primary insurer, transfers to another insurer, known as the **reinsurer**, some or all of the loss exposures accepted by the primary insurer under insurance contracts it has issued or will issue in the future. The primary insurer may also be referred to as the ceding insurer, ceding company, cedent, or reinsured. This text uses the term **primary insurer** to denote an insurer that provides insurance to the general public rather than to other insurers.

In almost all reinsurance agreements, the reinsurer does not assume all of the exposure of the primary insurer. The reinsurance agreement usually requires the primary insurer to keep a portion of the exposure, known as the insurer's **retention**. This portion can be expressed as a dollar amount, a percentage of the original amount of insurance, or a combination of the two. The reinsurance agreement usually contains an upper limit above which loss exposures are the responsibility of the primary insurer.

Reinsurers, like primary insurers, share loss exposures with other reinsurers. Those transactions are similar to the reinsurance agreements between the primary insurer and the initial reinsurer. In this way, loss exposures are shared globally in the reinsurance community. These transactions are known as retrocessions, whereby loss exposures are transferred from the retrocedent to the retrocessionaire.

FUNCTIONS OF REINSURANCE

At first, it might seem odd that an insurer would go to the trouble and expense of selling a policy and then pay a reinsurer to relieve it of some or all of the loss exposures assumed. Several practical business constraints are specific to the nature of the insurance business and the regulatory environment in which it operates. Reinsurance functions to alleviate these constraints.

Reinsurance
A contractual relationship in which a reinsurer reimburses a primary insurer for some or all of the claim payments made by the primary insurer under policies written for its policyholders.

Reinsurer
An insurance company that insures a primary insurer.

Primary insurer
An insurance company that provides insurance to the general public.

Retention
In reference to reinsurance, that portion of the exposure that the primary insurer assumes.

Reinsurance can provide the following functions to primary insurers:

- Stabilization of loss experience
- Large-line capacity
- Financing (surplus relief)
- Catastrophe protection
- Underwriting assistance
- Withdrawal from a territory or class of business

Stabilization of Loss Experience

An insurer, like any other business firm, must have a reasonably steady flow of profits to attract and retain capital and increase its capital and surplus to support growth. Insurance losses sometimes fluctuate widely because of demographic, economic, social, and natural forces, as well as simple chance. Smoothing the peaks and valleys of the loss experience curve is a major function of reinsurance. Stabilization of loss experience is closely related to the function of catastrophe protection, discussed later.

For example, a primary insurer might purchase reinsurance to limit the amount of any one loss it would pay. The primary insurer obtains stability in its underwriting results through the reinsurance transaction. How reinsurance provides stability is illustrated in Exhibit 8-1.

Large-Line Capacity

Large-line capacity refers to an insurer's ability to provide a high limit of insurance on a single loss exposure. For example, an insurer might be called on to write $150 million of coverage on a commercial office building or $160 million of physical damage (hull) coverage on a new jumbo jet. The liability coverage on a large passenger airplane could exceed $100 million.

Few primary insurers could write such a large amount of insurance on a single loss exposure without reinsurance. State insurance regulations prohibit an insurer from writing an amount of insurance in excess of 10 percent of its policyholders' surplus on any one loss exposure. An insurer can write a large line by keeping its retention within a reasonable relationship to its capital and surplus and reinsuring the balance of the risk.

An insurer might want to write a higher limit than it can retain for its own accounts for many valid reasons. For example, a primary insurer might consider accepting an application for hull coverage on a new jumbo jet valued at $160 million if it can minimize its retention to an acceptable level. Reinsurers, operating through pools or individually, take shares of the exposure. In turn, many reinsurers retrocede part of their exposure to other reinsurers. On large exposures like the jumbo jet, the participation of many reinsurers is common.

EXHIBIT 8-1

Stabilization of Loss Experience

Hypothetical Loss Experience of an Insurer for a Line of Business

Time Period (Year)	Losses (000)	Amount Reinsured (000)	Stabilized Loss Level (000)
1	$10,000	$ —	$10,000
2	22,500	2,500	20,000
3	13,000	—	13,000
4	8,000	—	8,000
5	41,000	21,000	20,000
6	37,000	17,000	20,000
7	16,500	—	16,500
8	9,250	—	9,250
9	6,000	—	6,000
10	10,750	—	10,750
Total	$174,000		

Average Annual Losses $17,400

The total losses are $174,000,000, or an average of $17,400,000 each time period. If a reinsurance agreement were in place to cap losses to $20,000,000, the primary insurer's experience would be limited to the amounts shown in the stabilized loss level column. The dark blue line that fluctuates dramatically shown in the graph below represents actual losses; the light blue line represents stabilized losses; the horizontal line represents average losses.

Graph of Hypothetical Loss Data

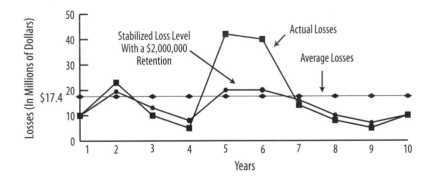

Financing (Surplus Relief)

An insurer is limited in the amount of premiums it can write. The limit for a given insurer is a function of policyholders' surplus. As a practical matter, an insurer is likely to be considered overextended if its net written premiums, after deducting premiums on reinsurance ceded, exceed its policyholders' surplus by a ratio of more than three to one. That is, a ratio below 3-to-1 is favorable.

A growing insurer might have difficulty maintaining an acceptable ratio because the premium-to-surplus ratio of a rapidly growing insurer is like a candle burning at both ends. As the premium volume grows, it causes the surplus to shrink. The shrinkage results when the prepaid expense portion of the unearned premium reserve, such as agents' commission and policy issuance, is charged against surplus.

In U.S. statutory insurance accounting, income and expense are mismatched. The insurer must establish an initial unearned premium reserve equal to the total premium for the policy and then recognize the income over the life of the policy. The insurer pays most of its expenses at the inception of the policy and is required to charge these expenses against income immediately rather than amortize them throughout the policy period. Because it has not yet earned any income, the insurer must take money from surplus to pay these initial expenses. This is referred to as the *surplus drain* caused by growth in written premium. This problem is illustrated in Exhibit 8-2.

Exhibit 8-2 illustrates the financing function of reinsurance—the reduction of surplus drain for a growing insurer that results from having to recognize all expenses when they are incurred. This function is usually called **surplus relief**. It is so important to poorly financed insurers that a special kind of reinsurance, sometimes called surplus-aid reinsurance, was offered in the past to insurers with inadequate surplus. A surplus-aid reinsurance agreement appeared on superficial examination to be a typical reinsurance contract, but it often contained an agreement requiring the primary insurer to reimburse the reinsurer for any claims paid under the reinsurance contract. The primary insurer would take credit for the reinsurance in setting its unearned premium reserve, even though no transfer of risk was involved. A similar device involved purchasing a normal treaty near the end of the year and canceling it early in the following year so that it would be in force on December 31 for Annual Statement purposes. Fortunately, these devices for circumventing solvency regulation have largely disappeared. Changes in accounting rules have eliminated the benefit that insurers sought in these arrangements.

A different form of reinsurance that provides surplus relief has recently received considerable attention, although it has been used on a limited scale for many years. Several forms of such reinsurance exist, but they are known collectively as **financial reinsurance**. The name results from the primary purpose of such contracts: to improve the financial status, or at least the apparent financial status, of the primary insurer. Financial reinsurance involves little transfer of risk; in some cases, no risk at all is transferred. Financial reinsurance is discussed in more detail later in this chapter.

Surplus relief
One of the functions of reinsurance. A growing primary insurer's surplus is drained as it pays for the initial expenses of acquiring new policies. Relief is provided by the ceding commission paid by the reinsurer that offsets some or all of the policy acquisition costs.

Financial reinsurance
A reinsurance agreement involving very little transfer of risk, with the objective of improving the actual or apparent financial status of the primary insurer.

EXHIBIT 8-2

Financing

Assume that Casualty Insurance Company opened for business on December 31, 20X1. On that date, it had $2 million of paid-in capital and surplus but no premiums. On January 1, 20X2, it wrote and collected $5 million of premiums on one-year policies. Its initial expenses for the policies were $1.5 million for producer commissions, premium taxes, underwriting expenses, policy writing, billing and collection, and so forth. Casualty also had to establish an unearned premium reserve, a liability, equal to the total amount of premium, $5 million. Consequently, the money for the expenses must be taken from surplus, leaving surplus to policyholders of only $500,000. Below is Casualty's balance sheet as it appeared on December 31, 20X1, before writing the premiums, and on January 1, 20X2, after writing the premiums and paying the initial expense resulting from them.

As shown in the balance sheet below, the shrinkage of the policyholders' surplus caused the ratio that originally was 2.5-to-1 ($5 million of premiums to $2 million of net worth) to become a ratio of 10-to-1 ($5 million of premiums to $500,000 of net worth). This is an extreme example, of course, but it does illustrate the problems a rapidly growing insurer can encounter.

Balance Sheets for Casualty Insurance Company
December 31, 20X1, and January 1, 20X2

	12/31/X1	1/1/X2
Assets		
Cash	$ 500,000	$4,000,000*
Investments	1,500,000	1,500,000
Total Assets	$ 2,000,000	$ 5,500,000
Liabilities		
Unearned Premium Reserve	$ 0	$ 5,000,000
Total Liabilities	$ 0	$ 5,000,000
Policyholders' Surplus		
Capital	$ 500,000	$ 500,000
Surplus	1,500,000	0
Total Policyholders' Surplus	$ 2,000,000	$ 500,000
Total Liabilities and Policyholders' Surplus	$ 2,000,000	$ 5,500,000
Ratio of Written Premium to Surplus		2.510

* The cash for 1/1/X2 was calculated by adding the premiums collected ($5,000,000) to the cash for 12/31/X1 ($500,000) and subtracting the expenses paid ($1,500,000).

Continued on next page.

Reinsurance, in various forms, can provide some relief to the premium-to-surplus ratio problem. First, the ratio is calculated on the basis of net premiums, after deducting premiums for reinsurance. Second, the unearned premium reserve is also calculated on the basis of net premiums. With some forms of reinsurance, the reinsurer pays a ceding commission to the primary insurer to cover its expenses in selling and issuing the policies, plus an override for profit. Thus, although the primary insurer takes credit for the full reinsurance premium in calculating its unearned premium reserve, it actually pays out only the net amount after deducting the ceding commission. The relief to surplus is therefore a direct result of the ceding commission received by the ceding primary insurer.

Balance Sheet for Casualty Insurance Company, January 1, 20X2,
Net After Ceding 50 Percent of Premiums and Receiving 30 Percent Ceding Commission

Assets

Cash	$ 2,250,000
Investments	1,500,000
Total Assets	$ 3,750,000

Liabilities*

Unearned Premium Reserve	$ 2,500,000
Total Liabilities	$ 2,500,000

Policyholders' Surplus

Capital	$ 500,000
Surplus	750,000
Policyholders' Surplus	$ 1,250,000
Total Liabilities and Policyholders' Surplus	$ 3,750,000

Ratio of Written Premiums to Surplus

* 50% of written premiums

Above is the balance sheet for Casualty Insurance Company on January 1, 19X2, as it would have appeared if Casualty had ceded half of its premiums to a reinsurer and received a 30 percent ceding commission on the *reinsurance premium*.

Casualty's premium-to-surplus ratio has fallen from 10-to-1 to 2-to-1, solely through the use of reinsurance. First, the net written premiums dropped from $5 million to $2.5 million because of the reinsurance cession. Second, the policyholders' surplus increased from $500,000 to $1.25 million because of the recapture of $750,000 of prepaid expenses. This arises from the 30 percent ceding commission paid by the reinsurer for the $2.5 million of written premium ceded.

Catastrophe Protection

Property-casualty insurers are subject to major catastrophe losses from earthquakes, hurricanes, tornadoes, industrial explosions, plane crashes, and similar disasters. These events can result in large property-casualty claims to a single insurer. Total industry losses have reached more than $16 billion for one hurricane and $13 billion for one earthquake, and winter storm losses in excess of $100 million are not uncommon.

Special forms of reinsurance, discussed in a later section of this chapter, have been developed to protect against the adverse effects of catastrophes. This purpose of reinsurance is closely related to the purpose of stabilizing loss experience, because catastrophes are major causes of the instability of losses.

Underwriting Assistance

Reinsurers deal with a wide variety of insurers in many different circumstances. Consequently, they accumulate a great deal of information regarding the experience of various insurers with particular coverages and the methods of rating, underwriting, and handling various coverages. This experience can be helpful to primary insurers, particularly small insurers or larger insurers planning to enter a new line. For example, one medium-sized insurance company reinsured 95 percent of its umbrella liability coverage over a period of years and relied heavily on the expertise of the reinsurer in rating and underwriting the policies. Without this technical assistance, many small and medium-sized insurers would be unable to write some coverages with which they have limited expertise.

This service of reinsurers is very important in both the life and the property-casualty fields. Of course, reinsurers must be careful when offering advisory service so that they do not reveal or use proprietary information obtained through confidential relationships with other primary insurers.

Withdrawal From a Territory or Class of Business

Occasionally, an insurer or a reinsurer decides to withdraw from a territory or a class of business, or to go out of business entirely. At least two ways are available to achieve either end. The insurer could merely cancel or nonrenew the unwanted policies and refund the unearned premiums to its policyholders. That process is unwieldy, expensive, and likely to create ill will among policyholders, producers, and insurance regulators. An alternative method is to reinsure the unwanted business with another insurer or a reinsurer. This method avoids the ill will resulting from terminating the insurance, and the cost of reinsurance might be less than the cost of processing and paying return premiums on canceled policies.

The process of reinsuring all losses for an entire class, territory, or book of business is known as **portfolio reinsurance**. This reinsurance process is an exception to the general rule that reinsurers usually assume only part of the

Portfolio reinsurance
The process of reinsuring all losses for an entire class, territory, or book of business after the primary insurer has issued the policies.

exposures of the primary insurer. In the absence of fraud, the portfolio reinsurer does not normally have any recourse against the primary insurer if the loss experience on the business does not turn out as expected.

POLICYHOLDERS AND REINSURANCE

Reinsurance involves a contractual relationship between a primary insurer and a reinsurer. The persons or firms insured by the primary insurer are not parties to the reinsurance contract and usually have no rights under that contract. For example, assume that the Manufacturing Company buys insurance on its factory for $1 million from the Insurance Company. Insurance Company, in turn, reinsures 90 percent of the exposure with Reinsurance Company. Fire destroys the factory. Since writing the policy, Insurance Company has become insolvent and is now unable to pay its claims. Because there is no contractual relationship between the insured and the reinsurer, Manufacturing Company cannot collect directly from Reinsurance Company. Reinsurance Company pays its share of the loss to the receiver of Insurance Company, and this money is distributed proportionately to all creditors of Insurance Company. Manufacturing Company must settle for only its proportionate share as one creditor of Insurance Company.

Some exceptions exist to the general rule that the policyholder has no direct right of action against a reinsurer. Occasionally, a reinsurer authorizes a primary insurer to attach to its policies an endorsement, executed by the reinsurer, called a cut-through endorsement. The **cut-through endorsement** generally provides that in the event of the insolvency of the primary insurer, the obligation under the policy becomes a direct obligation of the reinsurer. The cut-through endorsement is sometimes attached to fire insurance or homeowners contracts because a mortgagee has refused to accept the primary insurer's policies without it. Less frequently, it is attached at the request of the risk manager of a commercial policyholder or an industrial firm, and sometimes it is needed because the primary insurer is not rated by Best's.

Cut-through endorsement
An endorsement that provides that in the event of the insolvency of the primary insurer, the reinsurer directly assumes the obligations of the primary insurer.

Some other minor exceptions also exist to the rule that the primary insurer's policyholder does not have a right of direct action against the reinsurer. For example, when an organization purchases reinsurance for its captive insurer, of which it is a member, that organization may file a claim directly with the reinsurer.

The fact that the policyholders of the primary insurer have no right of direct action against the reinsurer does not mean that they receive no benefit from the reinsurance. Policyholders might, in fact, receive several benefits. The availability of reinsurance might enable them to obtain all of their insurance from one insurer instead of buying it in bits and pieces from several insurers, thus avoiding the potential problems of coverage gaps and loss collections when dealing with several insurers. Also, the availability of reinsurance helps to maintain the solvency of primary insurers, with obvious advantages to policyholders. The Best's rating of primary insurers is affected by the strength of their reinsurance. Finally, reinsurance allows small insurers to compete effectively against larger ones, thus increasing the options available to insurance buyers. Of course, reinsurers might, in some cases, reduce price and coverage competition, because their rating and underwriting practices influence the rates and policy forms used by their primary insurers.

TYPES OF REINSURANCE

Several different kinds of reinsurance have developed to serve the various functions listed in the first section of this chapter. No single kind of reinsurance serves all of the purposes effectively.

The section that follows discusses several forms of reinsurance as though they are standardized contracts. Although that method of presentation is necessary for clarity, each reinsurance contract is tailored to the specific needs of the primary insurer and the reinsurer. Consequently, a given reinsurance contract might include combinations of the reinsurance forms discussed here, or it might bear only a superficial resemblance to any of these forms.

Reinsurance contracts can be categorized in several ways. The first major categorization is between facultative and treaty reinsurance. In **facultative reinsurance**, the primary insurer negotiates a separate reinsurance agreement for each risk it wishes to reinsure. The primary insurer is not under any obligation to purchase reinsurance on a policy it does not wish to reinsure, and the reinsurer is not obligated to reinsure policies submitted to it.

Facultative reinsurance
A reinsurance agreement negotiated separately for each policy the primary insurer wishes to reinsure. The reinsurer retains the right to accept or reject each risk.

In **treaty reinsurance**, the primary insurer agrees in advance to reinsure certain lines of business in accordance with the terms and conditions of the treaty, and the reinsurer agrees to accept the business that falls within the treaty. Although the primary insurer might have some discretion in reinsuring individual policies, all of the policies that come within the terms of the treaty are expected to be placed with the reinsurer.

Treaty reinsurance
An agreement between the reinsurer and the primary insurer. The primary insurer agrees to reinsure certain lines of business, and the reinsurer agrees to accept the business that falls within the treaty.

Despite this seemingly clear-cut distinction between facultative and treaty reinsurance, some reinsurance contracts are a hybrid and are called facultative treaties.

On rare occasions, a facultative treaty might be called a facultative obligatory treaty, automatic facultative treaty, or another treaty with mixed nomenclature. Such a treaty might provide that the primary insurer has the option to submit risks within a specified class that the reinsurer is obligated to accept. Because of the obvious opportunities for adverse selection, reinsurers are careful in selecting the primary insurers for which they write facultative obligatory treaties.

Information regarding the relative importance of facultative and treaty reinsurance within the portfolios of reinsurers is limited. Some reinsurers specialize in facultative agreements, and others prefer treaty business.

Another system for categorizing reinsurance depends on the manner in which the obligations under contracts are divided between the primary insurer and the reinsurer. These two approaches to dividing losses are called pro rata reinsurance and excess of loss reinsurance.

Pro rata reinsurance
An agreement in which the amount of insurance, the premium, and the losses are divided between the primary insurer and the reinsurer in the same agreed portions. Also called proportional insurance.

Excess of loss reinsurance
An agreement that requires a reinsurer to pay that portion of a loss that exceeds the primary insurer's retention up to the reinsurance limit. Also called nonproportional reinsurance.

Under **pro rata reinsurance** (or proportional reinsurance), the amount of insurance, the premium, and the losses are divided between the primary insurer and the reinsurer in the same agreed proportions. That is, if the reinsurer gets 35 percent of the coverage under a given policy, it also gets 35 percent of the premium and pays 35 percent of each loss under the policy, regardless of the size of the loss. Under pro rata reinsurance treaties, the reinsurer usually pays a ceding commission to the primary insurer to cover its expenses and possibly an allowance for profit.

Under **excess of loss reinsurance** (or nonproportional reinsurance), no amount of insurance is ceded. Excess of loss reinsurance does not become involved until the primary insurer has sustained a *loss* that exceeds its retention under the contract and is covered by the excess of loss agreement. Both facultative reinsurance and treaty reinsurance can be written as pro rata or excess or a combination of the two. Exhibit 8-3 shows the various ways of categorizing reinsurance. Note the inclusion of financial reinsurance, which is a nontraditional and specialized type of reinsurance. Financial reinsurance and the other forms of reinsurance shown in Exhibit 8-3 are discussed in detail in the paragraphs that follow.

Treaty Reinsurance

Most insurers depend heavily on treaty reinsurance because it provides several advantages over facultative reinsurance. The reinsurer is obligated to accept all business that falls within the terms of the treaty. Consequently, the primary insurer can underwrite, accept, and reinsure such business without prior consultation with the reinsurer on each pending application. Also, because prior negotiation is not required, the handling expense for each policy reinsured is less under a treaty than under facultative reinsurance. Whether an insurer chooses to use a pro rata or an excess of loss treaty is determined by the kind of exposures to be reinsured, the financial needs of the primary insurer, and other factors.

Pro Rata or Proportional Treaties

Pro rata reinsurance is the choice for a thinly financed insurer, whether writing property or liability insurance, because it is more effective than excess of loss coverage in providing surplus relief. Its greater effectiveness in that respect stems largely from the practice of paying ceding commissions under pro rata treaties, a practice not common under excess of loss treaties. Also, the premium for a pro rata treaty is likely to be a larger percentage of the original premium than is the case with an excess of loss treaty.

The two kinds of treaties in the pro rata category are quota share and surplus share (sometimes simply called surplus). The principal difference between them is the way in which the primary insurer's retention is stated. (The term "surplus" should not be confused with the policyholders' surplus of either the primary insurer or the reinsurer.)

EXHIBIT 8-3

Categories of Reinsurance

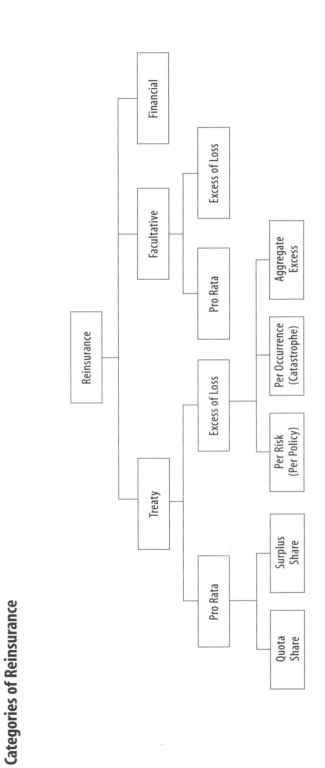

Excess of loss reinsurance written on a facultative basis is always on a per risk or per policy excess basis. Per occurrence and aggregate excess of loss reinsurance relate to a class of business, a territory, or the primary insurer's entire book of business rather than to a specific policy or a specific loss exposure. A financial reinsurance agreement can be written for any of the above types of reinsurance.

Adapted from Michael W. Elliot, Bernard L. Webb, Howard N. Anderson, and Peter R. Kensicki, *Principles of Reinsurance*, vol. 1, 2d ed. (Malvern, Pa.: Insurance Institute of America, 1995), pp. 5, 148.

Quota Share

Quota share treaty
Pro rata reinsurance agreement under which the primary insurer cedes a fixed, predetermined percentage of every risk it insures within a class or classes.

Under a **quota share treaty**, the primary insurer cedes a fixed, predetermined percentage of every risk it insures within the class or classes subject to the treaty. Even the smallest risks are reinsured.

The primary insurer's retention is stated as a percentage of the amount of insurance so that the dollar amount of its retention varies with the amount of insurance. The reinsurer assumes the amount of insurance less the primary insurer's retention, up to the reinsurance limit, which is expressed as a maximum dollar amount per one risk. The reinsurer receives the same percentage of the premium (less the ceding commission) as it does of the amount of insurance and pays the same percentage of each loss. An example of a quota share treaty is shown in Exhibit 8-4.

Quota share treaties can be used with either property or liability coverages, but property quota share treaties are much more common. They have the advantage of being simple to rate and simple to administer because the reinsurer receives the agreed percentage of all covered premiums. The principal disadvantage is that a quota share treaty results in ceding a large share of presumably profitable business. Because of this disadvantage, quota share reinsurance has been declining in popularity. However, it is still widely used, especially by small insurers and insurers that need surplus relief. Quota share is the most effective treaty for that purpose.

Quota share treaties are not effective in stabilizing underwriting results because they do not affect the primary insurer's loss ratio. Of course, a favorable ceding commission might affect the primary insurer's combined ratio, because reinsurance commissions received are credited against direct commissions paid in the primary insurer's Annual Statement. Over many years, one insurer showed a negative expense ratio on its Annual Statement because the ceding commissions on its reinsurance treaties were greater than all of its expenses paid. A reinsurer must anticipate an extremely low loss ratio in order to pay such a high ceding commission.

A quota share treaty can be reasonably effective in improving the primary insurer's large-line capacity, depending on the percentage retention required. However, it is not as effective in that regard as surplus share and per risk excess treaties.

Surplus Share

Surplus share treaty
A pro rata reinsurance agreement under which the reinsurer assumes pro rata responsibility for only that portion of any risk that exceeds the primary insurer's established retentions.

Surplus share treaties, like quota share treaties, are pro rata or proportional reinsurance. That is, the primary insurer and the reinsurers share the amount of insurance, the premium, and the losses in the same percentage. The difference between them is in the way the retention is stated. The retention under a quota share treaty is stated as a *percentage* of the amount insured, and the retention under a surplus share treaty is usually stated as a minimum *dollar amount*. However, the primary insurer might elect to retain more than the minimum retention stated in the treaty. If the amount of insurance under a given policy is less than the retention amount, no insurance under the policy is ceded. If the

EXHIBIT 8-4

Quota Share Treaty Example

Assume that Insurance Company has purchased from Reinsurance Company a quota share treaty with a $250,000 limit and a retention of 25 percent and a cession of 75 percent. Insurance Company has written three policies. Policy A insures Building A for $10,000 for a premium of $100, with one loss of $8,000. Policy B insures Building B for $100,000 for a premium of $1,000, with one loss of $10,000. Policy C insures Building C for $150,000 for a premium of $1,500, with one loss of $60,000. The table and graph below show how the insurance, premiums, and losses under these policies would be split between the primary insurer and the reinsurer. In each case, the primary insurer retains 25 percent of the insurance and the premium and pays 25 percent of the losses. However, the dollar amount of its retention increases as the amount of insurance increases.

Division of Insurance, Premium, and Losses Under Quota Share Treaty

	Insurance Company (25%)	Reinsurance Company (75%)	Total
Policy A			
Insurance	$2,500	$7,500	$10,000
Premium	25	75	100
Loss	2,000	6,000	8,000
Policy B			
Insurance	$25,000	$75,000	$100,000
Premium	250	750	1,000
Loss	2,500	7,500	10,000
Policy C			
Insurance	$37,500	$112,500	$150,000
Premium	375	1,125	1,500
Loss	15,000	45,000	60,000

amount of insurance under a policy exceeds the retention amount, the amount of insurance above the retention is ceded to the reinsurer, subject to the reinsurance limit and other limitations of the treaty. The reinsurer receives premiums and is responsible for all losses, regardless of size, in the same proportion that the amount ceded bears to the amount retained. Even though an individual loss might be less than the retention of the ceding company, it will be shared between the ceding company and the surplus share reinsurer if the amount of insurance exceeds the retention amount. The major distinction between quota share and surplus share is that although the same *percentage* of reinsurance applies to all eligible policies under quota share, the percentage *varies* from policy to policy in a surplus share treaty, depending on the amount of the insurance ceded. This is illustrated in Exhibit 8-5.

Surplus share reinsurance has been a common form of reinsurance for property insurers, though it has recently been losing ground to excess of loss reinsurance. It has seldom been used for liability insurance. If pro rata reinsurance is written for liability lines, it is done on a quota share basis.

The principal advantage to the primary insurer of surplus share treaties over quota share treaties is that surplus share treaties, because of their fixed dollar retentions, avoid ceding reinsurance on loss exposures so small that the primary insurer can afford to retain them. A surplus share treaty also provides a more logical approach to purchasing proportional reinsurance, because no reinsurance is purchased unless the risk is beyond the capacity of the primary insurer to absorb.

The principal disadvantage of surplus share treaties in comparison with quota share is the increased administrative expense. Because not all risks are reinsured,

---

EXHIBIT 8-5

Surplus Share Treaty Example

Assume that Insurance Company has purchased from Reinsurance Company a surplus treaty with a retention of $25,000 and a limit of $250,000. This would be referred to as a "ten-line surplus treaty," since the primary insurer will cede coverage up to ten times the retention amount. The table and graph in this exhibit show how this treaty would apply to the same three policies used previously to illustrate the application of a quota share treaty. For Policy A, no amount of insurance is ceded because the amount of insurance is less than the $25,000 retention. For Policy B, the proportion in which premiums and losses are shared is determined by the retention divided by the insurance amount. The same applies to Policy C. Under a quota share treaty (Exhibit 8-4), the percentage retention remains constant, and the dollar amount of retention increases as the amount of insurance increases. Under a surplus share treaty for insurance amounts above the retention, the dollar amount of retention remains constant while the percentage retention decreases as the amount of insurance increases.

Division of Insurance, Premium, and Losses Under Surplus Share Treaty With $25,000 Retention and $250,000 Limit

	Insurance Company (%)	Reinsurance Company (% Ceded)	Total
Policy A			
Insurance	$10,000 (100%)	$0 (0%)	$ 10,000
Premium	100	0	100
Loss	8,000	0	8,000
Policy B			
Insurance	$25,000 (25%)	$ 75,000 (75%)	$100,000
Premium	250	750	1,000
Loss	2,500	7,500	10,000
Policy C			
Insurance	$25,000 (16.67%)	$125,000 (83.33%)	$150,000
Premium	250	1,250	1,500
Loss	10,000	50,000	60,000

the primary insurer must maintain a record of those that are reinsured and furnish a report of them to the reinsurer each month or at some other regular interval. The listing of reinsured exposures, which usually includes premium and loss information, is known as a bordereau (of which the plural is "bordereaux"). Although reporting on a bordereau basis to reinsurers is not common practice today, the primary insurer must make records available to the reinsurer for audit purposes.

Surplus share treaties compared to quota share are of lesser importance in providing surplus relief, since no reinsurance is ceded on risks with limits of insurance less than the minimum net retention.

A surplus share treaty is superior to a quota share treaty in providing large-line capacity. Under a quota share treaty, the primary insurer's total *dollar exposure to loss* increases in direct proportion to that of its reinsurers, resulting in a limited line capacity. However, under a surplus arrangement, the primary insurer may cede several multiples of its net retention up to the limit of its treaty, providing significant risk capacity.

Because amounts of insurance ceded to a surplus treaty vary by risk, the financial results realized by the reinsurers can vary significantly from those of the primary insurer. In retrospect, the primary insurer may find that it has ceded very profitable business to the reinsurer. The loss of profit is part of the price the primary insurer pays in meeting a business objective through reinsurance.

Like the quota share treaty, the surplus share is not designed to protect the primary insurer from catastrophe loss occurrences. This function of reinsurance is satisfied by excess of loss treaties, described later. Until recently, *pro rata treaties generally did not have a per occurrence limit.* For example, some regional insurers wrote primarily large property exposures within a one- or two-state territory and used surplus share treaties as their major form of reinsurance. Severe earthquakes or hurricanes might damage or destroy many of the ceded exposures, resulting in large losses to reinsurers. Recent catastrophes such as Hurricane Andrew in 1992 and the Northridge, California, earthquake in 1994 have resulted in occurrence limits on most proportional treaties.

Excess of Loss or Nonproportional Treaties

Excess of loss treaties, sometimes referred to as nonproportional treaties, differ from pro rata, or proportional, treaties in that the primary insurer and the reinsurer do not share the amount of insurance, premium, and losses in the same proportion. In fact, *no insurance amount is ceded under excess of loss treaties, only losses and premiums.* The reinsurance premium is usually stated as a percentage of the primary insurer's premium income for the covered lines of business, but the percentage is subject to negotiation and varies by line and by insurer. Generally, ceding commissions are not paid under excess of loss treaties.

The excess reinsurer is responsible only for losses that exceed the retention and fall within the coverage provided by the reinsurance contract. Although coverage provided by the pro rata treaty is always concurrent (identical) with the coverage provided by the primary insurer's policy, the coverage provided by the excess reinsurance contract is not necessarily the same as that of the primary insurer.

Excess of loss treaties fall into three general classes: per risk or per policy excess, per occurrence excess (also known as per loss excess), and aggregate excess. They differ substantially in operation and are discussed separately below.

Per Risk or Per Policy Excess

Distinguishing between a per risk and a per policy excess of loss reinsurance treaty is important. A **per risk excess treaty** applies to property insurance in

Per risk excess treaty
An excess of loss reinsurance agreement applied to property insurance policies in which a retention and a limit of coverage apply separately to each risk insured by the primary insurer. A risk in this regard refers to each subject of insurance, which might include multiple buildings covered by one policy.

which the retention and limit apply separately to each risk insured by the primary insurer. A **per policy excess treaty** applies to liability insurance in which the retention and limit apply separately to each policy issued by the primary insurer. The retention under a per risk or per policy excess of loss treaty is stated as a dollar amount of loss (not an amount of insurance), and the reinsurer is liable for all or a part of loss to any one exposure in excess of the retention and up to the agreed reinsurance limit. In some cases, the reinsurer might agree to pay only a stated percentage, such as 90 percent or 95 percent, of the loss in excess of the retention.

The retention amount is usually set at a level to exclude a large majority, by number, of expected claims. This approach is consistent with the theory that excess of loss treaties are intended to protect the primary insurer against unusually large losses. However, the retention is sometimes set low enough so that reinsurance claims occur frequently. Treaties with such low retentions are frequently referred to as **working covers** (or working level excess treaties). Working covers permit the primary insurer to spread losses over a number of years so that profitable years can offset unprofitable ones. A small or inexperienced insurer might choose a working cover to minimize its exposure to loss until it gains confidence in the lines of business written.

The retention under a per risk or per policy excess of loss treaty *applies separately to each subject of insurance.* For example, if Insurance Company insured Company A at 1110 Main Street and Company B next door at 1112 Main Street, and they both burned, the retention under a per risk excess treaty would apply separately to each. If Insurance Company issued automobile liability policies to each of the above companies, and an auto accident occurred involving both policies, the retention under a per policy excess treaty would apply separately to each policy. As the next two sections explain, the retention applies differently for the other forms of excess treaty.

Unlike pro rata treaties, excess treaty reinsurers do not participate in all losses, but only in those that exceed the primary insurer's retention, and then only in the part that is in excess of the retention. This difference is emphasized here because it is a frequent source of confusion. Exhibit 8-6 shows how a primary insurer and a reinsurer would split losses under a per risk excess of loss treaty.

From the viewpoint of the primary insurer, the principal advantage of a per risk or per policy excess of loss treaty in comparison with pro rata treaties is that less premium is submitted to the reinsurer. This approach permits the primary insurer to earn income on the investment of these funds. Administration costs are also lower because fewer reinsurance claims are processed. Also, keeping track of the loss exposures reinsured, as is required under a surplus share treaty, might not be necessary. The excess of loss treaty is concerned only with losses.

Because the reinsurance premium is lower than for pro rata treaties and because commissions are normally not paid to the primary insurer, excess of loss treaties are not effective in providing surplus relief.

Per policy excess treaty
An excess of loss reinsurance agreement applied to liability insurance policies in which a retention and a limit of coverage apply separately to each policy issued by the primary insurer.

Working covers
Per risk or per policy excess treaties with such low retentions that the reinsurer expects moderate to heavy loss activity.

EXHIBIT 8-6

Per Risk Excess of Loss Treaty Example

Assume Insurance Company has purchased from Reinsurance Company a per risk excess of loss treaty with a $25,000 retention. The table and graph below show how losses will be split. Policy A and Policy B have losses below the retention amount, so the reinsurer is not involved. Policy A (see Exhibit 8-5) has a limit of only $10,000, so even a total loss will not come under this treaty. No mention is made here of policy limits or premium amounts because they are not relevant to the division of losses under an excess treaty.

Division of Losses Under Per Risk Excess Treaty With $25,000 Retention

	Loss Amount	Insurance Company	Reinsurance Company
Policy A Loss	$ 8,000	$ 8,000	$ 0
Policy B Loss	$10,000	$10,000	$ 0
Policy C Loss	$60,000	$25,000	$35,000

Policy C
$60,000 Loss

$35,000

$25,000

Policy A
$8,000 Loss

Policy B
$10,000 Loss

☐ Primary Insurer's Retention
▨ Reinsurer's Share of the Loss

Per risk or per policy excess treaties are effective in providing large-line capacity because they absorb the large losses that make large lines hazardous to the primary insurer. They are much more effective in this regard than quota share treaties and more effective than surplus share treaties, particularly if the reinsurance premium cost is considered.

Per risk or per policy excess treaties are effective in stabilizing the loss experience of the primary insurer because they lessen the effect of large losses, which contribute disproportionately to fluctuations of loss experience. The loss experience of the reinsurer is not the same as that of the primary insurer in any given year. However, over the long run, each primary insurer should expect to pay its own losses plus the reinsurer's operating expenses and profit. That is, the primary insurer gives up a part of its profits in the good years in order to transfer its losses to the reinsurer in the bad years, thus stabilizing its loss experience over time.

Per risk excess treaties are helpful in catastrophes because they pay the amount in excess of the primary insurer's retention on each individual claim. However, they are far less effective in this regard than per occurrence excess treaties, because a catastrophic loss from a hurricane, a tornado, or an earthquake can affect a large percentage of the insurers' policies written in a geographic area.

Per Occurrence Excess

Per occurrence excess of loss reinsurance provides indemnity against loss sustained in excess of the net retention of the primary insurer, subject to a reinsurance limit, regardless of the number of risks (number of separate policies or specifically scheduled items) involved in respect to one accident, occurrence, or event. Per occurrence excess of loss reinsurance applies to either property or liability coverages and is called catastrophe excess when applied to property coverages and clash cover when applied to liability coverages.

A liability per occurrence excess treaty is extremely important to primary insurers with very high limit requirements. Even insurers writing modest amounts of workers compensation, for example, might feel that having $5 million, $10 million, or more of per occurrence reinsurance protection is advisable.

The distinguishing feature of liability per occurrence excess is that auto liability, general liability, workers compensation, umbrella, and perhaps other coverages can be combined to form a single excess claim, and there might also be multiple claimants. When the per occurrence retention is set higher than the limit of any single liability policy, the coverage is sometimes known as a clash cover because it would take more than a single policy to involve the reinsurance coverage.

Another feature materially different from the property classes is the length of time required for the full development and settlement of all losses. The time between date of loss and notice to excess reinsurers might be several years. Final settlement of known losses may require many more years. In some cases, the time of the occurrence is not clear, such as carcinogenic exposures that might not manifest themselves for decades. Inflation and the late development of claims make this a difficult class to underwrite.

Property insurers are especially prone to large accumulations of losses arising from a single catastrophe, such as a hurricane or an earthquake that damages many insured properties. Most of the individual claims are relatively small, but the accumulated amount can be staggering. Catastrophe treaties are designed to cope with this problem.

Like the per risk and per policy excess treaties, the retention under a per occurrence excess treaty is stated as a dollar amount. The difference is that all of the net losses (that is, gross loss less deduction for all other per risk reinsurance) arising from a single occurrence are totaled to determine when the retention has been satisfied. The reinsurance limit also applies to the aggregate amount of losses from one occurrence. Consequently, the definition

Per occurrence excess of loss
Per occurrence excess of loss reinsurance indemnifies the primary insurer when the losses for an occurrence exceed the retention limit.

of occurrence becomes important. One catastrophe treaty defines an occurrence as follows:

C. The term "Loss Occurrence" will mean the sum of all individual losses directly occasioned by any one disaster, accident, or loss or series of disasters, accidents, or losses arising out of one event which occurs within the area of one state of the United States or province of Canada and states or provinces contiguous thereto and to one another. However, the duration and extent of any one "Loss Occurrence" will be limited to all individual losses sustained by the Company occurring during any period of 168 consecutive hours arising out of and directly occasioned by the same event except that the term "Loss Occurrence" will be further defined as follows:

(1) As regards windstorm, hail, tornado, hurricane, cyclone, including ensuing collapse and water damage, all individual losses sustained by the Company occurring during any period of 72 consecutive hours arising out of and directly occasioned by the same event. However, the event need not be limited to one state or province or states or provinces contiguous thereto.

(2) As regards riot, riot attending a strike, civil commotion, vandalism and malicious mischief, all individual losses sustained by the Company occurring during any period of 72 consecutive hours within the area of one municipality or county and the municipalities or counties contiguous thereto arising out of and directly occasioned by the same event. The maximum duration of 72 consecutive hours may be extended in respect of individual losses which occur beyond such 72 consecutive hours during the continued occupation of an assured's premises by strikers, provided such occupation commenced during the aforesaid period.

(3) As regards earthquake (the epicenter of which need not necessarily be within the territorial confines referred to in the opening paragraph of this Article) and fire following directly occasioned by the earthquake, only those individual fire losses which commence during the period of 168 consecutive hours may be included in the Company's "Loss Occurrence."

(4) As regards "Freeze," only individual losses directly occasioned by collapse, breakage of glass and water damage (caused by bursting of frozen pipes and tanks) may be included in the Company's "Loss Occurrence."

For all "Loss Occurrences," other than (2) above, the Company may choose the date and time when any such period of consecutive hours commences, provided that it is not earlier than the date and time of the occurrence of the first recorded individual loss sustained by the Company arising out of the disaster, accident, or loss and provided that only one such period of 168 consecutive hours will apply with respect to one event, except for any "Loss Occurrences" referred to in (1) above where only one such period of 72 consecutive hours will apply with respect to one event.

However, as respects those "Loss Occurrences" referred to in (2) above, if the disaster, accident, or loss occasioned by the event is of greater duration than 72 consecutive hours, then the Company may divide that disaster, accident, or loss into two or more "Loss Occurrences," provided no two periods overlap and no individual loss is included in more than one such period and provided that no period commences earlier than the date and time of the occurrence of the first recorded individual loss sustained by the Company arising out of that disaster, accident, or loss.

No individual losses occasioned by an event that would be covered by 72 hours clauses may be included in any "Loss Occurrence" claimed under the 168 hours provision.

The word "company" in the foregoing quotation refers to the primary insurer.

This definition of occurrence is important because it controls the application of the retention and the reinsurance limit. The retention would apply separately, but only once, to each occurrence, as would the reinsurance limit. For example, if a hurricane travels up the East Coast and causes wind damage over three days, all of the damage would be from a single occurrence. Consequently, the primary insurer would be required to absorb only one retention, and the reinsurer's liability could not exceed the amount stated in the treaty.

If the same hurricane brought heavy rains causing flooding in one river that drained into the Atlantic Ocean and another that drained into the Gulf of Mexico (not an uncommon circumstance), the floods in the two rivers would be two separate occurrences by the above definition. Consequently, the retention and the treaty limit would apply separately to each river, even though both floods originated from the same storm system.

The definitions quoted are merely illustrative. Different reinsurers, or even the same reinsurers in different treaties, might use different definitions.

Per occurrence excess treaties are effective in smoothing the fluctuations in loss experience to the extent that such fluctuations result from an accumulation of losses from a single occurrence. Such treaties do not contribute to the primary insurer's premium capacity (except to the extent that they stabilize loss experience) because they are not designed to cover individual losses, nor do they contribute to large-line capacity unless written to cover for a single large loss as well as an accumulation of losses.

Per occurrence excess treaties do not provide significant surplus relief. Because the reinsurance premium is a relatively small percentage of the direct premiums and the reinsurer usually does not pay a ceding commission, the benefit to surplus from this transaction is incidental.

Per occurrence excess treaties usually provide that the reinsurers will pay up to a stated percentage, that is, 90 or 95 percent, of the loss in excess of the retention. Therefore, not only does the primary insurer pay the losses up to the retention, but it also participates in the loss above the retention. This approach encourages the primary insurer to settle losses economically, because it will be participating in the loss even though the retention is exhausted.

Per occurrence treaties also differ from per risk and per policy excess of loss contracts in that they are usually written for a specific period of time (twelve months) and are usually noncancelable by either party.

Aggregate Excess

Aggregate excess treaties, sometimes called excess of loss ratio or stop loss treaties, are less common than the other forms of excess of loss treaties. However, they have been used with some frequency in connection with crop hail insurance and for small insurers in other lines.

Aggregate excess treaty
A form of excess of loss reinsurance under which the reinsurer begins to pay when all the primary insurer's claims for some stated period of time exceed the retention stated in the treaty.

Under an **aggregate excess treaty**, the reinsurer begins to pay when all the primary insurer's claims for some stated period of time, usually one year, exceed the retention stated in the treaty. The retention can be stated in dollars, as a loss ratio percentage, or as a combination of the two. The size of the retention is subject to negotiation between the primary insurer and the reinsurer, but it usually would not be set so low that the primary insurer would be guaranteed a profit. Also, the reinsurer normally does not pay all losses in excess of the primary insurer's retention, but only a percentage of the excess, usually 90 or 95 percent. This last feature is intended to discourage the primary insurer from relaxing its underwriting or loss adjustment standards after its retention has been reached.

Because the aggregate excess treaty limits the primary insurer's losses (or loss ratio), it would appear that no other reinsurance would be needed. However, when aggregate excess treaties are used, other treaties are commonly used to support the reinsurance program. In some cases, the reinsurer might insist on other treaties as a condition of providing the aggregate excess cover. In those cases, the other treaties would be written for the benefit of both the primary insurer and the aggregate excess reinsurer. That is, the primary insurer's retention and the aggregate excess reinsurer's liability would both relate to the net loss after the proceeds of all other reinsurance had been deducted.

The aggregate excess treaty is the most effective of all forms of reinsurance in stabilizing the loss experience of the primary insurer, particularly if the cost of reinsurance is ignored. It is also effective in providing large-line capacity and coping with catastrophes because the cap it puts on losses would apply equally to large individual claims and an accumulation of claims from a catastrophe.

However, an aggregate excess treaty usually does not involve ceding commission. Therefore, it does not provide significant surplus relief or premium capacity. Logically, it should increase premium capacity because the primary insurer would need less surplus to absorb the remaining fluctuation in loss experience. However, current regulatory techniques are not sophisticated enough to adjust premium-to-surplus ratio requirements to reflect the greater loss stability provided by aggregate excess covers.

A summary of the functions or purposes of reinsurance and how well each type of reinsurance serves those purposes is shown in Exhibit 8-7.

Facultative Reinsurance

Making specific statements about facultative reinsurance is difficult because each item of coverage is negotiated separately and can be in almost any form

EXHIBIT 8-7

Function of Specific Types of Treaty Reinsurance

Type of Reinsurance	Financing (Surplus Relief)	Large-Line Capacity	Catastrophe Protection	Stabilization of Loss Experience	Main Purpose
Quota share	Yes	Yes	Yes, but not purchased for this purpose	No	To provide surplus relief
Surplus share	Yes	Yes	No	No	Primarily to provide large-line capacity while providing some surplus relief
Per risk or per policy excess	No	Yes	Possibly to some extent, but not purchased for purpose	Yes	To provide large-line capacity while stabilizing loss experience
Per occurrence	No	No	Yes, sole purpose	Yes	To protect against an accumulation of losses from one event (property or casualty coverages)
Aggregate excess	No	Yes	Yes	Yes	To stabilize loss experience

and at almost any rate that is agreeable to both parties. In the past, facultative reinsurance on property was almost always written on a pro rata basis. Now, facultative excess is commonly used.

Regardless of the form, excess or pro rata, the approach to underwriting facultative reinsurance is substantially different from that for treaties. In underwriting a treaty, the principal emphasis is on the management of the primary insurer, the classes reinsured, the geographical spread, and the primary insurer's historical loss experience for the lines of insurance covered by the treaty. The reinsurer does not underwrite individual loss exposures under the treaty.

Under facultative reinsurance, the reinsurer underwrites each loss exposure individually as it is submitted for consideration. The primary insurer is required to furnish detailed information on each exposure (essentially the same information that a prudent primary insurer would require when underwriting an account).

The facultative reinsurer is not bound by the rates quoted or charged by the primary insurer. It may, if it chooses and if the primary insurer is willing, charge a higher rate for the reinsurance than was charged on the direct policy. For this reason, primary insurers that expect to depend heavily on facultative reinsurance frequently obtain a reinsurance commitment before they quote a premium to their prospective policyholders. Of course, primary insurers take this precaution only partly because of rates. They also want to be sure that reinsurance will be available. When an exposure is accepted, the reinsurer formalizes the agreement with a certificate of reinsurance.

In view of the uncertainty and handling burden of facultative reinsurance, why would a primary insurer use it? Why not rely solely on treaties? There are several reasons.

First, treaties have exclusions. Property treaties, for example, usually exclude reinsurance coverage for a list of so-called "target risks," such as large art museums, major bridges, tunnels, nuclear generating facilities, and other properties of high value. These properties are excluded primarily because their large values require them to buy insurance from a number of primary insurers. If they were not excluded in treaties, a reinsurer might find, after a loss, that its accumulated loss through several different primary insurers exceeded the amount it deemed prudent to accept. It would not know of such an exposure before a loss because the reinsurer does not underwrite each individual exposure under a treaty. Treaties might also exclude certain hazardous operations, either for property or liability lines. If an exposure is excluded under the primary insurer's treaties, it must turn to facultative reinsurers for protection.

Second, a primary insurer might use facultative coverage to protect its treaties, to protect a favorable commission allowance under its treaties, or to protect a profit-sharing agreement. A favorable reinsurance treaty is a valuable relationship for a primary insurer, facilitating its operations and contributing to its profits. However, the continuation of the treaty on favorable terms, or perhaps on any terms, depends on the quality of business placed with it. The ceding commission or rates under treaties are determined by loss experience under the treaty. Some treaties include retrospective rating plans or profit-sharing commission plans that tie the rates or commission directly to losses incurred under that treaty. The rates or commissions under other treaties are negotiated on the basis of past loss experience. If an insurer must write coverage on a loss exposure that might have an adverse effect on its treaty relationships, it can reinsure it facultatively instead. Because each facultative submission is an independent transaction and is underwritten separately, a loss under one facultative agreement has little or no effect on the terms or rates under subsequent transactions.

Another reason for using facultative reinsurance is to cover a loss exposure that exceeds the limits under the applicable treaties. The limit under a reinsurance treaty is one of the major determinants of reinsurance costs. Consequently, a primary insurer should set the limit at an amount that is adequate for the vast majority, say 98 percent, of the loss exposures it insures and rely on facultative coverage for the excess over treaty limits for the unusually large exposures.

The statement that each facultative submission is separately and independently underwritten has one exception. Reinsurers sometimes enter into what is called a facultative obligatory treaty. Under such a treaty, the primary insurer is not required to place any exposures, but the reinsurer is obligated to accept any business the primary insurer elects to place as long as it is within the class of business covered by the treaty. Under a facultative obligatory treaty, the reinsurer underwrites the management of the primary insurer at least as carefully as under the more common treaties, and possibly more carefully.

Facultative obligatory treaties are not common because of the opportunity for adverse selection against the reinsurer. Facultative treaties that are nonobligatory to the reinsurer are slightly more common. Such treaties merely set forth the conditions under which business will be placed and accepted if the primary insurer elects to place it and the reinsurer elects to accept it.

Pro Rata Facultative Reinsurance

As previously mentioned, facultative reinsurance for property exposures has traditionally been written on a pro rata basis, though excess of loss reinsurance has become more prominent in recent years. **Pro rata facultative reinsurance** functions similarly to a surplus share treaty except, of course, that each facultative agreement relates to a single subject of insurance. Exhibit 8-8 shows the operation of a pro rata facultative reinsurance transaction.

Pro rata facultative reinsurance
Reinsurance of individual risks in which the reinsurer shares a pro rata portion of the losses and premiums of the ceding company.

Excess Facultative Reinsurance

Excess of loss facultative reinsurance operates just like a per risk or per policy excess treaty. That is, the primary insurer pays all losses equal to or less than its agreed retention. The reinsurer is involved only if the loss exceeds the primary insurer's retention, and then it pays only the amount in excess of the retention, up to the reinsurance limit.

Excess of loss facultative reinsurance
Reinsurance of individual risks in which the primary insurer pays all losses up to its agreed retention. The reinsurer pays losses in excess of the retention up to the reinsurance limit.

Excess of loss reinsurance has been the traditional form of facultative reinsurance for liability and workers compensation coverages. As previously mentioned, it has been used with increasing frequency for property insurance.

For liability insurance, the per policy excess reinsurance premium is usually based on the increased limits factors used by the primary insurer. However, the reinsurance premium might be higher or lower than the primary insurer's increased limits premium, depending on the facultative reinsurer's judgment as to the adequacy of that premium for the particular exposure.

Specifying a method for rating excess of loss facultative coverage for property insurance is difficult. The rate would largely depend on the judgment of the facultative underwriter, reinforced to the extent possible by statistics from the reinsurer's experience with similar exposures, guides such as Lloyd's first loss scale, and what the competition is charging. Lloyd's first loss scale is used by property facultative underwriters in much the same way increased limit factor tables are used in liability lines.

EXHIBIT 8-8

Pro Rata Facultative Reinsurance Example

As an illustration, assume that Insurance Company has received an application from one of its producers to write $1 million of property insurance on the Foundry Corporation. Insurance Company has established its net retention limit on foundries at $100,000. In addition, it has automatic surplus share treaties that will cover five lines, or, in this case, $500,000. The surplus reinsurers pay Insurance Company a 35 percent ceding commission under the treaties.

Insurance, Premium, and Loss Division Through Surplus Share and Pro Rata Facultative Reinsurance

	Insurance	Premium	Loss	Ceding Commission to Insurance Company
Insurance Company	$ 100,000	$ 3,000	$ 2,000	$ 0
Surplus Share Reinsurers	500,000	15,000	10,000	5,250
Facultative Reinsurer	400,000	12,000	8,000	3,600
Totals	$1,000,000	$30,000	$20,000	$8,850

Insurance Company then approaches the facultative department of Facultative Reinsurer with a request for $400,000 of pro rata facultative reinsurance. After Facultative Reinsurer reviews all of the information furnished by Insurance Company, it agrees to provide the $400,000 of coverage, for which it will receive 40 percent of the direct premium and will pay Insurance Company a 30 percent ceding commission. The direct premium charged to Foundry Corporation by Insurance Company is $30,000.

Having obtained the necessary reinsurance, Insurance Company issued the policy to Foundry Corporation. A $20,000 loss occurred shortly thereafter. The insurance, premium, and loss would be divided as shown below.

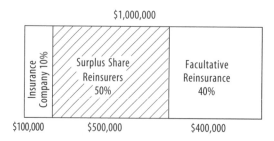

Functions of Facultative Reinsurance

The principal functions of facultative reinsurance, whether pro rata or excess of loss, are to provide large-line capacity, to cover those exposures specifically excluded from treaties, and to protect treaties from unusual or hazardous exposures. Facultative reinsurance can also be used to secure a second opinion from the facultative reinsurer as to acceptability, price, policy terms, and conditions. Because facultative coverage must be negotiated separately on each subject of insurance, it is not likely to provide significant surplus relief unless a very large number of facultative covers are purchased. The same characteristic prevents facultative reinsurance from effectively coping with catastrophes. It does help smooth the fluctuations in loss experience, however, by providing a means of limiting the effect of a single large loss.

FINANCIAL REINSURANCE

All reinsurance contracts are financial contracts. The characteristics that distinguish the traditional reinsurance contracts, discussed up to this point, from the so-called financial or finite reinsurance contracts, discussed here, are the kinds and amounts of risks transferred. Traditional reinsurance contracts are designed primarily to transfer underwriting risk—the risk that losses and expenses will exceed premium.

Financial reinsurance contracts usually transfer very little underwriting risk; some of them transfer no underwriting risk at all. They can also transfer some investment risk, some timing risk, or both. **Investment risk** is the chance that a reinsurer's investment portfolio will yield a lower return than expected. **Timing risk** is the risk that losses will be paid more quickly than expected, thus producing less investment income than expected.

A primary insurer's major motivation for purchasing financial reinsurance is to enhance its surplus position. However, because of accounting restrictions imposed in 1992, U.S. insurers are restricted from benefiting from some forms of financial reinsurance. According to these accounting guidelines, the following conditions must apply in order for a transaction to be considered "reinsurance":

1. The reinsurer must assume significant insurance risk under the reinsured portions of the underlying insurance contracts.
2. It must be reasonably possible for the reinsurer to realize significant loss from the transaction.

Although the term "insurance risk" is defined in the guidelines, the terms "reasonably possible" and "significant loss" are not. Thus, determining whether a financial reinsurance agreement meets these accounting requirements is complex.

Financial reinsurance agreements can be transacted using most types of reinsurance. Under a financial reinsurance treaty, the reinsurer's aggregate

Investment risk
The chance that a reinsurer's investment portfolio will yield a lower return than expected.

Timing risk
The risk that losses will be paid more quickly than expected, thus producing less investment income than expected.

liability under the contract is limited. That limit can be set equal to the reinsurance premium plus anticipated investment income, shielding the reinsurer from the underwriting risks.

The principal categories of financial reinsurance are as follows:

- Time and distance contracts
- Loss portfolio transfers

Many variations are possible within each of these categories.

Time and Distance Contracts

Time and distance contract
An agreement under which the primary insurer pays an agreed premium to the reinsurer in return for the reinsurer's promise to pay the primary insurer future payments.

Under a **time and distance contract**, the primary insurer pays an agreed premium to the reinsurer at the inception of the contract. In return, the reinsurer promises to pay to the primary insurer one or more future payments, with the date and amount of each payment specified in the contract. The payments to the primary insurer are not contingent on its underwriting experience. The premium paid by the primary insurer is determined by discounting the future payments to reflect the investment income that the reinsurer expects to earn on the premium it receives. A loading for the reinsurer's expenses and profit is added, either directly or by crediting interest at a lower rate than the reinsurer expects to earn. The only risk assumed by the reinsurer is the risk that it will not earn as much investment income as it anticipated in calculating the premium.

Time and distance contracts are no longer used much in the United States because regulatory authorities and auditors have judged them not to be reinsurance transactions. Instead, they are treated for accounting purposes in the same way as bank deposits. The major purchasers for such contracts are syndicates at Lloyd's of London.

Loss Portfolio Transfers

Loss portfolio transfer contract
An agreement under which the primary insurer cedes to the reinsurers its liability for a block of losses (or portfolio).

Traditional reinsurance contracts cover losses incurred by the primary insurer during the term of the reinsurance contract. By contrast, loss portfolio transfers cover losses incurred by the primary insurer before the inception of the loss portfolio transfer contract. Under a **loss portfolio transfer contract**, the primary insurer cedes to the reinsurer its liability for a block of losses (or portfolio) defined in the contract. Subject to the limits stated in the contract, the reinsurer then reimburses the primary insurer for any amounts paid to settle the covered losses.

Until recently, the advantage of loss portfolio transfers to U.S. primary insurers was an immediate increase in policyholders' surplus. The premium the primary insurer must pay is usually substantially less than the aggregate amount of loss reserves transferred because they are discounted in calculating the premium. Consequently, a primary insurer might transfer $100 million of loss reserves for a premium of $75 million. The difference of $25 million would be added to its policyholders' surplus. U.S. accounting standard changes have taken away this advantage for U.S.-domiciled insurers.

REINSURANCE THROUGH POOLS

Although there are some fine distinctions among pools, syndicates, and reinsurance associations, the three are discussed together here, and no distinction is made between them. A **reinsurance pool** (or syndicate or association) is an organization of insurers banded together to underwrite reinsurance jointly. Some pools write reinsurance only for member companies of the pool. Others write coverage only for nonmember insurers, and still others may write coverage for both members and nonmembers. Some reinsurance pools restrict their operations to relatively narrow classes of business, such as fire and allied lines coverages on sprinklered properties. Others write a wide variety of coverages.

Reinsurance pool
An organization of insurers that underwrite reinsurance jointly.

The initiative for the organization of a reinsurance pool can come from any of several sources. Several pools were organized because groups of relatively small insurers wanted to increase their capacity to write high-value properties. None of the insurers operating alone had sufficient skill and capacity, but the group could provide the needed capacity and hire technicians by combining financial resources through a reinsurance pool. Often, such pooling results in a lowering of total expenses. Examples of such pools are the Industrial Risk Insurers (IRI) and the United States Aircraft Insurance Group (USAIG). Governmental pressure or suggestion has been the initiating force in the formation of some pools. Among these are the nuclear energy pools and the reinsurance plans and joint underwriting associations that function in some states to provide automobile, fire, and workers compensation insurance for those who cannot obtain coverage in the voluntary market.

A reinsurance broker, also known as a reinsurance intermediary, might organize a pool as a means of providing reinsurance to clients of the brokerage firm. Such pools are likely to be fluid, with old member firms departing and new member firms entering on a fairly frequent basis. Needless to say, the broker would need to offer some inducement to entice an insurer to participate. The inducement might be an established book of desirable business, some special expertise on the part of the broker, or some similar benefit to the insurer. Although many broker-initiated pools have operated successfully over many years, a few have failed, with severe results for the participating companies. With increasing exposure for legal liability resulting from such pool operations, broker-oriented pools are not as prevalent today as in past years.

Pooling, by itself, does not necessarily improve the underwriting results of the pooled business. Poor business placed in the pool simply develops poor pool results.

The operating methods of reinsurance pools vary as widely as their purposes of organization, or perhaps more so. Automobile residual market mechanisms, discussed in Chapters 1 and 6, exemplify how the property-casualty industry has combined resources to address a market need. Similarly, insurance-industry-backed nuclear energy pools were created to protect the public from the peacetime use of nuclear energy.

THE REINSURANCE MARKET

The boundaries of the reinsurance market are difficult to define. It is a surprisingly international market, and a single large loss might be shared by reinsurers throughout the world. In 1995, U.S. insurers bought almost half of their reinsurance, measured by premiums, from nonadmitted alien reinsurers. These alien reinsurers are located in many countries of the world, including Russia and China. However, Britain, Bermuda, and Switzerland overwhelmingly account for the largest shares. The share of U.S. reinsurance premiums going to nonadmitted alien insurers does not fully indicate the international nature of the reinsurance business. Of the twenty largest U.S.-based reinsurers in 1995, four were owned by foreign reinsurers. Of course, some of the nonadmitted, alien reinsurers to which U.S. companies ceded premiums were owned by U.S. insurers, especially those reinsurers domiciled in the United Kingdom and Bermuda.

Insurers based in the United States sell much reinsurance abroad, but not nearly as much as they buy abroad. The United States is a net importer of reinsurance.

Exhibit 8-9 shows a list of the largest reinsurers in the world in 2000, along with their estimated written premiums. All of the reinsurers listed in Exhibit 8-9 are active in the U.S. market, either directly or through subsidiaries. Lloyd's of London is not included in Exhibit 8-9, but probably would rank near the middle if included.

Note the geographic diversity in top reinsurers, with eight headquartered in the United States, three each in Germany and Japan, two each in Switzerland and France, and one each in England, Italy, and Bermuda. Numerous smaller reinsurers are located in many other countries.

In addition to the geographic spread of the largest reinsurers, one other fact stands out in Exhibit 8-9. Many reinsurers are substantially smaller financially than the primary insurers to which they provide reinsurance protection. However, any one professional reinsurer does not write or retain for its own account all of the exposures assumed under a treaty with a major primary insurer. A major treaty is usually shared by several reinsurers on a percentage basis, or if one reinsurer initially writes the entire treaty, it might cede much of it to other reinsurers under retrocession agreements.

Multiplicity of Reinsurers

In addition to its geographic spread, the boundaries of the reinsurance market are difficult to define for another reason. Any insurer can provide reinsurance unless it is subject to statutory or charter prohibitions. Few such prohibitions exist, and many primary insurers also provide some reinsurance. Even relatively small insurers can engage in the reinsurance business by participating in

EXHIBIT 8-9

Top Ten Global Reinsurance Companies, by Gross Premiums Written, 2000

Company	Country	Gross premiums written[1] ($ millions)
Munich Re: Segment Reinsurance	Germany	$17,269
Swiss Re	Switzerland	16,176
GE Global Insurance Holdings	U.S.	10,149
Berkshire Hathaway	U.S.	9,270
Hannover Re Group	Germany	7,841
Lloyd's of London	U.K.	6,398
Zurich Financial	Switzerland	5,107
Gerling-Globale Reinsurance Group	Germany	4,897
SCOR	France	3,259
London Reinsurance Group	Canada	2,167

[1] Direct premiums plus assumed premiums; data include pro forma consolidations.

Insurance Information Institute, *The Fact Book 2002,* New York, 2002, p. 3.
Source: A.M. Best Company, Inc.

various reinsurance pools and syndicates, their participation sometimes being a very small fraction of a percentage point of the pool business. Such small companies are not major factors in the reinsurance market, either individually or collectively.

As a practical matter, the reinsurance market for U.S. insurers is composed of (1) U.S. insurers or licensed alien insurers that specialize in reinsurance, frequently referred to as professional reinsurers; (2) U.S. insurers or licensed alien insurers whose primary business is direct insurance with the public but that have professional reinsurance departments; and (3) nonlicensed (nonadmitted) alien reinsurers. U.S. reinsurance is almost evenly split between professional reinsurers and nonlicensed alien reinsurers.

Reciprocity

Another complicating factor in the measurement of the reinsurance market is the practice of reciprocal reinsurance among primary insurers. In **reciprocal reinsurance**, two (or possibly more) primary insurers enter into an agreement under which each cedes to the other an agreed percentage of its business. For example, a U.S. automobile insurer and a Canadian automobile insurer entered into an agreement whereby the U.S. insurer ceded approximately 80 percent of its business to the Canadian insurer in exchange for 30 percent of the Canadian insurer's direct premiums. Because of the sizes of the two insurers, the dollar amounts of ceded premiums were approximately equal. The transaction provided both insurers with some protection against fluctuations in loss experience both by sharing losses and by providing each insurer with a better spread of exposures geographically and in numbers.

Reciprocal reinsurance
An agreement under which two or more primary insurers cede to the other an agreed percentage of their business.

In this case, both insurers were writing substantially the same class of business—private passenger automobile insurance predominantly for blue-collar workers. Similarity of business is a prime consideration in any reciprocal reinsurance arrangement. If the exchanged business is not substantially similar, one insurer is likely to profit at the expense of the other.

The two insurers in this case also possess another characteristic that is highly desirable for successful reciprocal reinsurance. They do not compete in the same market area. Because each partner in a reciprocal arrangement must furnish the other partner with a great deal of proprietary information, such arrangements are generally not satisfactory in a competitive situation. This fact, perhaps more than any other, contributed to the decline of reciprocity as a major force in the reinsurance market.

In years past, when professional reinsurance was less available and few insurers operated nationally, reciprocity was an important reinsurance technique. Today, its use is relatively limited except for the special case of reciprocal reinsurance arrangements among several insurers under common ownership or common management or both. In that special case, reciprocity is still common.

SUMMARY

Reinsurance describes the contractual relationship between insurers when risk is transferred from one to another. Individual business enterprises purchase insurance to reduce the chance of financial loss. Likewise, insurers purchase reinsurance primarily to ensure financial stability. Specifically, these functions include stabilization of loss experience, large-line capacity, financing, and catastrophe protection. Additional functions include underwriting assistance and assistance provided to an insurer withdrawing from a territory or class of business.

The reinsurance relationship exists exclusively between the primary insurer and the reinsurer. The individual policyholder is *not* a party to the reinsurance contract unless an endorsement is attached to the primary insurer's policy. This endorsement permits the policyholder to cut through the primary insurer and present a claim directly to the reinsurer.

Several forms of reinsurance have been developed to serve the functions of reinsurance. A reinsurance agreement could contain several of the forms described in this chapter. The reinsurance program of a primary insurer might contain many agreements with many reinsurers, each comprising several forms of reinsurance. For instructional purposes, this text describes each reinsurance form separately, even though most insurer reinsurance programs would use several forms in combination.

Reinsurance is arranged in two general ways. Treaties are ongoing relationships between parties. The usual treaty arrangement obligates both parties to a specified transfer and acceptance of risk. Facultative reinsurance is usually a one-time negotiated arrangement between parties. Facultative arrangements often serve as a stopgap for treaty exclusions or when the treaty limits are lower than needed.

Financial reinsurance is a relatively new type of reinsurance arrangement in which the underwriting risk traditionally present is absent. Financial reinsurance contracts transfer the risks that the reinsurer's portfolio will yield a lower return than expected and that losses will be paid more quickly than expected.

In some instances, insurers have banded together into reinsurance pools. The composition, operation, and purpose of pools vary. Some pools were formed to meet the needs of small insurers, and others were formed to combine the technical resources needed to offer certain forms of insurance. The state and federal governments have been the initiating force of some pool organizations.

The market for reinsurance is international. Like primary insurers, reinsurers share risks with other reinsurers through retrocession. In this process, the effect of a reinsured loss is diluted. In addition, primary insurers might join together to meet the reinsurance needs of one another through reciprocal reinsurance arrangements.

Chapter 9

Direct Your Learning

The Reinsurance Transaction

After learning the subject matter of this chapter, you should be able to:

■ Evaluate the reinsurance needs of an insurer and recommend a program to satisfy those needs. In support of this educational objective:

- Describe the factors to consider in developing a reinsurance program.

- Explain the considerations in setting retentions and limits.

- Describe the cost components of reinsurance.

■ Explain how reinsurance agreements are negotiated. In support of this educational objective:

- Describe the information needed.

- Explain the role of the primary insurer, the reinsurance broker, and the reinsurer in the agreement's administration.

- Explain how claims subject to the agreement are handled.

■ Explain how the loss experience of the primary insurer affects the loss experience of the reinsurer.

■ Explain how reinsurance is priced.

■ Explain how the reinsurance transaction is regulated.

■ Explain the factors that affect the ability of reinsurers to provide capacity to primary insurers.

Develop Your Perspective

What are the main topics covered in the chapter?

An insurer's characteristics affect its reinsurance needs. Primary characteristics include its large-line capacity, its stability, its investments, and its need for surplus relief. The process of obtaining, administering, pricing, and regulating reinsurance is also described in this chapter.

Compare the sample profiles of insurance companies in the chapter to your own organization.

- Based on these examples, what insurance limits, retentions, and types of reinsurance might fit the needs of your organization?

Why is it important to know these topics?

Factors considered in planning an insurer's reinsurance program include the kinds and volume of insurance written, exposures to catastrophic loss, financial resources, and growth plans. In underwriting a reinsurance treaty, a reinsurer also considers the insurer's management, underwriting policies and results, and financial condition. A reinsurance policy is an individually tailored and priced contract.

Consider the factors involved in tailoring a reinsurance contract.

- How would a reinsurer view the characteristics of your organization in developing a reinsurance contract?

How can you use this information?

Investigate your own organization's reinsurance needs.

- How might your organization's current objectives change its reinsurance requirements?

Chapter 9

The Reinsurance Transaction

A well-planned and well-executed reinsurance program is a valuable asset to a primary insurer. It can help to stabilize loss experience, provide capacity, and provide surplus for growth. In periods of severe catastrophe, a good reinsurance program can mean the difference between survival and failure.

An optimal reinsurance program requires careful planning by the primary insurer, possibly with assistance from reinsurers, reinsurance brokers, and consultants. The persons planning and executing the plan must understand several aspects of reinsurance. Among them are the following:

1. How the characteristics of the primary insurer affect its reinsurance needs
2. The information needed to design a reinsurance program and negotiate the required reinsurance contracts
3. The administrative procedures involved in various forms of reinsurance
4. The methods reinsurers use in pricing their services
5. The effects of regulation on reinsurance at both the primary insurer level and the reinsurer level

This chapter provides an introduction to these subjects.

REINSURANCE PLANNING FOR A PRIMARY INSURER

Many kinds of reinsurance exist, and, with rare exceptions, any primary insurer can find a combination of reinsurance contracts that meets its needs. The development of such a reinsurance program requires careful analysis of the primary insurer's needs as well as a thorough understanding of the reinsurance market.

The principal purposes of reinsurance are to provide large-line capacity, to stabilize the primary insurer's loss ratio, and to provide surplus relief. The first step in planning a reinsurance program for a primary insurer is to determine how much large-line capacity, how much stability, and how much surplus relief are needed.

At a minimum, the loss ratio must be sufficiently stable so that it does not pose a threat to the insurer's continued solvency. The insurer should also be able to pursue its future growth plans. Beyond those considerations, managements of different insurers may differ in the degree of stability they demand and the amount they are willing to pay to obtain it. The reinsurance program for a given primary insurer must reflect the attitude of its management toward risk.

Mutual insurers, for example, may be willing to accept greater loss ratio volatility than stock insurers. Mutuals are controlled by their policyholders, who are likely to be less concerned with short-term profits than are the shareholders of stock companies.

Management must be concerned with the stability of operating profit, which consists of the sum of underwriting profit and investment profit. Reinsurance deals only with the underwriting profit, yet management must also consider the stability of investment profit when designing the reinsurance program. Stable investment profit permits greater variation in underwriting profit. Several large insurers have suffered severe financial strains when their under-writing experience and their investment experience turned unfavorable at the same time.

Although the stability of investment profit must be considered in designing a primary insurer's reinsurance program, the goals of the program will ordinarily be stated in terms of net loss ratios, that is, the primary insurer's loss ratio after adjustment for reinsurance premiums ceded and losses recovered under the reinsurance program.

Other goals in addition to loss ratio stability may be specified for the reinsurance program. They might include the following:

1. Avoid any increase in net loss ratio in excess of five percentage points as a result of chance variations in frequency or severity of losses, including catastrophes.
2. Provide single risk capacity of at least $20 million for commercial property insurance and $10 million for commercial liability insurance under automatic treaties.
3. Increase surplus by $10 million.

The goals might be much more elaborate, listing many lines of insurance and classes of risks within each line.

Achievement of the specified goals might not always be possible or practical because of market conditions and cost considerations. Also, one must recognize that reinsurance planning is largely judgmental. Although some actuarial tools may be used in the process, it is still far short of an exact science. Despite those limitations, setting goals or objectives provides valuable guidance in reinsurance planning and reinsurance negotiations.

Factors Determining Reinsurance Needs

The reinsurance needs of a primary insurer depend on several factors. Among the most important are the following:

1. Kinds of insurance written

2. Exposures subject to catastrophic loss
3. Volume of insurance written
4. Available financial resources
5. Stability and liquidity of investment portfolio
6. Growth plans

All of those factors must be considered in designing a comprehensive reinsurance plan.

Kinds of Insurance Written

The characteristics of the various lines of insurance that help to determine reinsurance needs include stability of loss frequency and stability of loss severity.

Catastrophe exposure, discussed below, is an element in both loss frequency and loss severity.

None of the common forms of reinsurance deals directly with loss frequency variations, but several forms of reinsurance can be used to reduce their financial effect. Perhaps the most effective form of reinsurance for handling loss frequency variations (especially if reinsurance costs are ignored) is an aggregate excess treaty. It puts a cap on the primary insurer's loss ratio (subject to percentage participations and treaty limits), whether such variations occur from catastrophes, other frequency variations, or variations in loss severity.

Reinsurance products are much more effective in reducing the effects of fluctuations in loss severity than they are for fluctuations in loss frequency. For large individual losses, both surplus share and per risk excess treaties are especially effective. The choice between them should be based on a consideration of cost and the need for surplus relief. Facultative cessions are also useful tools for controlling large losses from unusually hazardous or unusually large exposures. The delays and heavy administrative burden associated with facultative cessions limit their use to relatively unusual situations.

Exposures Subject to Catastrophic Loss

Several lines of insurance are especially susceptible to catastrophes, such as windstorm, earthquake, hail, and winter storms. Other lines have less serious catastrophe exposures.

Catastrophe exposures vary widely from one geographic area to another. For example, hurricane losses are more common along the Gulf Coast and the south Atlantic coast than elsewhere in the United States, although they do sometimes cause damage for some distance inland or along the north or middle Atlantic coast. Tornadoes, on the other hand, are more common in the middle of the country. Hail losses are more severe at higher altitudes. Earthquake losses tend to be concentrated around certain well-known geologic faults.

In designing a catastrophe reinsurance program, a primary insurer must carefully analyze the geographic distribution of its insured properties. Such an analysis should consider the number of properties that could be damaged in a single occurrence and the maximum aggregate amount of damage from such an occurrence. Extensive data are available to assist in such an analysis. Data concerning the occurrence and intensity of hurricanes, tornadoes, and earthquakes are available from various governmental agencies. Insurance loss data are available from industry organizations.

It is essential to consider such data in establishing retentions and coverage limits under catastrophe excess treaties. Several South Carolina insurers were forced into insolvency by losses from Hurricane Hugo. More thorough analyses of their hurricane loss exposures might have enabled them to obtain additional reinsurance to ensure their survival.

The analysis of hurricane loss exposures is fairly typical of the techniques that can be used to analyze potential catastrophe losses. The first step in the analysis is to plot on a map the distribution of the properties insured in areas subject to hurricane damage, showing both the number and value of properties insured. Those properties should be shown for the smallest practical geographic units, at least by county and preferably by postal ZIP Code area.

The second step is to superimpose on the map of insured properties a plot of historic hurricane tracks, showing both the path and the intensity of past storms. Insurance industry loss data for such storms should also be analyzed and adjusted to reflect inflation and increased population density since the past storms occurred.

Through such careful analysis, an insurer can derive a reasonable estimate of the largest amount of aggregate losses it is likely to sustain in a single storm. Similar techniques can be used for earthquakes, floods, or other natural disasters. Although such analyses are time-consuming and expensive, they are necessary to ensure that the primary insurer has adequate catastrophe reinsurance limits. Some reinsurers and reinsurance brokers have computer models to assist in the process. Because they have already collected the necessary historical data, the primary insurer need provide only its own data concerning the distribution of insured properties.

Volume of Insurance Written

The volume of insurance written is another major determinant of the primary insurer's reinsurance needs. According to the law of large numbers, an insurer with a large volume of insurance should have a more stable loss ratio than one with a small volume, all else being equal. The increased stability resulting from large volume reduces the need for reinsurance. Of course, the volume needed to provide stability differs from one line of insurance to another. A line of insurance that has frequent, small losses can achieve stability with a smaller volume than one that has infrequent, large losses.

For example, an insurer that specializes in physical damage coverage for private passenger automobiles could achieve reasonable stability with a relatively small premium volume. Some catastrophe reinsurance might be needed unless the insurance is widely distributed across the country.

On the other hand, it is doubtful that any attainable premium volume would provide acceptable stability without reinsurance for an insurer that specializes in property insurance on large industrial facilities. Such an insurer would likely need a relatively complex reinsurance program, involving both treaty agreements and facultative cessions, regardless of its premium volume.

Available Financial Resources

The financial resources available to the primary insurer affect its reinsurance needs in two ways: through its need for stability and through its need for surplus relief. An insurer with a weak surplus position needs a highly stable net loss ratio to avoid serious financial difficulties and possible insolvency. The weak surplus position may also require the use of pro rata reinsurance to provide surplus relief.

An insurer with a strong surplus position can afford to risk a more volatile net loss ratio because it has the financial strength to absorb some unanticipated losses. However, the absolute size of the insurer's surplus is not the only concern. The quality of the surplus, as indicated by the invested assets that stand behind it, must also be considered.

Stability and Liquidity of Investment Portfolio

The stability and liquidity of a primary insurer's investment portfolio are important considerations in designing its reinsurance program. If an insurer plans to rely on its surplus to absorb abnormal losses, that surplus must be invested in assets that are (1) readily marketable and (2) not subject to wide fluctuations in market price. Otherwise, the surplus might not be sufficient to pay losses in a timely manner.

An insurer that holds large amounts of common stock in its investment portfolio would need to be more heavily reinsured than an insurer that holds short-term bonds, all other things being equal, because the common stock might be marketable only at a substantial loss in an unfavorable market. A large portfolio of long-term bonds might also sustain substantial market losses. An insurer that invests a large part of its funds in wholly owned subsidiaries needs to have a substantial reinsurance program because the subsidiaries' stock might not be marketable when unusual losses occur.

Growth Plans

An insurer's growth plans also affect its reinsurance requirements. In general, an insurer that plans to grow rapidly needs to be reinsured more heavily than one that plans to grow more slowly. The rapidly growing company's greater need for reinsurance stems from the following two sources:

1. New business constitutes a larger part of the premium volume of a rapidly growing insurer. The loss ratio on new business is likely to be higher and less predictable than the loss ratio on business that has been seasoned through renewal underwriting.

2. A rapidly growing insurer is more likely to need surplus relief than an insurer that is growing more slowly. An insurer might earn a reputation for being an unreliable market if it has to discontinue writing new business because it has already written too much.

A primary insurer might reduce its long-term profits by entering into the reinsurance agreement because it has potentially ceded away profitable business. Sacrificing these profits is a short-term strategy that enables the primary insurer to continue to grow and possibly to earn greater profits in the future.

Examples

Some examples can help to clarify the reinsurance planning process. Although these examples are hypothetical, they are intended to be reasonably realistic.

Example 1—Large Personal Insurer

The first example is a very large insurer. It specializes in personal insurance, primarily private passenger auto and homeowners insurance. Its annual direct premium volume is $20 billion. Its business is spread across the country, with the proportion of its business in any one state being approximately the same as that state's proportion of the nation's population. Its policyholders' surplus is $12 billion. Its investment portfolio consists mostly of federal government bonds and high-grade industrial and utility bonds. The insurer normally holds about $500 million in treasury bills, high-grade commercial paper, and other short-term assets. Common stocks account for only about 5 percent of its invested assets and less than 10 percent of policyholders' surplus. The insurer has shown an operating profit every year for the past decade. An analysis of the geographic spread of its homeowners and auto physical damage exposures indicates that losses in excess of $500 million in any one catastrophe are very unlikely.

After reviewing all of the available data, the insurer has decided that it does not need any reinsurance. Its large premium volume; wide spread of small individual risks; strong surplus position; and stable, liquid investment portfolio would enable it to cope with any loss ratio variation it might reasonably expect to occur, including catastrophes.

Example 2—Small Multi-Line Mutual Insurer

The second example is near the other end of the spectrum of U.S. property-casualty insurers. It is a small mutual insurer whose business is confined to a single state. Its annual direct premium volume is $20 million, and its policyholders' surplus is $5 million. It writes homeowners coverage and property insurance for small commercial risks. It is headquartered in a city on the south Atlantic coast, and about half of its business is in or near the coastal region. Virtually all of its policies provide windstorm coverage; many also provide earthquake coverage. Minor quakes occur in or near its headquarters city several times each year. The most recent damaging quakes occurred in the nineteenth century.

An analysis of the geographic distribution of its business indicates that a major hurricane could cause losses of as much as $10 million to the properties currently insured. An earthquake could cause losses of as much as $5 million. Its investment portfolio consists primarily of U.S. government bonds, with some bonds issued by its home state and local governments within that state. The insurer has experienced moderate growth in the past and expects to continue to grow at about 5 percent each year. Although it has shown an operating profit in most years of the last decade and for the decade as a whole, its loss ratio fluctuated substantially from year to year even though no major catastrophes occurred during that period.

With a premium-to-surplus ratio of 4 to 1, this insurer needs surplus relief if it is to continue to grow. Consequently, a quota share treaty is needed. Management has decided to cede 25 percent of its business under a quota share treaty, and the reinsurer has agreed to pay a 25 percent ceding commission. That transaction would reduce its net written premiums to $15 million, and the ceding commission would increase its policyholders' surplus to $6.25 million, giving it a premium-to-surplus ratio of less than 3 to 1. That ratio is acceptable to the regulatory authorities in the insurer's home state.

Management has decided that an aggregate excess treaty offers the best solution to stabilizing the insurer's net loss ratio. A reinsurer has offered to provide such a treaty with the retention of an 80 percent loss ratio. The reinsurer would pay 95 percent of losses in excess of the retention along with its proportional share of loss adjustment expenses. However, the reinsurer is willing to provide that aggregate excess treaty only if the primary insurer purchases a per occurrence excess treaty with a limit of at least $8 million and a retention of $500,000 or less. The per occurrence excess treaty would apply only to the primary insurer's net losses after deducting amounts recoverable under the quota share treaty. The aggregate excess treaty would apply only to the primary insurer's net losses after deducting recoveries under both the quota share treaty and the per occurrence excess treaty. The per occurrence excess treaty would apply only to property losses. The other two treaties would cover liability losses under the homeowners policies also.

Example 3—Large Multi-Line Stock Insurer

The final example, typical of U.S. property-casualty insurers, is a stock insurer with annual direct written premiums of $1 billion and policyholders' surplus of $500 million. It has averaged 10 percent annual growth over the past decade and expects to continue to grow at about the same rate.

Its combined ratio has exceeded 100 percent each year for the last decade, averaging 102 percent for the period. It has reported an operating profit each year for the last decade, but the profit has been small in some years. A high-grade portfolio of bonds and other fixed-income securities accounts for about 95 percent of its invested assets. The balance consists of carefully selected preferred and common stocks.

The insurer writes commercial automobile insurance, general liability, commercial multi-peril, and commercial fire and allied lines insurance. It writes small to medium-sized commercial and industrial risks. A survey of its outstanding policies showed that about 95 percent of its liability policies had occurrence limits of $10 million or less, and about 95 percent of its property policies provided coverage of $15 million or less. Management has decided to set its treaty limits to cover those amounts and to depend on facultative reinsurance for the policies with greater limits.

The insurer does not need surplus relief, so no pro rata reinsurance will be purchased. Per risk or per policy excess treaties will be purchased for both liability and property insurance. Management has decided that the insurer can afford to assume individual losses up to 0.5 percent of direct written premium, or 1.0 percent of policyholders' surplus. Consequently, the retention under both the liability and property treaties will be set at $5 million per loss. Treaty limits will be $5 million for liability and $10 million for property losses. Thus, the primary insurer's retention and the treaty limits will fully cover about 95 percent of all policies issued.

The properties insured by the primary insurer are spread widely across the country, but several areas have high concentrations of values subject to catastrophe losses. The worst of those is a metropolitan area on the Gulf Coast, where management estimates that a direct hit by a major hurricane could cause losses of up to $50 million. A catastrophe treaty with a limit of $50 million and a retention of $5 million will be purchased to cover that exposure.

Setting Retentions

Although actuaries have experimented with mathematical methods for establishing reinsurance retentions, such methods have not been generally accepted. Setting retentions is still more a matter of judgment than an exact science. However, some general considerations apply to the process.

The method of setting retentions varies with the kind of treaty as well as with other factors. The reasons for buying a pro rata treaty differ from the reasons for buying an excess treaty, so the factors considered in setting the retention also differ.

The principal reason for choosing a pro rata treaty in preference to an excess treaty is to provide surplus relief. Consequently, the amount of surplus relief needed must be an important factor in the selection of the retention. The amount of surplus relief received will be a function of the percentage of premiums ceded and the percentage ceding commission received. Exhibit 8-2 (in Chapter 8) illustrates the effect of pro rata reinsurance on policyholders' surplus and indicates the general method of making such calculations.

The principal purposes of excess of loss treaties are to stabilize loss experience and to provide large-line capacity. Providing large-line capacity is a function of the treaty limit rather than the retention. Therefore, the principal consideration in setting the retention of an excess of loss treaty is the size of loss that the primary insurer can absorb without undue effect on the policyholders' surplus or the loss ratio for the line or lines covered by the treaty. That amount is, in turn, a function of the premium volume and the policyholders' surplus of the primary insurer.

Most states have a statutory provision that sets an upper limit on an insurer's retention under its reinsurance treaties. That provision usually states that an insurer cannot retain net for its own account an amount on any one loss exposure in excess of 10 percent of the insurer's policyholders' surplus. Thus, if an insurer has policyholders' surplus of $10 million, its legal maximum net retention for any one loss exposure would be $1 million. Very few insurers retain their legal maximum.

One of the principal purposes of excess reinsurance is to stabilize loss experience. It seems logical, therefore, that the primary insurer should retain that part of its aggregate losses that is reasonably stable and predictable and should cede that part that is not reasonably stable and predictable. However, that simple statement raises two complex questions. First, what is meant by "reasonably stable and predictable"? Second, given criteria for "reasonably stable and predictable," how does one determine what portion of aggregate losses meets those criteria?

Insurers' management differ in their criteria for what is reasonably stable and predictable. However, a general rule applies. Losses can be said to be reasonably stable and predictable if the maximum probable variation is not likely to affect the insurer's loss ratio or surplus to an extent unacceptable to management.

For example, the management of one insurer might conclude that it could accept a maximum variation of 3 percentage points in the loss ratio and 9 percent in policyholders' surplus due to chance variation in losses during the year. Another insurer with less surplus or less venturesome management might decide that it could risk only 2 percentage points of the loss ratio and 4 percent of surplus to policyholders. All other things being equal, the second insurer would probably elect a lower retention. Of course, the selection of a retention requires a balancing of the desirability of stability against the undesirability of high reinsurance costs. Lowering the retention increases stability, but it also increases reinsurance costs.

Based on the foregoing considerations, two methods have been used to select the retention level under an excess treaty. Both assume that the primary insurer should retain losses within the size category in which sufficient frequency exists for reasonable predictability. Consequently, both methods require an analysis of a loss-size distribution such as that shown in Exhibit 9-1, but the method of analysis differs somewhat. The losses in Exhibit 9-1 have been adjusted for inflation from the date of occurrence to the midpoint of the period for which the treaty will be in effect.

The simpler of the two methods is to examine a table such as the one shown in Exhibit 9-1 for the point at which the frequency trend shows a sudden change. For example, in Exhibit 9-1, the frequency of each size bracket is approximately one-half of the next lower bracket for losses up to $20,000. However, the frequency for the $20,001 to $25,000 bracket is only one-third of the next lower bracket. Consequently, a retention of $20,000 might be selected. A retention of $20,000 would include 97 percent of the number of claims and 94 percent of the dollar amount of losses (all of the losses up to $20,000 plus the first $20,000 of each loss in excess of $20,000).

EXHIBIT 9-1

Distribution of Losses by Size for Past Ten Years, Adjusted for Inflation

Loss Size	Losses		Percentage of	
	Number	Total Amount	Number	Amount
$ 1– 5,000	11,381	$ 23,774,909	48%	14.4%
5,001–10,000	6,639	48,033,165	28	29.2
10,001–15,000	3,557	43,804,455	15	26.6
15,001–20,000	1,423	24,664,859	6	15.0
20,001–25,000	474	10,564,986	2	6.4
Over 25,000	237	13,845,777	1	8.4
	23,711	$164,688,151	100%	100.0%

Alternatively, management might prefer a retention of $15,000, at which a smaller break in the trend occurs. That retention would include 91 percent of the losses by number and 89.6 percent by amount.

The second method of setting the retention under an excess treaty involves determining the largest loss for which underwriting results are acceptably stable. The first step is to restructure the loss distribution from Exhibit 9-1 into a new distribution as shown in Exhibit 9-2. This table shows the losses by size for each of the past ten years, but instead of showing the number or dollar amount of losses, it shows them as loss ratios. That is, the dollar amount of losses in each bracket has been divided by the earned premium for the year. The premiums and losses should be adjusted to reflect rate changes and inflation, respectively, before the loss ratios are calculated.

EXHIBIT 9-2

Loss Ratios by Loss Size for Past Ten Years, Adjusted for Rate Changes and Inflation

| | Loss Ratios by Year | | | | | |
Loss Size	1	2	3	4	5	6
$ 1– 5,000	8.6%	8.4%	8.8%	8.7%	8.9%	9.0%
5,001–10,000	16.9	17.4	17.4	17.6	17.0	18.1
10,001–15,000	15.0	16.1	16.3	16.9	17.3	14.8
15,001–20,000	8.4	9.7	9.3	5.8	10.8	13.4
20,001–25,000	1.3	3.5	4.6	5.4	2.1	2.9
Over 25,000	6.3	4.9	9.8	7.3	8.1	1.0
Totals	56.5%	60.0%	66.2%	61.7%	64.2%	59.2%

Loss Size	7	8	9	10	Mean
$ 1– 5,000	8.8%	8.5%	8.5%	8.8%	8.7%
5,001–10,000	18.3	17.1	17.3	17.9	17.5
10,001–15,000	16.0	16.3	15.2	16.1	16.0
15,001–20,000	12.1	6.0	5.5	9.0	9.0
20,001–25,000	1.1	1.0	9.7	6.4	3.8
Over 25,000	4.1	5.7	2.1	0.7	5.0
Totals	60.4%	54.6%	58.3%	58.9%	60.0%

The retention is set at the upper limit of the highest loss size class for which the variation in loss ratio is acceptable to management. In Exhibit 9-2, the statistics would probably indicate a retention of either $15,000 or $20,000, depending on the amount of variation management is willing to accept. In the $15,001 to $20,000 bracket, the difference between the worst year and the best year is 7.9 percentage points (13.4 – 5.5) of loss ratio, or about 84 percent of the mean loss ratio for that bracket for the ten-year period. In the $20,001 to $25,000 bracket, the difference between the best year and the worst year is 8.7 percentage points (9.7 – 1.0) of loss ratio, or approximately 229 percent of the mean loss ratio for that bracket for the ten-year period.

In these hypothetical illustrations, both methods resulted in the same retention, depending on the choice between the two possible retentions in the second method. They would not necessarily be in such close agreement in actual practice.

The first step in setting the retention for a catastrophe treaty is for management to decide how much policyholders' surplus and how many points of loss ratio the insurer can risk on one year's catastrophes. These numbers must, of course, be translated into dollars.

The second step is to estimate the maximum number of catastrophes that might reasonably be expected to occur in one year. That number would depend on the line or lines of insurance concerned, the territory in which the primary insurer operates, and the concentration of insured properties within the territory. For jurisdictions that have windstorm pools, the effects of such pools must be considered when setting windstorm retentions. The retention per catastrophe would be found by dividing the number of dollars from the first step by the number of catastrophes from the second step.

Retention setting is easier under an aggregate excess treaty than under any other kind of reinsurance. The primary insurer should select for its retention the lowest loss ratio (1) for which the reinsurance premium is affordable and (2) that is acceptable to the reinsurer. Those two considerations almost inevitably result in a retention loss ratio somewhat higher than the primary insurer's break-even loss ratio.

Most of this discussion of retention-setting has ignored the cost of reinsurance and the role of the reinsurer in setting retentions. However, those factors cannot be overlooked in actual practice. Most insurers purchasing excess treaties accept retentions higher than they would prefer, either to reduce reinsurance costs or because the reinsurer insists on it.

Under surplus share treaties, the position of the reinsurer may be reversed. That is, the reinsurer may sometimes insist on a lower retention than the primary insurer would prefer. Under a surplus share treaty, no reinsurance is ceded on properties for which the amount of insurance is less than the retention. Consequently, a very high retention would mean that the reinsurer is excluded from participating in a large part of the primary insurer's business. If the business below the retention is the most desirable part of the primary insurer's portfolio, the reinsurer may insist on a lower retention to enable it to participate in that business.

If the primary insurer carries several treaties that may cover the same loss, the retention under each of them should be set with due consideration for the relationships between them. For example, an insurer's reinsurance program might have a quota share treaty, a per risk excess treaty, and a catastrophe treaty. The retention under the catastrophe treaty should be higher if that treaty is written for the benefit of both the primary insurer and quota share reinsurers than if written only for benefit of the primary insurer.

To illustrate the difference, assume that the retention under the quota share treaty is 25 percent and the retention under the catastrophe treaty is $1 million. Assume further that a catastrophe causes losses totaling $3 million under coverages reinsured under the catastrophe treaty. If the catastrophe treaty is written for the benefit of the primary insurer only, the treaty will not pay any of the loss. The primary insurer's portion of the losses would be 25 percent, or $750,000, which is less than the catastrophe retention.

If the catastrophe treaty is written for the benefit of the primary insurer and quota share reinsurers, the catastrophe reinsurer would pay $2 million, assuming that the treaty limit is at least that high. The quota share reinsurer would then pay 75 percent of the remaining $1 million, leaving the primary insurer with a net retention of only $250,000.

A similar analysis could be made for the per risk excess treaty and the quota share treaty or, for that matter, for all three of them. This is another reason that an insurer's reinsurance program should be a carefully integrated program and not merely a collection of treaties.

Setting Reinsurance Limits

Setting reinsurance limits is only slightly less subjective than setting retentions. Pro rata and per risk or per policy excess treaties, in whatever combination carried, should have sufficiently high limits to cover, in combination with the primary insurer's retention, a substantial majority of the loss exposures insured by the primary insurer. Exactly how large a majority will be covered depends on cost considerations because reinsurance costs can be expected to increase as the limit increases and the retention remains constant. This increased cost for a higher limit must be weighed against the premium, administrative expense, and inconvenience of facultative reinsurance for those exposures not fully covered by treaties.

Limit-setting for a catastrophe treaty is even more subjective. The goal is to select a limit just adequate to cover the largest catastrophe that might reasonably be expected. The difficulty is in determining the potential loss amount in the largest catastrophe likely to occur. The primary insurer's past experience is not a satisfactory guide. Catastrophe losses are notoriously variable, and the largest catastrophe the insurer sustained in the past might not be the largest that is likely to occur in the future. In addition, circumstances change. For example, the insurer might now be writing more business in a catastrophe-prone area than it wrote in the past.

Perhaps the best way to set the limit for a catastrophe treaty is through a careful analysis of the concentration of loss exposures as previously explained.

The limit for an aggregate excess treaty should be set at an amount adequate to cover the highest loss ratio the primary insurer might reasonably expect to sustain, provided the reinsurance premium for such a limit is acceptable to its management. Unfortunately, there is no reliable method of accurately estimating this loss ratio. However, some general guidelines can be followed. The variation in loss ratios is, in part, a function of the lines of insurance written. A property insurer can expect a greater variation in loss ratios than a liability insurer can because of the catastrophe exposure in property insurance. The existence of a catastrophe treaty (in addition to the stop loss treaty) would lessen the variation from catastrophe.

The insurer's size is another important determinant of loss ratio variability. All other things being equal, a smaller insurer (measured by premium volume) can expect more variation in loss ratio than a larger one. The smaller insurer would, therefore, need a higher treaty limit relative to its premium volume.

Perhaps the most important factor is the geographic distribution of the insurer's business. An insurer writing property classes in one territory is much more vulnerable to loss ratio fluctuation than an insurer having a nationwide spread in its exposures. Again, this is primarily because of catastrophe possibilities.

In setting the limit for any kind of reinsurance, the interaction among all applicable treaties must be considered. For example, the limit for an aggregate excess treaty can be lower if the insurer carries adequate catastrophe reinsurance. Also, the limit of a catastrophe treaty can be lower if it applies only to the primary insurer's retention after recoveries from pro rata reinsurance, rather than to the direct losses.

Cost of Reinsurance

The cost of reinsurance might not be easy to determine in advance. The cost is not simply the premium paid to the reinsurer. Several other major factors must be considered. One of those factors is the losses recovered or to be recovered under the reinsurance agreement. The losses are an especially important factor under a pro rata treaty or a working cover for which substantial loss recoveries are anticipated.

A primary insurer is expected to pay its own losses and the reinsurer's expenses and profit under any treaty that is continued over a sufficiently long period of time. Consequently, the amount included in the premium for the reinsurer's expenses and profit becomes an important factor in assessing the cost of reinsurance.

Reinsurance transfers some loss reserves and unearned premium reserves from the primary insurer to the reinsurer. Because the assets offsetting these reserves are invested, this transfer results in some loss of investment income to the primary insurer. The loss of investment income is likely to be greater under a pro rata treaty than under an excess treaty because the reinsurance premium for a pro rata treaty is usually greater. However, some investment income is lost in either case, and the lost income is an additional cost of the reinsurance transfer.

The cost to the primary insurer of administering the reinsurance program must also be considered. Facultative reinsurance is especially expensive to administer because each reinsurance transaction must be negotiated individually. Pro rata treaties, especially surplus share, are generally more expensive to administer than excess treaties because of the more detailed record keeping and the greater frequency of reinsurance claims. In any case, the cost of administering the program must be considered in evaluating reinsurance costs.

Finally, one additional factor must be considered in a reciprocal reinsurance arrangement. The business assumed might not be as profitable (or more unprofitable) than the business ceded. This profit or loss on the assumed insurance under a reciprocal arrangement must be included in the estimated cost of the reinsurance program.

REINSURANCE NEGOTIATIONS

Reinsurance negotiations may be conducted in several ways, depending on the nature of the primary insurer and of the reinsurer, the kind of reinsurance concerned, and other factors. This section discusses in general terms some of the major factors involved in the negotiation of reinsurance agreements.

Information Needed

The primary insurer's first step in reinsurance negotiations is the compilation of necessary information. Depending on the kind of reinsurance involved, the required information might be voluminous, and compilation might require a substantial effort. Therefore, the task should not be taken lightly. Favorable reinsurance terms and rates might depend on the thoroughness of the data the primary insurer provides.

The information required in reinsurance negotiations varies with the kind of reinsurance arrangement under negotiation. In treaty negotiations, the reinsurer is interested primarily in information concerning the primary insurer's management and underwriting operations. Little attention is given to individual loss exposures insured; instead, the reinsurer is concerned with product mix and geographic spread. In negotiations for facultative cessions, the reinsurer is interested primarily in the details of the individual loss exposure and only secondarily in the primary insurer's general operations. Of course, if the subject of negotiation is an obligatory facultative treaty, the information needed would be essentially the same as any other treaty. However, the reinsurer might underwrite the primary insurer even more carefully because of the greater opportunity for adverse selection under an obligatory facultative treaty.

The reinsurer's principal considerations in underwriting a treaty are the primary insurer's management characteristics, underwriting policies, underwriting results, and financial condition. The integrity of the primary insurer's management is a major consideration. Numerous opportunities exist for fraud in the administration of a reinsurance treaty, and numerous cases of fraud have occurred.

The reinsurer is interested in more than just honesty. It is also interested in the demonstrated capability and stability of management and the experience and capabilities of the underwriting staff. Reinsurance treaties are intended to be long-term arrangements. Consequently, the reinsurer is concerned with the possibility of a change in management personnel, a change in management objectives, or both.

A reinsurer is also concerned with the primary insurer's financial strength. The insolvency of a primary insurer normally does not increase the reinsurer's liability, but it does complicate the administration of a treaty, and it could involve the loss of part of the reinsurer's premiums. The reinsurer's role might get especially complicated if many cut-through endorsements are outstanding because the reinsurer might be required to adjust losses under such endorsements directly with the original insured. Depending on state law, the reinsurer may be required to pay some losses twice: to the beneficiary under the cut-through endorsement and to the receiver of the insolvent primary insurer. If local courts permit, the reinsurer will offset net premiums due against claims payable. Otherwise, the reinsurer is just another general creditor of the insolvent primary insurer. Also, as noted above, reinsurance treaties are usually considered to be long-term relationships, and the insolvency of the primary insurer is hardly consistent with that concept.

The reinsurer would be especially interested in the solvency of the primary insurer if the treaty provides for payment of premiums as earned rather than as written or if the treaty permits the primary insurer to hold funds of the reinsurer so that the primary insurer can take credit for the reinsurance in calculating its unearned premium or loss reserves. The latter provision is fairly common if the reinsurer is unlicensed in the primary insurer's state of domicile.

Perhaps the most important considerations in reinsurance negotiations are the primary insurer's underwriting policies and underwriting results. Factors to consider in assessing an underwriting policy are shown in Exhibit 9-3.

The existence of and the terms of other reinsurance would also be important considerations. In property insurance, for example, pro rata reinsurers would be interested in the terms of any catastrophe treaty and other excess reinsurance. Are they written only for the interest of the primary insurer, or do they protect the interest of pro rata reinsurers as well?

The reinsurer would also be interested in the primary insurer's loss experience over the most recent several years. Loss ratio is especially important in connection with a pro rata treaty because it is used for underwriting selection, rating, and setting commission terms. The reinsurer is interested not only in the level of the loss ratio but also in its stability or volatility over time. For a per risk or per policy excess treaty, the reinsurer requires data concerning distribution of losses by size. A distribution of insurance amounts by size may also be required.

The discussion to this point has concentrated on the information the reinsurer is likely to require from the primary insurer. However, in most cases reinsurance negotiations are two-sided; that is, the primary insurer is also interested in obtaining information about the reinsurer. The information the primary insurer needs, while less detailed, is approximately the same as that any consumer needs in purchasing insurance. Is the reinsurer financially sound and well managed? Are its claims practices satisfactory?

EXHIBIT 9-3

Factors To Consider in Assessing the Underwriting Policy of a Primary Insurer

1. What classes of business is the primary insurer writing?

2. Is it writing primarily personal, small mercantile, industrial, or other lines?

3. What is its geographic area of operation?

4. Are the primary insurer's underwriting guidelines (e.g., acceptable, prohibitive, and submit-for-approval lists) satisfactory?

5. Are its gross line limits and net line limits in keeping with the financial strength of the primary insurer?

6. Are the primary insurer's loss control and loss adjustment practices adequate for the classes of business written?

7. Have the primary insurer's underwriting results been satisfactory in the lines covered by the proposed reinsurance treaty?

8. Does the primary insurer anticipate any substantial changes in its management, marketing, or underwriting practices?

9. Are the primary insurer's rates adequate for the risks covered under the treaty?

Can it offer the services needed by the primary insurer? Are its rates competitive? Is it licensed in the primary insurer's state of domicile, or can it make other arrangements so that the primary insurer can take credit for the reinsurance in calculating its unearned premium and loss reserves?

Use of Reinsurance Brokers

The first step in the negotiation of any contract is for the parties to get together. The primary insurer and reinsurer may get together directly or work through an intermediary called a reinsurance broker.

The function of a **reinsurance broker** is essentially the same as that of any other broker: to bring together two potential contracting parties and to assist them in reaching agreement on the terms of the contract. The reinsurance broker, in this case, is compensated for those efforts through a commission paid by the reinsurer. The percentage commission may be small in comparison with the commission rates paid to primary insurance brokers, frequently as low as 1 percent of the reinsurance premium. However, the premiums are often large, so the dollar amount of commission may also be large.

When reinsurance is handled by a broker, premium payments usually pass through the broker from the primary insurer to the reinsurer. Also, loss payments and premium refunds pass through the broker from the reinsurer to the primary insurer. The reinsurance broker may be able to earn substantial investment income on these funds in its custody, adding significantly to its income.

Reinsurance broker
The intermediary between a primary insurer and the reinsurance company who assists them in reaching an agreement on the terms of a reinsurance contract.

Should a primary insurer use a reinsurance broker in the negotiation of its reinsurance program even though many large reinsurers are willing to deal directly? No single answer applies to all cases. The answer depends on an insurer's own needs and circumstances.

If the primary insurer is well staffed with people who are thoroughly familiar with reinsurance markets and are capable of designing its reinsurance program and of negotiating its reinsurance contracts, it might not need a reinsurance broker. Consequently, it might be able to negotiate a slightly lower reinsurance cost because of the absence of a brokerage commission.

However, many insurers, especially the small and medium-sized ones, do not have the personnel needed to manage their reinsurance affairs effectively. They must rely on an outside person for advice. That person could be a consultant or an employee of a reinsurer, but frequently it is a reinsurance broker.

A broker handles the reinsurance needs of several primary insurers. That exposure to a variety of problems enables brokerage personnel to develop expertise in handling reinsurance problems. This expertise, when coupled with a knowledge of available reinsurance markets and access to such markets, can make a reinsurance broker a valuable ally for the negotiation of a reinsurance program.

Reinsurance brokers offer one other advantage. Some reinsurers might not be staffed to deal directly with potential reinsurance buyers. This is particularly likely with respect to small professional reinsurers and primary insurers with limited reinsurance operations. Also, some very large reinsurers deal only through reinsurance brokers. A reinsurance broker might provide the only practical means of access to such reinsurers, either through a pool managed by the brokerage firm or through individual negotiation.

Precise figures are not available to show the proportion of U.S. reinsurance handled by reinsurance brokers. One estimate places the market share of all reinsurance brokers combined at approximately 75 percent of U.S. reinsurance premiums. Most of the reinsurance premiums controlled by brokers are for treaty reinsurance. Many brokers prefer not to handle facultative reinsurance agreements because of the extensive amount of effort and paperwork involved in handling individual placements.

Historically, reinsurance brokers were small, independent business firms controlled by one or a few individuals. Most recently, the trend has been toward large reinsurance brokers controlled by even larger retail brokerage firms, such as Marsh and Aon Risk Services, or by insurance companies. Of the ten largest U.S. reinsurance brokers, five are controlled by large retail brokerage firms.

Whether the reinsurance broker is acting as a representative of the primary insurer or of the reinsurer is not always clear. The question is more than academic because it could determine, among other things, whether a reinsurance contract is void because of misrepresentation or concealment.

For example, the primary insurer might make full disclosure to the reinsurance broker, but the reinsurance broker might fail to transmit a material fact to the reinsurer. If the reinsurance broker is the agent of the primary insurer, the treaty might be voidable at the option of the reinsurer for concealment. If the reinsurance broker is the agent of the reinsurer, the treaty would not be voidable because the reinsurer would be charged with the knowledge of the reinsurance broker. Consequently, no concealment would have occurred.

In most cases, the courts have held that reinsurance brokers are agents for the primary insurer. However, a reinsurance broker may become the agent of a reinsurer either by specific contractual agreement or by actions of the reinsurer that lead the primary insurer to believe that the broker is the reinsurer's agent.

Reinsurance Commissions

Two kinds of commissions may be involved in reinsurance transactions: (1) ceding commissions that the reinsurer pays to the primary insurer and (2) brokerage commissions that the reinsurer pays to the reinsurance broker. **Ceding commissions** are intended to reimburse the primary insurer for the expenses it incurred in selling and servicing the business ceded to the reinsurer. Such commissions are common under pro rata treaties but not under excess treaties. The ceding commission is subject to negotiation between the parties and usually depends on (1) the primary insurer's actual expenses (including acquisition costs along with administrative, information system, and accounting costs); (2) the reinsurer's estimate of the premium volume and loss experience expected under the treaty; and (3) the competitive state of the reinsurance market at the time the treaty is negotiated. Treaties frequently provide for a retrospective adjustment of the ceding commission if the actual loss ratio under the treaty varies substantially from the expected loss ratio.

Brokerage commissions vary, but a typical commission scale might be 1 percent to 2 percent on pro rata treaties and 5 percent to 10 percent on excess treaties. The higher commission percentage on excess treaties reflects the fact that they produce lower premiums while requiring substantially the same amount of effort on the reinsurance broker's part. Thus, a higher percentage commission is needed to provide the same dollar remuneration. Some reinsurance brokers negotiate a fee for their services to the primary insurer instead of a commission.

Ceding commission
Fees paid to a primary insurer by a pro rata reinsurer. The commission is compensation for the primary insurer's acquisition costs such as state premium taxes, agents' commissions, and other operating costs.

REINSURANCE ADMINISTRATION

The administration of a reinsurance program is a joint effort by the primary insurer and the reinsurer. Each of the parties has specified duties, obligations, and rights under the reinsurance contract.

Role of the Primary Insurer

After the reinsurance agreement has been negotiated and has become effective, the heaviest burden of administration falls on the primary insurer; the reinsurer depends on the primary insurer's capabilities, good faith, and good luck. The primary insurer is obligated to conduct its underwriting and loss adjustment operations in the manner contemplated by both parties when they negotiated the reinsurance or to notify the reinsurer of any substantial changes.

Within the contemplated policies, the primary insurer is free to exercise its best judgment in underwriting individual risks or in adjusting individual claims, and the reinsurer is bound by the primary insurer's actions in such matters. In the words common to reinsurance, the reinsurer "follows the fortunes" of the primary insurer.

The treaty may require the primary insurer to notify the reinsurer promptly upon receiving notice of a large loss, and the reinsurer may reserve the right to participate in the investigation or defense of such claims. Such right is exercised only in unusual circumstances, but these are becoming more frequent.

The primary insurer should design its information system to capture and process the data required to fulfill its administrative duties. If the reinsurance program is a simple one, including only quota share and excess treaties covering all policies issued by the primary insurer with the same retentions and limits, the data requirements can be rather simple. In such a case, the primary insurer would need to collect only direct premium data to calculate the reinsurance premiums payable to the reinsurers. Data for individual losses would be needed to apply treaty limits and excess retentions. Such data are needed for other accounting purposes in any case, so there would be little additional burden for reinsurance administration.

If a catastrophe excess treaty is carried, the primary insurer must code losses so that those arising from catastrophes can be identified. Similarly, if casualty "clash" coverage is carried, occurrences must be identified so that all casualty losses arising from a single occurrence can be readily identified.

A surplus share treaty might have slightly more complex data requirements. The primary insurer must have sufficient data to determine the portion, if any, of each of its policies ceded to each surplus share reinsurer. Such information is essential for the calculation of both reinsurance premiums payable and reinsurance losses recoverable.

Extensive use of facultative reinsurance might also require a more elaborate approach to fulfilling data needs. Each facultative reinsurance cession is negotiated separately, so the retention, the limits, the rate, and even the reinsurer may be different for each policy. Even the nature of the coverage (excess or pro rata) may differ. The information system should be adequate to capture those differences.

Some of the primary insurer's underwriting practices might also require expansion of the data collection system. If the primary insurer writes risks that are excluded from one or more of its treaties, the policies covering such risks should be coded to avoid paying reinsurance premiums for them and submitting reinsurance claims for them.

If the primary insurer elects not to cede an otherwise eligible risk under a treaty (to protect its treaty or for other reasons), special coding is necessary to avoid errors in calculating reinsurance premiums or losses. Special coding is also needed if the primary insurer elects a retention or reinsurance limit different from the standard retentions and limits provided by its treaties.

A properly designed data collection and information system greatly simplifies the reinsurance administrative process. It also simplifies the process of compiling information for the negotiation of renewal or replacement treaties.

The primary insurer is required to report premiums and losses, and perhaps other data, to the reinsurer by bordereaux or by such other means as the treaty might specify. The reinsurance agreement might also require the primary insurer to make its books and records available to the reinsurer at reasonable times and places so that the reinsurer can verify the reported data.

Exhibit 9-4 shows a segment of a bordereau one primary insurer uses to report required information to its reinsurer. Exhibit 9-5 shows one form of current account statement one primary insurer uses to report reinsurance premiums and losses to a reinsurer that does not require a detailed bordereau.

Historically, bordereaux were required by virtually all reinsurers. That requirement is much less common today. Many reinsurers are willing to accept a current account statement such as that in Exhibit 9-5. They rely on their contractual right to audit the primary insurer's books to guard against incorrect information.

Traditionally, reinsurance treaties were considered "gentlemen's agreements" and contracts of utmost good faith. Disputes were to be settled by negotiation and arbitration rather than by legal action. Those concepts have been weakened by the competitive pressures and practices of recent years.

Role of the Reinsurer

Under a smoothly functioning treaty relationship, the reinsurer's duties, other than collecting premiums and paying claims, are minimal. Many reinsurers prefer to write excess treaties with very high retentions so that claims are rarely presented.

Yet, the reinsurer performs additional duties. Although it ordinarily does not become involved in the underwriting of individual insureds or the adjustment of individual losses, the reinsurer may audit the primary insurer's underwriting and claim practices to be sure they are being conducted as anticipated. Large, individual losses may be examined partly to verify that proper adjustment and reserving practices were followed and partly to extract whatever underwriting implications they provide. The primary insurer may also consult the reinsurer about individual underwriting or claim problems.

EXHIBIT 9-4

Illustrative Bordereau—July 20X1

Insured	Policy	Effective Date	Expiration Date	Premium Ceded	Ceding Comm.	Net Ceded Premium	Losses Paid	Loss Expense	Losses Out-standing	Balance due to Reins.
Boat Manufacturer	CPP99406	07/03/X1	07/03/X2	$17,953	$ 4,488	$13,465	$ 825	$ 75	0	$12,565
Book Store	CPP88431	09/07/X0	09/07/X1	0	0	0	7,593	487	0	−8,080
Restaurant	CPP89976	11/13/X0	11/13/X1	0	0	0	12,576	793	$8,541	−13,369
Delivery Service	CPP97865	07/01/X1	07/01/X2	24,581	7,374	17,207	0	0	0	17,207
Totals				$42,534	$11,862	$30,672	$20,994	$1,355	$8,541	$ 8,323

Summary

Gross Premiums Ceded	$42,534
Less Ceding Commissions	−11,862
Net Premiums Ceded	30,672
Less Loss and Loss Adjustment Expenses Paid	−22,349
Balance Due to Reinsurer	$ 8,323

EXHIBIT 9-5

Illustrative Reinsurance Current Account

Annual Statement Line	Premiums Ceded	Ceding Comm.	Net Premiums Ceded	Losses Paid	Loss Expenses Paid	Losses Outstanding
01-Fire	$ 40,560	$10,140	$ 30,420	$ 20,321	$ 2,503	$ 45,654
02-Extended Coverage	13,471	3,347	10,124	4,783	3,977	26,894
05-C.M.P.	180,478	45,140	135,338	97,728	10,539	140,000
09-Inland Marine	53,547	13,436	40,111	21,649	2,374	27,652
Totals	$288,056	$72,063	$215,993	$144,481	$19,393	$240,200

Summary

Gross Premiums Ceded	$288,056
Less Ceding Commission	−72,063
Net Premiums Ceded	215,993
Less Loss and Loss Adjustment Expenses Paid	−163,874
Amount Due to Reinsurer	$ 52,119

A substantial amount of litigation has involved the reinsurer's obligation to share in punitive damage judgments or judgments for bad faith against the primary insurer arising out of the primary insurer's handling of claims covered under the reinsurance contract. In most cases, the courts have held that the reinsurer is not liable for such judgments because they did not arise from the reinsured policy but from the primary insurer's errors or unfair practices. Coverage for those "extra-contractual obligations" is frequently provided under liability excess treaties.

Claim Settlement

The adjustment of claim under the primary insurer's contracts with its policyholders is usually left to the primary insurer's judgment. Reinsurance contracts usually permit the reinsurer to participate in the adjustment of direct claims that might result in reinsurance claims, but that right is exercised infrequently.

The procedure for claim adjustment between the primary insurer and the reinsurer may vary from one agreement to another and by type of treaty. Under a pro rata treaty, the primary insurer may be required to file a monthly bordereau showing premiums due to the reinsurer and claims due from the reinsurer. If the premiums exceed the losses, the primary insurer remits the difference. If the losses exceed the premiums, the reinsurer remits the difference. Exceptionally large individual losses may be paid individually before the end of the reporting period as a convenience to the primary insurer.

Losses under a working cover or per occurrence excess treaty may be handled by bordereau in the same manner outlined above for pro rata treaties, because a substantial number of losses is expected under a working cover treaty. For excess treaties with higher retentions, losses are reported individually as they occur. The contract usually requires the primary insurer to report all losses that are expected to exceed a specified amount, with that amount being somewhat less than the retention.

Per occurrence excess treaties are not involved until the accumulated losses exceed the retention. At that point, the primary insurer begins presenting claims to the reinsurer as soon as it has paid them. The reinsurer is usually obligated to pay the primary insurer as soon as reasonable proof of loss has been received. Proof of loss is often simply a statement of total claims paid and, as additional information, current reserve estimates.

Aggregate excess treaties usually provide for an initial payment a short time, perhaps sixty days, after the end of the year. If the primary insurer's loss ratio has not been finalized at that time, a subsequent adjustment may be made. Although usually no contractual requirement calls for it, most reinsurers would begin to make initial payments before the end of the year if it becomes clear that the primary insurer's loss ratio will exceed the retention.

LOSS EXPERIENCE IN REINSURANCE

Under excess treaties and facultative reinsurance, no inherent relationship exists between the loss experience of primary insurers and reinsurers. In times of rapid inflation (assuming a fixed retention), excess reinsurers are likely to have worse underwriting experience than the primary insurers. The poorer experience results from two factors. First, the excess reinsurer covers the top of the large losses, where inflation comes into play, while the primary insurer's payment is limited by the agreed retention. Second, inflation pushes more of the smaller losses over the retention amount, resulting in payment by the reinsurer. Of course, fluctuations in the number and size of catastrophes also affect the loss experience of reinsurers. In addition, competitive pressures may differ between the primary insurance market and the reinsurance market.

Consequently, reinsurers' loss experience of as a whole may be better or worse than primary insurers' experience in any given year. Exhibit 9-6 shows the combined ratios (loss ratio plus expense ratio) for reinsurers.

EXHIBIT 9-6

Combined Ratios Compared—1996–2000

Year	Combined Ratio All Lines of Property and Liability Insurance*	Combined Ratio U.S. Professional Reinsurers
1996	104.7	104.5
1997	99.9	102.7
1998	104.0	105.5
1999	106.4	114.8
2000	108.8	116.4

*Combined ratio before dividends to policyholders

Data obtained from *Best's Aggregates and Averages—Property-Casualty*, 2001 Edition, pp. 123, 139.

Combined ratios of individual reinsurers varied widely from the averages shown. The averages seem to follow the primary insurer experience reasonably closely. Historically, the combined ratios for reinsurers have been a few percentage points higher than those for primary insurers, but the magnitude of the difference has declined in recent years.

REINSURANCE PRICING

As one might expect, pricing methods for reinsurance vary with the kind of reinsurance. Pricing methods also vary from one reinsurer to another, so it is not practical to discuss here all of the methods in use. Consequently, the discussion in this chapter stresses general principles rather than detailed calculations.

Pro Rata Treaties

For quota share and surplus share treaties, the reinsurance rate is customarily the same as the rate the primary insurer used for the original policy. In other words, the pro rata reinsurer usually charges a pro rata part of the original premium, based on its pro rata share of the amount of insurance. However, the ceding commission paid to the primary insurer will vary according to the reinsurer's estimate of the loss ratio to be incurred on the premium ceded under the treaty. The ceding commission, in effect, "prices" the pro rata treaty because the net amount paid by the primary insurer is the premium less the ceding commission.

For example, if the pro rata reinsurer expects to incur a loss ratio of 60 percent under the treaty and is willing to accept 15 percent of the premium for expenses, profit, and contingencies, it would pay a ceding commission of 25 percent of reinsurance premiums. Alternatively, if it expected a loss ratio of only 50 percent with the same allowance for expenses, profit, and contingencies, it would allow a ceding commission of 35 percent.

Retrospective (or profit-sharing or sliding scale) commission arrangements are quite common. Under such arrangements, the ceding commission varies with the actual loss ratio incurred under the treaty. For example, in the first illustration given in the preceding paragraph, the treaty might provide for a provisional commission of 35 percent, to be adjusted after the end of the year according to the commission rates and loss ratios shown in Exhibit 9-7. Thus, if the actual loss ratio for the year is 50 percent, instead of the expected 60 percent, the primary insurer would receive an additional 5 percent ceding commission. In effect, the unexpected profit is shared approximately equally between the primary insurer and the reinsurer under the retrospective ceding commission scale in Exhibit 9-7.

The reinsurer's estimate of the loss ratio to be incurred is usually based primarily on the primary insurer's past experience. However, that experience may be adjusted for industry trends, changes in the primary insurer's underwriting practices, and other factors the reinsurer considers relevant.

Per Risk or Per Policy Excess Treaties

The ratemaking procedure for per risk or per policy excess treaties is somewhat more complicated than that for pro rata treaties. A traditional excess rating methodology prevalent among reinsurers is the burning-cost method. To compute a **burning-cost rate**, the underwriter divides the sum of known losses in the excess layer occurring over some time period, usually five years, by the premium for these policies during the same time period. To get a rate, this ratio is then multiplied by a selected loss development factor, perhaps multiplied by some selected trend factor, loaded by a factor to recognize exposure when no losses have occurred, and divided by an expected loss ratio. The problem with this approach is that it does not consider underlying exposure changes, rate changes, the emergence of incurred but not reported claims, adverse claim

Burning-cost rate
Rate for excess reinsurance treaties established by first dividing the sum of known losses in the excess layer for a particular period by the premium for these policies during the same period. This ratio is then multiplied by a selected loss development factor, loaded by a factor to recognize exposure when no losses have occurred, and divided by an expected loss ratio.

development, or claim growth caused by inflation. Burning-cost rating is not very accurate and, in fact, can be highly misleading, even for the working cover excess of loss property treaties for which it was designed.

EXHIBIT 9-7

Retrospective Ceding Commission Scale

Actual Loss Ratio	Commission Rate
60% or more	35.0%
59% but less than 60%	35.5
58% but less than 59%	36.0
57% but less than 58%	36.5
56% but less than 57%	37.0
55% but less than 56%	37.5
54% but less than 55%	38.0
53% but less than 54%	38.5
52% but less than 53%	39.0
51% but less than 52%	39.5
50% but less than 51%	40.0
Less than 50%	41.0

Catastrophe Treaties

In theory, the method of making rates for catastrophe treaties is the same as that for per risk or per policy excess treaties, except the loss distribution would show aggregate amounts per occurrence rather than for individual losses. In practice, reliable catastrophe data are not available on a company-by-company basis because of the large element of chance variation in catastrophic occurrences. Consequently, judgment plays a much larger role in the rating of catastrophe treaties than it does in per risk or per policy excess treaties. Of course, national, regional, and state catastrophe data are available and are used to the extent they are applicable. However, an individual insurer's catastrophe experience can be expected to differ from industry experience because of its geographic spread of business and the differing nature of insured exposures.

Aggregate Excess Treaties

Theoretically, the premium for an aggregate excess treaty can be calculated from a probability distribution of loss ratios. In practice, that method is seldom, if ever, used because the nature of the probability distribution is not known. In any case, the mathematical manipulations involved in such a calculation are beyond the scope of this text.

In practice, the premium for an aggregate excess treaty is likely to be based largely on the judgment of the reinsurance underwriter. Of course, the underwriter will reinforce judgment with an analysis of the primary insurer's loss ratios over the last several years, probably five or more. The primary insurer's class of business and territory of operation are important factors, as are the magnitude of the retention and the treaty limit. Beyond those general statements, it is difficult to describe ratemaking for stop loss treaties in terms that are not both highly mathematical and highly theoretical.

Effect of Competition

Reinsurance is a very competitive business, both domestically and internationally. This competitiveness results, in part, from the relative ease of entry into the market. For example, a new reinsurer in the broker market does not need to invest large sums in building a marketing force.

In the United States, with one or two exceptions, an insurer's charter to write primary business also includes reinsurance for the same lines. Thus, little or no additional funding is required to capitalize a reinsurer.

Finally, a new reinsurer using reinsurance brokers needs only a minimal staff. Services to the policyholder are furnished by the primary insurer, and the reinsurer need not become involved in them except in very unusual circumstances. Even the reinsurer's claim department can be minimal because the loss adjustment is handled by the primary insurer in the majority of cases.

Insurers move in and out of the reinsurance business as market conditions change. Those changes in the market tend to unsettle reinsurance rates and cause fluctuations in the availability of reinsurance coverage.

When reinsurance is profitable, new reinsurers may be formed, and primary insurers enter the market to sell reinsurance. Those new reinsurers must offer some incentive to prospective customers—usually price—either in the form of lower rates or higher ceding commissions. Established reinsurers must meet their new competitor's prices, leading to lower profits, or possibly to underwriting losses, and the resulting withdrawal of marginal reinsurers.

Effect of Inflation

For pro rata reinsurance, inflation affects the loss experience of both primary insurers and reinsurers about equally. That effect is discussed in the chapters on ratemaking for direct insurance.

Inflation affects excess of loss reinsurers to a substantially greater degree than pro rata reinsurers. The effects are felt at both ends of the treaty: the retention and the reinsurance limit. The excess reinsurer covers the top part of the claims in excess of the retention, and, as those claims increase from inflation, the increase is at the top. If a fixed retention is used rather than a variable one, the inflationary increase in losses above the retention does not affect the primary insurer's net loss.

If a fixed retention is used, the excess reinsurer also suffers at the lower end of the loss distribution. The inflationary increase in the smaller losses pushes more of them over the primary insurer's retention, so the reinsurer must pay part of them. The effect of inflation is illustrated in Exhibit 9-8.

REGULATION OF REINSURANCE

Traditionally, reinsurance has been subject to very limited regulation. The principal purpose of insurance regulation is to protect insurance consumers from unfair practices of some insurers and from the insolvency of insurers. That protection was deemed necessary because of the unequal knowledge and bargaining power of insurers and insurance consumers. Because the reinsurance business is conducted between two insurers, the knowledge and bargaining power of the parties were deemed to be relatively equal, so the protective shield of regulation was not considered necessary. Some also feared that rigid regulation of U.S. reinsurers would limit their ability to compete with alien reinsurers, both here and abroad.

Another factor that reduced the need to regulate reinsurance was the nature of the market and the participants in the market. Only a few reinsurers were in business, and they were well-financed firms with a long history of ethical and sound business dealings. The market situation has changed drastically in recent years. Many new firms, both reinsurers and reinsurance brokers, have entered the market. It is evident that some of them are lacking in ethical standards, financial strength, or both. The world of reinsurance has been shaken by several scandals in the United States, the United Kingdom, Panama, Bermuda, and other places. Those scandals have brought about increased pressure for more detailed regulation of reinsurance. The New York regulation dealing with reinsurance brokers, shown in Exhibit 9-9, arose from one of the scandals—the insolvency of a reinsurance broker with large losses to both reinsurers and primary insurers.

With the exception of New York Regulation 98, the regulation of reinsurance in the United States has changed little. Many changes have been proposed, and some of the proposals are discussed later in this chapter. First, a brief review of the current regulatory pattern is in order.

Present Reinsurer Regulation

Reinsurers domiciled in the United States and alien reinsurers licensed in the United States are subject to the same solvency regulations as primary insurers. They are required to file annual, and sometimes quarterly, financial statements with state regulatory authorities and to adhere to state regulations

EXHIBIT 9-8

Effect of Inflation on Reinsurance Losses

Assume that a primary insurer, reinsured under an excess reinsurance treaty with a $100,000 retention, sustains two losses: one for $95,000 and one for $225,000. These losses would be divided as shown below.

	Amount	Amount Paid by	
		Primary Insurer	Reinsurer
Loss 1	$ 95,000	$ 95,000	$ 0
Loss 2	225,000	100,000	125,000
	$320,000	$195,000	$125,000

Now assume that two losses causing the same amount of actual physical damage as those above occurred two years later. Although the actual physical damage was the same, higher prices caused the cost of repairs to increase to $115,000 and $270,000, respectively. These two losses will be divided as shown below.

	Amount	Amount Paid by	
		Primary Insurer	Reinsurer
Loss 1	$115,000	$100,000	$ 15,000
Loss 2	270,000	100,000	170,000
	$385,000	$200,000	$185,000

The total loss has increased by $65,000, and the reinsurer's share has increased by $60,000, but the primary insurer's share has increased by only $5,000. This simplified example somewhat overstates the relative effect of inflation, but it does illustrate the nature of the problem.

Reinsurers have attempted to combat problems caused by inflation by adopting treaties with variable retentions, sometimes called indexed retentions. Under such treaties, the amount of retention increases automatically with an increase in some price index, such as a construction cost index or a consumer price index. In the illustration used above, prices seem to have increased approximately 20 percent, so the retention would have increased from $100,000 to $120,000. The resulting division of losses would be as shown below. Thus, the inflationary increase has been spread more evenly between the primary insurer and the reinsurers.

	Amount	Amount Paid by	
		Primary Insurer	Reinsurer
Loss 1	$115,000	$115,000	$ 0
Loss 2	270,000	120,000	150,000
	$385,000	$235,000	$150,000

regarding reserves, investments, and minimum capital and surplus requirements. They must also undergo periodic examination by the appropriate state authorities. However, those regulations cannot be applied to unlicensed alien reinsurers because they are not within the jurisdiction of state (or federal) regulatory bodies. Much concern has arisen in recent years about the possible insolvencies of some unlicensed alien reinsurers, but U.S. regulatory agencies can do little to prevent such failures. Primary insurers and reinsurance brokers must rely on their own efforts to detect impending insolvencies of alien reinsurers. The solvency tests for reinsurers are the same as those applied to primary insurers.

Reinsurance rates are not regulated directly in this country. The regulation of primary insurer rates could indirectly affect reinsurance rates, however. The establishment of the primary insurer's rates might place an effective ceiling on the amount it can pay for reinsurance.

Reinsurance contracts are regulated to only a slightly greater degree. Such contract regulation is aimed at the primary insurer rather than the reinsurer because many reinsurers are not within the jurisdiction of regulatory agencies.

Primary insurers are usually eager to take credit against their unearned premium and loss reserves for premiums ceded to and losses recoverable from reinsurers. The availability of those credits reduces the drain on the primary insurer's surplus from writing new business. Regulators motivate primary insurers to require some desirable provisions in their reinsurance contracts by withholding permission to take credit for the reinsurance unless it contains the specified clauses. Note that those provisions are not mandatory. A primary insurer that is willing to forgo the reserve credits can enter into a reinsurance contract that does not include them.

Insolvency clause
A clause required in reinsurance contracts indicating that the primary insurer's bankruptcy does not affect the reinsurer's liability for losses under the reinsurance contract.

The first clause to be required was an insolvency clause. Before the insolvency clause was required, reinsurers sometimes escaped the payment of losses if the primary insurer became insolvent. The required **insolvency clause** provides that the primary insurer's insolvency does not affect the reinsurer's liability for losses under the reinsurance contract. The reinsurer pays the receiver or liquidator of the insolvent primary insurer for the benefit of its creditors.

Intermediary clause
A clause required in reinsurance contracts that provides that the reinsurance broker is the agent of the reinsurer for the collection of reinsurance premiums and the payment of reinsurance claims.

More recently, some states have required an **intermediary clause** in reinsurance contracts. This clause provides that the reinsurance broker is the agent of the reinsurer for the collection of reinsurance premiums and the payment of reinsurance claims. Thus, the reinsurer assumes the risk that the reinsurance broker will be unable or unwilling to pay over to it all of the premiums collected under its reinsurance contracts. It also assumes the risk that the reinsurance broker will not transmit to the primary insurer all claim payments made by the reinsurer. This clause is beneficial to primary insurers because courts have held in most cases that the reinsurance broker is the agent of the primary insurer. Consequently, in the absence of this clause, the risk of insolvency of the reinsurance broker would fall most often upon the primary insurer and not upon the reinsurer.

Insurance regulatory authorities can influence the activities of primary insurers and reinsurers. The value of most proportional reinsurance transactions lies in the transfer of the unearned premium reserve to the reinsurer. If state insurance regulators do not approve of a reinsurer, they can deny the primary insurer any benefit of a reinsurance contract with the unacceptable reinsurer. Some states permit the primary insurer to take the reserve credits only if the reinsurer is licensed in the state. Others permit the credit if the reinsurer is licensed in any state of the United States. Finally, some states permit the reserve credits even if the reinsurer is not licensed anywhere in the United States, provided the primary insurer obtains the state insurance department's permission before entering into the contract. Credit may also be permitted if reinsurance loss reserves are funded by a letter of credit or a trust fund.

Regulation of Reinsurance Brokers

Unlike primary insurance brokers, reinsurance brokers are neither required to be licensed in most states nor required in most states to demonstrate any special skill in their chosen field. The principal purpose of licensing primary insurance brokers, at least in theory, is to protect the public against being victimized by dishonest or incompetent brokers. Because reinsurance brokers deal only with insurers, that protection has not been deemed necessary in their case. Some discussion of licensing reinsurance brokers has occurred because of the much-publicized failure of a large reinsurance brokerage firm during the mid-seventies. Many reinsurance brokers are also excess and surplus lines brokers and must be licensed to write those lines.

New York requires licensing of reinsurance brokers and makes them subject to examination by the superintendent of insurance. Regulation 98, adopted by the New York Superintendent of Insurance, establishes the regulatory pattern for that state. **New York Regulation 98** is shown in Exhibit 9-9.

New York's requirements do not apply to managers of reinsurance pools, syndicates, or associations.

New York Regulation 98
Establishes requirements for reinsurance brokers regarding their handling of funds, authority, licensure, and record keeping. The regulation arose from the insolvency of reinsurance brokers resulting in large losses to both reinsurers and primary insurers.

Proposed Reinsurance Regulation

The present minimal regulation of reinsurance seems unlikely to continue. The NAIC has developed model reinsurance regulatory acts that have been submitted to the various state legislatures for possible enactment. One of the NAIC model acts deals with reinsurance ceded to nonadmitted reinsurers; the other is the NAIC Model Reinsurance Intermediary Act. The American Institute for Certified Public Accountants (AICPA) has promulgated guidelines for accountants to follow in auditing the reinsurance operations of either primary insurers or assuming reinsurers.[1] The Reinsurance Association of America (RAA) has also developed a model act. All of those documents are intended to solve essentially the same problems and take essentially the same approach to the solutions.

EXHIBIT 9-9

New York Regulation 98

(1) Reinsurance intermediaries act in a fiduciary capacity for all funds received in their professional capacity and must not mingle them with other funds without the consent of the insurers and reinsurers they represent;

(2) Reinsurance intermediaries shall have written authorization from the insurers and reinsurers they represent, spelling out the extent and limitations of their authority;

(3) The written authority above must be made available to primary insurers or reinsurers with which the intermediary deals;

(4) No licensed intermediary shall procure reinsurance from an unlicensed reinsurer unless the reinsurer has appointed an agent for the service of process in New York;

(5) The intermediary must make full written disclosure of

    (a) any control over the broker by a reinsurer,

    (b) any control of a reinsurer by the intermediary,

    (c) any retrocessions of the subject business placed by the intermediary, and

    (d) commissions earned or to be earned on the business;

(6) Records of all transactions must be retained for at least ten years after the expiration of all reinsurance contracts.

The principal problems that the proposed regulations address are as follows:

1. Potential losses to primary insurers and their policyholders resulting from the insolvency of alien reinsurers

2. Potential losses to primary insurers and their policyholders resulting from the insolvency or fraudulent activities of reinsurance intermediaries

3. The difficulties for U.S. primary insurers in litigating disputed claims against alien reinsurers not licensed in the United States

4. Potential losses to stockholders and policyholders of primary companies resulting from the fraudulent use of reinsurance by management

The regulatory acts use the leverage of reinsurance reserve credits to motivate primary insurers to require desirable provisions in their reinsurance contracts and to select reinsurers in sound financial condition. They generally provide that reserve credit will not be allowed for reinsurance unless the reinsurer meets one or more of the following conditions:

1. The reinsurer is licensed in the state concerned.

2. The reinsurer is licensed in another state of the United States and meets solvency tests similar to those required by the state concerned.

3. The reinsurer maintains a trust fund in the United States for the sole benefit of U.S. insureds, including primary insurers, of at least $20 million for insurers and of $100 million for associations of individual insurers (such as Lloyd's).

4. The primary insurer holds assets of the reinsurer or an irrevocable letter of credit issued by a U.S. bank in an amount at least equal to the reserve credit.

In addition to the preceding requirements, the reserve credits generally will not be allowed unless the reinsurance contract provides that:

1. The reinsurer will submit to the jurisdiction of U.S. courts and be bound by the decision of such courts in any dispute under the contract.
2. The state insurance commissioner is appointed the reinsurer's agent for the service of process.
3. The liability of the reinsurer for loss under the contract shall not be reduced by the insolvency of the primary insurer.

The RAA model act includes provisions to control the use of bulk reinsurance, in which an insurer cedes all or substantially all of its business to a reinsurer. Bulk reinsurance has sometimes been used to deprive the stockholders of a stock company or the policyholders of a mutual company of all or part of their ownership rights in the company.

The model act provides that no bulk reinsurance contract can become effective without the prior written approval of the insurance commissioner. The commissioner can approve such a contract only if it is found (1) to be fair and equitable to the primary insurer and (2) not to reduce the protection provided to policyholders of the primary insurer. In addition, no director, officer, agent, or employee of either the primary insurer or the reinsurer can receive any fee, commission, or other valuable consideration for aiding or promoting the bulk transfer. For mutual primary insurers, additional provisions apply regarding approval by policyholder vote and payment in cash to policyholders for their equity in the business ceded.

REINSURANCE AND THE CAPACITY PROBLEM

One of the principal purposes of reinsurance, as discussed earlier in this chapter, is to provide capacity both for large loss exposures and for premium volume. Without reinsurance facilities, primary insurers would find it difficult to meet the insurance needs of the public. However, the success of reinsurers in providing the needed capacity varies from time to time, depending on several factors.

A major factor in capacity availability is price adequacy. Both primary insurance and reinsurance are subject to pricing cycles in which rates vary from grossly inadequate to excessive. Those cycles result from competition, from inability to cope with inflation, and in the case of primary insurers, from excessive zeal on the part of state regulatory authorities in the control of rates. Of course, a reinsurer is less than eager to write business for which it has no reasonable expectation of profit.

Reinsurers can have poor loss experience for at least two reasons. One reason is inadequate rates. The other reason is chance fluctuation in losses, especially from catastrophes, which could cause poor loss experience in a single year even though rates are adequate for the long term. That is especially true, of course, of reinsurers that write a substantial amount of catastrophe coverages. One year or a few years of poor underwriting experience can restrict reinsurance capacity in two ways. First, existing reinsurers become less interested in writing new business and might even terminate some existing business, either because of poor profit expectations or because of shrinkage of surplus. Second, poor investment experience, especially sharp declines in the stock market, could have much the same effect because of the resulting drop in policyholders' surplus.

When capacity shortages in insurance and reinsurance have occurred, the insurance marketplace has sought new sources of capital. During the years when advisory organizations made rates and were successful in keeping primary insurance rates adequate by controlling competition, capacity shortages were less common. However, a return to that kind of rate control in the near future seems unlikely.

Any move by reinsurance to fix rates at a prohibitively high level would be certain to run afoul of federal antitrust laws and probably would not succeed even in the absence of antitrust laws. Rates fixed at an unrealistically high level would merely attract new reinsurers willing to write business at lower rates. The ease of entry into the reinsurance business virtually precludes effective price fixing. In addition, primary insurers have resisted excessive reinsurance rates by increasing their retentions.

It seems likely that reinsurers' shortages will continue to occur. Fortunately, they tend to be relatively brief and to cause fewer problems than might be expected from a casual reading of the speeches and magazine articles that usually accompany them.

SUMMARY

The reinsurance program of a primary insurer consists of a number of reinsurance transactions. A primary insurer's reinsurance relationship may be with a single reinsurer, but, more likely, many reinsurers are involved. Several reinsurers may be involved in achieving a specific objective of the primary insurer. Such is the case when many reinsurers commit to one multi-line surplus share treaty.

The reinsurance program of a well-managed insurer plays a key role in the attainment of specific insurer goals. The usual goals served by reinsurance were described as reinsurance functions or purposes of reinsurance in the previous chapter. Those functions fulfill needs—needs created by the desire to achieve specific insurer objectives.

In designing a reinsurance program, insurers or their reinsurance brokers compare existing reinsurance arrangements with their ever-changing needs. To be effective, reinsurance programs must be flexible enough to meet known and anticipated needs. Designing a reinsurance program involves determining the reinsurance needs, gathering information to establish the retention and limits, setting retentions, and setting limits.

After the reinsurance program is in place, it must be administered. The level of administration varies by the type of reinsurance used. The cost of administering the reinsurance program is an additional consideration in selecting the components of a program.

Reinsurance is less regulated than primary insurance. The premise state regulators use is that in the reinsurance transaction, both parties to the contract are knowledgeable concerning their rights and obligations. In reality, the traditional relationship of "utmost good faith" that permitted reinsurance to operate on a handshake has deteriorated because of unfulfilled promises. Insurance regulators have recognized that the insurance consumer could suffer if reinsurance contractual agreements are not met. In response, several proposals have been initiated to increase the level of regulatory supervision of reinsurers.

CHAPTER NOTE

1. Douglas McLeod, "New Guidelines to Spell Out Reinsurance Procedures," *Business Insurance*, October 8, 1983, p. 18; and William J. Kane, "Reinsurance Accounting: Whose Responsibility?" *National Underwriter*, Property & Casualty Edition, August 26, 1983, Part 2, p. 26.

Chapter 10

![Direct (watermark)]

Direct Your Learning

Ratemaking Principles

After learning the subject matter in this chapter, you should be able to:

■ Explain the principles underlying insurance pricing. In support of this educational objective, do the following:

- Describe the professional credentials required of actuaries.

- Describe the actuarial services required of insurers.

- Describe the actuarial functions performed by advisory organizations.

■ Compare the objectives pursued by insurers in ratemaking with regulatory standards.

■ Describe the assumptions required to make rates under a stable, idealistic set of circumstances and the assumptions required in the real world.

■ Contrast the development of rates by each of the following methods:

- Judgment

- Loss ratio

- Pure premium

■ Given a case, calculate a rate change.

■ Explain how investments are included in the ratemaking process.

■ Describe the administrative procedures used to file rates.

Develop Your Perspective

What are the main topics covered in the chapter?

The purpose of ratemaking is to develop rate structures that enable the insurer to compete while earning a reasonable profit. The simple ratemaking steps are complicated by the intricacy of the real world. Rate regulations layer additional complexities onto the process.

Consider a type of insurance policy that your company writes.

• What factors in the real world would complicate the ratemaking process for those policies?

Why is it important to know these topics?

Ratemaking is the projection of past loss experience into rates designed to develop future premiums that will pay for losses and expenses and provide a margin for profit and contingencies. Premiums based on inaccurate predictions can result in an underwriting loss for your organization.

Identify the ratemaking process for your own organization.

• Who is responsible for determining rates?

• How frequently are rates revised?

How can you use this information?

Compare your organization's rating structure with that used by a competitor.

• How do the risk classifications vary for the two organizations?

• How might the differences in the application of classifications attract or deter customers?

Chapter 10

Ratemaking Principles

Property-casualty insurers require many actuarial services to function effectively. Among them are ratemaking, verification of loss reserves, collection and analysis of company data to evaluate the insurer's profitability, analysis of data from other sources to determine the insurer's competitive position, and preparation of statistical reports for management and regulatory authorities. This chapter, the first of two that explore these actuarial services, focuses on the principles of ratemaking.

Actuaries usually supervise ratemaking activities. An **actuary** is trained in applying mathematical techniques to insurer operations and must demonstrate competence by completing written examinations administered by actuarial professional organizations. For property-casualty insurance, the principal actuarial professional organization in the United States is the Casualty Actuarial Society (CAS), which has two levels of membership. A person becomes an Associate of the Casualty Actuarial Society (ACAS) by successfully completing seven examinations. Successful completion of three additional examinations qualifies the Associate to become a Fellow of the Casualty Actuarial Society (FCAS). Most members of the CAS are also members of the American Academy of Actuaries (AAA). The AAA performs educational, public relations, government relations, disciplinary, and other types of functions on behalf of various actuarial professional bodies in the United States and Canada. Members of the Academy may use the designation MAAA after their names.

Actuary
A professional trained in applying mathematical techniques to insurer operations who must demonstrate competence by completing written examinations administered by actuarial professional organizations.

Regulatory authorities generally require an actuary to be a member of the CAS or AAA or to otherwise demonstrate actuarial competence before performing certain services for insurers, such as certifying the adequacy of loss and loss expense reserves.

ACTUARIAL SERVICES

Insurers retain actuarial services in several ways. Many insurers have one or more actuaries on staff, whereas smaller insurers rely on actuarial consultants. Insurers with actuaries on staff may also retain actuarial consultants, either because their staff actuaries lack adequate expertise in specific fields or because they believe that an outside consultant will provide greater objectivity than a staff actuary. Entities with which insurers negotiate, such as regulatory authorities and reinsurers, sometimes require the insurer to provide a consulting actuary's opinion verifying the accuracy and reasonableness of the staff actuaries' work.

Some actuarial services can also be obtained from advisory organizations, which perform the following actuarial functions:

1. Collection of ratemaking data
2. Analysis of the data and calculation of loss costs
3. Preparation of rate filings
4. Submission of rate filings to appropriate state regulatory authorities

Rate filing

A document containing rates and rating plans along with the necessary data and statistical analysis to show that the rates comply with regulatory requirements. Rate filings are submitted to regulatory authorities.

A **rate filing** is a document containing proposed rates along with data and statistical analysis to show that the rates comply with regulatory requirements. Advisory organizations maintain contact with regulatory authorities to facilitate approval of rate filings. If regulatory hearings or judicial proceedings are required, the advisory organization provides necessary actuarial and legal services. Advisory organizations also provide some services that are not actuarial in nature, such as drafting policy contracts.

Advisory organizations have move away from calculating final rates and toward providing prospective loss cost information to insurers. Each insurer must then add its own expense information to determine its final rates.

The principal advisory organizations are (1) Insurance Services Office (ISO), (2) American Association of Insurance Services (AAIS), (3) National Council on Compensation Insurance (NCCI), and (4) Surety Association of America. Several additional, more specialized advisory organizations also exist.

ISO performs actuarial services related to most lines of property-casualty insurance other than workers compensation insurance and surety and fidelity bonds. AAIS also provides services for several lines of insurance other than workers compensation and surety bonds. NCCI has jurisdiction over workers compensation insurance, and Surety Association of America specializes in fidelity and surety bonds.

PRINCIPLES OF RATEMAKING

The remainder of this chapter is devoted to the principles of the ratemaking process.

Objectives of Ratemaking

The primary objective of ratemaking is to develop a rate structure that enables the insurer to compete effectively for business while earning a reasonable profit on its operations. Several subsidiary objectives are imposed by corporate considerations or by regulatory requirements.

Corporate Objectives

From the insurer's viewpoint, rates should (1) be stable, (2) be responsive, (3) promote loss control, (4) provide for contingencies, and (5) be easy to understand and apply. Because some of these objectives conflict with others, compromises among them are necessary at several levels.

Stability of rates is highly desirable for several reasons. Changing rates is an expensive process and should be kept to a practical minimum. Also, large and sudden rate changes cause dissatisfaction among consumers and may lead to harsh regulatory actions and unfavorable legislation. The adoption of Proposition 103 in California in 1988 and similar rate regulatory legislation in several other states stemmed from public perception that insurance rates were not sufficiently stable.

Too much rate stability however, conflicts with the second objective that rates should change promptly in response to external factors that affect losses.

Rates that are too stable may also conflict with the fourth objective that rates should provide for contingencies. This objective means that a reasonable allowance should be made in the rates to cover unexpected variations in losses and expenses.

Rating systems encourage the third objective—loss control—by providing lower rates for policyholders who undertake loss prevention measures. For example, policyholders who install burglar alarm systems receive a reduction in their burglary insurance rates. Lower fire insurance rates are charged to policyholders who install sprinkler systems at their premises. Alternatively, policyholders who engage in activities that tend to result in higher losses, such as persons who use their cars for business, may pay higher rates.

The final objective, simplicity, is a relative one. Rating systems should be simple enough that agents, brokers, underwriters, and policyholders can understand them. Of these groups, policyholders are the least likely to be sophisticated in insurance matters. The level of insurance expertise among policyholders varies from personal lines consumers, who might know little about factors affecting insurance pricing, to large corporations with well-staffed risk management departments that have considerable insurance expertise. The insurance product should have a pricing methodology that the buyer can understand.

Regulatory Objectives

State law sets forth the regulatory objectives. These objectives specify that rates (1) must be adequate, (2) must not be excessive, and (3) must not be unfairly discriminatory. These requirements are discussed in greater detail in a later section of this chapter.

The Ratemaking Process

Insurance ratemaking techniques are frequently described by complicated mathematical formulas. Consequently, many people consider the ratemaking process to be complex and esoteric. Others liken it to the ancient art of reading the future from tea leaves or animal entrails. This chapter attempts to strip away the mystery and present the principles of ratemaking in nonmathematical form. The next chapter explores the ratemaking process in greater depth.

This chapter uses private passenger automobile insurance to illustrate the principles of insurance ratemaking, because more people are familiar with it. Also, the same ratemaking principles that apply to auto insurance apply in varying degrees to other lines of property or liability insurance. Finally, auto insurance is the largest line of property-casualty insurance written.

Ratemaking in a Stable World

In a stable world, where nothing ever changes, the insurance ratemaking process would be simple. It could be carried out in three easy steps:

1. Calculate the amount needed to pay claims.
2. Calculate the amount needed to pay expenses.
3. Add (1) and (2) to find the rate to be charged.

An Example

To illustrate this simple process, assume that an actuary has been commissioned to calculate auto insurance rates for the Kingdom of Everstable, a country ruled by a benevolent despot. The king believes that his people will be happy if nothing ever changes. Consequently, he has decreed the following:

1. There will always be exactly 100,000 cars in Everstable, and they will all be exactly alike and will never change.
2. All drivers in Everstable will be exactly equal in driving ability, temperament, and miles they drive.
3. All cars will be insured for exactly the same coverages and limits, which will never change.
4. Driving conditions will be uniform throughout the kingdom and will never change.
5. Laws governing compensation for auto accidents will be uniform throughout the kingdom and will never change.
6. There will be no inflation in the kingdom, so prices will never change.

The insurance companies in Everstable have paid out exactly $10 million in claims each year for the past ten years. All claims in Everstable are paid within an hour of the occurrence of the loss. Errors in estimating future loss payments are not a concern because no loss reserves need to be estimated.

The insurers in Everstable have paid out $100 in claims each year for each car insured (calculated by dividing the $10 million in claims by the 100,000 cars). Because nothing ever changes in Everstable, the same sum will be paid next year. The first step in the ratemaking process is now completed, and, to pay claims, the insurers will need $100 for each car insured, not including expenses.

The insurers' accountants tell the actuary that they have incurred the following expenses each year for the past ten years:

Loss adjustment expenses	$1,000,000
Acquisition expenses	1,500,000
General administrative expenses	800,000
Premium taxes	200,000
Total expenses	$3,500,000

Dividing the expenses by 100,000 (the number of cars) yields a total of $35 in expenses for each car insured. So the total premium for each car will be $100 loss plus $35 expense, or $135.

Terminology

Actuaries have names for the two elements included in this gross rate of $135. The $100 needed to pay claims is known as the **pure premium**. Loss adjustment expenses are sometimes included in the pure premium, in which case Everstable's pure premium would have been $110. It is important to determine whether a quoted pure premium includes or excludes loss adjustment expenses.

The amount included in the premium for expenses is known as an **expense loading**. In the example under discussion, the expense loading included loss adjustment expenses. As noted, loss adjustment expenses are commonly included in the pure premium, in which case those expenses would not be included in the expense loading. The sum of the pure premium and the expense loading is called the **gross rate**.

The insurers of Everstable were as benevolent as the king. They did not include anything in their rates for profit. In the real world, an allowance known as **profit and contingencies** is included in the expense loading. That amount protects the insurer against the possibility that actual claims or expenses will exceed the estimated claims and expenses included in the rates, either because of errors in estimation or because conditions change. If not needed for excessive losses or expenses, the funds generated by the loading become profit for the insurer.

Ratemaking in the Real World

Unfortunately (at least for actuaries), the real world bears little resemblance to the imaginary Kingdom of Everstable. This section examines the major differences.

Loss Reserves

Not all claims are paid immediately in the real world. In fact, for some liability lines, many years may elapse between the time a loss occurs and the time the resulting claims are paid. For example, many claims are in litigation now involving injuries allegedly sustained by workers using asbestos in shipyards during World War II, more than fifty years ago. Although this is

Pure premium
The amount included in a rate for the payment of losses. It may also include loss adjustment expenses.

Expense loading
The amount included in a rate to cover the insurer's expenses. It does not include investment expenses and may not include loss adjustment expenses.

Gross rate
The sum of the pure premium and the expense loading.

Profit and contingencies
An allowance included in the expense loading that protects the insurer against the possibility that actual claims or expenses will exceed estimates.

an extreme case, delays of ten to twelve years in the settlement of liability claims are not unusual.

Insurers are required by law (and by good business practices) to estimate the amounts that they will eventually pay on such claims. The estimated amounts of future payments for claims that have already occurred are shown as a liability on the insurer's balance sheet and are usually referred to as **loss reserves**. Unfortunately, all insurers are not equipped with perfect foresight, so these estimates are not always accurate. Errors in estimating claims payment amounts are reflected in rates calculated on the basis of such estimates. If claim estimates are too low, resulting rates will be too low. If claim estimates are too high, resulting rates will be too high.

To illustrate this effect, assume that rates are to be calculated for an auto liability insurance line for which 25 percent of losses are paid in the same year the accident occurs, 50 percent are to be paid in the next year, and the remaining 25 percent are to be paid in the second year following the year in which the accident occurs. The rates are to be calculated on the basis of the losses that occurred in the most recent three-year period. Exhibit 10-1 shows the losses for each year in the three-year period, with Year 1 being the earliest year and Year 3 the most recent year. The paid losses in Column (1) are the amounts paid up to and including December 31 of Year 3.

Loss reserves

A liability on an insurer's balance sheet reflecting the insurer's obligation to make future payments to settle open claims.

EXHIBIT 10-1

Paid Losses, Loss Reserves, and Incurred Losses for a Hypothetical Auto Liability Line Evaluated on 12/31/X3

Year	(1) Losses Paid	(2) Loss Reserves	(3) Incurred Losses
1	$10,000,000	$ 0	$10,000,000
2	7,500,000	2,500,000	10,000,000
3	2,500,000	7,500,000	10,000,000
Totals	$20,000,000	$10,000,000	$30,000,000

The loss reserves shown in Column (2) are the insurer's estimates, as of December 31 of Year 3, of the amounts it will pay in the future for losses that happened during the period. All losses that happened in Year 1 have been paid, so there is no reserve for that period. Column (3), which is the sum of Columns (1) and (2), is labeled *Incurred Losses*; this is a standard actuarial term. The **incurred losses** for a given period are the sum of (1) all amounts already paid for losses that happened during that period and (2) amounts that will be paid in the future for losses that occurred during that period.

Incurred losses

The sum of all amounts already paid for losses that happened during a specific time period and amounts that will be paid in the future for losses that occurred during that period.

If the insurer in Exhibit 10-1 insured 100,000 cars each year during the period, it would have provided 300,000 *car-years* of protection. (A car-year represents the exposure of one car insured for one year.) If the 300,000 car-years are divided into the $30 million of incurred losses, based on past experience only, the insurer will need a pure premium of $100 per car (the amount needed to pay losses).

Now assume that the insurer's loss reserves proved to be inadequate. When all claims were settled, the incurred losses turned out to be $33 million instead of the estimated $30 million in Exhibit 10-1. In that case, the pure premium actually needed was $110; the insurer's rates would have been too low.

In theory, an insurer could avoid the problem of incorrectly estimating loss reserves by waiting for all claims to be paid before calculating rates. However, major problems arise with this approach. Several years may elapse before all claims are paid. Delaying the rate filing for several years to permit all claims to be settled allows a greater length of time for inflation, changes in traffic conditions, and other factors to affect incurred losses. Errors in estimating these factors' effects may be greater than the errors in estimating loss reserves.

Exhibit 10-2 shows the payout pattern reported by one insurer for automobile liability insurance. In Exhibit 10-2, Year 1 is the year the accidents happened, Year 2 is the following year, and so forth.

EXHIBIT 10-2

Payout Pattern: Automobile Liability Insurance Losses Incurred in Year 1

Year	(1) Losses Paid	(2) (3) Losses Unpaid		(4) Estimated Losses Incurred in Year 1
		Reported	IBNR	
12/31/1	$ 5,051,145	$13,837,205	$9,592,239	$28,480,589
12/31/2	10,780,845	12,906,866	4,187,646	27,875,357
12/31/3	16,036,708	9,058,737	2,036,246	27,131,691
12/31/4	19,667,531	6,782,231	79,247	26,529,009
12/31/5	22,268,032	4,308,212	0	26,576,244
12/31/6	24,714,163	3,136,059	0	27,850,222
12/31/7	25,088,249	860,395	0	25,948,644

Column (1) of Exhibit 10-2 shows the actual amount the company paid to the end of the year indicated for claims arising from insured events that occurred during Year 1—$5,051,145. During Year 2, the company paid an additional $5,729,700 on such claims, bringing total payments to $10,780,845. At the end of Year 7, the company had paid a total of $25,088,249 for claims that arose in Year 1.

Column (2) of Exhibit 10-2 shows the company's annual year-end estimate of the amount it will pay to settle claims that occurred in Year 1 and have been reported to it but have not yet been paid. This figure drops each year as claims are settled; it has become a relatively small $860,395 at the end of Year 7.

Column (3) shows the company's estimates of future payments to settle claims that happened in Year 1 but have not yet been reported to it. These are known as **incurred but not reported (IBNR)** claims. The company assumed that all auto insurance claims incurred in Year 1 had been reported to it by the end of Year 5, so the IBNR figure is zero for Years 5 and later.

The figures in Columns (2) and (3) are estimates of future payments. The figures in Column (2) are usually estimates by claim department personnel of the amounts to be paid on individual claims. The numbers in Column (3) are usually calculated by actuaries on the basis of historical data. The methods used to arrive at these estimates are discussed in Chapter 12. The amounts ultimately paid are seldom, if ever, exactly equal to the estimates, and the differences are sometimes substantial.

The company in Exhibit 10-2 estimated at the end of Year 1 [see Column (4)] that it would eventually pay a total of $28,480,589 to settle all of the auto liability claims it incurred in Year 1. At the end of Year 7, it had reduced that estimate to $25,948,644. With only $860,395 outstanding at the end of Year 7, that estimate should be much more accurate than the original estimate at the end of Year 1.

If the company in Exhibit 10-2 had used its estimated incurred losses at the end of Year 1 for ratemaking purposes, the resulting rates would have been too high by approximately 10 percent. Such an error could cause it to become noncompetitive and lose market share. Of course, not all insurers overestimate their loss payments. Some underestimate them, which could lead to inadequate rates, underwriting losses, and possibly even insolvency.

Actuaries have developed methods for detecting and correcting consistent errors in the estimation of future loss payments. The method most commonly used is known as **loss development**, which is discussed in some detail in Chapter 11. It is based on historical data and assumes that the company is making the same errors in estimation now that it made in the past

Inflation

Errors in the estimation of loss reserves are not the only ratemaking errors that actuaries must guard against. Unlike the mythical Kingdom of Everstable, the real world is subject to inflation and, sometimes, to deflation. Inflation, especially rapid inflation, presents a substantial actuarial problem. An inevitable lag occurs between the time losses are incurred and the time those losses are reflected in rates charged to consumers. The delay can be as long as three years.

The lag in reflecting loss experience in rates stems from several sources. The principal sources of delay are as follows:

1. Delays by policyholders in reporting losses to insurers
2. Time required to analyze the data and prepare a rate filing

---

Incurred but not reported (INBR)
Estimates of amounts to be paid in the future to settle losses that have happened but have not yet been reported to the insurer. Insurers are required to establish reserves for such losses.

Loss development
A mathematical technique used in ratemaking to recognize consistent patterns over time in the accuracy of reserves based on a comparison of actual and expected loss ratios. Loss development is applied to detect and correct errors in the estimation of future loss payments.

3. Delays in obtaining approval of filed rates by state regulatory authorities

4. Time required to communicate the new rates to agents and brokers

In addition, rates are frequently in effect for one year. Thus, the last policy issued under a given set of rates is issued one year after the effective date of the rate filing, and coverage under those rates continues until the policy expires, possibly a year later. During periods of rapid inflation, these delays could result in substantially inadequate rates.

Exhibit 10-3 shows a reasonably typical schedule for the development, approval, and implementation of new auto insurance rates. Exhibit 10-3 assumes that the insurer is basing its new rates on its loss experience for a three-year period, called the **experience period**. All pertinent statistics from that period are collected and analyzed in the ratemaking process. The data items used are usually (1) earned exposure units, (2) earned premiums, (3) incurred losses in dollars, and (4) the number of claims incurred. An **exposure unit** is a measure of the risk assumed under an insurance contract. The premium for a policy is calculated by multiplying the number of exposure units by the rate for each exposure unit. For private passenger auto insurance, the unit of exposure is one car-year, or one car insured for one year.

Experience period
The period for which all pertinent statistics are collected and analyzed in the ratemaking process.

Exposure unit
A measure of the loss exposure assumed by an insurer. For example, a car-year in automobile insurance is an exposure unit.

The experience period in Exhibit 10-3 begins on January 1 of Year 1. Experience statistics are collected for the three-year period beginning on that date and ending on December 31 of Year 3. The midpoint of the experience period is July 1 of Year 2.

Exhibit 10-3 shows the analysis phase of the ratemaking process beginning only three months after the end of the experience period. Some insurers prefer to wait longer to permit claims information to mature. As noted earlier, many claims incurred during the experience period would not yet have been reported to the insurer.

Exhibit 10-3 assumes that the new rates will become effective on January 1 of Year 5, one year after the end of the experience period. They will remain in effect until December 31 of Year 5, two years after the end of the experience period. However, the policies issued on December 31 of Year 5 will remain in force until December 31 of Year 6. Consequently, the last claim under these rates will be incurred three years after the end of the experience period and six years after the occurrence of the first of the claims on which the rate calculation was based. Some insurers shorten this process slightly by filing new rates every six months or issuing six-month policies. Others may follow an even longer cycle.

In Exhibit 10-3, the lag between the midpoint of the experience period and the midpoint of the period in which losses are incurred under the rates is 3.5 years. In that length of time, substantial changes can occur in loss severity and frequency resulting from inflation, changes in laws, traffic density, or other factors. Rates calculated without regard to these potential changes could prove to be grossly inadequate or grossly excessive, depending on the nature of the changes taking place.

EXHIBIT 10-3

Chronology of a Rate Filing

January 1, Year 1	Beginning of the experience period, first claim incurred.
December 31, Year 1	
July 1, Year 2	Midpoint of experience period.
December 31, Year 2	
December 31, Year 3	End of experience period.
March 31, Year 4	Begin data collection and analysis.
July 1, Year 4	File rates with regulatory authorities.
September 1, Year 4	Receive approval of rates.
January 1, Year 5	Begin using new rates.
December 31, Year 5	Stop using rates from this filing. Also, midpoint of period during which losses are incurred under this filing.
December 31, Year 6	Last claim incurred under this rate filing.

Other Time-Dependent Factors

Inflation affects the average cost of a claim. Other time-dependent factors affect the number of claims that occur. Among them are the following:

1. Changes in traffic density (the number of vehicles per mile of road)
2. Changes in law enforcement efforts
3. Changes in legal rules governing claims settlement

Some of these factors may be difficult to identify and to reduce to mathematical expressions, but they nonetheless affect insurance claims. Ignoring them may result in inadequate or excessive rates.

Trending
A statistical technique for analyzing environmental changes, such as inflation, that affect insurance losses and for projecting such changes into the future.

The actuarial technique used to cope with these time-dependent factors is known as **trending**. Some of the factors that affect the size and frequency of claims cannot be identified or measured directly, but their aggregate effect on claims can be determined with reasonable accuracy by statistical means.

Trending uses statistical techniques to measure these effects in the past and to project them into the future. Trending is usually done separately for the average amount of a claim, called severity, and the average number of claims, called frequency. Trending is sometimes applied to pure premiums, which combine frequency and severity into a single number. Chapter 11 discusses trending in more detail.

Risk Classification

In the Kingdom of Everstable, all drivers and all cars are equal. In the real world, both cars and drivers vary widely, and their variations have important implications for the cost of insurance. No satisfactory way exists to directly measure the propensity of a particular driver to have accidents, but certain groups of drivers are known to have more accidents than others. For rating purposes, drivers are grouped into classes according to criteria that provide at least a rough measure of the claims they are likely to generate. This process of categorization is usually referred to as **risk classification**. Among the rating criteria frequently used for private passenger auto insurance risk classification are the following:

Risk classification
The process of categorizing insureds according to characteristics that affect their expected losses.

1. Age of the driver
2. Sex and marital status of the driver
3. Nature of the vehicle
4. Use of vehicle
5. Driving record of the driver
6. Risk classification rating

Age

When immaturity is coupled with inexperience, age becomes a good predictor of accident frequency. Both insurance statistics and statistics gathered by state motor vehicle departments show that young drivers have more accidents than older drivers. Perhaps youthful operators are more reckless than older drivers or more inclined to take chances that result in accidents. As young drivers gain more driving experience and develop more mature judgment, their accident records improve.

Sex and Marital Status of the Driver

A driver's sex also seems to be a factor in accident experience, though less so than age. Regulatory requirements in a few states prohibit the use of sex as a rating criterion. Marital status has been used to further subclassify youthful operators. The presumption is that young married operators are more settled than their unmarried counterparts. In Georgia, for example, the class factor used is 10 to 15 percent higher for unmarried youthful operators than for married youthful operators.

Nature of Vehicle

Cars differ as to (1) susceptibility to accidents, (2) damageability, and (3) protection provided to occupants. Several notable examples of accident susceptibility have in recent years drawn public attention in recent years. Some sports utility vehicles were found to be unstable and likely to overturn during sharp turns, for example, during emergency maneuvers to avoid collisions. High-powered sports cars, with rapid acceleration and high-speed capabilities, were also found to have been involved in more accidents than were more conservative vehicles, especially when operated by inexperienced drivers.

Cars also vary in their ability to resist damage when an accident occurs. Susceptibility to damage may result from weak bumpers, the complex shape of metal parts such as decorative fenders, or excessive use of materials that are difficult to repair, such as molded fiberglass-plastic.

Finally, cars differ in the protection they offer to passengers when an accident occurs. One car model became infamous because its gasoline tank frequently ruptured when the car was struck from the rear, causing serious fires and many deaths to occupants. Others were found to provide less than satisfactory protection to passengers in collisions. Many studies have shown that small cars provide less passenger protection than larger cars.

Accident susceptibility is an important rating consideration for all lines of automobile insurance except possibly theft. Damageability is important primarily for collision coverage rates. Passenger protection is important primarily for no-fault and medical expense coverages and also liability coverage because of possible injuries to passengers.

Auto insurance ratemaking practices differ among insurers. Some insurers might not take all of these factors into account in calculating their rates.

Use of Vehicle

The use to which a vehicle is put usually determines the mileage driven and is therefore an important determinant of losses. Consequently, it is an important factor in risk classification. Cars used for business purposes are likely to be driven more than those driven only for personal use. Cars driven to and from work are likely to be driven more than those used only for pleasure. There are exceptions to these general rules, but the rules are useful for risk classification despite the exceptions.

Although the use of the vehicle is an important classification criterion, mileage driven is sometimes used as a separate criterion. It may be specified in terms of total annual mileage driven or in terms of the one-way distance between the policyholder's home and place of employment.

Driving Record

Many auto insurers use the policyholder's driving record as an important risk classification criterion. They might use years of driving experience instead of age as a risk classification criterion, or they might consider past accidents and traffic violations for rating purposes. Some statistical compilations indicate that a driver who has had one or more accidents in the past three years is significantly more likely to have another accident in the next year.

Risk Classification Rating

Insurers use these and other risk classification criteria to categorize drivers into reasonably homogeneous groups in which all members of the class have substantially the same exposure to loss. A rate is then calculated for each class so that the members of each class pay a premium commensurate with the loss exposure of the class. Rates such as these applied to a class of individual insureds to reflect the loss exposures of the group are known as **class rates**. They are the most common kind of rates for private passenger auto insurance. Class rates are sometimes referred to as manual rates because they are usually published in rating manuals for the convenience of agents, underwriters, and others.

For some other lines of property or liability insurance, a separate rate is determined for each policyholder. Such rates are sometimes called **individual rates** or specific rates to distinguish them from class rates. As a general rule, individual or specific rates are used in connection with lines of insurance for which (1) each policy produces enough premium to justify the added expense of developing specific rates, and (2) the loss exposures are so varied that risk classification within the line is difficult or impossible. Class rates, on the other hand, are used in connection with lines of insurance for which the policyholders can be classified into groups with reasonably homogeneous loss exposures.

Merit rating is an intermediate step between class rates and individual or specific rates. Under most merit rating plans, the premium for a particular policyholder is first calculated by the use of class rates and then modified upward or downward to reflect one or more characteristics of the policyholder that affect the policyholder's loss exposures. The characteristics for which merit rating plans reduce or increase rates include past loss experience, loss control measures adopted by the policyholder, and similar factors.

Territorial Rating

In Everstable, driving conditions and laws were uniform throughout the kingdom. Elsewhere, the area where the vehicle is driven may be a factor in determining insurance rates. Accident rates may vary from one place to another for many reasons, including differences in traffic density, climate, road construction and maintenance, and law enforcement.

To provide an equitable distribution of insurance costs, states are divided into rating territories based primarily on loss experience. Urban areas usually have higher rates than rural areas for most auto insurance lines because the greater traffic density in urban areas results in more accidents. Also, the costs of medical treatment and car repairs are likely to be higher in urban areas.

The primary goal of both risk classification and territorial rating is an equitable allocation of insurance costs among the various groups that buy insurance. Failure to recognize these differences among groups of policyholders results in some buyers' paying more than their fair share of insurance costs, while others pay less.

Credibility

As noted, insured auto losses vary over time as a result of inflation, traffic density, law changes, and other identifiable, time-dependent changes in the

Class rates
Rates that apply without modification to all members of a group (or class) of policyholders. Also called manual rates.

Individual rate
A rate calculated to apply to only one policyholder.

Merit rating
A process for modifying a class rate, either upward or downward, to reflect characteristics of a particular policyholder that are expected to result in that policyholder's having greater than or less than the average losses for other members of the policyholder's rating class.

insurance environment. They may also change because of pure chance. Trending is used to adjust past data to future conditions by reflecting projected changes in time-dependent environmental conditions. However, some reasonably stable, identifiable rate of change must exist for trending to work properly. If inflation has been causing annual loss increases of 4 percent year, that rate of increase can be projected into the future in the absence of any indication that it will change.

Chance variations, however, may cause losses to rise sharply one year and fall sharply the next. Such random changes cannot be projected reliably into the future. Consequently, actuaries have developed a process for moderating the variations in rates that would otherwise result from purely chance variations in losses.

An essential element in this process is the law of large numbers. Stated in insurance terminology, the law of large numbers says that all other things being equal, the accuracy of loss forecasts improves as the number of exposure units in the database increases. In other words, the level of confidence an auto insurance actuary has in the projected losses (and the resulting rates) increases as the number of insured vehicles increases. The confidence level is known to actuaries as **credibility**. Credibility factors vary from zero (no confidence at all) to one (full confidence).

Credibility

The level of confidence that an actuary has in the available data as an indicator of future losses.

One simple way of applying credibility is to multiply the projected rate change by the credibility factor. For example, if the credibility factor is .30 and the data indicate that a rate increase of 10 percent is needed, a rate increase of 3.0 percent ($10 \times .30$) would be taken. The same approach would be used for rate reductions so that rates would be stabilized over time. Chapter 11 discusses credibility in more detail.

Additional Concepts

Written premiums

All of the premiums for policies and endorsements recorded on a company's books during a specific period of time.

Two fundamental concepts of insurance ratemaking are written premiums and earned premiums. The **written premiums** for a period consist of all of the premiums for policies and endorsements recorded on the company's books during the period. The **earned premiums** for the period consist of the premiums used to pay for protection actually provided during the period. For example, assume that a company writes only one policy during the year, a one-year policy with an annual premium of $100 written on October 1. The written premium for the year would be $100, the entire premium for the policy. The earned premium for the year would be $25, because only three months of protection would be provided during the year. The remaining $75 of the policy premium would be earned in the next year. The $75 not earned by December 31 would appear on the company's year-end balance sheet as a liability called the **unearned premium reserve**.

Earned premiums

The portion of the written premium for a particular policy that applies to the part of the policy period that has already occurred.

Unearned premium reserve

The total of an insurer's unearned premiums on all policies at a particular time; premiums that have been written but are not yet earned.

Similar concepts apply to losses. Incurred losses for a period consist of all losses arising from insured events that happened during the period. Paid losses for a period consist of all losses for which checks or drafts were issued during the period. Some of the paid losses may also have been incurred during the period, while others may have been incurred in earlier periods. The loss reserve on a given date consists of all amounts the insurer expects to pay in the future for losses incurred in the past.

The concept of an **earned exposure unit** is also important in ratemaking. An exposure unit is a measure of the loss exposure assumed by an insurer. For auto insurance, the most common exposure unit is a car-year. A car-year can consist of one car insured for one year, two cars insured for six months each, four cars insured for three months each, and so forth.

Earned exposure unit
Exposure unit for which a full year of coverage has been provided.

If ten auto policies, each covering one car for one year, are written on October 1, the written exposure units would be ten car-years. On the following December 31, the earned exposure units under the ten policies would be 2.5 car years, ten cars insured for 0.25 years each. Different lines of insurance use relevant exposure units. For example, workers compensation uses $100 of payroll, as do some general liability classes. Other lines of insurance use sales, square footage, or some other measure of exposure.

A loss ratio is calculated by dividing premiums into losses. Because two kinds of losses (paid and incurred) and two kinds of premiums (written and earned) exist, four different loss ratios are possible. Of those, the one that is most useful for ratemaking purposes is the incurred-earned loss ratio, calculated by dividing earned premiums into incurred losses. The incurred-earned loss ratio is the most appropriate loss ratio for ratemaking purposes because it provides the closest match between losses and the premiums intended to cover them.

This point can be illustrated by examining an extreme case—professional liability insurance for physicians and surgeons. Historical data indicate that fewer than 2 percent of losses for that line, when measured by dollar amount, are paid in the same year in which the related malpractice events occurred. Or, to state it differently, more than 98 percent of the losses paid in any given year were incurred in some earlier year. On the other hand, about half of the premiums written in any given year pays for insurance actually provided in the following year. Consequently, a paid-written loss ratio for this line of insurance would be comparing losses that happened in the past to premiums for the future. The incurred-earned loss ratio, in contrast, would compare losses and premiums for the same period.

Ratemaking Methods

There are three approaches to ratemaking:

1. Judgment method
2. Loss ratio method
3. Pure premium method

Judgment Method

The **judgment method** is the oldest of the three and is still used for some lines of insurance. With this method, the underwriter selects a rate on the basis of

Judgment method
A method for determining insurance rates that relies heavily on the experience and knowledge of an actuary or an underwriter with little or no use of statistics.

his or her experience and judgment and uses little or no statistical information. The judgment method is still used for ocean marine insurance, some inland marine lines, and aviation insurance. In general, underwriters use it when sufficient statistical information is unavailable to apply the other methods.

Loss Ratio Method

Loss ratio method
A method for calculating insurance rates based on a comparison of actual and expected loss ratios.

The **loss ratio method** is a method for adjusting an existing rate either upward or downward to reflect changing conditions. In its simplest form, the loss ratio method involves comparing two loss ratios—the actual loss ratio and the expected loss ratio. The actual loss ratio is the incurred-earned loss ratio achieved by the insurer during the selected experience period. The expected loss ratio is the loss ratio that the insurer would need to achieve its profit objectives. It is determined by subtracting the insurer's expense loading (including a profit allowance) from 100 percent. For example, an insurer with an expense loading (sometimes called an expense ratio) of 40 percent would have an expected (or permissible) loss ratio of 60 percent. The expected loss ratio and the expense loading always add up to 100 percent.

The following equation represents the loss ratio method in its simplest form.

$$\text{Percentage rate change} = (A - E)/E,$$

where A = actual loss ratio and E = expected loss ratio. If the answer is negative, it indicates a percentage rate reduction. If positive, it indicates a rate increase. For example, if A = 54 percent, and E = 60 percent, the answer would be –0.10, indicating a rate reduction of 10 percent.

The loss ratio method cannot be used to calculate rates for a new line of insurance because neither an actual loss ratio for the calculation nor an old rate to adjust is available. For a new line of insurance, either the judgment method or the pure premium method must be used.

Pure Premium Method

Pure premium method
A method for calculating insurance rates. A pure premium is first calculated, and an expense loading is added to it.

The **pure premium method** of ratemaking in its simplest form involves three steps: (1) calculating the pure premium, (2) calculating the expense loading, and (3) combining the pure premium and the expense loading into the gross rate.

The pure premium is the amount needed for each exposure unit for the payment of losses incurred. Loss adjustment expenses are frequently included in the pure premium, but they may be included in the expense loading instead. The pure premium is calculated by dividing the number of earned exposure units into the dollar amount of incurred losses. For example, if an insurer has 100,000 earned car-years and $4 million of incurred losses, including loss adjustment expenses, the pure premium would be $40 per car-year.

The expense loading, which usually includes a factor for profit and contingencies, is based on the insurer's past expenses. It includes an allowance for all of the insurer's expenses except investment expenses and possibly loss adjustment expenses. If loss adjustment expenses are included in the pure premium, they are excluded from the expense loading. Investment expenses are deducted from investment income and are not directly reflected in rate calculations.

Traditionally, the expense loading for property-casualty insurance has been stated as a percentage of the gross rate. Consequently, it cannot be added directly to the pure premium. The two must be combined by a simple algebraic formula. The formula can be derived as follows:

$$G = P + (L \times G)$$

where G = gross premium, P = pure premium, and L = expense loading.

Subtracting (L × G) from both sides of the preceding equation yields:

$$G - (L \times G) = P$$

or

$$(1 - L)G = P.$$

Dividing both sides by (1 – L) yields:

$$G = \frac{P}{(1 - L)}.$$

This final form of the equation indicates that the gross premium is calculated by dividing the pure premium by one minus the expense loading.

A pure premium of $40 and an expense loading equal to 20 percent of gross premium yield a gross premium of $50. The calculation is as follows:

$$G = \frac{\$40}{(1 - .20)} = \frac{\$40}{.80} = \$50.$$

Some insurers separated their expense loadings into two components: fixed expenses and variable expenses. Fixed expenses are stated as a dollar amount per exposure unit. Variable expenses are stated as a percentage of the gross rate. For example, the insurer in the preceding illustration might decide that its cost for issuing a policy and collecting the premium is $2.50 per car-year, which does not vary with the size of the premium, the rating class, or the rating territory. Its other underwriting expenses vary with the size of the premium, and the total of such expenses equals 15 percent of gross premium.

Based on these assumptions, its gross premium would be calculated by the formula:

$$G = \frac{P + F}{1 - V}$$

where F = dollar amount of fixed expenses, V = percentage of variable expenses, and the other symbols have the meanings previously assigned to them. Substituting the preceding numerical values yields the following gross rate:

$$G = \frac{\$40 + 2.50}{1 - .15} = \frac{\$42.50}{.85} = \$50.$$

In this example, both the percentage loading and the loading separated into fixed and variable expenses resulted in the same gross rate. That usually is not the case. A percentage loading results in policyholders in higher-rated classes and higher-rated territories paying more of the insurer's expenses than policyholders in lower-rated classes and territories. If some of the insurer's expenses do not vary with premiums, policyholders in the higher-rated classes and territories will pay more than their fair share of the cost of insurance. Adopting a fixed/variable expense loading may result in a more equitable allocation of expenses.

Investment Income in Ratemaking

Investment income

Interest, dividends, rents, and similar income that an insurer receives from its investment assets.

A property-casualty insurer operates two businesses. The insurance business writes policies, collects premiums, and pays losses. The investment business uses the funds generated by the insurance business to buy bonds, stocks, and other investment vehicles to earn an investment profit. Investment profits are derived from three sources: investment income, realized capital gains, and unrealized capital gains. **Investment income** consists of interest, dividends, rents, and similar regular income received from the invested assets held by the company. Investment income is the most stable source of income for most insurance companies.

Realized capital gains (losses)

The differences between the purchase price of an asset and the proceeds from selling it. This is usually applied to an insurer's investment assets.

Realized capital gains occur when an insurer sells an asset for more than its cost. If an asset is sold for less than its cost, a **realized capital loss** results.

Unrealized capital gains (losses)

The differences between the purchase price of an asset and its current market price.

An **unrealized capital gain** results when an asset's market price exceeds its cost and the insurer continues to hold the asset. If the asset's market price falls below its cost and the insurer continues to hold the asset, an **unrealized capital loss** results. An example of these sources of investment income is shown in Exhibit 10-4.

Traditionally, property-casualty insurers did not consider their investment profits directly in the calculation of insurance rates, though they may have considered investment profits informally in determining the allowance for profits and contingencies in the rates.

It is becoming more common to consider investment profits explicitly in the rate calculation. Some states now require the explicit consideration of investment income. Fewer states require the explicit consideration of capital gains; most of these focus on realized capital gains. One method for reflecting investment profits in ratemaking is to estimate the investment profits to be realized on the line of insurance and deduct that amount from the expense loading used in the rates. For example, if an insurer's expenses are expected to be 30 percent of the gross rate and its investment profit is expected to be 5 percent of earned premiums, it would include an expense loading of 25 percent in its rates.

EXHIBIT 10-4

Investment Income

On January 1, Insurance Company bought 1,000 shares of Publicly Held Corporation stock for $100 per share for a total cost of $100,000. During the year that followed, Publicly Held paid Insurance Company $5,000 in dividends on the stock. On December 30, the Publicly Held stock was quoted on the stock exchange at $160 per share, for a total market value of $160,000. On December 31, Insurance Company sold the stock for $160,000. Insurance Company's investment income for the year would be $5,000, the amount of the dividends.

On December 30, it had an unrealized capital gain of $60,000, the difference between the cost and the market value of the stock. On December 31, when it sold the stock, Insurance Company converted its unrealized capital gain to a realized capital gain.

The investment profit earned on a line of insurance depends largely on the loss reserves and unearned premium reserves generated. Consequently, including investment profits in ratemaking is likely to affect liability insurance rates more than property insurance rates.

RATE REGULATION

The ratemaking process is not entirely mathematical. Actuaries must also be cognizant of government regulation. All states regulate insurance rates to some degree, with some imposing more stringent regulations than others.

Statutory Standards

All of the states impose three standards by which rates are judged, although the methods of applying those standards vary. The three standards require that a rate be (1) adequate, (2) not excessive, and (3) not unfairly discriminatory.

A rate is considered adequate if it is sufficient to cover the probable losses and expenses of the insured. Most insurers would prefer to have something left for profits as well, but the statutory standard usually does not require a profit.

A rate is usually considered not excessive if it does not generate an unreasonable profit for the insurer. Much debate in recent years has centered on what constitutes an unreasonable profit.

A rate is considered not unfairly discriminatory if it equitably reflects the expected loss and expenses of the policyholder to whom it applies. Under this standard, to knowingly overcharge one policyholder and undercharge another would be unlawful.

Administration

Although all the states apply the same three standards for regulating insurance rates, they vary widely in how they administer the standards. The methods of administration various states use can be classified into the following five categories:

1. State-made rates
2. Mandatory bureau membership
3. Prior approval
4. File and use
5. No filing required

State-Made Rates

Massachusetts calculates the rates for compulsory automobile insurance coverages in that state. All insurers that write automobile insurance there must use the rates determined by the state. The only way they can compete on the basis of price is to pay dividends to policyholders. Texas follows a similar procedure for several lines of property-casualty insurance.

Mandatory Bureau Membership

Several states have statutory rating bureaus for one or more lines of insurance. The bureaus were created by state law but are owned and managed by insurance companies. They collect data from their member companies and calculate rates based on the data. All insurers that write the lines of insurance under the jurisdiction of the statutory rating bureaus are usually required by law to be members of the bureau and to use the bureau rates.

Prior Approval Laws

About half of the states have prior approval rate regulatory laws. Under a prior approval law, an insurer must file its rates with state regulatory authorities for approval before the rates can be used. In some states, prior approval laws include so-called "deemer provisions," which provide that if the authorities fail either to approve or disapprove the rates within some specified period, such as forty-five days, the rates are deemed to be approved.

File-and-Use Laws

Almost half of the states have file-and-use laws. Under these laws, an insurer must file its rates with—but need not obtain approval from—the authorities before the rates are used. However, regulatory authorities can order the insurer to stop using the rates if they find that the rates fail to meet statutory requirements. A variation of this category is the use-and-file law, under which an insurer can begin using rates before they are filed but must file them within some specified period, such as fifteen days, after they are first used.

No-File Laws

The most liberal of the rate regulatory laws are the no-file laws. These laws do not require rates to be filed with the state on a regular basis. However, regulatory authorities may require the insurer to provide data to support the rates if they have reason to believe that the rates do not comply with statutory requirements. Historically, California was the most notable of the no-file states. Proposition 103, adopted in 1988, converted California to a prior approval state beginning in 1991. The term "open competition law" is sometimes used to refer to no-file, file-and-use, and use-and-file laws, either individually or collectively.

To date, no credible evidence has been produced to show any great advantage of one type of regulation over the others for either consumers or insurers. However, the debate continues with unabated furor, and states frequently change from one regulatory form to another.

SUMMARY

An actuary is a person trained to use mathematical techniques to solve problems related to insurer management. The two most prominent actuarial functions for property-casualty insurers are ratemaking and verifying loss reserves. This chapter introduced the principles of ratemaking.

Insurance ratemaking would be simple if all insured persons and all loss exposures were identical and unchanging. The complexities of real-world ratemaking processes arise from variations in policyholders and loss exposures and time-related changes in the insurance environment.

There are three methods of determining insurance rates. The judgment method relies heavily on the knowledge and experience of an actuary or an underwriter, with little or no use of statistics. The loss ratio method determines a new rate by modifying an old rate, using a comparison of actual and expected loss ratios. The pure premium method involves calculating a pure premium, the amount needed to pay losses, to which an expense loading is added.

The ratemaking process is further complicated by various states' regulatory requirements. Rate regulation in all states is based on the statutory requirements that rates must be adequate, not excessive, and not unfairly discriminatory. However, the methods used to administer these basic requirements vary from the relatively liberal no-file laws to relatively rigid state-made rates. It is not unusual for a state to change from one form of rate regulation to another.

Chapter 11

Direct Your Learning

The Ratemaking Process

After learning the subject matter of this chapter, you should be able to:

- Given a case, apply the ratemaking process. In support of this objective, do the following:
  - Describe the data collection methods and their effect on ratemaking results.
  - Describe the importance of loss trending and loss development.
  - Given a case, calculate territory and class relativities.
- Explain how ratemaking methods compare with one another.
- Explain how experience period, loss development, trending, large loss limitation, and credibility vary in use by line of insurance.
- Describe the steps in the rate filing process.

Develop Your Perspective

What are the main topics covered in the chapter?

This chapter describes the processes applied in ratemaking. These processes include the methods of gathering statistics, adjustments for loss development factors and trending, and territorial and class relativities. Ratemaking methods and variations by line of insurance are illustrated.

Determine methods of ratemaking for a line of insurance that your company writes.

- How are statistics gathered and applied?

- What adjustments are made to the statistics?

- What relativity factors are applied?

Why is it important to know these topics?

Actuaries use the processes described to develop the rates that are documented and submitted to the states in rate filings. By understanding the processes involved, you can appreciate the importance of the development of statistics, which are the basis of rate development and future premium income.

Consider how errors in statistics can affect rate development.

- How might the use of inaccurate statistics or the choice of an inappropriate rating processes affect your organization's premium income?

How can you use this information?

Assess your own organization's ratemaking process.

- What statistics are used, and how are they gathered?

- Are the processes described in the chapter applied, or are other calculations required?

Chapter 11

The Ratemaking Process

Chapter 10 introduced a number of basic concepts in ratemaking for property-casualty insurance. This chapter integrates those basic concepts into a demonstration of the ratemaking process. Some additional, more advanced concepts are also introduced. As in Chapter 10, private passenger automobile insurance is used to illustrate the process.

DEVELOPMENT OF RATEMAKING DATA

Rates for most lines of insurance, including private passenger auto insurance, are determined separately for each state. This practice is reflected in the terminology used in this chapter. However, the ratemaking process is generally the same for the few lines of insurance for which rates are calculated nationally.

Exhibit 11-1 shows the major steps in the ratemaking process. The insurer's own staff might perform the steps, or an advisory organization might perform some or all of them.

EXHIBIT 11-1

Steps in the Ratemaking Process

- Collect statistics.
- Adjust statistics.
- Calculate statewide average rate.
- Calculate territorial relativities.
- Calculate classification relativities.
- Prepare rate filing.
- Submit rate filing to regulatory authorities.
- Follow up to obtain necessary regulatory action.

Collection of Statistics

With the possible exception of the judgment method of ratemaking, the first step in the ratemaking process is to collect the ratemaking statistics. The first step in collecting statistics is to determine the kinds of statistics to collect and the form in which to collect them.

The loss ratio method requires statistics for incurred losses, earned premiums, and the expense loading. The pure premium method also requires earned exposure units. If rates are to vary by rating class and territory, the statistics, with the possible exception of the expense ratio data, must be collected separately for each class and territory.

Ideally, the same group of insured entities should generate the incurred losses, earned premiums, and earned exposure units. In practice, such precise matching is not always practical, so approximation techniques are used.

Policy-Year Method

The policy-year method, sometimes called the policy-year statistical period, is the only method for gathering statistics that provides an exact matching of losses, premiums, and exposure units to a specific group of insured entities. A **policy year** consists of all of the policies issued in a given twelve-month period, frequently a calendar year. When the policy-year method is used to gather statistics, all premium transactions attributable to a specific policy are directly tied to that policy. These would include the original premium along with additional premiums or return premiums resulting from premium audits, retrospective rating plans, policy changes, and similar transactions. Exposure units are calculated in a similar manner. Incurred losses and allocated loss adjustment expenses are also tied back to the policies that cover them. With such data collected, the actuary need only add up the earned premiums, exposure units, and incurred losses attributed to the specific group of policies to obtain policy-year statistics.

Two major disadvantages apply to the policy-year method. First, and perhaps most important, it involves longer delays in gathering statistics than do the other two methods discussed next. Also, it involves some additional expense, because policy-year statistics are used only for ratemaking purposes. The statistics used in the other two methods are gathered, in part, as a byproduct of the company's accounting operations.

Delays are inherent in the policy-year method. For example, assume that the policy year begins on the first day of the calendar year. Then, the last policy in the policy year would be issued on the last day of the calendar year and, assuming it is a one-year policy, it would expire on the last day of the following calendar year. Thus, a policy year spans two calendar years.

These delays can be overcome in part by estimating the ultimate values of data for which final values are not yet available. However, potential errors in estimating such values reduce the "apples-to-apples" advantage of the policy-year method.

Historically, the additional cost of compiling policy-year statistics was a major disadvantage of that method. With the advent of computers, however, the extra cost of compiling policy-year statistics has become much less significant.

Policy year
All the policies issued in a given twelve-month period. All losses, premiums, and exposure units are tied back to the policies to which they are related.

Calendar-Year Method

The oldest and least accurate method of collecting statistics for ratemaking purposes is the **calendar-year method**, sometimes called the calendar-year statistical period. This method does have two advantages, however. The statistics are available quickly, and little expense is involved in compiling them. These advantages stem from the fact that the calendar-year statistics are derived from data that must be compiled for accounting purposes.

An insurer's accounting records do not show incurred losses, earned premiums, or exposure units. Earned premiums must be estimated from written premiums and unearned premium reserves. The formula usually used for that estimation is as follows:

Earned premiums = Unearned premiums at the beginning of the year
+ Written premiums for the year
− Unearned premiums at the end of the year.

This formula provides a reasonably accurate, but not exact, estimate of the actual earned premiums. The earned premiums may not be precisely matched to a specific group of insured entities because of additional premiums or refunds resulting from premium audits or retrospective rating plans on earlier policies, but these problems should be relatively small for most insurers.

Incurred losses must also be estimated by formula under the calendar-year method. The formula for that estimation is as follows:

Incurred losses = Loss reserves at the end of the year
+ Losses paid during the year
− Loss reserves at the beginning of the year.

That formula may sometimes result in serious errors in estimating the true incurred losses, especially for liability lines. When the formula is used, the estimated incurred losses for a given year may be distorted by changes in loss reserves for losses that occurred in earlier years. A simplified illustration may clarify the problem in estimating incurred losses, as follows:

Assume that at the beginning of 2002, Insurance Company had only one open claim. The claim arose for an accident in 2000, and Insurance Company showed a reserve for the claim at the beginning of 2002.	Claim A: $100,000 reserve in 01/2002
At the end of 2002, the claim was still open, and Insurance Company decided to increase the reserve.	Claim A: $500,000 reserve in 12/2002
During 2002, Insurance Company sustained two additional claims arising from two accidents that happened during 2002. One of these two claims was settled during 2002.	Claim B: $200,000 claim settled 06/2002
The other claim was still open at the end of 2002.	Claim C: $300,000 reserve in 12/2002

Thus, Insurance Company's actual incurred losses in 2002 were $500,000 for Claims B and C, but the formula would indicate estimated incurred losses of $900,000.

Formula:	
Loss reserve at the end of the year	$800,000
Loss paid during the year	+200,000
Loss at the beginning of the year	−100,000
Incurred losses	$900,000

It is unlikely that the estimating error would be so large proportionately for an actual insurer. However, errors can be substantial in lines of insurance for which delays occur in the payment of claims. Errors are not likely to be large for lines such as inland marine and auto physical damage, for which losses are paid rather quickly. For those lines, calendar-year statistics may be accurate enough for practical purposes.

Insurer accounting records usually do not contain exposure unit data. Consequently, calendar-year statistics usually do not include exposure unit data and cannot be used alone in the pure premium ratemaking method. Of course, exposure unit information can be collected separately from the usual accounting data if desired.

Accident-Year Method

Accident-year method
A method of collecting ratemaking statistics. The incurred losses for an accident year consist of all losses related to claims arising from accidents that occur during the year. Earned premiums are estimated by formula from accounting records.

The **accident-year method** of gathering statistics (or the calendar-accident year method) is a compromise between the policy-year method and the calendar-year method. It achieves much of the accuracy of the policy-year method while preserving most of the economy and speed of the calendar-year method.

Earned premiums for the accident-year method are calculated in the same way they are calculated for the calendar-year method. The only difference between the two methods is in the calculation of incurred losses.

In the accident-year method, incurred losses for a given period consist of all losses and claims arising from insured events that occur during the period. The claims may be either open or closed, but if they arose from an insured event that occurred during the period under consideration, they are included in incurred losses for that period.

Because incurred losses under this method consist only of claims arising from insured events that occur during the period, they are not affected by changes in reserves for events that occurred in earlier periods. Thus, the accident-year method avoids the largest source of error inherent in the calendar-year method.

However, neither earned premiums nor incurred losses are tied as directly to a specific group of policyholders under the accident-year method as they are under the policy-year method. The accident-year statistics are slightly more expensive to compile than calendar-year statistics, because accounting records do not distinguish between insured events that occurred during the period under consideration and those that occurred earlier.

Exhibit 11-2 illustrates several claims, indicating how each would be classified under the three methods of gathering statistics. All policies in Exhibit 11-2 are one-year policies. Each claim is assigned to only one year under both the policy-year and accident-year methods, though the year may not be the same for both methods.

The calendar-year method can result in the inclusion of parts of a single claim in several years, depending on the timing of loss reserve changes and the difference, if any, between the final reserve and the loss payment. These peculiar results under the calendar-year method make that method unsuitable for collecting ratemaking statistics for liability and workers compensation insurance, for which the delay in loss payment may be long and the loss reserves may be large relative to earned premiums. For those lines of insurance, either the policy-year or accident-year method should be used.

For some other lines of insurance, such as fire, inland marine, and auto physical damage, losses are paid quickly, and loss reserves tend to be small relative to earned premiums. For those lines, the calendar-year method may be satisfactory for ratemaking purposes, though still less accurate than the other two methods.

An insurer should decide which statistical method it will use early in its existence, preferably before it issues its first policy. The alternative is to adopt a statistical plan that is sufficiently flexible to permit the use of several statistical methods. Policy information is collected most conveniently when policies, endorsements, and invoices are issued. Claims statistics are collected when claims are reported, reserves are changed, checks or drafts are issued, or claims are closed. Each insurer must have a statistical plan to inform personnel about the statistics to be collected and the methods to be used for coding the data for computer compilation. Various advisory organizations provide such statistical plans, but some insurers may choose to develop or adopt statistical plans that collect more data than the advisory organizations require.

Adjustment of Statistics

The raw data, as initially collected, are not suitable for determining the adequacy of current rates or as a basis for calculating revised rates. The raw loss data reflect conditions from present and past periods, whereas the rates being developed will be used in the future. Also, the premiums in the raw data may have been written at several rate levels. Consequently, the actuary must adjust loss data and premium data to make a useful evaluation. In addition, the actuary must adjust the raw loss data to reflect systematic errors, if any, in the estimation of loss reserves. These adjustments are discussed next.

EXHIBIT 11-2

Illustrative Examples of Calendar-Year, Accident-Year, and Policy-Year Statistics—Hypothetical Data

(1) Claim Number	(2) Date of Occurrence	(3) Policy Effective Date	(4) Date Claim Reported	(5) Original Loss Reserve	(6) Change in Reserve	(7) Date of Reserve Change	(8) Amount Paid to Close	(9) Date Paid	(10) Policy Year	(11) Accident Year	(12) Calendar Year	(13) Calendar Year Reserve
1	7-1-00	1-1-00	2-1-01	$100,000	—	—	$100,000	6-3-02	2000	2000	2001	
2	11-1-01	12-15-00	1-1-02	200,000	—	—	200,000	9-1-03	2000	2001	2002	
3	10-3-00	2-4-00	12-20-00	100,000	+$200,000	3-1-02	300,000	4-6-03	2000	2000	2000	$100,000
											2002	200,000
4	9-13-00	2-2-00	3-14-01	50,000	+100,000	4-4-02	300,000	5-3-03	2000	2000	2001	50,000
											2002	100,000
											2003	150,000
5	12-1-01	12-15-00	1-10-02	100,000	−50,000	3-1-03	150,000	2-1-04	2000	2001	2002	100,000
											2003	−50,000
All policies are for one-year terms.											2004	100,000

Notice how each claim is charged differently under the policy year, accident year, and calendar year:

- Policy years (Column 10) reflect the year in which the policy was effective.
- Accident years (Column 11) reflect the year in which the loss occurred.
- Calendar years (Column 12) reflect the year in which the loss was paid or reserves were changed.

Loss Development Factors

Calculating the loss development factors is the first step in adjusting loss data. The purpose of loss development factors is to adjust the reported loss (paid losses plus unpaid loss reserves) data to correct for systematic errors in the estimation of reserves for unpaid losses.

Loss development factors are usually calculated through the use of a table of successive estimates of reported losses. Exhibit 11-3 shows such a table, using hypothetical data. Because of the shape of the table, it is sometimes called a **loss triangle**.

Loss triangle
A table of data used to calculate loss development factors.

The loss development factors to be used in this chapter are shown below the tables in Exhibit 11-3. The method used to calculate them is also shown.

Exhibit 11-4 shows the developed losses for the five-year period shown in Exhibit 11-3. No adjustment is made to the losses from Year 1, which are assumed to be fully mature. The losses for Year 2 are twelve months from maturity, so the one-year loss development factor is applied to them. Losses for Year 5 are four years from maturity, so the four-year development factor is used to adjust them. The losses from the other two years are similarly adjusted.

In this example, the developed losses are less than the reported losses both in total and for some individual years. However, that would not always be the case. Developed losses could be either more or less than reported losses, depending on the insurer's past record in estimating loss reserves.

If loss reserves have been consistently underestimated in the past, developed losses will be higher than reported losses. If loss reserves have been consistently overestimated in the past, developed losses will be lower than reported losses.

EXHIBIT 11-3

Reported Losses (000s omitted)

(1) Accident Year	(2) 12	(3) 24	(4) 36	(5) 48	(6) Final 60
		Months of Development			
1	10,000	11,000	12,000	11,500	11,000
2	9,000	10,500	11,000	10,750	
3	10,500	12,000	12,000		
4	9,750	11,000			
5	10,250				

- Each line shows successive estimates of reported losses for a different year.
- Year 1 is the oldest year, and Year 5 is the most recent year.
- Column (2) shows the company's estimate of its reported losses after twelve months of development.
- Column (3) shows the company's revised estimate at twenty-four months of development.
- Column (6) shows the actual losses reported at sixty months of development. The incurred losses are assumed to be known accurately at that point.

Only Year 1 has matured to sixty months. The other years are too immature, with Year 5 having developed only to twelve months.

Percentage Development

	12–24	24–36	36–48	49–60
	Months of Development			
1	1.100	1.091	0.958	0.957
2	1.167	1.048	0.977	
3	1.143	1.000		
4	1.128			
5	—			
Average	1.135	1.046	0.968	0.957

One-year loss development factor = 0.957.
Two-year loss development factor = $0.968 \times 0.957 = 0.926$.
Three-year loss development factor = $1.046 \times 0.968 \times 0.957 = 0.969$.
Four-year loss development factor = $1.135 \times 1.046 \times 0.968 \times 0.957 = 1.100$.

The figures in this lower part of the exhibit are calculated from the data in the top of the exhibit. They show the percentage change in the reported losses from one period to the next.
- For Year 1, the reported losses increased 10 percent from twelve months of development to twenty-four months of development.
- An additional 9.1 percent increase occurred from twenty-five months to thirty-six months.
- After thirty-six months, the estimate decreased each period.
- The bottom line, labeled "Average" shows the arithmetic change during the period for all years for which data are available. That is, it shows the average change during the period for all years for which data are available. For this example, these factors will be used directly to calculate the loss development factors. In practice, an actuary might make some modifications to the averages to reflect changing circumstances. For example, the claim department might have changed its reserving methods so that the past statistics are not a good indication of current reserve accuracy. Such adjustments are based largely on judgment.

EXHIBIT 11-4

Developed Losses

Year	(1) Reported Losses	(2) Loss Development Factors	(3) Developed Losses
1	$11,000,000	1.000	$11,000,000
2	10,750,000	0.957	10,287,750
3	12,000,000	0.926	11,112,000
4	11,000,000	0.969	10,659,000
5	10,250,000	1.100	11,275,000
Totals	$55,000,000		$54,333,750

- Reported losses (Column 1) and Loss Development Factors (Column 2) are taken from Exhibit 11-3.
- Column (3) = Column (1) × Column (2).

The loss development factors calculated in Exhibit 11-4 are for the dollar amount of losses. Development factors can be derived in the same manner for the number of claims.

Exhibit 11-5 shows for each year the developed number of claims, the developed amount of losses, and the average amount per claim severity.

EXHIBIT 11-5

Developed Losses and Developed Claims

(1) Year	(2) Developed Losses	(3) Developed Number of Claims	(4) Average Claim
1	$11,000,000	9,167	$1,200
2	10,287,750	7,913	1,300
3	11,112,000	7,880	1,410
4	10,659,000	6,995	1,524
5	11,275,000	6,860	1,644
Totals	$54,333,750	38,815	$1,400

- The developed number of claims in Column (3) would be derived through the use of loss triangles similar to those in Exhibit 11-3, using number of claims instead of loss amounts. The process is not illustrated in this chapter.
- The total in Column (4), $1,400, is a weighted average of the amount of claims, using the number of claims as weights. Alternatively, it can be calculated by dividing the total number of claims (38,815) into the total amount of losses ($54,333,750).

Trending

Loss development is an attempt to correct for errors in reporting past losses and to estimate the ultimate settlement value of reported losses. An estimate of losses for a future period is needed for ratemaking purposes. The purpose of trending is to adjust the developed losses from the experience period to reflect conditions that are expected in a future period. The current practice in the U.S. insurance business is to make the adjustment by projecting past trends into the future.

An examination of Exhibit 11-5 shows that severity (the average amount of claims) was on an upward trend during the experience period. However, as shown in Exhibit 11-6, the decrease in the number of claims resulted from a decline in earned exposure units over the period.

A statistical technique known as least-squares regression is frequently used to project these trends into the future. Two methods of trending are in general use in the United States: linear trending and exponential trending.

EXHIBIT 11-6

Calculation of Claims Frequency

(1) Year	(2) Developed Number of Claims	(3) Earned Car-Years	(4) Frequency
1	9,167	458,350	2.00
2	7,913	386,000	2.05
3	7,880	380,676	2.07
4	6,995	333,095	2.10
5	6,860	325,118	2.11
Totals	38,815	1,883,239	2.06

- Column (4) represents claims per 100 earned car-years (4) = (2) ÷ [(3) ÷ 100].
- The total in Column (4), 2.06, is the average frequency.

The actual claim frequency, measured in claims per 100 earned car-years, actually rose slightly, from 2.00 to 2.11.

Linear Trending

Linear trending assumes that the statistical series being trended will increase or decrease by a fixed amount each year. For example, frequency will increase by a fixed number of claims per unit, and severity (the average amount of claims) will increase by a fixed number of dollars each year.

Exponential Trending

Exponential trending assumes that the statistical series being projected will increase or decrease by a fixed percentage, rather than a fixed amount, each

Linear trending
A method of trending that assumes a fixed amount of increase or decrease for each period, the amount being either in dollars or number of claims.

Exponential trending
A method of trending that assumes a fixed percentage increase or decrease for each period.

year. Exponential trending will result in higher projected losses than linear trending in virtually all cases. Consequently, it will result in higher insurance rates in virtually all cases, all other things being equal. The differences can be substantial.

The choice between the two methods should be based on either theoretical grounds or observation of the trend indicated by the data to be projected. If the data series seems to be increasing or decreasing in a straight line, linear trending is recommended. If the rate of change appears to be accelerating, exponential trending may be appropriate.

Some theoretical basis exists for using exponential trending for claims severity. Inflation, which is an exponential process, is a major factor in increasing severity. However, generally little theoretical basis exists for using exponential trending for claims frequency. Its use for frequency should be supported by empirical data.

A detailed explanation of the mathematics of trending is beyond the scope of this chapter. Exhibit 11-7 shows the results of applying both linear and exponential trending to the frequency and severity figures from Exhibits 11-5 and 11-6.

Exponential trending produces both higher frequency and higher severity in comparison with linear trending. This is usually the case, but linear trending may produce higher results in some rare instances.

The projected frequency figures in Exhibit 11-7 show that the frequency for any data point is found by multiplying the preceding frequency by 1.0031. The comparable multiplier for severity (average claim) is 1.0202. Because aggregate claims result from both frequency and severity, a combined trend factor can be found by multiplying the two together. That combined factor is 1.023 (1.0031 × 1.0202), rounded to three decimal places. This indicates that aggregate losses increase by 2.3 percent each quarter, on the average.

Consequently, the percentage increase for sixteen quarters would be found by raising 1.023 to the sixteenth power.	$(1.023^{16})=1.439$
If the developed aggregate losses from the bottom of Column (2) in Exhibit 11-5 are multiplied by this increase...	× $54,333,750
the product is the developed and trended losses at Year 7 levels.	= $78,186,266
Dividing the earned car years from Exhibit 11-6 into the developed and trended losses...	÷ 1,883,239
yields the estimated statewide average pure premium for Year 7. An expenses loading must be added to arrive at the gross rate.	= $41.52

The insurer for which these rates are being calculated has the following underwriting expenses, all stated as a percentage of the gross rate:

Commissions and brokerage	15.0%
Other acquisition	1.0
General administration	5.0
Taxes, licenses, and fees	2.0
Profit and contingencies	2.0
Total	25.0%

In this example, loss adjustment expenses are included with losses. The gross rate is figured as follows:

$$\text{Gross rate} = \frac{\text{Pure premium}}{1 - \text{Expense ratio}} = \frac{41.52}{1 - 0.25} = \frac{41.52}{0.75} = \$55.36$$

This is the **statewide average rate**, which is used as the basis for calculating rates for various territories and rating classes. However, before those calculations are made, the statewide average rate is again calculated, using the loss ratio method. Only one of the two methods would be used in an actual rate filing. Both are used here for instructional purposes.

To use the loss ratio method, premium data are required. Exhibit 11-8 shows such data, along with the raw reported loss data, loss ratios, and statewide average rates for each year. Although Exhibit 11-8 shows premiums, losses, and loss ratios for the experience period, those figures must be adjusted before they are used in the formula for the loss ratio method. A new loss ratio will be calculated for use as the actual loss ratio in that formula. The losses used in that ratio will be the developed and trended losses as calculated previously in the pure premium method, $78,186,266.

The premiums in Exhibit 11-8 also cannot be used directly in the loss ratio method. The goal in ratemaking is to determine whether the present rates need to be changed, but the premiums in Exhibit 11-8 were based on several different rate levels used over time, not all on the current rate level. What is needed are premiums based on the *present* rate level, usually referred to in actuarial literature as "premiums on level" or "premiums on rate level." In this case, premiums on level are easy to calculate. The number of earned exposure units (1,883,239) and the current statewide average rate ($44.63) are known. Consequently, premiums on level can be determined by multiplying the two ($84,048,957). Therefore, the actual loss ratio is as follows:

$$\text{Actual loss ratio (A)} = \frac{78,186,266}{84,048,957} = 0.93 \text{ or } 93\%.$$

Because the company has an expense ratio of 25 percent, its expected loss ratio is 75 percent. Given the loss ratio method formula from the preceding chapter, the rate modification factor is calculated as follows:

$$\text{Rate change} = \frac{A - E}{E} = \frac{0.93 - 0.75}{0.75} = \frac{0.18}{0.75} = 0.24 \text{ or } 24\%.$$

EXHIBIT 11-7

Trending Results: Frequency and Severity

12-Month Period	Actual Frequency	Actual Severity
3/31/1	1.98	$1,125
6/30/1	1.97	1,175
9/30/1	2.02	1,195
12/31/1	2.00	1,200
3/31/2	2.04	1,210
6/30/2	2.02	1,290
9/30/2	2.06	1,275
12/31/2	2.05	1,300
3/31/3	2.03	1,295
6/30/3	2.06	1,325
9/30/3	2.08	1,400
12/31/3	2.07	1,410
3/31/4	2.11	1,420
6/30/4	2.08	1,405
9/30/4	2.07	1,490
12/31/4	2.10	1,530
3/31/5	2.09	1,560
6/30/5	2.08	1,620
9/30/5	2.10	1,670
12/31/5	2.11	1,660

| | Projected Frequency | | Projected Severity | |
	Linear	Exponential	Linear	Exponential
3/31/6	2.123	2.124	$1,668.95	$1,688.76
6/30/6	2.129	2.131	1,696.68	1,722.87
9/30/6	2.135	2.138	1,724.41	1,757.67
12/31/6	2.141	2.145	1,752.15	1,793.17
3/31/7	2.147	2.152	1,779.88	1,829.39
6/30/7	2.153	2.159	1,807.61	1,866.34
9/30/7	2.159	2.166	1,835.34	1,904.04
12/31/7	2.165	2.173	1,863.07	1,942.50

Both the frequency data and the severity data have been restated in this exhibit to show twenty moving twelve-month periods, one ending each quarter, in lieu of the five annual periods shown in earlier exhibits. This is a common practice in trending calculations. Also, the moving-average presentation of the data helps to smooth chance variations in data, making the true trend more apparent.

The data can be used to adjust the developed aggregate loss data to the levels anticipated during Year 7, the year when the new rates will be used. The midpoint of the experience period for which data were collected is 6/30/3, and the midpoint of the year in which the rates will be used is 6/30/7. Consequently, the developed loss data must be projected, on the average, four years (or sixteen quarters) in the trending process.

Projected frequency and severity were calculated using least-squares regression. The details of these calculations are beyond the scope of this text.

EXHIBIT 11-8

Data for Loss Ratio Method (000s omitted)

(1) Year	(2) Premiums Earned	(3) Reported Losses Incurred	(4) Reported Loss Ratio	(5) Statewide Average Rate
1	$14,286	$11,000	77%	$31.17
2	14,333	10,750	75	37.13
3	15,190	12,000	79	39.88
4	14,865	11,000	74	44.63
5	14,510	10,250	71	44.63
Totals	$73,184	$55,000	75%	$39.49

- Column (3) figures come from Exhibit 11-4.
- Column (5) figures were taken from prior rate filings.
- The statewide average rate for Year 6, the year during which the rates are being calculated for Year 7, has remained at $44.63, the same as for Year 4 and Year 5 (see highlighted numbers).

Therefore, the new rate is 1.24 × 44.63 = $55.34, which is virtually the same as the rate calculated by the pure premium. Actually, the two rates should be identical. The difference is due solely to rounding in the calculation.

It can be shown algebraically that the pure premium method and the loss ratio method are mathematically equivalent. However, the proof is beyond the scope of this chapter.

If earned exposure units were not available, as is frequently the case when the loss ratio method is used, the on-level adjustment of premiums would have been calculated by a different technique. Exhibit 11-9 and the paragraphs that follow illustrate that technique. Some simplifying assumptions have been made in this illustration to avoid undue complexity. These assumptions are (1) all rate filings are effective on January 1, and (2) all policies are one-year policies and are also effective on January 1. If these assumptions are not met, which is common, the technique would be somewhat more complex.

The purpose of this technique is to adjust reported earned premiums for all rate changes that occurred after the policies were written. The premiums for Year 5 and Year 6 did not require any adjustment, because no subsequent rate changes occurred.

Multiplying the actual earned premium for each year by the index for that year yields the estimated earned premiums at the present rate level. In this case, this technique provides a result that is very close to the exact calculation using earned exposure units. This high level of accuracy results in part from the simplified assumptions used in this example.

EXHIBIT 11-9

On-Level Premium Adjustment Using a Rate Level Index

(1) Year	(2) Reported Earned Premiums	(3) Statewide Average Rate	(4) Annual Rate Change	(5) Rate Level Index	(6) Premiums on Level	
1	$14,286,000	$31.17	—	1.431	$20,443,266	Column (4) shows the annual rate changes, and Column (5) shows a rate change index computed from the annual rate changes. The rate change index for Year 1 is calculated by 1.191×1.074 $\times 1.119 \times 1.000 \times 1.000$ $= 1.431$: for Year 2, it is 1.074 $\times 1.119 \times 1.000 \times 1.000$ $= 1.202$, and so forth.
2	14,333,000	37.13	0.191	1.202	17,228,266	
3	15,190,000	39.88	0.074	1.119	16,997,610	
4	14,865,000	44.63	0.119	1.000	14,865,000	
5	14,510,000	44.63	0.000	1.000	14,510,00	
6	—	44.63	0.000	1.000	—	
Totals	$73,184,000				$84,044,142	

- Column (2) figures taken from Exhibit 11-8.
- In Column (3), no rate change occurred in Year 5.
- Column (4) shows statewide average rate Year 2 ÷ Statewide average rate Year 1, etc. − 1.

Territorial Relativities

The next step in preparing a rate schedule is to determine territorial relativities. Insurers use several techniques for determining territorial relativities, including the much-used technique outlined here.

Exhibit 11-10 shows the basic data for this calculation. Three rating territories are in the state, and Exhibit 11-10 shows the data separately for each territory. Territorial relativities are calculated by comparing the estimated incurred loss ratio for each territory to the statewide average loss ratio. The earned premium figure used in the loss ratio is calculated on the basis of the statewide average rate currently in use, and not on the territorial rate now in use. In this instance, the premiums at statewide average rate level were calculated by multiplying the earned exposure units by the statewide average rate.

The initial territorial relativities are shown in Column (7) of Exhibit 11-10. Territory 3 is very small, with only 807 claims incurred during the experience period of Column (5). This is not a sufficient number of claims to give full confidence to the initial relativity. With that small number of claims, the loss experience could be expected to vary rather widely over time. To reduce chance variations in the relativity for Territory 3, a credibility factor has been introduced into the calculation. In this example, the statewide data and the data for Territories 1 and 2 are sufficient for full credibility. Consequently, no credibility calculation is required for them.

EXHIBIT 11-10

Calculation of Territorial Relativities

(1) Territory	(2) Developed and Trended Losses (Dollars)	(3) Premiums[1] on Level at Statewide Average Rate (Dollars)	(4) Earned Exposure Units	(5) Developed Number of Claims	(6) Loss[3] Ratio	(7) Initial[4] Terr. Rel.	(8) Cred. Factor	(9) Cred. Weighted Terr. Rel.	(10) Terr.[6] Average Rate
1	$43,283,841	$43,065,228	964,939	20,586	100.5%	1.086	1.00	1.086	$60.12
2	33,435,196	38,982,074	873,450	17,422	85.8	0.923	1.00	0.923	51.10
3	1,467,229	2,001,655	44,850	807[2]	73.3	0.788	0.80	0.830[5]	45.95
Statewide	$78,186,266	$84,048,957	1,883,239	38,815	93.0%	1.000	1.00	1.000	$55.36[7]

1. The premiums in this column were calculated by multiplying the earned exposure units in Column (4) by the current statewide average rate of $44.63.

2. Territory 3 is very small, with only 807 claims incurred during the experience period of Column (5). This is not a sufficient number of claims to give full confidence to the initial relativity.

3. (6) = (2) ÷ (3)

4. $(7) = \dfrac{\text{Territory loss ratio from Column (6)}}{\text{Statewide loss ratio from Column (6)}}$

5. $(0.788 \times 0.80) + (1.00 \times 0.20)$. See text for explanation.

6. $55.36 \times (9)$

7. Calculated on page 11.13.

Class Relativities

Class relativities are calculated in the same manner as territorial relativities. In this example, there are three rating classes. Exhibit 11-11 shows the calculation of class relativities. The final relativities are shown in Column (7) of Exhibit 11-11. A rate table showing rates for each territory and class can now be calculated, as shown in Exhibit 11-12. This completes the ratemaking process for this example. The principles illustrated here are applicable to most lines of property-liability insurance, but some modifications in the process may be needed in some lines. Those are discussed in later sections of this chapter.

Even for auto liability insurance, some variations are possible and may even be necessary in some cases. For example, consumer organizations and some regulators have objected to the expense loading technique used in the preceding example. When the expense loading is stated as a percentage of the gross premium, as was done in the preceding example, persons with higher expected losses pay a larger amount of expenses as well.

Using the rates calculated in Exhibit 11-12, a person in Territory 1, Rating Class C, would pay $30.51 (0.25 × $122.04) for the company's underwriting expenses, while a person in Territory 3, Class A, would pay only $8.49. One way to reduce this difference is to state some of the expenses as a flat dollar amount, which does not vary with expected losses. Assume, for example, that the company used in the preceding illustration concluded that it needed a flat $3.33 per car-year

EXHIBIT 11-11

Calculation of Class Relativities

(1) Rating Class	(2) Developed and Trended Losses	(3) Premiums on Level at Statewide Average Rate	(4) Earned Exposure Units	(5) Developed Number of Claims	(6) Loss Ratio	(7) Initial Class Rel.	(8) Cred. Factor	(9) Cred. Weighted Class Rel.	(10) Class Average Rate
A	$27,811,791	$40,484,676	907,118	15,421	68.7%	0.739	1.00	0.739	$ 40.91
B	26,670,223	31,011,513	694,858	13,897	86.0	0.925	1.00	0.925	51.21
C	23,704,252	12,552,768	281,263	9,497	188.8	2.030	1.00	2.030	112.38
Statewide	$78,186,266	$84,048,957	1,883,239	38,815	93.0%	1.000	1.00	1.000	$ 5.36

- The premiums in Column (3) were calculated by multiplying the earned exposure units in Column (4) by the statewide average rate of $44.63 currently in use.
- This formula is used to determine the Loss Ratio in Column (6): (6) = [(2) ÷ (3)] × 100.
- This formula is used to determine the Initial Class Relativity in Column (7):

$$\text{Class relativity} = \frac{\text{Class loss ratio from Column (6)}}{\text{Statewide loss ratio from Column (6)}}$$

- The final relativities are shown in Column (7).
- The text and Exhibit 11-11 explain the Credibility Factor in Column (8).
- The following formula is used to determine Column (10) Class Average Rates: $55.36 × (9).

EXHIBIT 11-12

Final Rate Table Showing Rates by Territory and Class

(1) Territory	(2) All Classes[1] Combined	(3) Class[2] A	(4) Class[2] B	(5) Class[2] C
1	$60.12	$44.43	$55.61	$122.04
2	51.10	37.76	47.27	103.73
3	45.95	33.96	42.50	93.28
All Territories Combined	$55.36	$40.91	$51.21	$112.38

Using a 0.25 underwriting expense loading, individuals would pay different amounts based on their territory and class for the company's underwriting expense:

- Territory 1, Rating Class C, would pay $30.51 (0.25 × $122.04).
- Territory 3, Rating Class A, would pay $8.49 (0.25 × $33.96). An alternative is to create a flat dollar amount.

1. From Exhibit 11-10, Column (10).
2. Calculated by multiplying the rate for all classes combined, Column (2), by the appropriate class relativity factor from Exhibit 11-11.

for general administration and other acquisition costs and 19 percent of gross premium for commissions, taxes, profit, and contingencies.

In that case, the class and territorial relativities would be applied to the pure premium, producing a table of pure premiums like the one shown in Exhibit 11-13. The pure premiums for each territory and class are then loaded for expenses. This calculation is shown in Exhibit 11-14. The state-wide average gross rate for all classes and territories combined is the same in Exhibit 11-14 as in Exhibit 11-12. The gross rates for the lowest-rated territories and classes have been increased slightly, while the rates for the highest-rated territories and classes have been reduced. In most states, the differences in gross rates between the lowest-rated territories and classes and the highest-rated ones would be much greater than in this example. Conse-quently, the changes in rates from using some fixed-dollar expense loading might be somewhat greater than shown here.

EXHIBIT 11-13

Pure Premiums by Class and Territory

(1)	(2)	(3)	(4)	(5)
		Rating Class		
Territory	All Classes Combined	Class A	Class B	Class C
1	$45.09	$33.32	$41.71	$91.53
2	38.32	28.32	35.45	77.79
3	34.46	25.47	31.88	69.95
All Territories Combined	$41.52[1]	$30.68	$38.41	$84.29

1. From page 11.13.

Another possible variation would be the selection of the experience period from which data were drawn. An experience period of five years was used in the preceding examples. A shorter period, ranging from one to three years, might be used. A longer period has the advantage of smoothing chance variations in losses and promoting rate stability. This advantage is offset, at least in part, because a long experience period tends to conceal important developing trends and, therefore, reduces the responsiveness of rates to environmental changes. Of course, the experience period should be sufficiently long so that the resulting data set is large enough to have substantial credibility.

COMPARISON OF RATEMAKING METHODS

The foregoing example relied primarily on the pure premium method of ratemaking. The loss ratio method was introduced briefly, partly to demon-strate that the two methods produce the same rates when the same data are

EXHIBIT 11-14

Gross Rates by Class and Territory

(1)	(2)	(3)	(4)	(5)
		Rating Class		
Territory	All Classes Combined	Class A	Class B	Class C
1	$59.78	$45.25	$55.60	$117.11
2	51.42	39.07	47.88	100.15
3	46.65	35.56	43.47	90.47
All Territories Combined	$55.37	$41.99	$51.53	$108.17

The rating class gross rates were calculated from the pure premiums by territory and class from Exhibit 11-13 using the formula:

$$\text{Gross rate} = \frac{\text{Pure premium} + 3.33}{1 - 0.19}$$

used in both. Despite their mathematical similarities, the pure premium method has some practical advantages over the loss ratio method. For example, using a mixed expense loading, part fixed dollar and part percentage, is difficult in the loss ratio method but simple in the pure premium method. Because mixed expense loadings are likely to be common in the future, the pure premium method may have a substantial advantage.

On the other hand, the pure premium method cannot be used unless meaningful exposure unit data are obtained. Therefore, the loss ratio method will likely continue in use for the foreseeable future for some property insurance lines, such as inland marine insurance, in which the insured exposures are so variable that they virtually preclude the collection of meaningful exposure unit data.

The judgment method of ratemaking, used alone, has limited application. It is used primarily in ocean marine, aviation, and some inland marine lines. However, judgment is an important part of the ratemaking process for all lines of insurance. For example, selecting an experience period is largely a matter of judgment, with statistical analysis playing only a minor role.

Although trending is based on statistical procedures, primarily regression analysis, the choice between linear trending and exponential trending (and possibly other variations) is based largely on actuarial judgment. Loss development factors are also heavily influenced by judgment in most cases.

Ratemaking processes for some lines of insurance use all three ratemaking methods to one degree or another. In workers compensation ratemaking, for example, the loss ratio method is used to determine the statewide average rate increase or decrease, while the pure premium method is used to determine class relativities. Of course, judgment is used in several phases of the process, such as trending and developing credibility factors. Such combination methods, using two or all three of the basic techniques, might become even more common as the insurance environment continues to increase in complexity.

OTHER LINES OF INSURANCE

The basic principles discussed up to this point and applied in the foregoing auto insurance example apply to all lines of property-casualty insurance. However, the details of application may vary widely from one line to another. These variations may result from characteristics of the loss exposures insured, regulatory requirements, political considerations, or other factors.

Experience Period

Although an experience period of one to three years is common for automobile insurance and other liability lines, a five-year experience period is used almost universally for fire insurance. The reason for that choice is simple: it is required by law in many states. However, the five years are usually not given equal weight. The most recent years in the experience period are given greater weight to promote rate responsiveness.

The experience period for extended coverage is even longer, frequently twenty years or more. The purpose of that long experience period is to avoid the large swings in insurance costs that would otherwise result when a major hurricane or a series of major tornadoes strike an area.

In summary, the factors to be considered in determining the appropriate experience period are (1) legal requirements, if any, (2) the variability of losses over time, and (3) the credibility of the resulting ratemaking data. Of course, items (2) and (3) are related to some degree.

Loss Development

The loss development technique illustrated in the preceding auto insurance example is applicable to all lines of insurance. However, the desirability of loss development varies from one line to another. Loss development is essential for most lines of liability insurance because of the long delay in loss settlement and the resulting large accumulation of loss reserves. An error in estimating the loss reserves could result in a substantial error in rates, because the incurred losses used in ratemaking may include a substantial proportion of reserves for open claims.

However, losses for fire, inland marine, and auto physical damage insurance are settled much more quickly. Consequently, the loss reserves for those lines tend to be a relatively small part of incurred losses. Also, open claims for those lines can be estimated more accurately than liability losses. Consequently, loss development factors are frequently not used in the ratemaking process for those lines.

Trending

Trending practices also vary by line of insurance. For liability lines, trending claims frequency and claims severity (as measured by the average claim amount) is common. For fire insurance, the frequency is low and generally very stable, so trending is restricted to severity. However, the average claim is not used as a measure of severity because the average fire insurance claim is likely to be distorted by infrequent, very large claims. Consequently, a composite index, composed partly of a construction cost index and partly of the consumer price index, is used for trending.

In fire insurance, trending both losses and premiums is necessary. Losses are trended in part to reflect the effects of inflation on claims costs. However, inflation also increases the values of the properties insured, and people tend to increase the amount of insurance to reflect the increased values. This increases insurer premium income. If the amounts of insurance kept pace perfectly with inflation, there would be no need to trend losses for inflation. However, the increases in insured amounts tend to lag somewhat behind inflation. Consequently, insurers have adopted the practices of trending both losses and premiums and offsetting the growth in premiums against the growth in losses. Premiums are also trended in other lines of insurance for which the exposure units are affected by inflation. Examples include workers compensation and some general liability lines.

A somewhat unique trending problem exists in workers compensation insurance. Because the benefits for that line are established by statute, they can change rather suddenly, and sometimes unexpectedly, when the legislature is in session. A law amendment factor is calculated to adjust rates and losses to reflect changes in the statutory benefits.

The law amendment factor is calculated on the basis of a standardized workers compensation injury table and a standardized wage distribution table. The injury table shows the probability of workers incurring specified kinds of injuries, the probabilities of their being disabled for specified periods of time, and the probabilities of their incurring specified amounts of medical expenses. The standardized wage table shows the probabilities that injured workers' wages will fall within certain ranges.

By combining the two tables, it is possible to estimate with reasonable accuracy the effects of a statutory benefit change on the losses insurers will incur under their policies. Unlike other trending, rate increases resulting from statutory benefit changes may apply to outstanding policies as well as renewals.

For boiler and machinery insurance, some expenses are trended. The loss control expenses for that line exceed the amount paid to settle losses. Thus, trending is desirable for those expenses because they constitute such a large share of the rate.

Large Loss Limitations

In using loss data for ratemaking purposes, one must guard against unusual rate fluctuations resulting from occasional large losses, whether from large individual losses or from an accumulation of smaller losses from a single event, such as a hurricane. In liability insurance, this problem is controlled by using only basic limits losses in calculating incurred losses. Basic limits losses are losses capped at some predetermined dollar amount, such as $25,000.

A similar practice is followed in ratemaking for workers compensation insurance. No basic limits exist for that line, so individual claims are limited to a specified amount for ratemaking purposes. In addition to the limitation on an individual claim, another limitation applies to multiple claims arising from a single event. Both limitations vary over time and by state.

Loss limitations also apply in ratemaking for property insurance. When a very large single loss occurs in fire insurance, only a part of it is included in ratemaking calculations in the state in which it occurred. The balance is spread over the rates of all the states. The amount included within the state depends on the total fire insurance premium volume in the state, so it varies substantially by state.

Most losses from catastrophe events, such as hurricanes, are excluded from ratemaking data and replaced by a flat catastrophe charge in the rates. The amount of the catastrophe charge is determined by data collected over a long period of time to smooth the fluctuations that would otherwise result from such catastrophes.

Credibility

The concept of credibility is the same for all lines of insurance, but the applications of that concept vary widely by line. In automobile insurance, it is usual to assume that statewide experience is fully credible. That assumption may not be appropriate for some small insurers who base their rates on their own data alone. Even some large territories and rating classes may not be fully credible. For those territories and classes that are not fully credible, rates are calculated as a weighted average of the indicated rate for the territory or class and the statewide average rate for all classes and territories combined, using the credibility factor as the weight in the weighted average. This is the procedure followed in the auto insurance example in a previous section of this chapter.

For fire insurance, even the statewide loss experience may not be fully credible. In that case, a three-part weighted average is used, combining the state experience for the rating class, regional experience of the rating class, and state experience of a major group encompassing several rating classes. Again, credibility factors are used as weights.

Pure premiums for workers compensation insurance are composed of three separate charges: a pure premium for medical costs, a pure premium for nonserious injuries, and a pure premium for serious injuries. A separate credibility table exists for each of these categories.

RATE FILINGS

The final product of the ratemaking process is a rate filing. A rate filing is a document prepared for and submitted to state regulatory authorities. The states vary as to the amount of information required in a filing and the form in which they require it to be prepared. In general, the filing must include at least the following:

1. A schedule of the proposed new rates

2. A statement about the percentage change, either an increase or a decrease, in the statewide average rate

3. If the same percentage change does not apply to the rates for all territories and rating classes, an explanation of the differences

4. Necessary statistics to support the proposed rate changes, including territorial and class relativities

5. If investment income is reflected directly in the rates, an illustration of the necessary calculations

6. Expense loading data

7. Sufficient explanatory material to enable state insurance regulatory personnel to understand and evaluate the filing

The rate filing may be transmitted to the authorities by mail or by hand delivery. Depending on state law, formal approval of the filing by regulatory authorities may not be required. In some states, approval must be obtained before the rates are used. In other states, formal approval is not required by law, but many insurers prefer to obtain approval before use to avoid the possibility of having to withdraw the rates later if the authorities decide that they do not meet statutory requirements.

An insurer should keep a log of all rate filings it submits to authorities. A log is especially necessary if formal approval of filings is required or desired. The log can be used to help keep track of filings so that the insurer can follow up if approval is not received in a timely manner. The log should show the date that the filing was submitted, the date of any follow-up by the company, the date any request for additional information or other contact is received from the authorities, and the date approval is received.

The actuarial department, either with or without assistance from the legal department, frequently conducts negotiations with the state insurance departments regarding rate filings. This seems like a logical approach, because actuaries are best qualified to answer any technical questions that the regulatory authorities may raise. However, some insurers prefer to delegate most of the contacts to the legal department and to call in actuaries only as needed.

Advisory Prospective Loss Costs

In the past, many insurers, especially smaller ones, depended on advisory organizations, sometimes called rating bureaus, to calculate rates, prepare rate filings, submit the rate filings to state regulatory authorities, and obtain approval of the filings. However, advisory organizations have now discontinued the calculation of rates in most states and calculate and file prospective loss costs instead. Prospective loss costs are simply loss data that have been modified by necessary loss development, trending, and credibility processes, not including expenses.

The advisory organizations calculate the advisory loss costs, prepare the necessary filings, and submit them to the state insurance departments as required. Each insurer that is a member of or subscriber to the advisory organization can then use the advisory prospective loss costs by adding its own expense loading, based either on its own expense data or on industry data.

This process requires most insurers, especially smaller ones, to take an active role in preparing and filing rates. Consulting actuarial firms are willing to perform such services, but the expense of such services encourages many companies to take a do-it-yourself approach to the task.

SUMMARY

The first step in the ratemaking process is the collection of data. The data to be collected include incurred losses, earned premiums, the number of claims incurred, and earned exposure units. Such data are best accumulated gradually as policies and endorsements are issued and as claims are reported and paid. Consequently, an insurer should decide early in its existence what data will be collected and the form in which that data will be collected.

The policy-year method is the most accurate method for collecting ratemaking statistics. It is also the most expensive method and involves a longer delay than the other methods. A policy year consists of all policies issued during a year. The incurred losses consist of all of the losses covered under those policies. The earned premiums consist of all premiums under those policies, including additional premiums under endorsements, premium audits, and retrospective rating adjustments. Thus, the incurred losses are tied directly to the premiums that were intended to pay them.

The calendar-year method is the least accurate method of collecting ratemaking statistics. However, the statistics are available quickly and with little additional expense because they are taken from the company's accounting records. This method is inaccurate primarily because incurred losses must be estimated from paid losses and loss reserves. Such estimates may be grossly inaccurate because of changes in reserves for outstanding losses.

The accident-year method of collecting ratemaking statistics is a compromise between the other two methods. It preserves most of the accuracy advantages of the policy-year method while achieving most of the speed and economy of the calendar-year method. The incurred losses for the accident-year method consist of all claims arising from insured events that occurred during the year, whether closed or open. The earned premiums are the same as for the calendar-year method.

After statistics have been collected, they must be adjusted before rates can be calculated. First, losses must be developed, a process intended to recognize consistent patterns in the accuracy of estimating loss reserves. Next, the trending process is applied to project the losses to the midpoint of the period in which the rates will be used. Earned premiums must also be adjusted to the current rate level.

When these adjustments have been made, the statewide average rate can be calculated, using either the loss ratio method or the pure premium method. Although the two methods can be shown to be mathematically equivalent, the pure premium method may enjoy some practical advantages. The pure premium method requires one additional step (the addition of an expense loading) in comparison with the loss ratio method.

Finally, territorial and class relativities must be determined so that rates for various classes and territories can be calculated. Credibility procedures may be applied at several stages of the ratemaking process to minimize the adverse effects of random fluctuations in losses.

The steps outlined above and the principles that underlie them are applicable to all lines of property-casualty insurance, although the details of application may differ by line.

Most advisory organizations no longer calculate final rates for the insurers they serve. Rather, prospective loss costs are developed by the advisory organizations. Insurers then load these loss costs with a provision for their expenses and profit requirements.

Chapter 12

Direct Your Learning

Insurer Financial Management

After learning the subject matter of this chapter, you should be able to:

- Explain the purpose of loss reserves.
- Describe the methods used to establish case reserves.
- Describe the methods used to calculate IBNR.
- Given a case, explain how loss triangles can be used for loss reserve analysis.
- Explain the debate over the use of discounted loss reserves.
- Explain the purpose of loss reserve analysis and verification.
- Explain how insurer planning can be supported by mathematical models.
- Explain the issues and factors an insurer must consider in aligning a reinsurance program with its goals.
- Explain the principal elements to be considered in an actuarial appraisal of an insurer.
- Describe the approach A.M. Best uses to evaluate insurers.
- Describe the operation and significance of the NAIC RBC model.
- Describe the components of the NAIC IRIS system.

Develop Your Perspective

What are the main topics covered in the chapter?

Important financial management activities, including loss reserve analysis, planning, and analysis of reinsurance requirements, are addressed in this chapter. Also addressed are the measurements by which insurers are evaluated for their financial strength, stability, and profitability.

Judge the financial management of an insurer.

- How can you determine the financial strength and stability of the insurer?

Why is it important to know these topics?

The financial management of an insurance company is crucial to its ability to effectively pay claims and expenses, invest to build financial strength, provide a return to investors and offer services to policyholders. Standard ratings of insurers help outsiders assess the insurer's ability to manage its finances.

Evaluate the necessity of the financial management activities as they are described in this chapter.

- What would be the consequences for an insurer if it failed to perform any of the activities?

How can you use this information?

Determine your own company's financial management actions and ratings.

- What financial management activities and methods are applied?

- Who in the organization performs these activities?

- What is the financial rating assigned to your company, and what does the rating mean?

Chapter 12

Insurer Financial Management

Insurance companies are financial intermediaries. Financial intermediation occurs when surplus funds from individuals, businesses, or governments are made available to others. Commercial and savings banks, savings and loans, credit unions, pension funds, and investment companies (mutual funds) are other examples of financial intermediaries.

At the end of 2000, the total assets under the control of U.S. property-casualty insurers totaled more than $912 billion. Total premiums written amounted to more than $299 billion. Policyholders' surplus was more than $317 billion.[1]

The magnitude of funds under the control of insurance companies and the public's dependence on the insurance product make the financial department an integral operation of an insurance company. This chapter focuses on financial management activities other than investment. These activities are primarily aimed at assisting insurer management in making better decisions. Many insurers rely on their actuarial staff to study these decisions because of the mathematics underlying them. The activities considered in this chapter are (1) loss reserve analysis and verification, (2) planning, (3) analysis of reinsurance requirements, and (4) evaluation of insurers. Closely related to those topics is how insurers are viewed by others. The rating system that A.M. Best Company uses and the tools regulators use are fundamental to this understanding.

LOSS RESERVE ANALYSIS AND VERIFICATION

Loss reserves represent the largest liability on the insurer's balance sheet. Accurate loss reserving is crucial, particularly as the property-casualty industry shifts from a predominately property insurance business to a predominately liability insurance business. Loss reserving consists primarily of establishing case reserves incurred but not reported, and of analyzing and verifying already established reserves.

Case Reserves

The analysis of loss reserves begins with the case reserves. **Case reserves** are reserves established on each individual claim as it is reported. The claim department usually establishes these reserves, but the actuarial department

Case reserves
Loss reserves established for individual claims as they are reported to the insurer.

may assist in some complex cases. Three methods, with variations of each, are used in establishing case reserves: (1) the average value method, (2) the judgment method, and (3) the tabular method. A fourth method, the loss ratio method, is also sometimes used. However, it is not properly classified as a case reserving method because it deals with aggregate reserves rather than individual cases.

The case reserving method used is determined to a large degree by the nature of the line of insurance concerned. More than one method may be used for the same line of insurance in some cases. For example, some companies may use an average value reserve for liability claims when they are first reported. That reserve is then adjusted upward or downward, based on judgment or the tabular method, as more information becomes available.

For some lines of insurance, it may be desirable to divide the losses into homogeneous groups and analyze each group separately. Commercial multiple peril coverage is one example of such a line. The property losses under this line are settled much more quickly than the liability losses. Also, the final payment is likely to differ from the original reserve by a smaller amount for property losses than for liability losses. Consequently, the accuracy of the reserve analysis is likely to be improved if the property loss reserves and the liability loss reserves are analyzed separately.

Average Value Method

Average value method
Method of developing case reserves that applies a predetermined dollar amount of reserve to each claim as it is reported.

When the **average value method** is used, a predetermined dollar amount of reserve is established for each claim as it is reported. This average value may apply to all claims within a line of insurance, such as physical damage for private passenger automobile insurance, or it may vary by risk class within the line. For lines of insurance with relatively small variations in loss size and relatively short delays in loss settlement, such as automobile physical damage, the average value reserve may not be changed during the life of the claim. For example, every physical damage claim may be reserved at $750 until the claim is closed. For other lines, an average value reserve may be established when a claim is first reported, and then later adjusted, either upward or downward, as more complete information becomes available. For example, every automobile bodily injury claim may be reserved at an average value of $2,000 when reported, with that reserve to be replaced with an individually estimated reserve within ninety days.

The average values used in this reserving method are usually based on the insurer's past average claims developed and trended to reflect current conditions. If the insurer's past data are not adequate for that purpose, the average factors may be based on judgment, or industry data may be used.

Judgment method
Method of developing case reserves that relies on claim department personnel to estimate the reserve for a claim.

Judgment Method

When the **judgment method** is used, a person in the claim department estimates the amount that will eventually be paid to settle the claim, and a reserve is set up in that amount. The reserve may be established solely on the judgment of the person involved, or management may establish some guidelines to assist in the process. Some insurers have recently used expert systems to assist in establishing case reserves. An expert system, in this application, is a computer program containing rules to assist in estimating loss and loss expense reserves. The details of a particular claim are entered into the computer, and the program applies the appropriate rules to estimate the amount of the claim and the amount of allocated loss expenses. An expert system provides greater consistency in reserving than a pure judgment-based system.

Tabular Method

The **tabular method** is based on the use of actuarial tables and an assumed interest rate to calculate the present value of a claim. This method may be used for claims that involve a series of fixed or determinable payments to the claimant over a prolonged period of time. For example, some disability insurance claims may require payment of a fixed sum over a period of many years, provided the claimant remains alive and disabled. That is, the payments will be terminated if the claimant dies or recovers from the disabling condition. Calculating the present value of the future payments requires assumptions about interest rates and the length of the disability. A mortality table may be used to estimate the probability of death and a morbidity table to estimate the probability of recovery. In some cases, such as widow or widower benefits under workers compensation, the claim may be terminated if the claimant remarries. A remarriage table, showing the probability of remarriage at various ages and periods of widowhood, is used to estimate the value of such claims.

To illustrate a tabular reserve calculation, assume that a thirty-year-old widow is receiving a widow's benefit of $300 per week for life, to be terminated on remarriage. The table of present values shows that the present value of her future benefit is 14.129 for each dollar of benefit, reflecting mortality, probability of remarriage, and interest. In this case, the tabular reserve would be as follows: ($300 per week) × (52 weeks) × 14.129 = $220,412.

The interest rate used should be one that the insurer can reasonably expect to earn during the expected life of the claim and should be based on the yield on low-risk investments, such as government bonds. It may be lower than the average yield currently earned on the insurer's investment portfolio.

The mortality, morbidity, and remarriage rates assumed in calculating tabular reserves will not be realized exactly in most individual cases. For example, most claimants will either live longer or die sooner than the mortality table shows. However, if an insurer has a large number of such claims, the average mortality, morbidity, and remarriage experience of all claims combined should approximate the tabular values rather closely.

Because the reserves have been discounted for interest, the average amount paid over the life of all claims combined should exceed the aggregate reserves. For any individual claim, the total amount paid may be more or less than the reserve, depending on how the mortality, morbidity, or remarriage experience of the person differs from the values shown in the tables.

Tabular method
Method of developing case reserves that calculates reserves on the basis of one or more actuarial tables, such as a mortality, a morbidity, or a remarriage table.

Loss Ratio Method

Loss ratio method
Method of developing case reserves that applies aggregate reserves for all claims within a line of insurance or a class of risks.

The loss ratio method is discussed here to provide a complete exposition of reserving methods, but it is not a method of case reserving. Case reserving is concerned with establishing reserves for individual claims. The **loss ratio method** establishes aggregate reserves for all claims within a line of insurance or a class of risks. In its simplest form, the loss ratio method assumes that aggregate losses will equal the amount included in the premium to pay them. That is, the aggregate losses for a given year will equal the earned premiums for the year multiplied by the permissible loss ratio used in calculating the rates that underlie the earned premiums. A loss ratio other than the one used in calculating the rates might be used if the rates are believed to be excessive or inadequate.

The loss ratio method is usually used only if the other methods prove to be inadequate. For example, in medical malpractice insurance for physicians and surgeons, under occurrence policies, only a very small fraction (1 percent to 2 percent) of covered claims are reported to the insurer during the year in which they are incurred. Therefore, the loss ratio method is commonly used to establish aggregate reserves at the end of the first year (at twelve months of development), and other methods are used thereafter. A similar approach has been used by reinsurers because of the long delays experienced in reporting and settling claims in that segment of the insurance business.

The NAIC Annual Statement requires minimum reserves (sometimes called "statutory" reserves) calculated by the loss ratio method for workers compensation and liability insurance. The loss ratio used to calculate the minimum loss reserve for liability lines varies from 60 percent to 75 percent, depending on the past loss ratios of the insurer. For workers compensation insurance, the percentage ranges from 65 percent to 75 percent.

Statutory minimum reserve
Loss reserves required by the NAIC Annual Statement for liability insurance and workers compensation insurance. They are calculated by the loss ratio method.

The **statutory minimum reserve** is found by multiplying the earned premiums for the year by the appropriate percentage and deducting losses and adjustment expenses already paid for the year. This statutory minimum reserve calculation applies only to the three most recent accident years.

IBNR Reserve

IBNR reserve
Pure IBNR reserve includes reserves for losses that have been incurred but not yet reported. The total IBNR reserve is the sum of the pure IBNR reserve and the reserve for case reserve deficiencies.

Insurers are required by law and good accounting practice to establish reserves for losses that have been incurred but not yet reported, the so-called **IBNR reserve**. Although the name of this reserve refers only to incurred but not reported losses, unreported losses account for only a part of the reserve in many cases. The balance of the reserve is for losses that have been reported but for which the case reserves that have been established are inadequate. A reserve for claims that have been closed and then reopened may also be included in the IBNR reserve. Of course, analysts usually cannot identify the specific claims for which inadequate case reserves have been established or the closed claims that will be reopened, nor can they determine the amount of inadequacy for specific claims.

In this chapter, the reserve for unreported claims is referred to as the *pure IBNR reserve*. The reserve for inadequate case reserves is called the *reserve for case reserve inadequacies*. The sum of the two will be called the *total IBNR reserve*.

Because the insurer does not know either the number or the amount of such unreported losses or case reserve deficiencies, the IBNR reserve must be based on estimates of some kind. There are two possible approaches to such estimates. One approach is to estimate the ultimate total amount of incurred losses for the period and subtract the paid losses and case reserves for reported losses. The remainder is the total IBNR reserve.

If the paid losses and case reserves are greater than the estimated ultimate losses, this calculation produces a negative total IBNR reserve. This result may indicate either excessive case reserves or an inadequate estimate of ultimate aggregate incurred losses. In any case, a negative total IBNR reserve likely indicates an error in the reserve calculation and calls for further analysis.

The second approach to IBNR estimation is to estimate the pure IBNR reserve independently, without reference to the case reserves. A separate calculation must then be made for the reserve for case reserve deficiencies to determine the total IBNR reserve. The report-year method discussed later may be used for this purpose. This approach requires that historic loss data files include both the occurrence date and the report date for each claim. With such data, it is possible to determine the proportion of incurred claims, both in number and amount, reported after some specified cutoff date (such as December 31) in past years. It is then assumed that the same proportion of claims for the year or years in question remains unreported. Of course, if environmental changes have occurred that would be expected to lengthen or shorten the reporting period, appropriate adjustments must be made. For example, the enactment of a shorter statute of limitations might cause some claims to be reported more quickly than indicated by historic data.

Some actuaries use both methods when sufficient data are available. If the two methods produce total IBNR reserve estimates that are consistent, the level of confidence in the result is increased. If the results are inconsistent, further analysis is needed to determine why and which, if either, is more likely to be correct.

In some lines of insurance, the total IBNR reserve may be a substantial part of an insurer's total liabilities. Consequently, insurers should take great care in estimating the IBNR reserve.

Loss Reserve Analysis and Verification Techniques

Insurers maintain two loss reserving systems. The case reserve system, discussed above, is concerned with individual losses and is primarily the responsibility of the claim department. Ideally, the case reserving system should provide a reserve for each claim that is equal to the amount that will be required to settle that claim. This ideal is seldom achieved and is probably impossible to achieve in most lines of insurance.

Actuarial reserving system
System that establishes the total of all outstanding losses for accounting purposes. These are the loss reserves shown on an insurer's balance sheet.

The second reserving system is the **actuarial reserving system** or the bulk reserving system. Its principal purpose is to determine the insurer's claim liabilities for accounting purposes. It is concerned with the insurer's total liability for all outstanding claims and not with the amount of reserve for individual claims.

The previous section of this chapter discusses the case reserving system. This section deals with the bulk reserving system.

The purpose of loss reserve analysis and verification is to determine whether the loss and adjustment expense reserves established by a company are adequate to cover the losses and adjustment expenses that have been incurred but have not yet been paid. Such a study may be commissioned by management as a normal part of management control by the company's auditors to determine whether the company's financial statement accurately indicates the company's financial condition, or it may be undertaken to comply with regulatory requirements. The NAIC Annual Statement instructions now require most insurers to have their loss reserves certified by an actuary or another qualified person. The NAIC's definition of a "qualified actuary" is shown in Exhibit 12-1.

EXHIBIT 12-1

Qualifications Required To Certify Loss Reserves

"Qualified actuary" is a person who is either:

1.   A member in good standing of the Casualty Actuarial Society, or

2.   A member in good standing of the American Academy of Actuaries who has been approved as qualified for signing casualty loss reserve opinions by the Casualty Practice Council of the American Academy of Actuaries, or

3.   A person who otherwise has competency in loss reserve evaluation as demonstrated to the satisfaction of the insurance regulatory official of the domiciliary state. In such case, at least 90 days prior to the filing of its annual statement, the insurer must request approval that the person be deemed qualified and that request must be approved or denied. The request must include the NAIC Biographical Form and a list of all loss reserve opinions and/or certifications issued in the last 3 years by this person.

Annual Statement Instructions—Property and Casualty, National Association of Insurance Commissioners, Kansas City, Mo., 1998, p. 7.

Signing such opinions or certifications creates an exposure to potential professional liability claims. Consequently, such opinions or certifications ordinarily would not be provided without a careful analysis of the reserves.

One actuarial technique for analyzing and verifying loss reserves is very similar to the loss development process discussed in the preceding chapter. In the first step of the process, the actuary must become familiar with the techniques the claim department uses to establish case reserves and must determine whether any changes have been made in case reserving methods.

The loss reserve verification techniques in common use measure past patterns in estimating case reserves and project these past patterns into the future. Consequently, a change in reserving practices, if it affects the pattern of case reserves, will result in an error in the evaluation of those reserves unless the change is detected and appropriate adjustments are made.

For example, a change in case reserving methods that resulted in an increase in case reserves could, if undetected, cause the analyst to assume that case reserves, having been inadequate in the past, are still inadequate. Actually, of course, the changed methods could result in reserves that are now adequate or even excessive.

Although this chapter emphasizes the mathematical methods for analyzing loss reserves, performing such an analysis is not an entirely mathematical process. The mathematical results must be carefully evaluated using nonmathematical information and common sense.

Accident-Year Loss Analysis Technique

One technique for loss reserve analysis uses loss triangles like those illustrated in Chapter 11 in Exhibits 11-3, 11-4, and 11-5. The triangles in Chapter 11 are accident-year loss triangles. Each line of data represents one accident year, with the various columns showing how the accident-year losses developed over time.

The number of accident years included in a loss development triangle for ratemaking purposes depends on the number of years in the experience period used for ratemaking purposes. There should be one line for each year in the experience period. However, the number of lines in a triangle used for loss reserve evaluation is determined primarily by the length of the delay between the occurrence of a loss and the time it is paid. Ideally, there should be one line for each accident year for which one or more reported claims remain open or for which one or more unreported claims are expected to be reported.

As a practical matter, it may be necessary to combine very old years with very few claims outstanding into a single line in the triangle. For example, the triangle might include a separate line for each of the last ten accident years plus a single line for the combined data for the eleventh year and all years before then.

Exhibit 12-2 shows the initial accident-year loss triangle for loss reserve verification. Exhibit 12-2 shows the dollar amount of incurred losses as reported for each accident year at various stages of development: twelve months, twenty-four months, and so on. The losses are presumed to be fully developed at ninety-six months, and do not change thereafter. As noted, Exhibit 12-2 differs from Exhibit 11-2 only in that it includes more accident years (ten plus a line for prior years instead of five years).

EXHIBIT 12-2

Loss Triangle: Accident-Year Method
Hypothetical Data

Accident Year	Months of Development							
	12	24	36	48	60	72	84	96
1992 & Prior	$279,554,361	$487,695,483	$498,712,348	$501,462,834	$507,832,541	$512,664,798	$515,447,632	$516,112,436
1993	26,443,738	44,658,934	46,112,869	47,355,873	48,586,914	48,967,324	49,116,736	49,214,873
1994	29,163,357	48,995,673	51,444,538	57,579,832	53,461,854	53,892,346	54,213,128	54,304,736
1995	32,561,477	54,564,783	52,668,598	58,234,768	58,977,654	59,541,632	59,843,486	59,925,726
1996	36,112,748	59,879,765	62,861,528	64,146,732	64,981,374	65,476,497	65,879,324	
1997	41,773,849	66,968,794	70,981,932	73,859,431	74,779,541	75,417,614		
1998	50,174,593	83,947,351	87,979,482	89,875,483	91,463,572			
1999	57,673,841	93,258,873	98,998,237	101,443,218				
2000	63,688,419	105,548,765	110,774,315					
2001	67,448,941	112,234,985						
2002	73,814,284							

Exhibit 12-3 shows loss development multipliers calculated from the data in Exhibit 12-2. The multipliers for each accident year were calculated by dividing the amount of losses for one development period from Exhibit 12-2 by the amount of losses on the same line for the immediately prior development period. For example, the multiplier for development from twelve months to twenty-four months for 1997 was calculated by dividing the losses at twenty-four months of development ($66,968,794) by the losses reported at twelve months of development ($41,773,849). The resulting loss development multiplier is 1.603. The other multipliers were calculated in the same manner.

The figures on the line labeled "Mean" in Exhibit 12-3 are the arithmetic means of the multipliers above them. The figures on the line labeled "Selected" are the ones chosen by the analyst to calculate the loss development factors on the line below. In this instance, the analyst has chosen to use the mean values without modification. In an actual analysis, the selected values might vary from the means. For example, if the accident-year multipliers indicated an increasing trend, the analyst might use selected values higher than the means. If the data were liability loss data from a state that had just adopted a shorter statute of limitations, the analyst might use selected values higher than average for earlier years and lower than average values for later years, indicating an expectation of earlier reporting in the future.

EXHIBIT 12-3

Loss Triangle: Accident-Year Method
Hypothetical Data

Accident Year	Months of Development						
	12–24	24–36	36–48	48–60	60–72	72–84	84–96
1992 & Prior	1.745	1.023	1.006	1.013	1.010	1.005	1.001
1993	1.689	1.033	1.027	1.026	1.008	1.003	1.002
1994	1.680	1.050	1.022	1.017	1.008	1.006	1.002
1995	1.676	1.057	1.010	1.013	1.010	1.005	1.001
1996	1.658	1.050	1.020	1.013	1.008	1.006	
1997	1.603	1.060	1.041	1.012	1.009		
1998	1.673	1.048	1.022	1.018			
1999	1.617	1.062	1.025				
2000	1.657	1.050					
2001	1.664						
Mean	1.666	1.048	1.021	1.016	1.009	1.005	1.002
Selected	1.666	1.048	1.021	1.016	1.009	1.005	1.002
Ultimate	1.840	1.105	1.054	1.032	1.016	1.007	1.002

The ultimate development factors are shown on the bottom line of Exhibit 12-3. The ultimate development factors for ninety-six months and later are not shown in Exhibit 12-3. However, all of them are 1.00, indicating that the losses are fully developed at ninety-six months, and no additional changes are expected after that time. The ultimate development factor for eighty-four months of development is simply the selected value from the line above. For each of the other periods shown, the ultimate development factor was calculated by multiplying the selected value for that period by the ultimate development factor for the following period.

Exhibit 12-4 shows the ultimate development factor for each twelve-month period from twelve months to ninety-six months and later. Exhibit 12-5 shows the ultimate projected losses for each year in Exhibit 12-2. These projected ultimate losses were calculated by multiplying the reported amount of losses for the latest period in Exhibit 12-2 by the appropriate ultimate loss development factor from Exhibit 12-4.

EXHIBIT 12-4

Ultimate Loss Development Factors: Accident-Year Method Hypothetical Data

Accident Year	Ultimate Loss Development Factors
1992 & Prior	1.000
1993	1.000
1994	1.000
1995	1.000
1996	1.002
1997	1.007
1998	1.016
1999	1.032
2000	1.054
2001	1.105
2002	1.840

The projected ultimate losses in Exhibit 12-5 include both paid losses and reserves, including IBNR reserves. The total loss reserve, including total IBNR, can be calculated by deducting the total paid losses of $972,213,944 (not shown in the tables) from the total projected losses of $1,395,724,850, shown at the bottom of Exhibit 12-5.

EXHIBIT 12-5

Developed Losses: Accident-Year Method
Hypothetical Data

Accident Year	Reported Losses	Loss Development Factors	Projected Ultimate Losses	IBNR	IBNR as % of Total
1992 & Prior	$ 516,112,436	1.000	$ 516,112,436	$ 0	.000
1993	49,214,873	1.000	49,214,873	0	.000
1994	54,304,736	1.000	54,304,736	0	.000
1995	59,925,726	1.000	59,925,726	0	.000
1996	65,879,324	1.002	66,011,083	131,759	.200
1997	75,417,614	1.007	75,945,537	527,923	.695
1998	91,463,572	1.016	92,926,989	1,463,417	1.574
1999	101,443,218	1.032	104,689,401	3,246,183	3.101
2000	110,774,315	1.054	116,756,128	5,981,813	5.123
2001	112,234,985	1.105	124,019,658	11,784,673	9.502
2002	73,814,284	1.840	135,818,283	62,003,999	45.652
Totals	$1,310,585,083		$1,395,724,850	$85,139,767	6.100

The total IBNR reserve can be calculated by deducting the total reported losses of $1,310,585,083 from the total projected ultimate losses of $1,395,724,850. Exhibit 12-5 shows this calculation along with the total IBNR for each of the accident years.

The loss triangles in this chapter include all reported claims, both closed and open. Some actuaries also use closed loss triangles in the reserve analysis process. Closed loss triangles are constructed and interpreted in exactly the same manner as reported loss triangles. The only difference is that only data for closed losses are used, whereas the reported loss triangles also include open losses. Using closed loss triangles has the advantage of eliminating the effects of errors in estimating case reserves. However, the delay between occurrence and closing losses can be substantially longer than the delay between occurrence and reporting. Consequently, the number of months needed until no further development in closed loss triangles occurs would be larger than for reported loss triangles. This longer delay introduces a greater chance for changing circumstances to lead to errors in interpreting the results.

Triangles for the number of claims are constructed in the same manner as those for loss amounts. The projected ultimate number of claims can then be cross-checked against the projected ultimate amount of losses to be sure they are consistent. Careful actuaries make many such cross-checks when certifying loss reserves.

Report-Year Loss Analysis Technique

The loss triangles discussed to this point have dealt with accident-year statistics. Loss data, either number of claims or dollar amount of losses, were grouped by accident year, the year in which the loss event occurred. This section discusses a technique in which the loss data are grouped by report year, the year in which the loss was first reported to the insurer. This technique can be used to calculate the reserve for case reserve deficiencies.

For some lines of property insurance, such as auto physical damage, a large majority of claims are reported in the same year in which the loss event occurred. For those lines, using the report-year technique for loss reserve analysis would add little information to the process.

However, for long-tailed liability lines, such as medical malpractice, the majority of claims may be reported to the insurer in years subsequent to the year in which the loss event occurred. Reporting such claims to the insurer ten years or more after the loss event occurred is not unusual. For such lines, claims included in *report-year* 2002, for example, would be quite different from those reported in *accident-year* 2002.

The report-year technique deals with a constant portfolio of claims. The dollar amount of claims within the portfolio may change as claims are settled or case reserves are amended, and claims may move from the open category to the closed category, but the total number of claims remains constant. Because only reported claims are considered, the exact number of claims in the portfolio is known on the last day of the report year and does not change thereafter.

This constancy of the portfolio is both a strength and a weakness of the technique. It is a strength of the technique because it permits the analyst to follow the development of a specific group of claims and to test the accuracy of early case reserving. This is not possible with accident-year data because new claims are added to the portfolio as they are reported to the insurer.

The constant portfolio of losses is a weakness of the report-year technique because it does not provide information needed to determine the amount of reserve required for losses that have been incurred but have not yet been reported to the insurer, the pure IBNR reserve. Note, however, that it does permit testing of a part of the total IBNR reserve: that part consisting of case reserve inadequacies for reported losses. Consequently, the report-year technique cannot be used as the sole technique for loss reserve testing. However, it can be used as an important tool to supplement the insight gained through the accident-year methods.

Adequacy of Case Reserves

The adequacy of case reserves is sometimes difficult to determine, especially for a relatively new insurer writing long-tailed liability insurance. Small claims, especially those settled without payment, tend to be settled quickly.

Because those are the claims for which excessive reserves are likely to be established, this pattern of settlement can give the appearance that all case reserves are excessive, especially for a company that has not been in business long enough to settle a representative number of larger, more complex cases.

In several cases, this phenomenon has misled the management of new companies into believing their reserves were adequate or even excessive when, in fact, they were grossly inadequate. The accident-year loss triangles, used alone, may not reveal this problem. Using the report-year technique may assist in avoiding the problem if sufficient data are available.

Report-Year Loss Analysis Example

Unlike accident-year loss triangles, which include loss data for several accident years, a report-year loss table includes data for only one report year.

Exhibit 12-6 shows a report-year loss table, using hypothetical data. Several such tables, one for each report year, would be needed for a typical loss reserve analysis.

Several things should be noted about Exhibit 12-6. First, the total number of claims never changes. At the end of the report year, all reported claims are known, so the number does not change thereafter. Claims move from the open column to the closed column when they are settled, even if they are settled without payment. Occasionally, a claim may move from the closed column back to the open column if it is reopened for some reason, but the total number of claims never changes. The total amount of losses does change. The change may be either upward or downward, depending on an insurer's reserving practices. The change is always upward in Exhibit 12-6, indicating

EXHIBIT 12-6

Report-Year Loss Table for 1995
Hypothetical Data

Report Year	Closed Claims			Open Claims			All Claims		
	Number	Amount	Average	Number	Amount	Average	Number	Amount	Average
1995	1,451	$ 5,117,677	$3,527	9,122	$49,597,598	$ 5,437	10,573	$54,715,275	$5,175
1996	4,794	18,562,368	3,872	5,779	41,111,644	7,114	10,573	59,674,012	5,644
1997	6,579	30,862,089	4,691	3,994	30,122,975	7,542	10,573	60,985,064	5,768
1998	7,841	40,059,669	5,109	2,732	20,967,687	7,675	10,573	61,027,356	5,772
1999	8,987	49,635,201	5,523	1,586	12,882,948	8,123	10,573	62,518,149	5,913
2000	9,898	57,814,218	5,841	675	6,057,275	8,974	10,573	63,871,493	6,041
2001	10,570	64,762,390	6,127	3	282,706	94,235	10,573	65,045,096	6,152
2002	10,573	65,097,961	6,157	0	0	0	10,573	65,097,961	6,157

that the insurer's case reserves were substantially inadequate initially. For many real companies, the change will be upward in some years and downward in others.

Both the average closed claim and the average open claim tend to increase as the claims mature. This results from the tendency for small claims to be settled first, with larger claims taking longer to settle. This increase in the average claims may not be as regular in real life as it is depicted in Exhibit 12-6, and a year-to-year decrease may occasionally occur. However, such a decrease calls for further checking to be sure that a data error has not occurred or to find the reason for the anomaly.

The report-year loss table in Exhibit 12-6 is for a *fully mature report year*, one for which all claims have been settled. Exhibit 12-7 shows a similar table for a year not yet fully mature.

A loss triangle similar to those used in accident-year analysis can be compiled from a series of report-year tables. The first step in compiling such a triangle is to calculate loss development multipliers from the total loss amount columns of the tables. Exhibit 12-8 shows the calculation of such multipliers from Exhibits 12-6 and 12-7.

Exhibit 12-9 shows a loss triangle using the data from Exhibits 12-6 and 12-7, along with additional data from other report years. The bottom line shows the ultimate development factors, the factors that can be used to project immature loss data to full maturity. In this illustration, the various twelve-month development factors in the next-to-last line of the table have been taken as the arithmetic mean of the multipliers above them for the report years. In actual practice, an analyst might elect a value greater or lesser than the arithmetic mean. Such a selection might be made because the data indicate an increasing or decreasing trend in the multipliers, or because of changes in case reserving practices. Other reasons might also exist

---

EXHIBIT 12-7

Report-Year Loss Table for 1998
Hypothetical Data

	Closed Claims			Open Claims			All Claims		
Report Year	Number	Amount	Average	Number	Amount	Average	Number	Amount	Average
1998	1,687	$ 6,677,146	$3,958	9,330	$57,474,845	$6,160	11,017	$64,151,991	$5,823
1999	5,135	24,139,635	4,701	5,882	43,559,830	7,406	11,017	67,699,465	6,145
2000	6,738	34,559,202	5,129	4,279	34,164,844	7,984	11,017	68,724,046	6,238
2001	7,953	43,590,393	5,481	3,064	26,653,999	8,699	11,017	70,244,392	6,376
2002	9,188	52,849,376	5,752	1,829	16,083,993	8,794	11,017	68,933,369	6,257

EXHIBIT 12-8

Report-Year Method
Development Multipliers

Months of Development	Report Year			
	1995		1998	
	Amount	Multiplier	Amount	Multiplier
12	$54,715,275		$64,151,991	
24	59,674,012	1.091	67,699,465	1.055
36	60,985,064	1.022	68,724,046	1.015
48	61,027,356	1.001	70,244,392	1.022
60	62,518,149	1.024	68,933,369	.981
72	63,871,493	1.022		
84	65,045,096	1.018		
96	65,097,961	1.001		

EXHIBIT 12-9

Loss Triangle
Report-Year Method

Report Year	Months of Development						
	12–24	24–36	36–48	48–60	60–72	72–84	84–96
1994 & Prior	1.065	1.031	1.023	1.022	1.034	1.016	1.003
1995	1.091	1.022	1.001	1.024	1.022	1.018	1.001
1996	1.084	1.019	1.025	1.023	1.026	1.017	
1997	1.071	1.021	1.018	1.019	1.027		
1998	1.055	1.015	1.022	.981			
1999	1.063	1.024	1.019				
2000	1.073	1.020					
2001	1.059						
Mean	1.070	1.022	1.018	1.014	1.027	1.017	1.002
Selected	1.070	1.022	1.018	1.014	1.027	1.017	1.002
Development Factors	1.182	1.105	1.081	1.062	1.047	1.019	1.002

for the analyst to conclude that the arithmetic mean was not the appropriate value to select in a given instance.

Exhibit 12-10 shows the ultimate development factors alone. The losses for report year 1998, which are sixty months developed in Exhibit 12-7, can be projected to ultimate value by multiplying by the ultimate development factor corresponding to sixty months, shown in Exhibit 12-10 ($68,933,369 × 1.047 = $72,173,237).

EXHIBIT 12-10

**Report-Year Method
Ultimate Development Factors**

Months of Development	Ultimate Development Factor
12	1.182
24	1.105
36	1.081
48	1.062
60	1.047
72	1.019
84	1.002
96	1.000

The report-year triangle shows that the company in question has consistently established inadequate loss reserves during the period being analyzed. In the absence of an indication that reserving practices have changed, an analyst looking at these data would assume that current reserves are inadequate by approximately the same percentage.

The foregoing analysis is based solely on claims reported to the insurer in the report year in question. Those claims would include some that were incurred during the report year and some that were incurred in earlier years. The data do not include any claims reported after the end of the report year, regardless of when they were incurred. Consequently, the claims projected to ultimate by this method do not include any amount for claims incurred but not reported. This part of the loss reserve must be computed separately when the report-year method is used.

As noted earlier, the IBNR reserve reported in the NAIC Annual Statement includes two elements, although the elements normally are not identified separately. The first of these elements is claims incurred but not yet reported, the pure IBNR reserve. The second element is composed of the deficiency (or perhaps redundancy) in the case reserves for reported losses. The report-year method does not provide an estimate of the first of these elements of the IBNR reserve, but it does provide an estimate of the second element.

Report-year triangles can be constructed using the number of claims as well as the amount of losses. However, such triangles are not as useful in the report-year method as they are in the accident-year method because the total number of claims for a given report year does not change in subsequent development. A triangle could be used to compile a distribution of lag times between the reporting and settlement of claims. Such a table is an important element in discounting loss reserves. The discounting process is discussed below.

In conclusion, the report-year method, standing alone, is not an adequate method for loss reserve verification. However, it is a useful tool when used in parallel with the accident-year technique. Because it deals with a fixed portfolio of claims, the report-year method is an excellent tool for measuring the past performance of the case-reserving process. One must rely on judgment to determine whether past performance indicates present performance.

Discounting the Loss Reserves

For workers compensation and liability lines, insurers accumulate large amounts of loss reserves. The funds that back these reserves are invested in income-producing assets, and the income they produce is a very important element in insurer profits.

Many people have suggested over the years that the loss reserves established by insurers should be reduced to reflect the future income to be received from these investments, a process known as **discounting the loss reserves**. This would be a substantial change from the industry's traditional practice of establishing reserves for NAIC Annual Statement purposes equal to the expected loss payments without any reduction for future investment income.

The proposal for discounting loss reserves has been controversial. Most insurers and most state regulatory authorities have opposed discounting. They point out that the practice of establishing full-value or gross (undiscounted) loss reserves provides an extra margin of safety to protect the solvency of insurers and is, at least to that extent, in the best interest of insurance consumers. They also question the desirability of discounting an estimated quantity that is subject to such a large margin for error. They say that discounting gives an appearance of precision that is not justified by the facts.

Proponents of discounting say that establishing full-value loss reserves understates an insurer's net worth and profits and, consequently, its tax liability. Most states permit insurers to discount some workers compensation insurance loss reserves, primarily those for which case reserves are calculated by the tabular method discussed previously in this chapter. Those are primarily long-term disability income and dependents' income benefits.

Some states also permit discounting loss reserves for some very long-tailed liability lines such as medical malpractice. This practice was adopted to

Discounting loss reserves
The process of reducing loss reserves to reflect future investment income produced by the assets backing the reserves.

facilitate the entry of newly formed insurers, primarily doctor-owned companies, into the medical malpractice market during the severe shortage of malpractice insurance in the 1970s. One small insurer specializing in medical malpractice insurance found that discounting reduced its loss and loss adjustment expense reserves by more than $40 million, or about 20 percent of the undiscounted reserve. Other insurers might experience either larger or smaller reductions, depending on the payout distribution and interest rate used.

With the exceptions noted above, the regulatory authorities in most states prohibit or strongly discourage the discounting of loss reserves. With the enactment of Section 846 of the Internal Revenue Code in 1986, discounting loss reserves became mandatory for federal income tax purposes.

Discounting loss reserves requires some assumptions regarding (1) the time lags between the time a loss occurs and the time it is paid, and (2) the interest rate that will be earned on the invested assets offsetting the loss reserves. The Internal Revenue Service publishes loss payout patterns for all lines of property-casualty insurance, along with discount rates to be used for discounting loss and adjustment expense reserves for federal income tax purposes.

For other purposes, the distribution of payment lags should be based on the insurer's own data if such data have sufficient credibility. If the insurer's own data lack credibility, other industry data can be used. The interest rate used in the discounting calculation should be related to the average yield on the insurer's own investment portfolio. However, that average yield may be adjusted to reflect future interest rate expectations. Also, if the insurer's investment portfolio includes high-risk investments, a lower interest rate may be used to discount loss reserves.

PLANNING

An insurer's planning operations include persons from several sectors of the company, including personnel involved with investments, marketing, underwriting, human resources, and others.

Actuaries often participate because they have been trained to have broad knowledge of insurer operations and the planning process. Additionally, they are adept at the mathematical phases of the process, such as the construction of mathematical models.

Planning includes both short-term (tactical) planning and long-term (strategic) planning. Planning inevitably involves collecting and analyzing voluminous statistical data. A comprehensive planning program almost inevitably includes the use of computer models for testing various alternative actions available to the insurer. Such models use mathematical equations to represent various functions within the insurer's structure and operations. The models vary from small and simple to very complex. A small model might represent only a small part of a company, even a single line of insurance. A more complex model might depict all of the operations of a company or group of companies. A small, simple model might take only a few seconds to run under spreadsheet software on a desktop computer. A complex model might take many minutes to run on a mainframe computer.

Regardless of their size or complexity, the models serve the same basic purpose: to permit planners to test various scenarios for the future operations of the company or group of companies.

Some of the kinds of questions that a computer model might answer include:

1. How is the profitability of various lines of insurance affected by an increase of one percentage point in the insurer's yield on invested assets?
2. What is the optimum mix of reinsurance for the insurer, considering its probable underwriting results, investment income, and policyholders' surplus?
3. What is the optimum mix of investments, considering investment income, taxes, regulatory requirements, and the insurer's needs for liquidity, stability, and solvency?

Many factors determine the answers to questions such as these, and the interrelationships among the factors are very complex. Few individuals understand all of the factors and their interrelationships. However, an interdisciplinary team, working together, can build an appropriate computer model to assist in the analysis.

When analyzing very complex systems, an analyst is not likely to follow the same path of analysis each time. A computer model, on the other hand, always follows the same path of analysis. Whatever factors and relations were programmed into it will be analyzed in the same manner each time.

This can be either a strength or a weakness of computer models. If the model was designed properly, its consistency is an advantage. If the model was not designed properly, it may give consistently incorrect answers.

Computer models fall into two general categories: deterministic models and probabilistic models. Each type of model has an appropriate role in insurance company planning.

Deterministic Models

Deterministic models are characterized by consistent results. If a deterministic model is run many times with exactly the same values for all of the input factors, it will produce exactly the same output each time. This is, of course, not representative of the real world.

Despite this substantial abstraction from the real world, deterministic models are useful in planning. They permit planners to experiment with changing a single factor while holding all other factors constant, something that is seldom possible in the business world.

Deterministic models
Mathematical models of a system, such as an insurance company, in which the outputs are determined solely by the inputs, without any element of chance variation. Such models are used for planning purposes and are characterized by consistent results.

Probabilistic Models

Probabilistic models
Mathematical models of a system, such as an insurance company in which the outputs are determined partly by the inputs and partly by chance variation.

Probabilistic models are sometimes called stochastic models. They may also be called Monte Carlo models, after the famous gambling casino in Monaco. This association with gambling stems from the fact that the output from such a model is not determined solely by the inputs but is also subject to some element of chance variation. The range of chance variation may be large in some models.

Two simplified examples that may help to clarify the difference between a deterministic model and a probabilistic model are shown in Exhibits 12-11 and 12-12.

Choosing the Best Model

Because the operating results of an insurance company are subject to chance variation, one might conclude that a probabilistic model would be the better planning instrument for an insurer. Actually, a deterministic model is likely to be more useful for most planning tasks. Because the output from a probabilistic model varies by chance, it is difficult to draw any firm conclusions from the model without running it many times and comparing the results of the many runs. This process can be expensive because it may involve substantial costs for both computer and employee time. In most cases, the additional expense of building and operating a probabilistic model is not justified by improved results.

One notable exception is the area of reinsurance planning. One major purpose of reinsurance is to protect the ceding insurer from excessive chance fluctuations in losses. The adequacy of a reinsurance program for that purpose can be tested adequately in advance only by using a probabilistic computer model. Investment operations may also be represented more realistically by probabilistic models. This is especially true for investments involving common stocks and real estate, for which market prices fluctuate widely and for which potential capital gains are a major consideration.

ANALYSIS OF REINSURANCE REQUIREMENTS

The goal of a primary insurer's reinsurance planning is to design a reinsurance program that provides the degree of stability the primary insurer needs while keeping reinsurance costs to a practical minimum. Of course, compliance with state regulatory requirements is also a concern.

The degree of stability needed is determined by the necessity for preserving the insurer's solvency and ability to function effectively and by the attitude of its owners and managers toward profit stability. The owners and managers of some insurers are willing to accept substantial fluctuations in profits from year to year, while others demand greater stability.

EXHIBIT 12-11

Deterministic Model Example

Assume that an insurer wants to estimate its loss ratio for auto liability insurance in a given state for a year five years in the future. It has an estimate that five million cars will be registered in that state in the year concerned. Based on its past trend in market share, it believes it will insure 3 percent of registered vehicles at that time. Its current average auto liability premium for the state is $300, and it estimates that rates will increase 7.5 percent each year for the next five years. Consequently, it estimates its earned premiums for the year five years in the future as follows:

Number of registered cars	5,000,000
Company's market share	$\times$ 0.03
Cars insured by company	150,000
Average premium: [$300 $\times$ (1.075)^5]	$\times$ $431
Total earned premium	$64,650,000

The company estimates that 2.5 percent of its insured vehicles will be involved in an at-fault accident each year. The average cost of claims arising from one accident is now $6,000, and the company expects that amount to increase at the rate of 8 percent each year. Consequently, the incurred losses for the year five years in the future will be calculated as follows:

Number of cars insured	150,000
Percentage of cars in accidents	$\times$ 0.025
Number of accidents	3,750
Cost per accident: [$6,000 $\times$ (1.08)^5]	$\times$ $8,816
Total incurred losses	$33,060,000

The company's projected loss ratio would be calculated as follows:

Incurred losses / Earned premiums

33,060,000 / 64,650,000 = 0.511, or 51.1 percent

Note that there is no element of chance in this model. If the number of registered cars, the market share, the average premium, the accident rate, the average claim, and the rates of increase remain constant, the model will always produce exactly the same answer, no matter how many times it is calculated. This is the characteristic that distinguishes a deterministic model from a probabilistic model.

EXHIBIT 12-12

Probabilistic Model Example

Assume that an insurer wants to estimate its hurricane losses under homeowners policies for the coming hurricane season. Past experience indicates that the number of hurricanes ranges from zero to five, with the following probabilities:

Number of Hurricanes	Probability	Mean
0	0.20	0.00
1	0.30	0.30
2	0.20	0.40
3	0.15	0.45
4	0.10	0.40
5	0.05	0.25
		1.80

The arithmetic mean is 1.8 hurricanes per year.

The total amount of the company's losses from a single hurricane varies from $100,000 to $15,000,000, with an arithmetic mean of $1,500,000 following a specified probability distribution.

The first step in simulating the hurricane losses is to select the number of hurricanes. The computer program would be designed to select a number from zero to five so that the probability of selecting zero would be 0.20, the probability of selecting one would be 0.30, and so forth. This is accomplished by using random numbers generated by the computer. Next, the total amount of losses for each hurricane is selected, again through the use of random numbers. For example, the first three runs might produce the following results:

Run Number	Number of Hurricanes	Total Amount of Losses
1	0	0
2	4	$3,500,000
3	2	$6,435,000

This process would be repeated many times, perhaps 10,000 times, and the arithmetic mean of all of the runs would be used as the estimate of the total losses to be expected. It is possible that no two of the 10,000 runs would produce exactly the same answer because of the element of chance introduced into the model.

An insurer must make many decisions in planning its reinsurance program. Among those decisions are the following:

- What kind or kinds of reinsurance should it buy?
- What retentions and limits should it have on each reinsurance contract?
- What is a reasonable price to pay for the reinsurance contracts it decides to purchase?

Among the factors the insurer must consider in answering these questions are the following:

- The size of the insurer's capital and surplus
- The sizes of the individual risks it insures and the limits of its coverage for them
- The total premium volume of the insurer
- The premium volume for each line
- The territory in which it operates
- The geographic concentration of risks insured
- The liquidity of the insurer's investment portfolio

Unfortunately, these factors cannot be evaluated individually and independently because substantial interactions occur among them. The most satisfactory method for considering all of these factors simultaneously is through the use of computer modeling. A reinsurance planning model is rather complex. Constructing such a model requires a thorough understanding of insurance, reinsurance, and company finance as well as mathematical techniques. Because a major purpose of reinsurance is to reduce chance fluctuations, a probabilistic model is appropriate for testing various reinsurance programs to find the one most advantageous to the particular circumstances under which the insurer operates.

For quota share reinsurance alone, the model can be rather simple, because the division of premiums and losses between ceding company and reinsurer is based only on aggregate premiums and aggregate losses. If only quota share treaties are to be considered, a deterministic model may be adequate.

However, for excess of loss and surplus share treaties, individual losses must be simulated. Both the number of covered losses and the amount of each loss must vary in the model in a manner similar to the way they vary in the ceding company's actual insurance portfolio. For surplus share, each loss must also be associated with an amount of direct insurance to properly apply the ceding company's retention.

For catastrophe reinsurance, the frequency of catastrophes (such as hurricanes, tornadoes, and earthquakes) must be simulated along with the aggregate amount of losses from each catastrophe. Depending on the terms of the proposed reinsurance contracts, simulation of individual losses within each catastrophe may also be necessary.

The number and amount of losses from catastrophes depend in part on the number and size of risks the insurer covers in areas subject to catastrophes. Consequently, a model to test catastrophe reinsurance must reflect the geographic distribution of insured properties as well as the probability of a catastrophic event and the probable magnitude of the forces unleashed by the event.

Another more complex probabilistic model would simulate the results on the insurer's financial statements of various kinds of reinsurance under various loss scenarios.

EVALUATION OF INSURERS

Insurers sometimes need to analyze another insurer financially. Such an evaluation may be made because of a proposed merger or acquisition, for tax purposes, or for other reasons. In the case of a merger or an acquisition, the evaluation may be conducted for either the acquirer or the acquiree. Due diligence requirements would mandate that an evaluation be performed by each side independently. Actuaries are frequently called on to perform that evaluation.

The Actuarial Standards Board listed the principal elements to be considered in an actuarial appraisal of an insurance company as follows:

> 5.2 *Estimated Value of Insurance Company*—Based on actuarial appraisal calculations, the value of an insurance company is normally expressed as the sum of the following three components as of the appraisal date:
>
> a. Adjusted Net Worth
>
> b. Appraisal Value of Business in Force
>
> c. Appraisal Value of Future Business Capacity
>
> 5.2.1 *Adjusted Net Worth*—This component consists of the following:
>
> • Statutory capital and surplus
>
> • Any statutory liabilities that, in essence, represent allocations of surplus (e.g., mandatory securities valuation reserves, statutory portions of casualty Schedule Preserves, etc.)
>
> • Any statutory non-admitted assets that have realizable value
>
> • Reduction for surplus items that represent obligations to others
>
> 5.2.2 *Value of Business in Force*—This component equals the present value of future earnings attributable to business in force on the appraisal date.
>
> 5.2.3 *The Value of Future Business Capacity*—This component is generally represented by the present value of future earnings attributable to business issued or acquired after the appraisal date and attributable to the existing structure of the enterprise. In certain cases, it could be based on the market value of the company's charters and licenses and similar components of goodwill.[2]

Of course, these broad categories include many items. Among the principal factors of an actuarial nature to be considered in evaluating an insurance company are the following:

1. Adequacy of loss reserves
2. Adequacy of the unearned premium reserve
3. Adequacy and competitiveness of rate structures
4. Adequacy of reinsurance arrangements
5. Adequacy of funding for employee benefit plans, especially health and pension plans

Item (5) above would most likely be evaluated by a person trained in life insurance and pension actuarial techniques. The methods used for that purpose are not explained here. The ratemaking techniques discussed in Chapters 10 and 11 would be used to test rate adequacy, along with an analysis of past loss ratios by line and territory.

Techniques discussed elsewhere in this chapter would be used to test the adequacy of loss reserves and reinsurance arrangements. A sample of claim files would also be examined to verify that case reserves were properly established. However, that task would probably be undertaken by claim personnel rather than actuaries. Testing loss reserves is also an important part of testing rate adequacy. Posting inadequate loss reserves results in an understatement of the loss ratio and, consequently, inadequate rates.

Rate testing for a contemplated merger or acquisition must consider not only the adequacy of rates but also their competitiveness. One proposed acquisition was dropped quickly after the acquiring insurer discovered that the company it proposed to acquire had priced itself out of the market. It had raised its rates well above its competitors. The result was high short-term profits but a rapidly declining market share and agency force. The acquiring company doubted that the damage could be successfully reversed.

Testing the unearned premium reserve is perhaps the least difficult part of the actuarial evaluation of an insurer. It involves checking to see that the records for policies in force have been maintained properly and that calculating the unearned premiums from the in-force file was performed correctly. Very little discretion is involved in calculating the unearned premium reserve, and significant misstatements of the reserve are rare. Because it is the second largest liability on an insurer's balance sheet, the reserve should be verified.

BEST'S RATINGS

The A.M. Best Company (Best's) has been in business for almost a century and has published financial-strength ratings of both life and property-casualty insurers during most of that time. Initially, its ratings were formulated only once each year, when insurers published financial statements.

Recently, the ratings have been reviewed quarterly, although mergers, catastrophe losses, the insolvency of reinsurers, or other unusual events may necessitate additional reviews.

Best's property-casualty insurance company ratings are published annually in two books, *Best's Insurance Reports—Property/Casualty Edition* and *Best's Key Rating Guide*. The discussion that follows is based on the Preface of the 2001 edition of *Best's Reports*.

Ratings that are changed during the year are reported in *Best's Rating Monitor*, a special section of the company's newsletter, *Best Week*. In addition, one can obtain up-to-the-minute ratings for a fee by calling *Bestline*, the company's telephone rating service. Changes in ratings for major insurers are often reported in the insurance trade press and sometimes in the popular press and on various computer on-line services. Best's prepares reports and ratings for almost all significant insurers. Small insurers that are exempted from filing the NAIC Annual Statement form, the primary source of rating information, are one exception.

Although the NAIC Annual Statement and quarterly statement forms are the principal sources of rating information, they may be supplemented by audit reports, SEC reports, reports of insurance department examinations, and internal company reports.

The A.M. Best Company publishes three types of ratings: a Best's Rating, a Financial Performance Rating (FPR), and a Financial Size Category rating. Each of these ratings is discussed in more detail below.

When a person within the insurance industry refers to a Best's Rating without further qualification, he or she is most likely referring to the financial strength rating, officially called a Best's Rating by the A.M. Best Company. The Best's Rating is generally considered to be the most important of the three ratings the A.M. Best Company publishes for most insurers. The company states the objective of the rating process as follows:

> The objective of Best's rating system is to provide an opinion of an insurer's financial strength and ability to meet ongoing obligations to policyholders. Our opinions are derived from the evaluation of a company's balance sheet strength, operating performance and business profile as compared to Best's quantitative and qualitative standards.[3]

In addition, Best's notes the following:

> While Best's Ratings reflect our *opinion* of a company's financial strength and ability to meet its ongoing obligations to policyholders, they are *not a warranty*, nor are they a recommendation of a specific policy form, contract, rate or claim practice (emphasis in original).[4]

Quantitative Tests

The quantitative phase of the rating procedure consists of more than 100 tests. The individual tests vary in importance from one insurer to another, depending on the characteristics of the insurer. However, the quantitative tests as a group are intended to measure the following characteristics of an insurer:

- Profitability
- Capital and leverage
- Liquidity
- Loss reserve adequacy

The tests are based on the insurer's reported data for at least the past five years. An insurer's test results are evaluated by comparing them to its peer group as established by the A.M. Best Company. The peer group standards are based on an analysis of the peer group's reported data for the past twenty years.

Profitability Tests

Profitability indicates management's ability to operate the company in such a way as to generate or attract sufficient capital to support its future operations and growth. The analysis of profitability encompasses underwriting profit or loss, investment profit or loss, and capital gains or losses. The insurer's profits and losses over the past five years are analyzed as to their magnitude and source. Profits are strongly affected by operational changes, so trends in premium volume and distribution, investment income, net income, and surplus are analyzed.

Capital and Leverage Tests

The company's ability to withstand losses from unfavorable management decisions, industry trends, and economic developments depends on its capital and leverage. An insurer's capital is measured by its surplus to policyholders. Its **leverage** is measured by its dependence on the use of money belonging to others to supplement its capital in financing its operations. Leverage can result from borrowing money from a bank or through a bond issue. The A.M. Best Company calls this **financial leverage**. Insurance companies rarely use financial leverage, but insurance holding companies do.

Leverage/financial leverage
The use of debt to increase returns.

Leverage from loss reserves, unearned premium reserves, or other funds generated by the insurance business is common and likely to be substantial, especially for an insurer that writes a great deal of liability insurance. A.M. Best Company calls this form of leverage operational leverage. Operational leverage increases as the insurer's written premiums increase.

Best's rating procedures identify and measure four kinds of operational leverage. The first of these is the leverage resulting from current premium writings. This form of leverage is measured by the ratio of net written premiums to the insurer's policyholders' surplus. Net written premiums are gross written premiums less reinsurance premiums ceded and less return premiums. Some analysts may calculate the premium-to-surplus ratio on the basis of the statutory surplus, as reported in the NAIC Annual Statement. The A.M. Best Company uses a modified surplus to policyholders, calculated by adjusting the statutory surplus to reflect the equity in the unearned premium reserve, inadequacy or redundancy in loss reserves, the difference between the reported value and the market value of assets, and other relevant factors. Best's considers a premium-to-surplus ratio unfavorable if it exceeds 2.0. In addition, a change in net written premiums greater than 10 percent is considered unfavorable.

The second form of operational leverage that Best's rating procedures recognize is the ratio of net liabilities to surplus. The net liabilities consist mostly of loss reserves and unearned premium reserves, which are adjusted to reflect relevant reinsurance transactions. A.M. Best Company considers this ratio unfavorable if it exceeds 2.0 for property insurers or 3.8 for liability insurers.

The third form of leverage analyzed is the insurer's dependence on reinsurers and exposure to credit losses, such as the possibility that it may not be able to collect amounts due from reinsurers. The analysis consists of two phases: (1) an assessment of the reinsurers' financial strength, and (2) measurement of the relationship between (a) surplus and (b) the premiums and reserves ceded to reinsurers and the related amount due or to become due from reinsurers. If the ratio of the ceded values to surplus exceeds 1.3, it is considered unfavorable.

The fourth form of leverage recognized in Best's rating procedures is investment leverage, which measures the risk that the insurer's surplus will be adversely affected by declining market prices of the insurer's investment securities. It measures the reduction in surplus that would result from (a) a 20 percent decline in the market value of the insurer's common stock portfolio and (b) the decline in the market value of the insurer's portfolio of bonds, preferred stocks, and mortgages that would result from an increase of two percentage points in market interest rates.

Liquidity Tests

Quick liquidity test
A ratio that compares quick assets (such as cash and short-term investments) to net liabilities (such as loss reserves and ceded reinsurance balances payable).

Liquidity tests measure an insurer's ability to meet unusual claims obligations without selling long-term investments or fixed assets that may be sellable only at a substantial loss during unfavorable market conditions. The emphasis in the liquidity tests is on cash and short-term securities that can be converted to cash with little or no loss in all but the most severe market conditions. One test of liquidity is the **quick liquidity test** ratio, which evaluates quick assets against net liabilities. The quick assets used in the ratio are (1) cash, (2) short-term investments issued by companies not affiliated with the insurer, (3) bonds maturing within one year and issued by companies not affiliated with the insurer, (4) government bonds maturing within five years, and (5) 80 percent of common stocks issued by corporations not affiliated with the insurer. Securities issued by companies affiliated with the insurer are excluded from quick assets regardless of their term or nature because they may not be marketable quickly without a substantial loss. Net liabilities consist primarily of loss reserves plus ceded reinsurance balances payable. A.M. Best Company considers a ratio below 30 percent for property insurers or 20 percent for liability insurers to be unsatisfactory.

The **current liquidity test** is the ratio of (1) the sum of cash, unaffiliated invested assets, and encumbrances on other properties to (2) net liabilities and ceded reinsurance balances payable, expressed as a percentage. If this ratio is less than 100 percent, the insurer may have to depend on the sale of its affiliated assets to cover its liabilities. A ratio lower than 120 percent for property insurers or lower than 100 percent for liability insurers is considered unsatisfactory.

The **overall liquidity test** is the ratio of (1) total admitted assets to (2) total liabilities less conditional reserves. A ratio below 140 percent for property insurers or 110 percent for liability insurers is considered unsatisfactory.

The **operating cash flow test** measures the funds generated by insurance operations, not including stockholder dividends, capital infusions, unrealized capital gains or losses on investment assets, and some noninsurance transactions among affiliated companies. A negative result is unsatisfactory and probably indicates poor underwriting results, poor investment results, or both.

The final test in the liquidity series is the ratio of (1) noninvestment grade bonds to (2) policyholders' surplus. The NAIC assigns a quality rating to all bonds held by insurers. The ratings range from 1 to 6, with 1 being the highest quality and 6 being for bonds that are in or near default. Bonds rated 3, 4, 5, or 6 are considered below investment grade. A.M. Best Company considers a ratio greater than 10 percent unsatisfactory for this test.

Loss Reserve Tests

The A.M. Best Company uses several measures of insurer loss reserves. It uses a proprietary model (details not disclosed) to measure the adequacy or inadequacy of the reserves. The needed reserves, as calculated by the model, are discounted for anticipated investment income to derive an economic loss reserve position. If the insurer's reported reserves are less than the calculated economic reserve, a deficiency in reserves is presumed to exist. If the reported reserves are greater than the economic reserve, a redundancy is presumed to exist. Any deficiency or redundancy is incorporated in the BCAR model discussed below.

Best's rating procedures also include the ratio of reported loss reserves to policyholders' surplus. A ratio greater than 150 percent is considered above the acceptable range for property insurers. A ratio above 300 percent for long-tailed liability writers is considered unacceptable.

Another test is the ratio of loss development to policyholders' surplus. The development of loss reserves (increase or decrease from previously reported values) is shown in Schedule P of the NAIC Annual Statement. If the reported development is positive and exceeds 25 percent of policyholders' surplus, the ratio is considered unacceptable.

Current liquidity test
A ratio that compares (1) the sum of cash, unaffiliated invested assets, and encumbrances on other properties to (2) net liabilities and ceded reinsurance balances payable.

Overall liquidity test
A ratio that compares (1) total admitted assets to (2) total liabilities less conditional reserves.

Operating cash flow test
A liquidity test that measures the funds generated by insurance operations.

The ratio of loss reserve development to net premiums earned is also calculated. The development figure used for this test is the same as that used for the above test. This ratio, like the others, is calculated for the most recent five years. If a comparison over time shows that the ratio is falling, it may indicate that the company is not establishing adequate reserves. However, the ratios over time will be affected by rapid growth (or shrinkage) of earned premiums and possibly by changes in the mix of business, so the ratio must be interpreted with care.

The four leverage measures, along with liquidity test and other tests discussed here, are combined in Best's proprietary model to calculate the insurer's capital adequacy ratio, which measures the adequacy of the insurer's capital relative to the risks it assumes in its operations. The capital adequacy ratio, in turn, is used to calculate Best's Capital Adequacy Relativity (BCAR), which measures the company's capital adequacy relative to the capital adequacy of its industry peers. In calculating BCAR, Best's divides insurers into thirteen broad categories reflecting the lines written, as follows:

1. Personal lines
2. Personal auto
3. Homeowners
4. Non-standard auto
5. Property
6. Commercial casualty
7. Commercial auto
8. Workers compensation
9. Medical malpractice
10. Excess and surplus
11. Fidelity and surety
12. Credit/accident and health
13. Reinsurance

In addition to this categorization by line, the industry peers are divided into three or four categories by size. A company's BCAR is calculated by dividing the company's capital adequacy ratio by the composite capital adequacy ratio of its industry peers.

The A.M. Best Company does not publish a detailed explanation of the BCAR calculation. Following is the explanation it provides:

> This absolute measure compares an insurer's economic surplus position relative to the required capital necessary to support its business risks. (Note: Prior to year-end 1999, A.M. Best had published relative BCAR results that compared a property/casualty company's capital adequacy ratio against industry composite values.)[5]

Qualitative Tests

In addition to the quantitative tests, several qualitative tests are used in evaluating these factors of the insurer's: its spread of risk and exposure to catastrophes; the quality and appropriateness of its reinsurance arrangements; the quality and diversity of its investments; the adequacy of its loss reserves; the adequacy of its surplus; the capital structure of the insurer and its affiliates; its management; and its market positions.

Spread of Risk

The analysis of an insurer's spread of risk includes (1) the size of its premium volume, (2) the geographic spread of its business, (3) the diversity of product lines written, and (4) the distribution systems used. The objective is to have a sufficiently diverse book of business so that the loss ratio will not be affected excessively by natural catastrophes, adverse economic developments, or other factors that might apply to a limited geographic area or a limited class of business. Insurers that operate in a limited geographic area may also be exposed to adverse underwriting experience resulting from regulatory actions.

Reinsurance Analysis

The reinsurance analysis includes a review of the appropriateness of the reinsurance contracts purchased and the financial strength of the reinsurers. The reinsurance program's appropriateness depends on the insurer's underwriting practices, including the lines written, the size of risks written, territorial spread of risks, and catastrophe exposures, as well as its other financial resources. The reinsurance contracts are also reviewed to see whether they provide true risk transfer or merely financial window dressing.

Quality and Diversity of Investments

The insurer's invested assets are carefully screened to determine whether they could be sold quickly in an emergency with minimal market loss. Particular attention is given to large individual investments constituting 10 percent or more of the insurer's policyholders' surplus and to large investments in subsidiaries or affiliates. Lack of diversification by industry or by geographic area is also cause for concern.

Loss Reserves

The analysis of loss reserves depends primarily on the quantitative tests discussed previously in this chapter. However, an estimate of the uncertainty in loss reserve estimates is also included. If the quantitative tests indicate that the estimated uncertainty is greater than any equity in the reserves as indicated by the quantitative tests, the insurer's rating may be adversely affected.

Surplus

An insurer's surplus is a proxy for its financial strength. Surplus serves as a cushion should unexpected events occur. The adequacy of any insurer's surplus must be evaluated relative to other factors specific to that insurer, such as its investment portfolio, reinsurance program, and underwriting book of business.

Capital Structure

The capital and surplus structure of the insurer and its holding company, if any, are analyzed to be sure that they are sound and able to meet their obligations. For example, if the holding company is heavily burdened by debt, the debt service costs may require large stockholder dividends from the insurer, thereby reducing its ability to accumulate surplus through retained earnings. In extreme cases, the dividend drain may hamper the insurer's efforts to provide efficient service to its policyholders.

Management

Although the experience, capabilities, and integrity of management cannot be measured with mathematical precision, they are crucial factors in assessing an insurer's future prospects. Those factors are analyzed partly on the basis of the insurer's past success if the present management has been in place for several years. Otherwise, the assessment is based on past experience of the managers in other positions and on the raters' opinions of the managers developed through extensive meetings with them.

Market Position

An insurer's market position depends on its ability to maintain or increase its market share. Market position, in turn, is based on factors such as a low expense ratio; superior service; strong recognition by buyers and producers in the insurer's selected market; access to plentiful and inexpensive capital; and control over distribution channels.

Best's Financial Strength Ratings

Based on the analysis outlined above, the A.M. Best Company assigns a letter rating, called a Best's Rating, to most significant insurers licensed and operating within the United States. The rating may be based on the data from a single insurer and apply only to that insurer, or it may be based on the consolidated figures for several companies operating under common ownership and management and apply to all insurers within the group. The fifteen letter ratings range downward from A++ to F. The rating of F is for insurers currently in liquidation.

Financial Performance Ratings

The A.M. Best Company assigns Financial Performance Ratings (FPR) to insurers that are too small to qualify for Best's Ratings or cannot provide data for five representative years as required for a Best's Rating. The process for determining an FPR is similar to that discussed above for Best's Ratings but is based on three years of data instead of five years. The FPRs range from "FPR=9," the most favorable rating, to "FPR=1," which indicates that at the insurer's request, no FPR is published. Before 1994, the Financial Performance Rating was known as the Financial Performance Index (FPI). Exhibit 12-13 shows all the Best's Ratings and Financial Performance Ratings along with a brief explanation of their meanings. It also shows the number of individual insurance companies that qualified for each rating as of July 10, 2001.

No Rating Opinions

At the bottom of Exhibit 12-13 is a list of Best's "no rating opinion" designations. These designations are applied to insurers that have not been assigned a Best's Rating. Some of them may qualify for the FPR. The reason for not assigning a Best's Rating is explained in the full report on the insurer in *Best's Reports*.

Rating Modifiers

Best's Ratings may be accompanied by one or more modifiers, indicated by lowercase letters. These modifiers are as follows:

- g—indicates that the rating is based on consolidated information for the rated insurer and one or more affiliated insurers under common ownership or management
- p—indicates a pooled rating based on data from two or more insurers operating under common ownership or management and pooling all of their business, with all premiums, expenses, and losses prorated among member insurers
- r—indicates that the rated insurer reinsures substantially all of its direct business with a single reinsurer and has been assigned the rating of the reinsurer
- q—indicates a rating that has been qualified because the insurer's rating may be adversely affected by state legislation or losses from residual market programs

Exhibit 12-14 shows the number of insurers to which the modifiers were assigned in 2001. As noted in Exhibit 12-14, two modifiers were assigned to the ratings of fifty-four insurers. The remaining ratings were subject to only one modifier each.

Best's Financial Size Category

The Best's Financial Size Category indicates the size of the company as measured by its reported policyholders' surplus plus conditional reserves. The fifteen financial size categories are indicated by Roman numerals. They range from Class I to Class XV, with Class I being the smallest

EXHIBIT 12-13

2001 Property/Casualty Rating Distribution Based on Individual Companies as of July 10, 2001

Best's Level	Rating /FPR Category	Number	Percent
	Secure Ratings		
A++	Superior	176	8.4%
A+	Superior	412	19.6
FPR 9	Very Strong	0	0.0
	Subtotal	588	28.0
A	Excellent	552	26.3
A–	Excellent	457	21.8
FPR 8	Strong	0	0.0
FPR 7	Strong	0	0.0
	Subtotal	1,009	48.1
B++	Very Good	163	7.8
B+	Very Good	152	7.2
FPR 6	Good	1	0.0
FPR 5	Good	2	0.1
	Subtotal	318	15.2
	Total Secure Ratings	1,915	91.3%
	Vulnerable Ratings		
B	Fair	77	3.7%
B–	Fair	24	1.1
FPR 4	Fair	1	0.0
	Subtotal	102	4.9
C++	Marginal	14	0.7
C+	Marginal	7	0.3
FPR 3	Marginal	0	0.0
	Subtotal	21	1.0
C	Weak	2	0.1
C–	Weak	5	0.2
FPR 2	Weak	0	0.0
	Subtotal	7	0.3
D	Poor	4	0.2
FPR 1	Poor	0	0.0
E	Under Regulatory Supervision	42	2.0
F	In Liquidation	7	0.3
	Subtotal	53	2.5
	Total Vulnerable Ratings	183	8.7%
	Total Rating Opinions	2,098	100.0%
	No Rating Opinions		
NR-1	Insufficient Data	418	55.2%
NR-2	Insufficient Size/Operating Experience	112	14.8
NR-3	Rating Procedure Inapplicable	195	25.8
NR-4	Company Request	18	2.4
NR-5	Not Formally Followed	14	1.8
	Total—No Rating Opinions	757	100.0%
	Total Rated Companies	2,855	

EXHIBIT 12-14

Assignment of Rating Modifiers, 2001

Rating Modifier	Number of Companies
g – Group	467
p – Pooled	545
r – Reinsured	393
q – Qualified	0
u – Under review	48
Subtotal	1,453
Dual Assignments	(34)
Total Modified Ratings	1,419

© A.M. Best Company. Used with permission, *Best's Key Rating Guide®—Property-Casualty, United States,* 2001 Edition, p. xviii.

insurers. Exhibit 12-15 shows the categories and the number of insurers assigned to each class in 2001. Exhibit 12-15 does not include insurers with a Best's Rating of E or F.

The Financial Size Category is not a measure of the insurer's financial performance or financial soundness. It is one measure of the insurer's capacity to assume large risks in either its insurance or its investment operations.

RISK-BASED CAPITAL

Risk-based capital (RBC) is a system developed by the NAIC to determine the minimum amount of capital an insurer needs to support its operations, given the insurer's risk characteristics. Before the implementation of RBC, state insurance codes made little or no allowance for risk differentials among insurers in the laws that specified minimum capital requirements. The NAIC RBC formula and the model law that authorizes it attempt to make the minimum capital required for a company a function of the risks assumed by that company.

The RBC model law enables insurance regulators to take regulatory action when it is warranted. The NAIC RBC formula prescribes four levels of regulatory intervention that permit state regulators to take decisive action before an insurer becomes too financially weak to be rehabilitated. Before the NAIC developed an RBC formula, state regulators were required to petition the courts and prove that the insurer was in financial difficulty before intervention was allowed, subjecting the insurer to regulatory control. The NAIC RBC formula offers an objective test of the insurer's solvency and matches regulatory action to the level of solvency concern. For example, the

Risk-based capital (RBC)
A system developed by the NAIC to determine the minimum amount of capital an insurer needs to support its operations.

first level of regulatory intervention is the Company Action Level. At this level, the insurer must submit a comprehensive financial plan that identifies the factors that caused the condition and proposes corrective action to solve the problem. At the fourth level of regulatory intervention, the Mandatory Control Level, the state regulators must seize control of the insurer.

EXHIBIT 12-15

2001 Financial Size Category

Financial Size Category	Adjusted Policyholders' Surplus ($ Millions)	Number of Companies
Class I	0 to 1	118
Class II	1 to 2	155
Class III	2 to 5	309
Class IV	5 to 10	273
Class V	10 to 25	303
Class VI	25 to 50	194
Class VII	50 to 100	224
Class VIII	100 to 250	322
Class IX	250 to 500	190
Class X	500 to 750	67
Class XI	750 to 1,000	103
Class XII	1,000 to 1,250	74
Class XIII	1,250 to 1,500	10
Class XIV	1,500 to 2,000	74
Class XV	2,000 or greater	390
Total Companies		***2,806**

* Does not include 49 companies rated E and F.

© A.M. Best Company. Used with permission, *Best's Key Rating Guide®—Property-Casualty, United States,* 2001 Edition, p. xix.

The nondiscretionary operation of the RBC model has benefits for insurers, state regulators, and the insurance-buying public. Insurers perform the RBC calculation themselves, so they know whether they will come under regulatory scrutiny. Before RBC was implemented, insurers performed the calculation, and many took early action to improve their total adjusted capital. Total adjusted capital is the result of an insurer's RBC calculation. State insurance departments that have been accredited by the NAIC do not have a choice about whether to implement the regulatory action specified; therefore, regulatory intervention is not arbitrary or motivated by political factors. State insurance regulators are given a clear mandate with RBC. Rehabilitation is no longer subject to delays caused by regulators' expectations that insurers' financial problems will solve themselves. The number of larger insurer failures in the 1980s increased public awareness that insurer solvency, the focus of insurance regulatory efforts, was not being achieved. RBC, part of a broader NAIC solvency policing agenda, is the insurance regulator's greatest weapon for ensuring solvency, which is fundamental to insurers' meeting obligations to policyholders and claimants.

The NAIC has been adamant since initial discussions about the creation of an RBC formula that the RBC level should not be construed to equate with financial strength. Even insurers with 150 percent to 200 percent of total adjusted capital are subject to state regulatory scrutiny at the company action level. The NAIC was equally concerned that its RBC formula not be used for making competitive comparisons among insurers. The result of an insurer's NAIC RBC calculation is shown in its NAIC Annual Statement. The NAIC RBC results for all insurers should not be ranked or used in insurer advertising. Comparisons among insurer RBC results are meaningless and could mislead the public. RBC is a regulatory tool designed to promptly redirect regulatory attention to financially distressed insurers.

The following sections, though not a comprehensive discussion, highlight the components of the NAIC RBC formula. The NAIC booklet entitled *1996 NAIC Property and Casualty Risk-Based Capital Report Including Overview and Instructions for Companies* provides a more thorough description. Although the main components of the NAIC RBC formula are well established, many of the factors used in the formula are regularly evaluated for their appropriateness and may change periodically. The NAIC formula was designed so that it could evolve into a more effective regulatory tool. As a result, the discussion that follows addresses only the main components of the NAIC RBC formula, not the details that support it.

The NAIC RBC formula has four main components: (1) asset risk, (2) credit risk, (3) underwriting risk, and (4) off-balance-sheet risk. Each component of the formula weighs the risks assumed by an insurer, because those risks vary by insurer. For example, one insurer might invest solely in short-term government bonds, while another holds a large portfolio of common stocks. The components of the NAIC RBC formula attempt to evaluate these risks and consolidate them into a single index. Because it is unlikely that all of the risks measured by the formula would befall an insurer simultaneously, the NAIC RBC formula tempers the amalgamation of components using a statistical adjustment called covariance. The covariance adjustment reduces the sum of the risk categories in the NAIC RBC formula.

Asset Risk

Asset risk is the chance that an asset's value will be lower than expected. Virtually all assets involve some such risk, though some assets are riskier than others. Under the RBC formula, the riskier assets require more underlying

Asset risk
The chance that an asset's value will be lower than expected.

capital than do less risky assets. The amount of capital required is determined by multiplying the NAIC Annual Statement value of the asset by a factor provided by the NAIC in the RBC booklet. Exhibit 12-16 shows some examples of the risk charges used. U.S. government bonds, for example, have a factor of 0.000. This indicates that they are considered risk-free; no underlying capital is needed to support them. On the other hand, bonds in default require $3 of supporting capital for each $10 of reported value of the bonds.

EXHIBIT 12-16

Sample of RBC Charges for Selected Asset Categories

Type of Investment	RBC Factor
U.S. government bonds	0.000
Highest-quality corporate bonds	0.003
Cash and short-term investments	0.003
High-quality corporate bonds	0.010 to 0.100
Bonds in default on principal or interest	0.300
Mortgages and collateral loans	0.050
Unaffiliated common stock	0.150
Real estate	0.100
Partnerships and joint ventures	0.200

Brian K. Atchinson, "The NAIC's Risk-Based Capital System," *NAIC Research Quarterly*, vol. 2, no. 4, October 1996, p. 7.

To determine the amount of risk-based capital required to support its asset risks, an insurer would multiply the NAIC Annual Statement value of each asset by the appropriate risk factor and sum the resulting products. Additional RBC charges are imposed if the insurer's investments are concentrated in securities issued by a small number of issuers; that is, if investments are not sufficiently diversified.

Credit Risk

Credit risk
Risk that reflects the possibility that the insurer will not be able to collect money owed to it.

Credit risk reflects the possibility that the insurer will not be able to collect money owed to it. One credit exposure is the chance that one or more of the insurer's reinsurers will not be able to pay amounts due under reinsurance contracts. Cessions to some reinsurers are not subject to the RBC charge. Such reinsurers include (1) state-mandated involuntary pools and federal insurance programs; (2) voluntary market mechanism pools that meet certain conditions specified in the RBC booklet; and (3) the insurer's U.S.-based affiliates, subsidiaries, and parents.

Other credit exposures that require RBC are (1) federal income tax recoverable; (2) interest, dividends, and real estate income due and accrued; (3) receivables from affiliates, subsidiaries, and parents; (4) amounts receivable relating to uninsured accident and health plans; and (5) aggregate write-ins for assets other than invested assets. For each of the categories above, the value shown in the NAIC Annual Statement is multiplied by the appropriate RBC factor to find the required RBC component for credit risk. The factor for reinsurance receivable is 0.100, and the factor for interest, dividends, and so forth is 0.010. The others in this category are all 0.050.

Underwriting Risk

Underwriting risk measures the volatility of the lines of insurance written by an insurer. For example, one insurer may specialize in physical damage insurance for private passenger automobiles, a line with virtually no exposure to large single losses and limited exposure to catastrophe losses. Another insurer may specialize in property insurance for large industrial risks, with an exposure to both large individual losses and catastrophe losses from earthquakes, tornadoes, and hurricanes.

Underwriting risk
Risk that measures the potential loss volatility of the lines of insurance written by an insurer.

The underwriting RBC varies by line of insurance. It is calculated by multiplying the written premiums and the loss and loss adjustment expense reserves for each line by their respective RBC factors. The RBC factors for each line can vary depending on the insurer's loss ratio (including loss adjustment expenses) and loss development experience for the line.

The experience adjustment to the RBC ratios is based on a comparison of the insurer's experience to the industry experience for the past nine years for most lines of insurance. Five years is used for special property, auto physical damage, and several other lines that do not have long loss development periods. This calculation reflects the underpricing of existing and future insurance products and the underestimation of loss reserves. Of all the components of an insurer's RBC, the formula places greatest emphasis on its underwriting risk.

Off-Balance-Sheet Risk

Off-balance-sheet risk recognizes those risks associated with contingent liabilities and excessive growth that do not appear on the insurer's balance sheet. If an insurer, for example, had significant investments in affiliates or had made financial guarantees on behalf of affiliates, the NAIC RBC formula would require additional capital to offset the risk present. Excessive growth is also penalized under the NAIC RBC formula. The excessive growth charge is based on a combination of the growth in gross premiums written for the most recent four years, the loss and loss adjustment expense reserves for the most recent year, and the net premiums written for the most recent year.

IRIS

The Insurance Regulatory Information System (IRIS) was developed by the NAIC in the 1970s, about two decades before the risk-based capital formula. It was originally known as the *Early Warning System*, a name that accurately indicates its original purpose. IRIS was developed to provide the regulatory authorities with an early warning that an insurer might be experiencing financial difficulty. An early warning might enable the regulators to rehabilitate the insurer or, if rehabilitation is not practical, to minimize the losses resulting from liquidation.

The Insurance Regulatory Information System consists of twelve tests. IRIS has two phases, statistical and analytical. In the statistical phase, key financial ratio results based on data submitted in insurers' annual financial statements is generated from NAIC's database. In the analytical phase, financial examiners and analysts review annual statements, financial ratios, and other automated solvency tools. Based on this review, each company is designated as either "Level A," "Level B," or "Reviewed—No Level." These levels are intended to assist states in prioritizing their workload so that potential problem companies are dealt with first. A "Level A" designation indicates the highest review priority but does not necessarily mean that the company is financially unsound. "Level B" companies may also have adverse financial results, but these companies do not require as immediate a response as those with a "Level A" designation. For a "Level A" company, the state regulators should perform a comprehensive analytical review of the company's financial condition to determine if closer regulatory attention is required.[6]

The twelve IRIS tests are listed below. The appearance of "(Best's)" after the test name indicates that the same test, possibly with some minor variations in calculation or interpretation, is used by the A.M. Best Company in formulating Best's Ratings. Detailed instructions for calculating the IRIS test ratios and more detailed explanations of their interpretation are given in the NAIC's publication *Insurance Regulatory Information System, Property and Casualty Edition*, published annually.

Gross Premiums Written to Policyholders' Surplus

The first test in the IRIS system is the ratio of gross written premium to policyholders' surplus, stated as a percentage. This ratio is a measurement of the adequacy of the insurers' policyholders' surplus, which provides a degree of protection in absorbing above-average losses. A ratio of 900 or less is considered acceptable. If this ratio is near 900 percent, it may be reviewed jointly with the Net Premiums Written to Policyholders' Surplus, described below.

Net Premium Written-to-Surplus Ratio (Best's)

The second test in the IRIS system is the ratio of net written premiums to policyholders' surplus, stated as a percentage. A ratio of 300 percent or less is considered acceptable. If this ratio is near 300 percent, it may be reviewed jointly with the ratio of surplus aid to surplus, described below, which shows the financial assistance provided to the insurer through its reinsurers.

Change in Writings (Best's)

Ratio 3 shows the percentage change in the insurer's net written premiums during the most recent year. Experience has shown that excessive growth in premium volume is frequently associated with financial problems. An increase or a decrease of 33 percent or less is considered acceptable for this ratio.

Ratio of Surplus Aid to Policyholders' Surplus

Ratio 4 is the ratio of surplus aid to surplus. Surplus aid, as used here, is the increase in the insurer's surplus that results from its purchases of reinsurance. The surplus aid is derived from ceding commissions on reinsurance ceded to nonaffiliated reinsurers. If the ratio exceeds 15 percent, it is considered unsatisfactory.

Two-Year Overall Operating Ratio (Best's)

Ratio 5 is calculated as the insurer's two-year loss ratio plus its two-year expense ratio minus its two-year investment income ratio. The loss ratio is the ratio of incurred losses and adjustment expenses and policyholder dividends to net earned premiums. The expense ratio is the ratio of underwriting expenses (all expenses except investment expenses) to net written premiums. The investment income ratio is the ratio investment income to net earned premiums. A ratio of less than 100 percent is considered satisfactory.

Investment Yield (Best's)

Ratio 6 is the ratio of net investment income to the average cash and invested assets for the year, stated as a percentage. A yield greater than 4.5 percent but less than 10.0 is considered satisfactory. A lower ratio may indicate excessive investment in home office facilities or subsidiaries and affiliates. A higher ratio may indicate investment in high risk instruments or extraordinary dividend payments from subsidiaries to the parent.

Change in Surplus (Best's)

Ratio 7 is the percentage change in adjusted policyholders' surplus during the year. Adjusted policyholders' surplus is the statutory policyholders' surplus (shown in the NAIC Annual Statement) plus equity in the unearned premium reserve. The ratio is considered satisfactory if it is in the range between a decrease of 10 percent and an increase of 50 percent.

Large increases in policyholders' surplus may result from an increase in surplus aid from reinsurance, from a manipulation of loss reserves development, or from other undesirable accounting techniques. Of course, large increases can also result from favorable developments, such as the issuance and sale of additional capital stock by the insurer. However, the reasons for any large change must be known and understood.

Liabilities to Liquid Assets (Best's)

Ratio 8 is the ratio of total liabilities to liquid assets. Liquid assets are computed as follows:

> Liquid Assets = Bonds, stocks, mortgage loans, real estate, other invested assets, receivable for securities
>
> + Installment premiums booked but deferred and not yet due
>
> + Cash and invested assets plus accrued investment income
>
> − Excess of real estate over five percent of liabilities
>
> − Investments in affiliated companies[7]

The ratio is considered satisfactory if it is less than 105 percent.

Gross Agents' Balances to Surplus

Ratio 9 is calculated by dividing agents' balances by policyholders' surplus, both as reported in the NAIC Annual Statement, with the result stated as a percentage. A ratio of less than 40 percent is considered satisfactory.

One-Year Reserve Development to Surplus (Best's)

Ratio 10 is the ratio of loss development during the past year to the insurer's policyholders' surplus at the beginning of the year (or the end of the prior year). The loss development is (1) the incurred losses for all years reported at the end of the year less incurred losses for the latest accident year minus (2) the incurred losses for all years reported at the end of the prior year. This figure is reported in Schedule P of the NAIC Annual Statement. The ratio is stated as a percentage, and a ratio of less than 20 percent is considered satisfactory.

A high ratio on this test may indicate that the insurer's loss reserves are inadequate and that its surplus has consequently been overstated. Ratios 11 and 12 also deal with the adequacy of loss reserves, indicating the importance attached to loss reserves as a factor in insurer insolvencies.

Two-Year Reserve Development to Surplus

Ratio 11 is calculated in the same manner as Ratio 10, except the loss reserves and surplus for the second prior year are used instead of those for the prior year. A ratio of less than 20 percent is also acceptable for Ratio 10.

Estimated Current Reserve Deficiency to Surplus

Ratio 12 is calculated by dividing the estimated current loss reserve deficiency by policyholders' surplus. The estimated reserve deficiency (or redundancy) is calculated by a rather complex formula based on the insurer's historical ratio of loss reserves to earned premiums. A work sheet for the calculation is included in the NAIC's publication *Insurance Regulatory Information System*. This ratio is considered satisfactory if it is less than 25 percent.

Other Tools

IRIS and RBC are merely two of the many tools available to regulators to avoid insurer insolvencies or reduce the losses that result from unavoidable insolvencies. Other tools, such as investment regulation, on-site examinations, and financial reporting, are equally or more important. However, understanding and complying with IRIS and RBC are important for insurers for reasons other than avoiding regulatory problems. These indicators of financial strength are also watched by sophisticated insurance buyers and producers, who may apply an even higher standard than the regulatory authorities.

SUMMARY

Insurance companies are financial intermediaries, and the assets controlled by U.S. insurers are considerable. The investment function of an insurer contributes significantly to its overall profitability. Although investment decisions are not discussed in this chapter, many other financially related management decisions are. Because of their analytical expertise, actuaries often participate in the decision-making process.

Establishing accurate loss reserves is crucial for an insurer. Loss reserves represent an insurer's largest balance sheet liability. Loss reserves established for liability lines of insurance are more volatile than those established for lines of property insurance. Most property claims are quickly settled, but liability claims might take years to resolve. Because liability loss reserves remain outstanding for several years, they are usually much larger than property loss reserves relative to earned premium. Interest in loss reserve analysis and verification have grown as the product mix of the U.S. insurance industry has transitioned from a predominately property-insurance industry to a predominately liability-insurance industry.

Success in marketing, underwriting, claims, and other insurer functional departments requires insurers to plan. Planning might be short- or long-term, and increasingly sophisticated models are used to project possible contingencies. Deterministic models are used when consistent results are expected. Probabilistic models are used when the results might be affected by some chance variation.

A key area of an insurer's financial well-being is the adequacy of its reinsurance program. Reinsurance provides an insurer with stability, yet that stability is obtained at a price. An analysis of an insurer's reinsurance program seeks to find the best balance between the stability afforded an insurer and the cost of reinsurance.

An insurer's promise to pay claims is no more valuable than its ability to do so. The A.M. Best Company established its ratings to simplify the complex task of evaluating insurer financial statements and to meet the needs of the unsophisticated public that needs that information. The A.M. Best ratings measure an insurer's financial strength in meeting policyholder obligations.

The primary purpose of insurance regulation is to monitor the solvency of insurers and safeguard the public from the effects of those insolvencies that do occur. The NAIC has developed several tools to assist in identifying financially weak insurers. The NAIC's Risk-Based Capital formula considers an insurer's asset risk, credit risk, underwriting risk, and off-balance-sheet risk and develops a minimum amount of capital each insurer should maintain. The Insurance Regulatory Information System (IRIS) consists of eleven financial ratios. Insurers that develop values outside an acceptable range on three of the ratios are subject to scrutiny by state regulators. Both NAIC tools serve the public interest by helping regulators address insurers with financial problems before they impinge on the insolvent insurer's claim-paying ability.

CHAPTER NOTES

1. A.M. Best Company, *Best's Aggregates and Averages, Property-Casualty Edition, United States*, 2001 Edition, pp. 4, 299.

2. *Exposure Draft of the Actuarial Standard of Practice, Actuarial Appraisals of Insurance Companies, Segments of Insurance Companies, and/or Blocks of Insurance Contracts* (Actuarial Standards Board, April 1990), pp. 4, 5.

3. A.M. Best Company, *Best's Key Rating Guide*®, *Property-Casualty, United States*, 2001 Edition, p. viii.

4. A.M. Best Company, *Best's Key Rating Guide*®, 2001, p. viii.

5. A.M. Best Company, *Best's Key Rating Guide*®, 2001, p. xii.

6. National Association of Insurance Commissioners, Insurance Regulatory Information System (IRIS), *2001 Property/Casualty Edition* (NAIC: Kansas City, 2002), p. 2.

7. National Association of Insurance Commissioners, Insurance Regulatory Information System (IRIS), *2001 Property/Casualty Edition*, p. 22.

Direct Your Learning

Claim Adjusting

After learning the subject matter of this chapter, you should be able to:

■ Illustrate how the performance of the claim department supports the insurance operation. In support of this educational objective:

- Explain the objectives of the claim department.

- Describe the environment in which the claim department must operate.

- Describe how the claim function can be organized.

■ Describe the claim adjustment process.

■ Explain the measures used to evaluate claim performance.

■ Explain how claim activities are regulated.

Develop Your Perspective

What are the main topics covered in the chapter?

Claim adjusting handles the demands for claim payment. In that role, the claim department fulfills the insurer's promises to the policyholders, and the claim department helps the insurer achieve its profit objectives. The structure of the department and its processes can vary.

Speculate regarding the outcome if a claim department failed to fulfill its role for an insurance company.

- How would an insurer's reputation and profitability change?

Why is it important to know these topics?

By understanding the objectives and functions of claim adjusting, you can appreciate the crucial role it plays within an insurance company. Adjusters are on the front line with customers and claimants. Adjusters represent the insurer in ensuring that claim payments are fair.

Judge the success of a claim department in fulfilling its function.

- What activities are required to be successful?

How can you use this information?

Compare your own organization's claim department with the one described in the chapter.

- Are the claim adjusters' objectives the same?
- What is the management structure and the settlement authority?
- Is the claim adjusting process similar?
- How might processes be improved?

Chapter 13

Claim Adjusting

Individuals and businesses purchase insurance to protect themselves from the financial consequences of loss and to alleviate the worry associated with the possibility of loss. Once a loss occurs, the insurer is expected to fulfill its responsibility to the policyholder and satisfy the demand for payment. **Claim adjusting** is the insurance company function that handles demands for claim payments.

This chapter lays the foundations for the study of claim adjusting by exploring the objectives of claim adjusting and the environment in which it is performed. The chapter also provides an overview of the claim adjusting process, focusing on aspects common to most types of claims. Issues particular to specific types of insurance are discussed in Chapter 14—Property Claim Adjusting and Chapter 15—Liability Claim Adjusting.

Claim adjusting
The insurance company function that handles demands for claim payments. Through claim adjusting, the insurer fulfills its promise to the insured, controls claim costs, and generates accurate claim information.

THE CLAIM ENVIRONMENT

The claim department exists to fulfill the insurer's promises to its policyholders. Because claim departments control more than half of what insurers spend, their proper and efficient performance is important to an insurer's profitability. The loss payments, expenses, and other information generated by the claim department is essential to the marketing, underwriting, and pricing of insurance products. Claim personnel are among the most visible of insurer employees to policyholders and the public. Claim adjusters must work well with a variety of people. Managing, organizing, and delegating settlement authority within claim departments contribute to their success.

Objectives of the Claim Department

Managing an efficient claim operation requires that senior management recognize the importance of the claim function to both the insurance consumer and the insurer itself.

Complying With the Contractual Promise

The primary function of claim adjusting is to satisfy the obligations of the insurer to the policyholder as set forth in the insurance policy. Following a loss, the adjustment process becomes the embodiment of the insurance policy, and, in the course of this process, the promise of the insuring agreement to "pay," defend, or indemnify in the event of a covered loss is fulfilled.

The insurer achieves that objective by providing fair, prompt, and equitable service to the policyholder, either (1) directly when the loss involves a first-party claim made by the policyholder against the insurer or (2) indirectly through the adjustment of a third-party loss to persons making a claim against the policyholder and to whom the policyholder may be liable. (Unfair claim practices laws have been enacted to ensure that policyholders and claimants are not being mistreated. An extensive discussion of the NAIC Unfair Trade Practices Model Act is presented later in this chapter.)

From the insurer's perspective, claims are expected, and adjusters must deal with them routinely. The occurrence of a loss and its consequences can be all-consuming. Adjusters must therefore deal with policyholders and claimants in extremely stressful circumstances. Insurance is marketed not only as a financial mechanism to restore policyholders to a pre-loss state but also as a way to ensure peace of mind. The manner in which an adjuster handles a claim can help soothe the policyholder who has suffered a devastating loss. This result may be most evident after a disaster such as a major storm or a serious accident in which multiple losses involve numerous people. Were it not for insurance, administered through the claim adjusting process, recovery would be slow, inefficient, and difficult.

Achieving the Insurer's Profit Objective

Most of the discussion about insurer profit objectives focuses on the marketing and underwriting departments—key contributors to an insurer's success. However, not recognizing the operation of the claim function as central to the success of the insurance operation would be shortsighted.

For example, overpaid claims result in lower profits. Policyholders are entitled to a fair settlement of their demands and nothing more. By overcompensating a policyholder or claimant, the insurer unnecessarily raises the cost of insurance for all of its policyholders.

Conversely, tight-fisted claim handling may result in angry policyholders, more litigated claims, or the wrath of insurance regulators. Policyholders and claimants are likely to accept the insurer's settlement offer if they understand the insurer's position on the claim and believe they are being treated fairly. If a claim adjuster treats a policyholder or claimant unfairly, the insurer may find itself in a lawsuit. Claims that are mishandled and that eventually lead to litigation erode goodwill and generate increased expenses for the insurer.

Insurers survive or fail to some extent on their reputation for providing the service promised. A reputation for resisting meritorious claims can invalidate the effectiveness of insurer advertisements or of goodwill earned over years of operation.

Uses of Claim Information

The claim function provides valuable information that helps other departments guide the insurer's operational direction. The three primary departments that receive management information from the claim department are the marketing, underwriting, and actuarial departments.

Marketing

The marketing department requires information relating to customer satisfaction, timeliness of settlements, and other factors that assist in marketing the insurance product. The marketing department recognizes that the other services the insurer performs for the policyholder are quickly forgotten if the insurer fails to perform well after the occurrence of a loss.

Many insurers that market commercial policies have developed "niche" products that address the needs of specific types of policyholders. The intent of these insurers is to become the recognized expert in certain business classes, providing a product and service that cannot be easily equaled elsewhere. Niche marketers recognize that the claim adjusting process can be a possible source for new coverage ideas and product innovations that can be incorporated into future policy forms.

Producers must also have policyholder loss information to prepare renewal policies properly. Many commercial policies are subject to rating plans that affect the policy premium, based, in part, on the policyholder's loss experience. In personal lines, personal auto policies may be surcharged when property damage claims are paid during the policy year.

Claim personnel must inform producers of court rulings that affect the insurer's exposure or pricing, such as interpretations of policy exclusions or application of limits.

Underwriting

Individual underwriters are interested in claim information for the specific accounts they have approved. A post-loss evaluation may reveal aspects of the risk that an underwriter should have detected when first reviewing an application. Even if obvious clues were not overlooked initially, reviewing the claim file can uncover operations and activities that the underwriter would have investigated more thoroughly had they been apparent on the application. In some instances, material aspects of the insured exposures have changed since the policy was first underwritten. Discovering these changes could prompt discussion about immediate policy cancellation or nonrenewal of the account. Underwriters also recognize that losses occur on even the best accounts. The occurrence of a minor loss could therefore create the opportunity to take corrective action, through the loss control department, that could prevent a subsequent major loss.

A number of similar claims may alert underwriting management to larger problems for a particular type or class of policyholder. These claims might be the result of new processes or technologies being used by the class of policyholders as a whole. For example, some roofing contractors may have tried to speed the process of replacing composite roofs by moving the tar smelter to the roof of the structure being repaired. This practice might have caused a number of fire losses. An adverse court ruling could also cause the loss experience of a class of business to deteriorate or could increase the number of claims presented.

Actuarial

Actuaries need accurate information not only on losses that have been paid but also on losses that have occurred and are reserved for payment. Such information helps actuaries establish reserves for IBNR losses and predict the development of open claims for which the reserves might change substantially over time before the claim is finally settled.

Claim Department Contacts

In addition to the producing agent, the claim department is the branch of the insurer most visible to the public. The claim department must therefore interact effectively with outside contacts, such as the general public, plaintiffs' attorneys, defense attorneys, regulators, and claim organizations and associations.

General Public

Although many insurance companies have a public relations department affiliated with advertising, the insurer's public image is largely determined by the behavior of the claim department. When Consumer Union surveyed 34,000 readers of its publication *Consumer Reports*, those surveyed reported that "promptness in claims handling was the single most significant factor in deciding how much they liked a company's service." For the most part, these respondents had been paid promptly for claims, with 70 percent saying they received their check within fourteen days.[1] Delay in receiving payment for a claim is the primary claim-related complaint; it causes many claimants and policyholders to seek attorney representation.

The nature of claim adjusting places the adjuster in a unique position to take advantage of unsophisticated policyholders and claimants. Adjusters must recognize that adjusting requires a high degree of integrity, involving more than just honesty. The adjustment process requires keeping a promise the insurer made, and the adjuster represents the insurer's sincerity to the policyholder.

Many states require adjusters to be bonded or to pass a written examination to become licensed, but this requirement is neither uniform nor universal. Exhibit 13-1 shows a list of states that require licensing of independent adjusters. Fewer states require licensing of company-employed adjusters.

Plaintiffs' Attorneys

In some areas of claims and in certain areas of the country, claimants are more likely to hire attorneys, often leading to costly litigation. Although attorney representation can result in a higher payment by the insurer, representation does not necessarily result in higher settlements to claimants, because they must pay expenses and attorney bills from the settlements. Attorney representation also does not guarantee a faster settlement.

EXHIBIT 13-1

Licensing of Independent Insurance Adjusters

States Requiring Adjuster Licenses

• Alaska	• Kentucky	• Oklahoma
• Arizona	• Maine	• Oregon
• Arkansas	• Michigan	• Rhode Island
• California	• Minnesota	• South Carolina
• Colorado	Mississippi	• Texas
• Connecticut	Montana	• Utah
• Delaware	• Nevada	• Vermont
• Florida	• New Hampshire	• Washington
• Georgia	New Mexico	• West Virginia
• Hawaii	• New York	• Wyoming
• Idaho	• North Carolina	• Puerto Rico (Terr.)

• States that require more than the payment of a license fee.

© A.M. Best Company. Used with permission, *Best's Directory of Recommended Insurance Attorneys and Adjusters*, 1996 Edition.

Litigation of third-party claims has become one of the most visible and expensive problems facing liability insurers. Although litigation of first-party claims is also a costly problem, the immediate costs associated with the tort system have led many insurers to realize that litigation prevention must be an active part of the claim function.

Defense Attorneys

The duty to defend under liability policies is as important as, or more important than, the duty to indemnify. Many insurers spend as much money on outside defense attorneys as they do on claim department staff salaries and independent adjusting fees combined. Managing defense expenses is an essential component of managing the claim function.

Insurers typically hire an attorney from the jurisdiction where the claim is presented. Most attorneys limit their practice to one or two counties within a state, affording them a familiarity with the local legal system. Lawyers from a particular jurisdiction are more likely to identify with the community and with potential juries. However, rising legal costs have made the use of in-house counsel for claim defense more attractive for many insurers, regardless of the advantages inherent in using local attorneys. Many insurers have created in-house law offices in major metropolitan areas to defend claims.

Defense attorneys usually work on an hourly fee basis. Typical fees range from $100 per hour to $250 per hour, with $100 to $150 per hour being the most common. Fees may vary based on geographical location, with higher fees in larger metropolitan areas. Because defense costs mount quickly at those rates, routine litigation can cost the insurer thousands of dollars.

The ideal situation for the insurer is to avoid litigation altogether through prompt investigation and resolution. A claim going to suit might indicate that some aspect of the claim adjusting process failed to operate properly. Perhaps the claim department was understaffed, or the individual adjuster did not recognize a legitimate claim or offered an unrealistic settlement amount. Alternatively, the adjuster may not have explained the merits of the insurer's case well enough for the plaintiff to recognize a valid settlement offer. Of course, even if the insurer presents a valid case, the plaintiff might still be convinced that the claim is worth more and might seek an attorney.

State Regulators

State insurance regulators monitor the insurer's activities in the claim settlement process. Regulators exercise controls through licensing adjusters, investigating consumer complaints, and performing market conduct investigations. Enforcement is usually handled through the Unfair Claims Settlement Practices Act or similar legislation.

Licensing

Not all jurisdictions currently license adjusters, and no standard procedure or uniform regulation exists for those that do. Some states require licensure only for independent adjusters, who work for many insurance companies, or public adjusters, who represent policyholders in first-party claims against insurers. In other states, staff adjusters must be licensed as well.

Most states or jurisdictions with licensing laws also require that the adjuster or his or her employer post a bond or show evidence of a fidelity bond. Many states with licensing laws also require the applicant to pass a written examination, which may be given either on a multiple-line basis or on specific lines of coverage. Some states also license vehicle damage or property appraisers, but others exempt such persons. A licensed attorney who is acting as an adjuster may be exempt from licensing requirements. Temporary permits or licenses are frequently granted to out-of-state adjusters brought in by insurers for major catastrophes, such as storms or other disasters.

Consumer Complaints

Claim departments must also pay attention to consumer complaints made to state insurance regulatory departments. Most states have a specific time limit within which inquiries by the department must be answered or acted on. Failure to respond can result in expensive fines and even in the loss of the adjuster's—or his or her employer's—license. Nevertheless, the relationship between state insurance departments and adjusters is usually positive.

Market Conduct Investigations

Insurance regulators periodically perform market conduct investigations either as part of their normal audit of insurance company activities or in response to specific complaints. The typical market conduct audit concerns more than just claim practices; it includes a review of all departments that directly interact with policyholders and claimants.

Claim Organizations and Associations

Although claim personnel represent one of the largest segments of those employed by the property-casualty insurance business, no single national organization or association exists for people who work in claims. However, there are several organizations whose focus is important to claim personnel. The National Association of Independent Insurance Adjusters (NAIIA) is open to independent adjusters who meet certain standards. The NAIIA promulgates adjusting standards; maintains communications with insurance companies; encourages ethical practices; and conducts national, regional, and state meetings. The NAIIA publishes the *Blue Book of Adjusters*, which lists its members throughout the country and maintains educational resources available to any interested party.

The Property Loss Research Bureau (PLRB) and the Liability Insurance Research Bureau (LIRB) are divisions of the Alliance of American Insurers. These organizations are primarily dedicated to education and research. They exist to provide expert research and analysis of claims and legal issues important to member companies. They also conduct an annual education conference that is open to anyone in the insurance business.

Property Claim Services, a division of American Insurance Services Group, provides catastrophe management and educational services to the industry. Its educational services include seminars, reference manuals, videos, and conferences.

The Loss Executives Association, consisting of claim experts in the property field, conducts seminars for its members. The Conference of Casualty Insurance Companies provides arbitration and educational services to its members. Arbitration Forums, Inc., administers through its many local offices various intercompany arbitration agreements, such as the Nationwide Intercompany Agreement and the Fire and Allied Lines Subrogation Arbitration Agreement.

The National Insurance Crime Bureau (NICB) was formed from the National Auto Theft Bureau (NATB) and the Insurance Crime Prevention Institute (ICPI). The NICB fights all forms of insurance fraud and crime, including automobile theft, medical fraud, and staged losses. It offers presentations on crime detection for claim representatives.

Local claim associations exist in most metropolitan areas. These groups are valuable sources of contacts within the local claim community and of information about local matters, such as defense law firms, public adjusters, plaintiff attorneys, and service providers. Most of the meetings held by these groups have both a social and an educational purpose. In fact, most meetings are organized around an educational presentation. Many state claim associations are likewise active and sponsor worthwhile educational programs.

Organization of the Claim Function

No ideal organizational structure exists for the claim function. What is best is generally what works. What works reflects the insurer's overall organization, its size, how it has grown, and its willingness to use outside providers of claim services.

Most claim departments can be distinguished by the degree of centralization and the division of labor along insurance product lines.

Centralized Versus Decentralized

Insurers can operate with either a centralized or a decentralized claim operation. Different insurers have been successful with each approach.

A centralized claim operation consists of one home office at which all claims are handled or a home office with few regional offices. Centralized operations can be more efficient than decentralized operations regarding the cost of office rental, supervisory overhead, information systems support, and support staff. This approach works well when supervision is important or when claims do not require personal inspection.

The advantages and disadvantages of decentralized operations are the reverse of those for centralized operations. Decentralization can be more costly and difficult to supervise, but it is preferable for claims that must be adjusted in person. Because many claim tasks, such as property inspections and witness interviews, cannot be done as well from a remote location, claims can never be centralized as effectively as can underwriting or processing support functions.

The line of business, the volume of business, the geographic location, and the density of risks an insurer writes may determine how it structures its claim operations, where it locates its field offices, and whether it uses inside adjusting procedures or a large number of staff or independent field adjusters. An insurer that writes a substantial amount of workers compensation insurance, for instance, may locate a workers compensation claim office in an area where its policyholders have many employees, or it may contract with a local independent adjusting firm in that area to handle claims.

By Product or Line of Business

Some companies divide their workload by product or line of business—a property claim department handles first-party claims, a casualty claim department handles third-party claims, a marine department handles marine claims, and so forth. Other insurers divide the tasks by commercial and personal lines. Responsibility for those lines of business is usually subdivided into geographic regions. As mentioned, some large personal lines insurers maintain a number of local claim offices, often several in a single metropolitan area. Some local offices may conduct a single activity, such as appraisal of automobile physical damage claims. These smaller claim offices report to the nearest regional service center. Many insurers also permit their producers to handle minor claims directly with their policyholders.

Management Structure and Settlement Authority

The claim department hierarchy and the flow of settlement authority within the department vary by insurer. Usually, the vice president of claims is a key member of the insurer's management team. Reporting directly to the vice president are one or more assistant vice presidents, who are responsible for individual coverage lines. Reporting to each of those may be one or more claim managers. The level of settlement authority required to settle or deny a claim usually follows the chain of command within the company. The settlement authority granted individual adjusters and examiners varies by experience, training, and education.

Beneath the senior level, claim adjusting personnel are organized by responsibility and authority into claim managers, examiners, supervisors, and adjusters. A diagram of an insurer's claim department structure is shown in Exhibit 13-2.

Claim Managers

In most claim organizations, the person below the top claim executive usually has the title of claim manager. Regardless of whether this individual works out of the home office of the insurer, a regional office, or a branch office, he or she is usually the senior person in the claim department involved with individual claim file decisions and loss management. The claim manager is often in charge of both claim files and the general administration and supervision of the claim department.

Examiners

Many insurers employ examiners at regional or home offices. Although an examiner's job description and title may vary among companies, the examiner is primarily a claim analyst, assessing the coverage, liability, and damage factors of any claim and extending settlement authority to adjusters or recommending a settlement amount or other authorization to a superior. The examiner may also be responsible for certain internal claim processes, such as preparing data input, reporting claims to a reinsurer, establishing a file reserve, or referring a claim file to counsel if a coverage or liability issue arises. Examiners are technical experts who do not usually supervise office staff.

EXHIBIT 13-2

Insurer's Claim Department Structure

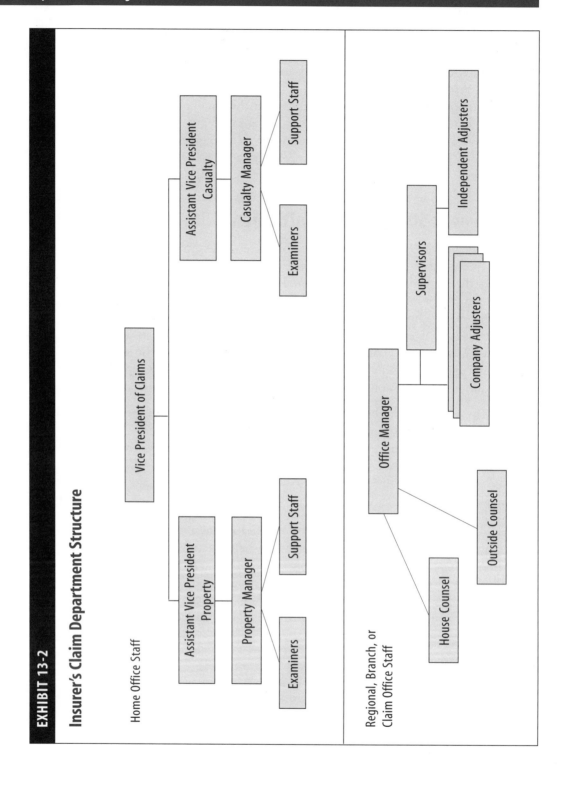

Supervisors

Most claim managers structure their departments into various units or subsections, either by line of coverage or by geographic location. Each unit is under the direction of a supervisor. The claim supervisor is usually responsible for the daily activities of the unit. The supervisor may serve in two capacities, both as a supervisor of claim personnel and as a supervisor of the claim files, giving guidance to as many as ten or more adjusters, appraisers, and other representatives on the routine investigation, evaluation, and disposition of the files. The supervisor's authority is usually also extended to the activities of defense attorneys, independent adjusters, appraisers, and other outside service personnel with whom the insurer may contract.

The supervisor may have certain levels of settlement or denial authority and may also be responsible for the supervision of the file if it goes into litigation and is referred to outside counsel. Supervision of outside defense attorneys may come from either the supervisor or the insurer's inside counsel, or in some cases from a staff adjuster. Many companies maintain a list of approved outside counsel in the localities where their losses are most likely to occur and often provide specific instructions and specify the authority granted to those attorneys.

Adjusters

The **adjuster** is responsible for investigating, evaluating, and negotiating the coverage, liability, and damages relating to each claim. Whether the adjuster's position is called "claim adjuster," "claim representative," or some other title, the adjuster is the insurer's direct contact with the policyholder, claimant, witness, or attorney; the liaison to the producer or broker; and the one, to a great extent, on whose shoulders the reputation of the insurer rests.

Adjuster (claim representative)
A person responsible for investigating, evaluating, and settling insurance claims.

An adjuster may be an employee of the insurer, an employee of an insurer-owned adjustment bureau or subsidiary firm, or an independent adjuster retained either on a contract basis or on an individual assignment basis. Staff adjusters usually have some authority to act and issue checks on behalf of the insurer without prior clearance once coverage has been confirmed, whereas the authority of an independent adjuster may be limited.

Adjusters are usually employed either as "field" adjusters who operate outside of the claim office or as "inside" adjusters who adjust claims by phone and mail. Field adjusters spend much of their time visiting the scene of a loss, interviewing witnesses, investigating damages, and meeting with policyholders, claimants, attorneys, and other persons involved in the claim. They may inspect damaged property themselves or work closely with damage appraisers and may attend trials and hearings on the claims assigned to them.

Inside claim adjusting is appropriate for claims whose costs are known or when additional investigation would not be beneficial. Examples of claims handled by inside adjusters are personal auto comprehensive claims resolving policyholder losses such as stolen hubcaps, broken windshields, and towing or workers compensation claims involving only medical expenses. Inside adjusters may also be responsible for cases in litigation in which outside investigation is no longer necessary.

Independent Adjusters

Independent adjusting
companies
Companies that provide claim adjusting services to a variety of insurers and self-insured companies. Independent adjusters handle claims on a case-by-case basis for a fee. They are not employees of insurers.

Independent adjusting companies provide claim adjusting services to a variety of insurers and self-insureds. Independent adjusting firms derive revenue by charging insurers a fee for claim settlement services. They may be owned by insurance brokers, insurance groups, or their own shareholders.

Two of the best-known national adjusting firms are GAB Business Services, Inc., and Crawford & Company. GAB Business Services was originally formed by several insurers to handle large property claims, but it is now independent of any insurer and handles all lines of claims. With its business divided almost equally between property and liability insurance loss handling, the firm also performs value appraisals and inspection surveys. Crawford & Company maintains about 700 offices domestically and internationally, offering loss adjustment services in liability, property, marine, environmental damage, flood, and aircraft insurance.

National adjusting firms serve not only insurance companies but also large self-insured corporations and government agencies. They may also offer related services, such as medical cost containment programs, health and vocational rehabilitation services, property and vehicle damage appraisals, loss data processing, and similar operations.

Many large insurer groups and brokerage firms own their own independent adjusting companies. These subsidiaries provide countercyclical revenue so that even during periods of heavy losses, fee income from adjusting services is available to partially offset losses. Whenever possible, the insurer-owner uses its own facilities. Additionally, most of these independent adjusters actively solicit nonrelated insurer accounts. Many independent adjusters operate in a specific geographic region. These adjusters cite their familiarity with the producers, policyholders, claimants, and legal environment as a reason to employ them when claims occur in their region.

Independent adjusters enable an insurer to have comprehensive coverage of a geographic area without the expense of leasing office space, hiring adjusters, and incurring other expenses associated with operating a claim office. Most companies use independent adjusters at some point in their claim program simply because claims can occur in places where the insurer does not have available staff. Many insurers keep full-time staff at minimal levels, so they must hire temporary employees or independent adjusters during periods of peak activity. In some instances, insurers hire independent adjusters to handle claims outside the normal expertise of the insurer's adjusters, such as pollution or asbestos claims. Access to specialized claim-handling expertise may be the deciding factor that wins the policyholder's account for the insurer.

In some "fronting" arrangements between businesses with a high self-insured retention (SIR) and the insurer, the insured may be instrumental in selecting the independent adjusting firm that will handle the claims on behalf of the insurer. Many of these adjusters operate autonomously, even maintaining trust accounts funded by the insured for payment of claims within the SIR and providing statistical data reports on the losses to the insurer and policyholders.

Insurance companies may also hire independent adjusters when they have been unable to hire skilled personnel on a permanent basis or to supplement staff during vacations. In the event of a catastrophic loss such as a hurricane or an earthquake, independent adjusting companies can supply claim adjusters to support the increase in claims.

An insurer that routinely employs an adjusting firm will usually provide instructions about where to report and how much authority the adjuster will have to act on behalf of the insurer. Many insurers supply settlement checks to their approved independent adjusters and expect them to operate within the scope of their authority.

Producer Claim Services

Most independent-agency insurers permit their producers to handle minor claims within specific settlement authority or to make assignments to independent adjusters. Extending settlement authority to producers expedites claim service. Producers like the opportunity to be the insurer's representative when the coverage purchased is finally needed. They can remind their clients of the value of their services and can reevaluate the policyholder's coverage. Additionally, many large commercial insurance brokers and agents employ claim personnel who assist policyholders with filing claims under policies serviced by the agent or broker.

Most large personal lines insurers have completely divorced their marketing and claim functions. Producers for these insurers may obtain the essential facts from the policyholder and forward the information to the regional service center for assignment to a local claim office. Some producers simply give the policyholder a telephone number of the insurer's claim service and a brief explanation of how the claim will be handled.

Public Adjusters

Many states permit the licensing of **public adjusters**, who represent policyholders in property claims against insurers. These adjusters assist their clients in preparing the verification of loss, negotiating values with the insurer's adjuster, and preparing the settlement documents, such as the proof-of-loss forms. Public adjusters are generally paid a percentage, such as 10 percent, of the settlement the policyholder receives from the insurer, which gives them an incentive to seek the highest possible settlement for their clients.

Many individuals and small businesses, without the time to deal with all of the documentation and negotiation required in a large fire or other property

Public adjusters
Adjusters who represent policyholders to negotiate a settlement with the insurer in exchange for a fee or a percentage of the settlement.

loss, find the services of the public adjuster convenient. When the insurance company is acting responsibly and in good faith, a public adjuster should not make a significant difference in the amount of the recovery. Any increase may be immediately offset by the public adjuster's fee. If policyholders believe that they are being treated unfairly, they should initially consult their producer for help.

Other Claim Adjusting Personnel

Insurers rely on other experts to handle a specialized type or a particular aspect of a claim. Among these are specialist adjusters, cause and origin experts, material damage appraisers, reconstruction experts, private investigators, accountants, health and rehabilitation experts, medical cost containment consultants, professional engineers, and other support personnel.

Specialist Adjusters

Both independent and staff adjusters tend to specialize in specific areas of claims. Those who have completed certain educational requirements and have a certain amount of experience may be granted a special title, such as "general adjuster." An adjuster who handles a single line of coverage may use that specialty in his or her title—for example, "property adjuster" or "marine adjuster."

One type of specialist adjuster is a catastrophe adjuster, who travels to the location of major disasters and remains there until all claims have been settled. Catastrophe adjusters are trained to handle natural disasters (such as floods, hurricanes, tornadoes, hail losses, earthquakes, and volcanic eruptions), man-made disasters, or multiple liability losses.

Some insurers and independent adjusting firms maintain special pollution liability teams that are prepared to go anywhere a major loss has occurred. These teams mitigate damages as well as adjust claims. Their quick action may help to improve policyholders' perception of the insurance company and reduce the likelihood of class action suits.

Another type of specialty line adjuster is the marine surveyor, or "average" adjuster, who exclusively handles loss to freight, cargo, vessels (including everything from small watercraft and yachts to oceangoing ships), and, occasionally, aircraft. ("Average" is a marine insurance term for loss.)

Cause and Origin Experts

Cause and origin experts attempt to determine where and how a fire began. These experts are often consulted for fires that have a suspicious origin or when the possibility for subrogation exists.

Material Damage Appraisers

Many adjusters are also trained as property or vehicle damage appraisers or evaluators. Others who work directly for insurers or for independent adjusters specialize only in the appraisal of damages. The appraiser inspects the damage and, if it is reparable, writes an estimate of the cost to repair. The appraiser then obtains an agreed repair price with a repair facility, contractor, body shop, or other organization that has been selected by the policyholder or claimant to make the repairs.

If an item is irreparable or missing because of theft or other loss, the appraiser assists the adjuster in determining the item's value or replacement cost and in disposing of salvage. Many insurers use wholesale replacement organizations that can obtain items commonly involved in losses at a lower price than can the policyholder. They also use automobile salvage "pools" to sell vehicles deemed to be a "total loss" to the highest bidder. Other companies assist adjusters in disposing of other salvage, such as merchandise from a commercial fire loss.

Reconstruction Experts

Some experts specialize in reconstructing the events of automobile accidents. They explain how an auto accident occurred and testify as to the rate of speed the vehicles were traveling, to the point of impact between the vehicles, and, in some cases, to what the various drivers were able to see before the accident.

Private Investigators

Many insurers also employ the services of detectives in the investigation of their claims for background and activity checks on claimants, surveillance of claimants who are allegedly injured, financial records checks, process serving, and other similar activities for which private investigators are licensed. Forensic engineers and highly trained arson investigators are also employed by insurers to investigate unusual or questionable losses. Many of these investigators operate as independent contractors. Most insurers also have their own special investigations unit (SIU).

Accountants

Accountants may be required to examine the books of a policyholder in first-party claims for loss of use and claims for damaged inventory. Accountants may also be used in liability claims to verify the financial losses demanded by claimants.

Health and Rehabilitation Experts

Liability insurers rely on a variety of medical specialists to assist in claim and medical management. Medical consultants and rehabilitation nurses also help arrange independent medical examinations (IMEs) and obtain second opinions before agreeing to a treatment or surgical process suggested by the attending physician.

Many states' workers compensation laws now mandate a variety of vocational rehabilitation services, such as employment consultation and job retraining for disabled workers. Large workers compensation insurers may operate their own rehabilitation firm as a subsidiary of the insurer, and some independent adjusting firms have health and rehabilitation divisions that provide such services.

Medical Cost Containment Consultants

The insurer's health experts also review medical reports and audit bills from physicians and other medical providers. In a process called "utilization review," the nurse or medical technician examines the physician's report to ascertain the diagnosis and then determines whether the treatment being provided is reasonable and necessary for that diagnosis. Because most claims are for a specific injury or illness, the insurer does not want to pay for unreasonable charges or for services that may be unrelated to the claim.

Professional Engineers

Many slip-and-fall cases involve steps, stairways, or sidewalks. Products liability cases often allege improper design. Professional engineers can help the insurer determine whether any OSHA requirement or a building code was violated.

Support Personnel

In addition to the experts already described, claim departments may employ a variety of support personnel for technical and clerical functions. Larger personal lines insurers may employ auto damage appraisers who inspect damaged vehicles locally and reach either an agreed price for their repair or an assessment of their value if they are a total loss. The insurer may also have other staff technicians who can assist in certain aspects of loss, including special fraud investigators, coverage analysts, research librarians (especially for legal issues), and even laboratory and engineering assistants.

Clerical assistants may include transcribers, file room assistants, mail room clerks, data entry clerks, check typists, and others who help the claim department run smoothly.

Unbundled Claim Services

Larger commercial businesses commonly have both the necessary attributes and the desire to retain, rather than insure, losses. Although many of these businesses may have the financial resources and sophistication to manage claims without the services of an insurer, they may not have or want to maintain the necessary in-house talent to handle their own claims.

Many insurers "unbundle" their services, permitting these firms to purchase loss control, data processing, or claim adjusting services separately. Independent adjusters or third-party administrators also offer their services directly to businesses choosing to self-insure their loss exposures. For the insurers involved in these programs, the unbundling of insurer services offers an opportunity for the claim department to generate revenue for the insurer without the exposure to underwriting risk.

THE CLAIM ADJUSTING PROCESS[2]

No universal, uniform process exists for adjusting all claims. The steps that an insurer takes to settle a claim vary significantly by claim. Although settling similar types of claims requires taking similar steps, so many challenges arise in settling claims that insurers have developed extensive procedures for claim adjusters to follow.

The manner in which property claims and liability claims are handled differs significantly. This difference is reflected throughout the claims organization in terms of how personnel specialize, which internal forms are used, and which procedures are followed. Although the distinction between property and liability underwriting has been gradually eroding since the introduction of package policies, this distinction remains in most claim operations. Policyholder claims can usually be categorized as either property (first-party) or liability (third-party). Chapters 14 and 15 present the property and liability claim adjusting processes in detail. This section deals with some of the common elements of both processes.

Virtually all claims are legitimate demands on the insurer to fulfill its obligations. In evaluating a claim, the adjuster must consider whether the claim in question should be paid and whether any defenses to the claim exist. This approach appears to be a negative process, but it usually has a positive result and is similar to the screening process that underwriters use in reviewing applicants.

In deciding whether to pay a particular claim, an insurer must have a clear reason for its decision. Therefore, virtually all of an individual claim adjuster's efforts revolve around three distinct questions:

1. Is the loss covered by the policy in question?
2. Is the policyholder or insurer legally liable for the loss?
3. What are the damages?

An adjuster investigates, evaluates, and answers each of these questions in the course of handling a claim.

Coverage

The clearest example of mishandling a claim is payment of a claim not covered by the policy. However, such a blunder may be only the second worst coverage mistake a claim adjuster can make. Wrongful denial of coverage when it exists is unfair and abusive towards policyholders and can result in bad faith suits and enormous verdicts of extra-contractual damages. A proper coverage decision is fundamental to good claim handling.

Claim departments typically have experienced personnel who each work on claims resulting from only one, or very few, types of coverages. Claim adjusters must have detailed knowledge of the policies with which they work. Every individual line and clause from a policy may affect the outcome of a claim.

Although experienced claim personnel have a well-developed sense of which situations are covered and which are not, good coverage analysis requires a methodical review of the specific policy on a given loss in light of the allegations and known facts.

Ultimately, coverage depends on (1) whether the loss or type of damage is within the insuring agreement and (2) whether any exclusion or condition in the policy eliminates or restricts coverage.

Insuring Agreement

Insuring agreements are usually brief, as the following examples illustrate:

From the Personal Auto Policy, Part A:

> We will pay damages for "bodily injury" or "property damage" for which any "insured" becomes legally responsible because of an auto accident.

From the HO-3, Section I:

> We insure against risks of direct loss to property described in Coverages A and B only if that loss is a physical loss to property. . . .

From the Commercial General Liability policy, Coverage A:

> We will pay those sums that the insured becomes legally obligated to pay as damages because of "bodily injury" or "property damage" to which this insurance applies.

From the Building and Personal Property Coverage Form:

> We will pay for direct physical loss of or damage to Covered Property at the premises described in the Declarations caused by or resulting from any Covered Cause of Loss.

Despite their apparent simplicity, these insuring agreements raise numerous issues. Terms that are defined, such as "bodily injury," "property damage," and "insured," implicitly exclude from coverage anything that is not within the definition. For example, "property damage" is generally not considered to extend to fines, purely financial loss, or the diminution in value of property unrelated to physical damage. The "insured" in an auto policy does not include every person who might be driving an auto owned by the named insured (for example, a thief is not covered). The distinction between actual damage and loss of use is important in property coverages because different provisions may apply for each. Finally, insuring agreements typically incorporate other portions of the policy that must be fully understood before the insuring agreement itself can be understood.

Exclusions

Exclusions from coverage are too numerous to present here. Claim adjusters must carefully read and understand every exclusion contained in the policy applicable to a given loss. The evidentiary burden of proof of the application of an exclusion is the insurer's. The rationale for most exclusions usually falls into one of four categories, discussed below.

Coverage Provided Elsewhere

Policies generally exclude coverage that is provided elsewhere. For example, auto and workers compensation losses are excluded from general liability policies because they are the subjects of separate policies.

Coverage Most Policyholders Do Not Need

Some exclusions exist because most policyholders do not need the coverage and thus save premium expense by not having it. For example, insureds whose property is located on flat and stable terrain have no need for earthquake or volcanic eruption coverage. Policyholders with out-of-the-ordinary exposures must cover them with endorsements or separate policies.

Occurrences Within Control of the Policyholder

Some exclusions are designed to ensure that the policyholder does not have control over the occurrence of the loss. For example, general liability policies exclude claims arising out of intentional wrongdoing on the policyholder's part and (with some exceptions) out of the failure of the policyholder to perform his or her contractual obligations.

Uninsurability

Other exclusions relate to events that are uninsurable because of the difficulty in spreading the risk. For example, losses caused by war, flood, and nuclear accident would affect many policyholders at once. Thus, the insurance business does not cover such exposures under normal policies.

Conditions

The most important policy conditions with which a claim adjuster must deal are those concerning duties and procedures in the event of a loss. The exact wording of those duties and procedures varies by policy, but certain conditions are common to almost every policy. For example, the policyholder must promptly notify the insurer of any loss or suit and must cooperate in investigating, settling, and defending any claim. These and other duties of the policyholder are conditions precedent to the insurer's obligation to pay the claim. However, the insurer, mindful of customer goodwill, cannot insist on a rigidly technical manner of performance because the courts will not allow it.

Response to Coverage Issues

When a coverage issue arises, a claim adjuster must protect the insurer's interests and resolve the issue quickly. If no coverage can be provided given the established facts, the claim adjuster must immediately inform the policyholder in writing, making reference to specific policy provisions.

Reservation-of-rights letter
Letter providing notice to the insured that the insurer is investigating a claim; it is issued to inform the insured that a coverage problem might exist and to protect the insurer so it can deny coverage if necessary.

Nonwaiver agreement
An agreement signed by the policyholder that the insurer may investigate a claim while reserving the right to deny coverage if necessary.

If coverage is uncertain, the claim adjuster must continue to handle the claim under a **reservation-of-rights letter** or **nonwaiver agreement** while taking immediate action to resolve the coverage issue. Reservation-of-rights letters and nonwaiver agreements serve the same purpose. They allow the claim adjuster to continue to handle the claim without voiding the insurer's right to later disclaim coverage. Otherwise, the insurer's continued handling of the claim could be legally construed as a waiver of its rights to deny coverage. The only difference between these instruments is that the reservation-of-rights letter is unilaterally issued by the insurer, and the nonwaiver agreement is signed and consented to by the policyholder.

Reservation-of-rights letters and nonwaiver agreements are not ends in themselves. They are means to allow the claim adjuster the time necessary to resolve the coverage issue. This resolution may require additional investigation or an opinion from an attorney experienced in insurance coverage matters.

Once a decision on coverage has been made, the policyholder should be advised immediately. Policyholders are naturally disgruntled whenever coverage for all or part of a claim is denied. Policyholders in this position have frequently sued their insurer for both the claim denial and the way in which the denial was handled. Damages in such cases, including compensation for the policyholder's emotional distress and punitive damages, may be enormous. Consequently, most claim departments restrict authority to issue coverage denials to the claim manager, supervisory personnel, or home office.

Declaratory judgment
A ruling by a court to determine whether an insurance policy provides coverage.

An alternative to the unilateral resolution of a coverage issue is the filing of a declaratory judgment action. A **declaratory judgment** action is a lawsuit that asks the court to declare the rights between parties rather than to award monetary damages as in a typical lawsuit. Courts have acknowledged that the resolution of insurance policy coverage is a suitable issue for a declaratory judgment action. The drawbacks of this procedure are that it is expensive and that, in some jurisdictions, the declaratory judgment action may not move through the court system any faster than the underlying suit that is the subject of the claim. In that case, the declaratory judgment action may not be decided until the underlying action has been decided.

Legal Liability

Legal liability
The legal responsibility of a person or organization for injury or damage suffered by another person or organization.

Legal liability is an important concept in third-party claims. The insuring agreements of the personal auto policy and the commercial general liability policy, quoted earlier, respectively refer to damages "for which any 'insured' becomes legally responsible" and "that the insured becomes legally obligated to pay." The phrases "legally responsible" and "legally obligated" are synonymous with the phrase "legally liable." **Legal liability**—the state of being legally liable for harm to another party—is thus a requisite of coverage under a liability insurance policy. The insurance company will not pay damages on behalf of the insured unless the insured is legally liable to pay such damages. Policyholders buy liability insurance to protect themselves against legal liability. A complete knowledge of legal liability requires an exhaustive knowledge of the law; it is difficult to achieve because of the many jurisdictions involved and the speed at which law changes. Nevertheless, the basics of legal liability are not difficult.

Sources of Liability

Other than from criminal acts, which are almost invariably not covered by insurance, legal liability arises from three sources:

- Statutes
- Contracts
- Torts

Statutes

An individual or a business may be required to do something or to refrain from doing something because a legislative body has enacted a law to that effect. For example, the obligation to pay taxes and file tax returns arises out of statute. Likewise, the obligation not to pollute the land, air, and water arises out of statute. Of great importance to insurance are traffic laws, which are primarily statutory. Many statutes are codifications of preexisting common law (judge or court-made law), and in such cases the statute preempts the common law. Breach of a statute is simultaneously a tort, in which such a breach is the proximate cause of damage to another.

Contracts

A legal liability to do something or to refrain from doing something can arise out of having made an agreement to that effect. The law enforces such agreements as long as the other party (or parties) incurs a reciprocal obligation and the agreement is not for an unlawful purpose. Contracts are common in both business and personal life. Generally, contractual obligations are not insurable. However, the exceptions to this general rule are common and important enough that claim adjusters need a good working knowledge of contract law. In particular, contracts are frequently used to transfer statutory and common-law duties from one party to another. Only a few special types of contracts must be in writing. The remainder can be, and usually are, strictly oral.

Torts

This category of legal liability encompasses all noncontractual civil wrongs. Many criminal acts, such as assault and battery and fraud, are also simultaneously torts. Claim adjusters must have a command of tort law because most torts are covered by insurance and because their possibility is the very reason most policyholders have insurance policies. Torts are categorized by the behavior of the wrongdoer (called a tortfeasor). They may occur when the tortfeasor has acted intentionally or negligently or, in some circumstances, regardless of how the tortfeasor has acted.

Intentional torts include assault, battery, false imprisonment, false arrest, trespass, nuisance (interference with the use of land), fraud, libel, slander, conversion (a legal term for stealing), and others.

Although most insurance policies exclude coverage for intentional wrong-doing, a claim adjuster cannot expect to escape these types of claims. The "personal injury" coverage contained in some liability policies covers damages that are frequently the result of intentional conduct. In any event, the insurer's duty to defend the policyholder exists if any part of a lawsuit is covered. Plaintiff attorneys include allegations of negligence, in addition to their allegations of intentional wrongdoing, to involve the insurer and its money in the case. Assault cases of this type are common. Furthermore, courts have interpreted intentional act exclusions narrowly, ruling that they apply only if the policyholder intends the specific harm that results, not just the act that caused the harm. This interpretation has enabled policyholders to involve their insurer in cases by maintaining positions such as, "I intended to punch him, but I didn't expect him to fall backwards and hit his head."

Negligent behavior is the source of most torts and most insurance claims. The law of negligence is almost entirely common law, although some of it, such as traffic laws, has been codified. Negligence is the failure to act as a reasonable and prudent person would act under the same circumstances. The "reasonable and prudent person" standard is not equivalent to what the average, or typical, person would do. The average person is often careless and thoughtless. The "reasonable and prudent person" standard is best understood as the behavior of someone who is always careful and prudent, a mythical person. The average person who is careless or thoughtless may be deserving of sympathy and understanding, but if that behavior causes damages to another, that behavior is negligent.

In some circumstances, tort liability may arise from an act regardless of how carefully the actor has behaved. These circumstances involve areas of absolute liability and strict liability. Absolute liability is found only in very narrow circumstances, such as blasting with dynamite. If the activity causes damage, liability exists, regardless of how much care was taken. The concept of strict liability arises from harm caused by products. A product manufacturer or seller is not absolutely liable whenever one of its products causes harm to someone. The manufacturer may have strict liability, however, if the product is somehow defective in a way that makes it unreasonably dangerous. Thus, liability depends on the nature of the product, not on the behavior of the manufacturer.

Investigation of Liability

Investigating liability is one of the claim adjuster's most important functions. It can also be one of the most challenging. Ideally, the claim adjuster should interview and obtain statements from all witnesses, inspect loss sites, review key documents, inspect products and advertising, and so forth. Witnesses include the parties directly involved and anyone else who knows anything about the case. Their statements should cover everything they know about the accident and the damages.

Claim adjusters take statements in one of two forms: handwritten or tape recorded. Handwritten statements have the advantage of forcing the claim adjuster to listen carefully to properly record what has been said. Tape recordings are more common today because of their convenience and accuracy. However, statements of either kind are rarely used in court. Most cases settle before they get that far. Even among the cases that do not settle, witness statements taken out of court cannot be used unless the witness tells a different story on the witness stand. Despite their infrequent use in court, witness statements are considered the heart of any investigation. They are essential to determining liability, a prerequisite to any settlement. Their existence helps to prevent witnesses from changing their story thereafter.

A problem for claim adjusters in liability investigations is inconsistency among witnesses. This inconsistency does not usually result from deliberate lies, although that is a possibility. More often, the witnesses had different opportunities and abilities to observe, have a different ability to remember, or were emotionally upset by the events in question. The "truth" of most events is not available. Only the evidence of such truth, in the form of witness statements, is available.

Damages

No claim is complete without damages. Both first-party and third-party insurance policies provide for indemnification against damages. No subject is of greater interest to claimants. Claim adjusters spend a great portion of their time investigating and evaluating damages. Insurance policies generally extend their coverage to damages consisting of property damage, bodily injury, or both.

Property Damage

In first-party coverages, the term "property damage" means the direct physical destruction of or damage to property. The measure of damages for such destruction or damage is usually specified in the policy as either replacement cost or actual cash value. Replacement cost is the cost to replace what has been damaged. Actual cash value is usually replacement cost minus depreciation. Arguments about depreciation are common. Courts have held that any relevant factor may be considered in determining depreciation, including cost to replace, cost when purchased, expected life span, technological or style obsolescence, market value, identifiable physical wear and tear, and anything else.

As an alternative to paying money to settle a property claim, the insurer can choose to conduct repairs or procure a replacement itself. This option may be exercised with personal property losses and with claims that raise suspicions.

Loss of use, which may be a result of property damage or destruction, is an element of damage but is not necessarily covered under first-party coverages.

Generally, homeowners policies have some coverage for loss of use. Many commercial property policies must have such coverage added separately. In both cases, loss of use is usually not covered by property insurance unless the loss results from a covered type of property damage or destruction. In other words, loss of use is not covered when property simply ceases to function without having been damaged or destroyed. The measure of damages for loss of use is specified in the policy.

Property damages in liability claims also include damages for the direct physical damage to the property and for loss of its use. When property has been totally destroyed, claimants are not entitled to replacement cost unless the property had not depreciated at all. With property that is only partially damaged and that can be repaired, the cost of repair is an accepted measure of damages. It is the least amount of money required to return the claimant to his or her original condition. Loss of use is measured by the cost of replacement services. However, all claimants in all liability claims are required to mitigate their damages. They cannot allow loss of use damages to accumulate beyond the value of damaged property or when destroyed property could be expeditiously replaced.

Bodily Injury Damages

Bodily injury damages may fall into at least nine categories: expenses for medical treatment, loss of earnings, pain and suffering, permanency, loss of consortium, future damages, punitive damages, survival and wrongful death, and extra-contractual damages. Punitive damages and extra-contractual damages can arise in property damage cases as well, but they are more often related to bodily injuries.

Expenses for Medical Treatment

These expenses include doctors' services, hospital expenses, nursing and rehabilitation treatment, medications, medical devices and equipment, and even transportation expense to receive medical care. All medical expenses must be (1) related to the injury resulting from the accident (preexisting problems and unrelated problems that develop after an accident are not the responsibility of the liability insurer unless the injury exacerbates a preexisting condition), (2) for treatment that is necessary (excessive treatment that accomplishes nothing is not the responsibility of the liability insurer), and (3) reasonable in amount (insurers need not pay unreasonable and excessive charges). Stating these parameters is easier than enforcing them. Medical care is usually controlled by the claimant and his or her doctor. Insurer arguments against the treatment prescribed are fruitless after the fact.

In many states, the defendant must pay the medical expense, even if it has been covered by another source of insurance, such as health insurance. This is known as the **Collateral Source Rule**. The rationale of this rule is that defendants should not benefit from the prudence of injured parties in insuring themselves. This rule also extends to other collateral coverage, such as disability

Collateral Source Rule
Rule that prohibits both the judge and the jury from considering the fact that the plaintiff has already been compensated for much of his or her financial loss, such as payment of medical costs through health insurance, or payment of income replacement benefits through a disability insurance plan or workers compensation plan.

insurance for lost earnings. Recently, some states have modified or abolished the Collateral Source Rule, thus allowing a deduction from a plaintiff's recovery for expenses covered by other insurance.

Loss of Earnings

Any amount that a claimant would have earned during a period of disability is recoverable. Determining what the claimant would have earned is usually not difficult, especially if the claimant worked a regular job for salary or wages. Claimants who are businessowners sometimes present a problem. Their incomes may vary seasonally; they might have poorly kept records; and they might have typical personal expenses, such as an auto, paid by the business. In addition, everyone supplying information to the claim adjuster works for the claimant. If the magnitude of a loss of earnings claim is significant, the insurer might employ the services of an accountant to review the claimant's business.

The most difficult aspect of lost earnings claims is the determination of whether the claimant is disabled. Doctors should perform a detailed analysis of the physical demands of the claimant's job and compare those demands to the claimant's physical capabilities to properly reflect the extent of the claimant's disability. Abuse of disability is one of the most serious problems in claims. In first-party no-fault and uninsured motorist claims, the insurer can compel the injured person to undergo a medical examination. However, in third-party liability claims, disability cannot be controlled until litigation has begun, at which time the claimant can be compelled to undergo independent medical exams.

Pain and Suffering

Pain and suffering is an intangible factor in every injury case and usually the biggest element of damages. It includes inconvenience, anxiety, and other types of distress. The amount awarded in a suit, or agreed on in a settlement, depends on the amount of the medical expense, the length of the disability, the severity and nature of the injury, the locale where the case is tried, the respective skills of the attorneys in creating sympathy and favorable impressions, the sympathies created by the parties, and many other factors in a given case. The question a claim adjuster faces in evaluating pain and suffering is, "What would a jury award?" Proper evaluation requires a good deal of experience, but even experienced claim adjusters are well aware of how inaccurate they could be in a given case. Claimant attorneys are also under the same pressure, and this mutual pressure causes many settlements. In clear or fairly clear liability cases, settlements for pain and suffering constitute the largest element of damages and are usually for amounts several times the medical expense, loss of earnings, or both.

Pain and suffering
Intangible injuries including inconvenience and anxiety as well as pain and suffering associated with the physical injury.

Permanency

In addition to having chronic pain, claimants sometimes suffer scarring or some loss of bodily function that may not cause pain but has reduced the quality of life. Permanent injuries and scars are evaluated in the same manner as pain and suffering: unscientifically. However, permanent injuries that reduce earning capacity can be accurately determined.

Loss of Consortium

Consortium
The legal rights of one spouse to the company, affection, and assistance of the other.

Loss of **consortium** is an element of damages that belongs to the spouse of the injured party. It consists of the three S's: sex, society, and services. "Sex" here refers to the loss of sexual relations because of the injury. "Society" means the loss of enjoyable companionship because of the injury. "Services" refers to the loss of useful services that the injured party formerly performed for the spouse. This element of damages is also difficult to evaluate. It is sometimes estimated as a percentage of the underlying injury. Plaintiff attorneys do not usually emphasize this aspect of a case with a jury because of the common attitude that spouses take each other "for better or for worse." Nevertheless, this element of damages and a spouse who inspires sympathy can increase the settlement and verdict value of a case.

Future Damages

Any of the previous elements of damage that can be expected to continue into the future should be included in a settlement or jury verdict. With serious injuries, future damages—such as future lost earnings and future pain and suffering—may exceed the damages incurred. Because of inflation, future damages may be larger, in their face amount, than present damages. However, any future damages that can be specified in amount should be adjusted to their present value. This procedure (explained in any elementary finance text) recognizes that a dollar received in the future is worth less than a dollar received today.

Punitive Damages

Special damages
Compensatory damages allowed for specific, out-of-pocket expenses, such as doctor and hospital bills. Also called specials.

General damages
Compensatory damages awarded for losses, such as pain and suffering, that do not have a specific economic value.

Damages that can be established in known amounts, such as for medical expenses and loss of earnings, are often called **special damages**, or the "specials." The other types of damages are **general damages**. Special damages and general damages together are called compensatory damages because they are designed to compensate the claimant for actual loss. Such compensation is generally all that a claimant can receive. However, in rare cases in which the defendant's conduct has been especially outrageous and wicked, the jury or court may award punitive damages. As the term suggests, these damages are levied against the defendant as punishment. Whether such damages are awarded and the amount awarded are unpredictable. Plaintiff attorneys request them far more often than they are awarded. In many states, such damages are uninsurable because the law or policy language prohibits insuring them. Other states do not prohibit insuring punitive damages, and some policies cover them.

Survival and Wrongful Death

This term refers to both the action and the damages. Like "pain and suffering" and "assault and battery," these two actions are so frequently mentioned in the same breath that it is difficult to distinguish them. **Survival actions** are those legal causes of action that existed for the deceased before his or her death. In other words, had the deceased lived, he or she could have pursued these actions like any other. The claims for the medical expense, lost earnings, and pain and suffering up to the time of death are elements of a survival action and are evaluated in the same manner as other cases are. However, actions that precede a death lose some value upon death because the claimant cannot testify on his or her own behalf.

A wrongful death action is different. In concept, a **wrongful death action** belongs to the survivors of the deceased. It is designed to compensate them for the loss of the deceased and arises only upon death. Evaluation of wrongful death actions is complicated. Only certain people are entitled to recover under a wrongful death claim. If none of these people exist, the wrongful death action may be worth very little. Most deaths involve eligible beneficiaries because most states allow spouses, parents, or children to recover, and most people have one or more such relatives. Even if eligible beneficiaries exist, their recovery may be limited to the benefits they would have received from the deceased. In the case of parents and adult children claiming for one another, the amount of the financial benefit from the deceased may be small. Many states allow recovery for loss of companionship, but this element of damages is usually moderate, except in the case of spouses. Financial dependence allows for the largest recoveries. Minor children are presumed to be financially dependent on their parents, and spouses are presumed to depend financially on one another. Some states provide for a loss-to-the-estate measure of damages to the eligible beneficiaries. Under these formulations, the deceased's future cost of maintenance is subtracted from future earnings to arrive at a net contributions figure, or the deceased's likely estate at death is estimated. Under both loss-to-the-beneficiary or loss-to-the-estate measures of damages, the future damages should be discounted to their present value.

Extra-Contractual Damages

The terms of insurance policies describe the circumstances in which and the amounts that the insurer must pay. However, in certain circumstances, insurers may be liable to their policyholders for amounts not called for in the policy or in excess of the policy limits. This situation can occur when the insurer has behaved improperly toward its policyholder. **Extra-contractual damages** are usually awarded in these cases because of an excess verdict or because of the wrongful treatment of a policyholder, such as a violation of the Unfair Claims Settlement Practices Act.

Reporting

The adjuster's reports are vital to the claim function. Whether the report is from a staff or an independent field adjuster to a supervisor, or from a defense attorney to the adjuster or examiner, it serves as an important part of the

---

Survival actions
Those causes of action that existed for the deceased before his or her death.

Wrongful death action
Those legal causes of action that exist for the survivor of the deceased.

Extra-contractual damages
Monetary awards against an insurer for its negligence to its insured. Such payments required of an insurer to its insured are extracontractual in that they are beyond the insurance contract between insurer and insured.

evaluation process, updating information about each claim so that the proper action can be taken. Adjuster file notes serve as the basis of the more formal types of reports discussed below. Reports can be categorized as preliminary, investigative, status, and concluding. With widespread use of computers and networks, insurers and adjusters can now prepare and transmit many reports entirely by computer.

Preliminary Reports

The ACORD form is used by many producers to report the occurrence of a claim to a company. A copy of the ACORD Property Loss Notice is shown in Exhibit 13-3. Once the insurer has assigned the case to an adjuster, many insurers require a first report to be filed within a certain number of hours or days from the time the loss is reported. Such reports usually identify the names and number of claimants and provide some initial evaluation of whether there are coverage issues that need to be explored, along with preliminary information on the liability factors involved. Above all, the report should guide the examiner in establishing the initial reserve for the claim.

Investigative Reports

The adjuster's next report is a detailed report on the claim investigation. Such a report is often called the "full formal" because it contains standard paragraph captions regarding coverage, liability, damages, and other factors involved in the loss. It also outlines the key information already obtained and the information that needs to be investigated. Each topic may be given a separate heading in the report.

Status Reports

After the preliminary investigation has been completed, the insurer will require periodic reports on the status of the claim. These reports may be sent every thirty days or over longer intervals if the claim is slow in developing, as is the case with many injury losses. One important purpose of status reports is to facilitate the constant reevaluation of the reserves being maintained on the file. As factors involved in the claim change, the reserves may need to be increased or decreased. Example status reports are shown in Exhibits 13-4 and 13-5.

Concluding Reports

The adjuster's final report usually outlines the basis of settlement or other conclusion of the claim. It also contains the documents necessary to close the file, such as a copy of the settlement check, the release or proof-of-loss document, dismissal of any litigation, and final billings for any other services performed in the settlement, such as the defense attorney's or independent adjuster's fees.

EXHIBIT 13-3

ACORD Property Loss Notice

ACORD™ PROPERTY LOSS NOTICE			DATE (MM/DD/YY) 8-24-00	

PRODUCER	PHONE (A/C, No, Ext):	MISCELLANEOUS INFO (Site & location code)	DATE OF LOSS AND TIME 7/29/00	AM PM	PREVIOUSLY REPORTED YES NO

PAUL PROCTOR
127 MAIN STREET
PLAINFEILD, OH

POLICY TYPE	COMPANY AND POLICY NUMBER	
PROP/HOME	CO: IIA INSURANCE COMPANY POL: HO 1894370	EFF: EXP:
FLOOD	CO: POL:	EFF: EXP:
WIND	CO: POL:	EFF: EXP:

CODE: 39542   SUB CODE:
AGENCY CUSTOMER ID:

INSURED

NAME AND ADDRESS	SOC SEC #:

LEONARD HILLMAN
156 SIXTH AVENUE
PLAINFIELD, OH

CONTACT   CONTACT INSURED

NAME AND ADDRESS	WHERE TO CONTACT
JULIA HILLMAN	
	WHEN TO CONTACT

RESIDENCE PHONE (A/C, No) 215-555-8181	BUSINESS PHONE (A/C, No, Ext) 215-555-5000	RESIDENCE PHONE (A/C, No) SAME	BUSINESS PHONE (A/C, No, Ext)

LOSS

LOCATION OF LOSS	POLICE OR FIRE DEPT TO WHICH REPORTED

KIND OF LOSS	FIRE THEFT	LIGHTNING HAIL	FLOOD WIND	OTHER (explain)	PROBABLE AMOUNT ENTIRE LOSS $

DESCRIPTION OF LOSS & DAMAGE (Use reverse side, if necessary)

WIND AND HAIL DAMAGED ROOF   **Sample**

POLICY INFORMATION

MORTGAGEE   PLAINFIELD FEDERAL SAVINGS AND LOAN ASSOCIATION

☐ NO MORTGAGEE

HOMEOWNER POLICIES SECTION 1 ONLY (Complete for coverages A, B, C, D & additional coverages. For Homeowners Section II Liability Losses, use ACORD 3.)

A. DWELLING	B. OTHER STRUCT	C. PERSONAL PROP	D. LOSS OF USE	DEDUCTIBLES	DESCRIBE ADDITIONAL COVERAGES PROVIDED
$100,000	$10,000	$50,000	$20,000	$500	None

COVERAGE A. EXCLUDES WIND
SUBJECT TO FORMS (Insert form numbers and edition dates, special deductibles)

FIRE, ALLIED LINES & MULTI-PERIL POLICIES (Complete only those items involved in loss)

ITEM	SUBJECT OF INS	AMOUNT	% COINS	DEDUCTIBLE	COVERAGE AND/OR DESCRIPTION OF PROPERTY INSURED
	BLDG ☐ CNTS				
	BLDG ☐ CNTS				
	BLDG ☐ CNTS				

SUBJECT TO FORMS (Insert form numbers and edition dates, special deductibles)   HO-290 REPLACEMENT COST COVERAGE

FLOOD POLICY	BUILDING: CONTENTS:	DEDUCTIBLE: DEDUCTIBLE:		ZONE	PRE FIRM POST FIRM	DIFF IN ELEV	FORM TYPE	GENERAL DWELLING	CONDO

WIND POLICY	BUILDING	DEDUCTIBLE	CONTENTS	ZONE	FORM TYPE	GENERAL DWELLING	CONDO

REMARKS/OTHER INSURANCE (List companies, policy numbers, coverages & policy amounts)
ROOF LEAKING AFTER STORM. WATER DAMAGE TO CEILING IN ADDITION TO ROOF DAMAGE.

CAT #	FICO #	ADJUSTER ASSIGNED		ADJUSTER #	DATE ASSIGNED
REPORTED BY LEONARD HILLMAN		REPORTED TO ANN ADAMS		SIGNATURE OF PRODUCER OR INSURED Ann Adams	

ACORD 1 (1/96)   NOTE: IMPORTANT STATE INFORMATION ON REVERSE SIDE   © ACORD CORPORATION 1988

Reserving

Reserving the claim file is a crucial adjusting task. The reserve represents the amount of money that the insurer anticipates may be needed to pay for a particular claim. The reserve includes both the amounts owed to the policyholder or claimant(s) and, with some insurers, the funds required to cover the insurer's expenses. Estimating ultimate losses is a key adjusting skill acquired with experience and training. Failure to reserve properly, by either underestimating or overestimating the final cost of claims, can accumulate, causing distortions on the insurer's financial statements. Underreserving is one of the major causes of insurer insolvency and bankruptcy.

The amount insurers pay on claims is a key element in the calculation of future premium rates. Actuaries base future rates not only on the amount of money the claim department has paid on both open and closed files, but also on the amount reserved on open files and reserved for incurred but not reported losses and reopened files. Accuracy in reserving eventually translates into premium rates that accurately reflect loss potential. Claim departments must reserve claims consistently. Claim department management must communicate to the actuarial department any change in reserving practices so that any abnormalities that develop in loss reserve data can be recognized.

Improper reserving can (but should not) affect the outcome of individual claims. Reserving a file at an amount higher than its real value may create a tendency to overpay the claim or to settle too quickly without adequate negotiation. An underreserved claim, on the other hand, may cause the insurer to take too firm a position, which may lead to litigation.

Allocated and Unallocated Expenses

In addition to the payment of the policyholder's loss, the insurer is responsible for the payment of the expenses associated with the claim. The NAIC Annual Statement requires that insurer claim expenses be apportioned between allocated and unallocated loss adjustment expenses. Claim costs that can be specifically identified with the settlement of a particular claim are **allocated loss adjustment expenses**. Specific charges that can be assigned to a claim include the fees paid to an auto appraiser to inspect a vehicle damaged in an accident, to a photographer to take photos of the scene, and to a private investigator who does a background check on the claimant, as well as fees for the report(s) of a physician who examines an injured claimant and assesses the injury. In addition, all of the costs related to the defense of the policyholder if the claim goes into litigation—including the attorney's bill and the fees for court reporters, copy services, process servers, and the appeal bond—can be allocated to the individual file.

Some independent adjusters may bill in bulk for a number of settled claims on behalf of the insurer rather than identify individual claim files. These expenses, though no longer attributable to specific claim files, are directly

Allocated loss adjustment expenses
Those costs associated with adjusting a claim that can be assigned to a specific claim.

EXHIBIT 13-4

Six-Month Supervisor's Reserve Adequacy Review—Property

Supervisor Jones	Policy No. CPP 6106442100	Insured Westwide Manufacturing	Loss Cause Fire	Suit ☐ Yes ☑ No	
Claim Rep Harrison	Amount of Coverage 500,000	Loss Date 4/5/0X	Date Reported 10/9/0X	Age (mos.) 6	LAE to date NA

ALL LOSSES	Y	N	N/A	A/N*
Scope—loss items defined in file content	☑	☐	☐	☐
Cause/Origin—clearly noted in file	☑	☐	☐	☐
Limiting Clauses Identified	☐	☐	☑	☐
Deductible Identified	☑	☐	☐	☐

BUILDING ONLY	Y	N	N/A	A/N*
ACV/RCV Calculated	☑	☐	☐	☐
Ownership Established	☑	☐	☐	☐
Coinsurance Noted	☑	☐	☐	☐
Mortgage Noted	☐	☐	☐	☐
R/C Holdback Applied	☑	☐	☐	☐
Statement Taken	☐	☐	☐	☐
CONTENTS				
Police Report Obtained	☑	☐	☐	☐
Property Verification of Items Involved	☑	☐	☐	☐

1. Are there any unresolved COVERAGE questions?   ☐ Yes ☑ No
    a. If yes, are all proper steps being taken to resolve them?   ☐ Yes ☐ No
    b. Needed actions:
    (1) <u>Report underinsurance to underwriting</u>
    (2) _____
    (3) _____

2. INVESTIGATION completed?   ☐ Yes ☐ No
    a. Specific investigation needed:
    (1) <u>Check for other property lines</u>
    (2) _____
    (3) _____

3. DAMAGES/EXPOSURE
    a. Is file properly documented to reflect the company's exposure?   ☑ Yes ☐ No
    b. If no, does file contain a plan to document damages/exposure?   ☐ Yes ☐ No
    c. If ALE/BI is involved, are steps being taken to control expense?   ☐ Yes ☐ No

4. REPORTING
    a. Are activity log notes clearly stated in file?   ☑ Yes ☐ No
    b. Does the file contain a 90-Day Status Report?   ☑ Yes ☐ No
    c. If defense attorney is involved, does the file contain an Initial
       Claim Analysis?   ☐ Yes ☐ No

5. Does the file contain a PLAN FOR RESOLUTION?   ☐ Yes ☐ No
    Additional steps needed to resolve:
    (1) <u>Arrange for salvage to be sold</u>
    (2) _____
    (3) _____
    (4) _____
    (5) _____

6. RESERVE ANALYSIS
    a. Have all reserve changes been posted in file?   ☑ Yes ☐ No
    b. In view of your analysis of liability and damages, is the reserve
       adequate?   ☑ Yes ☐ No

    Reserve: $ <u>300,000</u>   REVISED RESERVE: $ _____

Signature: _____   Date: <u>10/9/0X</u>

*A/N: Action Needed

EXHIBIT 13-5

Six-Month Supervisor's Reserve Adequacy Review—Casualty

Policy #: _____WC_____   Claim Rep: _____Harrison_____

Date of Loss: ___1238607___   Super: _____Jones_____

Age (Months): _____6_____   SUIT?   ☐ Yes   ☑ No

LAE to date: $ _____NA_____   Policy Limits Remaining: $ __200,000__

1. Are there any unresolved COVERAGE questions?   ☐ Yes   ☑ No
   a. If yes, are all proper steps being taken to resolve them?   ☐ Yes   ☐ No
   b. Needed actions:
      (1) _____
      (2) _____
      (3) _____

2. INVESTIGATION completed?   ☐ Yes   ☐ No
   a. Specific investigation needed:
      (1) Index claimant-to review past claim
      (2) Consider peer review of chiropractic bills
      (3) _____
      (4) _____
   b. LIABILITY Analysis:
      undisputed
      _____
   c. Is legal advice needed to assist in evaluating liability?   ☐ Yes   ☐ No

3. DAMAGES and INJURIES
   a. Are medicals and specials in the file?   ☑ Yes   ☐ No
   b. If not, have we obtained the information by phone?   ☐ Yes   ☐ No
   c. Has the claimant returned to work?   ☑ Yes   ☐ No
   d. DIAGNOSIS:
      (1) Cervical strain
      (2) full recovery   (3) _____
      PROGNOSIS:

      SPECIALS: $ 3,750

4. REPORTING
   a. Does the file contain 90-day report(s)?   ☐ Yes   ☐ No
   b. Does the file contain an Initial Claim Analysis?   ☐ Yes   ☐ No   ☐ N/A
   c. Does the file contain reports of depositions?   ☐ Yes   ☐ No   ☐ N/A

5. Does the file contain a PLAN FOR RESOLUTION?   ☐ Yes   ☐ No
   Additional steps needed to resolve:
   a. _____
   b. _____
   c. _____
   d. _____

6. RESERVE ANALYSIS
   a. Have all reserve changes been posted in file?   ☑ Yes   ☐ No
   b. In view of your analysis of liability and damages, is the
      reserve adequate?   ☑ Yes   ☐ No

   Reserve: $ _____   REVISED RESERVE: $_____

   Signature: _____   Date: _____

attributable to the settlement of individual claims and are considered allocated loss adjustment expenses.

Expenses related to the overall operation of the claim function are called **unallocated loss adjustment expenses**. These expenses include charges for the insurer's overhead expenses and adjustment expenses not included in the allocated adjustment expense category.

In some lines of insurance, certain aspects of medical coordination or vocational rehabilitation may also be allocated, but the use of rehabilitation and medical consultants for utilization review and other cost containment processes may be considered an unallocated expense.

The proper allocation of expenses between allocated and unallocated categories is significant because of state reporting requirements. Insurers frequently refer to these amounts to compare the efficiency of their claim operations with those of other insurers.

IBNR

Claim departments are involved in establishing case reserves. Case reserves are the ultimate loss expectations for each individual claim. Insurers also have bulk (or aggregate) reserves, used to estimate losses that are assumed to have happened but have not yet been reported to the insurer. Insurers also use those reserves to reflect workers compensation claims that are reopened after having been settled and closed and to compensate for a general inadequacy in reported case reserves.

These IBNR losses are significant to the insurer's overall expectation of profitability but are only slightly relevant to an individual adjuster. The connection between the two is that case reserves are often used as a basis for the methodology employed to calculate IBNR.

The claim department usually assists in establishing bulk reserves. Many insurers use a committee composed of underwriting, actuarial, accounting, claim, and senior management personnel to review recommendations for bulk reserves. The mathematical procedures used in this process are discussed in Chapter 12. Although a significant part of this procedure is an actuarial function, claim department management can provide valuable information on the validity of the individual case reserves (on which the IBNR estimates are based), changes in the methodology used to determine case reserves, catastrophic or large losses that could skew results, and changes in the legal climate and benefit levels that might affect the ultimate cost of claims.

Case Reserves

No system of bulk reserving can be accurate unless the underlying reserves on individual files are reasonably accurate. Ensuring their accuracy often falls to the individual adjuster, supervisor, or claim examiner who is responsible for setting the initial reserve or to a special committee set up for the primary purpose of reserve evaluation.

Unallocated loss adjustment expenses
Those costs in adjusting claims that relate to the overall operation of an insurer's claim function.

The three standard methods of establishing case reserves—the judgment, average value, and tabular methods—are discussed in Chapter 12 and are reviewed below. The effectiveness of these methods depends on how they are used and on recognizing their inherent weaknesses.

Judgment

In the judgment method, the ability of the adjuster is crucial in determining the appropriateness of the reserve selected. Depending on the nature of the claim, the adjuster needs to know medical treatment costs, average repair or reconstruction time, local pricing factors, local plaintiff attorneys, treating physicians, local contractors, and other factors that will influence the final cost of the claim. This type of reserve-establishing ability is influenced by the adjuster's experience. The subjective nature of the judgment method makes evaluating the adequacy of case reserves difficult, except in the aggregate.

Average Value

The average value method is suitable for types of claims that occur with regular frequency, such as automobile physical damage claims. The claim department can readily establish a reserve amount that can be used for all claims of this nature, recognizing that the reserve amount will be high or low in specific claims but will even out overall. Misinterpreting the average claim amount may cause problems. A low reserve may influence the insurer to ignore a potentially serious claim. Mishandled claims or claims that go to litigation usually settle for more than the average value.

For liability lines, the average value method is likely to produce inadequate loss reserves. This is especially true for those liability lines that usually do not settle readily, such as medical malpractice. In those situations, it is appropriate to use an average reserve when the claim is initially reported and to modify that average amount once the claim file can be reviewed in depth.

Tabular

The tabular method is similar in concept to the average value method of reserving. Instead of using a selected average amount, the tabular method provides an "average" amount for all claims that have similar characteristics in terms of the age, health, and marital status of the claimant.

Reserving Work Sheets and Software

Insurers employ various reserve work sheets that force the claim adjuster to consider all the factors concerning the claim. For a workers compensation or bodily injury claim, the work sheet will take into account not only the known or anticipated medical costs but also the length and cost of disability, the degree of permanency of the injury, and other special damage items that influence the claim. Sophisticated computer programs are now available to help claim adjusters consider all relevant factors in setting reserves.

For liability claims, the adjuster must also take into account the general damage factors, such as pain and suffering, that a jury would consider in deciding on an award. Reserving work sheets also require careful evaluation of liability. Comparative negligence factors must be applied if any are applicable. If joint tortfeasors will contribute or if the potential for subrogation exists, those cost-reducing factors must also be considered.

Property claims can also be systematically evaluated to include not only the direct damages that can be quickly appraised, but also the indirect damages, such as business interruption, extra expense, loss of use costs, and potential recoveries for salvage and subrogation, that will develop only after considerable time has passed.

Reserving Problems

Reserving becomes a problem when reserves are inadequate or redundant. During an investigation, it is expected that claims will be reevaluated and that reserves will be updated to reflect newly discovered facts.

Adjusters are often criticized for "stair-stepping" reserves, a practice that results when the claim is initially inadequately reserved and the reserves must be continually updated. **Stair-stepping** (or "reserve creep") often occurs in workers compensation or other types of claims in which periodic payments are made. The adjuster, instead of adequately establishing a sufficient reserve based on the realistic value of the claim, sets only enough reserve to cover costs for the immediate future. Then, when payments meet or exceed the established reserve, the figure is increased for another round of payments. The problem with such a method is that the true value of the claim does not become evident to senior claim management until perhaps years after the initial reserve was set, meaning that cost control procedures that might have helped to reduce the overall exposure were never considered. Further, stair-stepping methods may mislead the insurer into delaying a report to a reinsurer or, in a serious liability claim, notifying the policyholder of a potential excess loss situation.

Stair-stepping
Incremental increases in claim reserves by the claim representative without any significant change in the facts of the claim.

Few initial reserves on claims that are open for more than a few weeks will remain accurate over the long run unless the loss is reserved for policy limits, which is the limit of what the insurer could pay barring any extra-contractual obligations. Most claim reserves must therefore be reevaluated as additional information about the loss is received. This reevaluation may occur often enough that the file has the appearance of being stair-stepped, but the procedure is quite different, and the evaluation should more accurately represent both positive and negative factors of the loss.

Settlement

Even while the investigation of a claim is proceeding and the liability and reserves are being evaluated, the adjuster must establish personal relationships with a variety of people involved in the claim file in order to negotiate all of the factors that will be involved in the settlement.

Pre-Settlement Negotiation

Negotiation is a necessary step in the adjustment process at many levels. Aspects of coverage may need to be explored and agreed on by the policyholder and the insurer. Other insurers may be involved when more than one policy covers a loss or when more than one tortfeasor is responsible for the damages. All of the damages must be examined before any settlement can be reached. Disputes over the damages involved in a claim often require lengthy negotiations between not only the adjuster and the policyholder or claimant but also with repair facilities, public adjusters, and individuals or facilities providing care or treatment for the injured person.

Persons Involved in Claim Negotiations

The adjuster must become familiar with the producing agent, the policyholder, the third-party claimant or adverse party (if there is one), any witnesses, the specialists involved in repairs or damage restoration, the physicians, other experts who may be used, and the attorneys representing any parties involved in the claim. The adjuster's success in settling any claim depends on his or her familiarity and ability to negotiate with the persons involved in the claim. Whether the claim is for a first-party loss or for damages caused by the policyholder, the relationship established by the adjuster will determine whether the claim is settled with great difficulty, perhaps involving litigation, or directly with the individuals involved.

In most metropolitan areas, many attorneys specialize in representing parties involved in insurance claims. Over time, most adjusters establish either a relationship or a reputation with the local plaintiff bar, and vice versa. Most plaintiff's attorneys are sincerely interested in the welfare and best interests of their clients. Most adjusters are likewise interested in the best interests of all the parties concerned, primarily the policyholder, and those interests are best met when a claim can be quickly resolved by settlement rather than prolonged by litigation.

Negotiation of Settlements

Disposition of the claim is the final step in the adjusting process, whether the negotiation is carried on by the adjuster directly, through litigation, or by some other procedure such as appraisal or arbitration. Every claim must be resolved, and most means of resolution require some negotiation on the part of the adjuster, unless the claim simply involves payment of a fixed amount.

Accurate information is the key to settlements in which all the parties consider themselves to be winners. Unless the adjuster has adequately investigated and evaluated all of the factors involved, the negotiating position will be weak and ineffectual and may result in litigation. When the adjuster wants to pay $5,000, but the claimant is demanding $50,000, some means of position justification must be used. Both parties, in light of the facts of the loss, may need to reevaluate their positions. Adjusting requires a large measure of personal control and salesmanship, a friendly disposition, and a degree of tolerance for frustration.

Information must often be shared. Some adjusters may believe that they should not discuss or share information that supports their position with a claimant or opposing attorney, but unless they do, negotiations may suffer. The adjuster should not artificially set an opinion of value when intangibles, such as the value of pain or the loss of a loved one, are involved. Flexibility might be necessary if the claim is to be settled.

Some insurers now routinely use some form of advanced payments on both first- and third-party claims. On major property losses, the insurer will often advance the policyholder moneys toward additional living expenses and even reconstruction costs and supplies before settlement of the claim. On liability claims involving both property damage and bodily injury, the insurer will settle the property portion of the claim (without waiting for the bodily injury settlement in accordance with the Unfair Claims Settlement Practices Model Act).

Denial of Claims

Denying the entire claim, or partial denial based on individual factors in a loss, can be difficult unless the adjuster has thoroughly researched the claim. Denial of claims, to be successful and not result in litigation, must be based on accurate information about coverage, liability, and damages. When a loss is not covered, the adjuster must be prepared to show the policyholder why the loss is not covered. Denial of coverage must be made as soon as practical after all facts are known.

Denying payment to a third party on the basis that the policyholder is not legally liable must likewise be handled in a way that does not leave the claimant angry and vengeful. The adjuster must be certain that no liability exists. If the denial is based on a contract, being able to identify the applicable provision can be helpful. If the denial is based on a coverage exclusion, the adjuster must involve the policyholder to protect the policyholder's interests against the liability exposure.

Settlement Documents

Once the adjuster has received settlement authority from senior claim department personnel and the parties have agreed on the value of a claim, the concluding documents will be executed. Property claims are sometimes settled with a sworn statement in a proof-of-loss form. This document is submitted by the policyholder as a sworn presentation of the claim and as an offer to settle, whereupon it can either be accepted or rejected by the insurer. In questionable first-party claims or those with disputed facts, the policyholder may be provided blank proof-of-loss forms to use in submitting a claim. If the claim is known to be fraudulent, the insurer may deny coverage based on the insured's act of submitting the "sworn" proof. Although some insurers treat the proof-of-loss form as a settlement document, others waive the formal filing of the form entirely, simply issuing a check for the agreed-on amount.[3]

The final step in closing a third-party claim is obtaining a release from the claimant. A release is a legally binding document providing that, in exchange for the specific sums to be paid to the claimant, the claimant releases the policyholder from all claims arising out of the particular accident. There are a variety of release formats; the most commonly used is the **general release**. The general release is appropriate in almost all situations except when a specific type of release would be more appropriate. An example of a general release is shown in Exhibit 13-6.

General release
A legally binding document that provides that the insurer will pay specific sums to a claimant in return for the claimant's release of the policyholder from all claims arising out of an accident or injury.

Attorneys have drafted releases other than general releases to match certain situations, and, in many cases, the language of the releases varies to conform with individual state laws. These releases include joint tortfeasor release, covenant not to sue, high/low agreements, release for injury to a minor, parent's release and indemnity agreement, nominal or dollar releases, release draft, and telephone recorded releases.

Joint Tortfeasor Release

The joint tortfeasor release is used when a plaintiff is suing a number of different parties who are presumably responsible for the plaintiff's injuries. Under common law, the plaintiff cannot settle and release one tortfeasor without releasing all tortfeasors involved in the accident. Many states have adopted the Uniform Contribution Among Tortfeasors Act, which permits the plaintiff to release individual tortfeasors without releasing them all. The release shown in Exhibit 13-7 protects the insured from a possible claim for contribution if the claimant is successful in an action against the remaining tortfeasors.

Covenant Not To Sue

A covenant not to sue is not a release but an agreement not to bring a suit. Like the joint tortfeasor release, this agreement is used in situations with multiple tortfeasors.

In the event that the defendant does bring suit against the settling tortfeasor, the tortfeasor can sue for breach of contract and can recover the amount of legal costs for defense. As with the joint tortfeasor release, the use of this agreement varies by state based on the enactment of the Uniform Contribution Among Tortfeasors Act or similar legislation.

High/Low Agreements

High/low agreements are arrangements whereby the parties to the settlement agree to guaranteed minimum and maximum settlement amounts of claims in litigation or arbitration. A verdict below the minimum will result in payment of the minimum limit by the defendant. Likewise, a verdict above the maximum

EXHIBIT 13-6

Release in Full of All Claims and Rights (General Release)

For and in consideration of the sum of _____

_____ ($ _____), receipt of

which is acknowledged, I release and forever discharge _____

_____, their

principals, agents, representatives and insurance carriers from any and all rights, claims, demands, and damages of any kind, known or unknown, existing or arising in the future, resulting from or related to personal injuries, death, or property damage, arising from an accident that occurred on or about the _____ day of _____,

20____, at or near_____.

This release shall not destroy or otherwise affect the rights of persons on whose behalf this payment is made, or persons who may claim to be damaged by reason of the accident other than the undersigned or any other persons.

I understand that this is a compromise settlement of all my claims of every nature and kind whatsoever arising out of the accident referred to above, but is not an admission of liability. I understand that this is all the money or consideration I will receive from the above described parties as a result of this accident. I have read this release and understand it.

Signed this _____ day of _____, 20_____, at _____ .

_____   _____
WITNESS

_____   _____
WITNESS

will be capped at the maximum. Any verdict between the two limits becomes the settlement amount. These agreements are made with the understanding that neither party will appeal.

This type of agreement is appropriate when the plaintiff's case is doubtful but, because of the seriousness of the injuries, could result in a significant judgment. The high/low agreement ensures that the plaintiff will recover something even if the case is lost. The insurer can limit its liability and avoid the threat of a bad-faith claim for any excess verdict.

Release for Injury to a Minor

Minors cannot give effective releases for their injuries. Although parents can release their claim for expenses and loss of services, they cannot legally release the claim of their minor child. To effectively release a minor's injury claim, therefore, the release must be obtained in accordance with the statutory

EXHIBIT 13-7

Release (Joint Tortfeasor Act)

We, the Undersigned, in consideration of ___(amount of settlement)___ dollars, the receipt of which is acknowledged, do hereby forever release and discharge ___(names of insureds responsible for the loss)___ hereinafter called the Payor, their heirs, executors, administrators, employers, employees, principals, agents, insurers, successors and assignees, from any and all liability, damages, actions and causes of action on account of personal injuries, death, loss of services or consortium, property damage and any and all other loss and damage of every kind and nature sustained by or hereafter resulting to the undersigned, his heirs, successors and assigns or any person or persons for whom the undersigned is acting as executor, administrator or guardian from an occurrence on or about the _(loss date)_ day of ___(month)___, 20____ at ___(location of loss–address, street, city, county, state)___ .

It is further understood and agreed that all claims or damages recoverable by the undersigned against all other persons, firms, partnerships or corporations, jointly or severally liable to the undersigned in tort for injury to person or property as a result of said accidents are hereby reduced by ___(amount of settlement)___ .

The undersigned hereby warrant that I/we have not heretofore released any person, firm, partnership or corporation from any claims or liability for damages arising from said occurrence.

As inducement to the payment of the sum aforesaid, the undersigned declare that we fully understand the terms of this settlement, and that we voluntarily accept said sum for the purpose of making full and final compromise, adjustment and settlement of all claims against the Payor, and that the payment of said sum for this release is not an admission of liability by the Payor, but that the Payor expressly denies liability.

This release is not intended to nor shall it be construed as releasing or discharging any other tortfeasor who may be liable for the injury and damage sustained in the above occurrence.

It is agreed that distribution of the above sum shall be made as follows

_____

_____

In Witness Whereof, We hereunto set our hands and seals this _____day of _____, 20 ____ (today's date).

In presence of

Name _____(witness)_____   _____(claimant)_____ (Seal)

Address_____   _____ (Seal)

Name _____   _____(claimant's spouse)_____ (Seal)

Address_____   _____ (Seal)

          Witnesses sign here   Claimants sign here

provisions of the state in which settlement is made. In cases involving serious injuries, the claim should be closed only by means of a court-approved settlement through a guardian or by the procedure known as a "friendly suit." Ordinarily, the court will not approve the settlement unless it has reviewed a current medical report from the treating physician and is satisfied that the settlement fairly compensates the injured child. Because the procedure may vary by jurisdiction, adjusters should be familiar with the accepted procedure in their jurisdiction.

Parent's Release and Indemnity Agreement

When a minor's injuries are slight and a full recovery is anticipated, many insurers forgo the time and expense of the court approval process and use a Parent's Release and Indemnity Agreement.

Although specific criteria may vary by insurer, this release should be used only in the following cases:

- The injury is healed and medical expenses are not great, or the medical report indicates that the minor was examined by a physician and released.
- No fractures were involved.
- No scarring is involved.
- No likelihood exists of future disability or impairment.

This release contains an indemnity agreement that states that if the minor later makes a recovery against the policyholder, the parents will indemnify (or reimburse) the policyholder for any payment made. The legal effect of this release is rarely tested, but in situations in which this release is used, it probably does have the psychological effect of closing the issue.

Nominal or Dollar Releases

Some adjusters obtain a release from claimants who were involved in an accident but who sustained no injuries. A release without payment probably has no legal effect. When some liability exists, some adjusters settle for a nominal amount. Another approach to obtaining a claimant's release is to have the claimant make a "no injury" statement. In any case, the real value of these releases is to give the claimant some sense of finality and to preclude the claimant from later seeking damages.

Release Draft

Where legal, many insurers use a specific statement of release on the reverse side of drafts. Such releases are most commonly associated with small to moderate property damage claims. The claimant's endorsement of the draft or check serves as a release of the claim. Adjusters must remember that many unfair claims practice laws restrict the use of **release drafts**. Adjusters should be familiar with any such restrictions in their states.

Release draft
A statement appearing on the reverse side of a claim draft. When the claimant endorses the draft, he or she also releases the claim.

Telephone-Recorded Releases

Telephone-recorded releases are occasionally taken by adjusters in smaller claims in which the claimant is not represented by an attorney. The acceptability and use of telephone releases vary by company and, to some extent, by jurisdiction. Inside adjusters may find that releases are easier to obtain over the telephone, and a telephone release may occasionally be obtained instead of a telephone-recorded statement on smaller claims.

Litigation

Many insurers spend as much money on outside defense attorneys as they do for their entire claim department, yet defending policyholders is one of the key promises of liability insurance. It is essential to policyholders and to the insurer that claim personnel handle litigation well. Because of the enormous expense of litigation and the delays existing in many court systems, claim representatives should explore alternatives to litigation. When litigation cannot be avoided, claim representatives must carefully select and direct defense counsel. They must actively participate in litigation strategy to ensure proper defense of the policyholder and careful control of litigation expenses.

Alternatives to Litigation

Alternative dispute resolution (ADR)
Methods used to settle claims that avoid litigation.

Adjusters use various procedures called **alternative dispute resolution (ADR)** as alternatives to litigation, including negotiation, mediation, arbitration, appraisals, mini-trials or summary jury trials, and pre-trial settlement conferences. The insurance business and the courts encourage the use of these litigation alternatives. Approaches to alternative dispute resolution are discussed in Chapter 15.

Selection and Direction of Outside Attorneys

The selection of a defense attorney to handle a lawsuit against an insured is an important decision. For a routine claim in which the amount of damages is specific (as in property damage) or in which the action involves only subrogation collection, a new or unproved attorney who charges a minimum rate may be considered. But when the allegations against the policyholder are severe, liability is questionable, and the damages are so severe that a jury may award compensatory damages in excess of the policyholder's policy limits, the insurer must select an outstanding defense attorney.

The attorney's role is to be an advocate for the insured—regardless of how the attorney may personally view the policyholder's case or personal merits. The attorney must attack every aspect of the adverse party's claim, from the liability to the damages, seeking constantly to find something that will mitigate the claim against the policyholder and place the plaintiff in a position that will make settlement a more attractive option than an unknown award from an unpredictable jury.

Decisions Relating to Defense

The first decision that must be made is whether to defend the lawsuit at all. If the lawsuit is the first notice of the claim and liability is probable, the adjuster handling the claim may request an extension from the plaintiff's attorney while investigating and then try to settle the claim without incurring defense costs.

If the facts of the case are already known and the case is one of clear or probable liability, the adjuster should attempt to settle the case before incurring legal costs. The attorney may have filed the suit only to protect against a statute of limitations or to get the insurer's attention if settlement negotiations have failed to progress or have reached an impasse.

If, however, the claim is owed but the plaintiff is seeking more in the settlement than the insurer believes is justified, the adjuster may decide to allow discovery to proceed to learn whether the plaintiff has any proof that the damages are as severe as alleged.

When the previous investigation shows that insurer does not owe the claim because of either a lack of liability or damages or because another party owes the claim, the insurer may elect to defend. The defense attorney might move to have the case dismissed on summary judgment (a pre-trial verdict in favor of the party requesting it) or might file a cross action or third-party action against the party believed to be responsible to the plaintiff. This sort of defense can quickly become expensive as various motions are made before the court and the processes of discovery proceed.

Insurers often speak of "nuisance settlements" of a claim or lawsuit when either very little liability or no proof of damages exists. To save the cost of defending such a suit, the insurer may pay or contribute a minimal amount to a settlement to resolve the case. A valid argument might be made that nuisance payments produce more harm than good by encouraging unscrupulous claimants and attorneys to file more frivolous claims.

Selection of Experts

Whether or not a claim is in litigation, the adjuster may need a variety of experts to assist in the evaluation process. In complex claims involving traffic accidents, building or construction sites, products, mechanical processes, and other exposures that may require expert courtroom testimony, the adjuster must have available resources from which to draw the best witnesses. Someone with the most credentials may not be the best technical expert if he or she cannot adequately use lay terms to explain to the jury what happened. The adjuster must select a specialist who not only is an expert in his or her field but also is impartial and well-spoken.

Subrogation and Other Recoveries

Subrogation is the legal process through which an insurer assumes the right to pursue a legal action against a party who may be liable to the policyholder.

Subrogation
The insurer's right to recover payment for a loss it has paid to an insured from a negligent third party who caused the loss.

Subrogation is one of the most effective post-loss control processes, not just in first-party claims but also in liability and other types of claims. Most subrogation occurs in workers compensation, property insurance, and automobile physical damage claims. The insurer may include the policyholder's deductible in a claim but otherwise may not pursue other loss suffered by the policyholder that is not covered by insurance.

A physical damage insurer will frequently seek to recover collision damages it has paid to an auto owner from the liability insurer of the driver who struck the insured auto. Insurers that have signed the Nationwide Inter-Company Arbitration Agreement sponsored by Arbitration Forums, Inc., may use arbitration via panels of local claim adjusters to resolve disputes among themselves over liability issues related to their subrogation. This agreement also permits insurers to pursue the amount of the deductible on behalf of the insured. The decision of the panel is binding and generally cannot be appealed. Insurers can also subscribe to several other types of intercompany and special arbitration agreements. Disputed uninsured motorists claims are often settled using arbitrators affiliated with the American Arbitration Association.

Measuring Claim Performance

A community's recovery after a natural disaster is a testament to the success of claim activities. Yet insurers must have a more specific means of measuring the success of their claim departments and of individual adjusters.

There is no single convenient measure of the performance of an insurer's claim department. An insurer's claim-handling ability should be measured in terms of two categories: (1) financial measures and (2) measures that evaluate claim-handling performance.

Financial Measures

The insurer's loss ratio is one of the most commonly used measures of evaluating the financial well-being of an insurance company. A rising loss ratio may indicate that the insurer is improperly performing the claim function. Rising losses could also mean that underwriting failed to select above-average risks or that the actuarial department failed to price the insurer's products correctly.

When the expense ratio of the insurer rises, the claim department, along with other departments, faces pressure to reduce expenses. Management often relies on superficial and shortsighted solutions to controlling claim expenses. Claim personnel can quickly reduce claim adjusting expenses by offering policyholders and claimants the settlement demanded rather than the settlement they deserve. A proper claim settlement requires incurring expenses. Inflated claim demands should be resisted, researched, negotiated, and, if necessary, litigated.

One way to reduce the cost of claims is to reduce the number of claim adjusting personnel. Reduced claim staffs or restrictions on the use of independent adjusters usually increase the workload of claim personnel. Increased workload without changes in job standards will likely result in adjusters' taking short-cuts in handling claims.

The long-term consequences of not following acceptable claim procedures is an increase in the total cost of claims. So, although an immediate reduction in expenses results from these measures, claim costs are likely to rise as more claims go into litigation or are overpaid.

A better financial measure of claim performance is the accuracy with which claims are reserved. If the insurer must constantly transfer large sums on its financial balance sheet from surplus to reserves because of past underreserving, the claim department may be performing one of its primary jobs poorly.

Claim-Handling Performance

Claim-handling performance measures are internal standards by which claim departments and individual adjusters can be gauged. The criteria used to evaluate a claim department include the following:

- Turnover of claims
- Average cost of settlement
- Number and percentage of litigated files
- Litigation win/lose ratios
- Ratio of allocated to unallocated costs
- Average caseload per adjuster
- Turnover of staff

The performance of individual adjusters can be evaluated on the basis of the following factors:

- File turnover
- Ratio of litigated to settled files
- Average settlement costs compared to other adjusters with similar files

The adjuster's position, level of experience and education, and degree of supervision must be considered in the evaluation. An adjuster with a caseload that only grows, with few settled but many litigated files, is an adjuster in trouble. Overpaying claims is equally as troublesome, though it may reduce the caseload faster.

Unfair Claims Settlement Practices Legislation

The Unfair Claims Settlement Practices Model Act was developed by the National Association of Insurance Commissioners (NAIC) to establish standards for the proper handling of claims. Before its development, regulators relied on state unfair trade practices acts. These laws were often ineffective in protecting the public from insurer strategies to reduce or eliminate claims. Unconscionable insurer tactics included denying claims when liability was obvious or slowing down the settlement process until policyholders and claimants finally gave up.

In creating the Unfair Claims Settlement Practices Model Act, the NAIC incorporated many of the provisions already included in New York statutes. The act was added as a new section to the existing Unfair Trade Practices Act. In 1990, the NAIC separated the provisions of the act to clarify the distinction between general unfair trade practices and the more specific unfair claim settlement practices. The insurer activities prohibited by the Unfair Claims Settlement Practices Act are listed in Exhibit 13-8.

Under the provisions of the model act, if the insurance commissioner has reasonable cause to believe that an insurer is conducting business in violation of the act, the commissioner can issue a statement of charges to the insurer and set a hearing date. If it is determined after the hearing that the insurer has violated the act, the insurance commissioner will issue a cease and desist order and may impose a fine. The fine cannot exceed $1,000 for each violation and $100,000 altogether unless the violation was committed flagrantly and in conscious disregard of the act. In such cases, the penalty will not exceed $25,000 for each violation or $250,000 in the aggregate. The insurance commissioner may suspend or revoke the insurer's license if the insurer knew or reasonably should have known that the activity violated the act. Additional penalties exist for violation of cease and desist orders.[4] Some states may have adopted the model act but not the specific penalty provisions. Other states have altered the model act or deleted sections of it.

The Unfair Property/Casualty Claims Settlement Practices Model Regulation is a companion to the Unfair Claims Settlement Practices Act. As with the model act, individual state legislatures must choose to adopt the model law or some version of it and enact it into law. In states whose insurance commission has the power to devise insurance regulations to carry out the model act, the model regulation is available to serve as a basis for creating administrative guidelines.

The regulation defines procedures and practices that constitute unfair claim practices in the following specific areas:

- File and record documentation
- Misrepresentation of policy provisions
- Failure to acknowledge pertinent communications
- Standards for prompt, fair, and equitable settlements applicable to all insurers
- Standards for prompt, fair, and equitable settlements applicable to automobile insurance
- Standards for prompt, fair, and equitable settlements applicable to fire and extended coverage-type policies with replacement cost coverage

Forty-five jurisdictions have adopted either the Unfair Claims Practices Model Act or similar legislation. Twenty-one states have adopted the Unfair

EXHIBIT 13-8

Unfair Claims Settlement Practices

Committing or performing with such frequency as to indicate a general business practice any of the following:

A. Knowingly misrepresenting to claimants and insureds relevant facts or policy provisions relating to coverage at issue;

B. Failing to acknowledge with reasonable promptness pertinent communications with respect to claims arising under its policies;

C. Failing to adopt and implement reasonable standards for the prompt investigation and settlement of claims arising under its policies;

D. Not attempting in good faith to effectuate prompt, fair and equitable settlement of claims submitted in which liability has become reasonably clear;

E. Compelling insureds or beneficiaries to institute suits to recover amounts due under its policies by offering substantially less than the amounts ultimately recovered in suits brought by them;

F. Refusing to pay claims without conducting a reasonable investigation;

G. Failing to affirm or deny coverage of claims within a reasonable time after having completed its investigation related to such claim or claims;

H. Attempting to settle or settling claims for less than the amount that a reasonable person would believe the insured or beneficiary was entitled by reference to written or printed advertising material accompanying or made part of an application;

I. Attempting to settle or settling claims on the basis of an application that was materially altered without notice to, or knowledge or consent of, the insured;

J. Making claims payments to an insured or beneficiary without indicating the coverage under which each payment is being made;

K. Unreasonably delaying the investigation or payment of claims by requiring both a formal proof of loss form and subsequent verification that would result in duplication of information and verification appearing in the formal proof of loss form;

L. Failing in the case of claims denials or offers of compromise settlement to promptly provide a reasonable and accurate explanation of the basis for such actions;

M. Failing to provide forms necessary to present claims within fifteen (15) calendar days of a request with reasonable explanations regarding their use;

N. Failing to adopt and implement reasonable standards to assure that the repairs of a repairer owned by or required to be used by the insurer are performed in a workman-like manner.

NAIC Model Laws, Regulations, and Guidelines, Tab: Unfair Trade Practices, 1991, p. 900-2-3.

Property/Casualty Claims Settlement Practices Model Regulation or similar regulations. In states that have not adopted the model regulations, insurance regulators must decide case by case what is considered an "unfair" practice.

All state insurance codes contain various rules and regulations that govern the practice of claim adjusting. In addition, in many states, insurers, their adjusters, and independent adjusters are subject to the state's consumer-oriented Deceptive Trade Practices Act. These laws often leave the issue of what constitutes an unfair trade practice to juries, which can award triple damages.

Various states can interpret their laws and regulations differently. One state may require an adjuster to advise an unrepresented claimant of the statute of limitations, but in a state without such a rule, volunteering information might be construed as the unauthorized practice of law. In another example, one state may require a vehicle damage appraiser to list one or more shops that will agree to repair a damaged vehicle for the appraised amount, but in another state, recommending any repair facility is a violation of law. Many of these rules deal with misrepresentation of policy terms, refusal to settle, or lack of response to inquiries.

Recognizing the need to internalize the provisions of the model act into the procedures of the claim department, insurers have rewritten those provisions and have added specific standards for company adjusters when the regulations have provided none. Thus, even adjusters who may not be familiar with the act itself may be following company procedures that comply with the act. Enforcement of the Unfair Claims Settlement Practices Act is limited in most jurisdictions. In only a minority of states can individuals exert a right of action based on the act in first-party claims. Even fewer states permit a right of action in third-party claims. In the remainder of states, enforcement of the act is the full responsibility of the insurance department.

SUMMARY

The insurer fulfills its contractual promise to the policyholder through the claim settlement process. Adjusters screen requests for payment to distinguish valid from invalid claims. Claims that fall within the bounds of coverage are assessed to determine their value and are then paid.

Most policyholders have little or no contact with their insurer except when the initial policy is written or when the premium is due. When a claim does occur, the adjuster is responsible for the reputation of the insurance company. Fair and professional treatment of policyholders and claimants can do much to improve the image of the insurance industry, even on an individual, claim-by-claim basis.

Some insurers may think that any claim that goes to trial is a failure, even before the verdict is determined. When a claim does go to trial, the adjuster must manage the defense counsel and communicate to plaintiff's counsel the insurer's settlement philosophy. Internally, adjusters must provide information to several departments, including the marketing, underwriting, and actuarial departments.

The structure of an insurer's claim organization is typically described in terms of its geographic or physical organization and its management/settlement authority. Claim offices are usually located close to policyholders so that service can be provided easily. Often, when claims occur outside the normal geographic scope of the insurer, independent adjusters are employed to serve the policyholder. The management structure of a claim department is probably similar to the management scheme of any other insurer functional area. A distinguishing feature in a claim organization is that higher levels of settlement authority are assigned to individuals based on their responsible use of the claim authority already granted. Experience, knowledge, and the confidence of management are all factors considered in extending settlement authority.

In addition to handling claims outside the normal scope of operations, independent adjusters provide special expertise for complex or unusual claims. Many insurers employ independent adjusters as a normal part of their business rather than expanding their own staffs.

The claim adjusting process can be described in terms of investigation, evaluation, negotiation, and settlement of coverage, liability, and damage issues. The actual steps in this process may vary between property and liability claims. Specific claim-handling differences and the unique characteristics of individual lines of business are the subjects of Chapters 14 and 15.

CHAPTER NOTES

1. "A Guide to Auto Insurance," *Consumer Reports*, October 1995, p. 642.

2. The following section is based on Bernard L. Webb, Howard N. Anderson, John A. Cookman, and Peter R. Kensicki, *Principles of Reinsurance*, vol. 1 (Malvern, Pa.: Insurance Institute of America, 1990), pp. 185–196.

3. Robert J. Prahl and Stephen M. Utrata, *Liability Claim Concepts and Practices* (Malvern, Pa.: Insurance Institute of America, 1985), pp. 385–403.

4. NAIC Model Laws, Regulations, and Guidelines, 1991, Tab: Unfair Trade Practices, p. 900.

Chapter 14

Direct Your Learning

Property Claim Adjusting

After learning the subject matter of this chapter, you should be able to:

■ Given a property claim, identify the general issues that should be addressed.

■ Illustrate the challenges involved in adjusting claims involving each of the following:

- Residential dwellings
- Homeowners personal property
- Commercial structures
- Business interruption
- Merchandise
- Property in transit or held by bailees
- Property that has been stolen
- Property damaged by catastrophe

Develop Your Perspective

What are the main topics covered in the chapter?

This chapter describes how property claims are adjusted. The adjustment of property claims is distinctly different from that of liability claims. Property claim adjusters focus on detailed insurance policy provisions. These general provisions and those of selected property policies are included.

Examine the detailed level of policy examination required in property claim adjustment.

- What facets of this process would create challenges for a claim adjuster?

Why is it important to know these topics?

Property claim adjustment requires attention to policy content and application of that content to a specific claim situation. Insight into this process provides an opportunity to view the skill required for this function.

Estimate the knowledge and skills required to perform property claim adjusting and the adjusters' role in representing the company and safeguarding its profitability.

- Placing yourself in the role of an insurance company executive, what level of expertise would you hope to build in your property claim adjusting staff?

How can you use this information?

Investigate your own organization's property claim adjusting department.

- What type of policy losses do they adjust?
- How do the adjusters acquire their expertise?

Chapter 14

Property Claim Adjusting

Each of the final two chapters of this text addresses a specific type of claim: this chapter discusses claims for property losses (specifically claims for property damage under first-party insurance policies), and Chapter 15 discusses liability claims (primarily bodily injury claims under third-party insurance policies). This division is a natural one because claim adjusters are generally either property or liability specialists. Although claims for property damage can be asserted against third-party policies and injury claims can be covered by first-party policies, the majority of claim personnel do most of their work either in property-damage, first-party claims or in bodily-injury, third-party claims.

Property and liability claim specialists operate in different environments. Property claim adjusters are primarily concerned with the application of detailed insurance policy provisions to specific situations. Liability claim adjusters, on the other hand, are primarily concerned with how the legal system, which operates independently of insurance policy provisions, evaluates and compensates third-party claims. Property claim adjusters must indemnify losses that are supposedly objectively quantifiable, but liability claim adjusters must evaluate and settle claims that are largely subjective. "Pain and suffering," for instance, one of the major elements of damages in bodily injury liability claims, is highly subjective.

The first part of this chapter addresses general issues that arise in all property claims. Who has an interest in, and who is insured with respect to, damaged property? What property is insured under a policy and for what locations and for what time period? For what causes of loss does the insurance provide coverage? What is the dollar amount of the loss? What procedures must the insured and the claim adjuster follow to conclude the claim? As noted above, the answers to those questions are derived from applying the insurance policy provisions to specific situations.

The second part of this chapter discusses specific issues pertinent to specific types of claims and how claim adjusters must deal with those issues. Although the settlement of all claims includes each of the issues described in the first part of this chapter, certain issues predominate in certain types of claims. For example, issues that are paramount in homeowners claims may be much less important in commercial crime claims, and vice versa.

GENERAL ISSUES IN PROPERTY CLAIM ADJUSTING

The issues described herein pertain to every property claim and constitute a framework that property claim adjusters use to handle all kinds of property damage claims. The explicit language of insurance policies provides substantial direction and guidance to adjusters. For example, to determine who is insured, an adjuster can simply read the name on the policy. Although others may also be insured, the identification of the named insured is crucial. An adjuster can likewise resolve most of the issues described here by consulting the policy and applying the policy language to the given situation. The biggest exception to this approach is in determining the amount of loss. In contrast to the detail they provide concerning other matters, insurance policies are extremely general in how they state the value of insured property. Adjusters perform an in-depth analysis of property values on those policies that sustain a loss rather than on all policies insured by the company. The critical time for property valuation is at the time of the loss, not at the time the policy was issued.

Who Has an Interest? Who Is Insured?

Insurance protects people, not property. So-called property insurance protects people or organizations from loss of the value of their interest in property. Accordingly, an interest in property is a prerequisite to asserting a claim under an insurance policy.

Good underwriting practice requires a prospective policyholder to have an interest in property before an insurance policy can be issued. The underwriting standard is reinforced by language in the policy that limits all claims payments to the extent of the insured's interest. One might wonder why claim adjusters concern themselves with this requirement. A review of all interests that may exist in damaged property is an excellent means of determining with whom the adjuster must deal in settling a claim. Because property insurance exists to protect people, the adjuster's first questions on every claim should be, "Who is affected? Who has a right to assert a claim?"

Interests in Property

In general, anyone who would be harmed financially by the destruction of property has an interest in that property. The simplest and most obvious example of an interest in property is a sole owner with a complete interest in the property. However, numerous other interests, less than complete and sole, may exist in a particular property, often simultaneously.

Ownership may not rest with a sole person—there are various legal forms by which more than one person can own property simultaneously. Under **joint ownership**, two or more owners each have a complete, indivisible interest in the property. If one joint owner dies, ownership need not be transferred, because the other owner already has a complete interest in the

Joint ownership
Indivisible interest in property by two or more owners.

property. Joint ownership is often called "the poor person's will" because the property need never pass through the administration of the deceased's estate. Joint ownership between husband and wife is known as **tenancy by entireties**. **Ownership in common** involves two or more owners, each with an identifiable fractional interest in the property. This fractional interest is a financial interest and does not necessarily constitute any particular part of the physical property. Ownership in common is typical among partners.

A person or an organization can also have an interest in property that is not an ownership interest. Lessees of property have an interest in the use of the property for the life of the lease. Custodians of property, such as bailees, warehouse employees, and carriers, have an interest in the property to the extent of their fees and for their legal liability for the safe return of the property to its owner. Finally, security interests may exist in almost any property. The secured party is generally a creditor of the property owner. The existence of a security interest is usually not evident from an inspection of the property. The secured party usually does not have possession of the property, and the property is not marked physically to show the interest. Security interests are created by contractual agreement or by operation of law.

Policy Requirements for an Insurable Interest

Rather than listing the existence of an insurable interest as a precondition to coverage, insurance policies simply limit payment on any claim to the extent of the insured's interest. For example, the HO-3 policy states the following under Conditions 1:

> . . . we will not be liable in any one loss: a. to the insured for more than the amount of the insured's interest at the time of loss. . . .

Under Loss Conditions, paragraph 4.d., the business and personal property coverage form states:

> We will not pay you more than your financial interest in the Covered Property.

In addition, proof of loss forms usually require the insured to specify all interests in the property. Insurers typically provide these forms to insureds who have suffered losses and require that the insured sign and swear to the forms. Some insurance policies explicitly require that all interests be specified on a proof of loss form. Other policies may require the insured to file a signed, sworn statement listing all information required by the insurer. Invariably, the insurer will require complete information about interests in the property.

Because a proof of loss must be signed and sworn to, false information contained therein constitutes material misrepresentation that may void coverage. As noted later in this chapter, some insurers do not require a proof of loss on all, or even most, claims. However, any time the nature and extent of interests in the property are unclear, a proof of loss is invaluable to the insurer.

Tenancy by entireties
A form of joint tenancy in which the co-owners are husband and wife. When the husband or wife dies, the property passes to the surviving spouse.

Ownership in common
A form of ownership in which two or more owners each have an identifiable fractional interest in the property.

The limitation of claim payments to the extent of an insured's interest and the requirement that all interests existing in the property be specified are essential claim adjusting procedures. Allowing the insured to collect more than its interest in the insured property would provide a great incentive for the insured to deliberately destroy the property. Even when a policy has been properly underwritten, an insured's interest can change (for example, through divorce, marriage, or additional mortgages), thus creating opportunities for false claims if the insured's recovery is not limited to its actual interest.

Identifying all interests in the property enables the adjuster to treat every party fairly, without compromising the insurer's rights. It may also lead the adjuster to identify other coverage on the same property. Whenever multiple interests in property exist, each party might have its own insurance protecting its own interest. Another party's property or liability insurance may reduce the payments required of the investigating insurer. Policies contain provisions to uphold the indemnification concept. The other insurance and subrogation clauses reduce recovery or limit unjust enrichment.

Possibilities for Other Coverage

The most common situations in which parties with different interests have separate coverages are landlord-tenant, bailor-bailee, and mortgagor-mortgagee arrangements.

Landlord-Tenant Arrangements

The lease determines the relationship between a landlord and a tenant. The lease should specify precisely what property is subject to the lease; what rights of use or access, if any, the tenant has to the landlord's other property; the rights in the leased property that the landlord retains; the rights of the tenant to make improvements to the leased property; and the rights of the landlord to any improvements to the leased property upon expiration of the lease. The lease should also specify whether the landlord and tenant waive rights of recovery against each other and whether the tenant is obligated to provide insurance for the landlord. An adjuster cannot determine the interests of either a landlord or a tenant in property without reviewing the lease.

Although the lease determines the respective rights regarding the leased property, it does not determine coverage under an insurance policy. The landlord or the tenant may be named as an insured under the other's policy, or there may be coverage for the property of others in the insured's possession. Neither the landlord nor the tenant has any rights under the insurance coverage of the other unless the other's insurance policy so allows.

Thus, adjusters handling claims that potentially involve a landlord and a tenant must conduct a two-part analysis. First, what are the parties' respective interests in the property under the lease? Second, what rights does each party have under the insurance policy in question? To recover under an insurance policy, a party must have both the right to do so under the policy *and* an interest in some property that is covered by the policy.

Bailor-Bailee Arrangements

Bailor-bailee situations involve similar issues. The respective interests in the property are determined by contractual agreement or, in the absence of contractual terms, by the law. Rights under an insurance policy are determined solely by the terms of that policy. Because of their legal liabilities and because of industry custom, bailees such as warehouse employees, carriers, and repairers typically have some sort of coverage for the property of others while it is in their possession.

Adjusters handling claims for owners of property damaged in the hands of a bailee will usually look first to the bailee's insurer to handle the claim. Should the bailee's insurer fail to respond, or deny liability, the owner's insurer must handle the claim. Possible subrogation claims against the bailee may be waived or otherwise affected by the agreement between the owner and the bailee.

Mortgagor-Mortgagee Arrangements

The most common situation in which different interests are protected by common coverage is with owners and mortgagees. Mortgage agreements usually require the owner to name the mortgagee on the owner's insurance policy. Insurance policies grant rights to mortgagees that are separate and distinct from the owner's rights. Thus, adjusters may have to protect a mortgagee even when the owner's coverage under the property is void.

In most cases, the mortgagee's interest is protected by the use of the claim settlement proceeds to repair the property. The adjuster should include the mortgagee's name on any settlement draft. Failure to do so may render the insurer separately liable to the mortgagee. The adjuster should not become involved in disputes among the owner, the mortgagee, and the contractors over whether the property is reparable. Once the adjuster has agreed with the parties as to the amount of the loss and has named all parties on the settlement draft, the adjuster's task is complete.

Identification of Insureds

Adjusters must carefully distinguish among a variety of people with rights and duties under a policy. A policy may identify a "first named insured," "named insureds," spouse of a "named insured," "insureds," and people whose property may be covered under a policy.

Generally, only the "first named insured," "named insured," or spouse of the "named insured" is entitled to assert a claim. These specified individuals are likewise responsible for paying premiums and performing the insured's duties in the event of loss. In the event of the named insured's death, an adjuster can settle claims with the named insured's legal representative, either an executor or an administrator of the estate. These legal representatives are included in most policies' definition of "insured." Loss payees are parties, such as auto finance companies, that do not have any rights greater than or independent of the policyholder, but the loss payee's name must be included on any claim settlement check.

The adjuster must deal with the proper party or parties. Failure to do so may obligate the insurer to pay the claim more than once if the proper party appears or may render ineffective any legal notices the insurer has given. An adjuster should be able to determine easily the proper party with whom to deal. The policy declarations will identify the named insureds. The policy language can be consulted to determine exactly who can assert claims and who must perform the insured's duties in the event of loss.

In any case in which the insurer can deny coverage to the first named insured or to the spouse of a named insured, the adjuster must carefully check the policy for the rights the other insureds may still have. If the policy language is unclear about such situations, the adjuster should consult legal counsel.

What Is Insured? Where Is It Insured?

Policy provisions regarding what property is covered and where it is covered are straightforward and usually do not cause disagreement between the insured and the adjuster.

Buildings

Being stationary, most buildings are easy to describe and to identify. Most policies state the described buildings and structures at a given location. Other policies provide blanket coverage but still require a schedule of locations to identify the buildings to be insured.

Any inconsistency between the identification of an insured location on the declarations sheet and a purported insured location is probably caused by a clerical error that can be cleared up through research with the producer. The construction and the occupancy of a building described on a declarations sheet are *not* conditions of the policy coverage unless the policy explicitly says so. Thus, if a claim adjuster finds that a house described as "brick" construction is actually wood frame construction, the adjuster should report this discrepancy to the underwriter, but it will not void coverage unless the policyholder engaged in misrepresentation. Intentional misrepresentation is a basis for voiding the policy from its inception.

Personal Property

Other than the coverages provided by inland marine policies, most personal property is covered under insurance policies that are written for a fixed location (and that may be primarily concerned with coverage for a building at that location). Such policies provide different coverage, depending on the circumstances. In general, the insured's personal property at the insured location is covered; the insured's personal property away from the insured location may or may not be covered, depending on the policy; and personal property not owned by the policyholder is covered only at the insured location and while in the insured's care, custody, and control, often subject to a tight limit of coverage.

Adjusters handling claims for personal property must be alert to two situations in which coverage may be sought even though it may not apply: (1) a claim for the insured's property that may have been damaged away from the insured location, and (2) a claim for damage to the property of another. In the first case, an adjuster may become suspicious if the property has been damaged away from the insured premises because it is a certain type of property (for example, goods in the process of manufacture or goods that have been sold but not yet delivered). The cause of loss (for example, vehicle damage or theft without forcible entry) may also arouse suspicion. Additional documentation from, or investigation of, the insured is likely to confirm or disprove the suspicion. In the second case, the adjuster's job is easy if the insured acknowledges that the property in question belongs to another. The adjuster then need only check the policy to see what coverage pertains or whether other insurance covering the property is primary. The adjuster's job is more difficult if the insured tries to pass off the property of another as his or her own. The adjuster may suspect such a situation if the insured handles a great deal of other people's property without adequate coverage for this exposure. Careful research into the insured's records will usually reveal who owns the property. An adjuster may require assistance from an expert auditor for this task.

Fixtures are personal property that have become attached to and part of real property. In the event of a loss, the adjuster must determine whether a given "fixture" is real or personal property. Real property is land and everything attached to it, such as buildings. Personal property is everything not considered real property. The distinction between real property and personal property is important to adjusters. The two types of property may be valued differently (actual cash value versus replacement cost), may have different limits of coverage (which may not be adequate for one type of property), and may have different coinsurance requirements. Adjusters can distinguish fixtures as real property by means of the following guidelines:

1. How permanently attached to the real property it is (for example, a furnace is a fixture, but a window air conditioner is not)

2. Whether the property is well adapted to the real property (for example, draperies that have been selected to match the interior decorating of a particular room)

3. The intent of the owner (for example, something may be bolted or screwed onto the real property yet be personal property because the owner so intends)

Certain policy provisions are helpful because they relieve the adjuster from classifying certain property. For example, the business and personal property coverage form allows fixtures to be classed as either "building" or "business personal property." The ISO Homeowners Special Form (HO-3) requires that carpets, awnings, appliances, and antennae be valued as personal property, regardless of whether they might actually be fixtures. In any doubtful case, an adjuster should categorize property in whatever way is most favorable to the insured. Specialized policies for electronic data processing equipment address all computer-related exposures, whether the computer hardware is personal property or a fixture, and extend to additional expenses, such as reconstructing data.

Property Not Covered

Adjusters quickly learn the types of property that are typically not covered, but they should always check the exact policy wording before denying any claim. Failure to provide a reasonable explanation for a claim denial with references to the insurance policy and the facts of the case is a violation of the Unfair Claims Settlement Practices Act.

Insureds whose claims are denied usually accept a plausible and verifiable explanation from the adjuster. For example, the adjuster may simply have to explain that the property is the sort that is usually covered elsewhere (for example, motor vehicles) or through specialty lines of insurance (for example, valuable papers or livestock). Nevertheless, all claim denials should be in writing.

Additional Coverages

Following a loss, insureds frequently consult with the adjuster about whether, and to what extent, they can incur certain expenses under the various additional coverages. It is considered good practice for adjusters to respond to insureds' requests for authorization of additional coverage expense. Unless the insured is asserting a suspicious claim, the common-sense approach is to reach agreement about an expense before it has been incurred, rather than to argue about it afterward. The adjuster's authorization of an expense under the additional coverages is regarded as contractually binding on the insurer, even if the expense in question should not have been covered.

Against What Causes of Loss Does the Insurance Protect?

Determining whether a loss has resulted from a covered cause of loss is usually a simple matter for an adjuster. Causes of loss such as fire and windstorm, for example, lead to characteristic damage and are easy to verify. Adjusters may encounter problems verifying the cause of loss when certain perils or exclusions are involved. Water damage, collapse, theft, and vandalism, however, are troublesome perils to verify. The most troublesome exclusions are water damage (as an exclusion), wear and tear and other gradual causes of loss, ordinance or law causing increased cost to rebuild, faulty construction, and intentional acts on the part of the insured.

Direct and Indirect Physical Loss

Most property insurance policies provide coverage only for direct physical loss. Thus, adjusters must recognize indirect or nonphysical types of losses that may be presented for coverage.

The most important type of indirect loss is loss of use of property. Coverage for loss of use is provided as part of the package of coverages in the typical homeowners policy. In contrast, some commercial property policies do not automatically provide loss of use coverage. Unless the insured purchases such coverage, loss of use of property is not compensated.

Even when loss of use is covered, direct physical loss to property is essential to trigger such coverage and to measure its duration. For example, coverage for loss of business income applies only when the loss is caused by a direct loss to covered property or when civil authorities close the business because of a hazardous situation nearby. Such coverage begins after a brief waiting period after the covered property suffers direct loss and usually ends when the same property should be repaired or replaced.

Nonphysical losses include loss of value to property not caused by physical damage or destruction, such as obsolescence, loss of market, investment loss, and financial frauds. Loss of market is an important problem for claim adjusters. Insureds who operate seasonal businesses and who suffer losses at the busiest time of year frequently demand compensation for the diminished value of inventory that has gone unsold because of their loss. Assuming such inventory has not suffered physical loss, its diminished value is not compensable.

Water Damage

Property insurance policies that provide coverage for water damage generally limit such coverage to sudden and accidental overflow, breakage, or bursting of plumbing. In a given case, the exact wording of the coverage is crucial, because any type of water damage not within the defined cause of loss is not covered.

The most significant types of water damage that are usually not covered are gradual seepage and floods. Alone, these two types of water damage are easy to identify. Claim adjusters face difficulties, however, when these types of water damage are combined with covered losses. For example, a burst pipe may cause damage to property that has already suffered damage from gradual seepage. Except under certain "all-risks" policies that may cover seepage, the adjuster must separate property damaged by seepage from other property and must determine how much of the damage to the former was caused by the seepage and by the burst pipe, respectively.

Hurricanes frequently cause damage through a combination of wind, wind-driven water, and flooding. The typical property policy covers the damage caused by wind and wind-driven water (under specific circumstances), but not that caused by flooding. The adjuster must separate damages by cause even if the owner has purchased flood coverage through the National Flood Insurance Program (NFIP). Under the NFIP's Single Adjuster Program, one adjuster can handle both the wind and the flood claims at a single loss site. This is an important procedure because adjusters are usually in short supply following a major catastrophe. As a result, all claims in the affected geographic area can be handled sooner.

Collapse

Collapse is actually a type of loss, rather than a cause of loss. Recent Insurance Services Office policy forms treat collapse as an additional coverage. The effect of this treatment is to limit the coverage for collapse to the specific wording of the additional coverage. Collapse is covered only when it is caused by the perils specified in the additional coverage. Adjusters must be careful when handling claims involving two specific causes of collapse: hidden problems and defective construction.

Decay and insect and vermin damage are covered causes of collapse only if they are *hidden*. Conspicuous decay or insect or vermin damage should be repaired by the insured before further loss occurs. To determine whether the insured should have known of the damage that caused the collapse, claim adjusters must reconstruct how a structure looked before its collapse.

Defective construction is a covered cause of collapse only if the collapse occurs during construction. Policyholders have presented numerous claims to insurers for loss caused by defective construction. The underwriters of most property insurance policies do not intend to permit the policies to serve in place of a surety contract that would protect the structure's owner from the builder's mistakes.

Theft

Coverage for theft varies widely among property policies, from none to extensive. An adjuster handling a claim for loss caused by theft must be careful to thoroughly review the relevant policy provisions.

Assuming that the policyholder has theft coverage for the type and location of property concerned, the adjuster's most difficult task is verifying the loss. Both the loss itself and its amount must be verified. Theft claims are the easiest for a dishonest insured to fabricate because little or no evidence remains. Even in legitimate cases of theft, there is often no evidence that a thief acted, that the property involved ever existed, or of the values and quantities of property involved. The insured's statements as to the nature, quantity, and value of property allegedly stolen are admissible evidence in court. Thus, an adjuster cannot deny a claim simply because the insured fails to provide receipts.

Adjusters can (and should) require policyholders with theft claims to report such claims to the police. Most insurance policies require the policyholder to do so. Indeed, a policyholder's failure to do so will likely arouse the adjuster's suspicions. People who fabricate theft claims may be reluctant to involve the police because of the possibilities of criminal sanctions for false reporting. On legitimate claims, the police occasionally recover stolen property, thus mitigating the insurer's payment.

Disproving suspicious theft claims is difficult. Doing so usually requires statements from an unhappy spouse, a business partner, or an employee of the insured who turns against the insured. Without such statements, adjusters must judge theft claims by their reasonableness. Do the type and amount of property in question seem appropriate to the policyholder's standard of living? Does the policyholder claim unusual duplicates, such as two stereo systems or two sets of silver? Does the policyholder have documentation that is common, such as inventory records in a business or instruction manuals for consumer electronics? Ultimately, if the adjuster compels the policyholder to comply scrupulously with every duty following loss and the adjuster's suspicions remain unproven, the claim is likely to be paid.

Vandalism

Vandalism is the intentional or malicious destruction of property. Accidental or negligent destruction of property is not vandalism. Adjusters investigating unexplained damage to property cannot pay for such damage under the coverage for vandalism unless evidence of intentional or malicious wrongdoing exists. For example, landlords might report a tenant's abuse of property as vandalism. Unless evidence of maliciousness beyond mere carelessness is apparent, such abuse would not be vandalism.

Vandalism is likely whenever damage appears to have been caused by the actions of a person, rather than forces of nature, and the circumstances do not appear accidental. Examples include windows broken by rocks, spray-painted graffiti, and other deliberate defacement.

Gradual Causes of Loss

Exclusions from coverage concerned with gradual losses, such as those caused by wear and tear, rust, decay, deterioration, latent defect, and rot, are very important in claim handling. Losses from these excluded causes present the same problems as those caused by water seepage (described earlier).

Property that has suffered loss from any of these excluded causes may suffer a subsequent loss that is covered. In such a situation, the adjuster must separate property that suffered the gradual damage from that which did not. Gradual damage to property may be included in a claim for subsequent covered loss, but the claim for such property is limited to the extent its value has been further diminished by the covered cause of loss. The gradual cause of loss may have already diminished the property's value to nearly nothing.

Ordinance or Law

Local ordinances or laws may require the demolition of a damaged structure. The cost of demolition may be more than the cost to rebuild the structure. In addition, local ordinances or laws may require construction plans, methods, or materials that are different from, and more expensive than, what existed before the loss. In general, property policies do not cover these additional costs unless a special endorsement has been added to the policy.

An adjuster handling a claim in which these costs are added should have contractors prepare estimates as though the building were to be rebuilt as it was, even though such rebuilding is not legal. Alternatively, realistic and practical estimates can be prepared, as long as the added costs not covered are identified and segregated.

Faulty Construction

As noted previously with respect to collapse caused by faulty construction, property insurance policies are not designed to be surety contracts for construction work. Losses caused by faulty design, construction, or materials are generally excluded from coverage. The additional coverage for collapse, described earlier, actually "gives back" coverage for faulty construction in very limited circumstances, such as when the collapse occurs during construction, remodeling, or renovation. For example, if faulty construction caused a fire, the adjuster must segregate damage caused by the poor workmanship from that caused by the fire and might pursue subrogation.

Intentional Acts

The most obvious type of loss that should be, and invariably is, excluded from coverage is loss caused intentionally by the insured. For example, as noted earlier, theft claims can easily be staged by the policyholder.

Fires are the most common type of intentionally caused loss. Intentionally set fires are acts of arson, whether committed by the insured or not. Arson may also be committed for revenge, in the commission of a crime, or by vandals. In those cases, innocent property owners are entitled to insurance coverage. Nevertheless, in the insurance context, "arson" usually refers to a fire intentionally set by the insured. When arson by the insured is suspected, most insurers involve their special investigative units (SIUs) or outside legal counsel. The factors shown in Exhibit 14-1 are indicators of arson.

To prove arson, an adjuster must prove (1) an incendiary fire (one that has been set intentionally), (2) a motive on the insured's part, and (3) opportunity on the insured's part. A cause-and-origin expert, usually a scientist or an engineer with special expertise in identifying the cause of fires, can often determine the cause of the fire.

The insured's motive is usually financial, and it may be shown by demonstrating that the insured is better off financially with the insurance proceeds and a vacant lot than with an intact building. Examination of the policyholder's books and records may reveal such information. Irrational motives, such as hatred of a spouse or business partner, may also be the cause of an arson.

Opportunity to set the fire may be proven by demonstrating that the insured was in the vicinity of the building soon before the fire started or by proving that the insured hired someone to commit the act.

Once the investigation concludes that the insured committed arson, the insurer need only deny the claim for breach of the policy conditions against

EXHIBIT 14-1

Indicators of Arson

General Indicators of Arson-for-Profit or Fire-Related Fraud

*   Building or contents were up for sale at the time of the loss.

*   Suspiciously coincidental absence of family pet at time of fire.

*   Insured had a loss at the same site in the preceding year. The initial loss, though small, may have been a failed attempt to liquidate contents.

*   Building or business was recently purchased.

*   Commercial losses include old or nonsaleable inventory or illegal chemicals or materials.

*   Insured or insured's business is experiencing financial difficulties, e.g., bankruptcy, foreclosure.

*   Fire site is claimed by multiple mortgagees or chattel mortgagees.

Indicators at the Fire Scene

*   Building is in deteriorating condition and/or lacks proper maintenance.

*   Fire scene investigation suggests that property/contents were heavily over-insured.

*   Fire scene investigation reveals absence of remains of noncombustible items of scheduled property or items covered by floaters, e.g., coin or gun collections or jewelry.

*   Fire scene investigation reveals absence of expensive items used to justify an increase over normal 50 percent contents coverage, e.g., antiques, piano, or expensive stereo/video equipment.

*   Fire scene investigation reveals absence of items of sentimental value, e.g., family Bible, family photos, trophies.

*   Fire scene investigation reveals absence or remains of items normally found in a home or business. The following is a sample listing of such items, most of which will be identifiable at fire scenes except in total burns. Kitchen: major appliances, minor appliances, normal food supply in refrigerator and cabinets. Living room: television/stereo equipment, record/tape collections, organ or piano, furniture (springs will remain). Bedrooms: guns, jewelry, clothing, and toys. Basement/garage: tools, lawn mower, bicycles, sporting equipment, such as golf clubs (especially note whether putter is missing from otherwise complete set). Business/office: office equipment and furniture, normal inventory, business records (which are normally housed in metal filing cabinets and should survive most fires).

Indicators Associated With the Loss Incident

*   Fire occurs at night, especially after 11 P.M.

*   Commercial fire occurs on holiday, weekend, or when business is closed.

*   Fire department reports fire cause is incendiary, suspicious, or unknown.

*   Fire alarm or sprinkler system failed to work at the time of the loss.

Adapted with permission of the National Insurance Crime Bureau, Palos Hill, Illinois, 1992.

misrepresentations and because losses caused by intentional acts are excluded. The policyholder may then sue the insurer for the claim payment. Sometimes policyholders do not push the claim any further; this satisfies many insurance companies. Other insurance companies are more aggressive and will take every step possible to have the insured prosecuted by the criminal authorities, should the evidence be strong enough.

To prevail in a civil suit, the insurance company need have only the preponderance of the evidence in its favor. To prevail in a criminal action, the state must prove its case beyond a reasonable doubt. The criminal standard of proof is more difficult. Thus, even if the policyholder is acquitted of criminal arson or if the authorities have declined to prosecute, the arson defense may still be used successfully in a civil suit between the policyholder and the insurance company.

Amount of Loss

After determining that coverage is in order for the insured, the property, and the peril involved in a given loss, the adjuster must determine the amount of the loss. Although settlement of the amount paid may be the central event in claims work, insurance policies do not specify how adjusters should determine the amount. Policies usually value property at "replacement cost" or "actual cash value," without further guiding the adjuster as to how "replacement cost" can be determined or what "actual cash value" might mean (for example, does it differ from "cash value" or "value"?).

Replacement Cost

Replacement cost
The cost to repair or replace property using new materials of like kind and quality with no deduction for depreciation.

Replacement cost is the cost to replace property with identical property or with property of like kind and quality at the time of the loss. Replacement cost settlement provisions spare adjusters the difficulties of determining actual cash value and convincing the policyholder to agree with that value. Following the trauma of a loss, many policyholders are faced with actual cash value settlements that do not allow them to replace their lost property without substantial out-of-pocket expenditures.

Determining replacement cost is easier than determining actual cash value, yet several possibilities for disagreement with the policyholder exist. The adjuster and the insured must identify the property precisely. For personal property, the manufacturer's name, product description, and exact model or style numbers must be determined. For buildings, the exact measurements and descriptions and an exact specification of the type and quality of materials, including the manufacturer's name, are necessary.

Once the property is fully identified and described, the adjuster must determine the cost to replace it *at the time of loss.* The amount the insured originally paid for the property (generally less than the replacement cost or cost to replace) is irrelevant. The cost at the time of loss should be the amount at which the policyholder can buy the property. It is improper for an adjuster to argue for a lesser amount based on a bulk purchase price unless that option is also available to the policyholder or based on prices that may be available in other parts of the country but are unavailable in the policyholder's locale.

If the exact type of the property lost is no longer available, the adjuster can make settlement based on property of like kind and quality. Specific models and styles of goods are frequently discontinued. However, similar items are usually available, often from the same manufacturer. Settlement on the basis of such goods is rarely a problem with the policyholder, as long as the goods are of similar quality.

Adjusters obtain specific replacement cost information from catalogues, furniture retailers, and department stores. Retailers such as Sears, J. C. Penney, Macy's, Wal-Mart, K-Mart, and local department store chains provide a good gauge of costs for most clothes and household items. However, for specific losses, adjusters should consult the retailer from which a policyholder bought the property. Business personal property is normally replaced through the insured's usual suppliers and, thus, may be available at wholesale prices. Many replacement service vendors specifically service the insurance industry and can provide insurance companies the best price on items such as cameras. Insurance companies have the option to replace property rather than to pay money to settle claims.

Determining replacement cost for building damage requires construction estimates. Proper estimates are based on the following factors:

- *Specifications*. Specifications state precisely what must be done, including whether to repair or replace the property, the exact type of materials, and the quantity of materials in exact dimensions or count.

- *Materials*. The total quantity of materials is determined based on the specifications. Material prices are based on prevailing material costs for projects similar to what is required by the policyholder's loss. Bulk discounts cannot be considered unless such quantities are needed.

- *Labor*. The hours of labor required for a particular job depend on the amount and type of material to be installed and the working conditions. Skilled estimators can calculate labor amounts fairly accurately. In addition, there are published "standard" work rates that are generally regarded as fair. For example, such publications may indicate that a typical rate for hanging wallpaper is 200 square feet per hour. An estimate can be prepared using this rate, regardless of whether the paperhanger who does the job happens to be faster or slower. Wage rates for common laborers can be used in estimating tear-out and demolition work, provided enough work is available to justify separate hiring. Otherwise, a skilled craftsman's rate must be used. For example, a plumber's wage rate may be appropriate for tearing out a wall to gain access to a burst pipe.

- *Overhead*. Overhead represents the contractor's fixed costs of doing business or fixed specific costs attributable to the job. Examples include office space, telephones, insurance, permits, and job site offices and toilets. Generally, overhead is calculated as a percentage of the cost of the job, usually 10 to 15 percent, depending on a contractor's circumstances. Costs that are specific to the job, such as permits, may simply be added in.

- *Profit.* Contractors are in business to earn a profit. The amount computed for overhead is *not* profit. Overhead represents very real costs for the contractor. Once overhead costs have been added to the job, profit is calculated as a percentage of total costs, usually 10 percent.

Most adjusters simply ask or hire contractors to provide estimates. Policyholders, or public adjusters working for them, likewise engage contractors to provide estimates. Unless all contractors involved provide estimates with detailed specifications, material, and labor, resolving disparities is difficult. Round sum figures for an entire job are difficult for an adjuster to negotiate. Even when all parties have done detailed work, there is room for differences: Does property need to be replaced, repaired, or simply cleaned? Have measurements been rounded? What allowance is each contractor making for waste of materials or for difficult working conditions? What labor rate (dollars per hour) and rate of work does each contractor assume? Estimates may appear to be precise but may include a great deal of judgment and assume a great deal of background information.

Computer software is available to help adjusters or contractors prepare estimates. The adjuster or contractor specifies the work to be done, the measurements, and the quantities, and the computer calculates the total cost of materials and the total hours and cost of labor and determines the total estimate. Computerized estimating programs are quick and provide well-formatted output. The computer cannot, however, spot unusual circumstances. Computerized estimating programs are a useful tool for those who already understand estimating, but they cannot teach estimating to a novice.

Adjusters must be prepared to negotiate estimates in good faith and should be scrupulous in using only contractors who provide legitimate estimates and good workmanship. A policyholder who has suffered the loss of his or her home should not be put in the position of disproving fictitious estimates prepared by contractors with no intention of doing the work for the stated price.

Whenever losses are settled on a replacement cost basis, determining the insured's compliance with insurance to value requirements must likewise be done on a replacement cost basis. This task can be tedious if the loss is small relative to the total value of insured property. The adjuster must estimate the value of a great deal of property not affected by the loss. Fortunately, there are shortcuts. With business personal property, the insured's accounting records will usually show what items the business purchased, when they were purchased, and for how much. The services of an accountant may be needed to extract this information from the accounting records. An estimation guide, which uses factors such as square footage and construction quality to determine how much it would cost to rebuild a building, offers a shortcut for determining a building's value.

Insurance policies generally do not permit replacement cost settlements until the property is actually repaired or replaced. Such policy provisions exist to prevent unjust enrichment of the insured and to discourage intentional losses. Nevertheless, the insured may need funds to pay a contractor or merchant before repair or replacement is complete. The adjuster will either (1) release to the insured an actual cash value settlement, with the balance paid upon complete repair or replacement or (2) parcel out a replacement cost settlement as repair or replacement is gradually accomplished. Either of these approaches should be satisfactory to the policyholder.

Actual Cash Value

Actual cash value (ACV) is often defined as replacement cost minus depreciation. Claim adjusters applying this formula must have a sophisticated understanding of depreciation. Although the formula is generally appropriate, claims adjusters must realize when it is not.

Actual cash value (ACV)
The replacement cost of property minus depreciation.

Depreciation represents loss of value. It is not limited to physical wear and tear, although physical wear and tear is obviously an important consideration in determining the depreciation of certain property, such as carpeting. When physical wear and tear is the chief cause of depreciation, adjusters usually apply straight-line depreciation, by which a fixed percentage of the property's value is deducted for every year of the property's useful life that the owner has enjoyed.

Depreciation
The physical wear and tear or the technological or economic obsolescence.

Aside from physical wear and tear, obsolescence is the main cause of depreciation. Obsolescence is caused by changes in technology and fashion and can have much more sudden and dramatic effects on the value of property than physical wear and tear. Clothing in last year's fashions, even if untouched by wear and tear, will have lost significant value. Property for which technology advances rapidly, such as electronics and computers, will also quickly lose value.

Age alone, absent wear and tear or obsolescence, should not cause too much depreciation. For example, the frame carpentry (wall studs, floor joists, and so forth) of a 100-year-old house may be in as good a condition as when it was installed. Although some obsolescence may occur in such frame carpentry, obsolescence can be difficult to identify in residential construction. Although the copper pipes used today are superior to the lead pipes found in older homes, frame carpentry techniques have changed little in 100 years. Furthermore, certain features of older construction are considered desirable.

Adjusters frequently rely on published guides to determine depreciation. Individual insurance companies have created such guides based on their experience. Trade groups have published guides for items such as clothing and household furnishings. However, adjusters should consider the characteristics of the specific property in question when evaluating actual cash value. In every loss that is to result in an actual cash value settlement, the adjuster must determine depreciation for the specific property that has suffered loss.

In losses in which significant depreciation caused by obsolescence has occurred, guidebooks are likely to become obsolete sooner than the property in question. Guidebooks are primarily useful as a starting point for discussing depreciation caused by wear and tear. In many situations, the published rate of depreciation is perfectly appropriate. However, an adjuster who mindlessly applies guidebook depreciation to every loss will harm both policyholders and insurers. The reputations of the insurance company and the industry are harmed by such arbitrary and inflexible practices.

Other Definitions of Actual Cash Value

As long as depreciation is understood to represent loss of value of any type, the "replacement cost minus depreciation" definition of "actual cash value" is usually appropriate. However, it is not appropriate in all circumstances.

Application of the "replacement cost minus depreciation" definition requires an ascertainable figure for replacement cost. In some situations, no such figure exists. For example, antiques cannot be produced and sold new. Old buildings may feature construction methods that are no longer used. Finally, many adjusters mistakenly infer that the "replacement cost minus depreciation" definition allows only for deductions from the replacement cost. Certain property, such as some collectibles, is known to appreciate in value.

As a result of adjusters' misapplying the definition of actual cash value, some courts have defined the term to mean fair market value. The fair market value of an item reflects both the "replacement cost minus depreciation" approach and the possibility that an item is irreplaceable. The market valuation of antiques and objects of art is generally regarded as fair. In addition, a well-functioning market will consider obsolescence and any other factor that affects value. A well-functioning market for a type of property is key to determining market valuation. Unfortunately, no substantial secondary market exists for many common items of property, such as used clothing, which most people regard as completely valueless. Adjusters should not apply market valuation unless a well-functioning secondary market exists.

Other courts have avoided definitions based strictly on a formula of actual cash value. These courts have required adjusters to consider all pertinent factors, including physical wear and tear, obsolescence, market value, and any other relevant factors. This approach is known as the **broad evidence rule**.

Deductibles

When a loss is otherwise fully covered, applying a deductible is a simple matter. The deductible amount is subtracted from the amount of the loss, and the insured is paid the remainder. However, applying deductibles to a loss that is not fully covered is more difficult.

When the application of a coinsurance penalty results in a reduction of the recoverable amount of loss, the insured benefits by having the deductible applied first, as shown in the following example of the settlement of a $10,000 loss in which a policyholder maintained only $60,000 of coverage when $80,000 was required:

Broad evidence rule
Rule that requires claim adjusters to consider all relevant factors when determining the actual cash value of property. Factors that must be considered include replacement cost; physical wear and tear; economic, technological, or fashion obsolescence; market value; the circumstances of the property's use; the age of the property; and income that might be derived from the property.

Deductible Applied First

$10,000 loss − $100 deductible = $9,900

$$\frac{\$60,000}{\$80,000} \times \$9,900 = \$7,425$$

Coinsurance Applied First

$$\frac{\$60,000}{\$80,000} \times \$10,000 \; loss = \$7,500$$

$7,500 − $100 deductible = $7,400

Adjusters should use the first approach unless the policy explicitly states otherwise. The commercial building and personal property (BPP) form is an example of a policy that does state otherwise. The excerpt in Exhibit 14-2 shows that the BPP form requires the deductible to be applied after the coinsurance penalty.

A loss may also not be fully covered because of the application of a sublimit. The typical homeowners policy has numerous sublimits for specific types of property, such as cash, precious stones and jewelry, and firearms. Adjusters should first apply the deductible to any amount of the loss that is not covered because it exceeds a sublimit. For example, an insured with a $100 sublimit for cash and a $100 deductible who has lost $500 cash would recover only $100, and the deductible should not apply any further. The $400 loss in excess of the sublimit is more than sufficient to absorb the deductible. Although insurance policies do not explicitly require this approach, it is regarded among adjusters as good and proper practice.

Stated Values and Agreed Amounts

Some property policies are written on a scheduled basis, such as personal articles floaters and endorsements to homeowners policies designed for scheduled property. Individual property items may be listed separately with a value assigned for each, or the property may be listed by class, such as cameras, furs, or jewelry. Some coverages provided on personal articles floaters are on a stated amount basis. The **stated amount** is typically determined by appraising the policyholder's property or by reviewing a sales receipt for the property in question. In the event of a loss, the insured is entitled to no more than the *least* amount of (1) the actual cash value of the property, (2) the cost to repair or replace, or (3) the applicable amount of insurance.

Many policyholders believe that they are entitled to the stated amount regardless of the valuation provision of the policy. In fact, the stated value is designed as a maximum amount the insurer will have to pay.

Fine arts and valuable papers are usually insured on an **agreed amount** basis. In the event of a loss, the insurer agrees to restore the property to its condition before the loss or to pay the agreed amount. The distinction between

Stated amount
A method of valuing property often described in an insurance contract as the least of (1) the actual cash value, (2) the cost to repair or replace, or (3) the applicable amount of insurance listed for the property.

Agreed amount
A method of valuing property in which the insurer and the insured agree on the value of the property at the time the policy is written. That amount is stated in the policy declarations and is the amount the insurer will pay in the event of a total loss to the property. Also called agreed value.

EXHIBIT 14-2

Building and Personal Property Coverage Form Excerpt

1. Coinsurance

   If a Coinsurance percentage is shown in the Declarations, the following condition applies.

   a. We will not pay the full amount of any loss if the value of Covered Property at the time of loss times the Coinsurance percentage shown for it in the Declarations is greater than the Limit of Insurance for the property.

   Instead, we will determine the most we will pay using the following steps:

   (1) Multiply the value of Covered Property at the time of loss by the Coinsurance percentage;

   (2) Divide the Limit of Insurance of the property by the figure determined in step (1);

   (3) Multiply the total amount of loss, before the application of any deductible, by the figure determined in step (2); and

   (4) Subtract the deductible from the figure determined in step (3).

   We will pay the amount determined in step (4) or the limit of insurance, whichever is less. For the remainder, you will either have to rely on other insurance or absorb the loss yourself.

   Example No. 1 (Underinsurance):

   When:

The value of the property is	$250,000
The Coinsurance percentage for it is	80%
The Limit of Insurance for it is	$100,000
The Deductible is	$250
The amount of loss is	$40,000

   Step (1): $250,000 × 80% = $200,000 (the minimum amount of insurance to meet your Coinsurance requirements)

   Step (2): $100,000 ÷ $200,000 = .50

   Step (3): $40,000 × .50 = $20,000

   Step (4): $20,000 − $250 = $19,750

   We will pay no more than $19,750. The remaining $20,250 is not covered.

these properties and those covered on a stated amount basis is that the more valuable property is typically impossible to replace. Insurers recognize that owners of this type of property want the company to "preadjust" for potential losses in the underwriting process.

In dealing with agreed value losses, adjusters can become overly suspicious of fraud because the policyholder can readily fake a theft or mysterious disappearance. Underwriters recognize the increased chance of moral and morale hazards and scrutinize those applicants accordingly. If fraud is, in fact, evident, procedures should be followed just as in any fraudulent claim.

Repair or Replace Option

Claims are generally settled with money. Occasionally, adjusters prefer to settle claims by actually repairing or replacing the property as the policy allows. Adjusters might prefer not to repair or replace property because doing so opens up a new area for potential disagreement with the insured. The policyholder might expect the insurer to guarantee the repairs or certify the quality of a replacement item.

Adjusters choose the repair or replace option whenever it is significantly less expensive to do so. It may be less expensive to perform repairs or provide a replacement item when the insurer has discount purchasing arrangements through local contractors and retailers. Insurers frequently replace jewelry through wholesale channels. Repairing or replacing the property enables insurers to eliminate the financial incentive some insureds have to file claims.

Appraisal Clause

The appraisal clause found in every property insurance policy is used solely to settle disputes over the value of the property or the amount of loss. It is not used to determine coverage, to substitute for the proof of loss or the insured's examination under oath, or to preclude litigation between the parties.

Adjusters who work for years in property claims may never participate in an appraisal, but this does not mean that the clause is unimportant. The existence of the appraisal clause informally prompts the insured and the adjuster to do more formally what the appraisal procedure requires. The adjuster presents his or her position to the insured with estimates from contractors and other supporting documentation. The insured prepares similar information to present to the adjuster. The adjuster and the insured, or the contractors working for them, negotiate their differences and almost always reach an agreement. The possibility of an appraisal procedure in which an impartial umpire will settle the dispute gives both sides an incentive to negotiate in good faith.

Insured's Duties Following Loss

Every property insurance policy enumerates various duties the insured must perform following a loss. These duties are conditions of the policy. Thus, an insured is not entitled to payment for a loss unless these duties have been performed. The insured's performance of duties following a loss helps the adjuster to complete the loss adjustment, to verify the extent and the dollar amount of the loss, and to protect against fraudulent or exaggerated claims. Adjusters may waive certain duties if the circumstances so warrant, but they are likely to hold the policyholder to strict performance whenever unusual circumstances surround the claim or the claim seems suspicious. Enforcing all the insurer's procedures, without violating the Unfair Claims Settlement Practices Act, protects the adjuster from a critical review in a subsequent claim audit. Additionally, making the policyholder follow legitimate claim settlement procedures may unnerve fraudulent claim makers or reveal misrepresentations by the policyholder.

Notice

Obviously, nothing can be done with a claim until the policyholder notifies the insurer of the loss. The policyholder need not provide notice in any special form or in any special wording. Typically, the policyholder will telephone his or her agent and say, "I've had a fire." The policyholder does not have to give written notice that says, "I've suffered losses to the building and personal property and will suffer loss of use caused by the fire and smoke perils."

Although policies do not require the policyholder to give notice in any particular form, they do require that the notice be "prompt." An adjuster cannot properly investigate and evaluate a loss after too much time has passed. The prompt notice requirement rarely becomes an issue between insureds and insurers. Insureds are usually eager to report claims, and adjusters will generally not penalize delayed notice if a proper investigation is still possible. Courts generally require that the insurer suffer some prejudice to its rights before it can consider denying coverage. Nevertheless, lack of prompt notice (as well as breach of other policy conditions) is an issue, for example, when the insured repairs or replaces property before ever notifying the insurer of the loss.

In case of loss by theft, the insured is required to notify the police. In most states it is a felony to submit false reports to the police. Thus, the policyholder's duty to report thefts and other criminal violations discourages staged claims. The BPP requires the insured to notify the police if a law may have been broken, which includes the occurrence of a possible theft. The common-sense interpretation of the BPP limits this duty to violations of *criminal* law only.

Homeowners policies provide coverage for lost or stolen credit cards. In case of such an event, the insured must notify the credit card or funds transfer card company. Thereafter, the insured is not liable for improper and unauthorized charges. Should the insured fail to notify the credit card company, the insurer is not liable for any charges incurred after a reasonable time during which notice could have been given. An insured's lack of timely notice to a credit card company is rarely an issue between the insured and the insurer because most credit card agreements limit the cardholder's liability for unauthorized use to some small amount, such as $50.

Protection of Property

The insured is required to protect the property from further loss by making emergency repairs and implementing emergency safeguards. Such measures are a reimbursable part of the loss (subject to policy limits) as long as they are "reasonable" and "necessary." The insured will usually seek pre-approval of such measures from the adjuster. Adjusters are happy to cooperate with these requests to preclude any misunderstanding. Nevertheless, the insured is obligated to take "reasonable" and "necessary" measures regardless of whether the adjuster's approval has been obtained. Failure to do so may void coverage for any additional loss that results.

Assistance With the Loss Adjustment Process

Insureds have several duties that help expedite and conclude the loss adjustment process. They must inventory all damaged property and, under certain policies, all undamaged property as well. The inventory must include quantities, values, and amounts of loss and may be required as part of, or independent of, the proof of loss. Without such an inventory, the adjuster would have difficulty organizing and analyzing the loss to personal property and would have to deal with continual additions to the claim for personal property.

The insured must show the damaged property to the adjuster. The purpose of this requirement is to preclude claims based on photographic or verbal evidence, thereby discouraging exaggerated or fraudulent claims.

The insured must also allow an inspection of its books and other records. The adjuster might personally inspect the insured's books or might hire an accountant to do so. The evidence in a policyholder's books and records is often essential to verify the existence and value of property. For example, property is often destroyed in all-consuming fires or as a result of theft.

Some insurance policies generally require the policyholder to cooperate. For example, the BPP lists among the insured's duties in the event of loss the duty to "cooperate with us in the investigation or settlement of the claim." The absence of such a duty in other policies means that the insured has no general duty of cooperation, although the lack of such a duty does not usually create any problems for the adjuster. The specifically listed duties—and, in particular, the duty to submit a proof of loss—are sufficient for the adjuster to obtain whatever is necessary from the policyholder.

Proof of Loss

The proof of loss is a powerful adjustment tool, yet it is often not used, or is misused, by adjusters. A **proof of loss** is a written, signed, and sworn-to statement by the insured about the loss. Thus, it is the policyholder's official

Proof of loss
A written, signed, and sworn-to statement by the insured about the loss.

version of the loss. Because it is signed and sworn to, all statements it contains are material and, if false, are grounds to void the coverage. The formality of the proof of loss impresses policyholders with the importance of the statements made therein.

In a proof of loss, the insured is typically required to provide the time, place, and cause of loss; the interests in the property; any other insurance on the property; and detailed estimates, inventories, bills, and other documentation that prove the loss. The proof of loss should contain all the information necessary for the adjuster to settle the claim, including an exact dollar figure for the loss.

Once a proof of loss has been submitted, the adjuster must respond promptly. Many states have laws specifying the number of days following receipt of a proof of loss that an adjuster has to either accept or reject the proof of loss or to tell the policyholder specifically what is further required. An adjuster who rejects a proof of loss should do so in writing and state specific reasons for the rejection. The rejection letter should explain that the claim cannot be settled without a proper proof of loss and should invite the policyholder to submit a new proof if it is possible and still timely to remedy the original.

Many insurers routinely waive the proof of loss. On uncomplicated claims, doing so expedites the settlement and relieves the insured of a possibly tedious and intimidating exercise. The danger to insurers of routinely waiving proofs of loss on simple, straightforward losses is that adjusters may not spot nonroutine cases soon enough to implement the proof of loss requirement and will thereby waive valuable rights.

Some adjusters require the insured to complete a proof of loss only at the conclusion of the claim. At that point, the adjuster has presumably already agreed with the insured about the amount of settlement. Completion of the proof of loss form is likely to make little impression on the insured. To be most effective, the proof of loss should be required early in the adjustment process. A proof of loss that is completed after settlement is still a sworn statement of material fact and thus could be the basis of a fraud defense.

Examination Under Oath

Examination under oath
A statement given by a person who has sworn to tell the truth before an officer of the court.

An **examination under oath** is a statement given by a person who has sworn to tell the truth before an officer of the court. Insurers rarely require an examination under oath, but when they do, they usually suspect fraud by the policyholder.

The examination under oath is a policy condition that, if invoked by the insurer, the insured must fulfill. The insurer may require an examination even though the claim is not in litigation. The insured may have counsel present, but such counsel has no right to interrupt, object, or ask questions. Although adjusters can conduct examinations under oath themselves, they are almost invariably conducted by an attorney working for the insurer and helping the insurer prepare its fraud case.

An examination under oath is usually conducted after the insured completes and submits a proof of loss. The proof of loss commits the insured to a certain story, and the examination under oath allows the insurer to clarify that story.

Public Adjusters

Some state insurance departments recognize and license public adjusters. These adjusters work for policyholders and only rarely work for insurance companies. Public adjusters handle all of the insured's duties following loss (except that the insured must still sign and swear to the proof of loss and must appear for an examination under oath). The policyholder is free to engage a public adjuster just as the policyholder is free to engage an attorney. The adjuster is required to handle the claim with the policyholder's chosen agent.

Adjustment Procedures

Adjusters usually guide the policyholder through his or her duties following loss. The procedures the adjuster follows are not the same in every case, but all concern (1) verifying the cause of the loss, (2) determining the amount of the loss, and (3) documenting both the cause and the amount of the loss. Loss procedures vary according to the size and complexity of the loss.

Level of Investigation

Upon notice of a new claim, an adjuster must decide how to investigate. An adjuster can follow these three general procedures or some combination thereof:

1. The adjuster can accept the policyholder's word and settle the claim accordingly.
2. The adjuster can personally investigate the loss.
3. The adjuster can employ experts to investigate the loss or refer it to an SIU.

The smaller, simpler, and more straightforward a claim appears to be, the more likely an adjuster is to settle based on the policyholder's word. The larger, more complicated, and suspicious a claim appears to be, the more likely it is that an adjuster will hire experts or involve an SIU.

Experts may be consulted to determine the cause of a loss. Such experts include cause and origin scientists, accident reconstruction engineers, and private investigators. Other experts help to determine the value of a loss. These experts include contractors, accountants, and appraisers. Expert services are expensive but are essential when litigation is foreseeable, either following a claim denial or pursuant to subrogation.

Avoiding Waiver and Estoppel

Waiver
The voluntary and intentional relinquishment of a known right by an insurer that results in estoppel.

Estoppel
Principle that prevents the insurer from asserting a right that it has already waived. A party is estopped from asserting rights that are inconsistent with his or her words or behavior.

Waiver is the voluntary and intentional relinquishment of a right. It may be expressed explicitly or implied by conduct. **Estoppel** has a similar effect but results when one's words or behavior causes another to rely to his or her detriment on those words or behavior. Estoppel serves to bar the first party from asserting any rights inconsistent with his or her words or behavior. An estoppel can result from a waiver but can also be based on thoughtless, unintentional action on which the other party relies.

An adjuster's words and actions can cause waiver and estoppel of the insurer's rights. Although insurance policies require the insurer's written approval before they may be altered or amended, courts invariably deem adjusters to be agents of insurers with the power (if not the authority) to waive contractual conditions. Thus, an adjuster's words and behavior can undo policy requirements. The most significant way by which adjusters do so is by continuing to adjust *after* a coverage problem is revealed. Such behavior may be deemed by a court as waiver, or the policyholder may rely on such behavior, leading to estoppel.

Adjusters avoid the problems of waiver and estoppel with nonwaiver agreements or with reservation of rights letters. Exhibits 14-3 and 14-4 show a general nonwaiver agreement and a notice of reservation of rights, respectively. In each of these documents, the insurer makes clear that nothing it does (through the adjuster) in handling the claim is intended as a waiver of any of the insurer's rights.

The general nonwaiver is used whenever a great deal about the loss is unknown and the adjuster wishes to investigate without compromising the insurer's rights. The notice of reservation of rights accomplishes the same objectives as the general nonwaiver and also brings to the policyholder's attention any specific problems, such as property or perils that appear not covered or failure of the policyholder to perform any duties following loss or to comply with other policy conditions. A reservation of rights is the same in content as a nonwaiver agreement. It is sent (usually by certified mail) to the policyholder in the form of a letter, usually because the policyholder would not sign a nonwaiver or as a convenience by inside adjusters. Assuming that proof of receipt by the policyholder can be shown, a reservation of rights letter is as effective as a nonwaiver.

Once either a nonwaiver or a reservation of rights has been issued, the adjuster must promptly resolve the coverage issue and inform the policyholder. Should the adjuster fail to rectify whatever problem existed and proceed to settle the claim, the claim payment will constitute a waiver and the insurer will be estopped from ever again raising the problem.

Determining Cause of Loss

An adjuster who personally investigates the cause of a loss will inspect the property in question, take the policyholder's statement, or do both.

A personal inspection of the damaged property is a valuable adjusting practice. The adjuster sees exactly how the property has been damaged and can identify the property for purposes of verifying coverage. The effects of perils such as fire, smoke, lightning, windstorm, hail, explosions, and vandalism are usually obvious, and a quick inspection can verify coverage.

The adjuster will take the policyholder's statement to answer any questions about the cause of loss and to gather other information. Such a statement is informal, compared to the proof of loss or examination under oath, but it will be recorded. In some states, taking the policyholder's statement may preclude a subsequent proof of loss or examination under oath. When the policyholder's statement can be taken, the adjuster will ask about the cause of loss, any other interests in or liens on the property, other insurance, steps taken to mitigate loss, the documentation of the extent of loss, and any subrogation possibilities.

Determining the Amount of Loss

An adjuster who personally determines the amount of a loss must take careful, detailed inventories of personal property that specify the exact quantities and types of property and must prepare his or her own estimates for losses to buildings.

Most adjusters leave the item-by-item preparation of a personal property inventory to the insured. The adjuster will then spot-check the physical property or double-check with the policyholder's books and records. The adjuster must check the physical property sufficiently to determine appropriate depreciation.

An adjuster who prepares his or her own estimates must have extensive knowledge of construction practices and of the numerous resources concerning material prices and labor allowances. Indeed, such adjusters usually have their own library of materials catalogs, manufacturers' price lists, and construction trade association guides. Using these reference sources, they can determine, for example, the material and labor costs for applying a coat of paint, building a wall of cinderblocks, or installing a network of fire-extinguishing sprinklers.

Adjusters who write their own estimates must also develop a methodology for taking thorough specifications at a loss site. For example, an adjuster may take all outside measurements first, then go inside to take room measurements and, finally, determine all mechanical and electrical specifications. Completed estimates are usually also organized by trade, such as demolition, frame carpentry, finish carpentry, drywall, painting and decorating, plumbing, and electrical.

Documentation and Reporting

The ultimate service performed by claim adjusters for insureds is payment with the settlement check. While the adjuster investigates and gathers the information necessary to determine the amount of the settlement check, he or she should simultaneously create a file that would enable any other person to

EXHIBIT 14-3

Nonwaiver Agreement

Policy of insurance number ____HO 302 7648____ was issued to
__Michael Watson__ by __IIA Insurance Company__ to cover the period from____7-1-X6____
to ____7-1-X7____. Coverage under this policy of insurance has been requested for
occurrence which took place on ____12-21-X6____ at ____Malvern, PA____ .
A dispute has arisen about whether there is insurance coverage under the policy to
protect __Michael Doe__ for any liability which is a result of the reported occurrence.
The reason for the question of coverage is ____whether water damage was____
____caused by repeated seepage.____

Nevertheless, ____Leonard Phillips____ ____requests____ that the
__IIA Insurance____ Company investigate, negotiate, settle, deny, or defend any
claim or suit arising out of such accident or occurrence as it deems necessary.
__IIA Insurance____ Company agrees to proceed with such handling of this case
only on condition that such action taken will not waive any right the Insurance Company
may have to deny any obligation under the policy contract, or be considered an admission
of any liability on the part of the company. It is further agreed that such action will not
waive any rights of the insured.

There may be other reasons why coverage does not apply. We do not waive our right to
deny coverage for any other valid reason which may arise.

Nothing in this agreement precludes ____Leonard Phillips.____ from retaining personal
counsel for his or her own protection.

Either party to this agreement may at any time terminate the agreement upon notice in
writing and proceed under his/her own unrestricted rights.

Signed this ____4th____ day of ____May____, 20 _X2_ .

Jane Wilson	*Michael Doe*
Witness	Insured
	Additional Insured
Mary Harris	IIA Insurance Company
Witness	Insurance Company
	BY: *John Davis*
	For the Company

EXHIBIT 14-4

Notice of Reservation of Rights

_____5/8_____ , 20 _X2_

TO: RE: Insured: Ruth Andrews

                                                  Claimant:

                                                  Date of Loss:

                                                  Policy Number:

We have received notice of an occurrence which took place at   Malvern, PA   on
_____4-1-X7_____. As a result of this occurrence coverage has been requested under
policy number ___BOP 5612112___ which was issued to
_____IIA Insurance Company_____   by _____Ruth's Country Kitchen_____.
There is a question whether coverage under the policy applies to this occurrence.

The nature of the coverage question is as follows:_____whether it was lightning_____
____that caused the air conditioning unit to fail_____

_____IIA Insurance Company_____ will continue to handle this claim even
though a coverage question exists. However, no act of any company representative while
investigating, negotiating settlement of the claim, or defending a lawsuit shall be
construed as waiving any Company rights. The Company reserves the right, under the
policy, to deny coverage to you or anyone claiming coverage under the policy.

There may be other reasons why coverage does not apply. We do not waive our right to
deny coverage for any other valid reason which may arise.

You may wish to discuss this matter with your own personal attorney. In any event, we
would be pleased to answer any questions you might have concerning our position as
outlined in this letter.

                         Very truly yours,

                         _____IIA Insurance Company_____
                         Insurance Company

                         BY_____*John Davis*_____
                             For the Company

understand and follow the claim and agree with the amount paid. Every piece of pertinent information should be in the file. Insurers need thorough claim files to justify payments, to conduct audits of claim procedures and claim-handling quality, and to transfer cases from one adjuster to another. State insurance regulators and reinsurers are also interested in complete and thorough claim files.

Although an adjuster handles a claim, he or she must submit various reports to the insurer. A preliminary report usually only acknowledges receipt of the assignment, reports initial activity, suggests likely reserves, and raises any coverage issues that are found. Status reports are submitted on a regular basis thereafter, such as every fifteen to thirty days.

Investigative reports are longer, more formal, narrative reports in which the adjuster reports on all aspects of the claim to date and on expected future activity. Topics contained in such a report include the initial assignment, a description of insured and other interests and liens, coverage, any coverage questions, facts of the loss, official and expert reports, the investigation with the insured and witnesses, the scope of the loss, inventory, suggested reserves, subrogation or salvage, and work to be done.

Final reports account for payments made and describe any ongoing subrogation or salvage efforts. Most insurers have preprinted forms or general written guidelines for these various types of reports.

Salvage and Subrogation

Adjusters usually only disburse money for insurers. However, in salvage and subrogation activities, the claim adjuster can minimize the insurer's losses.

Whenever an insurer pays the insured the full value of personal property that has suffered loss, the insurer is entitled to take ownership of the property and can subsequently resell it. Any amount realized in the sale reduces the true cost of the claim. Taking the salvage value of property that has been "totaled" is the insurer's option. The policyholder cannot require the insurer to pay full value for damaged property and then take over the salvage. However, if damaged property might have some salvage value, insurers usually do not depend on the insured to realize that salvage value. Insureds are usually not familiar with salvage markets. It is also unfair for a claims adjuster to reduce the amount of a loss settlement because of the value of "expected" salvage that the insured could not be expected to sell. Instead, if salvage value is apparent, insurers will usually pay full value to the insured and will handle the salvage themselves.

Ordinarily, adjusters do not directly market salvage. They either sell or consign the property in question to professional salvage companies. The markets for salvaged goods are specialized, variable, and irregular. Even insurance companies that frequently see salvageable goods from their losses find that they cannot compete in salvage markets. Salvage companies typically sell goods on consignment for expenses incurred plus a percentage commission. Salvors can operate even when the insurance company has not taken title to the goods, as long as the insured agrees.

Salvors can provide more services to insurers than just selling damaged goods. They are expert in protecting and inventorying property. In certain cases when insureds are themselves merchants of the goods in question, a salvor can advise the insurer on the percentage of value remaining in the goods. In those situations, the insurer will settle the claim for the value of the goods less their remaining salvage value. Insureds accept such settlements when they are confident that their efforts can realize more value from a "fire sale" than could the efforts of anyone else.

An insurer may have subrogation rights when a party other than the policyholder is responsible for causing the loss. When an insurer pays an insured for a loss under a policy, the insurer is substituted (subrogated) for the insured and obtains the insured's rights against any responsible party. Handling a claim involving potential subrogation is no different for an adjuster than handling any other claim, except that the adjuster must be especially scrupulous in establishing and documenting the cause of loss and may put the responsible party on notice of the liability claim.

If the responsible party has liability insurance and the two insurers cannot agree on a settlement amount, a subrogation claim is likely to be handled through the nationwide arbitration system operated by Arbitration Forums Incorporated. A copy of the Property Subrogation Arbitration Agreement is reproduced in Exhibit 14-5. Although the jurisdiction of this agreement is limited to claims between signatory parties and amounts of $100,000 or less, this agreement keeps a vast number of cases out of the courts. The results insurers experience under this agreement are probably as fair as any court settlement and are far less expensive to obtain. Naturally, the claim adjusters for the two involved insurers are free to negotiate a settlement before arbitration.

When an insurer obtains an amount through subrogation efforts, it must first pay the attorney fees and other expenses of subrogation and then reimburse the insured for any deductible or any other amount of loss not covered. Finally, the insurer receives what is left.

CHALLENGES FACING SPECIFIC TYPES OF PROPERTY CLAIMS

Specific types of property loss claims raise specific issues. What is important in adjusting claims for residential structures may be unimportant when settling claims for common carriers, and vice versa.

The remainder of this chapter examines the challenges of adjusting losses to specific types of property. The general issues described in the preceding part of this chapter are not repeated, except when any such issue raises special concerns or is handled in special ways with regard to specific types of property.

EXHIBIT 14-5

Fire and Allied Lines Arbitration Agreement

PROPERTY SUBROGATION ARBITRATION AGREEMENT

WHEREAS, it is the object of companies which are now or may hereafter be signatories hereto to arbitrate disputes among themselves, the undersigned hereby accepts and binds itself to the following Articles of Agreement for the arbitration of property damage claims arising from fire and losses other than automobile:

ARTICLE FIRST:

Signatory companies are bound to forgo litigation and in place thereof submit to arbitration any questions or disputes which may arise from:

(a) any fire subrogation or property damage claim not in excess of $100,000;

(b) any extended coverage subrogation or self-insured extended coverage claim not in excess of $100,000;

(c) any additional extended coverage subrogation or self-insured additional extended coverage claim not in excess of $100,000;

(d) any inland marine subrogation to self-insured inland marine claim not in excess of $100,000;

(e) any first party property subrogation or self-insured claim not in excess of $100,000 that is not within the compulsory provisions of other industry inter-company arbitration agreements, except for subrogation or self-insured claims arising from accidents on waters subject to the International Rules of the Road, the United States Inland Rules of the Road, or the Great Lakes and Western Rivers Rules of the Road, provided the accident occurs on a body of water within the geographic limits of one state.

This Article shall not apply to:

(a) any claim for the enforcement of which a lawsuit was instituted prior to, and is pending at the time this Agreement is signed;

(b) any claim as to which a company asserts a defense of lack of coverage on grounds other than

   (1) delayed notice

   (2) no notice

   (3) noncooperation;

(c) subrogation claims arising out of policies written under Retrospective Rating plans, Comprehensive Insurance Rating Plans, or War Risk Rating Plans unless prior written consent is obtained from the companies in interest.

ARTICLE SECOND:

Any controversy, including policy coverage and interpretations, between or among signatory parties involving any claim or other matter relating thereto and not included in Article First hereof or which involve amounts in excess of those stated therein may also be submitted to arbitration under this Agreement with the prior consent of the parties.

For matters within Article First, if the law on the issue is in doubt and has not been interpreted by the courts of the jurisdiction, a party to the controversy may petition AF's Board of Directors to authorize the disputing party to proceed through litigation rather than arbitration. The Board's validation will be influenced by the effect on the industry through litigation to clarify the law. The decision to waive the mandatory provisions of the Agreement and proceed through litigation will be at the sole discretion of the Board.

ARTICLE THIRD:

Arbitration Forums, Inc. representing signatory parties is authorized:

(a) to make appropriate rules and regulations for the presentation and determination of controversies under this Agreement;

(b) to select the places where arbitration facilities are to be available, and adopt a policy for the selection and appointment of arbitration panels;

(c) to prescribe territorial jurisdiction of arbitration panels;

(d) to make appropriate rules and regulations to apportion equitably among arbitrating companies the operating expenses of the arbitration program;

(e) to authorize and approve as signatories to this Agreement such insurance carriers, self-insurers or commercial insureds with large retentions as may be invited to participate in the arbitration program and also to compel the withdrawal of any signatory from the program for failure to conform with the Agreement or the rules and regulations issued thereunder.

ARTICLE FOURTH:

Arbitration panels, appointed by the AF from among full-time salaried representatives of signatory companies, shall function in the following manner:

(a) Arbitration panel members shall be selected on the basis of their experience and other qualifications. They shall serve without compensation.

(b) No panel member shall serve on a panel hearing a case in which his/her company is directly or indirectly interested, or in which he/she has an interest.

(c) The decision of the majority of an arbitration panel shall be final and binding upon the parties to the controversy without the right of rehearing or appeal.

ARTICLE FIFTH:

Any signatory company may withdraw from this Agreement by notice in writing to the Arbitration Forums, Inc. Such withdrawal will become effective sixty (60) days after receipt of such notice except as to cases then pending before arbitration panels. The effective date of withdrawal as to such pending cases shall be upon final settlement.

Used with permission, Arbitration Forums, Inc.

Residential Dwellings

Probably no job in the property-casualty insurance industry is more important or more rewarding than adjusting losses to people's homes. Protecting people from the financial and emotional devastation that can follow the destruction of a home is perhaps the insurance industry's most important task.

Adjusters handling losses to homes must balance their concern for alleviating the policyholder's needs with their obligation to enforce the insurance policy and protect the insurer's rights. Generally, there will be little conflict between these concerns, provided the loss is not suspicious and the adjuster continually communicates and cooperates with the policyholder.

Insured's Concerns

Fortunately, most insureds who suffer a loss to their homes have never experienced such a loss before. However, as a result, the emotional trauma of seeing their home damaged is compounded by uncertainty and anxiety about their insurance and the loss adjustment process. Many policyholders fear that an inadvertent lapse on their part might somehow void their coverage.

Following a serious loss to a home, an adjuster's priorities should be (1) ensuring the physical safety of the policyholder's family; (2) ensuring the safety and security of the damaged home from further damage; and (3) explaining the coverage and adjustment procedure to the policyholder. Should there be any doubts about coverage, the adjuster can issue a reservation of rights letter and immediately begin with these priorities.

Sometimes a policyholder will escape from a burning home with nothing but the clothes on his or her back, which may be pajamas. An adjuster who deals with the insured at such a time can provide reassurance that the coverage extends to living expenses and replacement of personal property, and can issue an advance on the settlement on the spot. Exhibit 14-6 shows an advance payment receipt that incorporates a nonwaiver agreement. If no doubt exists about coverage, the second paragraph of this receipt can be deleted.

The insurance policy requires the insured to protect the property from further loss, yet the policyholder may be unsure about what that means. The adjuster should advise the policyholder of what is necessary and should recognize that such advice is equivalent to authorization of any attendant expense. Following a serious loss, the policyholder must usually turn off all utilities, drain all plumbing, secure or board up the windows and doors to keep out vandals and trespassers, and secure tarpaulins or plastic sheets over any openings in the roof or walls to keep out the elements. Policyholders can do this work themselves or can hire contractors to do it.

Once the insured's family and property are secure, the adjuster should thoroughly explain the coverage and the adjustment procedure and should answer any questions. Indeed, the adjuster should explain procedures and answer questions from the first moment of contact with the policyholder. For example, as noted, the adjuster should immediately communicate the existence of coverage for living expenses. The adjuster should reassure the insured that policy conditions are not highly technical and should emphasize the importance of the insured's good faith compliance with those conditions. The adjuster should welcome any questions the policyholder might have about the policy conditions and should be prepared to answer them. The policyholder should know what he or she should do the next day, the next week, and the next month. As long as the adjuster is not suspicious about the loss, such direction is perfectly appropriate and is welcomed by the insured.

Additional Living Expense

In the time immediately following a loss, policyholders appreciate additional living expense coverage because it helps normalize their condition by paying for increased living expense following a loss.

EXHIBIT 14-6

Advance Payment Receipt

Advance Payment Receipt and Reservation of Rights

I, the undersigned, hereby acknowledge the receipt of _____Five thousand_____

_____ Dollars ($ ___5,000___) in partial payment of the claim for insurance benefits which I have asserted in connection with a policy of insurance issued by __IIA Insurance Company__ (herein the Company) and bearing Policy Number __HP 721 1025__ . The claim I have made pertains to a ___fire___ loss which I reported as having occurred on or about the ___13th___ day of __May__ , 20 _X7_ .

I understand and acknowledge that the Company is continuing to investigate, in good faith, the claim I have made, that my claim has neither been accepted nor denied, that the advance payment is not an admission of liability whatsoever on the part of the Company, and that the payment should not be considered payment under the policy.

I further understand that the Company is making this advance payment in good faith reliance upon the claim I have made, the representations I made to the Company in support of that claim, and my express request for an advance payment.

I further understand that the Company reserves its rights under the policy and will require full compliance with all the conditions of the policy including, but not limited to, my submission of a proper Sworn Statement in Proof of Loss, the submission of receipts, invoices, books and records, and that the Company may exercise its right to require me to take an examination under oath, if deemed necessary.

I further understand that if the policy or the claim is not valid and payment is not required by the Company, I will repay the advance to the Company.

I further understand that if the policy and claim are deemed valid that the advance will be applied against any benefit due under the policy.

TO BE SIGNED BY ALL NAMED INSUREDS

Howard Elliot

Named Insured

Deb Elliot

Spouse or Partner

State of _Pennsylvania_

County of _Chester_

Subscribed and sworn to before me this ___15th___ day of __May__ 20 _X2_ .

Notary Public for _ABC Insurance Agency_   My Commission Expires: _1/1/X4_

Coverage paid under _C-Personal Property_

(specify)

The adjuster should try to explain the scope of additional living expense as clearly as possible. Misunderstandings about this element of loss can lead to anger and distrust that undermine all other aspects of the loss adjustment. Adjusters should emphasize to policyholders that they must get and keep receipts. Furthermore, although it is best to have receipts for everything, the policyholder must understand that he or she will be compensated only for *additional* living expense. Most policyholders can quickly grasp that normal living expenses for which they would be responsible even without the loss are not compensable. The adjuster should explain that coverage is limited to the policyholder's normal standard of living. Adjusters should not require people to live or eat in places that are beneath their previous standard of living. Policyholders will usually follow the adjuster's advice about what expenditures are appropriate and should be encouraged to check with the adjuster before making a doubtful expenditure.

The insured's residence must be uninhabitable (because of a covered loss) before additional living expense coverage is available. Fortunately, most losses are small. With large (total) losses, the inhabitability of a residence is obvious. With smaller losses, whether a home is inhabitable may be harder to judge. Adjusters can best approach this question by asking themselves whether they would expect their own family to live in a place damaged as badly as the insured's home. The stench of smoke may make a home uninhabitable, at least until it can be ventilated or fumigated. The loss of just a refrigerator or a stove probably does not make a home uninhabitable, but loss of an entire kitchen or an only bathroom probably would. Loss of a furnace (during a cold season) or loss of a hot water heater would likewise probably make a home uninhabitable.

Contractors

Damage to the policyholder's home is adjusted based on estimates. The insurance policy obligates the insured to prove and to present his or her damages. Contractors engaged by the insured should prepare detailed estimates that clearly show specifications, material costs, hours and costs of labor, and additional expenses such as overhead, permits, and demolition and debris removal. Estimates that show only grand total costs or trade-by-trade total costs are not suitable for loss settlements because it is impossible to see how such estimates differ from other estimates and to negotiate those differences in a meaningful way.

Most adjusters prefer to negotiate differences in estimates directly with contractors because they routinely handle construction issues. Estimates are likely to differ with respect to (1) specification of the work to be done; (2) quality of materials; or (3) hours of labor. Costs of materials and labor are generally well known, once the quality and hours have been specified.

Some insurance companies will recommend contractors to policyholders. Doing so is helpful to policyholders who might otherwise not know which contractors are honest, competent, and interested in insurance repair work.

However, making such recommendations creates some real dangers for the insurance company. The policyholder may interpret the adjuster's recommendation as a guarantee that the contractor's estimate will be accepted or that its work will be good. Furthermore, some insurance companies fear that allowing adjusters to make recommendations may lead to the adjusters' receiving kickbacks and gratuities from contractors.

Some contractors treat estimating for insurance repairs differently than other estimating. They may regard the work as more difficult or more complicated because it requires removing damaged sections and rebuilding. If all damaged property can be removed, estimating insurance repairs is identical to estimating new construction. Occasionally, access problems may justify more time and expense; or smoke, fire, and water damage may be hidden.

Restoration and Cleaning Services

Initially, many losses, especially losses caused by smoke and water damage, look far worse than they are. Although many types of water damage are not covered, water damage resulting from fire-fighting activity is covered (under the fire cause of loss) and is often a significant problem. Both smoke and water can cause increasingly worse damage to property if they are allowed to remain. Furthermore, smoke and water will cause little or no damage to certain types of property if they are quickly removed. Professional cleaning and restoration services are available to do such work.

Although the adjuster may take an "arm's-length" approach to the policyholder's selection of a contractor, the adjuster must quickly become involved in hiring a professional cleaning and restoration service. Adjusters and insurance companies should have existing contacts with such services so they can quickly be brought to the scene of a loss. The adjuster should agree on a price with the service providers and should obtain the policyholder's authorization for them to begin work immediately. Quick work by such services can save a great deal of property, minimize additional living expense, and reduce repair costs. In some cases, cleaning alone is sufficient when early observations might have indicated that repainting would be necessary, or repainting alone is sufficient when it was thought replacement would be necessary.

Homeowners Personal Property

Claims for loss to homeowners personal property present adjusters with some of their most difficult professional challenges. Proof that the property ever existed and that it was lost is frequently scarce. Evaluation is difficult to do with any confidence or accuracy and may provoke strong emotions from the policyholder. Finally, the dollar amount of such claims is frequently small, so the adjuster must be constantly aware of the adjustment costs relative to the value of the damaged property.

Inventory

Damaged personal property is usually available for the adjuster's inspection unless fire or theft caused the loss. Unfortunately, fire and theft are two of the most common perils affecting personal property. Even when personal property is burned beyond recognition or is stolen, the insured must prepare an inventory.

Most homeowners do not have written records of their personal property. Few people can even provide an accurate account of all the clothes they own. Often they cannot remember where or when various items were bought. Despite the often minimal evidence of personal property, adjusters cannot refuse to settle such claims. Most people own a collection of personal property that is consistent with their income and lifestyle. An adjuster would be unreasonable to deny a claim for a reasonable inventory of personal property just because the policyholder could not provide documentation. Large purchases can often be documented by bank statements or credit card bills. Personal photographs from relatives might show the policyholder's home and furnishings in the background. In most instances, the adjuster can jog the policyholder's memory by going through a checklist of types of property. Included in such a checklist might be major furniture in each room; clothes (by category) for each person in the household; drapes; rugs; towels and linens; kitchen appliances and utensils; food and liquor; pots and pans; dishes; televisions; radios; stereo equipment; tapes and compact discs; telephones; power tools and hand tools; gardening equipment; office supplies and books; home computers; toys; framed pictures and art objects; sports equipment; bicycles; firearms; and jewelry.

Depreciation

Homeowners generally can produce no better evidence of their property's depreciation than of its existence. Sometimes they can remember where they made major purchases, and those stores may have exact records to provide evidence of purchase dates.

In the absence of specific evidence of the age or condition of property, certain assumptions can be made. Clothes wear out and are subject to fashion obsolescence at a predictable rate. Carpets become threadbare after a certain number of years. Kitchen appliances may be good for only a few years; kitchen utensils and pots and pans last longer. Major furniture can last a long time if it is not subject to abuse and is of classic styling. Policyholders and adjusters can usually agree on reasonable assumptions. Policyholders cannot maintain that virtually everything they have lost was new or was never subject to use. Adjusters cannot maintain that everything had depreciated to near worthlessness or that everything beyond a certain age was "100 percent" depreciated.

Depreciating items of property by groups, such as clothing, kitchen utensils, books, and children's toys, is undesirable, but may be necessary when the property cannot be inspected. Whenever the property is available for inspection, an item-by-item determination of depreciation should be possible. The National Flood Insurance Program forbids depreciation by group or category.

Sublimits

Applying special sublimits is usually straightforward. Sublimits do not seriously affect most policyholders, but, when they do, the adjuster has a difficult human relations/customer service problem.

Because the application of sublimits is unambiguous, the adjuster cannot misrepresent or overlook the situation. The adjuster should first apply the deductible to the entire loss amount. The adjuster can then use the uninsured portion of the loss to absorb the policyholder's deductible. The adjuster should explain the rationale of sublimits: some property is especially vulnerable to theft (for example, cash, jewelry, and firearms), and large limit coverage for such property would tremendously increase the exposure to loss and cost; other property (boats, valuable papers, and business property) is often covered by specialized policies. Ultimately, the adjuster can only recommend that in the future the policyholder should increase coverage for special exposures.

Scheduled Property

When the policyholder has special coverage for individual items of property, the adjuster often has more loss settlement flexibility than with ordinary personal property.

Individual property usually gets scheduled coverage because it is valuable, and the policyholder wants the broader causes of loss or "all-risks" coverage typically associated with scheduled items. The scheduled coverage will usually identify the property precisely. Thus, the adjuster can contact merchants and appraisers who specialize in such property to determine whether it can be repaired, whether it can be replaced through a secondary market, how much its value has decreased because of a loss, and whether the insurer can buy at discount. Jewelry, camera equipment, and firearms are precisely the types of property for which the insurer is likely to exercise its "repair or replace" option, because the insurer might be able to buy an exact replacement for less than the policyholder paid originally. The high value of these items also makes repair far more feasible than it is with lower-value property.

Thefts

After reporting a theft to the insurer, the adjuster should insist that the insured also report the theft to the police so that they might catch the perpetrator and recover the property. Unfortunately for the policyholder victimized by an actual theft, insurers have experienced many fraudulent attempts to collect because of alleged theft. Adjusters may take extra steps to ensure that theft occurred by taking separate statements from residents of the household and requiring independent verification of the existence of the stolen property.

Commercial Structures

Adjusting losses to commercial structures is usually limited to highly skilled and experienced adjusters because the value of commercial structures can easily reach millions of dollars. Additionally, experienced adjusters are needed to deal with complex issues such as alternative methods of property repair and the value of depreciated property. Rarely can an adjuster handle losses to commercial structures without expert assistance. The complexity of losses to commercial structures extends to investigating arson and to considering the loss of use.

Architects and Contractors

Adjusters with substantial experience and expertise in estimating residential losses are not necessarily able to estimate losses in commercial structures. Construction principles, methods, materials, and available contractors are different for commercial structures. The adjuster usually must employ an architect to develop building specifications. The architect's fee is a legitimate element of the loss when architectural services are necessary.

Architectural plans dating from the building's construction are often still available. Those plans can provide valuable information about a building's details if a serious loss has occurred. They can also serve as the basis of a precise reconstruction of the destroyed building. Even with such plans, the adjuster may have to hire another architect to identify changes in building codes or to design alternatives to obsolete construction features and techniques. An architect can develop precise cost estimates or can hire professional estimators to do so.

Local contractors may not be adequate for reconstructing certain commercial structures. They may lack sufficient expertise, equipment, or staff for large or complicated work. The insured or his or her architect may have to solicit bids from contractors throughout the region or throughout the country. The adjuster cannot necessarily settle the claim based on the lowest bid for the work. The low bidder may be lowest because the contractor's lack of experience has resulted in a miscalculation. The adjuster should choose the lowest bidder who is both responsible and capable. The architect can help the adjuster identify which bidders meet those criteria.

The adjuster must remember that the insurance company's duty is to settle with the policyholder, not to engage a contractor to perform the actual reconstruction. Soliciting bids from contractors is done to help the adjuster evaluate the loss. Only the insured should enter into contracts for the construction work.

Determining Actual Cash Value

The value of commercial structures is more variable than that of residences. In addition, commercial structures are more likely than residences to experience significant depreciation caused by factors other than wear and tear.

The principle of supply and demand determines the value of a commercial structure. A portion of a structure's value depends on the profit a business derives from its use, or demand. The remainder of the structure's value depends on the cost of rebuilding that structure or of obtaining an alternative location, or supply. When demand is strong and supply is short, the value of commercial structures rises significantly. Alternatively, when demand is weak and supplies are glutted, values decline.

The demand for commercial structures fluctuates with the overall economy and with business conditions in particular industries. The more specialized a building is, the more the demand for its use will parallel economic conditions in a particular industry. For example, the value of an auto assembly plant corresponds more to the demand for autos than to the value of other commercial structures.

The supply of commercial structures is characterized by frequent shortages and oversupplies. This phenomenon is caused by the amount of time required to build commercial structures. In times of shortage, buildings are planned that may not be completed until an oversupply of similar buildings exists.

An adjuster evaluating the actual cash value at the time of loss of a commercial structure must consider market conditions. The market may be such that the replacement cost of a structure has significantly appreciated since it was built. If so, the insured should be appropriately compensated. Alternatively, the value of a building may have plummeted, so significant depreciation should be applied to the claim.

Although commercial structures experience wear and tear, other factors may be the prime causes of depreciation. Commercial structures are more susceptible than residences to economic and technological obsolescence. For example, an old warehouse may still be useful but less desirable than a newer warehouse because its floor space is broken up by pillars, its lighting is inadequate, its access roads and parking lots are in poor condition, its loading dock is not well designed, and its heating and ventilation are obsolete. Though still in use, the older, obsolete structure has far less value per square foot than a new structure. This difference is usually easy to document through commercial realtors. Realtors can quote the likely rental values of an old property and a new property. The difference in rental rates is a good gauge of depreciation.

The extent of depreciation a policyholder has taken in its financial records is irrelevant. Because financial depreciation reduces taxes, policyholders will take it as fast as the tax laws allow. Thus, most buildings will have less actual depreciation than the amount recorded in the policyholder's accounting records.

Problems With Mortgagee

The variability of the value of commercial structures, described previously, creates more potential for problems with mortgagees than residences create. Commercial mortgage agreements usually make the mortgage amount completely due and payable upon the destruction of the structure on the property. During depressed markets for commercial properties, mortgagees may see an insurance claim as their most likely chance of being paid. The mortgagee may resist the owner's wish to rebuild the property and may want to be paid in full.

The adjuster cannot solve this problem because it is between the owner and the mortgagee. The adjuster must put the names of both the owner and the mortgagee on the settlement draft and should keep both parties advised of the settlement. Beyond these actions, the adjuster has no obligation to either party.

Contamination and Pollution Cleanup

Serious losses at commercial structures, especially at manufacture and storage sites, may result in contamination and pollution. Adjusters should be concerned about such losses for several reasons.

First, the adjuster's own health and safety may be at stake from exposure to the loss site. Firefighters may be obligated to notify the Environmental Protection Agency (EPA) or state environmental agencies of contaminated loss sites. When such agencies are involved, the adjuster should avoid the site until notified that entry is safe.

Second, the coverage for pollution cleanup is tightly limited in most policies. The adjuster must be familiar with these limitations and must communicate them to the insured. Nevertheless, pollution caused by a covered peril is often covered.

Third, the adjuster should have contacts with specialized technical services that can help the policyholder to correct a contaminated site. The adjuster should not recommend such a service unless its cost will be covered or unless the insured provides clear acknowledgment (preferably in writing) that the insured is responsible for all costs. Although these technical services are expensive, they can often devise solutions that may be more practical, less expensive, and faster than the solutions of the EPA.

Arson Investigation

As in determining arson to a residence, the adjuster must prove three things to establish arson with a commercial structure: (1) incendiary fire, (2) motive, and (3) opportunity. As with suspected residential arsons, the incendiary fire can be proven by a cause and origin expert, and the insured's opportunity can be proven through an investigation of the insured and with SIUs. The only difference with commercial structures is that they experience a higher rate of incendiary fires not caused by arson. Commercial structures are frequently unoccupied at night and may be more tempting to vandals.

The main focus in cases of suspected arson to commercial structures is on the policyholder's motive. Such motive is almost always economic. Economic motive may exist even for a structure in regular use, provided the policyholder would be better off financially with the insurance settlement and vacant real estate. Usually in cases of suspected arson, the insured building is owned by a failing business in need of cash. Such circumstances can be established by having an accountant examine the policyholder's financial records. Indeed, considering the seriousness of the matter and the amount of money at stake, an adjuster should not consider asserting an arson defense without a solid accounting report that establishes motive.

Business Interruption

Adjusters regard business interruption claims as highly complex. Proper settlement of these cases requires detailed analysis of and considerable speculation about extensive financial records. Nevertheless, adjusters can organize and simplify their task by concentrating on just a few issues and reminding themselves that the ultimate effect of a business interruption settlement is to put the policyholder in essentially the same financial shape it would have been in without the loss. The few important issues concern the best approach to loss determination, the determination of business income, and the determination of the period of restoration.

Loss Settlement Approach

Claims for business interruption can be settled prospectively or retrospectively. **Prospective settlements** are those made before the property has been repaired. **Retrospective settlements** are those made after the property has been repaired and the policyholder has resumed operations.

Prospective settlements
Settlements made before property has been repaired.

Retrospective settlements
Settlements made after the property has been repaired and the policyholder has resumed operations.

Prospective settlements are desirable whenever the insured intends not to repair the property at all or intends to make significant alterations. Prospective settlement on any loss is also available at the policyholder's request. The policyholder is not required to wait until the property is repaired and operations resume to conclude a settlement with the insurer. Provided the policyholder and the adjuster agree on all data relevant to the loss, settlement can be made immediately.

Nevertheless, retrospective settlements are probably more common. Once the property is repaired and the policyholder has resumed operations, the amount of time taken to make repairs and the expenses incurred during the interruption are known. Furthermore, during the interruption of business, the policyholder is likely to be so preoccupied with issues involved in reopening that the business interruption loss settlement becomes a secondary concern. Unfortunately, retrospective settlements hold more possibility for argument and disagreement over what the period of restoration *should* have been. The insurance covers only the time in which repairs *should* be made, not necessarily the amount of time actually consumed.

Determining Loss of Business Income

"Business income" is a quantity the current ISO forms define as essentially net profit (or loss) plus continuing normal operating expenses. This term is most easily understood when it is placed within the basic framework of business accounting.

A business determines its profit (or loss) by subtracting its costs from its revenue. Revenue consists mainly of sales. Costs consist of the cost to acquire the goods the business sells plus all other expenses. For retailers, the cost of goods is called "cost of goods sold" and represents the cost to the retailers of acquiring goods from their suppliers. For manufacturers, the cost of goods is their own cost of manufacturing the goods.

Excerpts from the Business Income Report/Work Sheet for a manufacturer are shown in Exhibit 14-7. This is a somewhat more elaborate version of the preceding paragraph. A business that completes this work sheet can determine its likely "business income." This amount can be understood as either sales minus cost of goods sold minus operating expenses that discontinue or as net profit (or loss) plus operating expenses that continue. These two amounts should be equivalent. Typically, both claim adjusters and policyholders find it easier to approach a loss settlement with the former definition: sales minus cost of goods and discontinued expenses.

The adjuster cannot directly use the Business Income Report/Work Sheet to settle a claim. This work sheet lists projected amounts, and the claim should be settled based on actual loss. This principle might seem to conflict with the prospective approach to settlement. In case of a prospective settlement, the adjuster and the insured must make new projections of what the insured loss of business income is likely to be for the expected period of restoration. Any actual experience that has developed since the policyholder completed the work sheet should be used to make the best projection of the actual loss of business income.

Determining the Period of Restoration

The "period of restoration" is the time starting seventy-two hours after the loss and ending when the repairs should be completed. This period is so defined to compel the insured to make repairs and resume operations with due diligence and to allow for settlement when the insured neither makes repairs nor resumes operations.

The time in which repairs should be made can be determined by consulting with the contractors hired to do the work. Adjusters must remember that any such estimate from a contractor, even if made with the utmost good faith and honesty, is uncertain. Contractors cannot control weather, interruptions in the availability of supplies or of subcontractors, or subcontractor behavior.

Thus, many adjusters and insureds prefer to settle business interruption claims only after the repairs have actually been completed. However, at that point, the adjuster and insured may disagree over whether the insured used due diligence to get the work done. In general, adjusters do not penalize policyholders for delays caused by factors beyond their control. It is also good policy for adjusters not to penalize the policyholder for any delays caused by the settlement of the property damage claim. Delays in settling the underlying claim may be caused by the policyholder, the adjuster, or both.

EXHIBIT 14-7

Business Income Report/Work Sheet

Business Income Report/Work Sheet
Financial Analysis
(000 omitted)

Income and Expenses	12 Month Period Ending 12/31/X4		Estimated for 12 Month Period Beginning 4/1/X5	
	Manufacturing	Non-Manufacturing	Manufacturing	Non-Manufacturing
A. Gross Sales	$ 10,050	$	$ 10,350	$
B. Deduct: Finished Stock Inventory (at sales value) at Beginning ..	− 500	XXXXXX	− 550	XXXXXX
....	9,550	XXXXXX	9,800	XXXXXX
C. Add: Finished Stock Inventory (at sales value) at End	+ 533	XXXXXX	+ 480	XXXXXX
D. Gross Sales Value of Production	$ 10,083	XXXXXX	$ 10,280	XXXXXX
E. Deduct: Prepaid Freight—Outgoing	− 0	−	− 0	−
Returns & Allowances	− 20	−	− 21	−
Discounts	− 30	−	− 32	−
Bad Debts	− 25	−	− 27	−
Collection Expenses	− 0	−	− 0	−
F. Net Sales		$		$
Net Sales Value of Production	$ 10,008		$ 10,200	
G. Add: Other Earnings from your business operations (not investment income or rents from other properties): Commissions or Rents	+ 0	+	+ 0	+
Cash Discounts Received	+ 0	+	+ 0	+
Other	+ 10	+	+ 15	+
H. Total Revenues	$ 10,018	$	$ 10,215	$

       CP 15 15 06 95 ☐

Continued on next page.

Income and Expenses	12 Month Period Ending 12/31/X4		Estimated for 12 Month Period Beginning 4/1/X5	
	Manufacturing	Non-Manufacturing	Manufacturing	Non-Manufacturing
Total Revenues (Line **H**. from previous page)	$ 10,018	$ _____	$ 10,215	$ _____

I. Deduct:

Cost of goods sold (see next page for instructions)	− 5,725	− _____	− 5,900	− _____
Cost of services purchased from outsiders (not your employees) to resell, that do not continue under contract	− 0	− _____	− 0	− _____
Power, heat and refrigeration expenses that do not continue under contract (if **CP 15 11** is attached)	− N/A	XXXXXX	− N/A	XXXXXX
All ordinary payroll expenses or the amount of payroll expense excluded (if **CP 15 10** is attached)	− N/A	− _____	− N/A	− _____
Special deductions for mining properties (see next page for instructions)	− N/A	− _____	− N/A	− _____
J.1. Business Income exposure for 12 months ...	$ 4,293	_____	4,315	_____
J.2. Combined (firms engaged in manufacturing & non-manufacturing operations)	$_____		$_____	

The figures in **J.1.** or **J.2.** represent 100% of your actual and estimated Business Income exposure for 12 months.

K. Additional Expenses:

1. Extra Expenses—form **CP 00 30** only (expenses incurred to avoid or minimize & to continue operations) .... $ _____ $ _____

2. Extended Business Income and Extended Period of Indemnity—form **CP 00 30** or **CP 00 30** (loss of Business Income following resumption of operations, up to 30 days or the no. of days selected under Extended Period of Indemnity option) .... + _____   + _____

3. Combined (all amounts in **K.1.** and **K.2.**) . $_____

"Estimated" column

L. Total of J. and K. .... $

The figure in L. represents 100% of your estimated Business Income exposure for 12 months, and additional expenses. Using this figure as information, determine the approximate amount of insurance needed based on your evaluation of the number of months needed (may exceed 123 months) to replace your property, resume operations and restore the business to the condition that would have existed if no property damage had occurred.

Refer to the agent or Company for information on available Coinsurance levels and indemnity options. The Limit of Insurance you select will be shown in the Declarations of the policy.

Supplementary Information

	12 Month Period Ending 12/31/X4		Estimated for 12 Month Period Beginning 4/1/X5	
	Manufacturing	Non-Manufacturing	Manufacturing	Non-Manufacturing
Calculation of Cost of Goods Sold				
Inventory at beginning of year (including raw material and stock in process, but not finished stock, for manufacturing risks)	$ 1,050	$	$ 1,110	$
Add: The following purchase costs:				
Cost of raw stock (including transportation charges)	+ 5,715	XXXXXX	+ 5,820	XXXXXX
Cost of factory supplies consumed	+ 25	XXXXXX	+ 20	XXXXXX
Cost of merchandise sold including transportation charges (for manufacturing risks, means cost of merchandise sold but not manufactured by you)	+ 0	+	+ 0	+
Cost of other supplies consumed (including transportation charges)	+ 0	+	+ 0	+
Cost of goods available for sale	$ 6,790	$	$ 6,950	$
Deduct: Inventory at end of year (including raw material and stock in process, but not finished stock, for manufacturing risks)	− 1,065	−	− 1,050	−
Cost of Goods Sold (Enter this figure in item I. on previous page)	$ 5,725	$	$ 5,900	$

Extra Expense

Claims for extra expense can be settled only retrospectively. For extra expenses to be covered, they must be incurred to avoid or minimize the suspension of business. Thus, the policyholder could realize a windfall if the adjuster allowed extra expense based on projections. The adjuster cannot adequately monitor whether the insured incurred the expense legitimately or simply pocketed it.

Extra expense incurred to repair damaged property is covered *to the extent it reduces the business interruption claim.* Thus, as mentioned above, the adjuster can authorize expedited construction methods or relatively expensive contractors if the business interruption loss is thereby reduced.

Use of Accountants

Probably no type of claim requires as much use of professional accounting assistance as business interruption claims. Most adjusters have only a rudimentary knowledge of accounting, but they can follow a report from a professional accountant. Most adjusters are not competent to analyze the hundreds of entries that record individual transactions of an ongoing business. Adjusters cannot simply review historic data and determine the policyholder's "normal" operating expenses.

Some accounting firms specialize in claims work. These firms already understand the policy coverages and can explain them to the policyholder's accountant. Adjusters find that business interruption claims run smoothly when one of these accounting firms is hired to work with the policyholder's accountant.

Merchandise

Merchandise that the policyholder holds for sale is a special type of business personal property. Its valuation raises unique issues; it offers the best opportunities for salvage and use of salvor services; and claims for it must be settled in special ways.

Valuation of Merchandise

The replacement cost of merchandise is the cost to the policyholder of replacing that merchandise. The policyholder will usually have ongoing relations with its suppliers and can provide accurate information about their prices. If the policyholder regularly enjoys trade discounts and allowances from its suppliers, the effective cost to the policyholder will be less than what appears on supplier invoices. Replacement costs of finished goods in the hands of a manufacturer are the costs of manufacture.

Actual cash value standards can be difficult to apply to merchandise. In many cases, the goods have experienced no depreciation, and actual cash value is equivalent to replacement cost. Depreciation caused by ordinary wear and tear is not common, but many goods suffer "shop wear." They are picked over and handled by so many people that they are no longer presentable as first-quality goods.

Merchandise is also subject to significant depreciation caused by obsolescence. An adjuster can identify situations of obsolescence even when he or she is not familiar with the product. If, before the loss, the policyholder was offering the product to the public at a discounted price or had stopped offering it altogether, the product has likely suffered obsolescence. In fact, it is considered good accounting practice to reduce the inventory value of merchandise whenever its listed retail price is reduced. The adjuster should note such an accounting approach by the policyholder and should cite it as justification for settling claims at the reduced inventory figure. Fashion changes, technological changes, and seasonal selling patterns can all cause an inventory to become obsolete. Insurance is not designed to reimburse for such loss of value.

Salvage

Other than vehicles, merchandise is the only significant source of salvage for the insurance industry. As explained earlier in this chapter, adjusters and insurers rarely try to sell salvaged merchandise themselves; they employ professional salvage firms.

Salvage proceeds from the sale of damaged merchandise can be significant. Some merchants refuse to deal in damaged goods, no matter how superficial the damage is. These merchants will refuse to consider a loss settlement based on a percentage of the goods' value because in those merchants' markets the goods are "worthless." Adjusters find it easiest to settle with such merchants for 100 percent of the goods' value and to take the merchandise for salvage.

Professional salvage firms can act quickly to protect goods from further damage, can inventory and separate goods, and can give advice to claim representatives about the likely amount of residual value in damaged goods.

Reporting Form Losses

Inventories of merchandise are often insured under reporting form policies that require the policyholder to submit regular reports of value. Adjusters who handle claims for such merchandise must know what to do when the policyholder underreports its values or fails to report the values promptly. The following rules are based on ISO's value reporting form.

Following a loss to merchandise insured under a value reporting form, the adjuster must determine the value of the policyholder's inventory for the date of the last report. The adjuster is not concerned with the value of the inventory on the date of loss unless the inventory is totaled. Analysis of the inventory for a past date may require the assistance of an accountant. If the policyholder underreported the value of its inventory, it cannot recover the full amount of its loss. It recovers only a percentage of the loss equal to the percentage of inventory value it reported.

Should the policyholder fail to submit a report when due, the loss adjustment will be based on the last report submitted. The adjuster will not pay more than the amount last reported. This rule might penalize the policyholder. However, should the policyholder fail to submit even the first required report, the adjuster will not pay more than 75 percent of what would otherwise have been paid. Applying this latter rule always penalizes the policyholder.

Importance of Negotiation

As noted with respect to salvage, adjusters sometimes settle losses to merchandise based on a percentage of value. Under these settlements, the merchant keeps the merchandise and is reimbursed for its decreased value. The adjuster is not required to pay full value for the goods or to dispose of salvage. Adjusters should try to negotiate with policyholders towards such settlements because they offer mutual benefit.

For example, suppose that following a loss to merchandise, the adjuster believed that salvage of the damaged goods would yield about 35 percent of their insured value. It would not be unusual for the policyholder in such a situation to believe it could sell the goods for a much higher percentage of value, perhaps 55 percent. This assumption might be true because the policyholder is a merchant in the business and is already organized to sell such goods. On the one hand, the adjuster could total the goods and sell them as salvage for a net loss of 65 percent. Alternatively, the adjuster could try to negotiate settlement with the policyholder for some percentage less than 65 percent. The policyholder would be willing to take as little as 45 percent, because the policyholder believes it can still realize 55 percent by selling the goods itself. Any settlement figure between 45 percent and 65 percent is therefore fair *to both parties*.

This type of situation is common in losses to merchandise. Each party must assess the situation accurately to negotiate effectively. The adjuster can get advice from a salvor or can negotiate based on his or her personal experience with similar losses. Intelligent negotiating by the adjuster does not necessarily harm the policyholder. A policyholder, knowledgeable of the merchandise's value, can refuse unfavorable settlement proposals. If the adjuster is being unreasonable, the policyholder can invoke the appraisal clause or can challenge the adjuster to total the goods and try to realize the salvage value the adjuster claims still exists.

Transportation and Bailment Losses

Property is frequently in the possession of someone other than its owner. Losses to such property create complicated legal and insurance policy coverage issues. Adjusters may have to handle claims for either the owner or the party in possession of the property. An adjuster must carefully review the coverage, the law, and the contracts between the parties in these situations.

The most common circumstances in which property is in the possession of someone other than its owner are transportation and bailment situations.

Carriers such as trucking companies, railroads, and air freight companies are in the business of transporting other people's property. Bailments include situations in which owners entrust their property to bailees such as cleaners, repairers, processors, consignees, and warehousers. These relationships are contractual, and the pertinent contracts can affect both legal liability and insurance coverage.

Insurance Coverages

Adjusters handling transportation and bailment claims must orient themselves to the insurance policy under which they are working. Insurance policies exist for both the owner and for the other party involved. Policies written for motor truck carriers, bailees, warehouse workers, and so on, may provide certain coverage for other parties. Thus, adjusters may find themselves settling a claim for one party under a policy that names some other party as the insured. For example, an adjuster may settle losses under a dry cleaner's policy for the dry cleaner's customers rather than for the named insured—the dry cleaner.

Owner's policies typically provide limited coverage for property away from the insured location. Thus, the owner of the property may have significant uninsured exposures. An owner with predictable off-premises exposures should obtain special coverage under floater policies or shipper policies. Unfortunately, an owner's coverage is often inadequate. An adjuster handling a claim for an owner should check for off-premises coverage. If such coverage is inadequate, the adjuster should quickly settle for the available coverage and should place the carrier's or bailee's insurer on notice of the claim. Owner's policies typically have "no benefit to bailee" clauses. These clauses make clear that the owner's coverage does not extend to the carrier or bailee and that the owner's insurer retains its right of subrogation. However, as discussed later, subrogation rights may be affected by agreement between the parties.

Policies for carriers and bailees typically protect the interests of both the owner and the carrier/bailee. An adjuster handling claims under a carrier/bailee policy must usually settle two claims arising out of the same property loss: the owner's and the carrier/bailee's. The carrier/bailee has an interest in the property to the extent of its earned fees. In addition, the carrier/bailee may be legally liable to the owner for return of the property (the extent of a carrier/bailee's legal liability is discussed below). An insurance policy of a carrier/bailee that extends to liability for the owner's property requires the adjuster working for the carrier/bailee's insurer to settle the owner's claim. Most policies of this sort allow the adjuster to deal directly with the owner and also allow the insurer to defend the carrier/bailee against the owner's claim, rather than to pay it. Some carrier/bailee policies protect the owner regardless of the carrier/bailee's legal liability. Such policies are purchased to maintain customer goodwill. Owners expect to be reimbursed for damage to their property, without hairsplitting over legal liability. This quasi-first-party coverage allows the adjuster to deal immediately with the owner before conducting an investigation of legal liability.

Legal Liability

Even in the absence of agreement between the parties, the law provides for the extent of legal liability of the carrier/bailee to the owner. Because the relationship between the owner and the carrier/bailee is contractual, the specific terms of the contract between the parties also affect legal liability between them.

Bill of lading

A document that serves as a receipt for property being shipped. A bill of lading may also contain the contract of carriage between the shipper and the carrier.

Released bill of lading

A bill of lading that limits the carrier's liability for cargo loss in return for charging a lower freight rate than would be charged for carrying the cargo subject to full valuation.

In the absence of an agreement to the contrary, the law makes common carriers liable for damage to an owner's goods. The only exceptions to this liability are for acts of God, war, negligence of the shipper, exercise of public authority, and inherent vice of the goods. Carriers usually limit the dollar amount of their liability in their **bill of lading**, which is a receipt for the goods and a contract for transportation. A **released bill of lading** limits the carrier's liability to a specified dollar amount. Owners and shippers with greater exposures must pay higher rates for increased liability on the carrier's part. Adjusters handling losses in shipment *must* review the applicable bill of lading.

Other bailees are generally liable to the owner only for their negligence. Should a loss occur without any negligence on the bailee's part, the owner must bear the loss. Thus, owners with significant off-premises exposures must arrange special coverage. A bailee's coverage may not apply. As with a transportation contract, a bailment contract can modify the respective legal rights of the parties. A bailment contract might limit the dollar amount of a bailee's liability or make the bailee strictly liable. An adjuster handling an owner's claim against a bailee for legal liability must read and understand the contract between the parties. To the extent that the bailee's liability is limited, so too is any coverage for the owner that is based on liability. Furthermore, the subrogation rights of the owner's insurer may be limited. Most property insurance policies allow the insured to waive subrogation before a loss occurs. An adjuster who has paid a claim under an owner's insurance may find that the insured/owner has waived liability of the bailee beyond a certain dollar amount. Such a waiver likewise limits the insurer's subrogation rights.

Crime Losses

Property losses caused by crime present a significant challenge to adjusters. The property in question is usually gone. Thus, the best evidence that the loss occurred and of what the property was worth is absent. Adjusters handling such cases can usually expect a higher level of doubt and uncertainty than is considered acceptable and comfortable in other property losses.

On crime losses, the adjuster's most important duties are to verify the exact cause of loss, to verify the existence and value of the property, and to investigate any fraud possibilities.

Verification of Exact Cause

Because crime insurance is expensive, policy forms covering crime losses are narrowly tailored. The policyholder should have just the form or forms needed for that insured's significant exposures. For example, under the ISO crime program, Coverage Form C provides very broad coverage (theft, disappearance, or destruction) to a very specific category of property (money and securities), but Coverage Form D provides protection to broad types of property (anything other than money or securities) for very limited causes of loss (robbery of a custodian and safe burglary only).

Once the adjuster has carefully determined the policyholder's coverage, the adjuster must determine the exact cause of the loss. The insurance policy forms provide definitions of the various crimes that control whether a particular loss is covered. For example, burglary, by definition, requires signs of forcible entry or exit. This requirement may not exist under a particular state's definition of burglary in its criminal code. Nevertheless, for coverage to apply to a loss, the cause must satisfy the policy definition.

The adjuster must interview and obtain statements from every party with knowledge of the alleged crime. Although taking statements is not standard practice for ordinary property losses, it is for crime losses. A robbery victim should be able to furnish a complete account of the incident. The person who discovered a burglary should be interviewed in depth. The scene of a reported burglary must be inspected. The adjuster should require the policyholder to report the incident to the police and should obtain whatever report or investigation the police prepare. Unfortunately, police in many high-crime areas spend little time and effort tracking down burglars and may not conduct an investigation at all.

One of the most essential aspects of an adjuster's investigation into a crime loss is to conclude that the theft was not an inside job. "Theft" by the policyholder is not theft at all; it is fraud. Theft by employees is covered only by employee dishonesty (fidelity) policies. In the case of a reported burglary, the policy requirement of forcible entry or exit benefits the adjuster. In the absence of such evidence, the adjuster can deny the claim without necessarily accusing the insured or the insured's employees. In cases of employee theft, the policyholder is usually suspicious of employee involvement and may have good ideas about who is involved. Adjusters should not repeat unproven, slanderous accusations but should take statements from all suspects and then decide whether sufficient evidence exists to alert the police to likely suspects or to deny the claim.

Verification of the Property

It is difficult, but not impossible, for an adjuster to verify the existence and value of property that is gone.

Businesses should have inventory records that record the quantity and value of property in inventory. Although inventory records are not perfect, they are usually accurate within a few percentage points. Many crime policies preclude the use of inventory records to prove the occurrence of a crime because inventory "shrinkage" is a widespread phenomenon usually caused by unrecorded sales, discarding of damaged merchandise, and employee pilferage. However, inventory records can be used as part of the evidence concerning the quantity and value of property taken.

Should the adjuster be suspicious about the loss, he or she should check with the policyholder's suppliers. These suppliers should have complete records regarding the types, quantities, and values of goods shipped to the policyholder. The adjuster can also check with suppliers to determine whether the policyholder has submitted false inventory data to the adjuster claiming receipt and presence of goods that never existed.

Fraud Possibilities

Adjusters tend to be suspicious of all crime losses. Nevertheless, legitimate crime losses are the norm, so unless the adjuster can develop evidence to the contrary, insured crime losses must be settled.

The policyholder has a motive for fraud whenever its inventory is obsolete or not selling well. The adjuster should learn as much as possible about the policyholder's general business condition through credit reports, financial statements, and credit records. If those reports show deterioration in the policyholder's financial condition, the adjuster should further consider the possibility that the claim is fraudulent.

Employees are often the best sources of solid evidence of fraud on the policyholder's part. Employees may witness the removal of property that is subsequently reported stolen or may be aware of irregularities in the policyholder's bookkeeping. An adjuster investigating a suspicious loss may contact the employees at their homes, where they may feel more comfortable about discussing questionable business practices.

Catastrophes

Hurricanes, floods, tornadoes, earthquakes, and fires or explosions causing widespread damage affect entire communities at once. The insurance industry's role in helping communities recover from catastrophes represents the industry at its finest. Property adjusters are the specific individuals in the insurance industry who must respond to catastrophes. Such response includes preparation before loss and actions following loss.

Pre-Loss Planning

Claim departments would be overwhelmed by catastrophes if they did not plan for them. They must respond to catastrophes by having a sufficient number of adjusters in potential disaster areas while maintaining acceptable service throughout the rest of the country.

Certain areas of the country, such as the Gulf and Atlantic coasts during hurricane season, are most likely to "host" disaster recovery teams. Claim offices in these areas should prepare kits that include forms, maps, telephone directories, temporary licenses, tape measures, clipboards, calculators, and anything else a visiting adjuster would need to operate on the road. Although state insurance regulators vary as to how strictly they enforce licensing requirements following a catastrophe, every adjuster who is likely to be called into an area should be licensed.

The insurance company's administrative departments must be prepared to rent office space; to have telephones, copy machines, desks, and other equipment installed; and to procure temporary living quarters and rented cars on short notice.

Local agents or the underwriting department must establish a system by which adjusters can confirm coverage simply and reliably.

Post-Loss Planning

Adjusters on "storm duty" must work long hours and be separated from their families and normal lives for long periods. In addition, the circumstances of catastrophes will cause the adjuster to modify normal claim adjusting procedures. Adjusters often pay claims with less documentation than usual. They may also reimburse the insured for the insured's own labor in cleaning up the property, a circumstance that is especially common following catastrophes. Claims that would normally require an in-person inspection may be handled by telephone.

Local agents should be familiar with the insurer's claims practices so that they can advise policyholders on how to begin recovery from a loss. The agents should advise the policyholders of what documentation they must maintain and what actions they should take immediately following a loss.

Contractors' services may be at a premium following a major catastrophe. However, contractors from around the country will flock to the disaster area to help mitigate the shortage. Policyholders should be advised to be very careful about to whom they release money. Unscrupulous persons may take advantage of people who are shocked, confused, and suddenly holding cash.

SUMMARY

Several general issues pertain to every property claim and constitute a framework used by property claim adjusters to handle all kinds of property damage claims.

The first issue involves determining who has an interest in the property, interpreting policy requirements for an insurable interest, and identifying who is insured. Next, the adjuster must identify exactly what property is insured and at what location the coverage applies.

Although losses from fire and windstorm are fairly clear-cut, problems may arise from losses caused by water damage, collapse, theft, vandalism, wear and tear and other gradual causes, ordinance or law, faulty construction, and intentional acts on the part of the policyholder. Indirect losses are financial losses resulting from loss of income or extra expenses to remain in operation.

After determining that coverage is in order for the policyholder, the property, and the peril, the adjuster must address the amount of the loss. Policies usually value property at replacement cost or actual cash value without specifying how the adjuster is to determine those amounts. Determining replacement cost is usually easier than figuring actual cash value.

Every property insurance policy enumerates various duties the insured must perform following a loss. These duties include notifying the insurer of the loss, protecting the property from further loss, assisting the insurer with the loss adjustment process, providing proof of loss if required, and submitting to examination under oath if requested. Some policyholders hire public adjusters to handle the contractual duties imposed after a loss.

Loss adjustment procedures include verifying the cause of loss, determining the amount of loss, and documenting the cause and amount of loss. Salvage and subrogation activities offer the adjuster an opportunity to minimize the insurer's losses.

Claims for loss to homeowners' personal property present adjusters with some of their most rewarding, yet difficult, challenges. For example, adjusters helping homeowners after a devastating loss are able to help those traumatized by the loss of their home. Simultaneously, however, adjusters must control the adjusting process so that the insureds understand and follow adjustment procedures.

Losses to commercial structures can easily reach millions of dollars. In those cases, adjusters often confer with architects and contractors to determine the value of a commercial structure and the extent of the loss. Problems may arise with mortgagees. Serious losses at commercial structures may result in contamination and pollution. Suspected arson is also a concern.

Business interruption claims can be highly complex, and settlement often requires a detailed analysis of financial records by an accountant.

Merchandise that the policyholder holds for sale is a special type of business personal property. The valuation of merchandise for sale raises unique issues: it offers the best opportunities for salvage and the use of salvor services, and claims for it must be settled in special ways.

Transportation and bailment losses can create complicated legal and coverage issues. Adjusters may have to handle claims for either the owner or the party in possession of the property. A claim adjuster must carefully review the coverage, the law, and the contracts between the parties in these situations.

Property losses caused by crime are among the greatest challenges faced by adjusters. When handling crime losses, the adjuster's most important duties are to verify the exact cause of loss, to verify the existence and value of the property, and to investigate any fraud possibilities.

Catastrophes—hurricanes, floods, tornadoes, earthquakes, fires, or explosions—can cause widespread damage that affects entire communities. The adjuster's response to these losses should include preparation before the loss and actions following the loss.

Chapter 15

Direct Your Learning

Liability Claim Adjusting

After learning the subject matter of this chapter, you should be able to:

■ Given a liability claim situation, identify the general issues that should be addressed.

■ Illustrate the challenges involved in adjusting claims involving each of the following:

- Auto bodily injury
- Auto physical damage
- Premises
- Operations
- Products
- Workers compensation
- Professional liability
- Environmental and toxic tort

Develop Your Perspective

What are the main topics covered in the chapter?

Once coverage has been established, resolving liability claims depends on the law of liability and damages. These issues and challenges in handling specific types of liability are covered.

Examine the role of law in settling liability claims.

- What unique skills must liability claim adjusters possess to effectively perform their functional role?

Why is it important to know these topics?

Liability claim adjusting requires distinctly different skills than those required for property claim adjusting. By understanding the differences, you can appreciate why insurance companies typically divide these functional responsibilities.

Contrast the skills required for property and liability claim adjusting.

- What diverse skills are required? How might an insurance organization develop a claim department that supports the skills required and the tasks to be accomplished?

How can you use this information?

Consider the structure of the claim adjusting department in your own organization.

- What training, management, and support are provided?
- How might the structure be changed to enhance the activity required by adjusters to perform their functions?

Chapter 15

Liability Claim Adjusting

Liability claim work differs so significantly from property claim work that most insurance company claim operations are organized along property-liability lines. Within personal insurance companies, the liability side of claim work may consist primarily of auto claims. Within commercial insurance companies, the same personnel frequently handle auto liability and general liability claims, and auto physical damage and workers compensation claims may be organized into separate units within the claim department. (Although not traditional liability-based claims, auto physical damage and workers compensation are treated in this chapter.)

The specialization among claim personnel between property and liability claims exists because those claims differ from one another in several important respects. Once coverage is established, resolving liability claims depends more on the law of liability and damages than on the contractual terms of an insurance policy. The law of liability and damages exists apart from insurance policy terms. Liability insurance policies protect the policyholder against the financial consequences of liability law and the policyholder's own legal liability. Thus, liability claim adjusters spend most of their time and effort investigating and evaluating the legal aspects of liability and damages and relatively less time than property claim adjusters enforcing and performing insurance policy terms.

In liability claim situations, the policyholder is really not the person with the claim. The party with a liability claim *against* the insured is the real claimant. This party is referred to as the "third party" or "claimant." Thus, the insurer has no contract with, and the liability adjuster has no contractual obligations to, the claimant. Although most insurance companies consider it to be both ethical and in their own best interests to deal with claimants promptly and responsively, the adjuster has more leeway in dealing with a third-party claimant than with a policyholder. Most insurance department regulations and market conduct studies, for example, are more solicitous of the interests of first-party insureds than of third-party claimants. In addition, third-party claimants are more frequently represented by an attorney than are first-party insureds.

Liability claims include both property damage and bodily injury liability. Although liability claims for property damage exist, they represent a relatively minor percentage of the total dollars paid on all liability claims. The predominantly injury-oriented nature of liability claims distinguishes their settlement from the settlement of property damage claims. The evaluation of injuries by both claimants and adjusters is more subjective and uncertain than the evaluation of property claims, and, thus, negotiation plays a greater role in settling injury claims than it does in settling liability claims.

This chapter begins by describing the issues that exist in all liability claims. Coverage for the claim in question must first be verified. The adjuster must investigate and evaluate both legal liability and damages. Finally, the adjuster must settle the claim, either through negotiation or through the courts. The second half of this chapter describes issues that are important in the settlement of specific types of claims, including auto liability and physical damages, premises, operations, products, workers compensation, professional liability, and environmental impairment liability.

GENERAL ISSUES IN LIABILITY CLAIMS

In every liability claim, the adjuster must determine coverage, liability, and damages and must make settlement. The adjuster may have to investigate to determine coverage, liability, and damages; rarely are all three of these issues quickly and easily determined. Most of an adjuster's time is thus devoted to investigation and documentation. However, knowing how, when, and for what amount to settle provides the most difficult challenge to a liability adjuster's skill and judgment. This section describes how liability adjusters perform the core functions of determining coverage, liability, and damages and of making settlements.

Coverage

The essential coverage clause of most liability insurance policies is a simple one. For example, Coverage A of the commercial general liability (CGL) policy states, "We will pay those sums that the insured becomes legally obligated to pay as damages because of 'bodily injury' or 'property damages' to which this insurance applies." Thus, any type of bodily injury or property damage for which the insured is allegedly liable is covered, unless it is specifically excluded. When determining coverage, adjusters are primarily concerned with the possible application of exclusions. Nevertheless, the essential coverage clause raises important issues. Under Coverage A of the CGL, the claim must be for "bodily injury" or "property damage." Under most auto liability coverages, the claim must also arise out of the use of certain autos by certain individuals. Thus, a claim that is not for "bodily injury" or "property damage" or that does not arise out of the use of certain autos is not within the essential coverage provisions.

This section describes how claim adjusters determine whether a claim is covered. Although it is not a comprehensive exposition of coverage, this section addresses the major issues that adjusters face.

Claimants' Allegations

When a claim is first presented to an adjuster, the facts may be unknown or in dispute. Without knowing the facts, how can an adjuster determine coverage?

The claimant's allegations determine coverage, even if those allegations are disputed and even if they are eventually proven untrue. Liability policies protect the policyholder against legal claims and their cost to defend, regardless of whether the claims are valid or groundless. Protection against false, unproved, and unprovable claims is a crucial part of the protection provided by liability insurance policies. An adjuster evaluating coverage must first consider the claimant's allegations at face value. However, sometimes the claimant's allegations may not be covered, or coverage may be doubtful.

Coverage Problems

Adjusters face difficulty whenever coverage for a claimant's allegations is doubtful. This difficulty occurs when some aspects of a claim are covered and others are not or when coverage for the entire claim is questionable. Clear communication with the policyholder and prompt action on the part of the adjuster are essential to protect both the policyholder's and the insurer's interests. Whenever coverage is doubtful or not applicable to part of a claim, the adjuster must explain clearly, in writing, why this is so and what both the adjuster and the policyholder must do.

If part of a claim is clearly not covered, the adjuster must explain to the policyholder why not, with reference to specific policy provisions. The adjuster must explain that the insurer will continue handling the claim but that the policyholder may have to contribute to an eventual settlement or judgment. This being so, the adjuster should invite the policyholder to involve a private attorney in the claim. Often, in these situations, the policyholder neither involves private counsel nor contributes to a settlement. This is so because part of the claim *is* covered, and the insurer must continue to conduct the defense of the claim and must pay any settlement unless part of the settlement is clearly not covered. Because most liability claims are settled without a clear specification of the basis of liability or of the elements of damages, the insurer usually pays the entire settlement.

When coverage for the entire claim is doubtful, the adjuster must explain to the policyholder why, in writing, and must explain what the adjuster will do. The adjuster must usually conduct a further investigation. Pending this investigation, the adjuster will reserve the insurer's right to deny coverage should the facts so indicate. Upon issuing a letter advising the policyholder of a coverage problem and reserving the insurer's rights, the adjuster must promptly investigate and make a decision. If coverage is found to apply, the policyholder should be informed. If coverage is found not to apply, the policyholder should receive a prompt letter of denial.

Insurers can resolve coverage questions through declaratory judgment actions in court. As the term suggests, these lawsuits result in a court declaration of the rights between parties. Many jurisdictions allow the courts to declare rights between parties whenever a controversy surfaces in the investigation of the claim. Unfortunately, declaratory judgment actions have practical drawbacks. They are likely to consume thousands or tens of thousands of dollars of legal expense; thus, they are not feasible for small and moderately sized claims. Furthermore, in many jurisdictions, declaratory judgment actions do not move through the courts any faster than other cases. A declaratory judgment that takes years may not serve its purpose. The insurer will have to pay to defend the policyholder throughout that time and may have had to settle the case in the meantime. Filing a declaratory action, if unsuccessful, will also complicate the defense of the underlying action.

Whenever coverage does not apply to a claim, the policyholder should receive a written explanation, and a copy should go to the producer. If a lawsuit has been filed, the policyholder must be told exactly how much time he or she has to file a response with the court. Additionally, an adjuster should direct the policyholder to seek personal counsel.

Bodily Injury and Property Damage

As noted, liability insurance policies usually apply only to claims for bodily injury or property damage. The most likely exception to this rule is the personal injury coverage of the CGL, which extends to damages that are not limited to bodily injury and property damage. Attorneys use the term "personal injury" to refer to "bodily injury" claims as defined in insurance policies. In insurance, "personal injury" refers to specific policy coverage for defamation, false arrest, advertising injury, and malicious prosecution.

Generally, policyholders will submit claims for only bodily injury or property damage. However, not all policyholders have a clear idea of what their insurance covers and will submit any claim in the hope that it might be covered. Thus, adjusters occasionally see claims for damages other than bodily injury or property damage.

Money damages are an appropriate remedy for both bodily injury and property damage and are normally included in the relief sought in a lawsuit. Lawsuits that seek only an injunction, and not money damages, are generally not for bodily injury or property damage. An adjuster must be careful not to deny coverage too hastily in a suit seeking injunctive relief. A number of such suits concern ongoing injuries and seek an injunction to stop further injury. This situation is especially true for claims of interference with use of property. Because loss of use of property is included within the definition of "property damage," a suit based on such an alleged injury may be covered.

Suits involving breach of contract resulting in financial harm only or suits alleging financial fraud are more clearly not covered, because they do not concern claims for "bodily injury" or "property damage." Likewise, regulatory fines or minor criminal fines do not constitute "property damage" and are not covered.

Claims for emotional injury alone, without physical injury, present more difficult coverage issues. Generally, if the court cases of the jurisdiction in question allow a tort claim based on emotional injury only, then an emotional injury will constitute a bodily injury for purposes of coverage. Increasingly, more jurisdictions accept emotional injury as bodily injury.

Intentional Acts

Consistent with the notion that insurance is designed to cover accidental events, liability insurance policies generally exclude coverage for the policyholder's intentional acts. This is an important exclusion for adjusters because claimants often allege that the policyholder acted intentionally. Unfortunately, the application of this exclusion is difficult, because adjusters must uncover the answers to two questions: (1) whether the policyholder intended the result of his or her action or merely intended to commit the action without contemplating the injurious outcome and (2) whether intentional acts can be excluded when the claimant also alleges negligence or strict liability on the policyholder's part. An additional issue can involve vicarious liability in which a principal, the policyholder, may be liable for the intentional acts of an agent or a servant.

Adjusters cannot rely on the intentional act exclusion unless they are familiar with the law in their jurisdiction regarding its meaning. For example, in some states, an assault might not be excluded as an intentional act unless the policyholder intended the harm that resulted. This standard makes the exclusion much harder to apply than in states that consider an assault intentional as long as the policyholder intended to commit the assault. States that require a showing that the policyholder intended the harm do not require a showing that the policyholder intended the precise harm that occurred. Furthermore, the intent to cause harm may be inferred from the commission of the assault. Unfortunately, an insurer cannot deny coverage in the hope that a court will infer intent.

The distinction between intending the act and intending the harm has been at the center of numerous suits by policyholders seeking coverage under their homeowners liability insurance for acts of sexual molestation. Many of these cases involve victims who are small children. The policyholders in these cases have alleged that they were insane or severely emotionally disturbed or that they did not believe they were causing harm. Some courts have accepted those arguments and awarded coverage. Other courts have rejected the policyholder's arguments and have ruled that the intent to harm exists, as a matter of law, regardless of what the policyholder says about his or her subjective state. As a result, most homeowners policies now have a specific exclusion for sexual molestation.

Application of the intentional act exclusion is difficult when the claimant also alleges negligence or strict liability on the policyholder's part. Based on the claimant's allegations, part of the claim is covered, and part is not. In such situations, the insurer must defend the policyholder. If the opportunity arises, the adjuster may also have to settle the claim completely. Upon settlement, no distinction is made between which parts of the settlement are for which allegations. The case is settled as a whole, and coverage issues cannot be resolved in a settlement. The same problem exists even when a case is litigated to a verdict. In a few states, courts require juries to identify damages awarded count by count. Otherwise, the verdict will be expressed as a single sum of money and will not resolve any coverage issues. Sometimes the insurer can prove through a lawsuit's discovery process that the policyholder must have intended the behavior, and this evidence may be the basis for denying coverage. However, an insurer taking this approach is acting contrary to the policyholder's best interests and must do so through separate attorneys. The attorney hired by the insurer to defend the policyholder cannot simultaneously work for the insurer toward proving that the policyholder acted intentionally.

Contractual Obligations

In general, liability insurance does not exist to guarantee that policyholders will perform their contractual agreements. However, adjusters cannot deny coverage for all claims based on breach of contract. Contractual obligations are frequently involved in covered claims.

The consequences of a breach of contract may be covered even if the breach itself is not. For example, a contractor may be hired to erect a wall. Should the contractor do the work negligently and the wall collapse on a person, the cost of rebuilding the wall (the subject of the contract) would not be covered, but injuries to the person would be covered. Adjusters frequently see claims of this nature.

Certain contractual obligations may be directly insured by liability policies. For example, the CGL excepts from its contractual exclusion (therefore leaving coverage in place) liability assumed in a lease and the contractual assumption of liability for another's torts for bodily injury or property damage. Both of these contractual obligations play significant roles in claim work.

As with claims involving alleged intentional acts, claims of contractual breach may be joined with claims of negligence or strict liability. Such claims generally involve products or professional liability. The breach of contract aspect of these cases is usually incidental. Adjusters handling such cases often realize that they will not try to differentiate between the intentional act and the contractual breach so that they do not inform the policyholder that part of the claim should technically not be covered. Failure to so advise the policyholder is equivalent to granting coverage for the entire claim, which is probably what the adjuster intends.

Property Under the Policyholder's Control

Policyholders often submit claims for property damage to another's property that has been damaged while in the policyholder's care, custody, or control or while the policyholder was working on it. Such property damage is clearly excluded from coverage by the typical liability insurance policy.

Policyholders are usually not aware of what is or is not covered. They often do not read or understand their policy exclusions. Adjusters can identify care, custody, or control situations with a minimum of investigation. The adjuster can then usually direct the policyholder to the first-party coverage that deals with these situations.

Property damage to the policyholder's product itself, to the policyholder's work itself, or to property that the policyholder has sold or given away is likewise excluded from typical liability policies. However, consequential bodily injuries or damage to another's property are usually covered. Adjusters frequently encounter these situations and must carefully distinguish between damages that are covered and those that are not.

Legal Liability

Once coverage has been determined, the adjuster must determine legal liability and damages. This section describes the procedures an adjuster follows and explains the bases for legal liability.

Proper investigation is essential in determining legal liability. The ability to conduct a complete and proper investigation is one of the core skills of claim adjusting. The adjuster's investigation is guided by the essential facts that must be established to determine legal liability. These facts are dictated by the legal principles applicable to the situation. Many legal principles are relevant to claim work, including tort liability, criminal liability, contractual liability, statutory liability, and vicarious liability. This section explains these principles as they apply to claim work and explains the defenses that may be asserted against liability claims.

Investigation

The initial report of a claim will usually state nothing more than, "Insured involved in auto accident at 10th and Washington," or "Claimant fell at insured's store." The adjuster must develop the additional facts.

The adjuster will organize the investigation according to what information is needed and what is most important. For example, regarding the loss reports cited above, the adjuster would want to know the potential claimants' names, addresses, and telephone numbers and whether any of them are injured. On learning these facts, the adjuster would want to know each claimant's version of the story. When a person's account of an accident is committed to a statement, he or she cannot easily change his or her story later.

It is as important for an adjuster to obtain a claimant's story as to obtain the insured's story. The policyholder is required to cooperate and will usually be eager to do so. The claimant may exaggerate, embellish, or falsify his or her story if not questioned promptly. In addition to preserving evidence, prompt contact reassures the claimant about the insurer's responsiveness and greatly reduces the chance that the claimant will hire an attorney.

Taking statements is standard practice with liability claims. A good statement has a proper introduction of both the witness and the adjuster and systematically covers all relevant factual issues in the case. An adjuster should even cover areas with which the witness is likely to be unfamiliar. Having a witness respond "I don't know" prevents that witness from later inventing evidence on the same point. As long as a witness is available to testify, a statement given out of court cannot be used as evidence, except for impeachment.

Most statements are recorded on audiotape. This process is convenient for the adjuster, and it preserves the witness's words. Tapes are easy and inexpensive to reproduce should the witness want a copy.

Adjusters also collect evidence in other forms, such as police reports, photographs and diagrams of accident scenes, and products or objects involved in claims. Information should be collected promptly to preserve the accident scene before changes occur. For example, skid marks wear away quickly. Such evidence is useful for checking the credibility of witness statements and as direct evidence of what happened. Police reports should never serve to substitute for the adjuster's own investigation unless all parties agree as to the facts of the accident.

The most important aspect in any investigation is to obtain all of the relevant evidence. Once all of the evidence has been gathered, the adjuster must evaluate its credibility and decide what most likely happened. Adjusters should be constantly evaluating the credibility of evidence as it is received.

Adjusters quickly learn that in many cases, the "truth" is never known for sure. All that is available is evidence, and one set of evidence may contradict another. The best the adjuster can do is to evaluate the relative credibility of the evidence. Although the credibility of evidence and "truth" may not be the same in every case, credibility of evidence decides the outcome of cases.

For witnesses to be completely credible, they must have had the opportunity to observe the facts in question, must remember those facts accurately, must have the ability to communicate what is in their memory, and must have no motive to distort. Most witnesses are deficient in at least one of those respects. They may have had a good chance to observe but may have a poor memory. They may have a good memory but are so inarticulate that the adjuster must lead them through their entire statement, thus introducing the possibility of distortion. An adjuster must also remember that a witness may be biased but honest or may be articulate without having really seen what happened.

Tort Liability

A tort is a civil wrong not arising out of breach of contract. Some torts, such as assault, may also be crimes, and others, such as professional malpractice, may also be breach of contract. Generally, though, the law provides a remedy for torts because the wrongdoer (called a tortfeasor) has behaved in a manner that falls below acceptable legal standards and has caused damage to another.

Negligence is the usual basis of tort liability. Adjusters and attorneys use the term "negligence" to refer both to negligent behavior and to a cause of action in negligence. A claimant has a cause of action in negligence whenever all elements required for negligence exist. Those elements are a duty of care; a breach of that duty (these first two elements together are sometimes referred to as "negligence," meaning negligent behavior); proximate cause; and damages.

Whenever someone has failed to behave carefully and prudently, he or she has likely breached a duty of care. Negligent behavior is common; few people are always careful and prudent. An adjuster investigating a situation of potentially negligent behavior will usually proceed by investigating what the policyholder could have done differently to prevent the accident. If the policyholder could have reasonably avoided the accident, the policyholder is probably negligent. Violations of certain laws, such as traffic laws, are deemed negligence per se. These laws are designed to fix the standard of behavior for all people subject to the law. Anyone who drives must observe the traffic laws, and failure to do so is negligence.

It is not enough for the injuries of a person to be "caused by" another for compensation to result; **proximate** (or legal) **cause** must also exist. This legal concept requires that an unbroken chain of events must link the "cause" and the injurious "event." Although "proximate" means close, a proximate cause is not necessarily physically close or close in time to its outcome. The proximate cause requirement protects a wrongdoer from responsibility for remote, unforeseeable consequences. Proximate cause is most likely questioned when the injurious outcome is also caused by intervening negligence. The intervening negligence may eliminate proximate causation between the original negligence and the eventual outcome.

Proximate cause
The event that sets in motion an uninterrupted chain of events contributing to a loss.

Damages are an essential part of an action in negligence. Unless negligent behavior causes damage to another party, the wrongdoer escapes any legal consequences. Damages are virtually inevitable in liability claims, however; if no damage was done, then the claimant would not be complaining.

Tort liability may also be based on behavior other than negligence. **Intentional torts** include assault, battery, false arrest, false imprisonment, conversion (theft), defamation, trespass, and fraud. Although many of these torts are crimes and all involve intentional conduct, an adjuster cannot assume they are not covered. Indeed, personal injury coverage extends to many of these torts. Convicting the policyholder of a crime is generally conclusive evidence that a tort was committed.

Intentional torts
A deliberate act (other than a breach of contract) that causes harm to another person.

Torts may also be based on absolute (or strict) liability, which is liability that exists regardless of whether the policyholder was negligent. The term strict liability is often used in regard to products liability claims. Agreement is lacking in the insurance and legal fields as to the proper use of the terms "strict liability" and "absolute liability." Some use the terms interchangeably. Others try to distinguish between the two and the situations to which they apply. A major distinction some use is that the term "absolute liability" implies that no defenses are available. Those who hold this view believe that some defenses to strict liability situations are available.

An adjuster investigating tort liability must know all of the elements of the tort(s) in question so that instances of tort liability can be recognized. Claimants are unlikely to say, "I have an action in negligence against your insured." Instead, they say, "I fell and was injured at your insured's store."

Crimes

Criminals are legally liable in civil courts to their victims. As noted, criminal acts are generally intentional, but that does not automatically mean they are not covered by insurance.

Anyone, including a convicted criminal, who seeks insurance coverage for a victim's claim is required by the insurance policy to cooperate with the insurer. Adjusters frequently find that convicted criminals are not cooperative even though they have a duty to be so. Those accused of crimes are often unable to cooperate with the adjuster if doing so will jeopardize their Fifth Amendment rights.

A convicted criminal's lack of cooperation may have little practical significance. A conviction is conclusive evidence that the crime was committed. Therefore, the criminal's cooperation would not help to defend the claim. An adjuster handling a claim filed against a convicted criminal must often concede liability, but not necessarily coverage.

In the case of an accused, the adjuster can usually wait until the criminal proceedings are concluded before demanding the insured's cooperation. Criminal court dockets generally move much faster than civil court dockets, so the insurer is generally not prejudiced by the adjuster's waiting.

Contractual Liability

A party who breaches a contract is legally liable to the other party to the contract. If such breach causes bodily injury or property damage, the breaching party's liability insurance may cover the claim. As noted earlier in this chapter, certain contractual obligations may be covered by liability insurance.

In cases of alleged breach of contract, the adjuster must thoroughly review the entire contract and understand all of its terms. The adjuster must investigate the policyholder's behavior to determine whether it constitutes a breach of the contract. Finally, the adjuster must investigate all potential contractual defenses. Did the claimant breach the contract first, thereby excusing further performance by the policyholder? Has a precondition for the policyholder's contractual obligations not occurred or not been met? Have the policyholder and the claimant substituted a newer contract for a previous one?

In cases of contractual hold harmless agreements and assumptions of liability, the adjuster must carefully scrutinize the contractual language to determine whether it applies to the situation in question. Courts read such agreements narrowly, and an adjuster should do so as well. For example, in many hold harmless agreements, the policyholder agrees to hold another harmless for claims that arise out of the policyholder's conduct. Should the situation in question involve negligence on the part of others, especially the party seeking protection under the agreement, the agreement may not apply. Courts may also invalidate contracts that are against public policy, that attempt to transfer liability for a nondelegable duty, or that contain ambiguous language.

Statutory Liability

Except for workers compensation, insurance is generally not designed to cover a policyholder's statutory obligations. (Workers compensation laws create an obligation for employers even when negligence is not an issue.) Nevertheless, should violation of a statute cause bodily injury or property damage, the policyholder's liability coverage may apply to a resulting claim. For example, violating a traffic law and injuring someone would be covered by auto liability insurance.

Not all statutory violations that cause bodily injury or property damage are covered by liability insurance. For example, intentionally dumping pollutants would be excluded. The adjuster handling a case involving an alleged violation of statutes must determine exactly what the statute requires, exactly what the policyholder did, and whether any exclusion in the insurance policy is applicable.

Vicarious Liability

Adjusters must frequently investigate the possibility of vicarious liability, which is liability imposed on a party because of that party's relationship to a wrongdoer. For example, employers may be liable for the acts of their employees, and principals may be responsible for their agents. Most claims against commercial policyholders involve vicarious liability because corporations are simply legal entities that act through human employees.

For adjusters, the most important issue with respect to vicarious liability is the scope of employment or agency. An employer is liable for the acts of its employees only while they are acting within the scope of their employment. For example, if an employee goes home and assaults a neighbor, the employer is not liable. Unfortunately for adjusters, cases in which the "scope of employment" issue arises are not so clear-cut. For example, employees often make brief deviations from their employer's business to attend to personal matters. Whether such a deviation occurred and when it ended are difficult questions. An adjuster handling such a situation must thoroughly investigate. Another difficult situation for determining scope of employment arises when an employee attempts to conduct the employer's business by prohibited means, such as driving at illegally high speeds from one appointment to another. Usually, the law deems these situations to be within the scope of employment. The adjuster handling such situations often faces difficulty because the employer may overstate the extent to which it made its rules and prohibitions known.

Defenses to Liability Claims

Adjusters are interested in possible defenses to any claim they handle. As they investigate liability, adjusters also investigate possible defenses. The most useful defenses are absence of negligence, comparative or contributory negligence, assumption of risk, and statute of limitations. Other available defenses, such as exculpatory notices and hold harmless agreements, are not discussed here because they are less commonly encountered.

Absence of Negligence

Strictly speaking, absence of negligence is not so much a defense as it is a failure to prove the claimant's case. Nevertheless, adjusters should consider absence of negligence as a possible defense. Many accidents occur through no fault of anyone. Claimants often assert claims based on the notion that the mere occurrence of the accident entitles them to compensation. For example, a claimant who twists an ankle while walking through undeveloped land may expect the owner to compensate him or her. Yet it is not due to the negligence of the owner that the surface of the undeveloped property is uneven. Nature does not provide smoothly paved walkways, and anyone walking through natural terrain cannot expect to find them. Another unfortunately common example is auto accidents involving child pedestrians who dart into traffic. In many of those situations, it would have been impossible for the driver to have seen or anticipated the child's behavior or to have stopped the car in time. Defending these cases requires careful preparation, however, because any hint of negligence on the driver's part might render the driver liable. Children involved in these cases are frequently under seven years old and are thus legally incapable of negligence.

Comparative or Contributory Negligence

Comparative or contributory negligence exists whenever a claimant's own fault contributes to causing his or her injuries. This situation is common. In the few states that recognize contributory negligence, any fault on the claimant's part completely bars the claimant from recovery. Under comparative negligence laws, the claimant's recovery is reduced in proportion to the claimant's share of fault. In other words, if a claimant's negligence is a 25 percent cause of the accident, the claimant's recovery is reduced by 25 percent. Under some comparative negligence laws, claimant fault in excess of 50 percent completely bars the claimant from recovery. However, in "pure" comparative negligence states, a claimant can be 99 percent at fault and still recover 1 percent of the damages.

Assumption of Risk

The assumption of risk defense applies whenever a claimant knows of a risk and voluntarily encounters that risk anyway. For the defense to be valid, the claimant's behavior must be both knowing and voluntary. Assumption of risk is frequently confused with comparative negligence. Although assuming a risk may be negligent in many specific circumstances, it is not necessarily negligent. For example, participating in sports such as downhill skiing includes an unavoidable risk of injury, but it is not negligent to participate. Knowing that risk, many people choose to participate anyway.

Statute of Limitations

Each state has enacted time limitations on the right to bring suit. The amount of time varies by state and by the type of legal claim; time limits can range from two to fifteen years, depending on the circumstances. Failure to file a suit within the allotted time waives any obligation on the part of the tortfeasor so that an expired statute of limitations can serve as an absolute defense.

Damages

Adjusters must determine and document damages before a claim can be settled. Doing so usually requires less legwork but takes more time than the investigation of liability. A liability investigation often concludes within days, whereas determining damages can take weeks, months, or longer. Adjusters usually rely on outside experts for damage information, such as doctors on bodily injury cases; appraisers, contractors, or repairers on property damage cases; and accountants or economists for determining financial factors.

Damages in bodily injury liability cases are usually proven with medical reports and bills, hospital records, and employer information. The adjuster must assemble this documentation throughout the time in which the claimant continues to receive treatment. Thus, settling an injury claim often does not occur until treatment is concluded or until a clear prognosis and course of future treatment are known. Damages in property damage cases are proven with estimates for repair or with actual bills for repair and rental. Most of this section concerns damages in bodily injury cases because those cases account for the majority of claim dollars spent in liability cases. The latter part of this section describes property damage cases and how they differ from first-party property damage claims.

Elements of Damage in Injury Claims

Adjusters must understand every element of damages for which the law provides compensation to investigate and document the claims properly. The claimant has the burden of proving the damages. Nevertheless, the adjuster should take the initiative in investigating them to remain aware of the nature and value of the claim.

Medical expenses include all bills incurred for emergency care, visits to doctors, surgery, hospitalization, drugs, medical equipment, nursing care, and medical transportation. Both medical expenses already incurred and future medical expenses that are reasonably expected and provable are allowable elements of damages.

Lost earnings for the period of time the claimant is disabled can also be recovered. If loss of earnings is expected to extend into the future, it too can be compensated. Future lost earnings may be expected for either a limited time or indefinitely and may be partial or total. A partial loss of earnings is likely to exist when a claimant has lost some of his or her ability to earn but also retains some of that ability. Total loss of earnings exists when the claimant is unable to perform any work.

The damages for medical expenses and loss of earnings are called out-of-pocket expenses, or special damages. Special damages are recoverable even if they do not actually come out of the claimant's pocket. Many claimants have health insurance and disability insurance that cover these items. Nevertheless, special damages are recoverable despite these other sources of payment. The principle of the law is that a claimant should not be penalized, nor should a wrongdoer be rewarded, because of the claimant's prudence in having insurance coverage. This principle is called the collateral source rule, a rule that is phrased in the negative: any collateral source is *not* to be considered when settling third-party claims. Many accident and health insurers have policy provisions that allow them to recover their payments from a tort recovery from the accident.

In addition to special damages, claimants can recover general damages. General damages are compensation for intangibles such as pain and suffering, and scarring or disfigurement. Special and general damages together are called "compensatory damages" and are the damages for which claimants are usually compensated.

If a claimant is married, the claimant's spouse can assert his or her own claim for loss of consortium. Consortium is the companionship, household services, and sexual relations one spouse provides the other. Depending on the liability policy wording, a claim for loss of consortium may involve a separate per-person policy limit, a circumstance that can be important in cases of serious injury.

Should a claimant die, two other types of claims are possible. In a survival action, the claimant's estate is able to assert whatever claim the deceased claimant had during his or her life. In other words, a bodily injury claim that the claimant could have asserted during his or her life may be asserted by the claimant's estate. The estate will be compensated for the same damages, special and general damages, but they do not continue to increase past the date of death. A survival action may be asserted even if the death is completely unrelated to the bodily injury.

If the bodily injuries cause death, the deceased's survivors may assert a wrongful death claim. A wrongful death claim belongs to the survivors, not to the deceased. It may be prosecuted by the administrator(s) of the deceased's estate, but the beneficiaries are the survivors. Laws vary by state as to who is an eligible beneficiary and how damages are measured. In general, damages in a wrongful death claim should compensate the beneficiary for the support and benefits formerly received from the deceased.

Evaluation of Special Damages

A liable party is not required to compensate a claimant for special damages that *might* be incurred. Certain rules and limitations exist.

Medical expenses must be related to the injury, necessary to heal the injury, and reasonable in amount. Although unrelated medical expenses should not be compensable, adjusters often have them submitted for payment. Many people who become claimants have preexisting medical conditions for which they were already or should have been receiving treatment. Bills for these treatments are often included with bills for accident-related treatment.

Medical treatment must be necessary to be compensated. Second-guessing the treating physician is not easy, but with a solid case, an insurer can avoid payment for unnecessary work.

Finally, medical treatment must be reasonable in amount and cost. Although insurers do not have any statutory, regulatory, or contractual controls over doctors and hospitals, they are neither required to reimburse a course of treatment nor pay bills that they can show are excessive.

Because adjusters lack the experience and expertise necessary to evaluate the necessity and frequency of medical treatment, insurers have begun to employ utilization review services. These services represent a recognized specialty within the medical field. By assessing medical treatment and bills, they are able to advise when a course of treatment is unnecessary, unrelated to the specific injury, or redundant with other treatment.

Lost wages must be established by verifying the extent and period of disability and the earnings of the claimant. The extent and period of disability are medical issues that must be addressed by doctors with reference to the physical demands of the claimant's job. A physician who expresses an opinion about disability without knowing the demands of the claimant's job cannot be reliable, unless the claimant's condition would disable the claimant from any work at all. The adjuster must usually rely on a doctor's written report to evaluate a claimant's disability. Should the adjuster doubt the alleged disability, the claimant can be examined by a physician of the adjuster's choosing. An independent medical exam can always be obtained when a case is in suit. If not, the claimant might consent. Those who refuse to consent should raise the adjuster's suspicions.

Earnings are easily verified for a claimant who receives a salary or works regular hours for wages. The claimant's employer can verify earnings, or the claimant's tax returns can be used as evidence. Earnings of self-employed claimants and claimants who own their own businesses are more difficult to determine. Tax returns can be helpful, but business conditions for such claimants change yearly. The issue in every case is what the claimant would have earned during the period of disability, not what was earned just prior. It may be necessary to contact customers and clients of the claimant or to hire an accountant to review the claimant's books. A businessowner's lost time is especially difficult to evaluate because the business can often carry on temporarily without the owner.

Evaluation of General Damages

General damages are highly subjective, but they are the largest, and thus most important, element of damages in injury claims. Adjusters, claimant attorneys, and claimants often do not agree about how to evaluate general damages. Nevertheless, they regularly negotiate and settle claims involving general damages.

Both sides of an injury claim face the same pressure. If they cannot agree with the other side on an amount to settle the claim, a jury or judge will eventually evaluate the case. For a claimant, the jury's evaluation may be less than the insurer was offering before trial. For an adjuster, the jury's evaluation may be more than the claimant was willing to accept before trial. The possibility of a relatively bad outcome at trial, in addition to the expense, effort, and trouble of a trial, is a powerful incentive for both sides to negotiate.

Assuming liability is unquestioned, general damages are generally considered to be several times as great as special damages. Some adjusters consider only medical expense (often referred to as "medical specials") in determining a multiple for general damages and then add in the unmultiplied amount of lost earnings. Other adjusters multiply all specials.

The multiple-of-specials approach to general damages is often condemned as inappropriate in most cases. It has no logical basis nor any "official" recognition in case law. Nevertheless, both claimant attorneys and adjusters widely practice it.

The nature of the injury is a significant factor in determining general damages. Pain and suffering, disability, and disruption of daily routine are considered as relatively more or less severe for various injuries. For example, a broken tibia (the weight-bearing bone of the lower leg) is widely regarded as worse than a broken wrist, even of the dominant hand. Likewise, scars on the face are widely considered worse than scars on the abdomen.

In ordinary cases, loss of consortium is not usually evaluated separately. It may be regarded as worth some fraction of the value of the underlying injury. In more serious cases, the loss of consortium may be significant and worth a separate evaluation. It is difficult to defend a claim for consortium unless there is a separation or divorce pending.

Property Damage

In some respects, determining damages in property damage liability cases is easier than in first-party claims. The adjuster need not worry about deductibles, special sublimits, coinsurance, or damage being caused by both covered and noncovered causes.

The law allows a deduction for depreciation from replacement cost. Determining depreciation can be as complex as it is in first-party claims. The adjuster must consider physical wear and tear; obsolescence because of fashion, seasonal, and technological changes; market value; and any other relevant factors. However, as in first-party claims, depreciation may be negligible, and a replacement cost settlement may be appropriate in many cases.

One important difference between first-party claims and property damage liability claims is that the property owner's own negligence is irrelevant in first-party claims, but it can be a major factor in settling liability claims. In contributory negligence jurisdictions, the owner's fault in causing the loss is a complete bar to recovery. In comparative negligence jurisdictions, the owner's fault reduces the recovery by a proportionate percentage or may even completely bar recovery.

A property damage claimant is in a relatively weaker bargaining position with the adjuster than a bodily injury claimant because of the smaller or more definite value of property damage claims and the expense of litigating them. Some restrictions on adjusters exploit this situation. For example, adjusters do not wish to incur unnecessary legal expense. If liability and value are clear, most adjusters prefer to pay the claim and close their file rather than litigate. Claim managers strongly discourage having a property damage claim go into suit, and such a suit would be closely scrutinized to see whether the adjuster had neglected to make legitimate settlement efforts. Furthermore, the Unfair Claims Settlement Practices Act, a version of which is in effect in most states, requires adjusters to attempt settlement when liability is reasonably clear and forbids stalling on the settlement of one claim to influence the settlement of another. This latter rule is especially applicable to auto accident cases in which the property damage claim may be ready for settlement while the bodily injury case is still a long way from being complete.

Many property damage liability cases first appear as subrogation claims from other insurers. The adjuster for the liability insurer should respond to the claim like an adjuster would respond to a claimant. Should the adjusters for the respective insurers be unable to negotiate a settlement, the claim may be resolved by intercompany arbitration. As mentioned in Chapter 14, the Property Subrogation Arbitration Agreement covers most first-party subrogation claims. The Nationwide Inter-Company Arbitration Agreement covers subrogation of auto physical damage claims. The arbitrators in these cases decide issues of both liability and damages, and their decision is not appealable. The vast majority of insurers in the United States subscribe to these agreements.

Negotiation and Settlement

Everything an adjuster does on a claim should be directed towards settlement. The vast majority of liability claims are settled without going into suit. The vast majority of claims that go into suit are settled before trial. Settling liability claims is the most valuable service liability claim adjusters perform for policyholders, claimants, insurers, and society. The courts would be overwhelmed if even a small percentage of cases that are settled were tried. It is also in the best interests of the insurers for adjusters to settle liability claims. Insurers would pay more in legal fees and verdict amounts than they would pay in settlements if they were to try all the claims that they could settle.

An insurer's obligation to settle claims arises out of its duty to defend and indemnify its insured. Both the insurer and the claimant face pressure to settle without litigation or trial. The negotiation process may seem like a game to outsiders, but failure has its repercussions. Once negotiations have been completed, claims can be settled in several ways.

Duty To Settle

Liability policies usually give insurers the right to settle claims, but they do not express a duty to settle because insurers may want to litigate a case to conclusion. The insurer must have the right to litigate in order to protect itself against frivolous, fraudulent, or unfounded claims. The threat that a claim may be litigated probably keeps many dubious claims from ever being asserted.

Adjusters tend to believe that settling claims is expedient and in the best interests of policyholders and claimants. However, a legal obligation to settle arises when the value of a liability claim approaches, or clearly exceeds, the insured's policy limit.

Policyholders buy liability insurance for peace of mind. Almost nothing disturbs that peace of mind as much as being party to a lawsuit and enduring a court trial. Even if they are ultimately successful, most people are unsettled by the experience of a trial. A settlement shields the insured from this experience. Indeed, a settlement protects the insured from even being sued. Policyholders generally want claims to be handled without troubling or involving them too much. Because settling is also in the best interest of the insurer, it seems to be the best option for all concerned.

When the value of a claim approaches or exceeds the insured's policy limit, making settlement becomes a legal obligation and is no longer just good judgment. The insurer, rather than the policyholder, controls the defense and settlement of a claim. If a verdict exceeds the insured's policy limit, however, the insured would have to pay the excess. This situation creates a potential conflict. Absent a duty to settle the claim and once the value of the claim approaches or exceeds the policy limit, the insurer has little to lose by trying the case to verdict. The insurer might be surprised by a low verdict. If not, the policyholder will end up paying everything over the policy limit.

To prevent insurers from exploiting this situation and gambling with the policyholder's fortunes, courts have required insurers to make reasonable efforts to settle within policy limits and to accept settlement offers within policy limits whenever the value of a claim exceeds the limits. An insurer that rejects a settlement offer within policy limits does so at its own risk. Although courts have not made insurers absolutely liable for excess verdicts following the rejection of a settlement, convincing a court that the excess verdict was unforeseeable after it has been rendered is difficult. If a court thinks an insurer unreasonably rejected settlement, it will probably hold the insurer responsible for the excess amount. This type of action against insurers is known as a **bad faith claim**.

Pressures To Negotiate

As mentioned, both sides to a claim are pressured to negotiate by the possibility of a worse outcome at trial. This pressure is probably felt more strongly by insurers than by claimants, except when claimants face a serious risk of a defense verdict.

Even claimants who face little chance of losing at trial overwhelmingly prefer to settle than to litigate. Indeed, the typical liability claimant probably underestimates his or her claim for settlement; claimants typically settle for less than they could reasonably expect after trial. This outcome is probably true because claimants are far less able than insurers to risk an adverse result and because claimant attorneys make much more money for their time by settling cases than by trying them.

For most liability claimants, a claim may be a once-in-a-lifetime event. The claimant's injury may be a major trauma for that person. Claimants make an enormous emotional investment in their claims and can be devastated by an adverse result at trial. An adverse result need not even be a complete loss, but simply a verdict amount much less than anticipated. In contrast, for insurers, each claim is just one more case or a piece of business to be disposed of as readily as possible. With such differing emotional investments, claimants and insurers will approach settlement differently. Claimants are generally much less willing to risk a bad result than are insurers.

Claimant attorneys and defense attorneys face similar professional pressures. It is almost always in their clients' best interests to settle. Yet to develop their professional skills and present a credible threat to the other side, they must gain trial experience. Trying cases, however, is enormously stressful. Juries are unpredictable, clients can be unforgiving, and professional reputations can be made or destroyed by a single case. In addition, during the course of a trial, the attorneys spend all day in court and then must return to their offices for a full day's work. It is no wonder that many attorneys seem eager to settle cases and that many so-called trial attorneys rarely try cases.

Adjusters are highly motivated to limit and control legal expense. Both claim department management and corporate management closely monitor legal expenses. Adjusters are reprimanded for allowing cases to go into suit unnecessarily and for failing to pursue settlement throughout the course of litigation.

Bad faith claim
Claim that implies or involves actual or constructive fraud, a design to mislead or deceive another, or a neglect or refusal to fulfill some good faith duty or some contractual good faith obligation.

Negotiation Strategies

In the settlement of a typical claim, negotiations begin with a demand by the claimant's attorney for a specific sum of money. The opening demand is usually a high evaluation of the case. The adjuster will sometimes make the opening settlement offer to "adjust" the attorney's expectations. Usually, however, the adjuster responds to the attorney's demand with a settlement offer that is a lower evaluation of the case. The attorney and the adjuster discuss the merits of their case and the weaknesses of the other side's case and exchange further counterdemands and counteroffers. If they believe they can settle, they continue to negotiate until they agree on a specific settlement amount. With an unrepresented claimant, the adjuster is much more likely to make the first settlement offer. Claimants are often bewildered by or uncomfortable with the negotiation process. Typically, adjusters must establish trust and should try to make realistic initial offers with unrepresented claimants. Thereafter, if the claimant and the adjuster believe they can agree on a settlement, they continue to discuss the case until they reach settlement.

Neither adjusters nor attorneys consider willingness to negotiate a weakness. Both sides know that the vast majority of cases settle. Anyone who avoids or refuses negotiations looks inexperienced or disorganized. Good negotiators can take strong positions and encourage the other side to continue the process.

Proper preparation and intelligent evaluation of a claim are essential prerequisites to good negotiating. Proper preparation consists of the adjuster's investigation and documentation of liability and damages. The final step of proper preparation is the adjuster's review of the file to ensure that he or she can discuss all aspects of the case. Simultaneously, the adjuster must evaluate the claim intelligently. The adjuster should determine both a good first offer and a probable range of settlement. Every adjuster can settle cases without consultation only up to a specified dollar limit. Beyond that limit, the adjuster must obtain settlement authority from higher level personnel. Requests for settlement authority are usually presented in writing and summarize the facts, the liability picture, the injuries, and the special damages.

Adjusters want to communicate several messages with their first offer and throughout the negotiation process. They want to communicate an intelligent evaluation of the case; nothing discredits an adjuster faster than being obviously unaware of the value of a claim. They also want to communicate their confidence in their position and their willingness to litigate the case. In this respect, both the adjuster and the insurer should have experience litigating cases. The adjuster must also be sure that a credible defense attorney is involved should the case already be in suit. Finally, it is important to communicate some flexibility in one's position. Undervaluing a case and being inflexible risk stalling the negotiations and incurring needless litigation expense. However, overly generous offers and concessions may make an opponent too optimistic and inflexible.

Most adjusters and attorneys negotiate cooperatively and constructively. Such a negotiation style is safe and effective. Nevertheless, this is not the only style

of negotiation. Some parties negotiate in a hostile, competitive, and belliger-
ent manner, which can also be effective but is much riskier. Hostile, competitive negotiating works when it destroys the confidence of an opponent or
extracts concessions from an opponent who wants to placate his or her
adversary. The danger of hostile negotiating is that it can destroy the negotiation process. Because both sides benefit from negotiated settlements, most
attorneys and adjusters prefer to avoid a hostile style.

Settlement Techniques

Most claims are settled with a general release, in which the claimant releases
the insured of all liability for the accident in question and the insurer agrees to
pay the claimant the agreed settlement amount. Other types of releases exist
to handle particular situations, such as those concerning joint tortfeasors and
minors. Those are discussed in Chapter 13 along with other settlement tools.

In cases of claims by married individuals, the claimant's spouse should also be
a party to the release to dispose of his or her consortium claim. In cases in
which suit has been filed, the settlement must include dismissal of the suit by
the claimant. This action can be taken by the claimant's attorney, who files a
simple notice in the court records that the case has been settled.

Claims are usually settled with a lump-sum payment. Sometimes, the settlement
instead calls for payments at both the time of settlement and into the future.
These are called **structured settlements**. Structured settlements are usually
made on high-value claims, but there is no minimum-size claim below which
they are inappropriate. Structured settlements are especially useful when the
claimant is likely to experience regular damages into the future, such as loss of
income, or when the claimant is likely to squander a large settlement. Experience shows that most claimants tend to squander large settlements.

Structured settlements are attractive to insurers because they enable them to
offer more dollars in the total settlement at a lower present cost than with a
lump-sum payment. This is true because insurers can fund their future obligations with annuities purchased from other insurers, usually life insurance
companies. The present cost of an annuity is less than what the annuity will
pay in the future.

Many insurers use **advance payments** to control claimants and to discourage
them from hiring attorneys. Advance payments are made as the claimant
incurs medical or other expenses. They are paid without receiving a release in
return, but the claimant must sign a receipt acknowledging payment and that
the advance payments will count towards final settlement.

Some insurers practice **walk-away settlements**, in which the insurer pays the
claimant a lump-sum settlement and takes no release. These settlements are
most appropriate in smaller claims. Insurers that advocate this practice
consider it excellent public relations, assertive claim handling, and encourage-
ment to claimants not to consider bringing suit. In cases in which the claimant does sue, the insurer is entitled to credit for what it has paid.

Structured settlement
An agreement in settlement of a
lawsuit involving specific
payments made over a period of
time. Property-casualty insurance
companies often buy life
insurance products to pay the
costs of such settlements.

Advance payment
A payment made by claim
representatives to insureds
following a loss to cover the
immediate expenses resulting
from the loss.

Walk-away settlement
A settlement that involves lump-
sum payments made by insurers
to settle claims. No release is
taken from the claimant.

Litigation

All liability claim adjusters should be familiar with litigation. Ultimately, courts will determine both liability and damages for any claim that is not settled. Claimants may have to go to court to obtain compensation. Insurers and adjusters must understand how courts operate and how courts balance the rights and interests of plaintiffs and defendants.

Defense of lawsuits is a significant aspect of the protection policyholders buy through liability insurance policies. Insurers have both the right and the duty to defend the policyholder. Adjusters must understand and properly handle this right and duty.

Civil procedure
The rules by which courts conduct civil trials. Civil trials concern the judicial resolution of claims by one individual or group against another.

The conduct of lawsuits is governed by **civil procedure**, that part of the law that establishes rules for litigation in civil cases. Adjusters must understand civil procedure to contribute to case strategy and to control defense attorney conduct.

Because attorney fees are a major expense for liability insurers, adjusters implement a variety of controls designed to moderate legal expense. Thus, adjusters must simultaneously make certain the insured is properly defended, develop strategy, direct litigation, and manage legal expense. Properly handling litigation is one of the most challenging tasks within claim work and one of the most important of any insurance jobs.

Role of Courts in Resolving Claims

Although the majority of claims are settled before suit is filed and the majority of suits are settled before trial, the courts play an essential role in settling claims. Without the courts, there would be no incentive to negotiate. Policyholders could not be held legally liable without a determination from the courts. Insurers would not be needed to protect policyholders without the threat of legal liability.

Nevertheless, courts are not fast, inexpensive, or predictable. Claimants who might otherwise rely on courts to determine their rights against policyholders have an incentive to negotiate. Claimants who do rely on courts find that they wait many years, spend considerable sums on legal expense, and often end up with a result no better than they could have achieved in settlement.

The psychological effects of litigation tend to mount as time goes by, thus increasing incentives to settle. Leading up to trial, the pace of depositions and motions usually increases. These pretrial matters place great stress on the parties and their attorneys and give everyone involved a taste of what trial will be like. Following pretrial efforts, many parties conclude that they would prefer a settlement for a definite amount, with relief from the aggravation and stress of litigation, to the difficulty and uncertain outcome of a trial.

The values that attorneys and adjusters place on cases are derived from actual results of cases litigated to conclusion. Cases that are litigated to conclusion therefore have important effects on all other cases. Although only a small percentage of cases are decided by court verdicts, those verdicts influence the price of all cases.

Duty To Defend

In addition to paying amounts for which the insured is legally liable (up to policy limits), insurance companies are also obligated to defend their policyholders against suits. This protection is a valuable aspect of liability insurance. In many cases, the insurance company's duty to defend is more important to the policyholder than the duty to indemnify. The insurance company may have to spend exorbitant amounts defending a case if the case cannot be settled.

Many cases take a long time and a great deal of effort to settle. Other cases cannot be settled at all and are concluded by a trial and verdict. In both of these types of cases, legal expense can be extraordinary. Thousands and then tens of thousands of dollars of legal expense can quickly accumulate on ordinary cases, such as auto accidents and premises liability claims. Complex cases can result in legal expenses well into six figures.

Cases can be difficult to settle because of unreasonableness on the part of plaintiffs or defendants. Plaintiffs may make settlement demands so unreasonably high that the insurer for the defendant is not even tempted to settle. Likewise, insurers can make settlement offers far below what the plaintiff is likely to win in a trial or can simply fail to evaluate a case meaningfully. (Usually, once a case is in suit, the defense attorney hired by the insurer will realistically evaluate the case, even if the claim adjuster has failed to do so.) Another type of suit that is difficult to settle involves cases of multiple codefendants, all of whom insist they have no liability and refuse to offer anything. Complete mutual refusal by a group of codefendants to offer any settlement can ruin negotiations, even in cases involving clearly innocent and severely injured plaintiffs. The better practice, in such cases, is for the defendants to work in concert to settle the plaintiff's claim and then to arbitrate or to negotiate their respective shares of liability for the settlement. Unfortunately, this rational approach is often difficult to adopt because of the number of claim adjusters and attorneys involved.

The insurer's duty to defend is especially important in cases that are frivolous, fraudulent, or without merit. Absent the insurer's duty to defend, plaintiffs would be in a strong position to coerce settlements from defendants who lack the resources or the ability to resist lawsuits. In claims involving insurance coverage, plaintiffs face an opponent with tremendous resources and experience in defending lawsuits: the insurance company. When insurers defend frivolous suits to a verdict, they spend far more on defense than on indemnification of the claim. When insurers settle frivolous suits, they usually do so because settling saves an equal or a greater amount of legal expense.

The insurer's duty to defend is also its right. The insurer can select the defense attorney, and the insured is then obligated to cooperate with whichever attorney is chosen. As long as it is solely liable for the claim, the insurer can dictate defense strategy. The insurer can unilaterally decide to settle or to continue the defense of a claim. Although the defense attorney is professionally obligated to serve the insured's interests above all, the insurer pays the defense attorney and thus can dictate all defense decisions. As long as the insured is not financially exposed to the claim, the defense attorney will take direction from the insurer. Taking direction from the insurer in this situation does not compromise the insured's interest, as long as the defense attorney is not involved in matters in which the insured and insurer may be adverse, such as a coverage issue. Defense attorneys hired to defend the insured should never be used to advise the insurer on coverage in the same case.

The insurer's right and duty to defend lawsuits is complicated in cases in which coverage is doubtful or in which part of the case is clearly not covered. The general rule is that an insurer must provide defense to an *entire* claim whenever a plaintiff's allegations in *any part* of the claim are covered. Coverage applies according to the plaintiff's allegations, not according to the merits of the case. Otherwise, policyholders would be without coverage when they need it the most—when faced with unfounded claims. However, plaintiffs often assert claims that are clearly not covered (such as intentional wrongdoing) in the same lawsuit as claims that are covered (such as ordinary negligence) or assert claims that may not be covered at all (for example, a case in which it is doubtful whether the injury or damage occurred during the policy period). In these cases, the insurer must defend the entire lawsuit, but the policyholder has a right to involve an attorney of the policyholder's choosing at the policyholder's expense. When two attorneys are involved in the defense, the attorney selected by the insurer will have the right to control the case as long as the insurer's money is at stake. The insurance company's attorney will attempt to involve and get the approval of the policyholder's private counsel in all major decisions. Should the insurance company's attorney ever disagree with the policyholder's private attorney, the insurer is likely to be financially responsible for any consequences.

Civil Procedure

Court cases proceed according to rules of civil procedure. Although details may vary somewhat by state and county, the basic framework of civil procedure is the same throughout the United States. The principal stages of a lawsuit are pleadings, discovery, motions, trial, and appeal.

Pleadings

The **pleadings** are papers filed with the court clerk in which each side tells its story. A lawsuit is initiated with either a **summons**, a simple notice to the defendant that suit has been filed, or a **complaint**, a listing of allegations in which the plaintiff sets forth his or her case. Jurisdictions vary as to the extent of detail required in a complaint, but in all jurisdictions a complaint must notify the defendant of the nature of the case. Within a specified time, usually twenty or thirty days, the defendant must file an **answer** in which the defendant responds to each of the plaintiff's allegations and may raise affirmative defenses. The defendant may join additional defendants by filing

---

Pleadings
Formal written statements of the facts and claims of each side in a lawsuit.

Summons
A legal document issued by the clerk of court requiring the sheriff or other officer to notify the person named that an action has commenced against him or her and that he or she must answer the complaint.

Complaint
A document listing what the defendant has done to harm the plaintiff and the amount of money the plaintiff wants to recover.

Answer
A document that provides the defendant's initial response and defenses to the complaint.

a cross-complaint in the same manner that the plaintiff filed and served the initial complaint against other parties who may be ultimately responsible for the defendant's cause of action. Additional defendants must file an answer to the cross-complaint. The initial pleadings that join a party to a suit, whether a summons, complaint, or cross-complaint, are served on the party (usually personally) by a court officer called the "sheriff." Sheriffs' deputies may likewise serve court papers. In the federal courts, this task is performed by U.S. marshals. Thereafter, court rules usually allow papers to be served by private parties or through the mail.

Discovery

Once all parties have filed their pleadings, the issues in a case are clear, and discovery can begin. **Discovery** is the formal process by which each party obtains the evidence and information known to the other parties. Discovery may be by written **interrogatories**, a series of questions the other party must answer in writing; by **deposition**, a session of oral questions and answers that are recorded by a court reporter; by requests for documents, whenever documentary evidence is at issue; or by requests for admission, written statements that the receiving party must either accept or dispute. Because depositions are the most expensive and time-consuming form of discovery, most attorneys prefer to use first the other forms of discovery to narrow the issues. Nevertheless, depositions are usually essential to the preparation of a case. Discovery may also include a right of inspection, whenever the physical makeup of an object or a place is important in a case, or a right of independent medical examination, whenever a party's health and physical condition are at issue. Once all discovery is complete, each side should thoroughly know the opposing side's case and what evidence the opposing side will use at trial.

Motions

Motions are not really a distinct phase of litigation, because they can occur at any point from the initiation of suit to the appeal. A **motion** is a formal request to the court for a decision or ruling. A motion can be narrow and specific, such as a request to the court to allow or disallow a specific item of discovery, or comprehensive, such as a request to the court to terminate the suit in favor of the moving party. An example of the latter is a **motion for summary judgment**, in which the moving party asks the court to decide the case in its favor, usually after only pleadings or discovery has been completed and before trial. A motion for summary judgment is essentially an argument that there are no real issues in the case and that, as a matter of law, the moving party is entitled to judgment.

Trial

Barring summary judgment or a settlement, a case goes to trial. At **trial**, each side presents its evidence and has the opportunity to cross-examine and counter the evidence of the other side. The trier of fact, either a judge or a jury, decides which party's case is more persuasive and renders a verdict

Discovery
The exchange of all relevant information between the plaintiff and defendant before the trial.

Interrogatories
Specific written questions or requests that the opposing party must answer in writing.

Deposition
The recorded and transcribed testimony of a witness obtained through oral questions or written interrogatories that is used in preparation for a lawsuit.

Motion
Formal requests for a court to take a particular action.

Motion for summary judgment
A pretrial request to enter a judgment when no material facts are in dispute.

Trial
A formal judicial examination of evidence and determination of legal claims in a court of jurisdiction.

accordingly. When a case is decided by jury, the judge explains to the jury the relevant law and explains what factual issues the jury must resolve.

Appeal

Appeal
A request to a higher court to overturn the trial decision made by a lower court.

Following a verdict, the losing party can file an appeal. An **appeal** is a request to a higher court to overturn the trial decision. On appeal, the case is *not* heard again in its entirety. Only alleged errors of law, not issues of fact, may be argued on appeal. Examples of errors of law would be that inadmissible evidence was admitted or that the trial judge misstated the law to the jury. Occasionally, on appeal a party will ask the higher court to change the law or announce new law. Courts have the inherent power to change, add to, or interpret the law. Thus, the common law evolves. Common law is court-made law, as opposed to statutory law, which is enacted by legislatures. Because appeals can succeed only in cases of legal error, most trial verdicts are not appealed. The trial marks the end of most cases.

Control of Legal Expense

The defense of liability lawsuits is tremendously expensive. Consequently, insurers are extremely sensitive to legal expense and have adopted a number of strategies to control it. Adjusters are responsible for implementing and enforcing those strategies.

Most claim departments use only certain preapproved law firms to defend liability suits. Those law firms usually specialize in insurance defense work and are familiar with the types of cases insurance companies have and their needs. In exchange for a volume of business, such law firms usually work at a somewhat lower hourly rate than other attorneys and law firms with comparable skills and experience.

Claim departments usually require monthly or quarterly bills on active cases. These bills must be broken down by tenth of an hour or quarter-hour segments and must show exactly which attorney did what work in the time billed. Adjusters or specialized legal auditing firms can check these detailed bills against the actual file and the attorney's original time sheets to verify all charges.

Many claim departments require law firms to submit budgets for each case or quote a fixed price for the entire case. Sometimes fixed prices can be established for predictable work, such as completing pleadings (such as the complaint and answer in a lawsuit) or conducting a deposition. Many claim departments require adjusters to preapprove all depositions or motions. Adjusters must have a sophisticated understanding of trial evidence and strategy to exert such controls in a way that does not jeopardize the defense.

Ultimately, the best control of legal expense is complete avoidance of the legal process. Adjusters should settle cases that can be settled before they go into suit or before discovery and trial have caused enormous expenses to accumulate.

Alternative Dispute Resolution

For various reasons, potential litigants are often unable to resolve their disputes without the assistance of a third party. Traditionally, the courts were used in this role to resolve conflicts. The rising costs of allowing the courts to decide these cases and the enormous backlog of cases in the court system have caused potential litigants to search for alternative ways of resolving their disputes. Alternative dispute resolution (ADR) is an all-encompassing term used to refer to any number of methods for settling claims outside the traditional court system. The most common ADR forums are negotiation, mediation, arbitration, appraisals, mini-trials, and pre-trial settlement conferences. The courts have recently annexed some of these forums as a way of relieving the backlog of cases in the court system.

The most effective way of controlling litigation expenses is to resolve the dispute before litigation. Negotiation is the principal form of resolving claims outside litigation. **Negotiation** involves discussing all issues and arriving at a mutually satisfactory disposition of the case. Litigation is sometimes the sign of a poorly functioning negotiation process. Because of improper training or supervision, a claim representative might make inadequate offers to claimants. Claimant attorneys might also abuse the legal system by filing frivolous lawsuits in the hope of receiving a settlement because of the sheer "nuisance value" of the claim. Claim supervisors and managers should monitor the negotiation process to ensure that it is working properly. If the parties in dispute have acted in good faith, they should have fully explored the possibilities of resolution by direct negotiation before commencing a lawsuit.

Negotiation
Voluntary communication between two or more people to resolve differences and reach an agreement.

When direct negotiations fail, disputants may turn to mediation. **Mediation** can be considered a negotiation conference with a referee, called a mediator. In mediation, the parties in dispute present their case to the mediator, whose role is to facilitate an amicable resolution. The mediator will listen to each side present its case, point out the weaknesses in the arguments or in the evidence presented, propose alternative solutions, and help improve the relationship between the participants. The mediator does not normally decide the case for the parties but instead assists the parties in reaching a mutually agreed settlement. The fact that both sides must agree with the ultimate outcome makes mediation an attractive choice for disputants. The downside to mediation is that disputes sometimes do not get resolved. The opposing parties must then, after investing time and money in mediation, consider some other ADR forum or litigation.

Mediation
A negotiation process in which a neutral outside party helps participants examine the issues and develop a mutually agreeable settlement.

In **arbitration**, the participants present their cases to a disinterested third party (the arbitrator) who acts as a judge (and in many cases is an active or a retired judge) in weighing the facts presented and making a decision based on the evidence. The advantage of arbitration is that a decision is made. Whether the participants must accept this decision depends on the type of arbitration agreement the parties entered into. Binding arbitration requires the participants to accept the arbitrator's decision. In nonbinding arbitration, neither party is compelled to accept the decision of the arbitrator. However, the

Arbitration
A process in which the parties in a dispute agree to submit their controversy to a private body that will make a decision that can be final and binding.

arbitrator's decision provides the "winner" with leverage in future negotiations. Arbitration Forums, Inc., is one well-known national organization that insurance companies use to resolve intercompany disputes. Its most popular forum is the Nationwide Inter-Company Arbitration Agreement, which is used to resolve automobile subrogation claims.

Appraisals are a unique form of ADR. (They should not be confused with the damage estimates of an automobile or a property damage appraiser.) An appraisal, in this context, is a method of resolving disputes between insurance companies and their policyholders. The process of the appraisal and its scope are specifically described in the policy. Exhibit 15-1 shows the appraisal provision from the ISO HO-3 policy. The appraisal provision is designed to resolve disputes over the *amount owed* on a covered loss, but it is not used to determine whether coverage exists.

Appraisals
A policy condition used to settle disputes between insurers and insureds over the amount owed on a covered loss.

Mini-trials or **summary jury trials** closely resemble the traditional legal system in that representatives (usually attorneys) present an abbreviated version of their case to a jury. The decision of the jury can be binding or nonbinding, depending on the agreement. The rules of evidence and procedure law will normally coincide with that of traditional courts. Critics argue that little cost saving is achieved with this forum. The main advantage is that the litigants do not have to wait months or years to have their cases heard.

Mini-trials (summary jury trials)
Abbreviated versions of cases that allow parties to present evidence and arguments to a panel or an advisor. The advisor has no authority to make a binding decision but can pose questions and offer an opinion on the outcome of a trial based on the evidence.

A **pre-trial settlement conference** is an ADR forum that almost all states now require. The conferences are sanctioned by the court and are normally conducted by the judge who is presiding over the case. In these cases, a lawsuit has already been filed. The purpose of the settlement conference is to force litigants to make one last effort to resolve the case in lieu of going to trial. The judge's role is similar to that of a mediator, but sometimes the judge will subtly express to the litigants his or her opinion of their positions.

Pre-trial settlement conference
A meeting of the judge and the parties' lawyers in a judge's chamber two or three weeks before the trial to narrow the issues to be tried, to stipulate the issues and evidence to be presented at trial, and to help in settling the case.

CHALLENGES FACING SPECIFIC TYPES OF LIABILITY CLAIMS

The adjuster's general duties to investigate; to determine coverage, liability, and damages; and to settle are present in all liability claims. The challenges that exist in performing these duties vary by claim. General principles of liability and damages apply somewhat differently to different factual settings.

The remainder of this chapter describes the challenges that exist in various types of liability claims. This section first addresses auto bodily injury and auto physical damage, the two most common liability claims. It then discusses claims arising out of premises, operations, and products, the situations typically covered by general liability insurance. This section concludes by addressing the specialized areas of workers compensation claims, professional liability claims, and environmental and toxic tort claims.

EXHIBIT 15-1

Appraisal Provision From ISO HO-3 Policy

Appraisal. If you and we fail to agree on the amount of loss, either may demand an appraisal of the loss. In this event, each party will choose a competent appraiser within 20 days after receiving a written request from the other. The two appraisers will choose an umpire. If they cannot agree upon an umpire within 15 days, you or we may request that the choice be made by a judge of a court of record in the state where the "residence premises" is located. The appraisers will separately set the amount of loss. If the appraisers submit a written report of an agreement to us, the amount agreed upon will be the amount of loss. If they fail to agree, they will submit their differences to the umpire. A decision agreed to by any two will set the amount of loss.

Each party will:

a. Pay its own appraiser; and

b. Bear the other expenses of the appraisal and umpire equally.

Copyright, Insurance Services Office, Inc., 1999.

Auto Bodily Injury

Auto accidents are the most common type of liability claim. Nevertheless, auto accidents can cause some of the worst injuries and most expensive claims. New adjusters begin in auto claims because, fortunately, there are a majority of relatively minor claims and because the liability principles are so well known.

Although auto claims are a traditional training ground for liability adjusters, auto claims can be complicated in regard to coverage; accident reconstruction; and coordination with no-fault, workers compensation, and uninsured motorists claims.

Coverage Problems

Analysis of coverage is simple only when the accident involves the named insured as the driver and a vehicle specifically listed on the policy. More complicated are situations in which the named insured, or some other insured, has coverage while driving a vehicle not listed on the policy or when someone other than the named insured is using a covered vehicle.

Usually, when an insured is driving the vehicle of another, that other vehicle's coverage covers any loss. However, the other vehicle's coverage sometimes does not apply or is inadequate. In the event of the insolvency of the vehicle's insurance company or the exclusion of coverage for any reason, the insurance company for the driver must be prepared to take over the claim. Adjusters who "inherit" cases under these circumstances often find the investigation and other management of the case completely absent.

Inadequate policy limits are more common than the inapplicability of the vehicle's coverage. The adjuster working for the driver's insurer may adopt different strategies, depending on the circumstances. If the underlying coverage is far less than the value of the case, the adjuster for the driver's insurer should become heavily involved in the case or should take over its handling. If the underlying coverage is adequate to pay the claim, the adjuster for the driver's insurer is likely to take a less active role.

Accident Reconstruction

The facts of most auto accidents are not difficult to ascertain. The points of impact on each vehicle indicate at what angle and from what direction the two vehicles came into contact. The extent of damage to the vehicles provides some indication of the speeds of the vehicles. The parties to an accident usually differ more over how blameworthy they think each party is than over what happened. Fortunately for adjusters, clear right-of-way rules apply when two vehicles converge on the roads. Also, whenever the parties disagree about what happened, adjusters or accident reconstruction experts may be able to determine the facts.

Accident reconstruction experts are most helpful in determining the speed of a vehicle and what a driver should have been able to see at the time of an accident.

Vehicle speed is determined by examining skid marks and vehicle damage. Skid marks are reliable indicators of speed because once the brakes are locked, vehicles will stop according to their weight, the road grade, the road surface, and speed. All of these factors except speed are known or can be precisely measured following an accident. When, instead of coming to a complete halt, a vehicle collides with another vehicle, an accident reconstruction expert can determine that the vehicle was traveling no slower than a certain speed based on the skid marks. This information may be sufficient to disprove a party's statements or to establish liability. The point at which skid marks begin can establish when and where the driver first reacted to a danger, an essential piece of evidence when driver inattention is an issue.

Accident reconstruction experts can also determine what a driver should have been able to see just before impact. The exact time of day and weather conditions at the time of the accident can usually be established. The driver's lines of sight can be determined according to the type of vehicle and the height of the driver. The effects on visibility of curves or hills in the roadway are also considered. All of this information can be combined to determine whether a driver reacted promptly to a hazard or was slow and inattentive. That determination is essential in cases in which the driver alleges a sudden and unavoidable emergency or in which the claimant's comparative negligence is at issue. Comparative negligence is frequently an important issue in auto accident cases. In many cases, the policyholder may be primarily at fault, but the claimant is also substantially negligent for failing to respond to a hazard.

Coordination With No-Fault and Workers Compensation

An adjuster handling auto liability claims must frequently deal with other insurers that provide no-fault or workers compensation benefits to an injured claimant. The presence of another insurer can be either helpful or problematic to a liability claim adjuster.

Another insurer can provide the adjuster with detailed medical information. The adjuster can stay abreast of the claimant's injuries to be sure that the liability claim reserves for the case are adequate. The other insurer may provide medical information because it has a subrogation claim for the amount of the medical expense. In jurisdictions in which subrogation is possible, the other insurer is obligated to submit medical information to support its claim.

Difficulties may arise between the adjuster and the other insurer whenever subrogation rights do not exist or comparative negligence is an important issue. In the absence of subrogation rights, the other insurer should not turn over to the adjuster any medical information about the claimant without an authorization. Eventually, the claimant must reveal medical information to the adjuster, but the claimant is likely to want control over any such release. As a professional courtesy, another adjuster may be willing to comment on the adequacy of the liability claim reserves, but the other adjuster might be accused of invading the claimant's privacy should any medical information be revealed.

Uninsured Motorists Claims

Policyholders purchase uninsured motorists (UM) coverage to protect themselves against motorists who fail to carry liability insurance. An awkward aspect of the coverage is that the policyholder must be treated in the same manner as a claimant; the uninsured motorist is often an unavailable and uncooperative party who must be treated like an "insured." Denying a claim under uninsured motorists coverage might have immediate legal ramifications for the insurer that would not be present if the claimant were a third-party.

Attorney representation in an uninsured motorists claim is almost inevitable in many parts of the country. Once policyholders realize the opposing driver is uninsured, they assume that legal representation is essential. Unfortunately, dealing with the policyholder as a claimant leaves the adjuster with no favorable witness. The uninsured party is usually unavailable or uncooperative. A person who drives without insurance or causes hit-and-run accidents is usually not a credible witness, even if he or she is available and cooperative. Thus, uninsured motorists cases are extremely difficult to defend with respect to liability or on the basis of comparative negligence.

The adjuster has limited powers to defend uninsured motorists claims. In the event of any disagreement over the settlement amount, the policyholder can compel an arbitration. The arbitration is less expensive and time-consuming than litigation in the courts. Furthermore, arbitrators selected for these proceedings are usually attorneys who are aware that the claim involves the policyholder versus the insurance company. Arbitrators tend to give the policyholder the benefit of every doubt. Unfortunately, most adjusters believe that fraud and exaggeration are at least as common in uninsured motorists claims as they are in third-party liability claims.

In many states, purchase of uninsured motorists coverage is required in order to meet state financial responsibility laws. As is the case with any statutorily required coverage, the claim representative must be aware that some exclusions and other policy provisions might contradict the statutes. Courts have ruled that whenever policy language and state law conflict, state law controls. For example, in some states requiring uninsured motorists coverage for every vehicle, courts take the position that policyholders should be entitled to stack the limits of liability. Thus, if an insured has three cars with $100,000 uninsured motorists coverage on each, then the insured would be entitled to a total of $300,000 coverage despite the fact that this was not permitted by policy wording. Claim representatives must therefore be familiar with any state laws that might affect the coverage interpretation of the claims they are handling.

Underinsured Motorists Coverage

Uninsured motorists coverage rarely applies to claims in which the responsible motorist has some liability insurance coverage, even if that coverage is woefully inadequate. Because states' minimum liability limit requirements have not kept pace with rising medical costs, insurance companies have offered underinsured motorists (UIM) coverage to help counter that problem. The ISO Underinsured Motorists Coverage endorsement PP 03 11 defines an "Underinsured motor vehicle" as "a land motor vehicle or trailer of any type to which a bodily injury liability bond or policy applies at the time of the accident but its limit for bodily injury liability is less than the limit of liability for this coverage."

The following provides an example of an underinsured motorist:

- Allen, a policyholder for Company A, has a $100,000 UIM policy. He is involved in an accident with Bob, a policyholder for Company B.
- Bob, who is responsible for the accident, has a $25,000 bodily injury limit on his PAP.
- Bob's motor vehicle would be considered "underinsured" with respect to Allen's UIM policy.

Using the same scenario, the following explains how UIM coverage applies in most states:

- Allen suffers bodily injury with $200,000 in damages.
- Allen collects $25,000, the bodily injury limit, from Bob's policy.
- The ISO UIM endorsement limits coverage by the following provision, ". . .the limit of liability shall be reduced by all sums paid because of the 'bodily injury' by or on behalf of persons or organization who may be

legally responsible. . . ." So, Allen is entitled to $75,000 from his own UIM coverage (Allen's $100,000 UIM limit *minus* Bob's $25,000 bodily injury limit).

The purpose of the UIM coverage is to guarantee the policyholder a specific limit of protection (in this example, $100,000). In this scenario, Allen would be left uncompensated for his damages over $100,000. For that reason, courts in some states have construed the policy wording differently to provide additional coverage above the liability limit collected from the responsible party's insurance policy. Courts that take this alternative view might find a total of $125,000 in compensation for Allen's injuries (Allen's $100,000 UIM limit *plus* Bob's $25,000 bodily injury limit).

Auto Physical Damage

Auto physical damage claims are not like liability injury claims, even when they are asserted by third parties. Many auto physical damage claims are, in any case, first-party claims. Claim departments usually have auto damage specialists handling auto damage claims. Determining damage in auto damage cases requires expert knowledge of auto body repair methods and costs.

Proper handling of auto damage cases is an essential part of good relations with both policyholders and third parties. Calculating constructive total losses correctly and obtaining agreed repair prices are key tasks in the proper adjustment of auto damage claims.

First-Party Claims

Proper handling of first-party auto damage claims is one of the most fundamental and important services insurers provide to their policyholders. Cars represent a significant investment without which the policyholder may have difficulty commuting to work or satisfying family needs.

Adjusters who handle first-party auto damage claims should contact the policyholder and arrange to inspect the vehicle promptly, explain the complete procedure, and remain in contact with the policyholder throughout the claim process should any problems develop. The adjuster should not require the policyholder to pursue a liability claim against another party who may be liable for the damage. Should the insurer successfully subrogate against a responsible party, the policyholder's deductible amount should be reimbursed promptly.

Policyholders are sometimes upset to learn that personal property lost when their car has been stolen is not covered by their auto insurance. Adjusters should cite the language of the policyholder's auto and homeowners policies to explain the proper source of recovery. Policyholders are usually unhappy about absorbing two deductibles, especially when both coverages are through the same insurer.

Auto thefts represent a significant percentage of all claims that are questionable. A claim denial can be made only upon proof that the policyholder had the motive and opportunity to stage the claim or upon proof that the policy-holder still has the car. Adjusters who handle auto damage claims must guard against excessive suspiciousness. Real thefts of autos are more common than staged thefts.

Liability Claims

Adjusters handling third-party auto damage claims are much less prone to policy provisions and state insurance regulations dictating how they must act than when dealing with first-party claims. In addition, in liability claims, the adjuster can argue comparative negligence. Thus, although adjusters should handle first-party claims with a primary emphasis on customer service, they can adopt a more critical attitude on liability claims, should it be necessary.

Nevertheless, good reasons often exist to provide good service to liability claimants. If the claimant is injured, prompt, courteous service in handling the auto damage may prevent a bodily injury claim from being asserted. In cases in which the claimant is not injured, the law may require the adjuster to negotiate with the claimant. Although the law is not as solicitous of claimants as it is of insureds, adjusters cannot completely ignore the claimant when liability is clear. An adjuster is permitted to make good faith comparative negligence arguments but should be willing to negotiate with claimants.

Constructive Total Losses

Constructive total loss
A loss that occurs when the cost to repair damaged property plus its remaining salvage value equals or exceeds the property's pre-loss value.

When the cost to repair a vehicle plus its remaining salvage value equals or exceeds the vehicle's pre-loss value, the vehicle is a **constructive total loss**. It is financially senseless to repair a constructive total loss, even if it is physically possible to make satisfactory repairs. By paying the pre-loss value of the vehicle and taking the salvage, the insurer pays less overall. For example, assume a car worth $3,500 before loss suffers $3,000 of damage and retains $1,000 of salvage value. Rather than pay $3,000 for repairs, the insurer should pay $3,500 for the title to the car and obtain $1,000 in the salvage market, for a net loss of $2,500. Insurers have frequent contact with salvage dealers and are in a better position to dispose of salvage efficiently than is the average person.

Neither policyholders nor claimants are required to "sell" their cars to insurers, as the preceding example implies. Should the insured want to keep the car, the adjuster is entitled to take account of the salvage value. For example, using the numbers above, the actual cash value of the vehicle before loss ($3,500) minus the ACV of the vehicle following loss ($1,000) equals the amount of the loss ($2,500).

Agreed Repair Prices

If a vehicle can be repaired, the adjuster should obtain an agreed repair price with the body shop selected by the policyholder (or claimant). This agreement demonstrates that the adjuster's evaluation of the loss is legitimate and prevents disputes between the insurer and the auto owner or between the owner and the body shop. Although the adjuster should try to reach an agreed price, the choice of a body shop should be left to the vehicle owner.

Premises Liability

Businesses that regularly have members of the public on their premises, such as retail stores, restaurants, banks, and hotels, probably experience more premises claims than any other type of claim. Premises liability claims are usually relatively minor fall-down cases but are nevertheless important to both the claimant and the policyholder. Responsive handling of such claims can reduce their cost to the insurer and can preserve goodwill towards the policyholder.

Adjusters handling premises cases must establish good rapport with the claimant, both to establish the cause of the accident and to determine comparative negligence. Witnesses and employees of the policyholder can often help the adjuster in these efforts.

Determining Cause of Accident

Legal liability in premises cases is determined by negligence theories. The claimant asserts that the policyholder failed to maintain the premises in a reasonably safe condition. Under the law of negligence, the policyholder should be judged by how a reasonably prudent person would behave under the same circumstances.

The standard of care for property owners is traditionally qualified by the claimant's status on the premises. An owner owes only slight care towards a trespasser, primarily a duty not to intentionally injure. An intermediate level of care is owed to licensees, a group that includes social guests, letter carriers, and solicitors. A property owner owes a high duty of care towards business invitees, those who are on the premises at the invitation of the owner to do business with the owner. This group includes the customers of the various businesses that regularly have members of the public on their premises. Some jurisdictions have moved away from this classification scheme, requiring instead that reasonable care is the duty owed to all. Nevertheless, in substance, the law of these jurisdictions may differ little from the traditional classifications. What is "reasonable" in each situation largely depends on the claimant's status on the property.

Upon learning that a customer has had an accident on the premises, most policyholders are genuinely solicitous of the injured person, out of both human decency and a sense of self-protection. Most policyholders want to preserve their customers' goodwill and forestall possible legal actions against them. Injuries to pride and dignity are as common as bodily injuries, and policyholders find that injured customers respond well to genuine concern. Some policyholders in these circumstances will insist that the customer be seen by a doctor and will promise to pay whatever medical expense is incurred. Policyholders that take this approach should have medical payments coverage. Medical payments coverage is usually obtained for exactly this situation: taking care of a customer without regard for liability. Policyholders that do not have medical payments coverage probably violate their liability insurance policy conditions by making promises of payment, yet such promises do not usually cause trouble with insurers. If doing so will settle the case, adjusters are usually willing to pay for minor medical expense, regardless of fault, under liability coverage.

Maintaining rapport with claimants in premises cases is important. A dissatisfied claimant who seeks legal representation will usually cost much more to settle with. Thus, most adjusters handling premises claims do not push liability issues if a case can be settled for medical expenses only.

When premises cases cannot be quickly and easily settled, liability issues are important. In the case of business invitees, the policyholder owes a high duty of care. Thus, almost any factor in the environment of the insured premises contributing to the accident could indicate negligence on the policyholder's part. The floor may be uneven, slightly defective, or too slippery. The lighting may be insufficient or the environment too distracting. The policyholder may have failed to warn the public of a hazard or to barricade the hazard. The policyholder may have failed to conduct sufficient inspections of the premises to be aware of a new hazard. Sometimes (but rarely) claimants fall down on smooth, even, dry, clear, well-lit, and unobstructed surfaces. Usually, the claimant can blame something for the accident.

Adjusters investigating premises cases should solicit statements from the claimant and all witnesses who can testify about either the accident or the condition of the accident scene. If the scene is substantially the same as when the accident occurred, the adjuster should take photos. The adjuster should also determine the policyholder's cleaning, maintenance, and inspection practices and should get copies of any logs or records of such. Should the policyholder use an independent contractor for cleaning or maintenance work, the adjuster should determine the scope of that contractor's duties, obtain copies of the contracts, and determine what role in the accident the contractor may have played.

Determining Comparative Negligence

With respect to liability for their accident, claimants in premises cases are often in a difficult position. Unless their accident was caused by a hidden hazard, claimants must usually admit that (1) they have no idea what caused their accident; (2) they know the cause, but failed to observe and avoid it; or (3) they were aware of and observed the cause before the accident but encountered it anyway. With respect to liability, these three alternatives amount to (1) no negligence on the policyholder's part; (2) comparative negligence on the claimant's part; or (3) assumption of the risk by the claimant. A common example of the first situation is a fall down smooth, even, well-lit stairs. Most policyholders that have the public on their premises maintain their stairways well, and a fall on the stairs is usually the claimant's fault. An example of the second situation is a claimant who falls on an obvious hazard, such as debris on the floor. The defense of claims of this sort is weaker whenever something in the environment, such as a sales display, was a conspicuous distraction or whenever the policyholder should have known of the hazard and eliminated it before the accident. An example of the third situation is a claimant who voluntarily walks across an obvious hazard, such as a torn-up or an icy sidewalk. The defense of this third situation will be weakened if the claimant had no choice. The assumption of risk defense cannot be applied unless the claimant acted voluntarily.

The adjuster handling a premises case should get the claimant's statement as soon as possible. Immediately following an accident, a claimant is usually eager to talk about it and will often give candid statements that may suggest one of the preceding three defenses.

Operations

With respect to the liability theories and defenses that apply, claims arising out of a policyholder's operations are similar to premises cases. The key difference is that operations claims usually focus on an unsafe act rather than an unsafe condition. In addition, the policyholder in operations claims is typically a contractor rather than an establishment open to the public.

Bases of Liability

A policyholder's operations are alleged to be responsible for an accident whenever the accident results from an unsafe or improper act by the policyholder or the policyholder's employees; whenever the policyholder fails to properly supervise another party for which it is responsible; or whenever the policyholder has contractually assumed liability.

Construction sites and construction operations are inherently dangerous. Unsafe acts and conditions are common in this environment. As a result, many contractors and construction companies face very high costs for workers compensation and general liability insurance. Such organizations often devote great effort to safety, to control costs, to avoid unfortunate injuries, and to comply with OSHA. As a result, following an accident, the adjuster will often find that determination of liability is an extremely sensitive issue. The policyholder's workers may not be forthcoming, honest, and complete in response to the adjuster's inquiries. The policyholder's supervisors may be defensive, brusque, or irrational.

When investigating claims arising out of operations, the adjuster should begin by establishing exactly how the claimant's accident occurred. Exactly where did the accident occur? What workers were in the vicinity? Who employs and supervises these workers? Exactly what were these workers doing at the moment of the accident? What equipment were they operating? What did each of them see? Even in the face of evasion and reluctance from the witnesses, an adjuster can usually establish what happened through a thorough and methodical investigation.

A contractor may be responsible for its own employees as well as the supervision of others. Under many construction contracts, a general contractor has duties to ensure workplace safety, and individual contractors may be responsible for their own subcontractors. The duty to supervise may be an explicit contractual obligation, a custom of the trade that is implied in the contract, or required under general tort principles. When faced with a case of potential improper supervision, an adjuster will usually take the position that the primarily responsible party is the employer of the workers who caused the accident or its insurer. Nevertheless, the adjuster should thoroughly investigate what supervisory steps the policyholder actually took. Did the policyholder communicate with its subcontractors about safety? Did the policyholder conduct inspections, give warnings, withhold payments, or otherwise enforce safe practices?

Contractual Assumptions of Liability

In addition to their direct responsibility for their workers and their duty to supervise others, contractor-insureds are often liable for the faults of another because they have assumed liability by contract. Liability assumed by contract is different from liability for failure to supervise. When a contractor assumes liability for another, it is responsible for that other party's liabilities. In contrast, liability for failure to supervise is based on the contractor's own failures, not the failures or liabilities of another.

The legal interpretation of contractual assumptions of liability can be complex. Generally, courts recognize contractual assumptions of liability as valid but interpret them narrowly. An adjuster examining an assumption of liability clause must determine whether it requires defense and indemnity or just indemnity. Does the assumption of liability extend to all liabilities of the indemnified party or just liabilities that arise out of the indemnifying party's behavior? Does the assumption of liability extend to the owner of the project site or to subcontractors of the indemnified party? If the adjuster has any doubts about interpreting the assumption of liability clause, he or she should seek the advice of supervisors, managers, or counsel.

Insurance coverage for contractual assumptions of liability varies. Thus, adjusters with cases of contractual liability must check their policy wording carefully. Again, if coverage is unclear or in doubt, the adjuster should seek an opinion from superiors or staff advisers and should issue a reservation of rights letter to the policyholder until the matter is resolved.

When an adjuster handles a case of assumed liability, the adjuster must investigate with the indemnified party and its employees as though it were the insured. If the indemnified party has been sued, the adjuster may consider providing for its defense, even if the contract does not strictly require it. If the adjuster's insurer must indemnify the party in question, it may be sensible to provide for its defense as well. Whether to do so is a question of company policy that may also depend on the strength of the case and the willingness of the party in question to relinquish control of its defense.

Preservation of Accident Scene

In a claim involving operations, the adjuster should immediately try to preserve the accident scene through photos, diagrams, and detailed measurements. Construction sites change rapidly, and witnesses' memories can become confused and vague.

In addition to preserving the precise scene of an accident, photos can provide many important incidental details. Photos can show the exact stage of the project at the time of the accident, including the exact stage of each subcontractor's work. Photos can show which contractors were on the scene on the day of the accident. Photos can also show the presence or absence of safety measures and precautions. On large or well-organized projects, the owner, architect, or general contractor may have daily records of progress, including photos.

Products Liability

Any party that manufactures or sells a product that causes harm to another may be liable for that harm. Products liability claims may be based on traditional negligence theories, but also on other bases. An adjuster handling products claims must investigate all possible bases of liability and all defenses that apply to those bases.

Bases of Liability

Other than traditional negligence theories, products liability may be based on breach of warranty or strict liability in tort.

A **warranty** is any contractual promise about the product that accompanies the sale. The warranty that guarantees performance or durability is one type of warranty. An alleged breach of warranty may be based on an express warranty (described below) or on a warranty implied by law. Many written sales contracts explicitly disclaim any warranties, express or implied, unless set forth in the written contract.

Warranty
A promise, either written or implied, such as a promise by a seller to a buyer that a product is fit for a particular purpose.

An **express warranty** is any explicit statement about the product that accompanies the sale. For example, a statement that reads, "These hedge clippers can easily cut through branches up to a quarter-inch thick," could be the basis of liability if the hedge clippers failed to so perform and caused damage as a result. Express warranties may allow a claimant to assert a products claim that might not be sustainable on negligence or strict liability grounds. In the absence of an express warranty, the principal advantage to claimants of a warranty suit is that the statute of limitations is usually longer than for tort-based claims.

Express warranty
An explicit statement about a product. Such a warranty may accompany the sale of a product.

Strict liability in tort differs from negligence, yet the factual investigation for each theory is similar. Under strict liability theory, the nature of the product is the issue, not the behavior of the defendant. Specifically, the issue is whether the product is "defective" in a way that makes it "unreasonably dangerous," not whether the defendant was negligent. Yet asking whether a product is "defective" is very much like asking whether it should have been made differently by the defendant, and determining whether a product is "unreasonably dangerous" depends on how much less dangerous it might have been made.

Identification of Product and Manufacturer

The defense of products liability claims is significantly different for manufacturers than for those who merely sell the product. If a wholesaler or retailer resells a product in the same condition in which it left the manufacturer, the manufacturer is responsible for indemnifying the wholesaler or retailer from any products liability claim. An adjuster handling claims for a wholesaler or retailer can usually withdraw from the claim once the manufacturer's insurer is involved. Nevertheless, because the wholesaler or retailer is liable as far as the public is concerned, an adjuster for a wholesaler or retailer should be prepared to handle the claim should the manufacturer be out of business, not identifiable, insolvent, uninsured, or unwilling for any reason to handle the claim. Usually, however, manufacturers want to defend their products and their retailers for business reasons, over and above the law.

The product in question must be carefully identified in order to verify the manufacturer. Many retailers sell products with a store label that are manufactured elsewhere. Many products have component parts that come from sources other than the assembling manufacturer. Unless the manufacturer can be identified, the retailer will be responsible to the claimant. A retailer can usually verify whether it sold a particular type of product at a particular time. The retailer can usually also identify the source from which it bought its merchandise.

Use of Experts

Once a product has been identified, the issue of liability depends on whether the product could have been made safer otherwise and still perform its intended function. Some products are inherently dangerous. For example, power tools cannot perform their intended function without simultaneously being capable of severe bodily damage.

Determining liability in products cases often involves redesigning the product after the occurrence of an accident. The feasibility of redesign can be determined only through expert testimony. Both the plaintiff and the defendant must hire an engineer or other expert who can provide an opinion. Resolving products liability claims is thus very expensive. Most manufacturers consider the expense worthwhile because they might face potentially millions of claims from every user of the same products. Because the policyholder has often been in the business for years, it can be a good source of references for design engineers. However, adjusters must consider any financial stake such an engineer may have in his or her relations with the policyholder and whether the engineer is defending his or her own design.

Review of Warnings and Instructions

Often, in products liability claims, the product itself cannot realistically be redesigned, so the plaintiff argues that the warnings and instructions that accompanied the product were inadequate and that the product was thus defective.

When faced with such an allegation, the adjuster must review all literature accompanying the product. The adjuster should determine whether the warnings and instructions provided, if followed, would have prevented the claimant's accident. If not, the adjuster should try to determine what additional warning would have been necessary to prevent the claimant's accident. In all such cases, the adjuster should investigate whether the claimant ever read the instructions. If the claimant asserts that he or she did, the adjuster should ask the claimant to repeat whatever he or she remembers. Should it appear that the claimant never read the instructions, or forgot everything that he or she read, the claimant will have a difficult case to prove. Any alleged shortcomings in the manufacturer's instructions cannot be a cause of the claimant's accident if the claimant never read or cannot remember them.

Improper Use

Claimants are often injured while using products in ways that are not intended or foreseeable. For example, claimants may suffer injuries by using a lawn mower to trim hedges or by using prescription drugs for conditions other than those for which they were prescribed.

Adjusters who suspect an improper use should obtain a careful and thorough statement from the claimant. If the claimant is not available for a statement, the adjuster may be able to obtain an honest account of what happened from the claimant's emergency room records or from an initial report by the claimant to a state or federal consumer products regulatory agency.

Workers Compensation Claims

The workers compensation system is an exception to the liability system. Work-related injuries are compensated without regard to fault and usually without resorting to the courts. Although the compensability of work-related injuries is usually straightforward, adjusters handling workers compensation cases must investigate them diligently. In addition, the medical aspect of workers compensation cases may be extraordinarily complex and expensive.

Investigation of Compensation Cases

Workers compensation cases that involve only medical expenses, such as a single visit to the emergency room, are usually processed with no real investigation. The policyholder's word is accepted as proof that the accident happened on the job and that the injury is work-related.

Should an accident involve lost time from work, the adjuster is likely to conduct an investigation. Statements are obtained from the claimant, the employer, and any witnesses. The purpose of these statements is to establish that the injury is work-related, that the injury was not preexisting, what the likely period of disability will be, and whether relations between the employee and employer are such that the claimant might have staged the claim or might be inclined to exaggerate the disability. The adjuster must also obtain documentation of the employee's earnings so that the employee's disability compensation can be properly calculated.

The adjuster's investigation into the circumstances of the accident may be an important part of the employer's loss control program. Many policyholders are concerned about their workers compensation costs. In addition, these policyholders are interested in reducing workplace injuries for humanitarian reasons, to forestall any OSHA or state labor department investigation, and to maintain productivity in their business. Many insurers take an active role in loss control and depend on their adjusters' investigations for guidance as to where to devote their efforts.

Control of Medical Expenses

Workers compensation medical expenses are potentially unlimited. The law requires the employer (or its insurer) to pay all necessary and reasonable medical expenses related to the injury sustained on the job. Thus, workers compensation policies have no policy limits. A small percentage of workers compensation cases account for an enormous percentage of the medical expenses paid out by compensation insurers.

Compensation adjusters have limited tools with which to challenge medical expenses. The employee-patient is not required to co-pay any portion of the expenses, as is common with health insurance. Compensation insurers often do not have the bargaining power that health insurers have with medical providers. Furthermore, in many states, there are no fee schedules or other controls over medical bills. As a result, workers compensation medical costs have risen faster in the past decade than health costs in general.

Some compensation insurers have entered into agreements with **preferred provider organizations (PPOs)** by which the insurer receives a discount on the usual medical charges in exchange for a volume of referrals. This type of arrangement is feasible only in states that allow the employer or insurer to select the treating physician.

Most compensation insurers conduct **bill audits** to identify charges that are excessive, fabricated, or redundant. Specialized bill auditing firms can perform this service for compensation insurers. Bill audits usually result in more than enough savings to justify the expense of the audit.

Utilization review services, discussed previously, are also a valuable tool in determining whether medical treatment is necessary. However, before an insurer can deny reimbursement for a course of treatment, it must be certain

Preferred provider organizations (PPOs)
Administrative organizations that meet the common needs of healthcare providers and clients of healthcare. The PPO identifies networks of providers and contracts for their medical services at discounted rates. In turn, the PPO offers its clients access to these providers and discounts for a small access fee.

Bill audits
Investigations of medical invoices performed by workers compensation insurers to identify charges that may be excessive, fabricated, or redundant.

that experts from the utilization review service are willing and able to testify on its behalf. Because workers compensation laws are designed to protect workers regardless of fault, insurers should not deny claims without clear grounds for doing so.

Claims for psychological injuries are very expensive. The causes of psychological problems are complex and may include a mixture of work-related and nonwork-related factors. Furthermore, the recovery from and cure of psychological conditions are often vague and unclear. Thus, claims for psychological conditions are expensive to investigate and difficult to terminate. Claims for allegedly work-related stress disability may involve a complex interaction of employer-employee difficulties, preexisting personality disorders, and current difficulties outside the workplace. Adjusters are generally not competent to evaluate these cases. However, experts in the fields of psychology and psychiatry specialize in defense evaluations of psychological conditions.

The most sophisticated form of medical cost control is **medical management**. Medical management is devoted to controlling medical expenses on the small percentage of cases that involve high medical costs. Those cases usually involve permanent injuries that require tens of thousands of dollars of medical expenses annually for the remainder of the claimant's life. Medical management ensures that the claimant receives care in appropriate facilities with appropriate specialists. Rehabilitation facilities may specialize in certain injuries, such as brain trauma, quadriplegia, burns, or blindness. Medical management may enable an injured claimant to live independently rather than in an institution. By specializing in the care of serious permanent injuries, medical management specialists can both ensure optimum treatment for claimants and control costs for insurers.

Medical management
A cost control measure that involves directing and coordinating the efforts of healthcare providers to meet the needs of the patient and insurer.

Control of Disability

Controlling disability expenses is probably the foremost issue for compensation adjusters. Cases in which the claimant loses no time from work and cases in which the claimant returns to work promptly are relatively simple and straightforward. Cases in which disability extends over a long or an excessive period are the biggest problem and expense for compensation insurers.

Compensation insurers generally do not have the legal power simply to cease making payments on cases in which they believe the disability should have ended. Once a case has been initially accepted as compensable, the insurer can end disability payments only by agreement with the claimant or by order of the compensation commission. If the claimant does not agree, cases before the compensation commission can take months to resolve. Compensation commissions generally decide in favor of the claimant and will probably resolve doubtful cases against the insurer. Should the commission find in favor of the insurer and allow disability payments to cease, the claimant is not required to reimburse past payments. Thus, in jurisdictions in which compensation cases take months to resolve, the claimant is assured of compensation for those months, no matter what the outcome.

Some claimants in difficult disability cases are antagonistic towards the employer or hate their work. The adjuster can do little about those circumstances. However, such circumstances usually become obvious during the adjuster's investigation and act as "red flags" to the adjuster that the case in question could be difficult.

Adjusters can control disability by insisting that the treating physician explain why the claimant cannot perform the demands of his or her job. Many treating physicians will certify disability without any real understanding of the physical demands of the claimant's work. For almost any physical impairment, some jobs, or aspects of jobs, can be performed by someone with that impairment. Thus, physicians cannot simply assume disability because of the existence of certain impairments.

Adjusters can also work with the employer to modify the employee's job by removing the most physically demanding parts of it. Claimants who return to limited-duty work are usually on the road to recovery. Adjusters handling disability claims can encourage claimants to think in terms of returning to work by constantly asking them what aspects of their work they are still incapable of performing. Adjusters can then suggest job modifications to the employer.

Professional Liability

Liability claims for professional malpractice are generally handled by specialized insurance companies and adjusters. These cases require a specialized determination of liability and a complex determination of damages. Because of the importance of these cases to the professional reputation of the policyholder, the policyholder is usually involved in his or her own defense, and these cases are likely to be litigated to verdict rather than settled.

Professional liability claims can be asserted against people who provide professional services, such as physicians, engineers, architects, attorneys, accountants, or insurance agents. Most of the law of malpractice has developed from claims against physicians, not because they are more careless than other professionals, but because they work with people's health in an environment in which a negative outcome is always possible.

Determining Standard of Care

Physicians cannot guarantee a complete cure for every patient. Attorneys cannot win every case. Accountants cannot guarantee the financial health of a business or an investment. Professionals are not necessarily at fault for negative outcomes.

Professionals are required to exercise the standard of care accepted in their profession. In other words, professionals should perform their services in the manner of a competent, careful member of their profession. Malpractice cases are usually proved by expert testimony to the effect that the defendant should have behaved otherwise or should have made a different decision, given the facts and circumstances known when the professional services were rendered. An adjuster investigating a malpractice case should constantly ask what could have and should have been done differently at every point.

Laws in certain jurisdictions require that physicians be judged by the standards of their community. This means that a physician practicing in a rural community should be judged by a lower standard of care than a (presumably) more sophisticated urban physician. Probably in most jurisdictions, the once-significant differences in care between rural and urban communities have diminished. Physicians are part of a nationwide profession with professional journals and modern communications readily available. However, no physician is held to the standard of the leading expert in the field. If appropriate care of a patient would require leading-edge expertise, the average physician should not be judged as negligent for failing to provide such expertise.

Many physicians are found at fault for failing to obtain a patient's informed consent. Physicians are required to explain their care to their patients; they should explain the treatment options and risks associated with each. Should a physician fail to explain the risks inherent in a course of treatment, the physician may be liable to the patient, even if the adverse outcome is an unavoidable risk. Physicians must exercise judgment in how much they tell patients because exhaustive explanations would confuse most patients. Nevertheless, a physician who fails to fully inform a patient of the risks of treatment runs the risk of being responsible for any negative outcome. Obtaining informed consent is a difficult area to defend because many physicians do not document their discussions with their patients, or do so in very brief fashion. After a negative outcome, patients will often claim not to have understood the risks they faced, and the physician cannot prove otherwise.

Determining Damages

Damages in medical malpractice are similar to those in other bodily injury cases, except that the physician is not liable for the underlying condition that caused treatment initially. Determining damages requires expert testimony about how much the patient's condition would have improved or progressed with proper treatment. Often these issues can be determined only as matters of probability.

In cases of alleged attorney malpractice, the underlying legal matter from which the malpractice claim arose must be relitigated or reconsidered in the professional liability claim. The damages in the malpractice case depend on how much better the result obtained in the underlying matter should have been.

Determining damages in other types of malpractice cases is similar. Expert testimony must be used to establish what the claimant's condition would have been had proper professional services been rendered.

Defense of Malpractice Cases

In general, malpractice cases are litigated by only the most sophisticated plaintiff and defense attorneys. The insured professional is also likely to be heavily involved in the defense of the case.

As malpractice suits became more common, the insurers that handled them resisted easy settlement. In many of those cases, the insured professional had to consent in writing to any settlement. Absent such consent, the verdict had to be litigated. As the strength of the opposition became obvious, only the most talented plaintiff attorneys would accept these cases. To match the skills of the plaintiff bar, insurers increasingly relied on specialized defense attorneys. It is currently rare for a general practice attorney to handle a malpractice case.

Many professional malpractice policies require the policyholder's consent to settlement. The insured professional is more personally concerned about the outcome of professional malpractice claims than about the outcome of other claims because the professional's reputation is at stake. Some policies require the professional who rejects a proposed settlement to be responsible for any verdict in excess of the proposed settlement.

An adjuster involved in a professional malpractice case must investigate the possibility of defenses. In medical malpractice cases, for example, the patient could be responsible for failing to divulge all relevant information to the physician, for failing to follow the prescribed course of treatment, or for failing to report complications.

Environmental and Toxic Tort

Liability claims for environmental impairment and cleanup and for injuries caused by toxins are a growing area of claims work. Like professional malpractice, these areas are handled by specialists. The typical adjuster never handles such cases. Insurance companies that face significant exposures in these areas have usually established special units to handle them, have referred them to outside attorneys, or have consulted adjusting firms with the skills and experience needed.

All aspects of these cases are complicated. Determining coverage, liability, and damages may require the assistance of outside experts. The complexity of these cases has often resulted in multiple levels of litigation: litigation between the plaintiff and various defendants, between the various defendants and their insurers, and among the insurers. Some environmental and toxic tort cases also include bankruptcies of one or more of the parties, thus involving another court and adding complexity to each case.

Determination of Coverage

The specifics of the coverage issues involved in these cases are beyond the scope of this course. However, adjusters handling these cases must understand that coverage problems revolve around both a determination of the correct policy period and certain substantive coverage issues. The adjuster must understand company policy for handling those issues. Some insurers handle coverage issues with inside staff, and others always use outside legal counsel.

When different policy periods are at issue, coverage may be determined by when the harmful exposure occurred, by when the damage or injuries first occurred, or by when the damage and injuries were first discovered. Some jurisdictions require coverage to apply whenever any of these criteria exist. Thus, numerous different insurers are usually involved in the same claim, often with different policy limits or terms.

Aside from difficulties with policy periods, these cases also involve substantive coverage issues, such as the application of intentional act or pollution exclusions or the meaning of the phrase "property damage." Given the amount of money at stake in these claims, insurers that face a significant number of them usually litigate the meaning of their policy provisions through the courts. Courts, however, have generally resolved any coverage ambiguity against the insurer.

Determination of Liability

Liability for release of pollutants or other toxins depends on state and federal laws. Common law may have a role in determining liability, but the specially enacted environmental statutes are more significant. The specifics of those laws are beyond the scope of this course.

Adjusters with questions about environmental or toxic tort liability are usually required to consult with outside law firms that specialize in these issues. The typical insurance defense law firm does not have any expertise in environmental matters.

The law firm that consults about liability or that defends the policyholder should be different from the attorney or law firm that the insurer consults regarding coverage issues. When coverage questions exist, it is a conflict of interest for a law firm or an attorney to serve both the insurer and the policyholder simultaneously.

Determination of Damages

Because of environmental statutes, especially the federal Superfund law, few commercial firms are willing to perform environmental cleanups. As a result, the services of firms that do such work are expensive. More firms provide environmental consulting. Those organizations can provide expert opinions on the scope and cost of a cleanup effort, whether valid alternatives exist to the cleanup procedure required by the government, and whether a particular policyholder's chemical waste can be identified and segregated in a general dump site. These consulting firms are also expensive, even though they do not perform the cleanup.

In toxic tort cases, the plaintiff usually has a difficult burden of proof unless the cause-and-effect relationship between the toxin and the injury has been well established in scientific literature. Generally, in these cases, the plaintiff alleges exposure to a toxin caused by the defendant that results in a physical malady, such as cancer. Pioneering plaintiff attorneys do not mind losing a long string of these cases if they can eventually win one. Once a jury has decided in favor of a plaintiff, all subsequent cases have a certain settlement value. Courts have begun to recognize that this roulette-like approach to what is supposedly a scientific issue is inappropriate. Courts have therefore disallowed purported expert testimony on behalf of plaintiffs unless it would be acceptable in scientific literature.

SUMMARY

Liability claim adjusters are primarily concerned with the laws of liability and damages, which exist apart from the insurance policy. Once coverage has been verified in a liability case, the insurance policy plays a much smaller role than in the settlement of property loss claims.

The basic law of negligence applies to most cases that liability adjusters handle, but adjusters must be alert to other possible legal theories, such as strict liability for products and specific statutory liability for certain auto accidents.

Damages in injury cases include medical specials, loss of earnings, and general damages. Determining and evaluating general damages are essential skills for liability claim adjusters, because general damages are the main element of the claimant's case. Because general damages are subjective, great room for negotiations exists in liability claims. Most successful liability claim adjusters are excellent negotiators who enjoy the challenge of negotiation.

Should negotiations not prove successful, liability claim adjusters must know how to steer cases through the court system. Doing so requires knowledge of court procedures and the ability to deal with and manage attorneys.

Specific types of liability claims present their own unique challenges. Experienced liability claim adjusters are familiar with the difficulties that can arise in various types of cases.

Index

Page numbers in boldface refer to definitions of key words and phrases.